SAP PRESS e-books

Print or e-book, Kindle or iPad, workplace or airplane: Choose where and how to read your SAP PRESS books! You can now get all our titles as e-books, too:

- By download and online access
- For all popular devices
- And, of course, DRM-free

Convinced? Then go to www.sap-press.com and get your e-book today.

SAP® BusinessObjects™ Design Studio

SAP PRESS

SAP PRESS is a joint initiative of SAP and Rheinwerk Publishing. The know-how offered by SAP specialists combined with the expertise of Rheinwerk Publishing offers the reader expert books in the field. SAP PRESS features first-hand information and expert advice, and provides useful skills for professional decision-making.

SAP PRESS offers a variety of books on technical and business-related topics for the SAP user. For further information, please visit our website: *www.sap-press.com*.

Palekar, Patel, Shiralkar
SAP BW 7.4—Practical Guide (3rd edition)
2015, 852 pages, hardcover and e-book
www.sap-press.com/3733

Christian Ah-Soon, Peter Snowdon
Getting Started with SAP Lumira
2015, 540 pages, hardcover and e-book
www.sap-press.com/3645

Merz, Hügens, Blum
Implementing SAP BW on SAP HANA
2015, 467 pages, hardcover and e-book
www.sap-press.com/3609

Brogden, Sinkwitz, Marks, Orthous
SAP BusinessObjects Web Intelligence:
The Comprehensive Guide (3rd edition)
2014, 691 pages, hardcover and e-book
www.sap-press.com/3673

Dwain Chang, Xavier Hacking, Jeroen van der A

SAP® BusinessObjects™ Design Studio

The Comprehensive Guide

Rheinwerk® Publishing

Bonn • Boston

Editor Sarah Frazier
Acquisitions Editor Kelly Grace Weaver
Copyeditor Julie McNamee
Cover Design Graham Geary
Photo Credit Shutterstock.com/274400990/© Kike Fernandez
Layout Design Vera Brauner
Production Kelly O'Callaghan
Typesetting SatzPro, Krefeld (Germany)
Printed and bound in the United States of America, on paper from sustainable sources

ISBN 978-1-4932-1297-2

© 2016 by Rheinwerk Publishing, Inc., Boston (MA)
2nd edition 2016

Library of Congress Cataloging-in-Publication Data
Chang, Dwain, author.
 SAP BusinessObjects design studio : the comprehensive guide / Dwain Chang, Xavier Hacking, Jeroen van der A. --
2nd edition.
 pages cm
 Includes index.
 ISBN 978-1-4932-1297-2 (print : alk. paper) -- ISBN 1-4932-1297-4 (print : alk. paper) -- ISBN 978-1-4932-1298-9 (ebook)
-- ISBN 978-1-4932-1299-6 (print and ebook : alk. paper) 1. BusinessObjects. 2. Business intelligence--Data processing.
3. Dashboards (Management information systems) 4. SAP ERP. I. Hacking, Xavier, author. II. Van der A, Jeroen, author. III.
Title.
 HD38.7.H33 2015
 658.4'038028553--dc23
                                                            2015034421

All rights reserved. Neither this publication nor any part of it may be copied or reproduced in any form or by any means or translated into another language, without the prior consent of Rheinwerk Publishing, 2 Heritage Drive, Suite 305, Quincy, MA 02171.

Rheinwerk Publishing makes no warranties or representations with respect to the content hereof and specifically disclaims any implied warranties of merchantability or fitness for any particular purpose. Rheinwerk Publishing assumes no responsibility for any errors that may appear in this publication.

"Rheinwerk Publishing" and the Rheinwerk Publishing logo are registered trademarks of Rheinwerk Verlag GmbH, Bonn, Germany. SAP PRESS is an imprint of Rheinwerk Verlag GmbH and Rheinwerk Publishing, Inc.

All of the screenshots and graphics reproduced in this book are subject to copyright © SAP SE, Dietmar-Hopp-Allee 16, 69190 Walldorf, Germany.

SAP, the SAP logo, ABAP, Ariba, ASAP, Duet, hybris, SAP Adaptive Server Enterprise, SAP Advantage Database Server, SAP Afaria, SAP ArchiveLink, SAP Business ByDesign, SAP Business Explorer (SAP BEx), SAP BusinessObjects, SAP BusinessObjects Web Intelligence, SAP Business One, SAP BusinessObjects Explorer, SAP Business Workflow, SAP Crystal Reports, SAP d-code, SAP Early-Watch, SAP Fiori, SAP Ganges, SAP Global Trade Services (SAP GTS), SAP GoingLive, SAP HANA, SAP Jam, SAP Lumira, SAP MaxAttention, SAP MaxDB, SAP NetWeaver, SAP PartnerEdge, SAPPHIRE NOW, SAP PowerBuilder, SAP PowerDesigner, SAP R/2, SAP R/3, SAP Replication Server, SAP SI, SAP SQL Anywhere, SAP Strategic Enterprise Management (SAP SEM), SAP StreamWork, SuccessFactors, Sybase, TwoGo by SAP, and The Best-Run Businesses Run SAP are registered or unregistered trademarks of SAP SE, Walldorf, Germany.

All other products mentioned in this book are registered or unregistered trademarks of their respective companies.

Contents at a Glance

PART I Getting Started

1 Introduction to SAP BusinessObjects Design Studio 29
2 SAP BusinessObjects Design Studio vs. SAP BusinessObjects Dashboards vs. BEx Web Application Designer 49
3 Usage Scenarios 69
4 Installation and Configuration 91

PART II The Basics

5 The Integrated Development Environment 143
6 The Application Design Process 195
7 Components and Properties 217

PART III Advanced Concepts

8 Scripting for Interactivity 305
9 Planning Applications 385
10 Enhancing Applications with CSS 401
11 Design Principles and Visualization Options 429

PART IV The Software Development Kit

12 Using SDK Extensions in SAP BusinessObjects Design Studio 469
13 SDK Installation and Deployment 491
14 Building Components Using the SDK 507

PART V Examples

15 Building a Real-Time Production Dashboard 617
16 Building a Sales Dashboard Application 639
17 Building an OLAP Application Using a Template 675
18 Outlook 699

Dear Reader,

As the saying goes: "Everything's better the second time around!" For this hefty second edition, this certainly holds true. Much as Design Studio has matured as a software, so has this book. From a new co-author to a new title, we've moved on from simply getting started and have taken a deep dive into the feature-rich world of Design Studio.

Adding close to 300 more pages, Dwain Chang, Xavier Hacking, and Jeroen van der A have provided a comprehensive guide to the latest release of Design Studio. From installation and configuration steps to detailed usage scenarios for creating example applications, you'll find information on everything from the application design process to advanced concepts for scripting and using Design Studio's SDK. Having worked closely with these authors over the last few months, I'm proud to have been able to take part in this book's second edition transformation.

What did you think about *SAP BusinessObjects Design Studio: The Comprehensive Guide*? Your comments and suggestions are the most useful tools to help us make our books the best they can be. Please feel free to contact me and share any praise or criticism you may have.

Thank you for purchasing a book from SAP PRESS!

Sarah Frazier
Editor, SAP PRESS

Rheinwerk Publishing
Boston, MA

sarahf@rheinwerk-publishing.com
www.sap-press.com

Contents

Foreword 17
Introduction 19
Acknowledgments 25

PART I Getting Started

1 Introduction to SAP BusinessObjects Design Studio 29

1.1 What Is SAP BusinessObjects Design Studio? 30
    1.1.1 Development Environment 32
    1.1.2 Components 32
    1.1.3 Data Sources and Platforms 33
    1.1.4 Scripting 34
    1.1.5 Cascading Style Sheets 34
    1.1.6 Templates and Themes 34
    1.1.7 Application Execution 35
1.2 SAP BusinessObjects Design Studio and Existing SAP BusinessObjects BI Environments 37
    1.2.1 SAP BusinessObjects BI Tool Categories 38
    1.2.2 Content Creation and Consumption 44
1.3 Recent Developments 46
1.4 Summary 48

2 SAP BusinessObjects Design Studio vs. SAP BusinessObjects Dashboards vs. BEx Web Application Designer 49

2.1 SAP BusinessObjects Dashboards 49
    2.1.1 Setting Up a Dashboard 51
    2.1.2 Components 53
    2.1.3 Data Connectivity 56
    2.1.4 Publishing 57
    2.1.5 SDK 57
2.2 BEX Web Application Designer 58
    2.2.1 Setting Up a Web Application Template 60
    2.2.2 Web Items 62
    2.2.3 Publishing 64

2.3	Key Differences		64
2.4	Summary		68

3 Usage Scenarios ... 69

3.1	Real-Time Production Dashboard		69
3.2	Sales Dashboard Application		75
	3.2.1	Main Screen	75
	3.2.2	Detail Screen	77
	3.2.3	Quotes	79
3.3	OLAP Application		81
	3.3.1	Starting the Application	82
	3.3.2	Customizing the Application	83
3.4	Summary		89

4 Installation and Configuration ... 91

4.1	Architecture, Components, and Prerequisites		92
	4.1.1	SAP BusinessObjects BI Platform	94
	4.1.2	SAP Business Warehouse	95
	4.1.3	SAP Enterprise Portal	95
	4.1.4	SAP HANA	95
	4.1.5	SAP BusinessObjects Design Studio Client Tool	96
	4.1.6	Browsers	96
4.2	Preparing for Installation		96
	4.2.1	Accessing Document Guides	96
	4.2.2	Downloading Software Components	97
	4.2.3	Helpful SAP Notes	98
	4.2.4	Extracting Installation Files	98
4.3	Installing the SAP BusinessObjects BI Platform Add-On		100
4.4	Configuring the SAP BusinessObjects BI Platform		108
	4.4.1	Initializing the Analysis Application Service	109
	4.4.2	Setting the Number of Client Sessions	113
	4.4.3	Assigning User Authorizations	114
	4.4.4	Creating a Mobile Category	118
	4.4.5	Creating an SAP BW OLAP Connection	120
	4.4.6	Creating an SAP HANA OLAP Connection	123
4.5	Configuring SAP Enterprise Portal and SAP Business Warehouse		124
4.6	Configuring SAP HANA		131

	4.7	Configuring Connections via Universes and Custom Data Sources	133
		4.7.1 Universes	133
		4.7.2 Custom Data Sources	134
	4.8	Installing the SAP BusinessObjects Design Studio Client Tool	135
	4.9	Summary	140

PART II The Basics

5 The Integrated Development Environment ... 143

	5.1	Menu	143
		5.1.1 Application	143
		5.1.2 Planning	155
		5.1.3 Edit	156
		5.1.4 Layout	157
		5.1.5 Search	158
		5.1.6 View	160
		5.1.7 Tools	162
		5.1.8 Help	175
	5.2	Toolbar	177
	5.3	Layout Editor	179
		5.3.1 Components View	180
		5.3.2 Outline View	181
		5.3.3 Properties View	186
		5.3.4 Additional Properties View	190
		5.3.5 Error Log View	192
		5.3.6 Script Problems View	193
	5.4	Summary	193

6 The Application Design Process ... 195

	6.1	Setting Up the User Interface and Visualizations	197
	6.2	Adding the Data	202
	6.3	Making It Interactive	208
	6.4	Formatting and Fine-Tuning	211
	6.5	Executing the Application	214
	6.6	Summary	216

7 Components and Properties 217

7.1 Application Component Properties 217
7.1.1 Custom CSS 221
7.1.2 Global Script Variables and On Startup 225
7.2 Data Source Alias Component Properties 227
7.3 Visual Component Properties 229
7.3.1 Common Properties 229
7.3.2 Analytic Component Properties 231
7.3.3 Basic Component Properties 261
7.3.4 Container Component Properties 283
7.4 Technical Component Properties 293
7.4.1 Backend Connection Component 294
7.4.2 Context Menu Component 296
7.4.3 Global Scripts Object Component 298
7.4.4 PDF Component 300
7.4.5 Text Pool Component 301
7.4.6 Action Sheet Component 301
7.5 Summary 302

PART III Advanced Concepts

8 Scripting for Interactivity 305

8.1 BI Action Language 305
8.1.1 Syntax 306
8.1.2 Expressions 309
8.1.3 Script Variables 311
8.1.4 Calling the Event Handler 312
8.1.5 Global Scripts 312
8.2 Creating a Script 313
8.2.1 Using the Content Assistance Screen 314
8.2.2 Creating Predefined Statement Templates 317
8.2.3 Finding Script Errors 320
8.2.4 Creating a Global Script 321
8.3 Methods 322
8.3.1 Convert Component 323
8.3.2 Data Source Alias Component 324
8.3.3 Application Component 329
8.3.4 ApplicationInfo Object Component 331

		8.3.5	Bookmark Component	331
		8.3.6	Math Component	332
		8.3.7	Planning Component and Planning Function Component	333
		8.3.8	Context Menu Component	335
		8.3.9	Visual Components	335
	8.4	Example: Building Navigation Items	350
		8.4.1	Menu Navigation	350
		8.4.2	Popup Navigation	353
		8.4.3	Navigating between Applications	357
	8.5	Example: Manipulating Data Output	359
		8.5.1	Presenting Data in Text Components	359
		8.5.2	Preparing Data for Variable Input	361
		8.5.3	Data Binding	363
		8.5.4	Changing the Chart View	367
	8.6	Example: Building a Scorecard	370
	8.7	Example: Building an OLAP Application	373
		8.7.1	Initial Setup	373
		8.7.2	Adding Charts	376
		8.7.3	Selecting a Data Source	379
		8.7.4	Bookmarking	380
	8.8	Summary	383

9 Planning Applications 385

	9.1	Prerequisites for Planning	385
	9.2	Adding a Planning Connection	387
	9.3	Manual Planning: Crosstab and Spreadsheet Components	390
	9.4	Automated Planning: Planning Functions and Sequences	392
		9.4.1	Planning Functions	392
		9.4.2	Planning Sequences	393
	9.5	Planning Functionality Options	394
	9.6	Building a Planning Application	395
	9.7	Summary	399

10 Enhancing Applications with CSS 401

	10.1	CSS Themes	401
	10.2	Using CSS Classes and Styles	404
	10.3	Adding Custom CSS Classes	408
	10.4	Making Applications Responsive	414

		10.4.1	Hiding Panels Based on Screen Size	416
		10.4.2	Rearranging Blocks	418
	10.5	Modifying Standard Components		421
	10.6	Summary		427

11 Design Principles and Visualization Options ... 429

	11.1	General Design Principles		429
		11.1.1	Don't Make Users Think	430
		11.1.2	Don't Make Users Wait	430
		11.1.3	Managing User Focus	431
		11.1.4	Emphasizing Features	431
		11.1.5	Keeping It Simple	432
		11.1.6	Using Conventions	432
		11.1.7	Getting the Most Out of Screen Room	432
	11.2	Choosing a Visualization Method		434
		11.2.1	Single Number	436
		11.2.2	Line Chart	436
		11.2.3	Bar Chart	437
		11.2.4	Column Chart	440
		11.2.5	Area Chart	442
		11.2.6	Crosstab	443
		11.2.7	Bubble Chart	444
		11.2.8	Waterfall Chart	444
		11.2.9	Pie Chart	446
		11.2.10	Radar Chart	448
		11.2.11	Scatter Chart	450
		11.2.12	Chart Comparison	450
		11.2.13	International Business Communication Standards	451
	11.3	Building Complex Applications		453
		11.3.1	Building Principles	453
		11.3.2	Application Building Tips	454
		11.3.3	Scripting	457
		11.3.4	Managing the CSS Layout	461
	11.4	Designing for Performance		463
		11.4.1	Creating Row-Based Data Models	463
		11.4.2	Ensuring Calculations Are Done in the Backend	463
		11.4.3	Avoiding Variable Usage in Queries	463
		11.4.4	Be Thoughtful When Loading Data Sources	464
		11.4.5	How to Navigate	465
	11.5	Summary		465

PART IV The Software Development Kit

12 Using SDK Extensions in SAP BusinessObjects Design Studio   469

12.1	Extensions: What They Are and How They Work	469
12.2	Installing, Updating, and Removing SDK Extensions	471
	12.2.1 Installing	471
	12.2.2 Updating	478
	12.2.3 Uninstalling the SDK	480
	12.2.4 Falling Back to a Lower SDK Version	481
12.3	Moving an SDK through the System Landscape	482
	12.3.1 Promoting in SAP BusinessObjects BI	483
	12.3.2 Transporting with SAP Business Warehouse	483
	12.3.3 Transporting with SAP HANA	484
12.4	Testing Changes to an SDK Extension	484
12.5	Third-Party SDK Extensions	485
12.6	Summary	489

13 SDK Installation and Deployment   491

13.1	Installing Eclipse	491
	13.1.1 Java Development Kit	491
	13.1.2 Eclipse	494
13.2	Registering the XML Definition	498
	13.2.1 Downloading SAP Templates	498
	13.2.2 Setting Up XML	499
13.3	Importing the Project	500
13.4	Setting the Target Platform	502
13.5	Summary	506

14 Building Components Using the SDK   507

14.1	Understanding the SDK Framework	507
14.2	Languages Used in an SDK	509
	14.2.1 JavaScript Overview	509
	14.2.2 XML Overview	524
	14.2.3 HTML Overview	525
	14.2.4 CSS Overview	526
14.3	Building Blocks of an SDK Extension	527
	14.3.1 Contribution.xml	527
	14.3.2 Component JavaScript	528

	14.3.3	Additional Properties	529
	14.3.4	Script Contributions	530
	14.3.5	Component CSS	531
	14.3.6	Icon	532
14.4	Configuring the SDK Extension		533
	14.4.1	Extension Level	533
	14.4.2	Component Level	535
	14.4.3	Creating Data Bound Properties	540
14.5	Building Internal Functionality		544
	14.5.1	Function Calls	544
	14.5.2	Functions	546
	14.5.3	Data Runtime JSON	549
14.6	Creating Methods		557
14.7	Using the JavaScript Libraries		559
	14.7.1	jQuery	559
	14.7.2	D3	561
	14.7.3	SAPUI5	571
14.8	Example: Building a Bullet Graph SDK Extension		573
	14.8.1	Overview	573
	14.8.2	Setting Up the Project and Structure	574
	14.8.3	Setting Up the Base Folder Structure	575
	14.8.4	Expanding the Bullet Graph Component	586
	14.8.5	Creating the Component JavaScript	592
	14.8.6	Creating Additional Properties	607
	14.8.7	Adding Methods	611
14.9	Summary		613

PART V Examples

15 Building a Real-Time Production Dashboard — 617

15.1	Application Overview		617
15.2	Building the Application		618
	15.2.1	Views	620
	15.2.2	CSS Classes	622
	15.2.3	Components and Layout	623
	15.2.4	Adding Data to the Views	628
	15.2.5	Interaction	630
	15.2.6	Applying Filters at Startup	633
	15.2.7	Timer Component	636
15.3	Summary		638

16 Building a Sales Dashboard Application ... 639

16.1 Application Overview ... 639
16.2 Building the Application ... 642
  16.2.1 Main Page ... 642
  16.2.2 Detail Screen ... 660
  16.2.3 Quotes ... 666
16.3 Summary ... 674

17 Building an OLAP Application Using a Template ... 675

17.1 Creating the Application ... 675
17.2 Application Properties ... 682
17.3 Application Components ... 685
  17.3.1 Header ... 687
  17.3.2 Body ... 688
  17.3.3 Buttons ... 690
  17.3.4 On Startup ... 695
  17.3.5 Adding Filters ... 697
17.4 Summary ... 698

18 Outlook ... 699

18.1 SAP Analytics and Platform Strategy ... 699
18.2 Roadmap ... 702
  18.2.1 Planned Innovations ... 704
  18.2.2 Future Direction ... 705
18.3 Summary ... 705

Appendices ... 707

A Tips for Using SAP BusinessObjects Design Studio and
   SAP BusinessObjects Analysis, Edition for Microsoft Office ... 709
B SAP BusinessObjects Mobile and SAP BusinessObjects Design Studio ... 715
C The Authors ... 723

Index ... 725

Foreword

SAP BusinessObjects Design Studio is one of the core applications in the SAP Analytics portfolio and is designed entirely in HTML5 for a mobile first focus for interactive analytical applications and dashboards. Using SAP BusinessObjects Design Studio, you can ensure that your users will be able to access the insights they need to make better decisions wherever and whenever they want—connecting natively to data stored in SAP BW, SAP HANA, or any semantic layer. SAP BusinessObjects Design Studio was first released in November 2012. Since then, new releases have come every six months, as SAP continues to make significant investments in this software.

SAP BusinessObjects Design Studio is the heart of the dashboard and application functionality for analytics. This book is an excellent guide for both a beginner and advanced user of SAP BusinessObjects Design Studio. It covers a wide range of topics, from installing SAP BusinessObjects Design Studio to building add-ons through the SDK. This book is a step-by-step guide that teaches you how to build SAP BusinessObjects Design Studio applications via hands-on training. By reading and following along with the steps, you'll get a complete overview of the functionality, how to make CSS enhancements, build add-ons with the SDK, and best practices for making your applications both mobile and interactive. In addition, the book also covers some important strategic topics such as design principles, visualization options, and use cases for SAP BusinessObjects Design Studio.

Three of the top SAP BusinessObjects Design Studio experts have collaborated to make this book an excellent reference. Xavier Hacking, Jeroen van der A, and Dwain Chang all work for a top European consulting firm, Interdobs, out of the Netherlands. Xavier Hacking has been working with SAP business intelligence tools since 2007 and is an active blogger on *www.hackingsap.com*, which I have been following for years. In addition to his expertise in SAP BusinessObjects Design Studio, he also has been a long time SAP BusinessObjects Dashboards expert and is the author of the "SAP BusinessObjects Dashboards 4.1 Cookbook" which you can find on his website. Jeroen van der A is a platinum contributor on the SAP Community Network, freely answering questions and blogging to help build knowledge inside the community. Jeroen is an international speaker, and spoke at the SAP Insider conference on the "Ask the Experts" sessions in 2015. Dwain has been involved with a number of SAP BusinessObject Design Studio projects as a consultant at Interdobs for the last five years. He has a master's degree in economics and informatics and marketing from Erasmus University Rotterdam.

Don't forget to utilize SCN (*http://scn.sap.com/community/businessobjects-design-studio*) as a resource for any additional questions and to stay abreast of the latest news. If you have ideas you'd like to share with us at SAP for future releases, you can submit them and vote on other ideas at Idea Place (*https://ideas.sap.com*). I'd love to hear about the SAP BusinessObjects Design Studio applications you create, so don't hesitate to reach out to me either via Twitter (*@AnitaGibbings*) or SCN.

Anita Gibbings
Senior Director Product Marketing, Business Intelligence at SAP

Introduction

SAP BusinessObjects Design Studio (hereafter, Design Studio) was first released in November 2012 and has been placed in the SAP business intelligence product portfolio as a primary tool for creating interactive analytical applications for the web and mobile devices. Over the past few years we've seen Design Studio expand to support a wide range of scenarios. We expect this trend to continue in the future.

Given these circumstances, it is time to learn more about this new tool.

Target Group and Prerequisites

This book is intended for anyone who wants to learn more about Design Studio. It can be used by developers who are familiar with dashboard or application development with BEx Web Application Designer or SAP BusinessObjects Dashboards, or readers who are new to these tools. No pre-existing knowledge is required, as the book will explain every aspect of Design Studio in a step-by-step way, building up from easy-to-understand overview chapters to chapters that are dedicated to creating complex applications and building custom components.

Structure of the Book

This book is divided into five parts. Part I, Getting Started, begins with a broad overview of the Design Studio tool. In the first chapters, we introduce you to the product, compare it with other SAP products, and show several use case scenarios. We then walk you step-by-step through the installation procedure.

In Part II, The Basics, we go through every detail of the Design Studio application. First, we describe the application environment. Then we guide you through the general process of building an application. We then describe every available component and its properties in detail.

Once you have mastered the basics, we go into more depth about how you can enhance an application in Part III, Advanced Concepts. In this part of the book, we describe how to add interactivity, set up planning, format and enhance applications, and finally give you a set of guidelines for creating applications.

In Part IV, The Software Development Kit, we dive into creating custom components using an SDK in Design Studio. First, we show how to install ready-made components. Then we teach you how to set up your environment to create custom components. Finally, we provide the steps for creating a custom component.

In the final part of our book, Part V, Examples, we provide three example applications and the steps you need to build them. Our example applications include: a real-time production dashboard, a sales dashboard application, and an OLAP application built using a template.

Now that you have a general sense of the book's layout, the following addresses the topics covered in each individual chapter:

- **Chapter 1: Introduction to SAP BusinessObjects Design Studio**
  We start the book with a general introduction to Design Studio. We give a high-level overview of what the tool is, what application developers are able to do and build with the tool, and how Design Studio is positioned within the SAP business intelligence portfolio.

- **Chapter 2: SAP BusinessObjects Design Studio vs. SAP BusinessObjects Dashboards vs. BEx Web Application Designer**
  This chapter offers a discussion on how Design Studio differs from SAP BusinessObjects Dashboards and BEx Web Application Designer.

- **Chapter 3: Usage Scenarios**
  In this chapter, we walk through a variety of examples to show you how applications developed in Design Studio can be used in different business scenarios. Each scenario tells a story of an end user who is using an application designed for their particular role or task. The scenarios show that Design Studio is able to deliver process support in very different situations, varying from real-time operational support to in-depth strategic analysis.

- **Chapter 4: Installation and Configuration**
  After the broad overview chapters, we focus more on Design Studio itself. In order to get started with Design Studio, we take you through the steps to install and set up Design Studio within your SAP business intelligence environment. We also give an overview of Design Studio's architecture, discuss system

requirements, and explain how to gather all the installation material. The chapter ends with your first login with the Design Studio client tool.

▶ **Chapter 5: The Integrated Development Environment**
Once you've installed the Design Studio components and opened the Design Studio client tool for the first time, you will notice a whole lot of elements. This chapter explains Design Studio's integrated development environment, including the menus, toolbar, Layout Editor, and views for its components. After reading this chapter, you will be ready to dive into building applications.

▶ **Chapter 6: The Application Design Process**
This chapter introduces you to the general process of building a Design Studio application. It serves as a tutorial to guide you through the steps in creating a simple Design Studio application, and serves as a basis for the more detailed chapters that follow.

▶ **Chapter 7: Components and Properties**

In this chapter, we look at all the components and properties of Design Studio. Components are the building blocks of Design Studio, and an essential part of developing effective applications.

▶ **Chapter 8: Scripting for Interactivity**
In this chapter, we take it to the next level and introduce you to the scripting language you will use to create advanced interactive applications in Design Studio. We take a close look at the script language, and show examples of how to use these scripts in your applications.

▶ **Chapter 9: Planning Applications**
Design Studio can integrate planning scenarios into applications. This chapter will show how to include these scenarios into a Design Studio application. We take a look how to invoke automated planning functions and enable manual planning.

▶ **Chapter 10: Enhancing Applications with CSS**
There are many ways to improve formatting within an application. Design Studio applications can be enhanced using CSS. This chapter will show you the effect of applying standard themes in Design Studio. It will also teach you how to insert your own CSS, make applications responsive, and customize standard components.

- **Chapter 11: Design Principles and Visualization Methods**
  Before diving into the development of complex applications, we devote a chapter to the importance of user experience. In this chapter, we provide some general principles that will help you build applications that have a greater chance of actually being used by the user base. We also describe each Design Studio visualization method, and give tips for when these methods may or may not be appropriate.

- **Chapter 12: Using SDK Extensions in SAP BusinessObjects Design Studio**
  Design Studio has an SDK that allows for the design of custom extensions to enhance standard functionality. In this chapter, we will take pre-made SDK extensions, and walk through the steps to install an SDK component and how to make it available throughout the full SAP landscape.

- **Chapter 13: SDK Installation and Deployment**
  In this chapter, we will go through each step to install Eclipse and make it ready so we can create our own SDK components for Design Studio.

- **Chapter 14: Building Components Using the SDK**
  In this chapter, we are going to build a custom SDK extension. We'll introduce the SDK framework, programming languages, and building blocks. In the final section of this chapter, we will walk through the building process for a bullet graph.

- **Chapter 15: Building a Real-Time Production Dashboard**
  In Chapter 3, we described the usage scenario for a real-time production dashboard. In this chapter, we will guide you through the steps involved for designing and building this application. This chapter integrates many of the topics that you have already seen in this book, like setting up the data source, using scripts for interactivity, and CSS classes and styles. We will even show you how you can use one of the many available SDK components in Design Studio.

- **Chapter 16: Building a Sales Dashboard Application**
  In this chapter, we show a sales dashboard application that reports on worldwide sales. In this worldwide sales scenario, we track the sales data of seven global companies and their local markets.

- **Chapter 17: Building an OLAP Application Using a Template**
  OLAP applications are great applications for users who want to discover insights in their datasets by slicing and dicing through data and applying filters and calculations. In Chapter 3, we described such a scenario. In this chapter, we

Acknowledgments

First, I want to thank my co-authors Jeroen van der A and Dwain Chang for the very pleasant teamwork we had the past year creating this book. I also want to thank the SAP PRESS coordinators and editors Sarah Frazier and Kelly Weaver for all the great discussions on the content and the setup of the book.

Being able to write a book such as this also requires an environment that offers support and the necessary resources. A special word of thanks to Rob Huisman and Leon Huijsmans of our company Interdobs for doing absolutely everything possible to help us succeed in this project.

Of course, the SAP BI community on Twitter and the SAP Community Network shouldn't be forgotten. Here all the new ideas, solutions, and updates on SAP BusinessObjects Design Studio are shared and discussed (join us!).

Finally, I want to thank my girlfriend, Marieke, for all of her support.

Xavier Hacking

Writing a book is a journey that you cannot take alone. Over the last months, I relearned some of the lessons of the first book. Most importantly that you depend on the people around you.

I want to thank co-authors Dwain Chang and Xavier Hacking for undertaking this journey with me. Thanks for the dedication you guys showed in writing and reviewing.

I also want to thank my colleagues at Interdobs—especially Rob Huisman and Leon Huijsmans—who did everything they could to support us. We were also very fortunate that we could rely on René van Es for access to the demo systems when we needed them.

Finally, I want to thank my family, Susanne, Michael, and Tobias, who were all very supportive, even when I disappeared every weekend to continue writing the book. I owe my father-in-law Hans-Ludwig Wendler a special thanks. During the

Christmas holidays, I had to commandeer his work room to finalize the book and he generously allowed me to do so.

Jeroen van der A

I want to take this opportunity to say thank you to a couple of people who made this journey possible. First, my colleagues and co-authors of this book Jeroen and Xavier: Thank you for asking me to get involved in this project and for your valuable feedback and guidance over the last couple of months.

Thank you Rob Huisman and Leon Huijsmans at Interdobs for providing us the time and resources that we needed to complete this book. In addition, special thanks goes out to Sander van Gemert for doing the installation for us, when we were racing against our deadlines.

I would also like to thank Sarah Frazier for all of the good feedback she gave us on the chapters. Having now read all of them, I think she may know more about Design Studio then myself at this time. :)

And last, but not least, I want to say thank you to my dear family, Gisèle and baby Jamie. Thank you for your support, understanding, motivation, and most of all your patience.

Dwain Chang

PART I
Getting Started

Design Studio is a data visualization tool that allows you to create interactive applications with content ranging from high-level dashboards to very detailed OLAP analysis that can be run on any device.

1   Introduction to SAP BusinessObjects Design Studio

In this chapter, we provide a general introduction to Design Studio. We'll provide a high-level overview of what the tool is, what application developers are able to do and build with the tool, and how it should be positioned within the SAP BusinessObjects Business Intelligence (BI) portfolio. For users who are already familiar with previous versions of Design Studio, we list the most recent developments in Section 1.3.

Design Studio 1.6 is the latest major release of this relatively new tool. Design Studio was first released in November 2012 with releases following approximately every six months. Following the release of version 1.1 in June 2013, version 1.2 (November 2013), version 1.3 (May 2014), version 1.4 (November 2014), and version 1.5 (May 2015) were subsequently released. As of the writing of this book (February 2016), we are in version 1.6.

As you'll notice in this chapter and throughout this book, we refer to *applications* as the output from Design Studio. We don't use terms such as *reports* or *dashboards.* The reason for using this terminology is that the products or output you can create with Design Studio go far beyond the classic, standardized reports you're used to and that make up the majority of the documents in a business intelligence environment. These traditional reports are executed within reporting tools such as SAP Crystal Reports or SAP BusinessObjects Web Intelligence. In these tools, the report user has to know how to use the particular reporting tool in order to use the reports.

With Design Studio, you can create your own user experience by completely developing the user interface (UI) of your applications yourself. This means that you can keep the application as simple as you want by including only those interactivity elements (e.g., buttons or filters) that you really need in the UI. In addition, you can adjust the applications specifically to the devices with which the end user is working. An application interface should look different on an iPhone than on a desktop computer browser; for example, the iPhone application may need relatively bigger buttons to tap with your fingers, while the desktop computer browser version can be more detailed because you're using a cursor to navigate. On the other hand, you can add as many features (and as much complexity) as you want to! It's possible to create applications that consist of multiple tabs, pages, and/or layers that in turn are filled with multiple charts, tables, filters, and buttons that can trigger all sorts of interactive functionality. You can even include your own images to create an exact interface.

All these points are also true for dashboards, especially those created with SAP BusinessObjects Dashboards. However, the dashboards you create with this tool are only good at working with highly aggregated data. If you want to display or even process large amounts of data, you'll probably run into all kinds of performance problems. Design Studio doesn't have these limitations.

Shifting from reports to applications means that the work of a business intelligence developer is changing. It's moving away from creating reports that run within standard business intelligence tools and moving toward designing applications with completely independent and user-specific/purpose-specific interfaces. The developer should be well aware of how a user will deal with such an application interface when working with Design Studio.

Without further ado, let's get started. In this first chapter, we'll discuss three main topics: first, we'll explain what Design Studio is (Section 1.1); second, we'll talk about how Design Studio relates to the other products in the SAP BusinessObjects BI portfolio (Section 1.2); and, finally, we'll discuss some of the important recent developments that have taken place (Section 1.3). All the topics that are mentioned in this chapter will be discussed in more detail later in the book.

1.1 What Is SAP BusinessObjects Design Studio?

Design Studio is a tool that enables application designers to create analysis applications and dashboards based on the following data sources:

- SAP Business Warehouse (BW)
- SAP HANA
- Universes (UNXs)

Besides analysis applications, application designers can also create planning applications that support both manual and automated data entry and changes to data. With the use of a real-time package, application designers can create applications that have a real-time (push-based) or near real-time (pull-based) connection to the data source.

Following SAP's *mobility first* approach, Design Studio applications, which are created in an Eclipse-based application design environment, are fully HTML5-compatible and therefore can be executed on any device, whether it's a PC with a browser or a mobile device such as an iPad or iPhone.

In addition to allowing users to design analytic content that is centrally governable and that ranges in complexity from simple templates to feature-heavy applications, Design Studio also enables the building of applications that have built-in iPad support and are immediately compatible with standard web browsers and mobile devices (using HTML5). With Design Studio, application designers can easily create (drag and drop) interactive applications without any knowledge of HTML5 or iOS/Android programming. Figure 1.1 shows the integrated development environment (IDE). On the left, you see the component panel, where you can drag and drop components such as charts and filters. In the middle you see the preview of what your application will look like, and on the right, you see all the properties that can be set for a component that is selected. In Chapter 5, we'll discuss the IDE in more detail.

Design Studio can be used locally and can be integrated in the following platforms:

- SAP BusinessObjects BI
- SAP BW
- SAP HANA

1 | Introduction to SAP BusinessObjects Design Studio

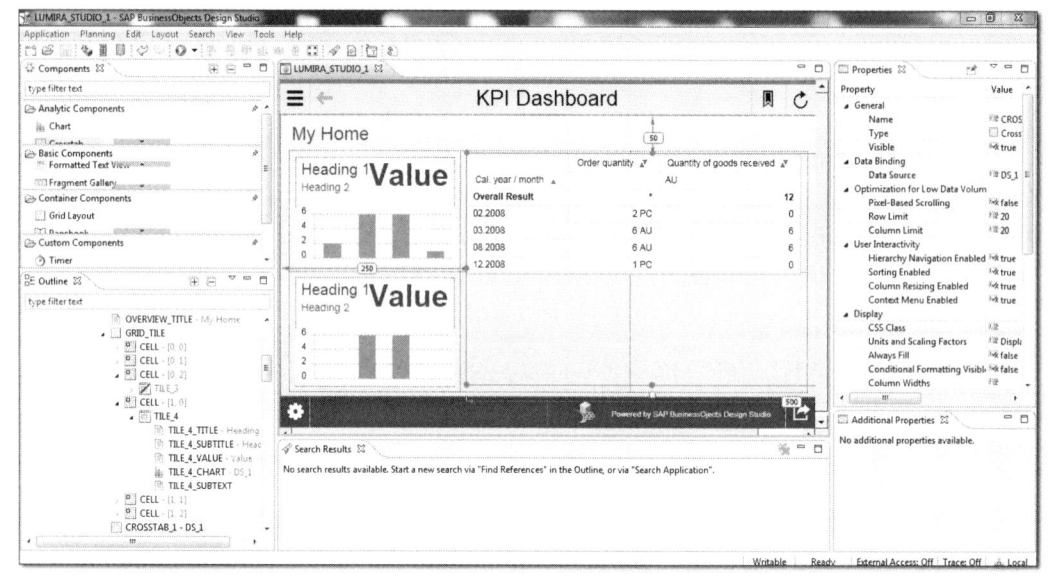

Figure 1.1 Design Studio Integrated Development Environment

1.1.1 Development Environment

The Design Studio development environment provides a what you see is what you get (WYSIWYG) toolset in which you can drag and drop the components that you want to use in an application and edit the layout with pixel-precise detail. This kind of toolset allows you to have a constant understanding of how the application is going to look, without having to execute and test the application in a browser or on a mobile device every time you make a change.

1.1.2 Components

A wide range of design components come pre-delivered with Design Studio. These components are the building blocks of your applications. Design Studio offers analytical components such as charts and tables to display and visualize data from data sources. Additionally, a number of filter, text, image, and button components can be used to add interactive features to the application. A set of container components are also available to group other components and to create applications with multiple pages. We'll discuss these components in more detail in Chapter 7.

In addition to these standard components, third-party developers can create their own components with the Design Studio software development kit (SDK). A lot of SDK components are already available, allowing for the creation of things such as new charts, connections to new data sources, and web services. In Part III of this book, we'll explain in more detail what you can do with the SDK in Design Studio. We'll also show you how to install and set up the SDK development environment as well as how you can create your own SDK components.

1.1.3 Data Sources and Platforms

As stated previously, Design Studio can be used with the SAP BusinessObjects BI platform, SAP BW, or SAP HANA.

When connected to an SAP BW environment, Design Studio can connect to SAP BW InfoProviders, BEx queries, and BEx query views. Applications can be saved to the SAP BW system and can be executed on the SAP BW Java stack.

When connected to an SAP BusinessObjects BI platform, Design Studio can use SAP BW data sources, as well as SAP HANA analytic and calculation views. These are defined on the SAP BusinessObjects BI platform in the OLAP CONNECTIONS screen. As of version 1.2, Design Studio also supports UNX as a data source. Created applications can be saved to the SAP BusinessObjects BI platform and executed from there.

When Design Studio is connected to SAP HANA, you can use analytical and calculation views as data sources. Also, the applications that you create in Design Studio are stored on the SAP HANA repository.

> **Local Scenarios**
>
> Design Studio can be used locally without a connection to a platform. Applications can then be run locally on the developer's computer for testing purposes. However, if you want to show data in those local apps, you still need a source system (SAP HANA or SAP BW) connected. Design Studio in local mode will use the connections that are defined on your computer, either in SAP Logon for SAP BW or in the ODBC Data Source Administrator for SAP HANA. We'll show you how to set this up in Chapter 4.

Once connected to a data source, the application developer has the option to change and format the output from within Design Studio. We'll discuss data sources in more detail in Chapter 6 and Chapter 7.

1.1.4 Scripting

Adding user interactivity to an application requires some scripting. Whenever the user performs a certain action, a script can be triggered to execute a specific task. For example, if the user clicks a button, a pop-up screen should appear on the application. With a little script in the BUTTON component, this functionality can be realized. As a scripting language, Design Studio uses a subset of JavaScript called the *BI Action Language* (BIAL). A wizard is included to help developers write these scripts in Design Studio. We'll discuss scripting in more detail in Chapter 8.

1.1.5 Cascading Style Sheets

Cascading Style Sheets (CSS) are developed to separate the layout and content in web page design. In Design Studio, you can use CSS in your applications. If you want to change the specific look of the components, custom CSS can be used to set, for example, the color and font size of a component. Such a CSS setup can even be used throughout the application for multiple components where the definition of the CSS class is maintained in a single place. These CSS files can be stored in a central location and be reused by multiple applications. We'll discuss the usage of CSS further in Chapter 10.

1.1.6 Templates and Themes

Design Studio comes with a set of predefined templates and themes for desktop, iPhone, and iPad applications; the goal here is to ease and quicken the development process. The *themes* influence the way components—and thus the applications—look. For example, in the mobile-specific theme, the components are designed to be pressed by fingers instead of clicked by a mouse.

Templates are preformatted Design Studio applications in which a layout is already defined and a number of components are included. These templates can be used as a starting point to develop a custom application. Figure 1.2 shows one of the ready-to-run templates in Design Studio.

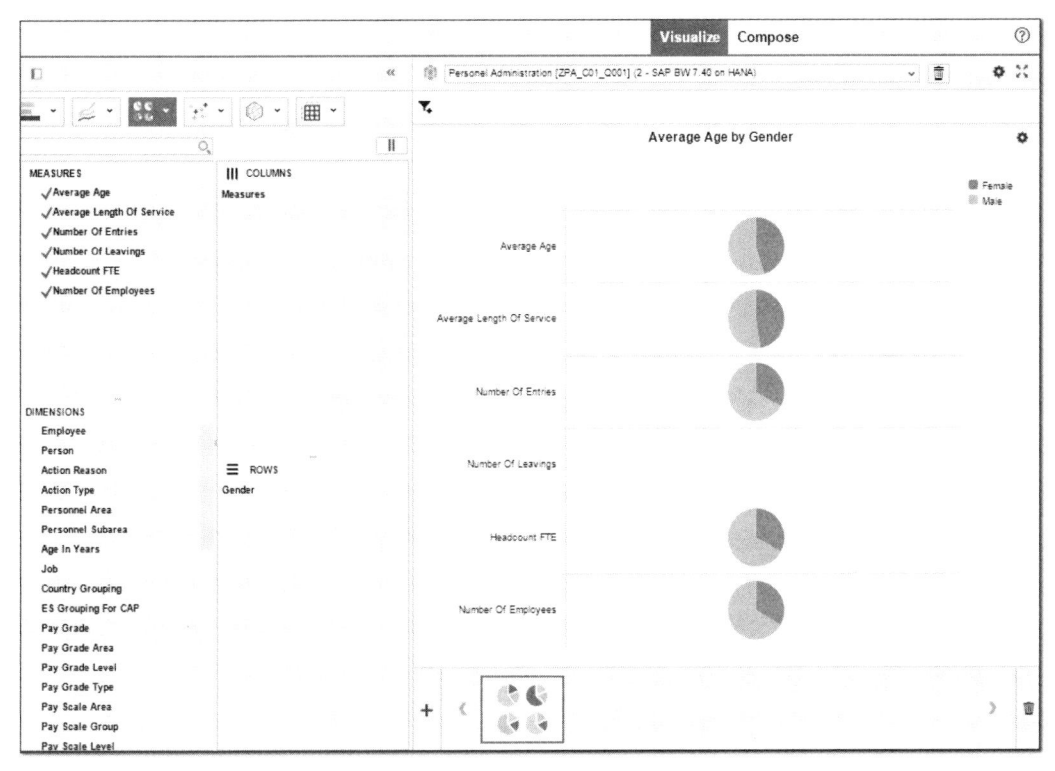

Figure 1.2 Design Studio iPad Template

1.1.7 Application Execution

As mentioned at the beginning of this section, in line with SAP's "mobility first" strategy, Design Studio applications are fully supported to run on mobile devices. You can run applications in a mobile web browser (Figure 1.3) by entering the URL of the application, or you can open them within the SAP BusinessObjects Mobile application (Figure 1.4). We'll discuss the SAP BusinessObjects Mobile application in Appendix B.

Using the Design Studio applications on a desktop computer is, of course, also possible. Applications can be started using the direct URL of the application or from within the SAP BusinessObjects BI Launch Pad portal environment.

1 | Introduction to SAP BusinessObjects Design Studio

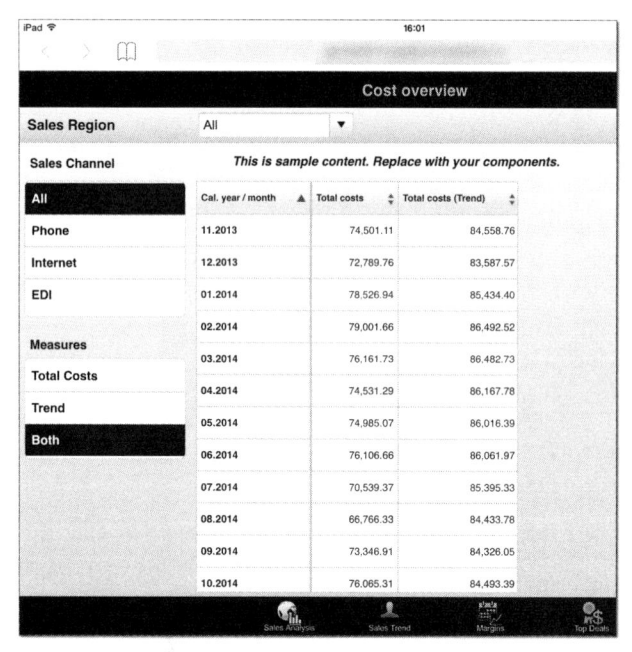

Figure 1.3 Design Studio Application Running in a Mobile Web Browser

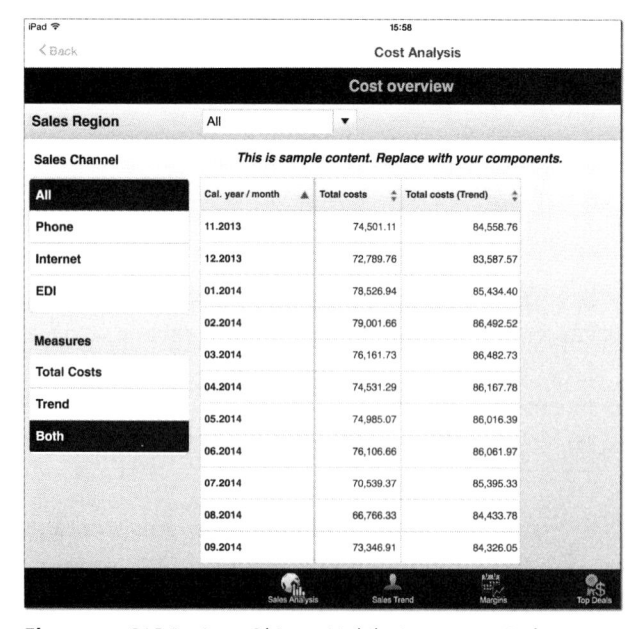

Figure 1.4 SAP BusinessObjects Mobile App on an iPad

1.2 SAP BusinessObjects Design Studio and Existing SAP BusinessObjects BI Environments

Since the acquisition of BusinessObjects by SAP in 2007, the SAP business intelligence frontend portfolio has changed dramatically. Before the acquisition, there were only a few options in the SAP BW toolset to present data from the SAP BW system to the end user. With BEx Analyzer, you could create workbooks in Microsoft Excel, and with BEx Web Analyzer, you could run BEx queries in a web-based environment. BEx Web Application Designer allowed you to develop interactive web applications based on SAP BW InfoProviders and BEx queries.

The SAP BusinessObjects BI portfolio added a set of new tools and brought in a complete business intelligence enterprise environment. This web-based platform integrates the SAP BusinessObjects BI tools and, with the BI Launch Pad, offers a single place for end users to create, store, and execute their reports. The new tools include the following:

- SAP Crystal Reports
- SAP BusinessObjects Web Intelligence
- SAP BusinessObjects Dashboards (formerly known as Xcelsius)
- SAP BusinessObjects Analysis, edition for Microsoft Office
- SAP BusinessObjects Analysis, edition for OLAP
- SAP BusinessObjects Explorer

However, SAP didn't stop with the BusinessObjects acquisition—it continues to broaden its analytical product suite. Since the introduction of SAP HANA, new tools such as SAP Lumira (formerly known as SAP Visual Intelligence) and SAP Predictive Analytics, which are able to use the power of SAP HANA, were presented. And now, last but not least, there is also the product that is the focus of this book: Design Studio.

Design Studio is being positioned as the premium successor to BEx Web Application Designer and BEx Web Analyzer. As you'll see in Chapter 2, Design Studio also has considerable overlap with SAP BusinessObjects Dashboards.

> **Note**
> SAP customers that currently have a license for SAP BusinessObjects Dashboards automatically have a license to use Design Studio as well.

37

1 | Introduction to SAP BusinessObjects Design Studio

In this section, we'll take the opportunity to put Design Studio in context with the rest of the SAP BusinessObjects BI portfolio. Specifically, we'll briefly discuss the purposes of the different SAP BusinessObjects BI tools and then talk about how these tools fulfill different content creation and consumption needs.

1.2.1 SAP BusinessObjects BI Tool Categories

The SAP BusinessObjects BI portfolio can be divided into four categories of tools:

- Reporting
- Discovery and analysis
- Dashboards and applications
- Microsoft Office integration

Figure 1.5 shows an overview of all the current tools and the future tool of use per category.

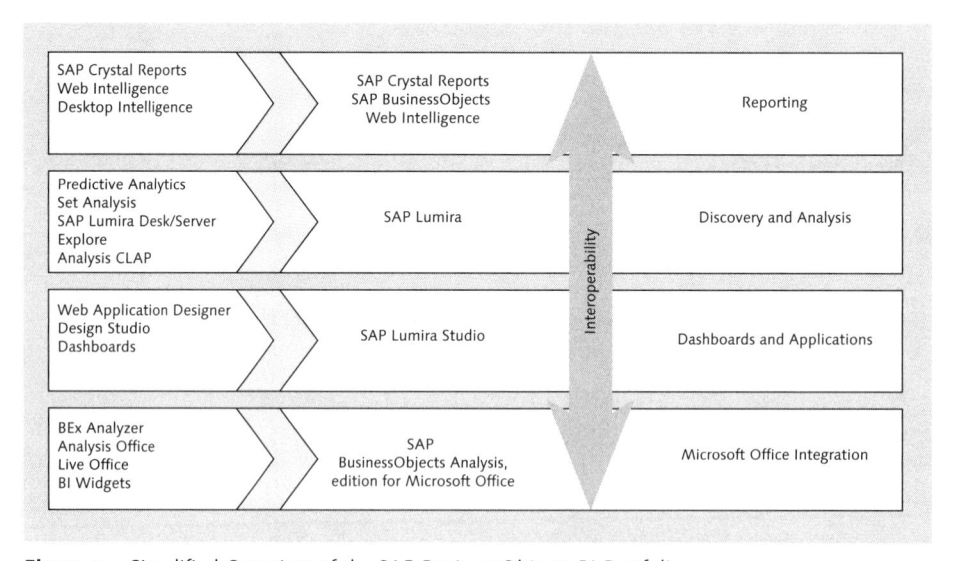

Figure 1.5 Simplified Overview of the SAP BusinessObjects BI Portfolio

Reporting Tools

The purpose of reporting is to share information, which includes distributing information across an organization, giving users the ability to ask and answer questions, and building printable reports.

SAP BusinessObjects Design Studio and Existing SAP BusinessObjects BI Environments | **1.2**

The reporting tools in the SAP BusinessObjects BI portfolio are SAP BusinessObjects Web Intelligence and SAP Crystal Reports. With these two tools, standard, highly formatted, pixel-perfect reports can be created. End users can refresh and distribute these reports from the BI Launch Pad platform or schedule them to do this automatically. Using SAP BusinessObjects Web Intelligence, users can create their own reports based on UNX or BEx queries to which they have access.

Whereas SAP Crystal Reports is more focused on delivering predefined, highly formatted reports that present very detailed information, SAP BusinessObjects Web Intelligence offers a more self-service approach that allows the end user to create and edit reports in an ad hoc way. Figure 1.6 shows an example of a highly standardized report created with SAP Crystal Reports.

Figure 1.6 SAP Crystal Reports Report

39

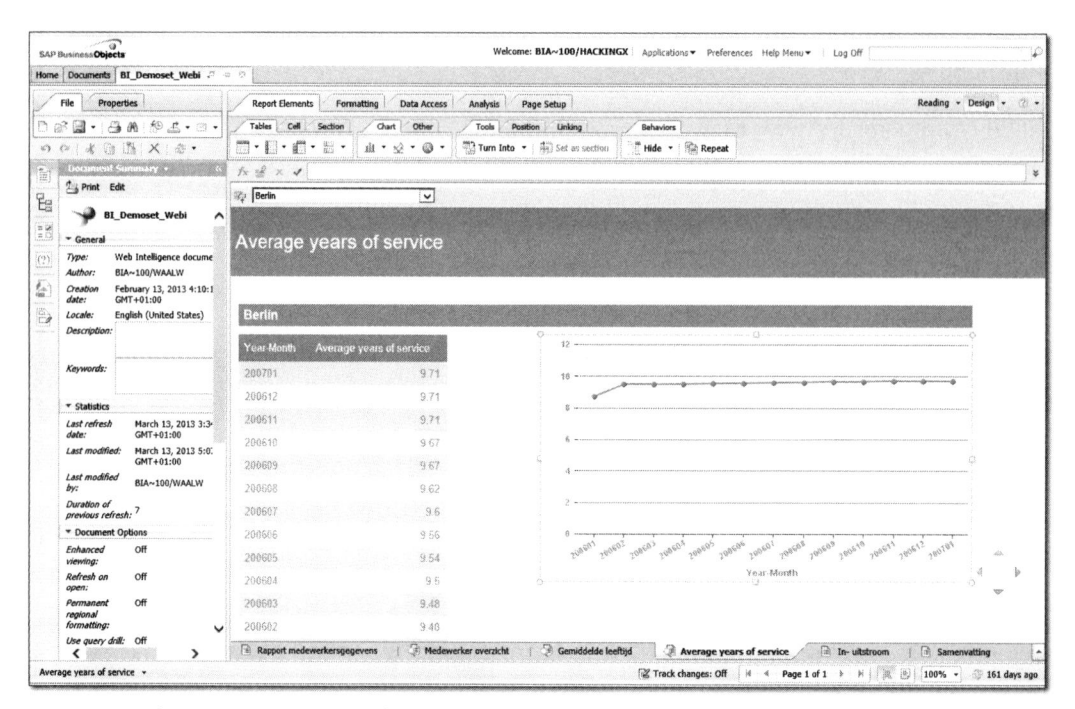

1 | Introduction to SAP BusinessObjects Design Studio

Figure 1.7 shows an example of an SAP BusinessObjects Web Intelligence report.

Figure 1.7 SAP BusinessObjects Web Intelligence Report

Discovery and Analysis

The purpose of discovery and analysis is to discover, predict, and create. The discovery and analysis category in the SAP BusinessObjects BI portfolio consists of four tools: SAP Lumira; SAP BusinessObjects Explorer; SAP BusinessObjects Analysis, edition for Microsoft Office; SAP BusinessObjects Analysis, edition for OLAP; and SAP Predictive Analytics. These tools give end users the freedom to perform their own analyses. The user starts with a set of data and some questions about that data and uses the tool to find and eventually present the answers.

SAP Lumira is a locally installed tool that can connect to several types of data sources, such as SAP HANA and CSV files. It offers an interface to select, clean, combine, manipulate, and enrich data from multiple data sources and finally visualize it with tables and charts. SAP Predictive Analytics (Figure 1.8) has a similar looking UI. With SAP Predictive Analytics, you can perform various statistical methods to gain hidden insights into your dataset.

40

1.2 SAP BusinessObjects Design Studio and Existing SAP BusinessObjects BI Environments

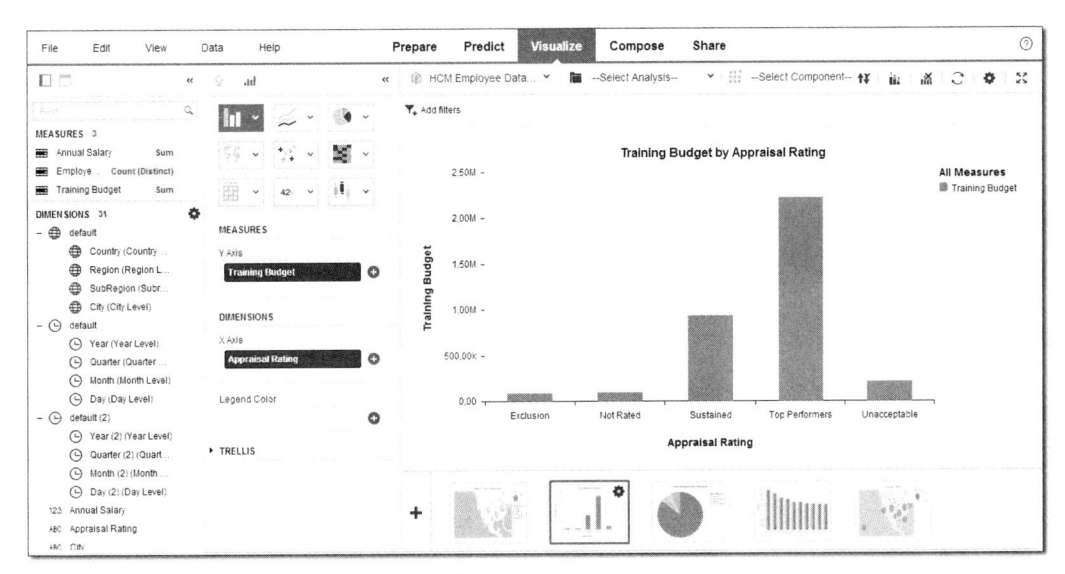

Figure 1.8 SAP Predictive Analytics User Interface

SAP BusinessObjects Explorer is an easy-to-use, web-based environment that allows you to retrieve answers to your business questions from corporate data quickly (Figure 1.9).

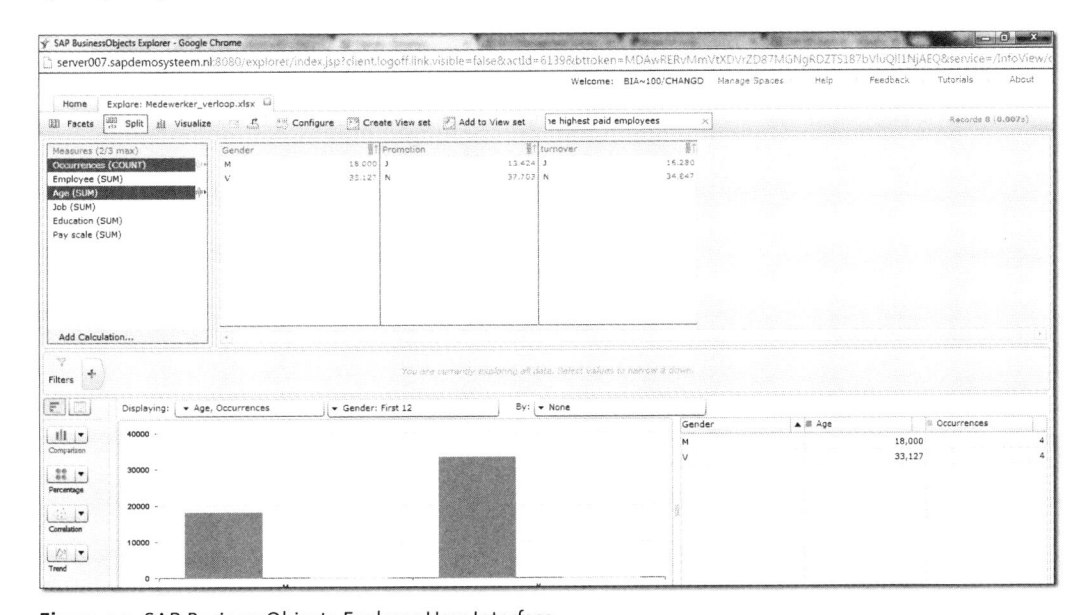

Figure 1.9 SAP BusinessObjects Explorer User Interface

41

1 | Introduction to SAP BusinessObjects Design Studio

SAP BusinessObjects Analysis is the successor to BEx Analyzer and is the tool used to perform OLAP analyses on multidimensional data sources such as SAP BW InfoCubes (Figure 1.10). The product is delivered in a Microsoft Office and a web-based variant. The Microsoft Office version integrates this reporting tool in Microsoft Excel and Microsoft PowerPoint; the web-based variant is integrated in the BI Launch Pad.

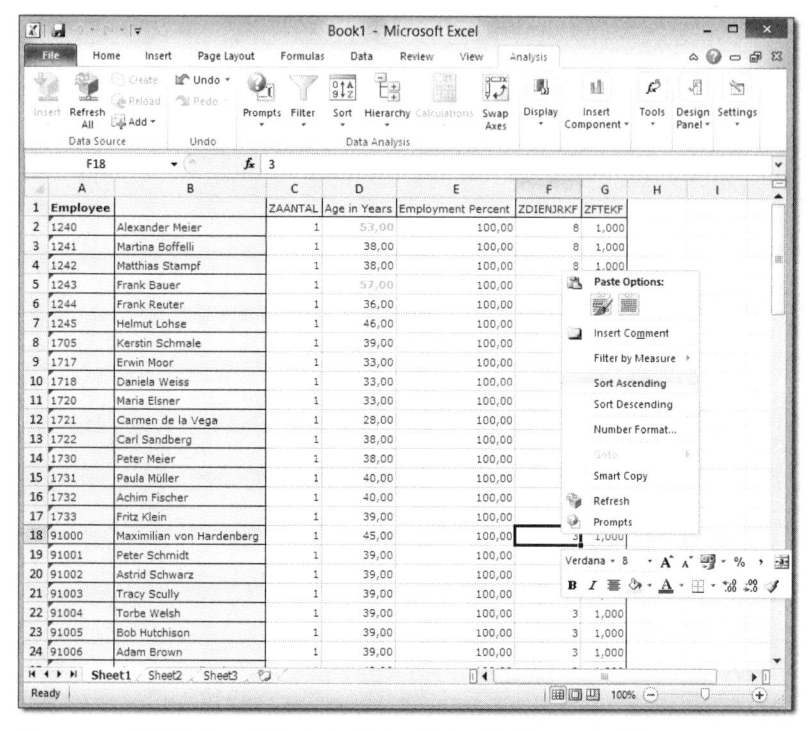

Figure 1.10 SAP BusinessObjects Analysis, Edition for Microsoft Office

SAP BusinessObjects Set Analysis enables organizations to define sets and track their success and contribution to overall performance. It also offers the following:

- Ease of segmentation
- Set membership tracking to help you monitor set growth
- Analytic templates to help you understand set behavior and contribution to business performance
- The ability to turn analysis into action so you have the information you need for effective decision making

Dashboard and Application Creation Tools

Dashboards and applications are used to build engaging experiences. This includes delivering the right information to users, tracking key performance indicators (KPIs) and summarizing data, and building custom experiences that suit a user's needs.

The dashboarding and application category includes Design Studio and SAP BusinessObjects Dashboards. With SAP BusinessObjects Dashboards, you can create highly visualized dashboards, showing data with a high level of aggregation. Such a dashboard might, for example, display the company's or department's KPIs. Dashboards created with SAP BusinessObjects Dashboards have a fixed layout and can't be edited by the end user. Just as with Design Studio, the complete interface has to be designed by the dashboard developer. Figure 1.11 shows an example of a dashboard created with SAP BusinessObjects Dashboards.

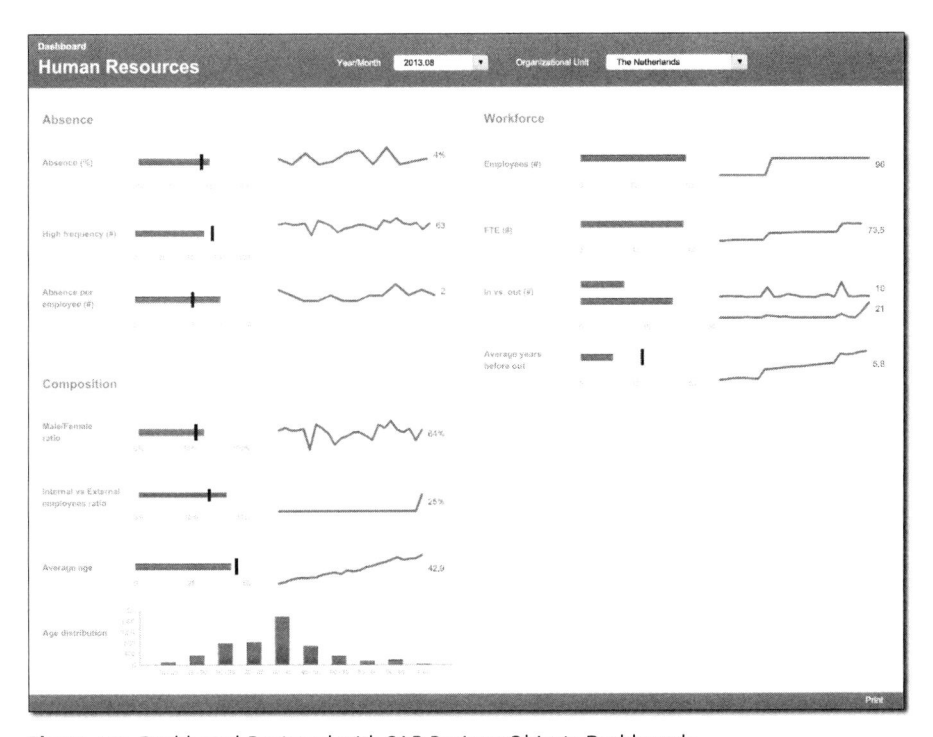

Figure 1.11 Dashboard Designed with SAP BusinessObjects Dashboards

In Chapter 2, we'll discuss SAP BusinessObjects Dashboards in more depth and compare it to the functionality available in Design Studio.

Microsoft Office Integration

Microsoft Office integration tools are usually Excel plug-in tools that allow you to consume various SAP BusinessObjects BI data sources, such as BEx queries and SAP HANA views. These tools allow the user to perform easy analyses on the data, usually by dragging and dropping dimensions and key figures into rows or columns in Excel.

The following tools are classified as Microsoft Office integration tools:

- BEx Analyzer
- SAP BusinessObjects Analysis, edition for Microsoft Office (also mentioned as a discovery and analysis tool)
- SAP BusinessObjects Live Office
- SAP BusinessObjects BI widgets (this is actually an OS integration tool, as widgets can be consumed straight from your desktop)

SAP is currently positioning SAP BusinessObjects Analysis, edition for Microsoft Office, as the current Microsoft Office integration tool.

1.2.2 Content Creation and Consumption

As you may already have noticed in the previous section, not all tools are used by end users. Table 1.1 shows this clear distinction, where the very fixed reporting outputs (e.g., the SAP Crystal Reports documents, the dashboards from SAP BusinessObjects Dashboards, and the Design Studio applications) are completely created by developers from the IT department. The business users work with the other tools to create their own reports and make custom analyses on their own.

SAP determines four levels of business users: executive, senior management, business analysis, and individual contributors. In Table 1.2, the products that present more aggregated data in a fixed way are toward the top of the table, and the products that provide more detailed and ad hoc reporting solutions are on the bottom. The broad scope of Design Studio is clearly highlighted here—as you can see, the solution is mentioned for all the user groups in the dashboarding and applications segment, as well as the top two user groups in the discovery and analysis segment.

	Reporting	Dashboarding and Applications	Discovery and Analysis
IT	SAP Crystal Reports	▶ Design Studio ▶ SAP BusinessObjects Dashboards	Design Studio
Business Users	SAP BusinessObjects Web Intelligence	Exploration views	▶ SAP BusinessObjects Analysis ▶ SAP BusinessObjects Explorer ▶ SAP Lumira

Table 1.1 Content Creators by Category

	Reporting	Dashboarding and Applications	Discovery and Analysis
Executives	None	▶ Design Studio ▶ SAP BusinessObjects Dashboards ▶ Exploration views	▶ Design Studio ▶ SAP BusinessObjects Explorer
Senior Management	SAP BusinessObjects Web Intelligence	▶ Design Studio ▶ SAP BusinessObjects Dashboards ▶ Exploration views	▶ Design Studio ▶ SAP BusinessObjects Explorer ▶ SAP BusinessObjects Analysis
Business Analysts	None	Design Studio	▶ SAP BusinessObjects Explorer ▶ SAP BusinessObjects Analysis ▶ SAP Lumira
Individual Contributors	▶ SAP Crystal Reports ▶ SAP BusinessObjects Web Intelligence	Design Studio	SAP BusinessObjects Analysis, edition for Microsoft Office

Table 1.2 Content Consumption by Category

Table 1.3 shows the various options for content consumption environments and the SAP BusinessObjects BI tools. The options are a desktop computer with a local installation of the tool, a web-based version of the report through the BI Launch Pad, and a mobile device. As you can see, almost all the solutions offer reports that are accessible through mobile devices with SAP BusinessObjects Mobile, which is available for iOS and Android devices.

	Reporting	Dashboarding and Applications	Discovery and Analysis
Desktop	▸ SAP Crystal Reports ▸ SAP BusinessObjects Web Intelligence	SAP BusinessObjects Dashboards	▸ SAP BusinessObjects Analysis, edition for Microsoft Office ▸ SAP Lumira
Web-Based	▸ SAP Crystal Reports ▸ SAP BusinessObjects Web Intelligence	▸ Design Studio ▸ SAP BusinessObjects Dashboards ▸ Exploration views	▸ Design Studio ▸ SAP BusinessObjects Explorer ▸ SAP BusinessObjects Analysis, edition for OLAP
Mobile	▸ SAP Crystal Reports ▸ SAP BusinessObjects Web Intelligence	▸ Design Studio ▸ SAP BusinessObjects Dashboards ▸ Exploration views	▸ Design Studio ▸ SAP BusinessObjects Explorer

Table 1.3 Content Consumption Environment by Category

1.3 Recent Developments

Design Studio has developed rapidly over the past couple of years. The most notable developments are listed here:

▸ **Updated charts and additional chart properties**
Users now have access to many more charts, as compared to version 1.0 of Design Studio. Design Studio allows you to customize almost every property of the available charts, from line sizes and colors to font sizes and colors. We'll discuss these properties further in Chapter 7.

- **All new components**
  Application designers can now use brand-new components such as SPREADSHEET, SCORECARD, and TREE.

- **Application behavior**
  The application designer can make the application remember the navigation steps, so that the end user can undo his steps in the application. We'll explain how this option can be used in Chapter 5.

- **Calculations**
  You now have the ability to calculate measures with the existing measures in your data source. You can use one measure to calculate the share of the total value, or you can use two measures to perform simple calculations such as multiplying and dividing.

- **Filter by measure**
  End users can apply filters on measures during the runtime of an application. For instance, an end user can apply a Top or Bottom 10 filter on a specific measure.

- **Bookmarking**
  End users can save bookmarks (navigation states) of the application. The benefit of this is that users can set their own filter values and save the application in this state. The next time the user opens the application, it won't be necessary to apply all the filters again.

- **Global scripts**
  Code can be centralized in global scripts. Scripting will be discussed in Chapter 8.

- **Integrated Planning**
  It's now possible to use Integrated Planning (IP) in applications. We'll look at a detailed scenario in Chapter 9.

- **Brand-new (analysis) templates**
  The application designer can make use of new templates to get a quick start when creating a new application. For instance, with the Generic Analysis template, you can easily create an OLAP application. We'll go into more detail on this in Chapter 16.

- **New component library**
  Application designers can choose from two component libraries: the SAPUI5 library, which is the common library that is also used in previous versions of

Design Studio, or the SAPUI5 m library, which looks and feels more like SAP Fiori and is developed with mobility in mind.

- **Parallel processing**
A huge new feature is the ability to process multiple data sources in parallel. This feature wasn't available until version 1.5, and it will boost applications with multiple data sources dramatically. In Chapter 7, where we discuss data sources and their properties, we'll show you how to use this option.

- **Better prompt handling**
Previously, when a value was set for a BEx variable, all the queries would be executed using that variable. It's now possible to "unmerge" variables. The benefit of this is that the application designer can now control the data sources that need to be refreshed when a variable value changes.

1.4 Summary

In this chapter, we provided a high-level introduction to Design Studio. We went through the most important features of the tool, discussed its position within the SAP BusinessObjects BI portfolio, and outlined many of its recent developments.

Because Design Studio has such a great overlap with SAP BusinessObjects Dashboards and BEx Web Application Designer, the next chapter is dedicated to comparing these three applications.

Design Studio isn't the only option in the SAP BusinessObjects BI portfolio to create interactive apps. In fact, there are three! It's time to introduce them to you and make some comparisons.

2   SAP BusinessObjects Design Studio vs. SAP BusinessObjects Dashboards vs. BEx Web Application Designer

The number of tools in the SAP BusinessObjects Business Intelligence (BI) portfolio increased significantly over the past couple of years, and, inevitably, some tools contain features that are also included in other tools. Because the objective of Design Studio overlaps with two of SAP's existing products, it's important to identify the differences among the three.

This chapter offers a discussion of how Design Studio is different from SAP BusinessObjects Dashboards and BEx Web Application Designer. If you're already familiar with the basic functionality of SAP BusinessObjects Dashboards and BEx Web Application Designer, you'll want to skip down to Section 2.3 for an understanding of how they differ from Design Studio. If you're new to the toolset or would like a quick refresher, you can read Section 2.1 and Section 2.2 for an overview of their functionalities.

2.1   SAP BusinessObjects Dashboards

Since the acquisition of BusinessObjects by SAP in 2007, SAP BusinessObjects Dashboards has been a core part of the SAP BusinessObjects BI portfolio. With SAP BusinessObjects Dashboards, you can create dashboards with great-looking data visualizations and design interactive scenarios without much programming knowledge.

2 | Design Studio vs. Dashboards vs. BEx Web Application Designer

Dashboards are visual displays of information that are able to support the user of the dashboard in making decisions (Figure 2.1).

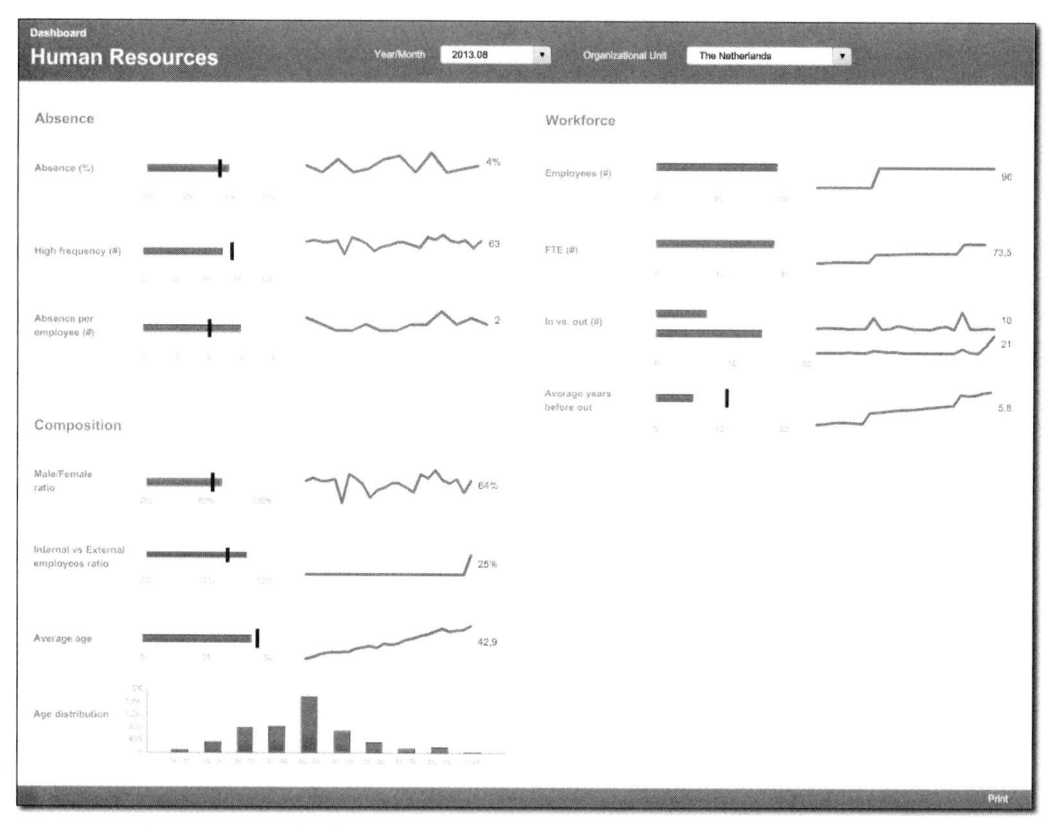

Figure 2.1 Example of a Dashboard Created with SAP BusinessObjects Dashboards

The user should be able to see this information at a glance, without having to perform many manual activities (clicks) before he can find the information he is looking for. Therefore, a dashboard should focus on only those performance indicators that are relevant for the user to make a certain decision. A dashboard can be used, for example, to provide a sales manager with a high-level overview of sales performance over time for all the sales regions. He can compare regions with each other, discover the high and low performers, see trends over time, and so on. Such a dashboard might trigger the sales manager to take action in a specific region if sales were headed in the wrong direction.

A dashboard shows the course of a dataset over a certain time period in a series of performance indicators. To visualize the data, dashboards use components such as charts, tables, gauges, and maps. Colors can be used to separate data series from each other or to highlight a certain result (alerting). Some basic level of drilling down and filtering data is provided in a dashboard; however, a lot of the information is fixed. Other reporting tools are often more suited for highly detailed reporting, data analysis, and data exploration.

Interactive scenarios—often referred to as *what-if scenarios*—let the user interact with the dashboard by adjusting one or more variables to see how the output changes. A simple example is a dashboard that can calculate the monthly interest payments on a mortgage loan. There are three variables in the formula to calculate the monthly payment: the loan amount, the interest rate, and the repayment period. The dashboard can, for example, consist of three input controls—let's say some sliders—to input the values for these variables. The monthly payment amount can be displayed in a gauge. When the user moves any of the sliders, the payment amount changes too, based on the underlying data model (formula). Increasing the interest rate will also increase the monthly payment amount.

In this section, we'll give you a brief overview of SAP BusinessObjects Dashboards by walking you through some of the most important things you should know about the tool. Again, if you're already familiar with the SAP BusinessObjects Dashboards tool, skip on ahead.

2.1.1 Setting Up a Dashboard

Developing a basic dashboard with SAP BusinessObjects Dashboards is straightforward and doesn't require much knowledge or training to get started. It's all about dragging and dropping the components—charts or maps—in the right place, tweaking the look and feel of the components, and using some Microsoft Excel magic to connect the data to these components. Yes, you read that right: Excel. Before SAP changed the product name to SAP BusinessObjects Dashboards, the tool was called Xcelsius, which—you may notice—sounds a lot like Excel. In fact, SAP BusinessObjects Dashboards was originally developed to turn Excel spreadsheets into interactive dashboards with visualizations that couldn't be provided with standard Excel charts. Even in the current version of SAP BusinessObjects Dashboards, the Excel spreadsheet still has a very important position.

Figure 2.2 shows the SAP BusinessObjects Dashboards design environment, including the Excel spreadsheet. Not only can this spreadsheet fill cells with data, but it also enables the use of a wide range of Excel formulas. This means you can make calculations, use if/then statements, and look up values (i.e., with the `VLOOKUP` formula). These formulas stay active when you run the dashboard. Therefore, if a value in a certain spreadsheet cell changes, it will have a direct effect on the outcome of any formula that uses this cell.

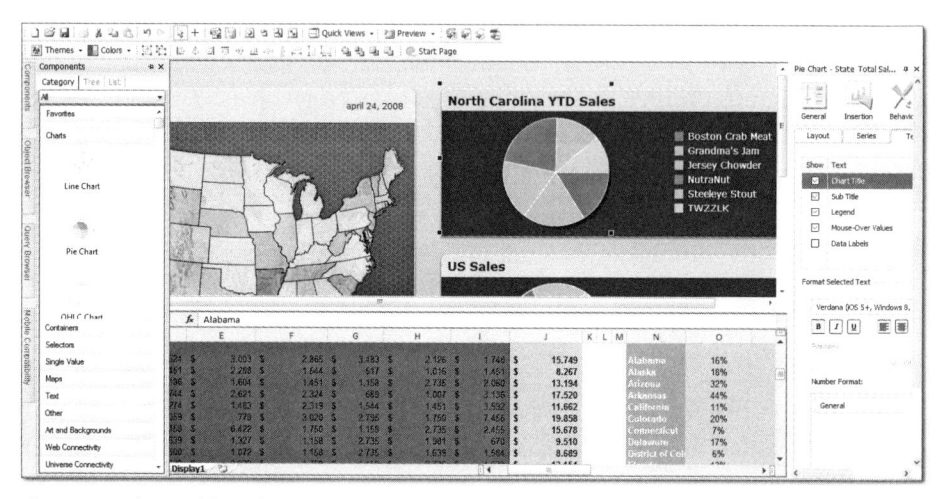

Figure 2.2 The Dashboard Design Environment

Handy features such as formatting and multiple spreadsheet tabs are also available, just as in the actual Excel software.

The left side of the screen shows a list of all available components. To use a component, you can simply drag it to the canvas in the middle of the screen and use the mouse to adjust the size and the position of the component.

On the right side of the screen are the properties of the selected component. Here the developer can connect the component to the data that are put into the spreadsheet. After executing this *data binding*, the component—in the case of Figure 2.2, a MAP and LINE CHART component—will put the dataset in a visual format. The trick is that you can change the values of the bound cells to make the dashboard interactive. In the PROPERTY tabs, you can use a legion of settings and tweaks on the component, such as adding labels and titles and setting up the formatting and positioning for these text items. Furthermore, you can adjust the look and feel of the component in terms of color and size (i.e., thickness of lines and markers). You can even activate alerts on a certain group of components. With these alerts, the color of a country on a map or a bar in a bar chart can change based on the value it represents; for example, good results can be shown as green, while bad results can be shown in red.

2.1.2 Components

SAP BusinessObjects Dashboards comes with a large set of standard components. Let's go through them so you get an understanding of the visualization and interactivity possibilities this tool offers.

Charts

The following standard chart types are available. These charts work more or less in the same way and have the same properties overall:

- Area chart
- Bar and column chart
- Line chart
- Pie chart
- Column chart
- Stacked area chart
- Stacked column chart
- Stacked bar chart
- Combination chart (both lines and columns are possible)

In addition to these charts, a number of more advanced charts are available to choose from. These charts are unique in their purpose and setup:

- Bubble plot
- Candlestick chart
- Horizontal and vertical bullet chart
- Marimekko chart
- Open High Low Close (OHLC) chart

- Radar chart and Filled radar chart
- Scatter plot (previously known as XY chart)
- Sparkline chart
- Tree map
- Waterfall chart

Selectors

Selectors provide interactivity options to set filters on data, make selections, push a certain value to a spreadsheet cell, or create menus in the dashboard user interface. The following selector components are available for these purposes:

- Accordion menu
- Checkbox
- Combo box
- Filter
- Fisheye picture menu
- Hierarchical table
- Icon
- Label-based menu
- List box
- List builder
- List view
- Play selector
- Push button
- Radio button
- Scorecard
- Sliding picture menu
- Spreadsheet table
- Ticker
- Toggle button

Single Value

Single value components are used to display or input single values of data. For this purpose, SAP BusinessObjects Dashboards delivers a set of dials, gauges, horizontal and vertical progress bars, and single and dual sliders.

Maps

One of the most interesting categories of components is the maps category. Map components create models with geographical representations that can display data by region. Each map is subdivided into regions, and for each region, a mouseover value can be shown. The user can also click on a region to explore the data in more detail. When activating alerts, you can color the regions based on their performance.

Containers, Text, Art, and Background

Container components can contain multiple other components. When you move the container, all components within this container move as well. SAP BusinessObjects Dashboards has three containers: the panel container, which is a panel with a title on top; the tab set container, which has multiple tabs with panels; and the canvas container, which is invisible when the dashboard is running but can be handy during development.

You can use text components to add labels and allow users to add text to the model. The three text components that are available are INPUT TEXT AREA, LABEL, and INPUT TEXT.

Art components provide visual enhancements to your model. You can use the following components: BACKGROUND, ELLIPSE, IMAGE COMPONENT, LINE, and RECTANGLE.

Other Components

Besides all the categories of components already mentioned, a set of more specific components is included. Examples include the PRINT button, the URL button, a TREND icon, and a CALENDAR component.

After going through this list of components, it should be clear that SAP BusinessObjects Dashboards offers a wide range of data visualization and interactivity features to tackle most dashboarding challenges.

2.1.3 Data Connectivity

We already talked a bit about the role of the Excel spreadsheet in SAP BusinessObjects Dashboards. But in a business environment, you want a dashboard or report to show fresh or even live data directly loaded from a business system or a data warehouse such as SAP Business Warehouse (BW)—and, of course, without having to perform repetitive manual activities every time the dashboard needs updated data. Therefore, using Excel to store the data and upload it into a dashboard isn't a workable solution.

SAP BusinessObjects Dashboards comes with a number of connectivity options to load data from a data source into the dashboard. In the Data Manager, the following connection types can be set up with data sources:

- SAP BW connection (Business Intelligence Consumer Services [BICS]) to a BEx query or BEx query view
- Universe published as a web service query (Query as a Web Service [QaaWS])
- Web service connection
- XML data and Excel XML maps
- Flash variables
- Portal data
- LiveCycle Data Services (LCDS) connections
- External interface connection
- SAP BusinessObjects Live Office connections
- Web Dynpro Flash Island

These connections can read values for variables from spreadsheet cells and return the output of the data request to a range of cells in the spreadsheet. From there, the data can be further processed and eventually be bound to the components.

In addition to these connectivity options, SAP BusinessObjects Dashboards also supports the creation and usage of SAP BusinessObjects BI 4.x queries. These queries correspond with the SAP BusinessObjects BI 4.x queries that can be created in the other SAP BusinessObjects BI tools such as SAP BusinessObjects Web Intelligence and SAP Crystal Reports for Enterprise. They also use the same workflow. SAP BusinessObjects UNX and SAP BW BEx queries can be used as data sources.

The big advantage here is that the query results can be bound directly to the components, without having to use the spreadsheet. In the SAP BusinessObjects BI 4.x query, one or more filters with prompts can be created. With the QUERY PROMPT SELECTOR component, the dashboard user can change the input value for such a prompt.

2.1.4 Publishing

When the dashboard is finished, it's published so the users can start using it from their own computers. To do this, you have to export the dashboard from the design environment. This export results in an SWF (Flash) file. If the dashboard developer exports the dashboard locally (on his own computer hard drive), the file can also be embedded into a PDF, Microsoft PowerPoint, Microsoft Word or Microsoft Outlook file, an HTML website, or an Adobe Air application. A nonembedded SWF file can run with a browser that has Adobe Flash Player installed.

Besides exporting locally and distributing the exported file, you can publish the dashboard to the SAP BW environment and the SAP BusinessObjects BI 4.x platform. When published to the SAP BW environment, the dashboard becomes an object that can run from the SAP BW Java portal, in the same way that you can execute BEx queries as web queries. The dashboard can run from a web URL address. When published to the SAP BusinessObjects BI platform, the dashboard will be available in the BI Launch Pad.

Adobe Flash has become a huge barrier to running dashboards on mobile platforms and devices such as the iPad because they don't support Flash, and there are no signs that they will in the near future. With the release of SAP BusinessObjects BI 4.0 SP 05, it's now possible to export a dashboard into HTML5 format. This HTML5 dashboard can be run from SAP BusinessObjects Mobile, which is available for Apple iOS and Android. In SAP BusinessObjects Dashboards 4.1 SP 06, not all components can be exported into the HTML5 format yet. All query browser connections can be used, as well as web service query and flash variables.

2.1.5 SDK

The SAP BusinessObjects Dashboards software development kit (SDK) enables Adobe Flex developers to create components for SAP BusinessObjects Dashboards.

2 | Design Studio vs. Dashboards vs. BEx Web Application Designer

These *add-ons* can provide additional functionality to SAP BusinessObjects Dashboards on top of the default set of components and connectivity options.

In previous years, a small number of third parties provided a number of interesting add-ons. There are add-ons available that achieve additional connectivity options, for example, to load data from CSV files, SAP BusinessObjects Web Intelligence reports, or Salesforce.com accounts. Other add-ons provide more advanced data visualization possibilities, such as adding more specific charts to the list of components, and adding a Google Maps integration component (see Figure 2.3). There is even a specific add-on available with advanced dashboard printing features.

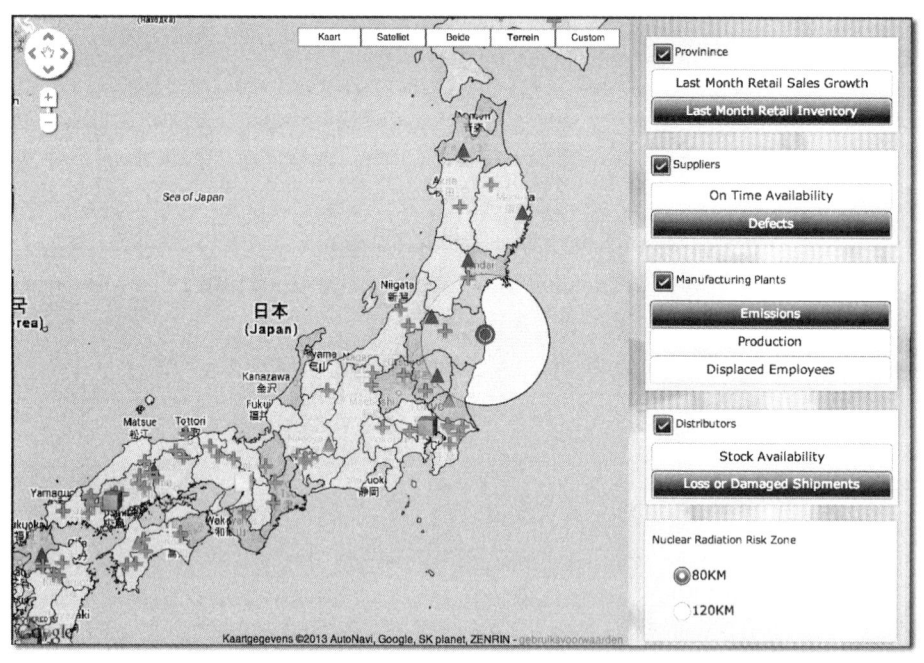

Figure 2.3 Dashboard Created with SAP BusinessObjects Dashboards and the Google Maps Plugin Add-On

2.2 BEX Web Application Designer

BEx Web Application Designer is part of the SAP Business Explorer (BEx) toolset and is used to create web applications. Figure 2.4 shows an example of such an application. You can compare these web applications to the BEx Web Analyzer workbooks that are created with the BEx Web Analyzer. This tool is based on the same principles, only now the report/application runs not as an Excel workbook, but as an HTML web application in a web browser.

A web application can contain objects such as analysis tables, charts, or maps to present data. Buttons can be used to create a navigation menu to control which objects should be shown or hidden. With the help of filter and navigation panes, the data can be filtered and the layout can be adjusted.

An example of a web application is the standard template that used when executing a BEx query in BEx Web Analyzer (see Figure 2.4). BEx Web Analyzer is actually a BEx Web Application Designer template (0ANALYSIS_PATTERN) offering an analysis table, a navigation pane, a series of buttons with functionalities such as exporting to Excel and opening another report, and a dropdown box to switch between an analysis table and a chart.

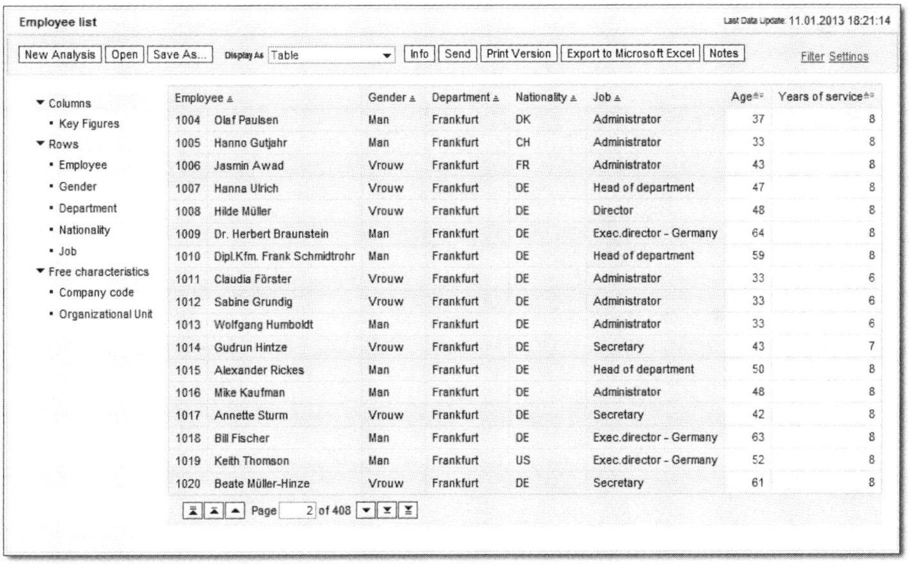

Figure 2.4 Bex Web Analyzer

In this section, we'll give you a brief overview of BEx Web Application Designer by walking you through some of the most important things you should know about the tool. As with SAP BusinessObjects Dashboards, if you're already familiar with BEx Web Application Designer, skip on ahead.

59

2.2.1 Setting Up a Web Application Template

Let's have a look at BEx Web Application Designer to get some basic knowledge of how this tool works. BEx Web Application Designer looks a bit like the development environment of SAP BusinessObjects Dashboards (see Figure 2.5). On the left, there is a list of available web items dragged into the web application layout. In contrast to adding components to the SAP BusinessObjects Dashboards canvas from the components list, here it isn't possible to place a web item precisely where you want it. If you add a second web item, it's positioned right next to the first component. To adjust the positioning of the web items, you can use special container web items. You can also add HTML tables in which to arrange web items. (Note that it's quite a challenge to create advanced application layouts.) A web application is saved as a web template, and the result of these actions is saved in a web template object.

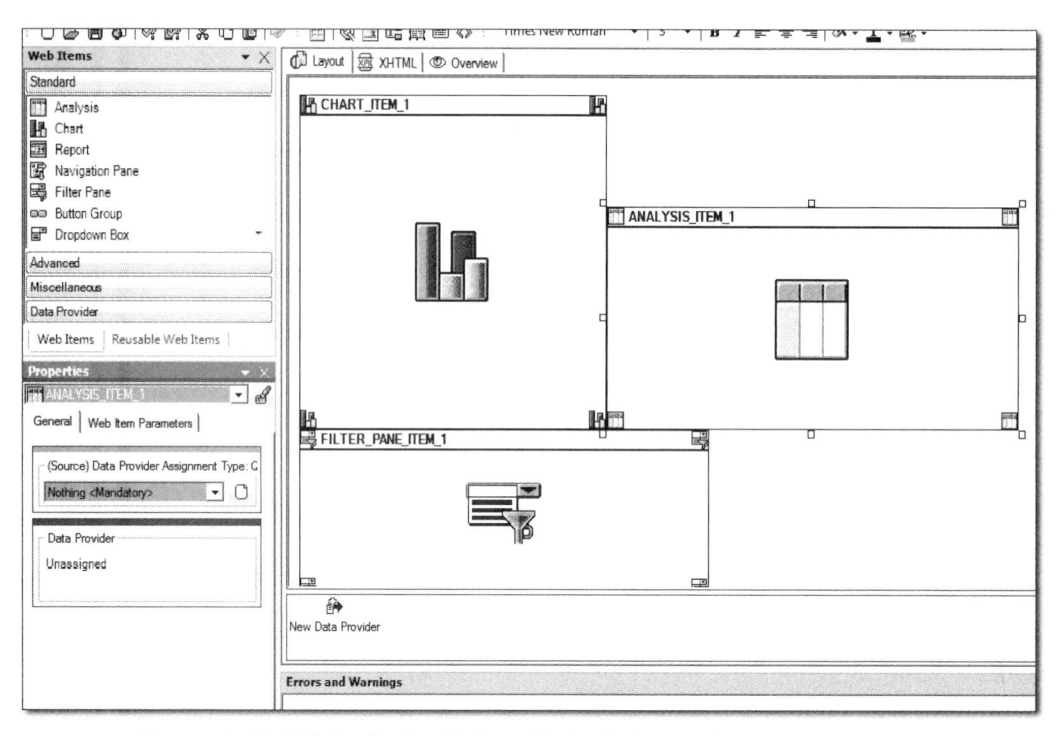

Figure 2.5 BEx Web Application Designer Design Environment

The data provider plays a central role in the creation of web applications. After you drag one of the web items to the layout, the web application only contains a placeholder. No data will be shown because no connection with a data source has been defined yet. A data provider will bring the web application to life and provide it with data from the SAP BW system. The source for such a data provider can be a BEx query, a BEx query view, or an SAP BW InfoProvider such as an InfoCube or InfoSet. A web application can have multiple data providers, and a data provider is connected to multiple web items in a web application (see Figure 2.6). For example, a data provider connected to a BEx query on HR data can provide an analysis table with data and a filter pane with filter options. When the user of the web application sets a certain filter (e.g., his own organizational department) in the filter pane, the data provider updates the query result with this input. Accordingly, the analysis table will be updated and now show only data on the user's organizational department. So changing the input on a web item can affect all the web items connected to the same data provider.

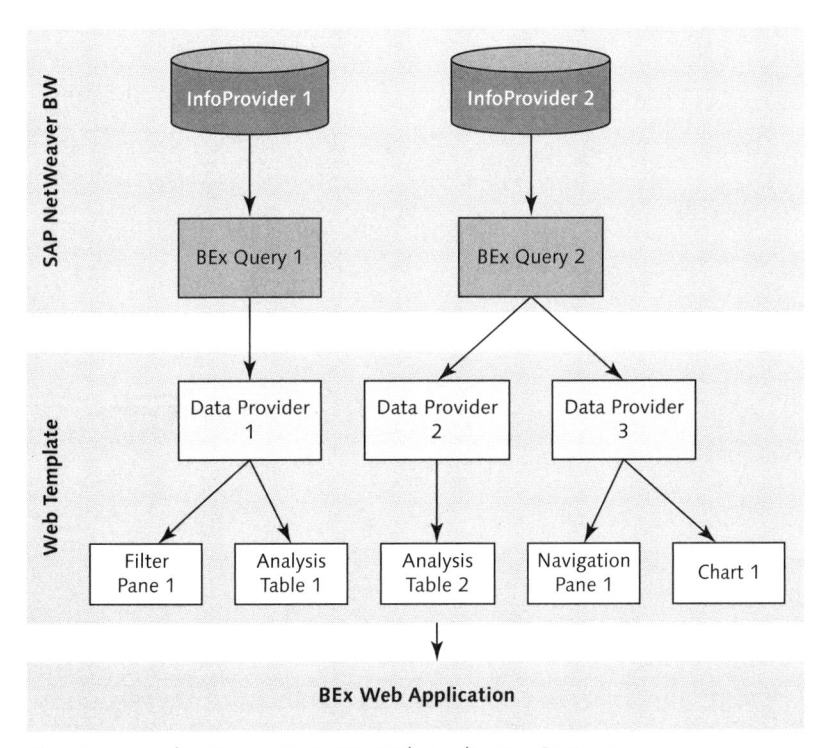

Figure 2.6 Application Layers in BEx Web Application Designer

The properties of the selected web item are shown under the list of web items in BEx Web Application Designer (refer to Figure 2.5). A new data provider can be created here, and existing data providers can be connected to the web item. In the web item parameters, some web-item-specific settings can be adjusted, such as the width and height of the web item and the maximum number of displayed values.

The XHTML tab shows the web items and some corresponding settings. This XHTML is fully editable, so this is used to edit a web application. All used objects are listed in the OVERVIEW tab.

2.2.2 Web Items

BEx Web Application Designer provides a number of web items, divided into three categories: standard, advanced, and miscellaneous web items. These web items are comparable to the components in SAP BusinessObjects Dashboards and are the building blocks of a web application. Next, we briefly outline the three categories of web items.

Standard Web Items

The standard web items are as follows:

- **Analysis**
  This is a table-like item that presents the data provider results in rows and columns.

- **Chart**
  BEx Web Application Designer offers a wide range of chart types:
    - Horizontal line chart
    - Vertical line chart
    - Bar chart
    - Column chart
    - Horizontal area chart
    - Vertical area chart
    - Pie chart
    - Doughnut chart
    - Split pie chart
    - Polar chart

- Radar chart
- Scatter
- Time scatter
- Speedometer (gauge)
- Portfolio chart
- Histogram
- GANTT chart
- MTA chart
- Heat map
- Delta chart

▶ **Report**
Reports created with BEx Report Designer can be embedded into a web application using this web item.

▶ **Navigation pane**
This item shows the available characteristics and their positions (columns, rows, free). A characteristic can be dragged from this pane into the analysis table.

▶ **Filter pane**
This item allows the user to easily set up filters on one or more characteristics.

▶ **Button group**
Buttons can be programmed with standard commands or a custom script.

▶ **Dropdown box, radio button group, checkbox group, list box**
These web items function as custom filters.

▶ **Hierarchical filter**
This item lets a user navigate through a hierarchy for a specific characteristic and set up filters on hierarchical nodes.

Advanced Web Items

The advanced web items are, in contrast to the standard web items, more focused on grouping and placing web items than on displaying data. For this purpose, a container item, a container layout item, a tab pages item, and a group item are available. All these web items are able to arrange other web items in a certain layout.

With the map item, the BEx map feature can display data in a map. There are also web items for displaying system messages and info fields to show all kinds of BEx query-related information (i.e., the most recent data update date of the InfoProvider).

The input field item is interesting because it can be used for SAP BW Integrated Planning (SAP BW-IP) web applications to enter values. It can also be used to enter a filter by typing the filter value in a field.

Miscellaneous Web Items

With the list of conditions and list of exceptions items, all conditions and exceptions that are available in the connected BEx query can be displayed. The user of the web application can activate and deactivate the conditions and exceptions from this web item.

A ticker item can present data as a moving ticker, like the ones news channels use at the bottom of the screen. There is a text item to add text objects to the web application, and, with the menu bar item, a number of buttons with commands can be created. Furthermore, this category consists of web items that work on the background and can, for example, add custom scripts to the web application and select which options should be shown in the context menus (right-click) of the other web items.

2.2.3 Publishing

A web template for a web application has to be published to the SAP BW environment. The web template then becomes an object that can be run from the SAP BW Java portal, the same way you can execute BEx queries as web queries or, as you've seen earlier, dashboards from SAP BusinessObjects Dashboards. The web application can be run from a web URL address.

2.3 Key Differences

Now that you have a basic understanding of the features of SAP BusinessObjects Dashboards and BEx Web Application Designer, we can compare them with Design Studio. Table 2.1 compares the three tools in a number of categories.

2.3 Key Differences

	SAP Business-Objects Dashboards	BEx Web Application Designer	Design Studio
Platform	SAP BW Java Portal, SAP BusinessObjects BI Launch Pad, SWF file (standalone or embedded in PDF, HTML, Adobe Air, Word, Outlook, PowerPoint)	SAP BW Java Portal	SAP BW Java Portal, BI Launch Pad, SAP HANA
Output Format	SWF file or HTML5 (mobile)	Java	HTML5
Components	Very wide range of charts, maps, containers, and selection and other graphical components.	Large set of charts, containers, and customizable buttons; limited graphical components.	Wide range of charts, containers, and selection components. Also available is a geo map component.
Component Adjustment Options	Very high: All components have a lot of options to tweak their functionality, looks, and interactivity options. In an Excel spreadsheet, Excel formulas can be used for custom calculations.	High: Components can be adjusted with high detail.	Very high: A lot of tweaking options are available for charts and other components. Interactivity has to be scripted. Developers can use Cascading Style Sheets (CSS) to change the layout of a component.
Layout Development Flexibility	High flexibility: Drag and drop components to the exact preferred position, that is, what you see is what you get (WYSIWYG).	Low flexibility: Containers and HTML tables/code are used for positioning.	High flexibility: WYSIWYG is used, including relative positioning of components.

Table 2.1 Key Differences

	SAP Business-Objects Dashboards	BEx Web Application Designer	Design Studio
Data Connectivity	UNX, BICS, web service query (QaaS), web service connection, XML data and Excel/XML maps, SAP BusinessObjects Live Office connections, Flash variables, Portal data, LCDS connections, external interface connection, Web Dynpro, Flash Island.	BEx query, BEx query view, SAP BW InfoProvider.	BEx query, SAP BW InfoProvider, SAP HANA, and UNX (relational and single source) that are defined on the SAP BusinessObjects BI 4.1 platform.
Data Input Options	Interactive scenarios can be developed using the Excel spreadsheet.	SAP BI-IP options can be incorporated.	SAP BI-IP options can be incorporated.
Scripting Options	Excel spreadsheet.	XHTML, JavaScript, and ABAP coding.	JavaScript and CSS coding.
SDK	SDK available for development of custom components and connectivity options.	No SDK available.	SDK available in Design Studio version 1.2.
Mobile	HTML5 export for a limited number of components and connectivity options. These dashboards are viewed via SAP BusinessObjects Mobile.	No options for mobile.	Applications are viewable on any device with an HMTL5 browser or via SAP BusinessObjects Mobile.
SAP HANA	No support for direct access to SAP HANA data sources.	No support for direct access to SAP HANA data sources.	Direct access to SAP HANA analytic views and calculation views.

Table 2.1 Key Differences (Cont.)

The remainder of this section describes three images of dashboards/applications created with the three tools we compared in this chapter. As demonstrated here, the three versions look a lot alike and have the same functionality. Each dashboard/application contains two charts, a number of filters, some tabs, and a text object that shows the latest refresh date of the data.

Figure 2.7 shows the SAP BusinessObjects Dashboards version, Figure 2.8 is the BEx Web Application Designer version, and Figure 2.9 displays the Design Studio application.

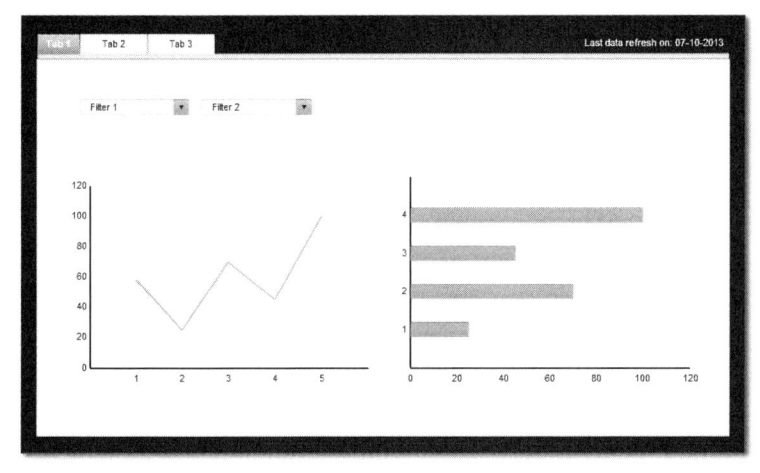

Figure 2.7 Simple Dashboard in SAP BusinessObjects Dashboards

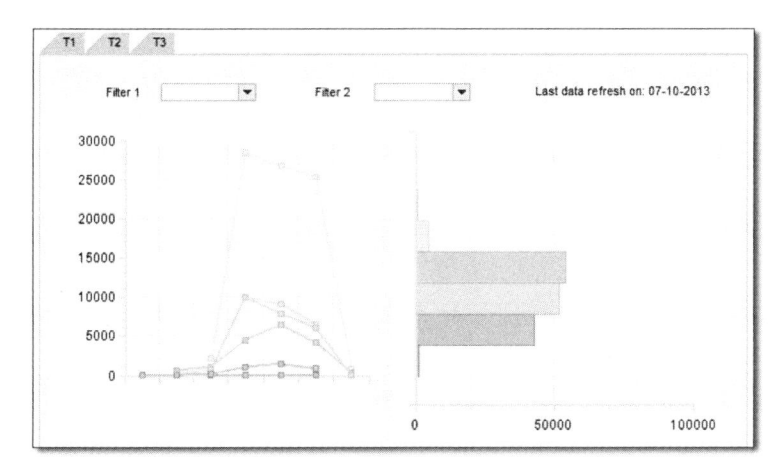

Figure 2.8 Simple Application in BEx Web Application Designer

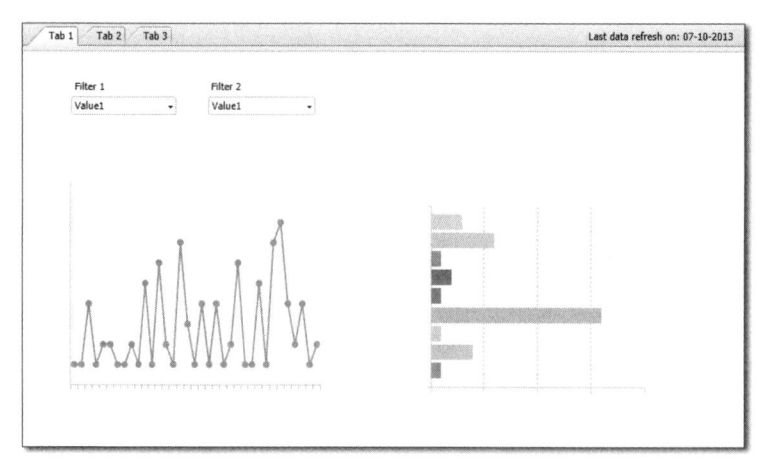

Figure 2.9 Simple Application in Design Studio

2.4 Summary

In this chapter, we introduced two tools from the SAP BusinessObjects BI portfolio that overlap with the features and purpose of Design Studio: SAP BusinessObjects Dashboards and BEx Web Application Designer. We took a quick dive into the steps and activities required to create a report, dashboard, or SAP BusinessObjects BI application. Next, we reviewed the different components of the tools that form the building blocks of the development process. Additionally, we examined the data connectivity options and the publishing possibilities for each tool. Finally, we discussed the key differences among the three tools.

In the next chapter, we'll take a look at some real-life examples of how Design Studio applications are used.

This chapter shows use case scenarios featuring applications developed in Design Studio that are used by end users in diverse business scenarios.

3   Usage Scenarios

In this chapter, we'll walk through three examples that show you how applications are developed in Design Studio and how they can be used in different business scenarios. Each scenario will tell a story of an end user who is using an application designed for his particular role or task. The scenarios will show that Design Studio is able to deliver process support in very different situations, varying from real-time operational support to in-depth strategic analysis.

We'll begin by discussing how a real-time production dashboard is used in Section 3.1. In Section 3.2, we'll provide an overview of a sales dashboard application built in Design Studio. Finally, we'll show you how users can explore data by using an Online Analytical Processing (OLAP) application in Section 3.3.

The information provided in this chapter will be used in Chapter 15, Chapter 16, and Chapter 17, where we'll describe how to create the different parts of the example applications in this chapter.

3.1   Real-Time Production Dashboard

One of the most common key performance indicators (KPIs) for production is the *Overall Equipment Efficiency (OEE)* KPI. The OEE gives an indication of the performance for a given production unit. The score of the OEE is represented in percentages. Often companies define an acceptable target OEE and use a dashboard to monitor this KPI.

The OEE score is calculated using three sub-KPIs:

- **Availability**
  This is the percentage of time that a machine is available for production.

- **Performance**
  This provides the difference in time between the actual speed of production and the designed speed of production for a certain amount of products. This is also expressed in percentages.
- **Quality**
  This shows the percentage of good products that are produced.

In this section, we'll demonstrate the use of a real-time production dashboard with particular attention to the OEE KPI. The sub-KPIs are defined out of other KPIs such as unscheduled and scheduled downtime, actual speed, target speed, good quantity, and target quantity. For simplicity, we'll only focus on the OEE, availability, performance, and quality KPIs in this example.

There are various ways this dashboard can be used. Consider the following scenarios:

- On one big screen or multiple big screen monitors in the production area. The manufacturer receives (almost) real-time information concerning the OEE on a specific day. When the OEE starts to drop below a certain level, the manufacturer can easily identify which sub-KPI has caused this.
- Managers can use this dashboard to analyze trends in the OEE. They can analyze which machines do well and which machines may need to be replaced. They use this dashboard for trend analysis over time (daily/monthly). This doesn't have to be in real time.

In our first example use case, we have a production facility where a supervisor wants to use a real-time dashboard to track certain KPIs. Production at the company starts at 9 a.m. and ends at 5 p.m. The company has three plants and five machines. The production supervisor starts up the real-time dashboard and activates the real-time functionality in the morning. Each of the five available machines delivers the data for the dashboard to the data warehouse once an hour.

At 10 a.m., the supervisor sees that the OEE started off low. At the moment, he isn't worried because he knows that some of the machines need time to warm up before they reach optimal production speed. However, at 11 a.m., he checks the dashboard again and sees that the OEE is still dropping (Figure 3.1). This time he does want to know what caused this drop and investigates further.

Real-Time Production Dashboard | **3.1**

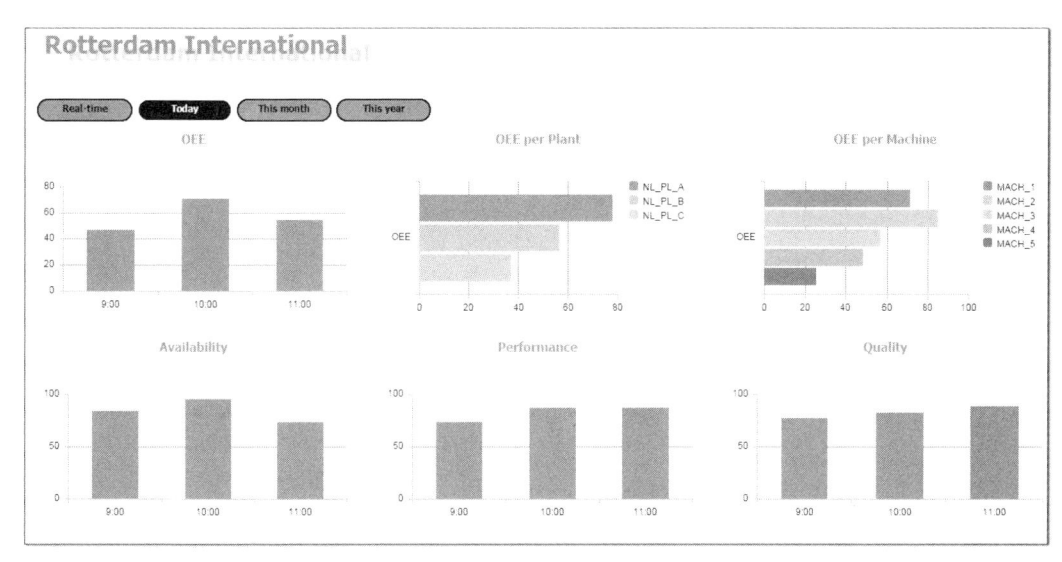

Figure 3.1 Real-Time Dashboard

The supervisor checks the dashboard and sees in the second chart that the OEE in plant NL_PL_C has dropped to an unacceptable level (Figure 3.2).

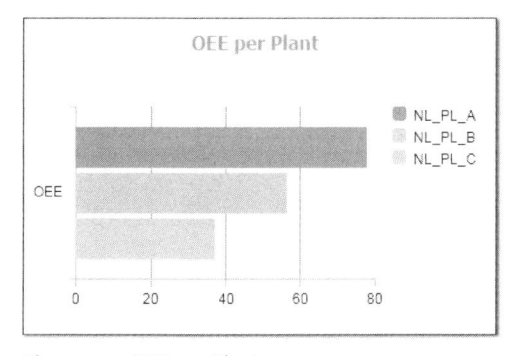

Figure 3.2 OEE per Plant

On the touch-screen monitor on the production floor, he selects plant NL_PL_C in the chart to see what is happening in the plant. As soon as he selects plant NL_PL_C in the chart, the dashboard is updated. Now the supervisor can see how well the machines in this plant are doing (Figure 3.3) and which of the sub-KPIs are causing the OEE to drop (Figure 3.4).

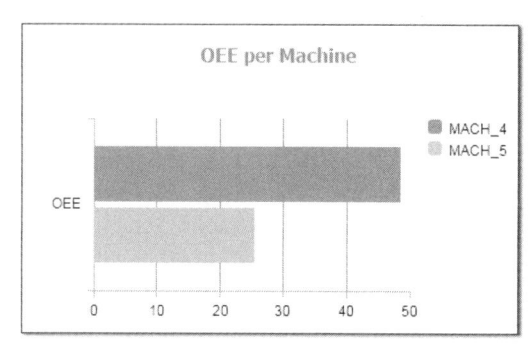

Figure 3.3 OEE per Machine

Figure 3.4 gives an overview of the sub-KPIs Availability, Performance, and Quality. In Figure 3.4, these measures are an average of MACH_4 and MACH_5 (both machines in plant NL_PL_C).

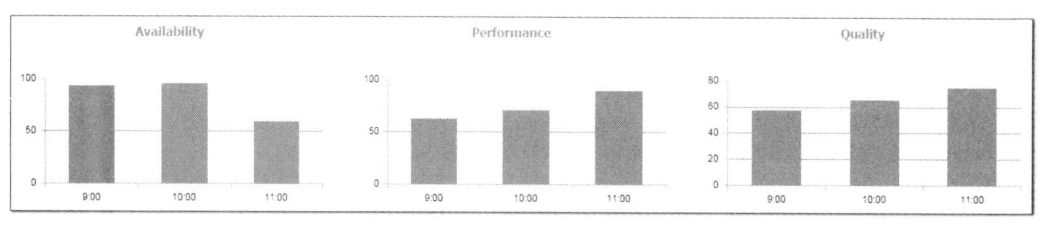

Figure 3.4 Sub-KPIs

The supervisor sees that the OEE for both machine MACH_4 and MACH_5 are very low and wants to evaluate each of these machines separately. To do this, he clicks on the first machine in his dashboard. Again, the sub-KPIs are updated immediately. When he observes the KPIs, he sees that the availability for MACH_4 is very low (Figure 3.5). Seeing this information, he can call the machine operator and handle the problem accordingly.

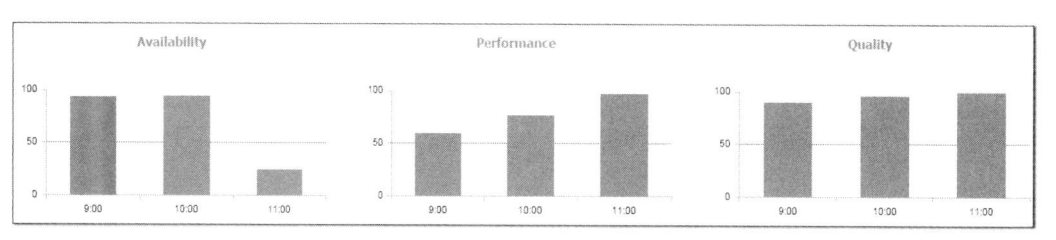

Figure 3.5 Low Availability for MACH_4

Real-Time Production Dashboard | 3.1

Because the OEE for MACH_5 was also very low, the supervisor decides to check out what is happening with this machine by selecting it within the dashboard. He sees that the Availability and Performance are reasonable for this machine but the Quality is just above 40% (Figure 3.6). Again, the supervisor can now quickly call the operator for this machine and investigate what is going on.

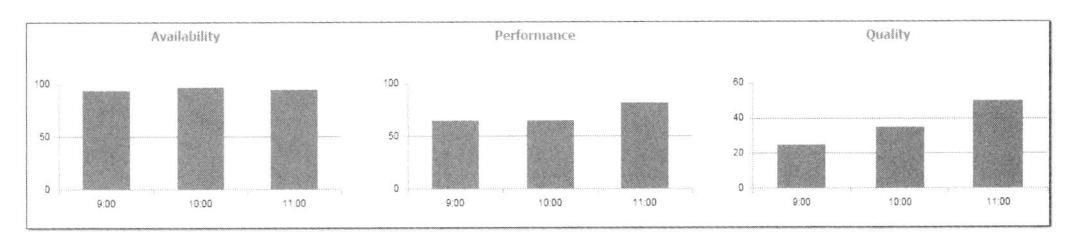

Figure 3.6 Low Quality for MACH_5

As time passes, the OEE dashboard is updated automatically. At the end of the day, the dashboard will give an overview, as shown in Figure 3.7. Here the manager can see data for each hour between 9 a.m. and 5 p.m.

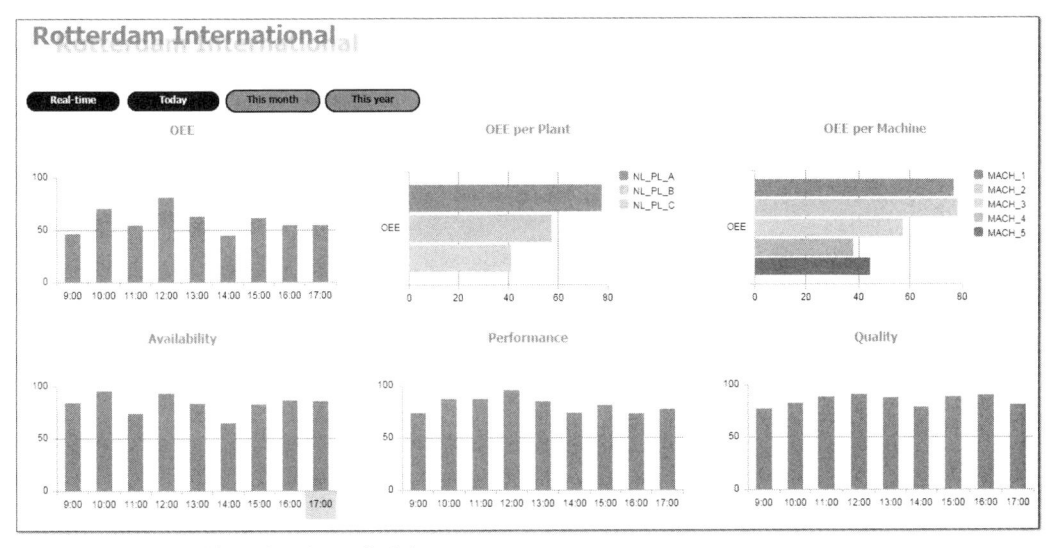

Figure 3.7 OEE Dashboard at the End of the Day

This dashboard can also be used to follow the trend of each KPI for the current month. When the supervisor wants to compare the OEE for each day of this month, he simply selects the THIS MONTH button. The overview changes from an hourly overview to a daily overview, as shown in Figure 3.8.

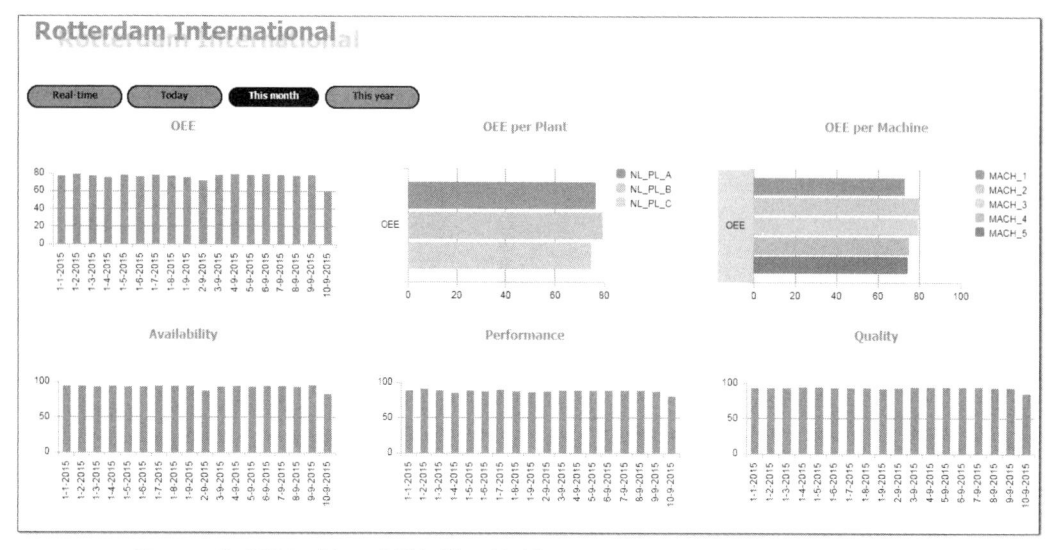

Figure 3.8 OEE Dashboard: This Month's View

The supervisor can filter the data for either one of the plants by clicking on a specific plant in the dashboard or on one of the machines by selecting one in the dashboard. At the end of the day, the supervisor has a meeting with his manager to discuss whether or not to replace certain machines.

The manager wants to know how well production was this year up to the present. The supervisor switches to the THIS YEAR'S view by selecting the THIS YEAR button and gets an overview of the year thus far, as shown in Figure 3.9. The supervisor and his manger see that the OEE is steady across the whole company; all plants and individual machines are doing quite well. The manager decides that an extra investment isn't needed at this point in time.

In this section, we demonstrated how the real-time production dashboard can enhance decision making and give key insight into performance. Using the dashboard, the supervisor and his manager were able to make informed decisions on the maintenance of their machines and plants.

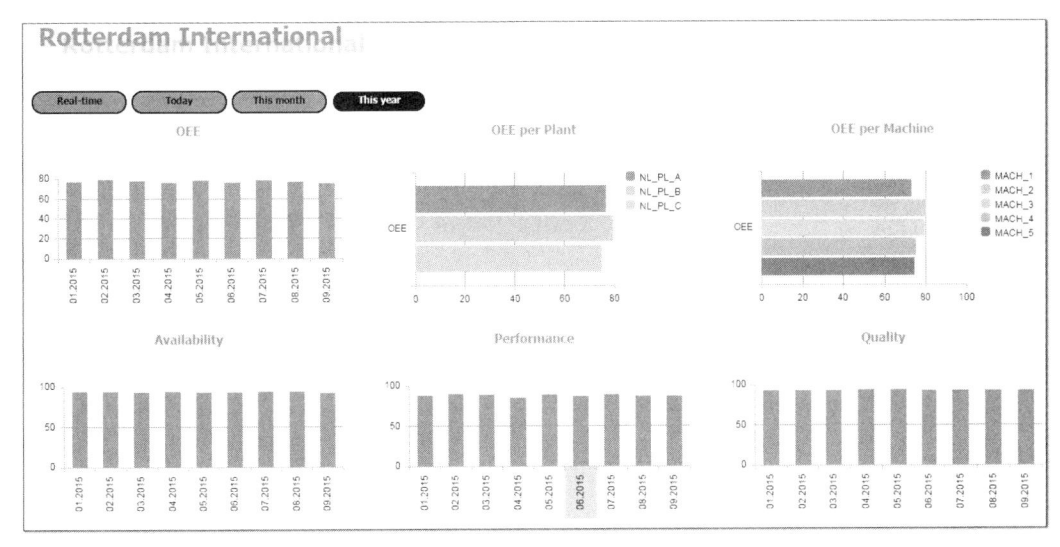

Figure 3.9 OEE dashboard: This Year's View

3.2   Sales Dashboard Application

Tracking sales and customer satisfaction is a vital task within a company. In this section, we'll look at a solar installation company that is using a sales dashboard application created in Design Studio. For this use case, we'll assume the role of the sales director.

As part of the job, the sales director has to not only look at the state of sales but also customer satisfaction. Using the sales dashboard application, the sales director can monitor these areas during and post-installation, as maintenance or services may be needed after install. In addition to monitoring this data, the sales director will also be able to create a price quote for a new customer.

In the following sections, we'll discuss how the sales director can utilize the different areas of the sales dashboard application.

3.2.1   Main Screen

The main screen of the application (Figure 3.10) has a number of important areas that the manager has to oversee. In addition, the KPIs highlighted at the top of the main page indicate that those KPIs need extra attention.

3 | Usage Scenarios

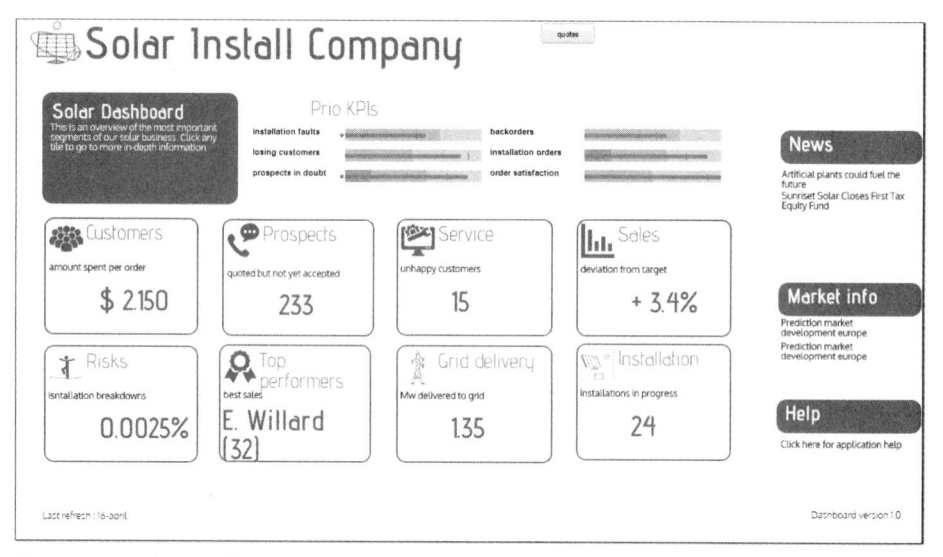

Figure 3.10 Solar Install Company Main Dashboard

On the right-hand side of the main screen, there are informative sections that have news items on solar panels, supply market information, and help for using the application.

The largest part of the screen shows eight tiles, each depicting an area relevant to the company. Each tile contains one KPI that is most important to that area. In the Customers tile (Figure 3.11), you see the KPI used to display the amount spent per order. On the top left, you see an icon symbolizing the company's customers. When the sales director clicks this tile, a details page appears in which he can drill down on customers (see Section 3.2.2).

Figure 3.11 Single Tile with KPI

Looking again at the main page, you see several KPIs visualized using bullet graphs (Figure 3.12).

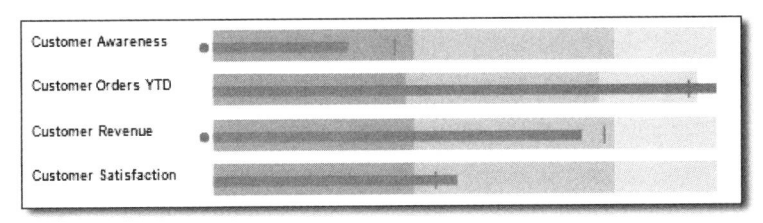

Figure 3.12 Bullet Graphs

These graphs show the current realization (the horizontal blue bar) and compare it to thresholds in the form of gray blocks and to previous periods in the form of vertical lines. A circle appears next to the KPI name when extra attention is needed, for example, if certain targets aren't met.

> **Building a Custom Chart Component**
>
> The bullet graph shown in this example isn't included in the default Design Studio installation. In Chapter 14, we explain how to build such a custom chart yourself using the SDK extension options.

3.2.2 Detail Screen

If the sales director clicks on one of the tiles, the application will open a detail screen that shows more in-depth data about the chosen area. For this example, we'll look more closely at the customer detail screen (Figure 3.13).

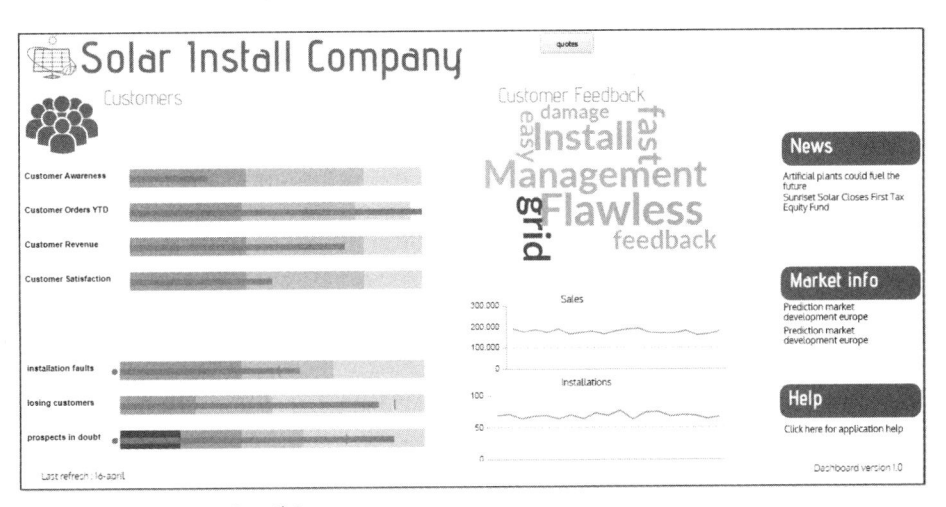

Figure 3.13 Customer Detail Screen

On the left side of the screen, you see multiple bullet graphs that highlight a number of KPIs. Customer-related subjects such as awareness, orders, and satisfaction are some of the KPIs that are highlighted on this screen.

On the right side, you see a *word cloud* (Figure 3.14). A word cloud is a way to visualize the impact of texts, in this case, the comments from users. Instead of reading through all the comments, you get an overview of the frequency of words within comments. Additionally, you can color code the words. By giving positive words a different color from negative words, the sales director can easily decipher customer feedback. In the backend, the system reads each comment and counts the occurrences of each word. The higher the number of occurrences of a word, the bigger the word appears in the word cloud.

Figure 3.14 Word Cloud

Under the word cloud on the detail screen, you see the trend graphs. These trend graphs indicate the sales and installations (Figure 3.15). A dependency should be evident between the sales and installations graphs. First, there has to be a sale where a date for installation is agreed upon. Following the sale, at some point, is the installation. An uptick in sales should result in an increase in installations later on.

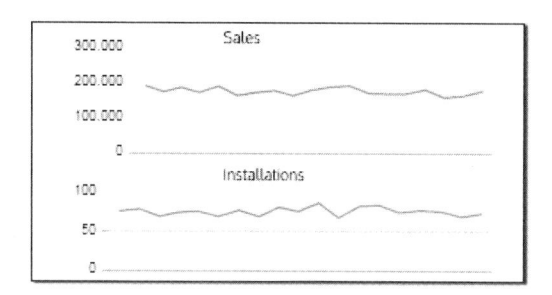

Figure 3.15 Sales and Installations Trend Graphs

Finally, on the right-hand side of the detail page, you see the same items that are present on the main screen: links to news, market insights, and help.

3.2.3 Quotes

Besides analyzing the sales and customer satisfaction, the sales director can also create a quote within the sales dashboard application. As an example, we've provided a form that the sales director can fill in and use to create a document. At the top of both the main screen and the detail screen, there is a QUOTE button. Clicking this button will open a form where the sales director can select products, set the delivery date, and provide the name of the potential customer (Figure 3.16).

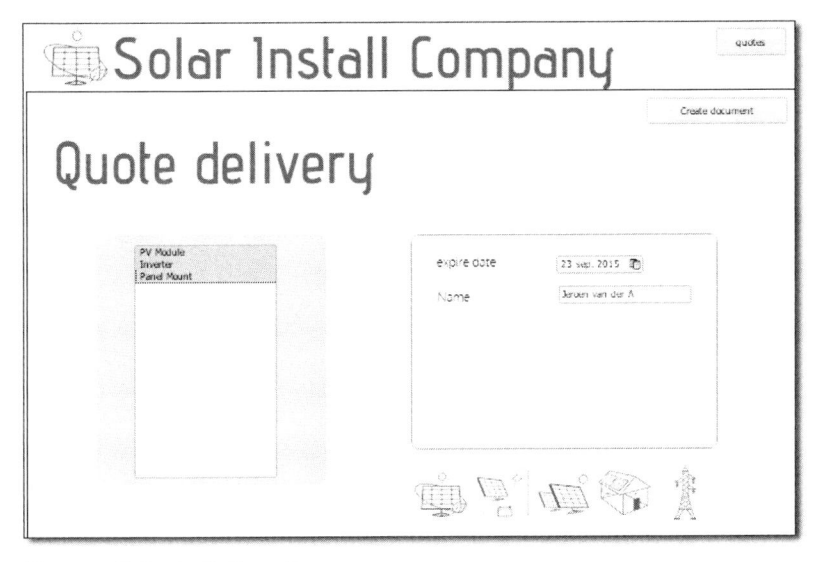

Figure 3.16 Quote Delivery Form

For this example, we kept the number of editable items at a minimum, but you can imagine how this can be expanded further to create a fully functional quote form. After all the products have been selected, and the fields are filled, the sales director can select the PRINT button. A popup screen appears where you can set headers and footers (Figure 3.17).

When the sales director clicks the PRINT button, a PDF document is created with the information entered in the form (Figure 3.18).

3 | Usage Scenarios

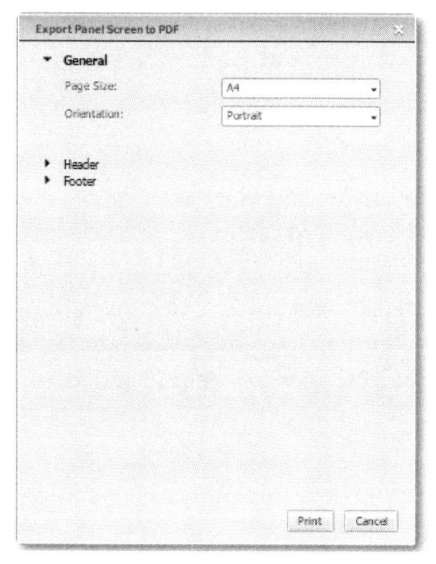

Figure 3.17 Export Panel Screen to PDF

Figure 3.18 PDF Document

Figure 3.19 shows the layout of the printed quotes page.

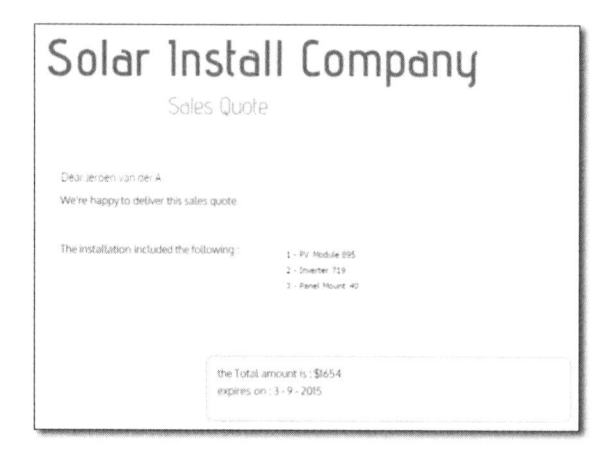

Figure 3.19 PDF Document Layout

In this section, we discussed how an end user, in our case, a sales director, can take advantage of a sales dashboard application. In this example, the dashboard has a drill-through functionality and the option to create quote documents. We used a number of visualization types to communicate information such as a word cloud, a bullet graph, trend graphs, and numbers.

3.3 OLAP Application

Online Analytical Processing (OLAP) is used to answer business questions from multidimensional data sources interactively. Using an OLAP application allows users to slice and dice through data and create totals or other calculations.

A number of OLAP tools are available, such as SAP BusinessObjects Analysis, edition for Microsoft Office; SAP BusinessObjects Analysis, edition for OLAP; and SAP Lumira. With Design Studio, you can create your own OLAP application, as you'll see in Chapter 17. In Design Studio, you can create a fully customizable OLAP application to follow the same look and feel as other reports and dashboards within your company.

For our final use case, we'll discuss a company that wants to use an OLAP application to explore data in more detail. In this scenario, the application will consist of two tabs. On the first tab, the user will see some charts containing relevant information. When the user clicks on a certain point in the chart, the second tab in the application will be shown. On this second tab, the user will be able to slice and dice through the data using OLAP capabilities.

In Chapter 17, we'll explain in more detail how this application is built. For now, it's important to know that we started the development of this application using the default GENERIC ANALYSIS template that is provided with the installation of Design Studio (ready-to-run template). Although the application consists of many components and scripts, it's basically ready for use, meaning relatively small changes were needed for the application.

In this section, we'll discuss how the user can navigate to the OLAP application to get purchasing information.

3.3.1 Starting the Application

When the user starts the OLAP application, the user will see a simple dashboard containing purchasing information (Figure 3.20). In the first chart of this screen, invoiced amounts and the number of purchase order items are shown per month in a combination chart (columns and lines) with two Y-axes. In the second chart, a tree map is used to display the months in the year 2015. A bigger square indicates a longer total delivery time. The darker color of the square indicates a higher number of purchase order items.

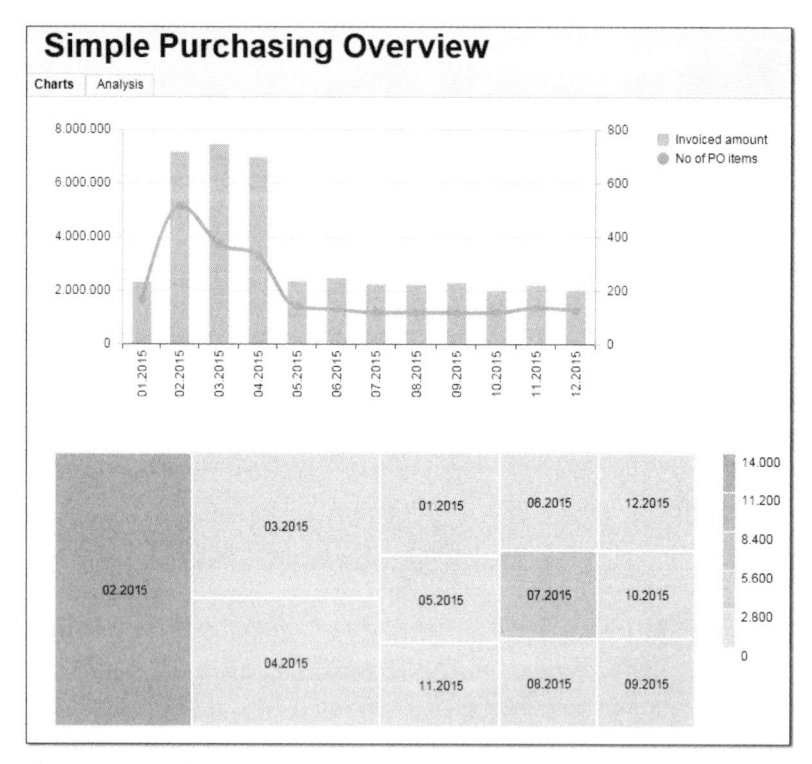

Figure 3.20 Purchasing Dashboard

As shown in Figure 3.20, the application consists of two tabs: CHARTS and ANALYSIS. The CHARTS tab displays charts with purchasing information.

Using the ANALYSIS tab or by clicking on a chart, users can explore the reasons behind, for example, a strange dip in one of the charts. By using slicing and dicing within the ANALYSIS tab, users can obtain more details. Figure 3.21 shows the information found under the ANALYSIS tab of the application.

OLAP Application | 3.3

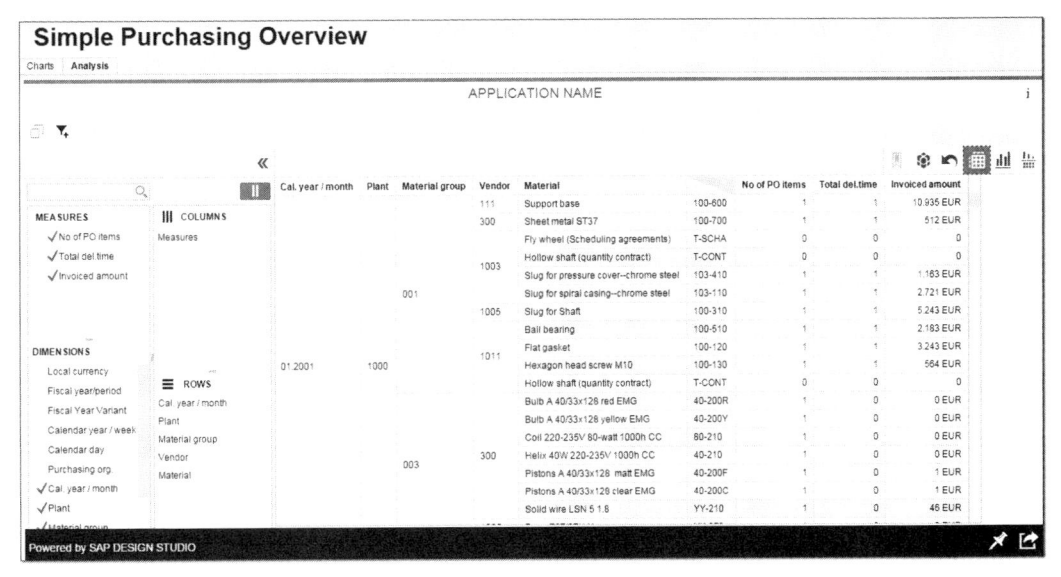

Figure 3.21 Analysis Tab

The first tab of the application is very straightforward and only consists of two charts. In this section, we'll focus on the second tab, namely the ANALYSIS part of our application. The main components that you see on the screen are a navigation panel and a CROSSTAB component. As shown in Figure 3.21, the columns and rows of the navigation panel and CROSSTAB component correspond to each other initially.

3.3.2 Customizing the Application

Users can customize different aspects of the OLAP application to suit their needs. In this section, we'll look at the different options available.

View

Within this application, you can edit the view of the data within the navigation panel (Figure 3.22) on the left of the screen.

You can drag and drop available DIMENSIONS and MEASURES to the ROWS or COLUMNS part of the screen to add them to the CROSSTAB. Note the PAUSE button in the top-right corner of the screen. You can use this button to freeze the refreshing of a view in your CROSSTAB component. This means that you can edit the way the view looks first in the navigation panel and after that refresh the actual view in the CROSSTAB component.

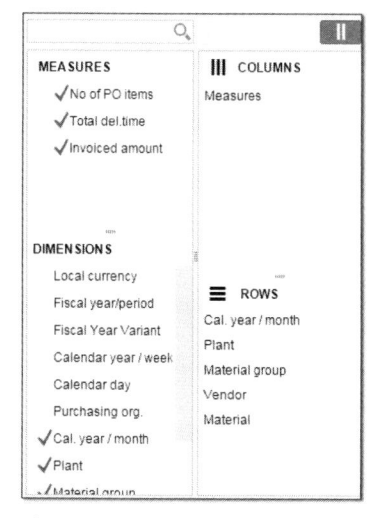

Figure 3.22 Navigation Panel

Crosstab and Context Menu

After you've edited the view of your data, the results will appear in the CROSSTAB on the screen (Figure 3.23).

Figure 3.23 Edited View of the Data

By right-clicking on a dimension in the CROSSTAB, a context menu will open. This menu offers various options to alter the view in the CROSSTAB. For instance, you can use the SORT option to sort the values of a dimension by either TEXT or KEY, in ascending or descending order. You can also display the values of a dimension as KEY, TEXT, or both (Figure 3.24).

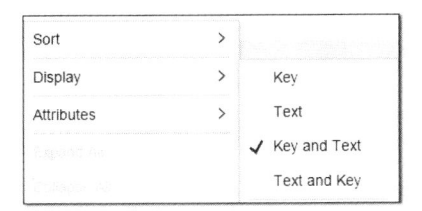

Figure 3.24 Context Menu Display Options

With the context menu, you can also filter dimensions or add some extra dimensions to the drilldown of the data (Figure 3.25).

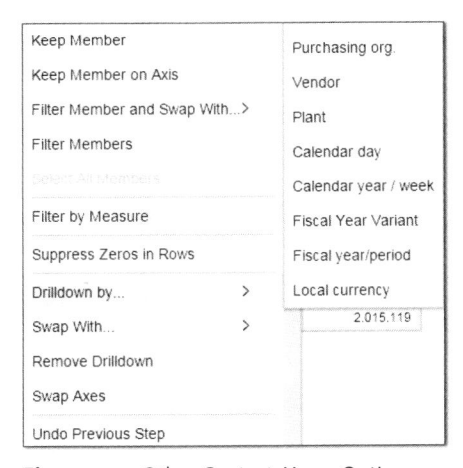

Figure 3.25 Other Context Menu Options

Output

You've seen the data presented in a CROSSTAB component. The user can change this view with the options found in the upper right of the screen (Figure 3.26).

Figure 3.26 View Options

3 | Usage Scenarios

The first button shows the data in a CROSSTAB, the second button shows the data graphically (in a CHART component), and the third button shows the data both graphically and in a table (Figure 3.27).

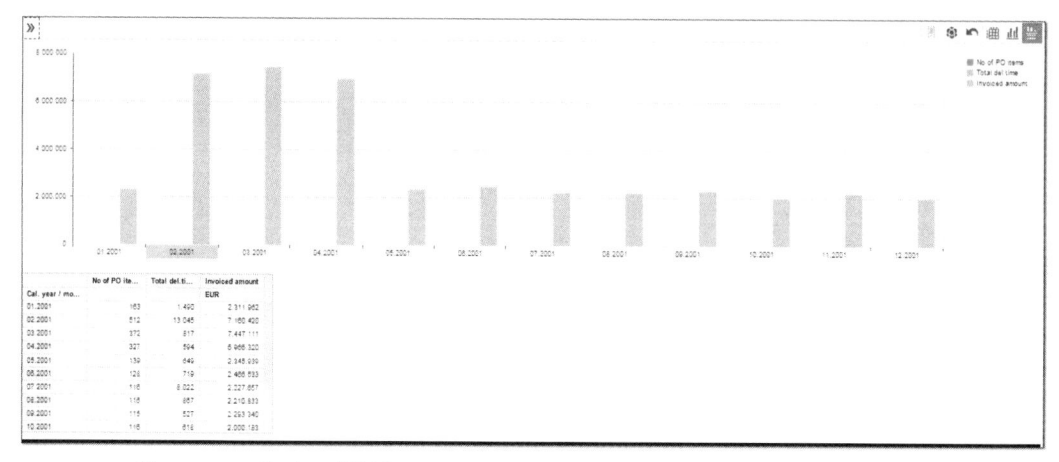

Figure 3.27 Chart and Table

The user can even choose to display the data in another chart type. When they click on the arrow at the top-left corner of the screen (Figure 3.27), a panel containing additional options will open (Figure 3.28). All available charts are grouped together by chart types.

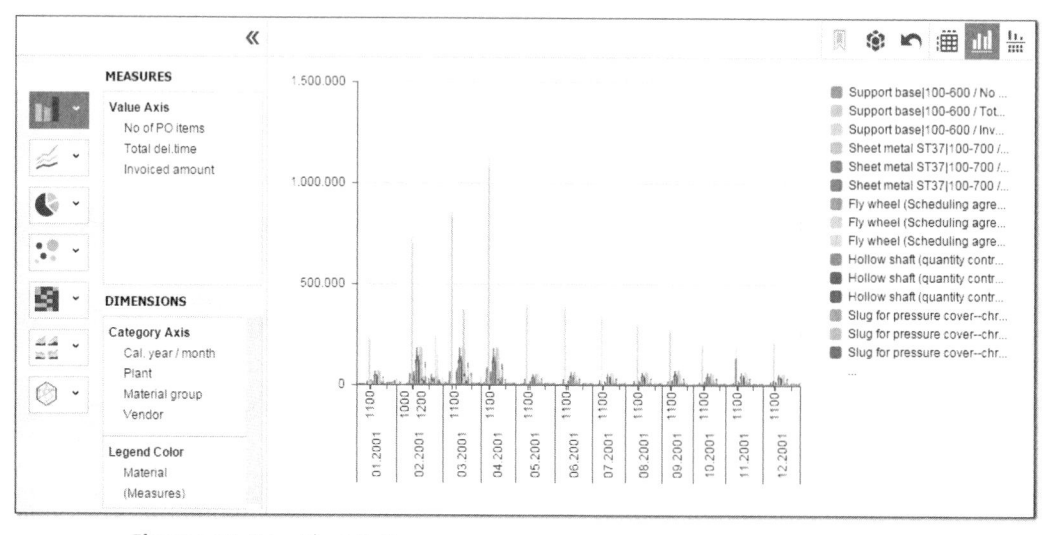

Figure 3.28 Extra Chart Options

Filters

You've already seen that you can apply filters on the data by using the context menu of the CROSSTAB on the screen. However, there is another way to apply filters as well within the OLAP application. As shown in Figure 3.29, you can click on the ADD FILTERS icon in the top-right corner of the screen to show the available dimensions. Select one of the dimensions to apply a filter on that dimension.

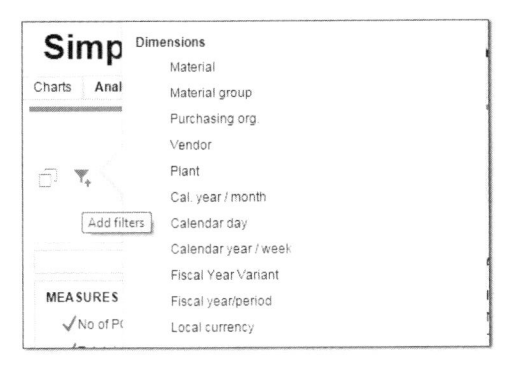

Figure 3.29 Add Filters

After you've selected the dimension on which you want to apply the filter, a new window will open where you can select filter values (Figure 3.30). The filters will be activated when you click the APPLY button.

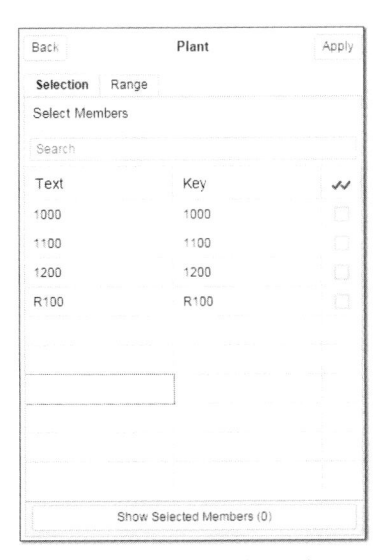

Figure 3.30 Selecting Filter Values

After you've applied the filters, the filter bar will look like Figure 3.31. You can see what filters are applied, and you can remove the applied filters by clicking on the x button in the upper-right corner of the filter.

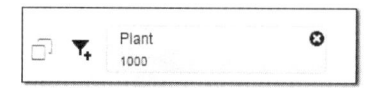

Figure 3.31 Applied Filters

Additional Options

Figure 3.32 shows additional options the user has in this application. The first icon (far left) is the BOOKMARK icon. Clicking this icon opens the bookmark menu, which users can use to save and share bookmarks of their OLAP application (Figure 3.33 and Figure 3.34).

The second icon is the cube browser. With this option, users can choose a different data source for their OLAP application. A new window will open, showing all available connections and queries. The last icon is the UNDO button, which undoes one navigation step at a time.

Figure 3.32 Other Options

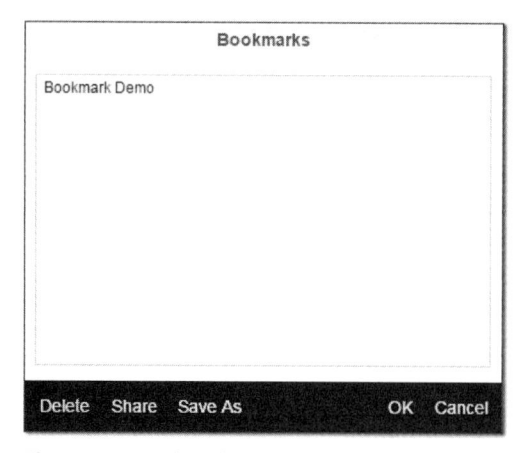

Figure 3.33 Bookmark

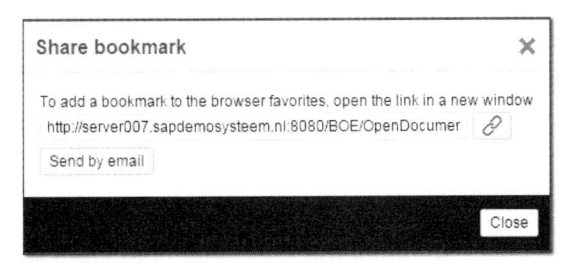

Figure 3.34 Share Bookmark

3.4 Summary

With these three examples, we've shown you some of the many possible usage scenarios for Design Studio applications. The production and sales dashboard show the different ways users can display KPI values in a dashboard application. Users can also take advantage of an OLAP application for dashboarding and for data analysis.

In the next chapter, we'll guide you through the installation of the Design Studio add-on for SAP BusinessObjects BI, SAP HANA, and SAP BW. In addition, we'll show you how to configure connections with Universes and custom data sources.

This chapter guides you through the steps to install and configure the Design Studio server-side add-on components for the SAP BusinessObjects BI platform, SAP BW, and SAP HANA, as well as the Design Studio client tool. We'll also look at how to configure connections via Universes and custom data sources.

4   Installation and Configuration

In this chapter, we'll take you through the steps to install and set up Design Studio within your SAP BusinessObjects Business Intelligence (BI) environment. We'll start with an overview of the Design Studio architecture, including system requirements (Section 4.1). Then we'll explain how to gather the material you need for the installation (Section 4.2).

Depending on your current SAP BusinessObjects BI landscape, you can choose to install Design Studio on one of the following platforms:

- SAP BusinessObjects BI
- SAP BW
- SAP HANA

In Section 4.4, we'll guide your through the steps involved to install and configure the Design Studio add-on for the SAP BusinessObjects BI platform. In Section 4.5, we'll go through the steps to install the Design Studio add-on on the SAP BW system, and, in Section 4.6, we'll use a step-by-step approach to show you how to install and configure the SAP HANA platform to run Design Studio. We'll then look at configuring connections via Universes (UNX) and custom data sources in Section 4.7. The last part of the chapter covers the installation of the client tool itself (Section 4.8). After everything is installed and configured, you'll perform your first login with the Design Studio client tool.

> **Version**
>
> This chapter is based on Design Studio 1.6, patch level 0. The content of the following sections is aligned with this software version and might change in future editions of Design Studio.

4.1 Architecture, Components, and Prerequisites

Figure 4.1 shows a high-level overview of the Design Studio architecture in which three layers can be defined. Starting at the bottom is the first layer with the data sources that contain the data, that is, an SAP BW or SAP HANA system.

As stated earlier, Design Studio can be integrated in three platforms: SAP BusinessObjects BI, SAP HANA and SAP BW. This is the second layer, where the connections to the data sources are set up, and the Design Studio applications can be stored here.

On the top layer, the end users of the Design Studio applications can run the applications in a browser or on a mobile device. In addition, from this layer application, developers can use the Design Studio client tool for development purposes.

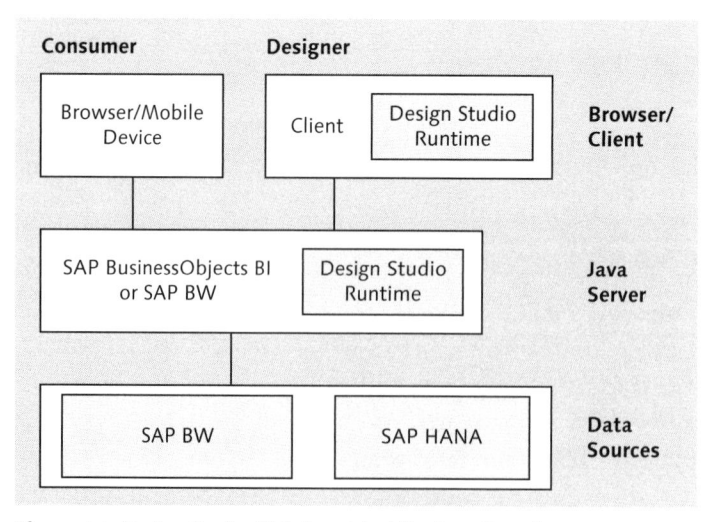

Figure 4.1 Design Studio High-Level Architecture Overview

Design Studio consists of four components that can be installed and/or configured:

- **SAP BusinessObjects BI platform and add-on**
  In addition to the platform itself, there is an add-on for Design Studio that must be installed. Connections via UNX and custom data sources can be published on the SAP BusinessObjects BI platform.

- **SAP BW and SAP Enterprise Portal**
  To integrate Design Studio in SAP BW, some configurations need to be made in the system. To deploy Design Studio applications to SAP Enterprise Portal, you need to install a component and perform some additional configurations.

- **SAP HANA add-on**
  You can use SAP HANA as a repository to run, store, and deploy Design Studio applications. To do this, you need to install some components and deploy them using SAP HANA Studio.

- **Design Studio client tool**
  The Design Studio client tool is an application that has to be installed locally on a Microsoft Windows computer.

Note that when you choose to use SAP BusinessObjects BI as the platform for Design Studio, you don't need to set up SAP BW and SAP Enterprise Portal, or SAP HANA. Similarly, if you want to connect directly to the SAP BW system and host your Design Studio applications there, you don't need to set up the SAP BusinessObjects BI platform or SAP HANA.

With the SAP BusinessObjects BI platform, you can use the data connections that are defined in the Central Management Console (CMC) as OLAP connections. (Later in in Section 4.4.5 and Section 4.4.6, we'll set up such OLAP connections to connect to an SAP BW system and an SAP HANA system, respectively.) When you connect directly to an SAP BW system, the data connections are defined in your local SAP Logon. In this scenario, you can only connect to a single SAP BW system at a time. When you use SAP HANA as the platform, you can use calculation views and analytical views as data sources in your applications.

To move Design Studio applications and files from the development environment to other environments (quality, production), the SAP BusinessObjects BI platform uses SAP Promotion Management. In SAP BW scenarios, the SAP Transport

Management System (TMS) can be used. In a scenario where you use SAP HANA as platform, you can use delivery units to move files to other environments.

Running Design Studio on the SAP BusinessObjects BI platform has a few advantages over running the application on one of the other platforms. The SAP BusinessObjects BI platform is the only platform where you can use and combine multiple sources of data. With the SAP BusinessObjects BI platform, you can also easily link Design Studio applications to reports built in other tools such as SAP BusinessObjects Web Intelligence and SAP BusinessObjects Analysis, edition for OLAP. Another advantage is that you can use the SAP BusinessObjects Mobile app to run reports on iOS or Android devices.

SAP BusinessObjects Mobile app can be downloaded from the Google Play store at *https://play.google.com/store/apps/details?id=com.sap.mobi* or from the Apple App store at *https://itunes.apple.com/us/app/sap-businessobjects-mobile/id441208302?mt=8*.

Of course, these components all have some landscape prerequisites, and the actual execution of Design Studio applications has browser requirements. We'll look at all of these next.

> **Product Availability Matrix**
>
> An updated list of all supported operation systems, browsers, and mobile devices for Design Studio is available in the Product Availability Matrix (PAM) on the SAP Service Marketplace at *http://service.sap.com/pam*.

4.1.1 SAP BusinessObjects BI Platform

For the SAP BusinessObjects BI platform, the following versions are supported:

- SAP BusinessObjects BI platform 4.0 with at least SP 05
- SAP BusinessObjects BI platform 4.1
- SAP BusinessObjects BI platform 4.2

The following conditions must be met:

- Your account for the operating system has administrative rights.
- The machine has a 64-bit operating system.

- The Adaptive Processing Server is installed.
- The MULTIDIMENSIONAL ANALYSIS SERVICE component is installed.
- The SAP BusinessObjects BI platform WEB APPLICATIONS component is installed.
- The MOBILE SERVICES component is installed.

> **SAP BusinessObjects BI Platform Services**
> Section 4.4 will further discuss how to set up these necessary services in the CMC.

4.1.2 SAP Business Warehouse

The following versions of SAP BW are supported:

- SAP BW 7.30 with at least SP 09
- SAP BW 7.31 with at least SP 07
- SAP BW 7.40 with at least SP 02

4.1.3 SAP Enterprise Portal

To use SAP Enterprise Portal with Design Studio, the following conditions must be met:

- SAP Enterprise Portal is installed with the BI Java or SAP Enterprise Portal core usage type.
- BI Java is configured for use with SAP BW.

4.1.4 SAP HANA

To use SAP HANA as a platform, make sure the following are in place:

- SAP HANA (SPS 10) is correctly installed.
- `SAPUI5_1` delivery unit is installed and working properly on the SAP HANA system.
- The `HCO_INA_SERVICE` delivery unit is installed and working properly.
- A suitable version of SAP HANA is installed on the local computers of the application designers.

4.1.5 SAP BusinessObjects Design Studio Client Tool

To install the client tool for Design Studio on your local machine, you need the following (minimum) components to be installed:

- Microsoft Windows Vista SP 2 or Windows 7 SP 1, 32-bit or 64-bit
- Java Runtime Environment (JRE) 1.6 or 1.7, 32-bit
- Microsoft Internet Explorer 9.0

It's also recommended to have SAP GUI 7.30 installed on your local machine to prevent possible problems with connections to SAP BW systems that communicate through a message server.

4.1.6 Browsers

Finally, as we mentioned, there are browser requirements for running Design Studio applications. The following browsers are supported:

- Internet Explorer 8
- Internet Explorer 9
- Internet Explorer 10
- Google Chrome 21.0 and higher for Windows
- Firefox 17.0 and higher for Windows
- Apple Safari 5.1 and higher for Mac

4.2 Preparing for Installation

In this section, you'll find all the material that you need to install Design Studio in your SAP BusinessObjects BI environment.

4.2.1 Accessing Document Guides

Table 4.1 provides a list of the standard SAP product documentation guides for Design Studio. To access these documents, you need an SAP Service Marketplace account (*http://support.sap.com*).

Material	Location
Administrator Guide: Version for SAP BusinessObjects Business Intelligence (BI Platform)	SAP Help Portal *http://help.sap.com/boad* • INSTALLATION, CONFIGURATION, SECURITY AND ADMINISTRATION INFORMATION • ADMINISTRATOR GUIDE
Administrator Guide: Version for SAP NetWeaver	SAP Help Portal *http://help.sap.com/boad* • INSTALLATION, CONFIGURATION, SECURITY AND ADMINISTRATION INFORMATION • ADMINISTRATOR GUIDE
Application Designer Guide	SAP Help Portal *http://help.sap.com/boad* • APPLICATION HELP • ADMINISTRATOR GUIDE
What's New Guide	SAP Help Portal *http://help.sap.com/boad* • APPLICATION HELP • WHAT'S NEW
Business Intelligence Platform Administrator Guide	SAP Help Portal *http://help.sap.com/bobip40* • SYSTEM ADMINISTRATION AND MAINTENANCE INFORMATION • ADMINISTRATOR'S GUIDE
SAP BusinessObjects Mobile Administrator and Report Designer's Guide	SAP Help Portal *http://help.sap.com/bomobil-eios* • INSTALLATION, ADMINISTRATION, CUSTOMIZATION AND REPORT DESIGNING INFORMATION • ADMINISTRATOR'S GUIDE

Table 4.1 Standard SAP Product Guides

4.2.2 Downloading Software Components

Table 4.2 shows the paths to the download locations for the Design Studio software components. To download these files, your SAP Service Marketplace account needs to be linked to an SAP customer number that owns a license for the Design Studio software.

To check which SAP software your company has access to, you can go to the SAP Software Download Center at the SAP Service Marketplace Support Portal. Go to *http://support.sap.com/swdc*, and choose SAP SOFTWARE DOWNLOAD CENTER • INSTALLATIONS AND UPGRADES • MY COMPANY'S APPLICATION COMPONENTS • MY COMPANY'S SOFTWARE. A complete list of authorized software is provided there.

4 | Installation and Configuration

Software Component	Download Location
SAP GUI for Windows 7.40	SAP Software Download Center *https://support.sap.com/swdc* • SOFTWARE DOWNLOADS • SAP SOFTWARE DOWNLOAD CENTER • INSTALLATIONS AND UPGRADES • BROWSE OUR DOWNLOAD CATALOG • SAP FRONTEND COMPONENTS • SAP GUI FOR WINDOWS • SAP GUI FOR WINDOWS 7.40 CORE • INSTALLATION
SAP BusinessObjects Design Studio 1.6 Design tool and SAP BusinessObjects BI platform, SAP NetWeaver and SAP HANA add-on	SAP Software Download Center *https://support.sap.com/swdc* • SOFTWARE DOWNLOADS • SAP SOFTWARE DOWNLOAD CENTER • INSTALLATIONS AND UPGRADES • BROWSE OUR DOWNLOAD CATALOG • ANALYTICS SOLUTIONS • SBOP DESIGN STUDIO SBOP DESIGN STUDIO 1.6 • INSTALLATION

Table 4.2 Software Components Locations

4.2.3 Helpful SAP Notes

Table 4.3 shows a number of important SAP Notes that are related to Design Studio. To access the SAP Notes, you need an SAP Service Marketplace account. You can find SAP Notes at *http://support.sap.com/notes*.

SAP Note Number	SAP Note Title
2180026	SAP BusinessObjects Design Studio 1.6: Release Note for First Delivery
1177020	SAP BusinessObjects Design Studio: Sizing Information
1760372	SAP BusinessObjects Design Studio: Release Schedule
1773751	SAP BusinessObjects Design Studio Support
1894504	Design Studio – Support Note for BIP Add-On
1894594	Design Studio – Support Note for NetWeaver Add-On
2239525	SAP BusinessObjects Design Studio 1.6: Release Limitations

Table 4.3 Important SAP Notes

4.2.4 Extracting Installation Files

Before installing the various components, you have to download and extract the Design Studio software. Follow these steps:

1. Make sure you've downloaded all the files you need from the SAP Software Download Center (see Table 4.2 for the exact download location). As you can see in Figure 4.2, you can choose to download the Design Studio Client, or either one or all of the three Design Studio platform add-ons. Note that the SAP HANA and SAP NetWeaver platform add-ons are platform-independent. Make sure that when you download the Design Studio client or the SAP BusinessObjects BI platform add-on, you select the download for the correct operating system.

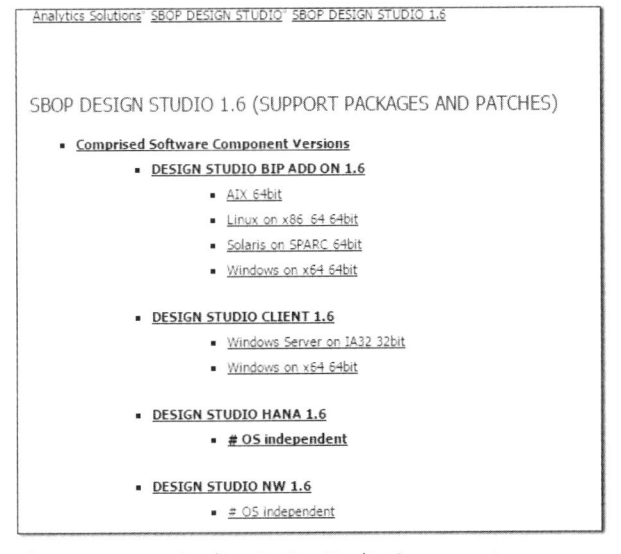

Figure 4.2 Downloading Design Studio Components

2. Download the Design Studio client to a folder on the PC that you'll use for development.

3. If you're installing the SAP BusinessObjects BI platform add-on, download the software to a folder on the server where you have the SAP BusinessObjects BI platform running.

4. If you're installing the SAP NetWeaver platform add-on, download the software to a folder on the server where you have SAP NetWeaver running.

5. If you're using SAP HANA as a platform, download the required software to a folder on the PC that you'll use for development.

4.3 Installing the SAP BusinessObjects BI Platform Add-On

In this section, we'll discuss the installation steps for the SAP BusinessObjects BI platform add-on for Design Studio.

> **Operating Systems**
>
> In this book, we'll only follow the installation steps for installing Design Studio on a Microsoft Windows environment. In the latest Design Studio 1.6 roadmap, SAP encourages customers to deploy Design Studio on the SAP BusinessObjects BI platform because future developments will focus on this platform. You can view the roadmap (S-user required) at *https://websmp201.sap-ag.de/~sapidb/011000358700000390622012D.pdf*.

To complete this server-side installation, follow these steps:

1. Extract the zip file to a folder on the server (Figure 4.3). Open folder DSBIPADDON00_0-70001269.ZIP. If you're running version 4.0 of the SAP BusinessObjects BI platform, open the 40 folder. If you're running version 4.1 open the 41 folder, and if you're running version 4.2, open the 42 folder.

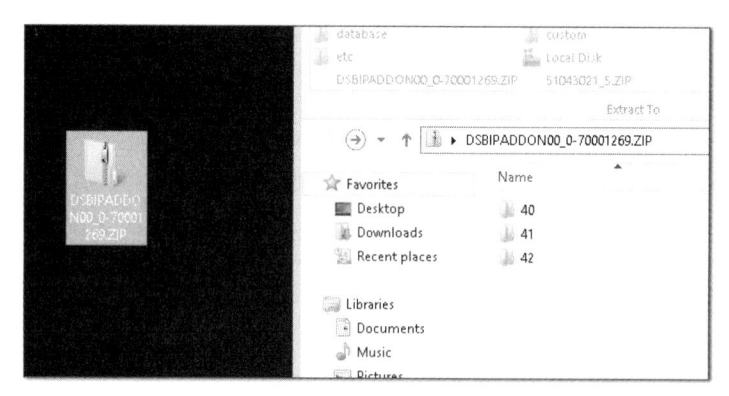

Figure 4.3 Downloading and Extracting Files

2. Double-click SETUP.EXE to start the installation (Figure 4.4).

3. Select a setup language, and click OK (Figure 4.5). This is the language for the Installation Wizard only, not for the Design Studio installation itself. In this example, select ENGLISH as the setup language.

4. A prerequisite check is performed on the SAP BusinessObjects BI platform and server environment (Figure 4.6). The installation can't start unless all of the critical prerequisites are met.

Installing the SAP BusinessObjects BI Platform Add-On | **4.3**

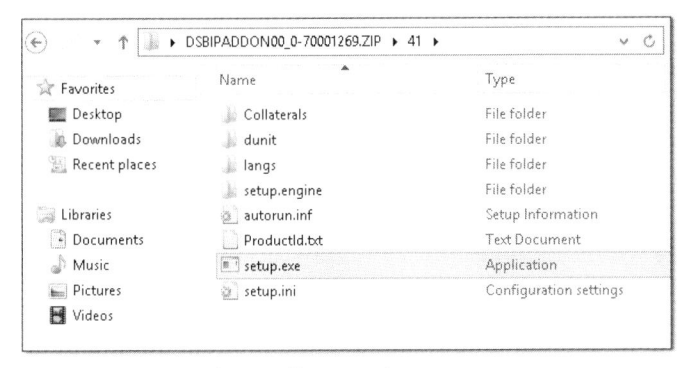

Figure 4.4 Starting the Installation with Setup.exe

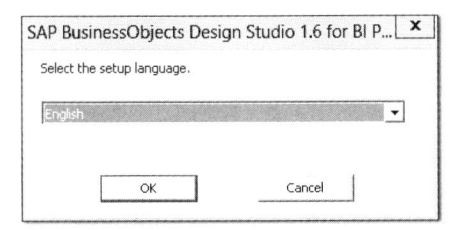

Figure 4.5 Language Selection

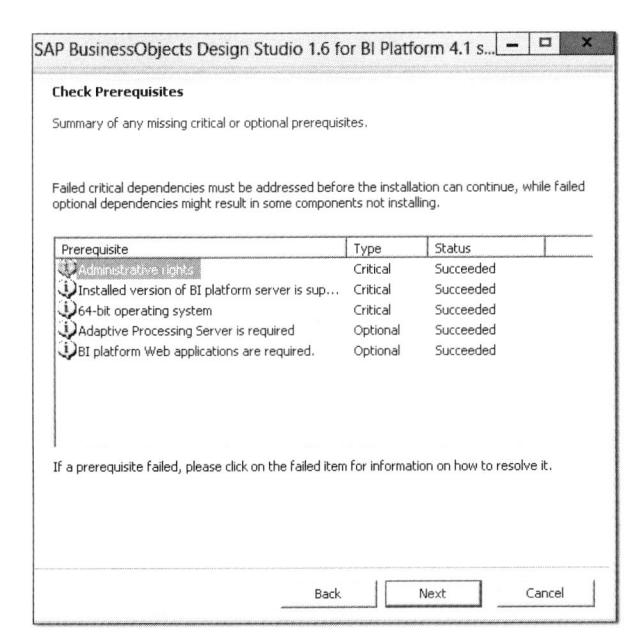

Figure 4.6 Prerequisite Check

101

> **Optional and Critical Prerequisites**
>
> Some of the optional prerequisites might become critical, depending on the specific SAP BusinessObjects BI platform installation and the installed components.

5. The next screen shows the Installation Wizard (Figure 4.7). Click NEXT to start the installation.

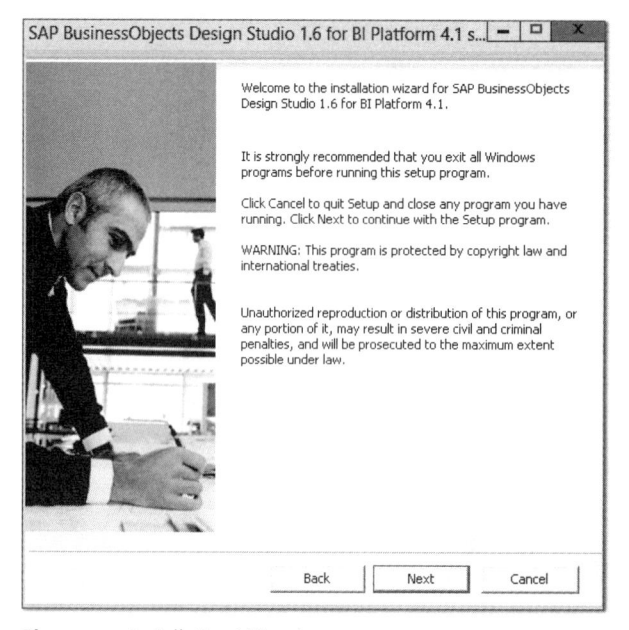

Figure 4.7 Installation Wizard

6. The SOFTWARE LICENSE AGREEMENT is displayed (Figure 4.8). If you accept the terms, click the I ACCEPT THE LICENSE AGREEMENT line and the NEXT button to continue.

7. The destination folder location for the installation opens next (Figure 4.9). Because this directory is based on the SAP BusinessObjects BI platform installation directory, and it can't be changed, the only thing you can do here is click NEXT.

Installing the SAP BusinessObjects BI Platform Add-On | 4.3

Figure 4.8 Software License Agreement

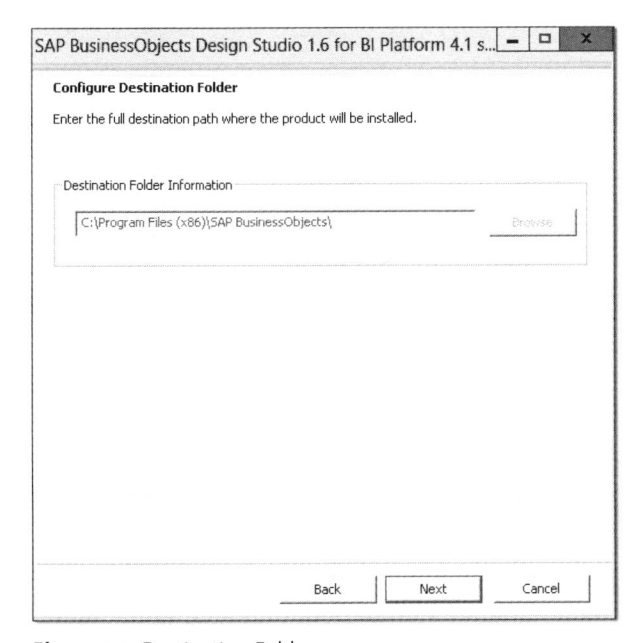

Figure 4.9 Destination Folder

103

8. In the SELECT FEATURES screen (Figure 4.10), you have the choice to perform either a full installation or an installation including only some specific features:
    - ANALYSIS APPLICATION WEB COMPONENTS
    - ANALYSIS APPLICATION SERVICE
    - ANALYSIS APPLICATION SUPPORT FOR MOBILE SERVICES

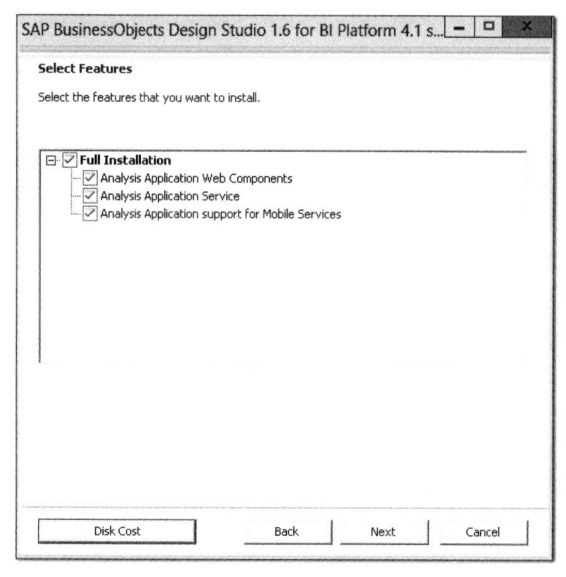

Figure 4.10 Installation Features Selection

Table 4.4 describes these features. By clicking on the DISK COST button, you can calculate the required amount of disk space. Select the features you want to install, and click NEXT to continue.

Feature	Description
ANALYSIS APPLICATION WEB COMPONENT	This feature enables the integration of Design Studio applications in the BI Launch Pad environment, so they can be used like any other SAP BusinessObjects BI document. OpenDocument links are supported. The feature also allows the Design Studio client tool to communicate with the SAP BusinessObjects BI platform to save and execute Design Studio applications.

Table 4.4 Installation Features

Installing the SAP BusinessObjects BI Platform Add-On | 4.3

Feature	Description
ANALYSIS APPLICATION SERVICE	This feature enables the execution of Design Studio applications. It includes the Analysis Application Service in the Adaptive Processing Server.
ANALYSIS APPLICATION SUPPORT FOR MOBILE SERVICES	This feature includes mobile support for Design Studio applications. It enables users to access Design Studio applications through SAP BusinessObjects Mobile on mobile devices such as the iPad.

Table 4.4 Installation Features (Cont.)

9. Now you're asked to enter some information on the SAP BusinessObjects BI platform you're using for this installation (Figure 4.11):

    - CMS NAME
    - CMS PORT NUMBER
    - CMS administrator user/password

   After entering the right credentials, click NEXT to continue.

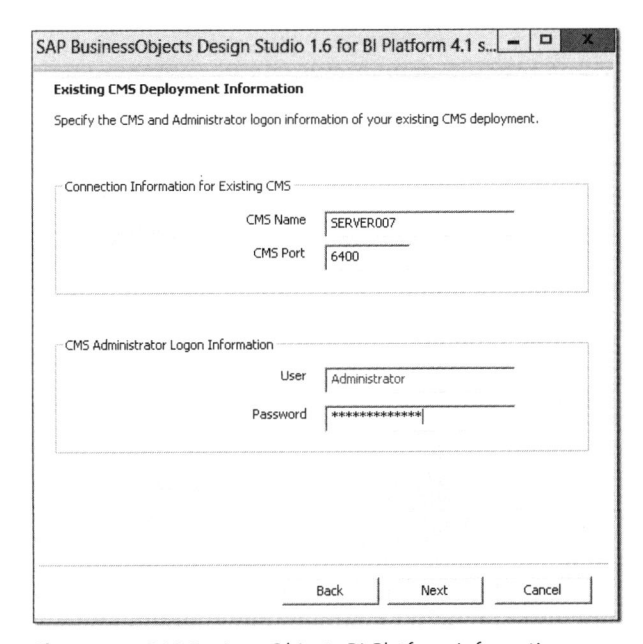

Figure 4.11 SAP BusinessObjects BI Platform Information

4 | Installation and Configuration

10. You're one NEXT click away from the installation finally starting (Figure 4.12). Click NEXT on the START INSTALLATION screen.

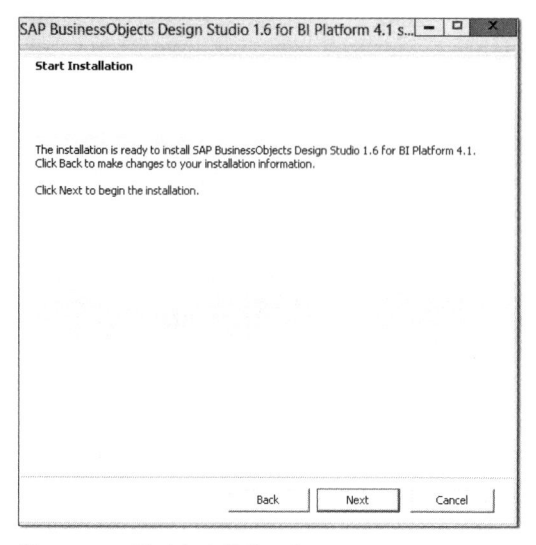

Figure 4.12 Start Installation Screen

Now you can sit back, enjoy something to drink, and let the machine do its work (Figure 4.13).

Figure 4.13 Running the Installation

11. When the installation is finished, a post-installation instruction is displayed (Figure 4.14). If you use multiple Web Application Service nodes, or you don't use the default Tomcat server or Web Application Container Services (WACS), you need to perform a post-installation step using the WDeploy tool.

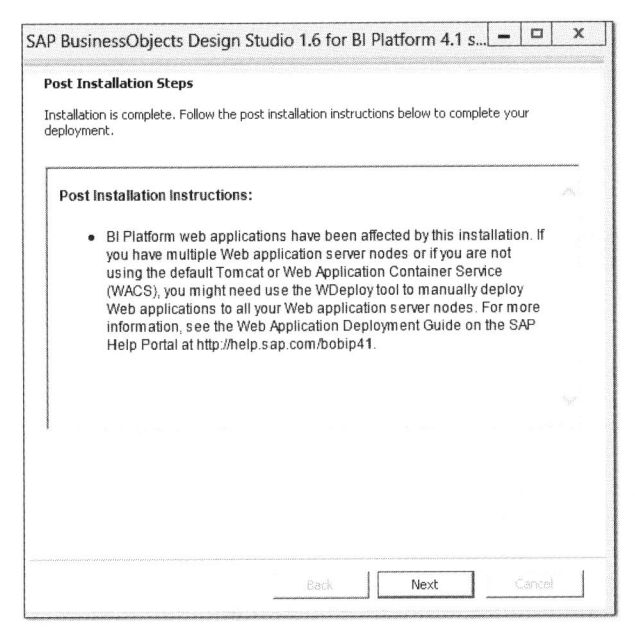

Figure 4.14 Post-Installation

12. You've now successfully installed the SAP BusinessObjects BI platform add-on for Design Studio (Figure 4.15). If you want to launch the WDeploy tool, just select the AUTOMATICALLY LAUNCH WDEPLOY TOOL AFTER INSTALL checkbox.

> **WDeploy**
>
> For more information on the WDeploy tool, see the SAP BusinessObjects BI *Web Application Deployment Guide* on SAP Help at *http://help.sap.com/bobip*.
>
> If you choose to run the WDeploy tool later, you can find it via START • ALL PROGRAMS • SAP BUSINESS INTELLIGENCE • SAP BUSINESSOBJECTS BI PLATFORM 4 • WDEPLOY.

Next, we'll continue the installation process with the configuration of the SAP BusinessObjects BI platform.

Figure 4.15 Installation Finished

4.4 Configuring the SAP BusinessObjects BI Platform

Now that the SAP BusinessObjects BI platform add-on for Design Studio has been installed, you can set a number of configurations on the platform itself. These configurations include the following:

- Initializing the Analysis Application Service
- Setting the number of client sessions
- Assigning user authorizations
- Establishing a MOBILE category

After these steps are accomplished, we'll show you how to set up OLAP connections to an SAP BW and SAP HANA environment.

4.4.1 Initializing the Analysis Application Service

To run Design Studio applications from the SAP BusinessObjects BI platform, the Analysis Application Service has to be successfully initialized. You can check this in the CMC.

1. Log in to the CMC via START • ALL PROGRAMS • SAP BUSINESS INTELLIGENCE • SAP BUSINESSOBJECTS BI PLATFORM 4 • SAP BUSINESSOBJECTS BI PLATFORM CENTRAL MANAGEMENT CONSOLE. This is a shortcut to the CMC's URL, which is *http://<host>:8080/BOE/CMC*.

2. Go to SERVERS.

3. Check if there is an Adaptive Processing Server available under SERVICE CATEGORIES • ANALYSIS SERVICES (Figure 4.16).

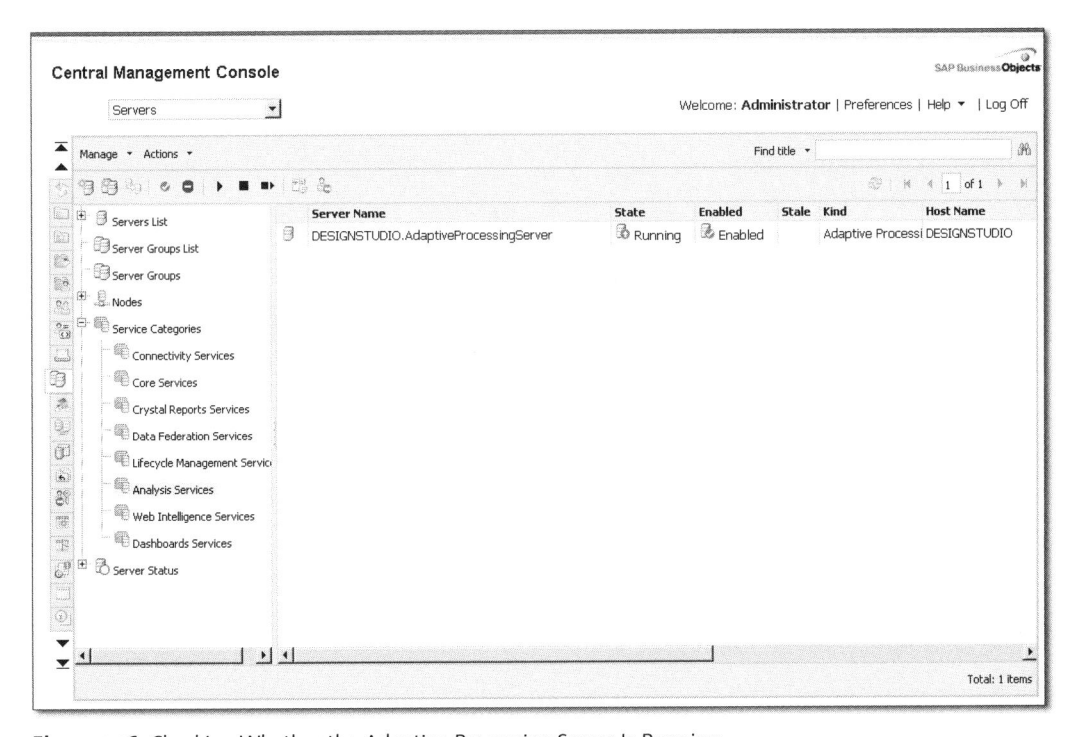

Figure 4.16 Checking Whether the Adaptive Processing Server Is Running

4. If this Adaptive Processing Server isn't available, you have to add one. To do this, go to MANAGE • NEW • NEW SERVER (Figure 4.17).

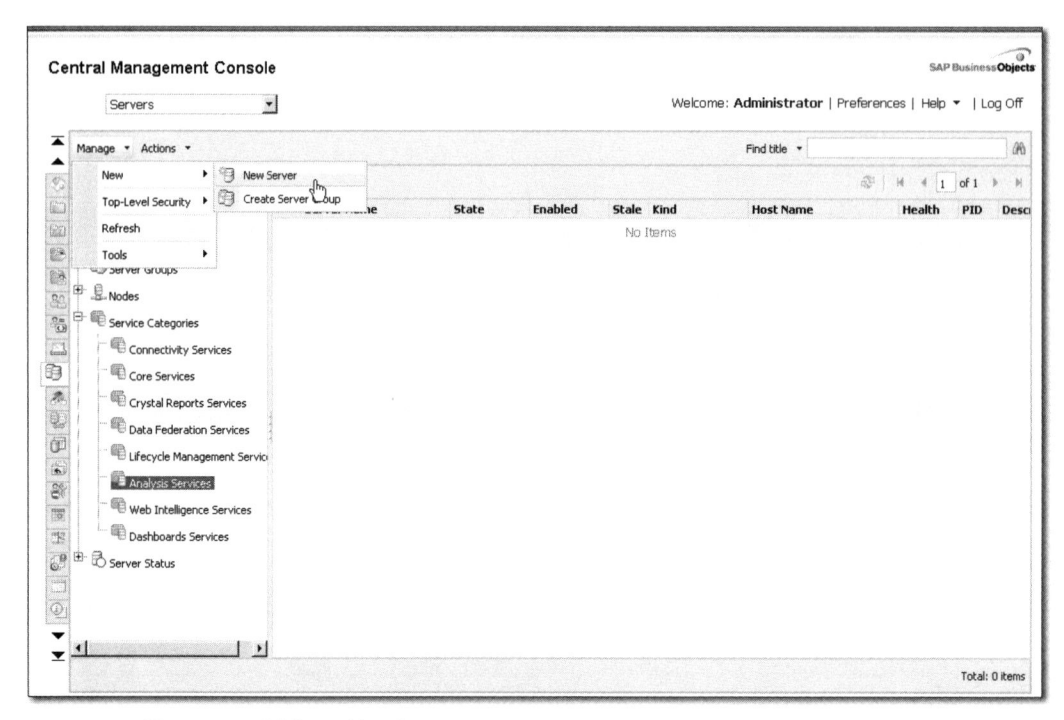

Figure 4.17 Adding a New Server

5. Select ANALYSIS SERVICES from the SERVICE CATEGORY field (Figure 4.18).

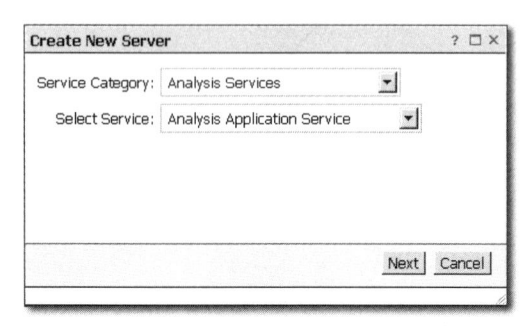

Figure 4.18 Selecting the Service Category

6. Select the ANALYSIS APPLICATION SERVICE from the SELECTED SERVICES list, and click NEXT (Figure 4.19).
7. You can edit the server name if you like. Click CREATE to continue.

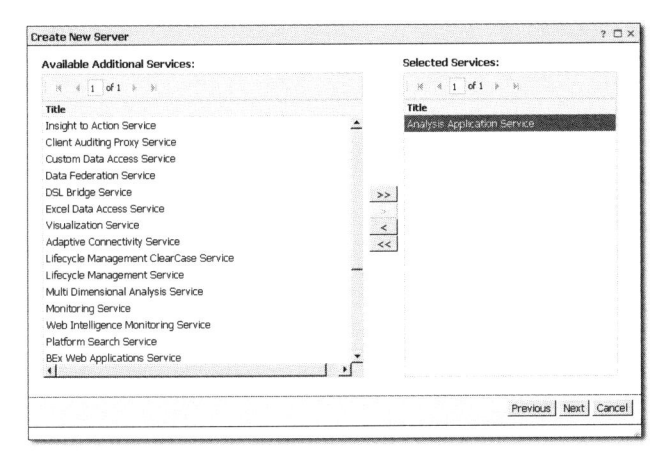

Figure 4.19 Selecting the Service

8. As you can see in Figure 4.20, the Adaptive Processing Server is now available, but it's still inactive. Right-click on the Adaptive Processing Server name and select ENABLE SERVER (Figure 4.21).

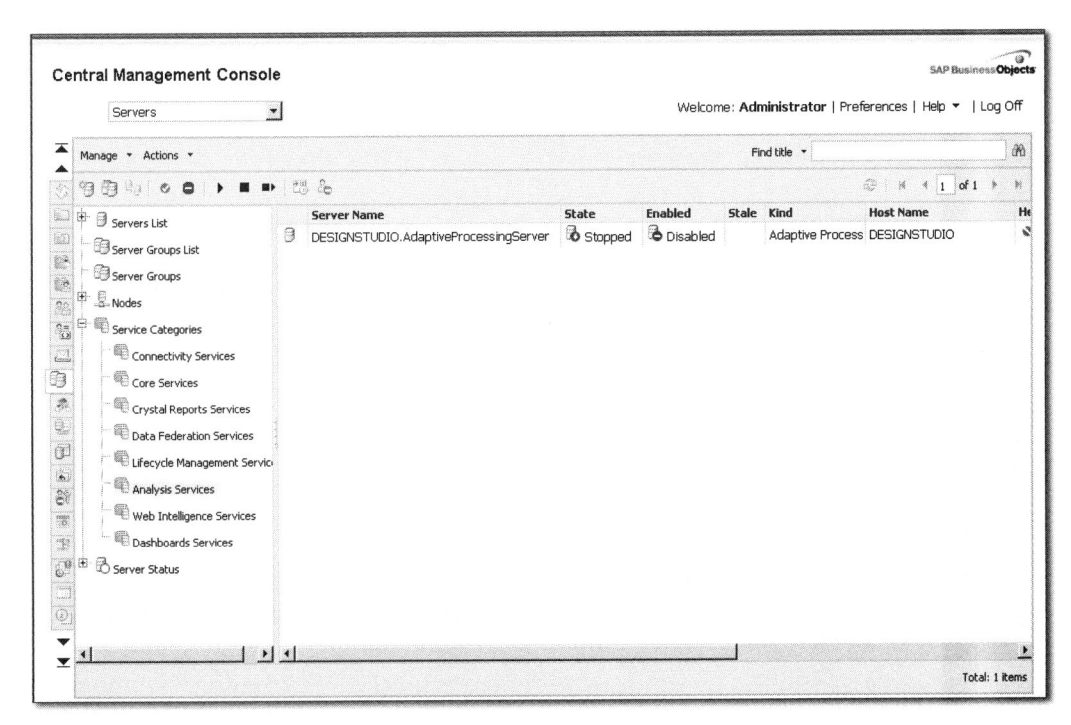

Figure 4.20 The Newly Created Adaptive Processing Server

4 | Installation and Configuration

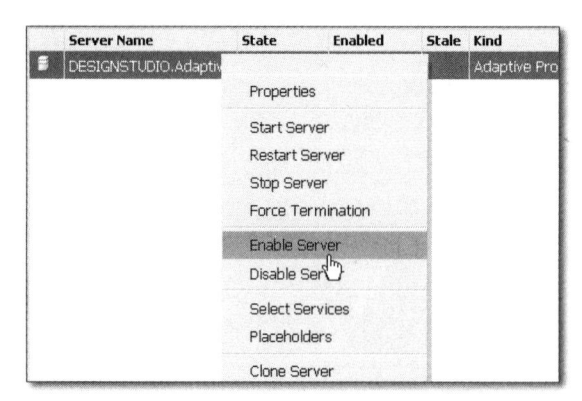

Figure 4.21 Choosing Enable Server

9. When the server is enabled, you can start it. Right-click the Adaptive Processing Server name, and choose START SERVER (Figure 4.22).

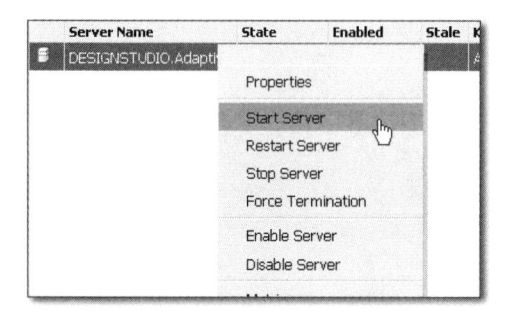

Figure 4.22 Choosing Start Server

10. Right-click the Adaptive Processing Server name again, and choose PROPERTIES to check the initialization status of the server. Scroll all the way down to the ANALYSIS APPLICATION SERVICE area of the screen (Figure 4.23).

11. The message that should appear here is SERVICE IS HEALTHY. If the service isn't successfully initialized, it shows SERVICE INITIALIZATION FAILED. In this case, you should check the server log files to fix the issue.

12. Click SAVE & CLOSE to finish.

Configuring the SAP BusinessObjects BI Platform | **4.4**

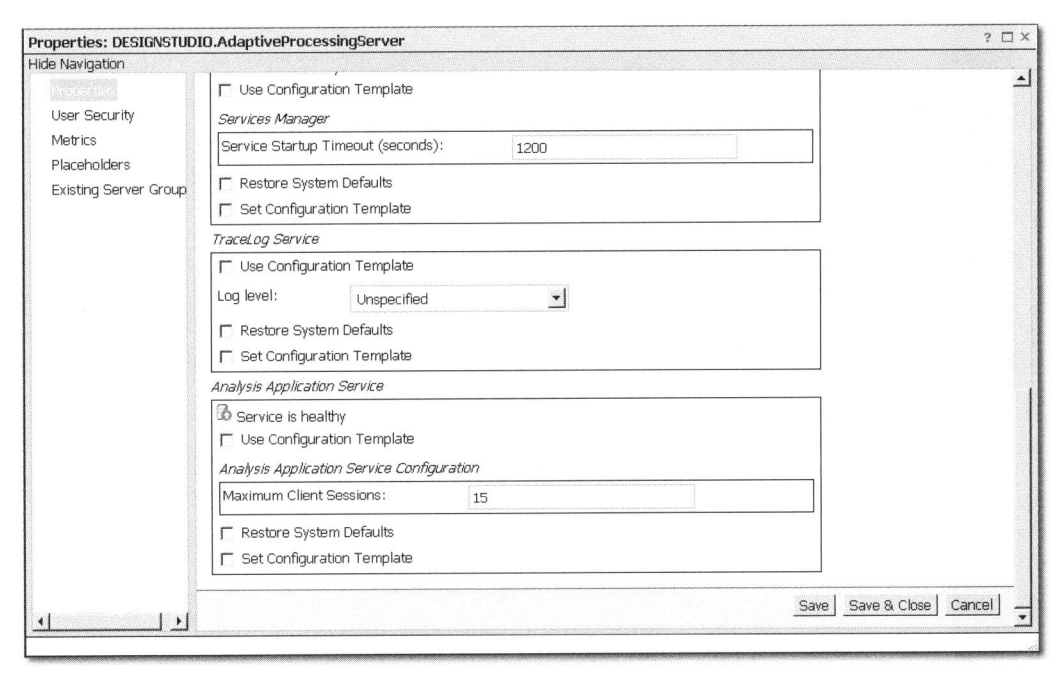

Figure 4.23 Checking the Server Status

> **Managing and Configuring Logs in the SAP BusinessObjects BI Platform**
>
> For more information about logging traces, you can check the "Managing and Configuring Logs" chapter in the *Business Intelligence Platform Administrator Guide*, which can be downloaded from *http://help.sap.com/bobip*.
>
> For more information about SAP BusinessObjects BI administration in general, see *SAP BusinessObjects BI System Administration*, by Greg Myers and Eric Vallo (2nd ed., SAP PRESS, 2014).

4.4.2 Setting the Number of Client Sessions

The maximum number of client sessions that can be active simultaneously can be altered for the Analysis Application Service. When the number of active sessions reaches this number, any further attempts to use Design Studio applications will be canceled. You'll see an error message like the one shown in Figure 4.24.

113

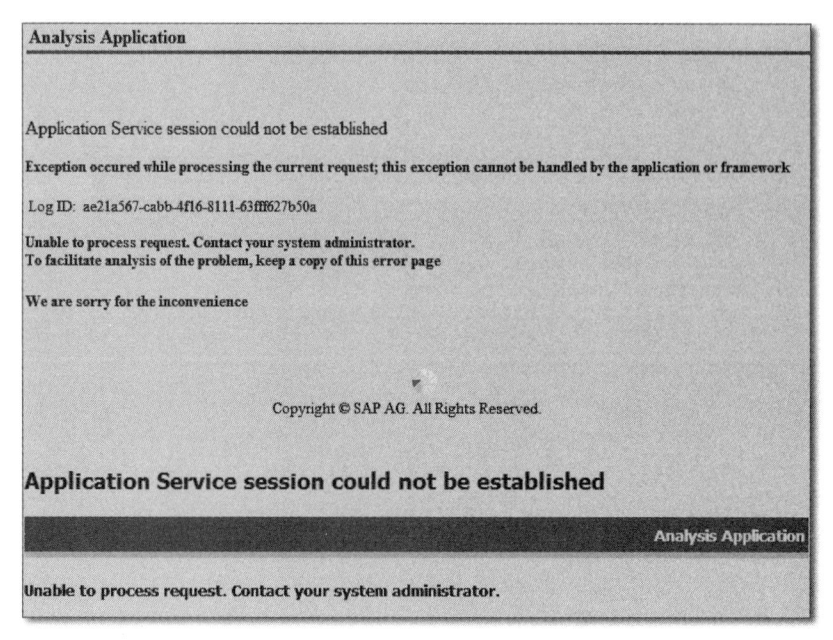

Figure 4.24 Error Due to Reaching the Maximum Number of Client Sessions

To change the number of sessions, follow these steps:

1. Log in to the CMC, and go to SERVERS.

2. Go to SERVICE CATEGORIES • ANALYSIS SERVICES (refer to Figure 4.16).

3. Right-click on ADAPTIVE PROCESSING SERVER, and choose PROPERTIES. Scroll all the way down to the ANALYSIS APPLICATION SERVICE area (refer to Figure 4.23).

4. Check the MAXIMUM CLIENT SESSIONS field, and change the default value if required.

4.4.3 Assigning User Authorizations

Design Studio application designers and users need specific authorizations to access and work with applications. We'll now describe the steps required to create a new user group for these Design Studio users and assign the appropriate authorizations to it. Follow these steps:

1. First, you need to create a new user group. Log in to the CMC, and go to USERS AND GROUPS.
2. Select MANAGE • NEW • NEW GROUP, and enter a group name, for example, "Design Studio Users" (see Figure 4.25). Click OK to save the new user group.

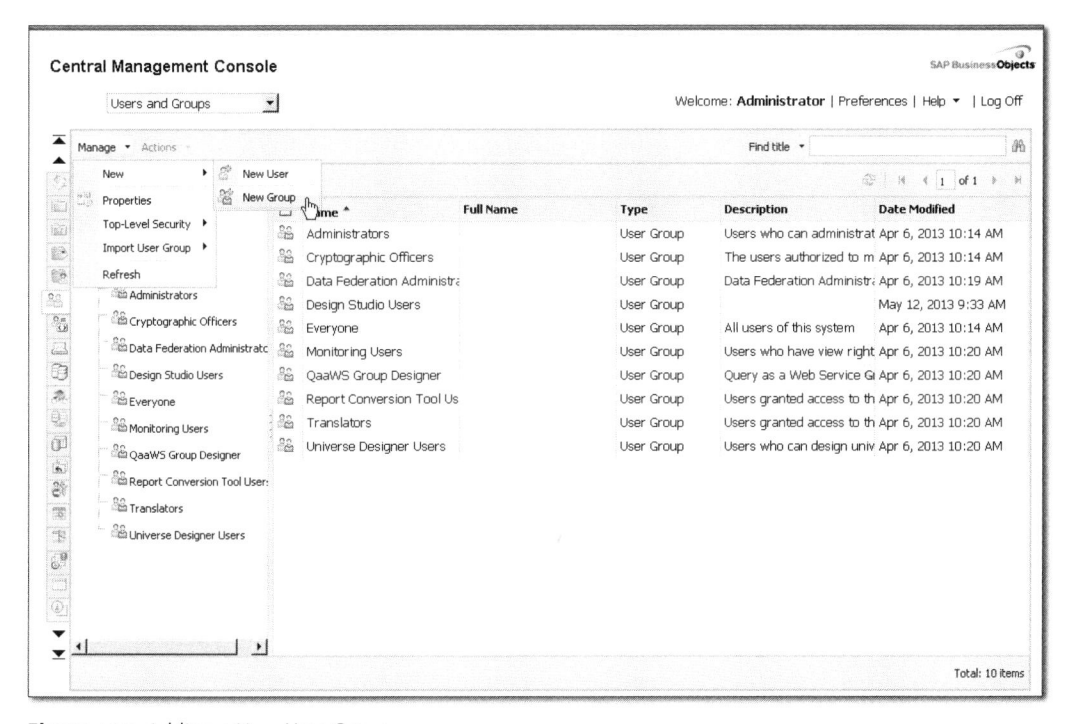

Figure 4.25 Adding a New User Group

3. You can add existing users to this group by right-clicking on the group and selecting ADD MEMBERS TO GROUP (see Figure 4.26). Select the users you want to add, and click OK to finish.
4. Now go to the APPLICATIONS menu in the CMC.
5. Right-click on DESIGN STUDIO RUNTIME, and select USER SECURITY (see Figure 4.27). Now you'll add the group you just created to this application's user security configuration.

4 | Installation and Configuration

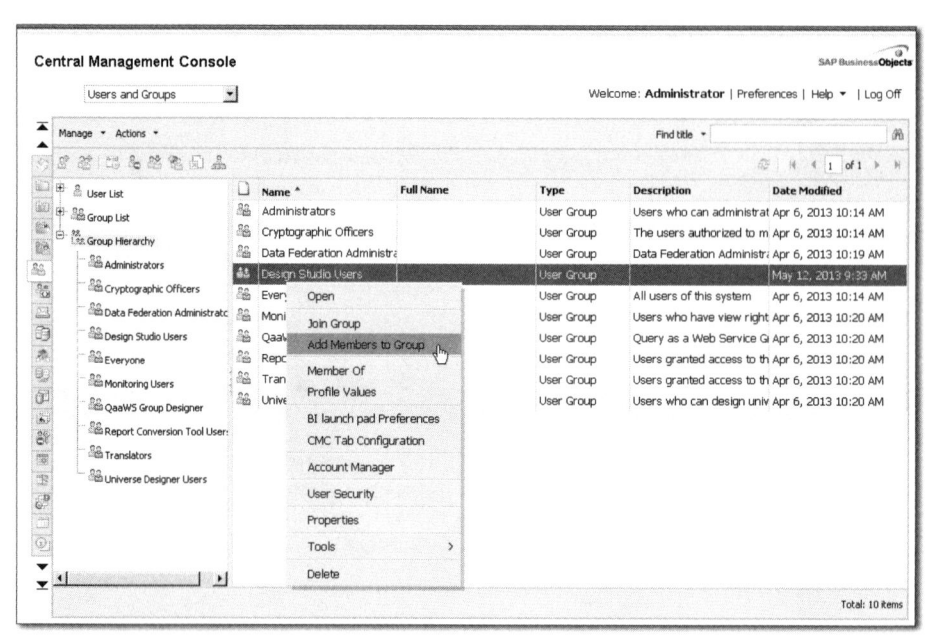

Figure 4.26 Adding Members to a User Group

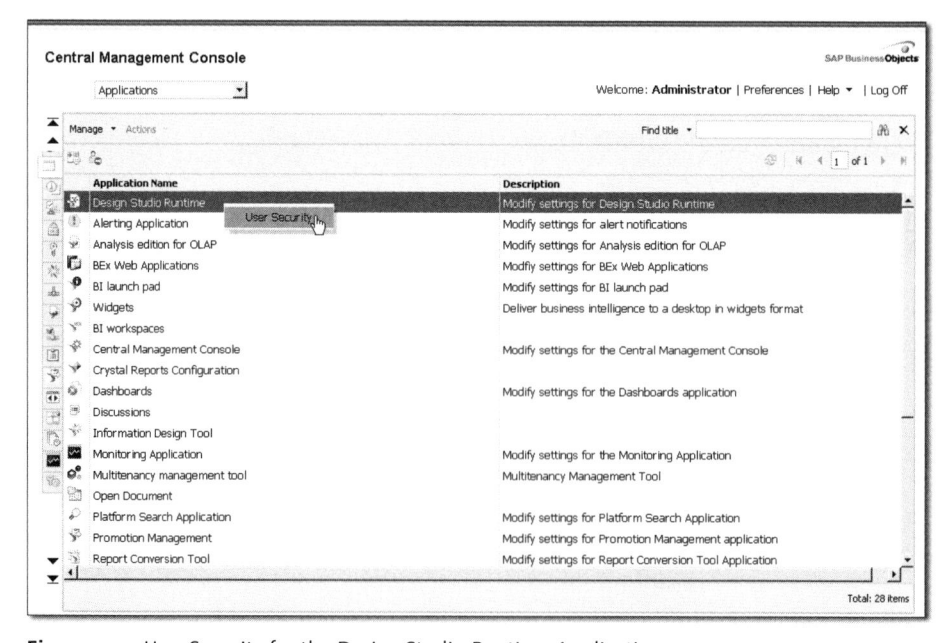

Figure 4.27 User Security for the Design Studio Runtime Application

6. Click ADD PRINCIPLES.
7. Select GROUP LIST, and add the DESIGN STUDIO USERS group to the SELECTED USERS/GROUPS (see Figure 4.28). Click ADD AND ASSIGN SECURITY.

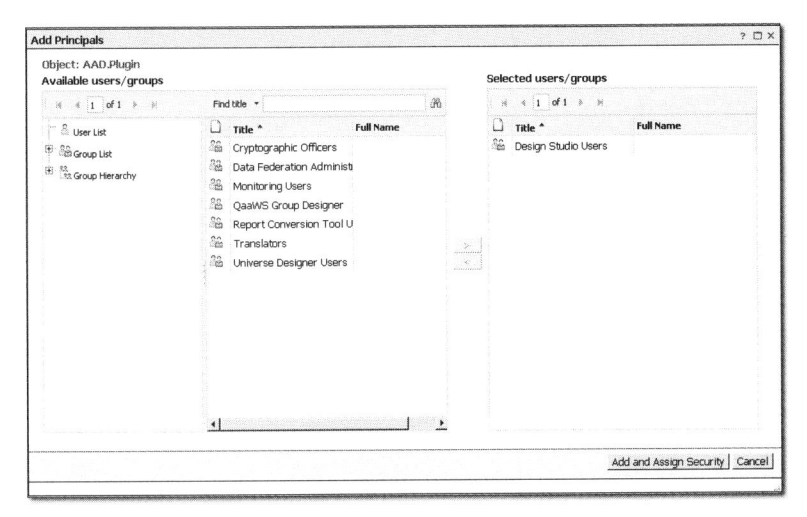

Figure 4.28 User Group Selection

8. Select the VIEW access level, and add it to the ASSIGNED ACCESS LEVELS (see Figure 4.29). Click OK to finish.

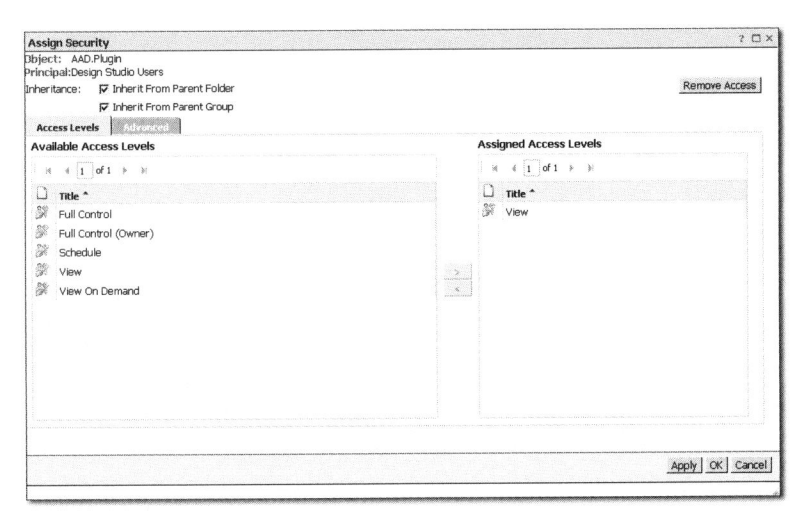

Figure 4.29 Access Level Selection

Your users have been granted the authorization rights for Design Studio. Remember, however, you'll also have to configure the authorizations for other parts of the SAP BusinessObjects BI platform, such as the OLAP connections and the document folders you want this user group to use.

4.4.4 Creating a Mobile Category

Design Studio applications can be accessed through the SAP BusinessObjects Mobile application on mobile devices (see Appendix B). To enable this feature, a Design Studio application should be filed to the MOBILE category on the SAP BusinessObjects BI platform. In this section, you'll check whether this category exists, and, if not, you'll create it. Follow these steps:

1. Log in to the CMC, and go to CATEGORIES.
2. Check if there is a MOBILE category.
3. If not, select MANAGE • NEW • CATEGORY (Figure 4.30).

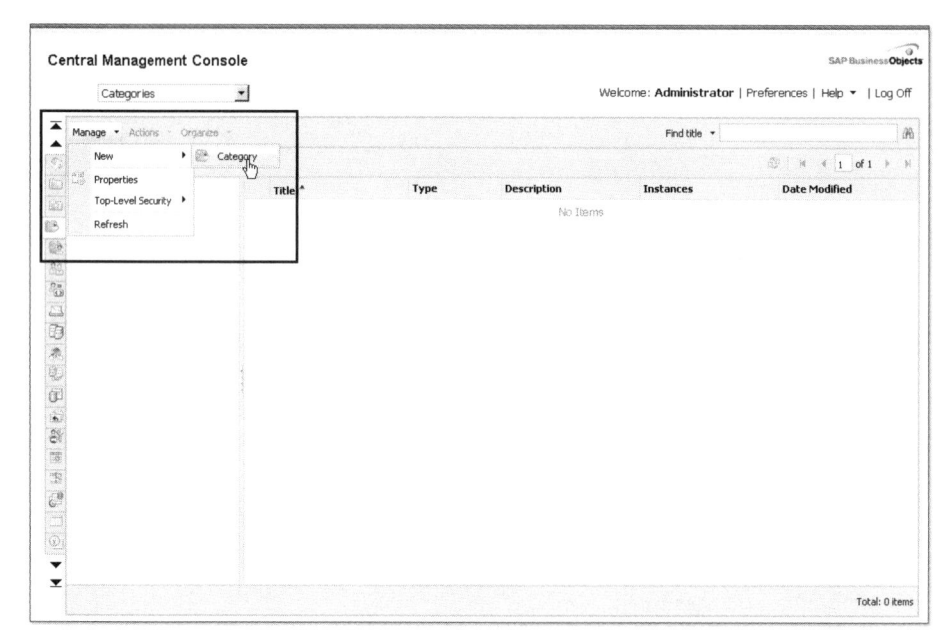

Figure 4.30 Adding the New Category

4. Enter "Mobile" as the new category name, and click OK (see Figure 4.31).

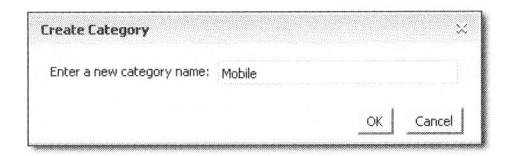

Figure 4.31 Mobile Category Name

5. The MOBILE category is now available (Figure 4.32).

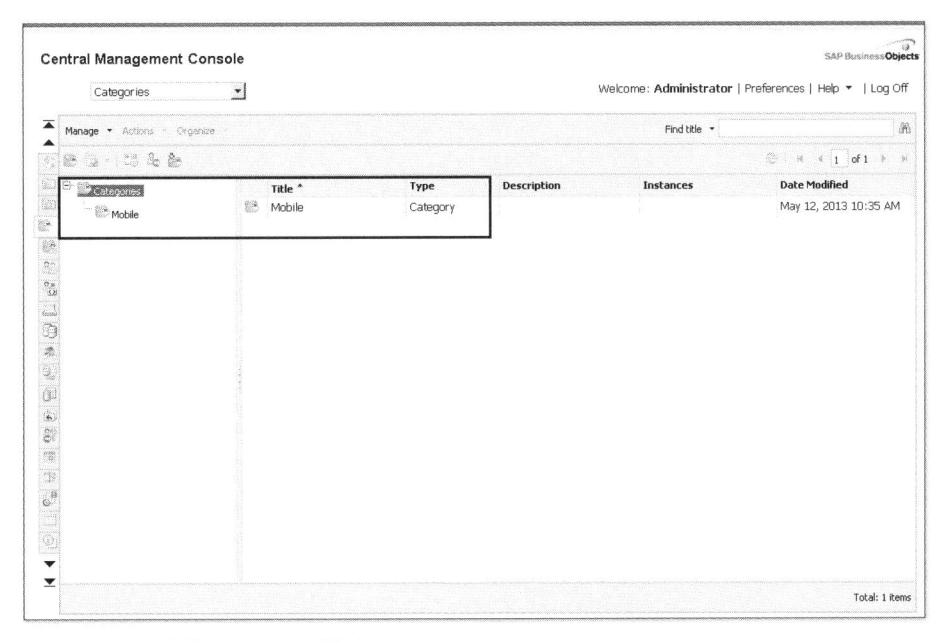

Figure 4.32 Mobile Category Added

6. You can add Design Studio applications to this category by right-clicking on the MOBILE category and choosing ADD TO CATEGORY. You can also right-click on the Design Studio application document itself and choose CATEGORIES.

> **Configuring Categories on the Mobile Server**
>
> The default name for the mobile category is MOBILE. For more information on how to change this category name and organize and display the mobile content, check the "Configuring Categories on the Mobile Server" section in the *SAP BusinessObjects Mobile Administrator and Report Designer's Guide*. You can download this document from *http://help.sap.com/bomobileios*.

4.4.5 Creating an SAP BW OLAP Connection

To connect to an SAP BW system and its BEx queries and InfoProviders, an OLAP connection has to be created on the SAP BusinessObjects BI platform. Such an OLAP connection can give access to the whole SAP BW system or to a specific BEx query, BEx query view, or SAP BW InfoProvider (e.g., an InfoCube or DataStore Object [DSO]). To set up an OLAP connection, follow these steps:

1. Log in to the CMC.
2. Go to OLAP CONNECTIONS, and click NEW CONNECTION (Figure 4.33. This is the third icon in the menu on the top left, just below the ACTION menu).

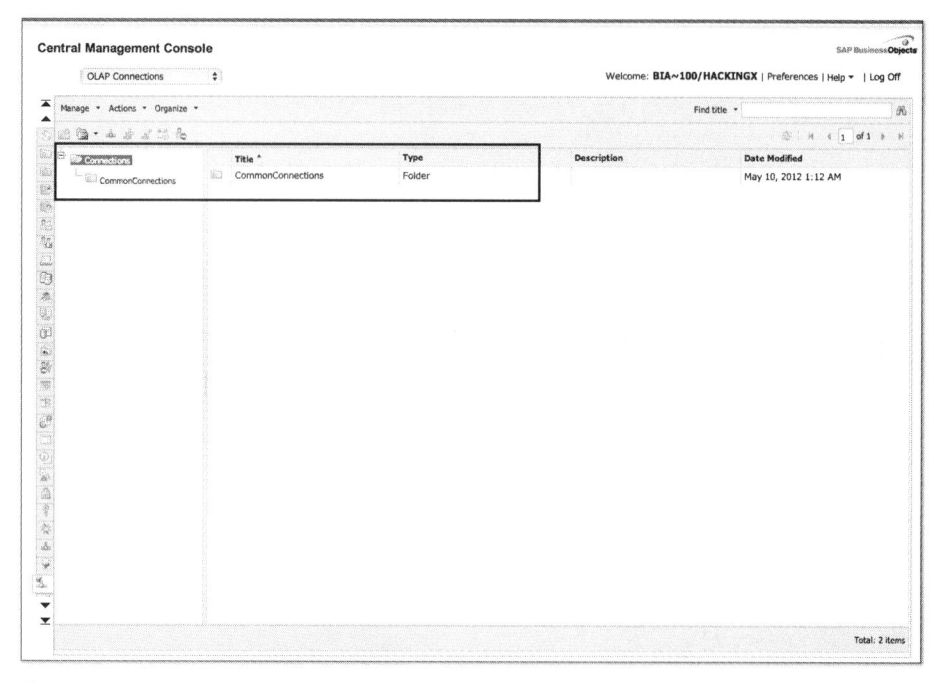

Figure 4.33 OLAP Connections in the CMC

3. In the configuration screen that appears, enter the appropriate text into the NAME and a DESCRIPTION (OPTIONAL) fields for the connection.
4. Choose SAP NETWEAVER BUSINESS WAREHOUSE as the PROVIDER for the OLAP connection.
5. Enter the SAP BW SERVER INFORMATION of the server to which you want to connect (Figure 4.34).

Configuring the SAP BusinessObjects BI Platform | **4.4**

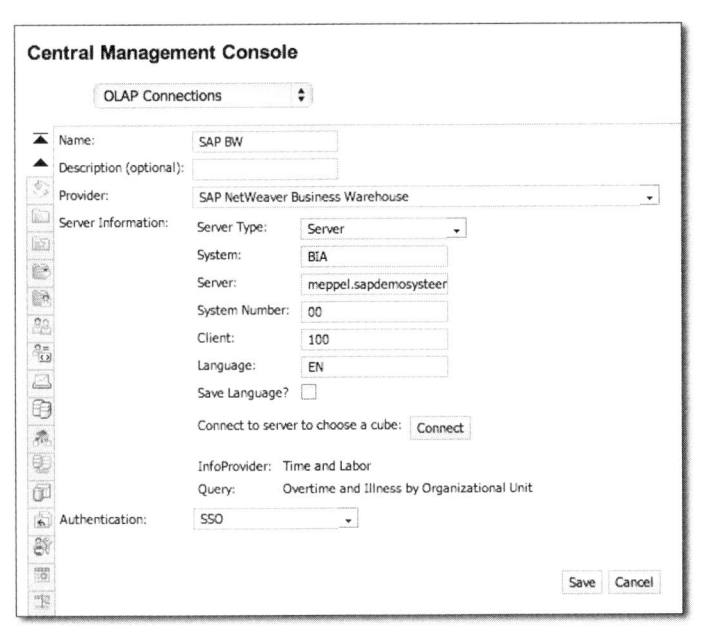

Figure 4.34 OLAP Connection Settings for SAP BW

6. To define an OLAP connection to a specific SAP BW object, click the CONNECT button. Enter your SAP BW credentials in the popup to log on here, and click OK (Figure 4.35).

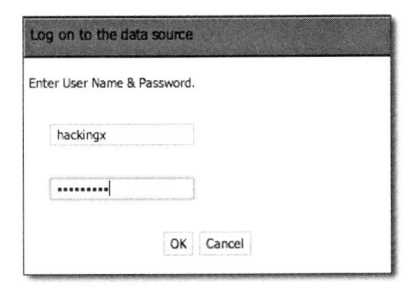

Figure 4.35 Logging On to the Data Source Popup

7. With the CUBE BROWSER, you can now browse to a BEx query, BEx query view, or SAP BW InfoProvider. Click SELECT after you make your selection (Figure 4.36).

4 | Installation and Configuration

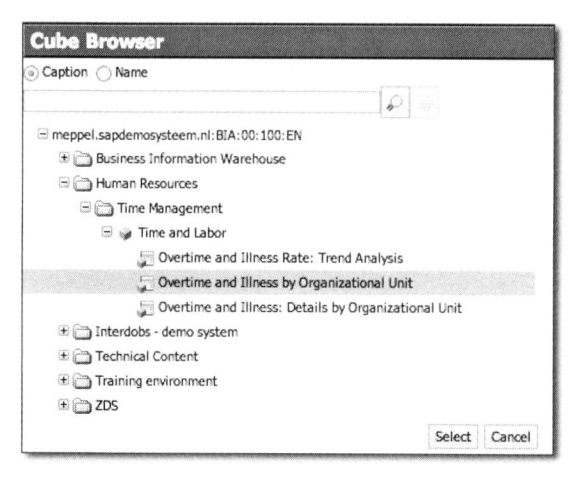

Figure 4.36 Cube Browser

8. Finally, the authentication method has to be defined. There are three possible options here:

   ▶ PROMPT: The users have to log on with their own user credentials. They can change the client and the language in the logon screen.

   ▶ SSO: The users don't have to enter their credentials with single sign-on (SSO), but they still can change the client and language in the logon screen. The users of an application can access the SAP BW objects and data for which they are authorized by the SAP BW authorization concept.

   ▶ PRE-DEFINED: The credentials of a specific user account have to be entered, which means the authorization profile of this user will be used whenever this connection is used.

9. Click SAVE to save the new OLAP connection. The OLAP connection is now added to the list of available connections (see Figure 4.37).

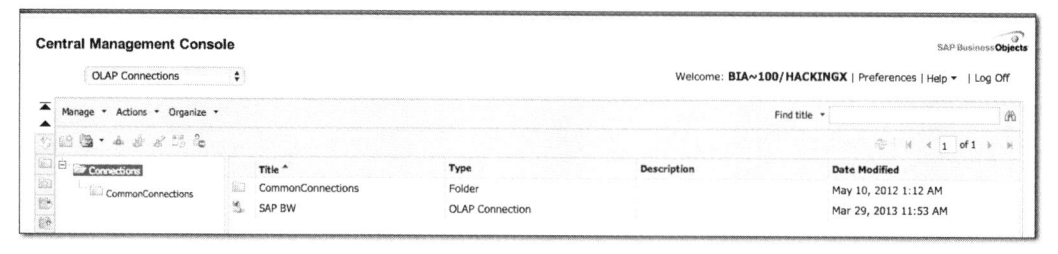

Figure 4.37 OLAP Connections

122

4.4.6 Creating an SAP HANA OLAP Connection

Setting up an OLAP connection from the SAP BusinessObjects BI platform to an SAP HANA system requires most of the same steps as in the previous section. You can connect to an SAP HANA system as a whole, to an analytic view or to a calculation view. Follow these steps:

1. Log in to the CMC, go to OLAP CONNECTIONS, and click NEW CONNECTION (refer to Figure 4.33).
2. Enter a NAME and a DESCRIPTION (OPTIONAL) for the connection.
3. Choose SAP HANA as the PROVIDER for this OLAP connection (Figure 4.38).
4. Enter the server address and port in the SERVER INFORMATION fields.

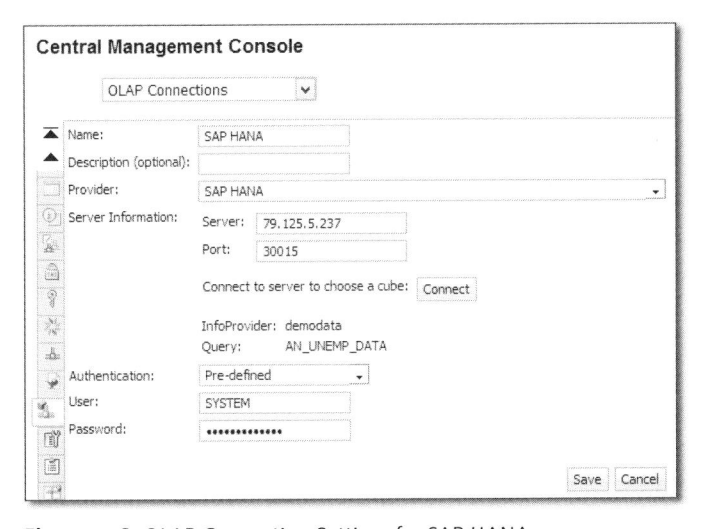

Figure 4.38 OLAP Connection Settings for SAP HANA

5. To define this OLAP connection for a specific SAP HANA object, click the CONNECT button. Enter your SAP HANA credentials in the popup to log in, and click OK.
6. Use the CUBE BROWSER to browse to the analytic or calculation view you want to use in this OLAP connection. Click SELECT to continue (Figure 4.39).

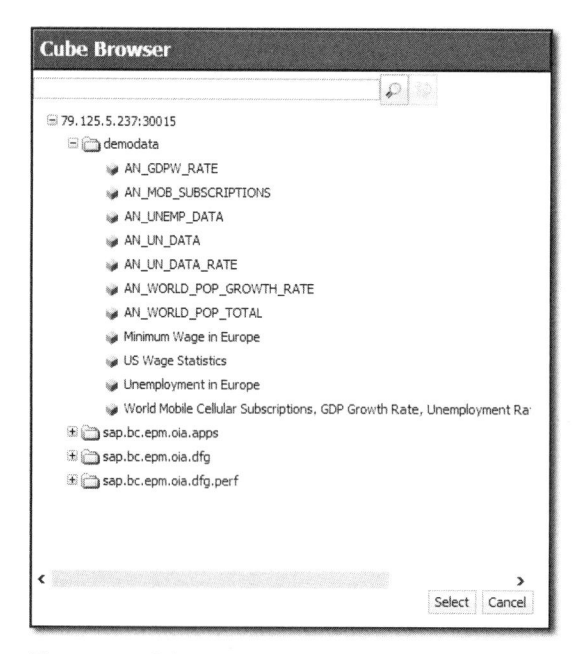

Figure 4.39 Cube Browser

7. Next, you have to set the authentication method. Depending on the version of the SAP BusinessObjects BI platform you're running, you'll see different options here:

   ▶ SAP BusinessObjects BI platform 4.0: PROMPT and PRE-DEFINED.
   ▶ SAP BusinessObjects BI platform 4.1: PROMPT, PRE-DEFINED, and SSO.
   ▶ SAP BusinessObjects BI platform 4.2: PROMPT, PRE-DEFINED, and SSO.

8. Click SAVE to store this OLAP connection.

4.5 Configuring SAP Enterprise Portal and SAP Business Warehouse

In this section, we'll walk through the installation steps to enable the use of Design Studio within an SAP BW environment. To do this, you have to set some configurations and installations on SAP Enterprise Portal and set up the authorization objects in SAP BW.

SAP BW 7.30 SP 09 and 7.31 SP 07

When running SAP BW version 7.30 with SP 09 or version 7.31 with SP 07, SAP Note 1811747 must be applied. This is necessary to save, delete, and load Design Studio applications from the SAP BW system. Later service packs already include these features.

If you try to log on to an SAP BW environment that doesn't have the correct service pack level, an error message like the one shown in Figure 4.40 will appear, preventing you from continuing with the logon.

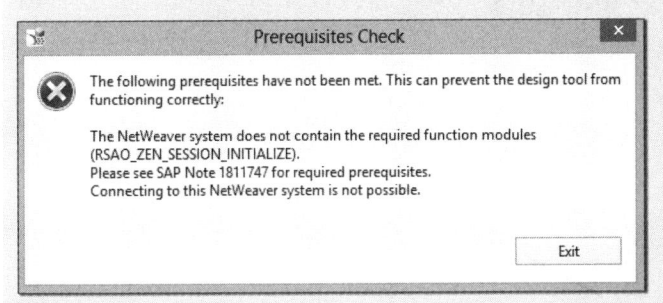

Figure 4.40 Prerequisites Check Error When Logging On to SAP BW 7.30

Connecting to Multiple SAP BW Systems

When using the SAP BW platform, you can only use a single SAP BW system as a source for your Design Studio application's data sources. If you want to connect to multiple SAP BW systems, you should use the SAP BusinessObjects BI platform.

You've seen where you can download the files you need for the Design Studio SAP BW add-on installation in Section 4.2.2. The component that you'll download for Design Studio 1.6 is named DESIGNSTUDIONW00_0-70001237.SCA. To deploy the Design Studio add-on, you have to install this file on the SAP BW portal using the Software Update Manger by following these steps:

1. On the Windows server, start the command line (Figure 4.41), and to extract the Software Update Manager, use the command: `sapcar -xvf D:\SUM10SP15_620006676.SAR` (D:\ is the path to the Software Update Manger located on this server).

2. Next, start the Software Update Manger by right-clicking on the STARTUP.BAT (this will become available after step 1) file (Figure 4.42), and then select RUN AS ADMINISTRATOR from the context menu.

Figure 4.41 Extracting the Files

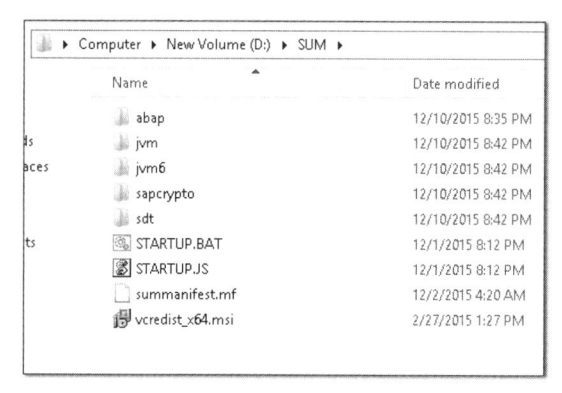

Figure 4.42 Start Software Update Manager

3. A browser window starts up and asks how the file should be opened. Open the file with JAVA WEB START LAUNCHER (Figure 4.43).

4. In the login screen that appears next, use your administrator credentials to log in to the system.

5. You're now ready for the actual installation. Figure 4.44 shows the progress steps, starting with the welcome screen.

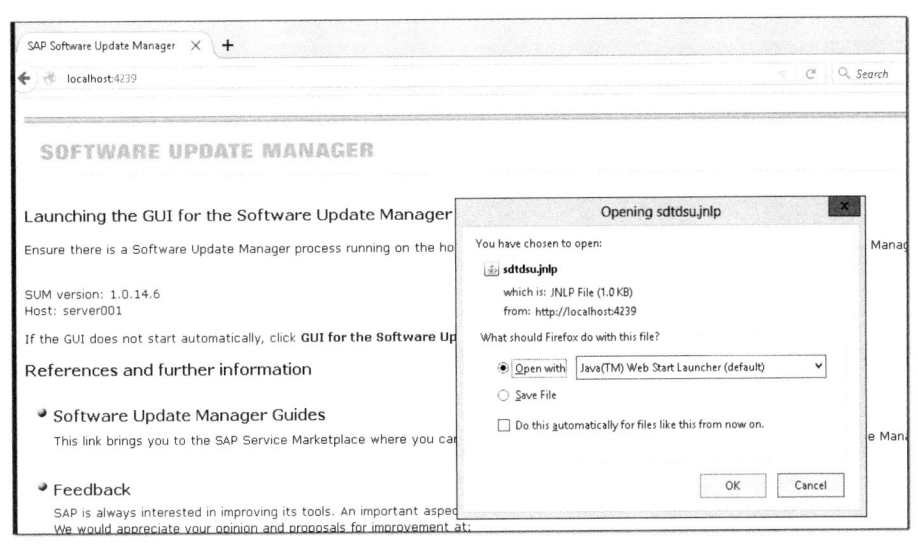

Figure 4.43 Starting Software Update Manager with JAVA

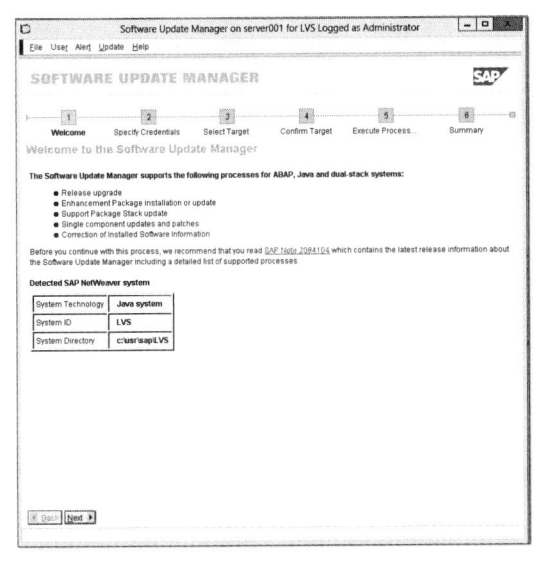

Figure 4.44 Software Update Manager Progress

6. In the next step, the update manager asks for credentials. Enter the credentials for the LVSADM user, and click NEXT (Figure 4.45).

4 | Installation and Configuration

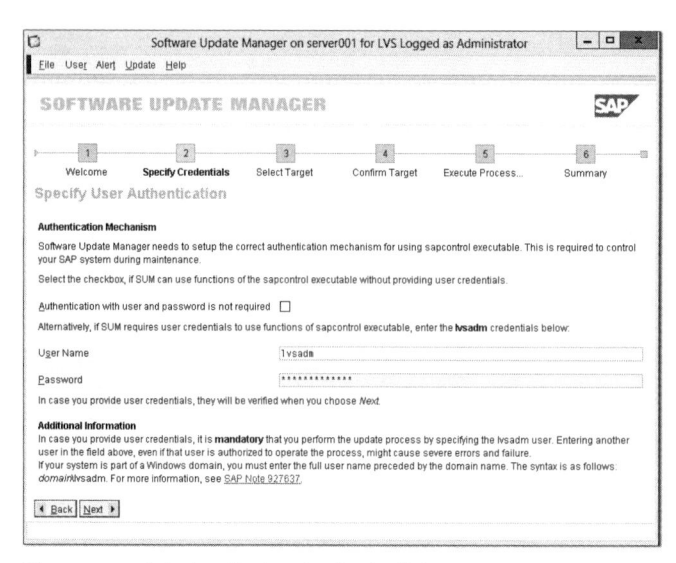

Figure 4.45 Entering the lvsadm Credentials

7. In the following screen, add the path to where the SCA file is located (Figure 4.46). You downloaded this file earlier.

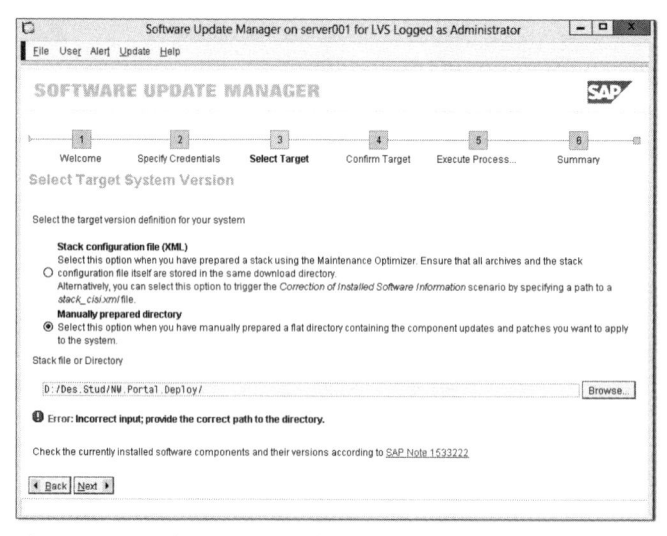

Figure 4.46 Deploying the SCA file

8. Choose NEXT. The files will now be extracted. Choose NEXT again. This time you have to supply your Java administrator user name and password (Figure 4.47).

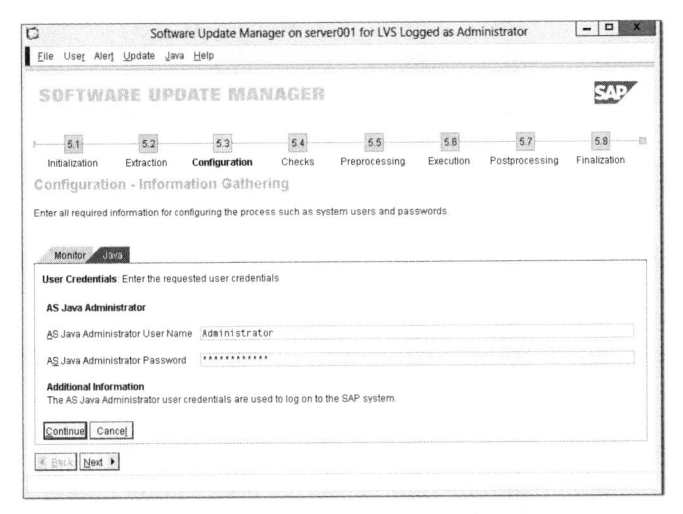

Configuring SAP Enterprise Portal and SAP Business Warehouse | **4.5**

Figure 4.47 Entering the Java Administator Credentials

9. Click NEXT, and go through all the following processing steps. You won't be prompted again to input information. When you reach the last step in the installation (Figure 4.48), click EXIT. The Design Studio add-on is now successfully installed on the SAP BW system.

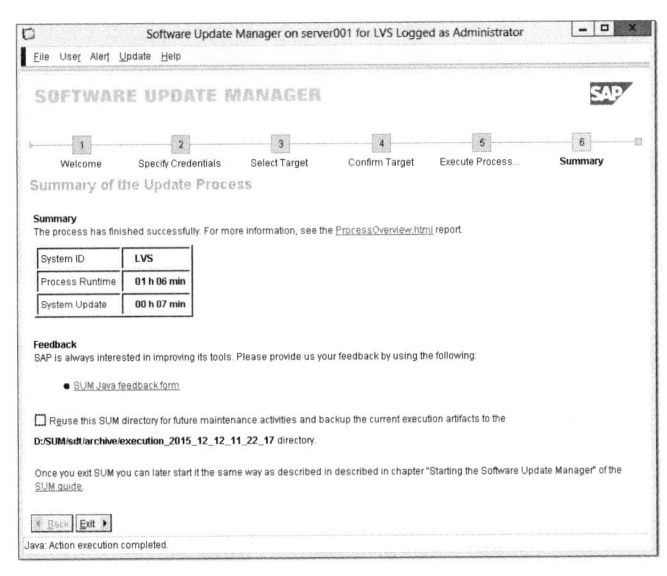

Figure 4.48 Installation Finished

129

4 | Installation and Configuration

Now that you're finished with the installation and configuration of SAP Enterprise Portal for Design Studio, a new iView template for Design Studio is available (Figure 4.49). This can be used to integrate Design Studio applications in SAP Enterprise Portal.

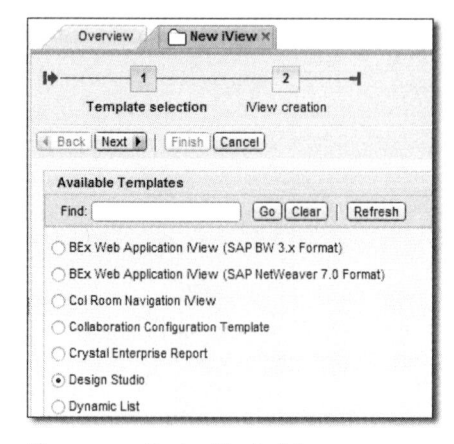

Figure 4.49 Design Studio iView

To provide Design Studio application users and developers with the correct authorizations, the authorization object S_RS_ZEN can be used (Figure 4.50). Table 4.5 explains the authorization fields.

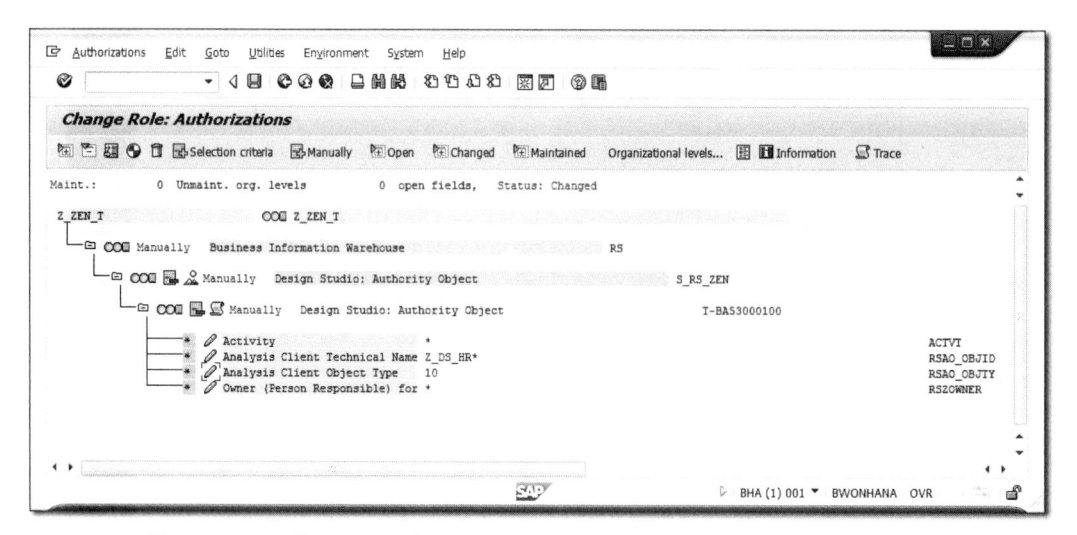

Figure 4.50 Authorization Object S_RS_ZEN Settings

Authorization Field	Description
ACTVT (Activity)	Design Studio application developers need all activity values. Application users only need DISPLAY (03) and EXECUTE (16).
RSAO_OBJID (Analysis Client Technical Name)	Technical name of the Design Studio application. You can use an asterisk (*) to limit the access to a specific range of applications (e.g., Z_DS_HR_*).
RSAO_OBJTY (Analysis Client Object Type)	The object type value should be 10 (ANALYSIS APPLICATION) for Design Studio applications.
RSZOWNER (Owner [Person Responsible] for a Reporting Component)	With this option, you can limit access based on the owner of the Design Studio applications.

Table 4.5 Authorization Object S_RS_ZEN Settings

4.6 Configuring SAP HANA

In Section 4.1.4, you can read the prerequisites for installing the Design Studio add-on on the SAP HANA system. When you've met all of these prerequisites, follow these steps:

1. Open SAP HANA Studio, and connect to your SAP HANA system.
2. Select FILE IMPORT • DELIVERY UNIT (Figure 4.51).

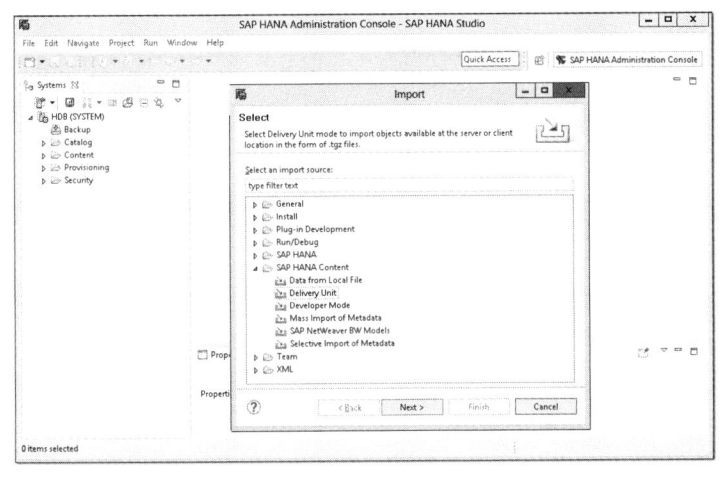

Figure 4.51 Delivery Unit

4 | Installation and Configuration

3. Select your SAP HANA system, as shown in Figure 4.52.

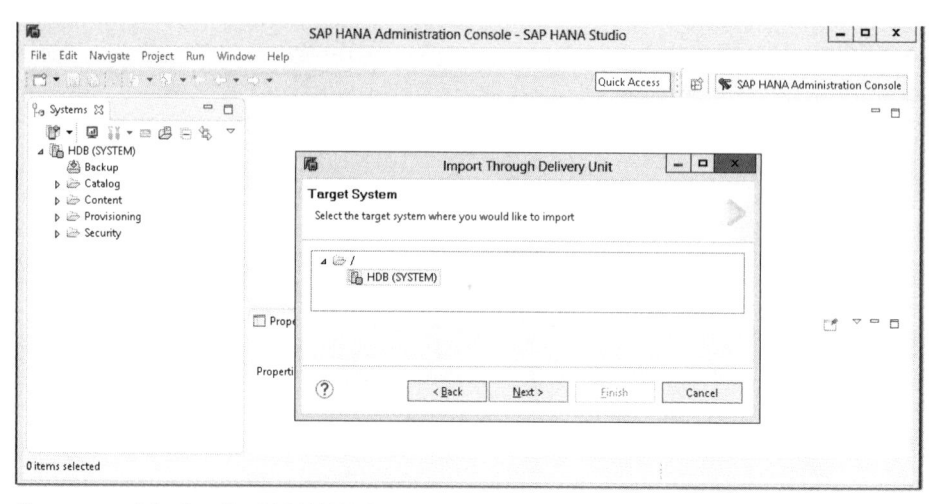

Figure 4.52 Selecting the SAP HANA System

4. Import the HCOBIAAS.TGZ file that you've previously downloaded (Figure 4.53).

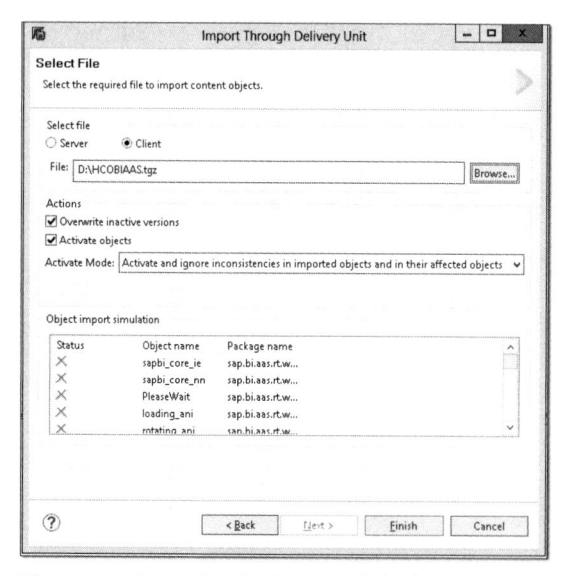

Figure 4.53 Importing the Downloaded File

5. Wait for the installation to complete. When the status indicates no errors, than the installation is successful (Figure 4.54).

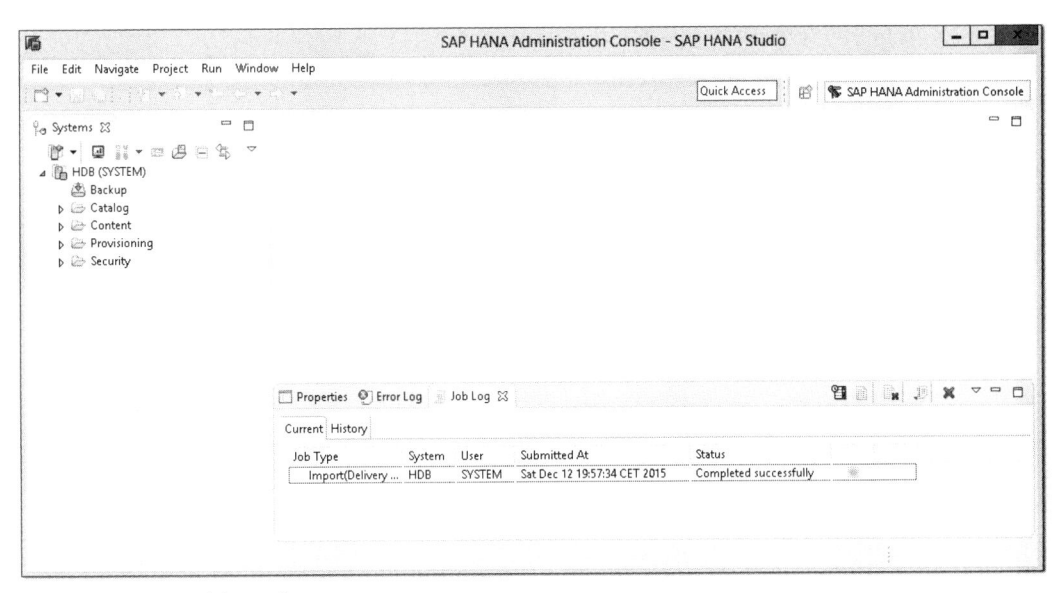

Figure 4.54 Succesful Installation

4.7 Configuring Connections via Universes and Custom Data Sources

As mentioned in Section 4.1, one advantage of using the SAP BusinessObjects BI platform is that you can combine multiple data sources in your application. On the SAP BW platform, you can only use SAP BW data sources, and on an SAP HANA platform, you can only use SAP HANA views.

In this section, we'll discuss how you can configure Design Studio to connect to other non-SAP BW and non-SAP HANA databases using UNX and custom data sources.

4.7.1 Universes

You can set up a connection to an external data source using UNX, which can be published to the SAP BusinessObjects BI platform. After a universe is published to the SAP BusinessObjects platform, it can be accessed and used by Design Studio as a data source in your application.

The following types of UNX can be used:

- Relational UNX
- Single-source UNX
- Multisource relational UNX

UNX can be created using the Information Design Tool (IDT). For more information about IDT, check out the SAP Community Network site at *http://scn.sap.com/docs/DOC-8461*.

You can add UNX in your application the same way you would add a BEx query:

1. In the OUTLINE view, right-click on DATA SOURCES, and select ADD DATA SOURCE (Figure 4.55).

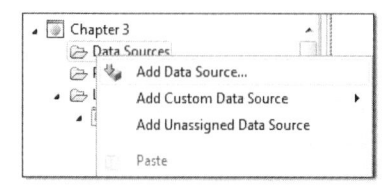

Figure 4.55 Adding a Data Source to the Application

2. Select the UNX that you want to use from the list of available connections.
3. When needed, you can also change the query definition of the selected UNX.

Universe Access

If you want to use UNX in your application, you have to make sure that the SAP BusinessObjects BI platform is at least version 4.1.

4.7.2 Custom Data Sources

Besides BEx queries, SAP HANA views, and UNX, you have some other options you can use to add data to your application. For example, you can use a streaming data source to create real-time applications. A streaming data source can be added in the OUTLINE view by right-clicking on the DATA SOURCES folder and selecting ADD CUSTOM DATA SOURCE • STREAMING DATA SOURCE (Figure 4.56).

Installing the SAP BusinessObjects Design Studio Client Tool | **4.8**

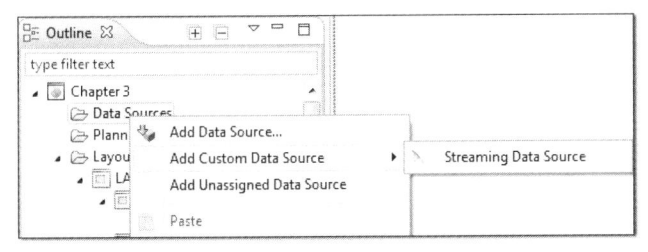

Figure 4.56 Streaming Data Source

The streaming data source uses a connection, which you have to set up using either SAP HANA Smart Data Streaming or SAP Event Stream Processor (ESP). For more information, see *http://help.sap.com/hana_options_sds/*.

SAP HANA Smart Data Streaming

To learn more about SAP HANA Smart Data Streaming, check out *SAP HANA Smart Data Streaming and the Internet of Things* by Eric Du (SAP PRESS, 2015) at *https://www.sap-press.com/3956*.

4.8 Installing the SAP BusinessObjects Design Studio Client Tool

In this section, we'll cover the installation of the Design Studio client tool.

Technical Prerequisite

The user account used for the installation should have administrative rights on the local client system.

To install the Design Studio client tool, follow these steps:

1. Double-click on the installer that you've previously downloaded (DS_CLIENT00_0-70001266). The necessary files are extracted, and the frontend installer starts (Figure 4.57).

2. Click NEXT to continue to the following screen. Select the Design Studio component (Figure 4.58), and click NEXT to advance to the following screen.

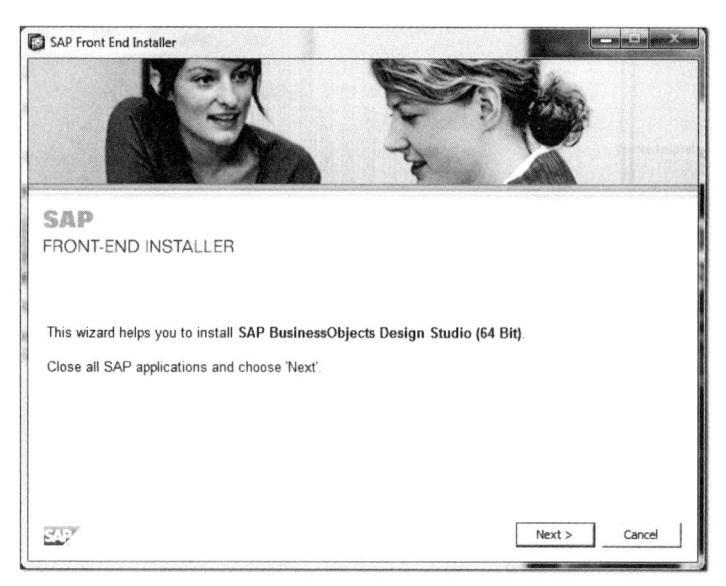

Figure 4.57 Installation Wizard

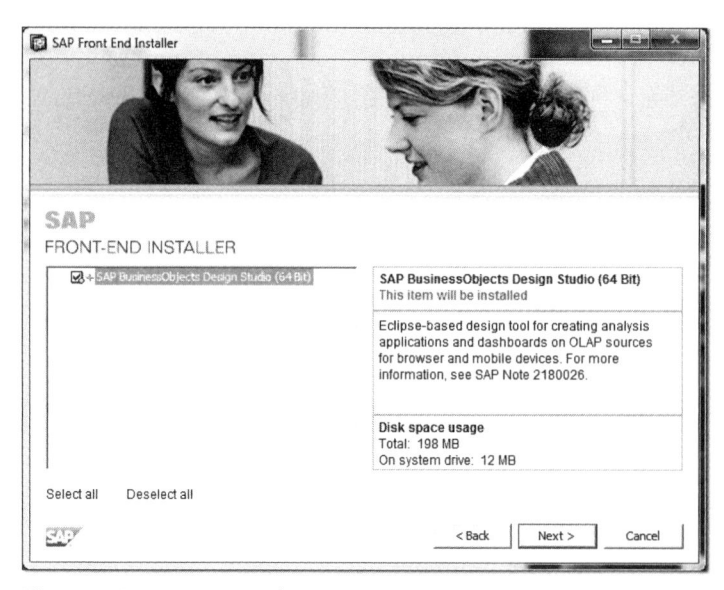

Figure 4.58 Component Selection

3. Click the BROWSE button to configure the target directory for the installation files (Figure 4.59).

Installing the SAP BusinessObjects Design Studio Client Tool | 4.8

Figure 4.59 Target Directory for Installation

4. After you click the NEXT button, the installation will start (Figure 4.60).

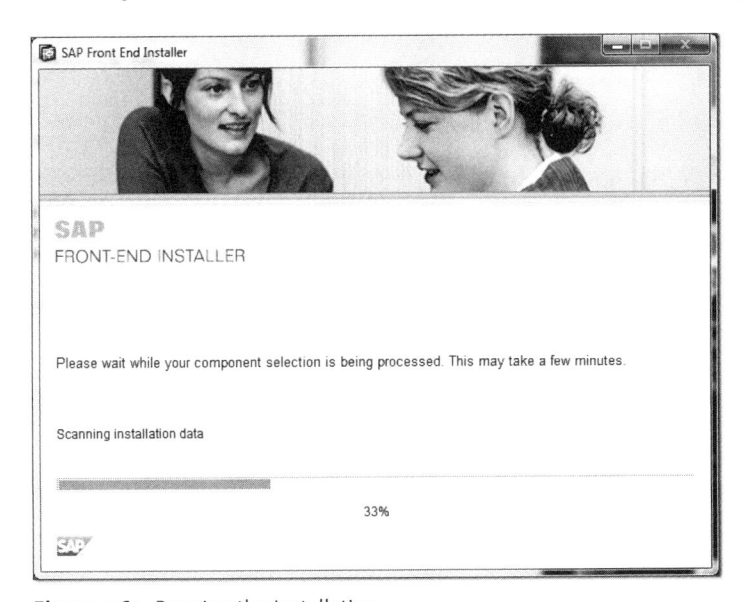

Figure 4.60 Running the Installation

5. If the installation executes successfully, the installer will show a screen like the one shown in Figure 4.61. Click the CLOSE button to exit the wizard.

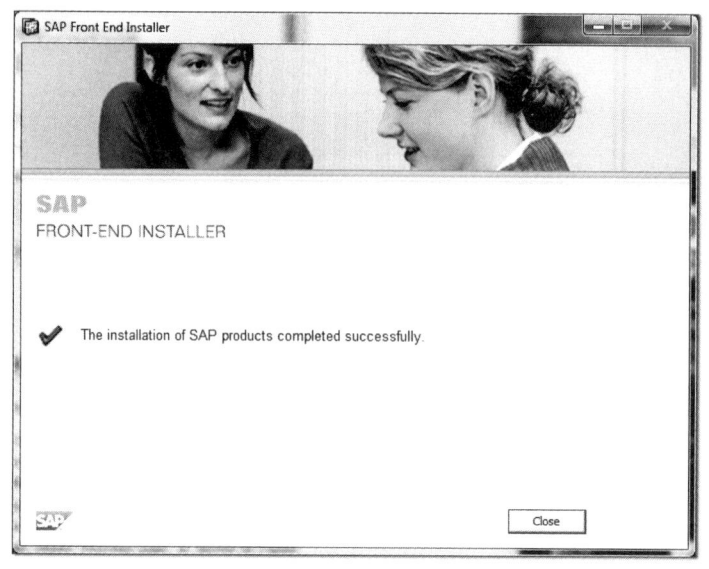

Figure 4.61 Installation Completed Successfully

Congratulations! Design Studio is officially installed. The next step is to run the client tool and log in for the first time. Follow these steps:

1. Open Design Studio via START • ALL PROGRAMS • SAP BUSINESS INTELLIGENCE • SAP BUSINESSOBJECTS DESIGN STUDIO • DESIGN STUDIO. Design Studio starts as shown in Figure 4.62.

Figure 4.62 Design Studio Starting Up

2. The LOGON TO SAP BUSINESSOBJECTS BI PLATFORM screen appears (Figure 4.63). Enter your USER NAME and PASSWORD, as well as the WEB SERVICE URL. This

URL describes the connection to the SAP BusinessObjects BI platform and has the following format: *http://<host>:<port>/dswsbobje/services/Session*.

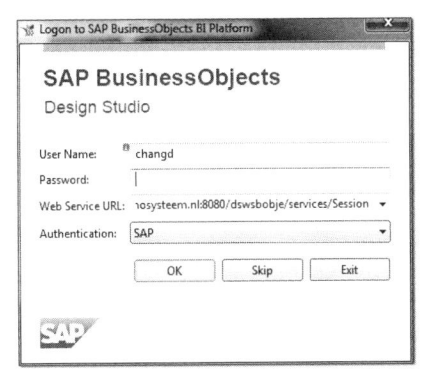

Figure 4.63 Logging On to the SAP BusinessObjects BI Platform

3. Select the AUTHENTICATION type you want to use for your connection. Remember that for access to SAP BW objects, you'll need to use the SAP authentication method.
4. Click the OK button to log in. If you choose SKIP, the Design Studio client tool will start in local mode, with no active connectivity. You should now see the Design Studio welcome page, as shown in Figure 4.64.

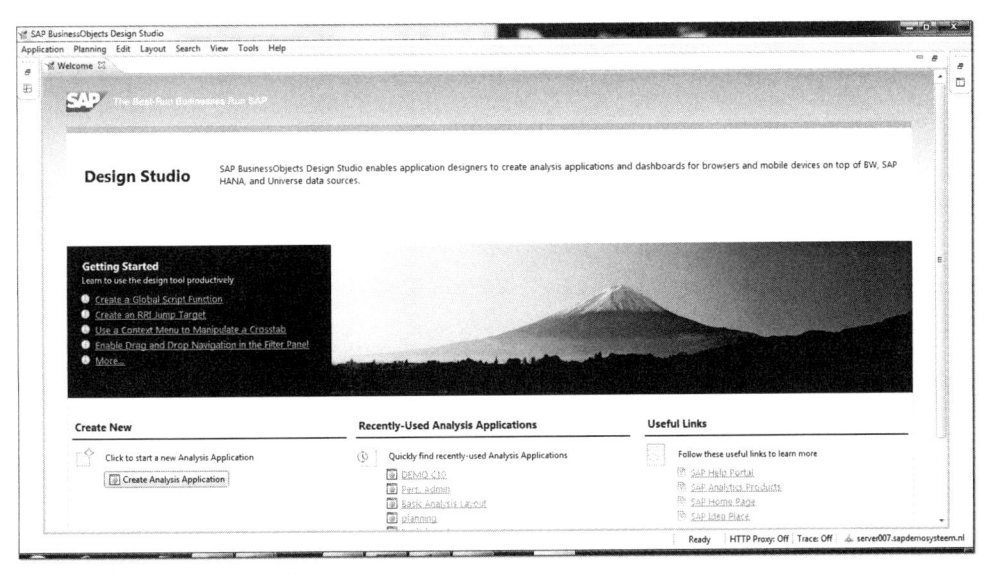

Figure 4.64 Design Studio Welcome Page

4.9 Summary

In this chapter, we went through all the preparation steps required to start using Design Studio to build applications. We started with an architectural overview of Design Studio, including its components, environments, and prerequisites. Then we provided some information about what you need to do and have to prepare for installation. In the heart of the chapter, we provided step-by-step instructions for installation, configuration, and your first logon.

In the next chapter, we'll discuss the integrated development environment (IDE).

PART II
The Basics

Before you can start building dashboards and applications with Design Studio, you should know your way around the development environment. This chapter introduces the Design Studio workspace and its elements.

5   The Integrated Development Environment

Design Studio allows developers to create interactive applications and dashboards. With its integrated development environment (IDE), the developer can create a user interface (UI) using components from a predefined library, configure the properties of these components, and set up data connections with the source systems. Finally, the application can be published to SAP Business Warehouse (BW), SAP HANA, or the SAP BusinessObjects Business Intelligence (BI) platform. Design Studio is fully what you see is what you get (WYSIWYG), which eases the development process.

Figure 5.1 shows the Design Studio development environment, including the menus, toolbar, and Layout Editor. The views for COMPONENTS, OUTLINE, PROPERTIES, ADDITIONAL PROPERTIES, ERROR LOG, SEARCH RESULTS, and SCRIPT PROBLEMS are also visible. This chapter will introduce you to all these features of the Design Studio IDE and help you get familiar with the menus, toolbars, and views available in this tool.

5.1   Menu

The menu bar is located at the top of the Design Studio window, and contains eight dropdown menus. We'll discuss each of these menus and their items next.

5.1.1   Application

The APPLICATION menu has the most options in Design Studio. Here you can create, open, save, or execute a Design Studio application. You can even import and export applications from this menu, as shown in Figure 5.2.

5 | The Integrated Development Environment

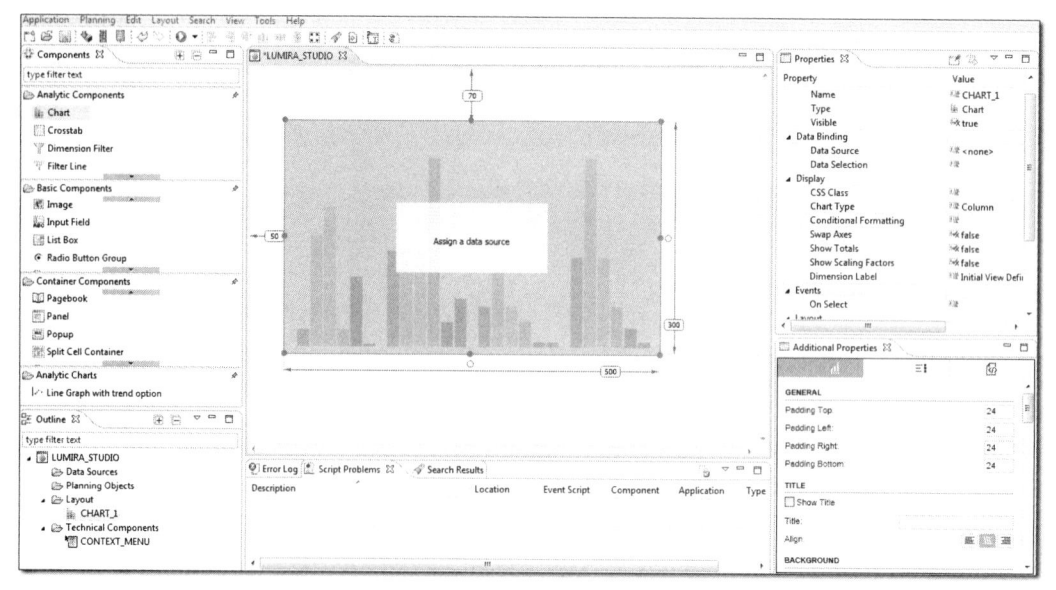

Figure 5.1 Design Studio Development Environment

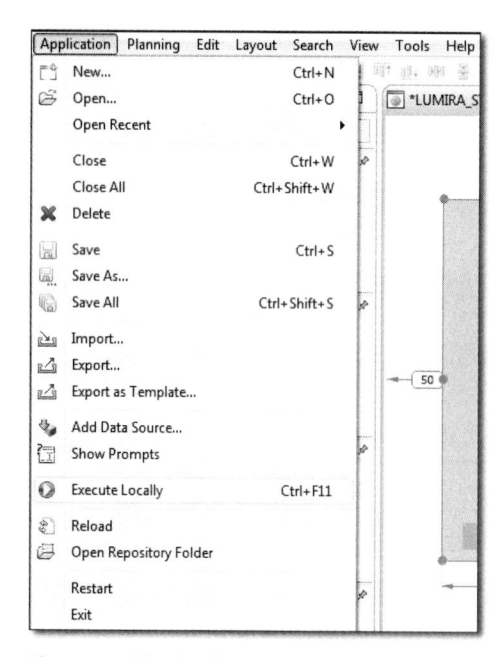

Figure 5.2 The Application Menu

144

5.1 | Menu

New...

With the NEW command, you can create a new Design Studio application from scratch or start with one of the device-specific templates. The keyboard shortcut for this option is [Ctrl]+[N].

If you're logged in to an SAP BusinessObjects BI platform, the BROWSE button will be shown, which can be used to select the folder in which to store the application. (If you started in local mode, this option isn't available.) Here you also can enter a unique name for the application in the APPLICATION NAME field (see Figure 5.3). You can also choose to start with one of the available templates in Design Studio. If you want to start from scratch, select the BLANK template.

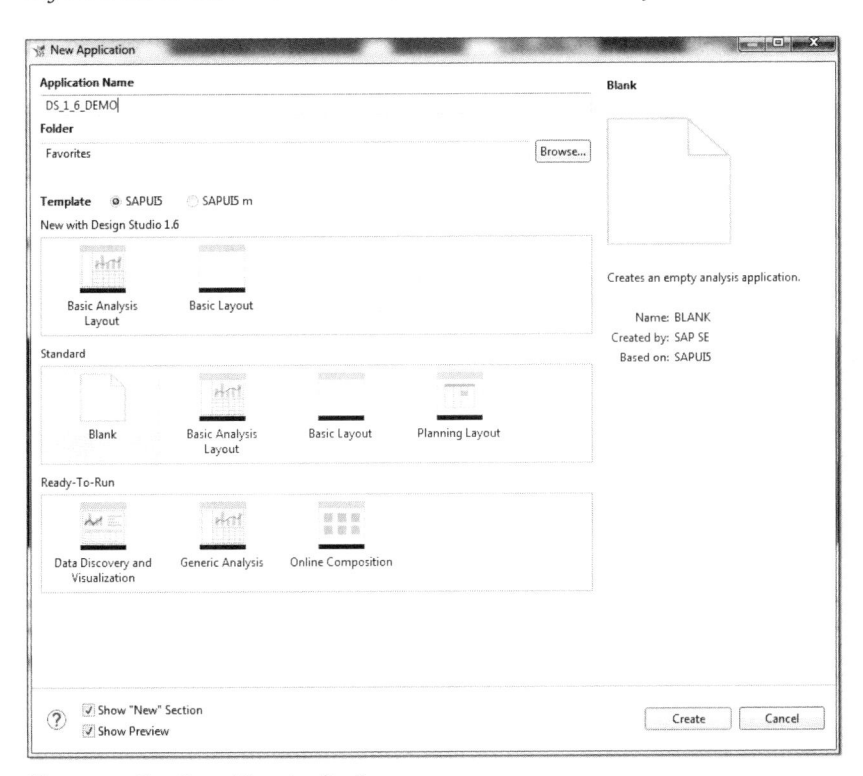

Figure 5.3 Creating a New Application

You can click the CREATE button to create a blank application instantly. It's worth the effort to check out the other available templates. Some of these templates offer a ready-to-run application, and the others are great starting points for developing your own applications.

145

When creating an application, you can choose to use one of the predefined templates. After you've entered a name for your application, you can choose a rendering mode. You have two options here, the SAPUI5 common mode or the SAPUI5 m mode. The SAPUI5 common components are built using a library that is already familiar from previous versions of Design Studio. The SAPUI5 m components are built with a focus on mobility. The components also have a look and feel that is similar to SAP Fiori.

Most of the components are available with both rendering options. However, some components are only available in one or the other. The following are components exclusive to SAPUI5 common mode:

- POPUP
- FILTER LINE
- SPLIT CELL CONTAINER
- FRAGMENT GALLERY
- CHARTS

The following component is exclusive to SAPUI5 m mode: ACTION SHEET

If you select the SAPUI5 common mode, the following template categories are available:

- STANDARD
  This includes the following templates:
  - BLANK: You can use this option to start building your application from scratch.
  - BASIC ANALYSIS LAYOUT: You can use this template to create an analysis application where the user can slice and dice through the data. The main components used in this template are a NAVIGATION PANEL and a CROSSTAB component. The user can drag and drop dimensions from the NAVIGATION PANEL into the CROSSTAB component.

- BASIC LAYOUT: In this template, the screen is divided into three parts (containers), namely a header, body, and footer. No ANALYTICAL components are placed in this template.
- PLANNING LAYOUT: This template can be used as the basis for a planning application. The main components used here are the NAVIGATION PANEL component and the new SPREADSHEET component, where the user can copy and paste data.

- READY-TO-RUN
This includes the following templates:
  - DATA DISCOVERY AND VISUALIZATION: This template creates an application that has the same look and feel of SAP Lumira. The user can select a dataset (SAP BW or SAP HANA) and perform data discovery (apply filters and drill up/down) as well as visualize and present the data as they choose. Users can choose between all available chart types to present their data.
  - GENERIC ANALYSIS: This template creates an application that resembles SAP BusinessObjects Analysis, edition for OLAP. Users can select a dataset and perform slice-and-dice operations by using the drag and drop functionality.
  - ONLINE COMPOSITION: This template creates an application that allows users to compose their own dashboard. The building blocks for this composition are pieces of other applications that have been previously bookmarked.

If you select the SAPUI5 m category, you can choose from the following two templates:

- BLANK
Again, this is just an empty starting point to create your own application from scratch.
- BASIC LAYOUT
This is the same as the BASIC LAYOUT mentioned previously in the STANDARD templates.

After you select a template and click the CREATE button, the application is generated. Figure 5.4 shows the Layout Editor and the OUTLINE view for the BASIC ANALYSIS LAYOUT template.

5 | The Integrated Development Environment

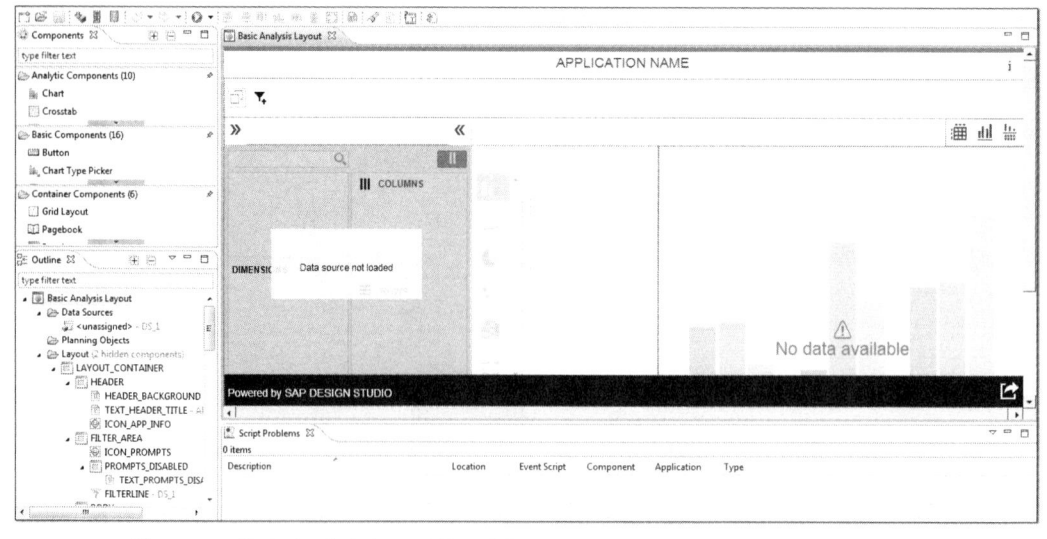

Figure 5.4 Basic Analysis Layout Template

Open, Open Recent

You can use the OPEN command to open existing applications that have been saved previously. Depending on how you logged in, you can open these applications from an SAP BusinessObjects BI platform, SAP BW, SAP HANA, or your local system. Figure 5.5 shows this OPEN APPLICATION window for the SAP BusinessObjects BI platform. The keyboard shortcut for this option is Ctrl+O. The OPEN RECENT menu item shows the eight most recently edited applications. From here, you can quickly open these applications. The CLEAR LIST option erases this list.

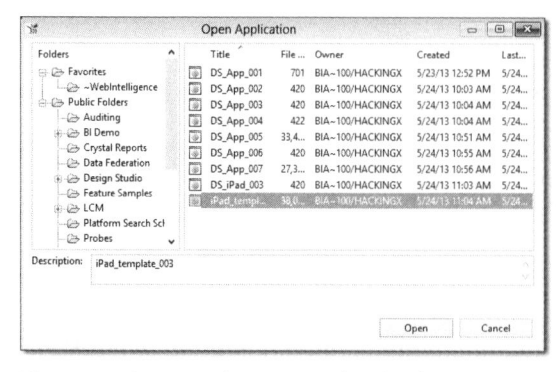

Figure 5.5 Open Application Window for the SAP BusinessObjects BI Platform

148

Close, Close All

To close the application you're working in, you can select the CLOSE command or press ⌈Ctrl⌉+⌈W⌉. If you made some changes to your application, a popup will appear asking if you want to save these changes before closing the application.

The CLOSE ALL option has the same purpose as the CLOSE command, but it closes all of your open applications. The keyboard shortcut for this option is ⌈Ctrl⌉+⌈Shift⌉+⌈W⌉.

Delete

The DELETE command completely removes your application from either the platform that you're connected to or your local system. Make sure you use this option with care because after you click the confirmation button, there is no way back. Probably for this very reason, there is no shortcut available for this command.

Save, Save As, Save All

If you want to keep the changes you've made to an application, you can use the SAVE command to overwrite the original saved file with the newer version. The keyboard shortcut for this command is ⌈Ctrl⌉+⌈S⌉.

If you don't want to overwrite your original saved file, you should use the SAVE AS option. You'll be prompted for a new (unique) technical name and a description (optional), and you have to select the location on the SAP BusinessObjects BI platform where the application will be saved.

When you're working with multiple applications at the same time, the SAVE ALL command can save changes for all these applications at once. The keyboard shortcut for this option is ⌈Ctrl⌉+⌈Shift⌉+⌈S⌉.

Import, Export, Export as Template

You can import applications from one platform to another or to your own local system. The same goes for exporting applications. Application designers can export applications from their own local system or from the platform they are working on. Exported applications can be shared with others (can be imported on other systems).

5 | The Integrated Development Environment

You can use the application that you've created as a template (see Section 5.1.7), which can be useful when you want to make sure that the layout of all your applications is consistent.

Add Data Source

A *data source* is a gateway to get data from a certain part of your SAP BusinessObjects BI source system to the components in your Design Studio applications. Data sources are very important objects in Design Studio because without at least one data source, there wouldn't be any data to present in your application. Depending on the kind of platform you logged in to when starting up Design Studio, you can use different objects as data sources. If you're logged in to an SAP BW system, you can use SAP BW BEx queries, query views, and InfoProviders. If you're connected to an SAP HANA platform, you can use analytic views and calculation views. If you're logged in to the SAP BusinessObjects BI platform, you can use all the OLAP connections that are defined there, including SAP HANA views and Universes (UNX).

If you click the ADD DATA SOURCE command, a popup window will appear giving you a few options (see Figure 5.6). First, you need to select a CONNECTION with the top-right BROWSE button. The SELECT CONNECTION window (Figure 5.7) lists all connections that are defined on the SAP BusinessObjects BI platform. Click the RELOAD ALL CONNECTIONS button to refresh the list.

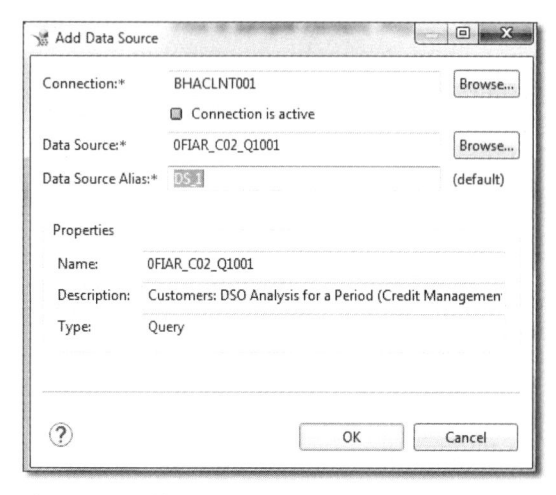

Figure 5.6 Add Data Source Window

150

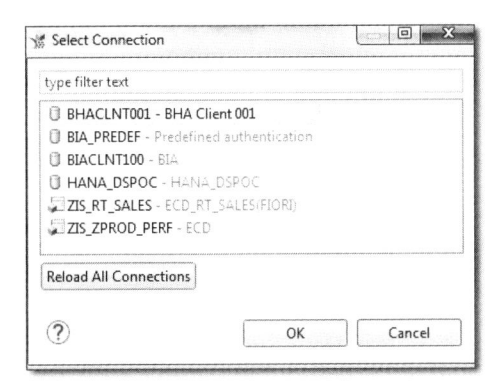

Figure 5.7 Select Connection Window

Next, you can choose a data source. If you already know the exact name of the data source that you want to use, you can enter this in the DATA SOURCE field. Otherwise, click the BROWSE button to search for and select it. For SAP BW systems, you can browse through ROLES or INFOAREAS, or use the SEARCH option. In the FOLDERS tab, you can select a data source from a hierarchical structure. This is grouped by either SAP BW InfoAreas or roles (Figure 5.8). In the SEARCH tab, you can search by the technical name and description of the available data sources.

To find a data source in SAP HANA, you can either look in the FOLDERS tab, where the data sources are displayed in a hierarchical structure, or search for the data source in the SEARCH tab.

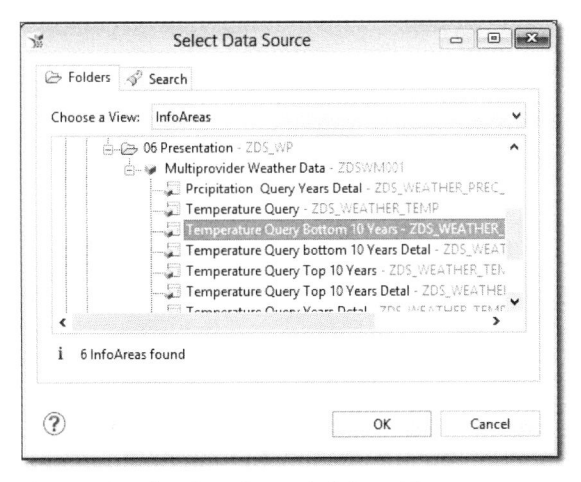

Figure 5.8 Select Data Source InfoAreas View

After you select a data source, the NAME, DESCRIPTION, and TYPE fields in the PROPERTIES area of the screen are filled in (refer to Figure 5.6). In the DATA SOURCE ALIAS field, a default name for the data source is entered, starting with DS_1 and counting up every time you add another data source. If you want to change this default name, make sure you use logical names for your data sources because you might use the data source name later in scripts.

After you click OK, the data source is defined and can be assigned to one or multiple components.

> **Tip**
>
> To quickly assign a data source to a component that is already added to the application, you can drag and drop the data source on top of either the item in the OUTLINE view or the component in the Layout Editor.

Show Prompts

If you added a BEx query as a data source for the application and that BEx query contained one or more input variables, these prompts can be displayed by choosing the SHOW PROMPTS option. Figure 5.9 shows a BEx query with the input variable SELECT MONTH on the characteristic CAL. YEAR / MONTH. This same variable is shown as a prompt in the Design Studio prompt window (Figure 5.10).

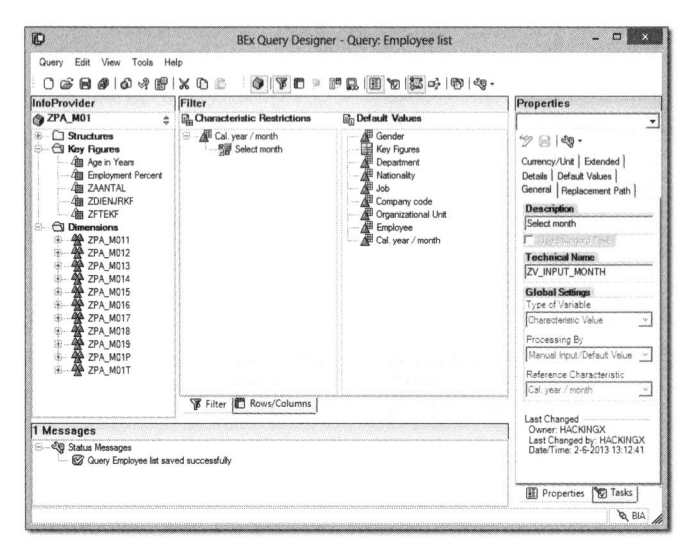

Figure 5.9 BEx Query with Input Variable

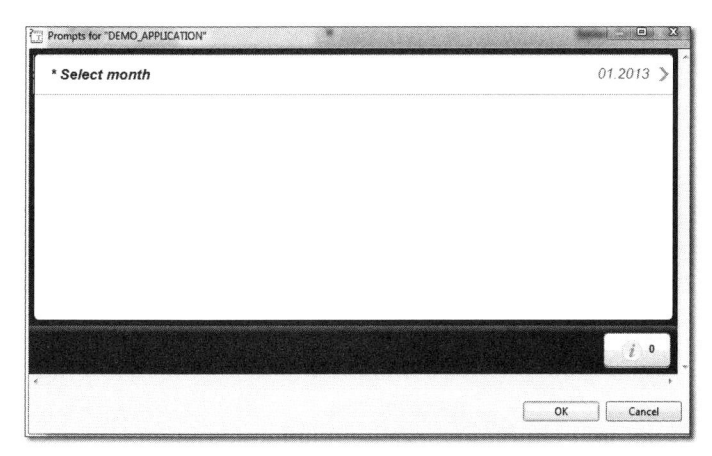

Figure 5.10 Prompt Window

In the prompt window, you can also edit the selected values for each prompt by double-clicking the selected values. The selection window shown in Figure 5.11 will appear.

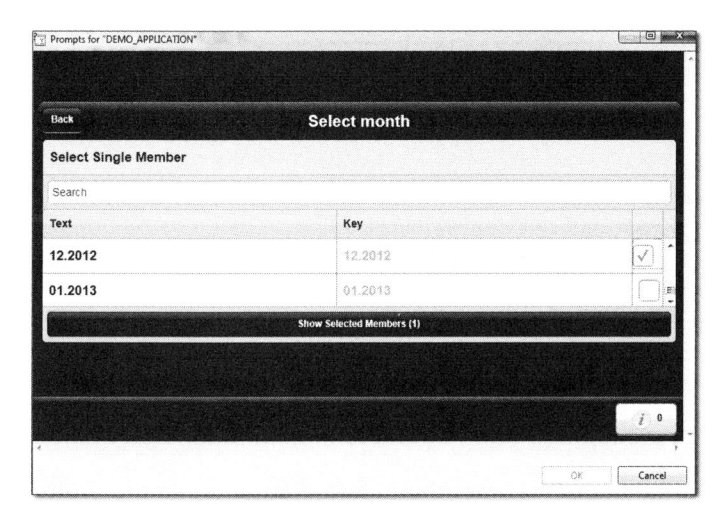

Figure 5.11 Selecting the Prompt Value

Execute Locally

You can execute your application to see what it looks like and how its interactive features work. If you choose the EXECUTE LOCALLY option, a local web server embedded in Design Studio will run the application. A new window of your default web browser will open and load the application. With this option, there is no need to save changes you made to the application before executing it. The keyboard shortcut for this command is [Ctrl]+[F11].

Execute on SAP BusinessObjects BI, SAP HANA, and SAP BW

If you want to execute the application on the SAP BusinessObjects BI platform you're connected to, you can use the EXECUTE ON BI PLATFORM option. The application will be run in a new browser window and is executed with the login credentials you used when logging in to Design Studio. If you haven't saved your application before using this command, Design Studio will ask you to save. If you decline, the last saved version of the application will be executed.

Consequently, when you're connected to SAP HANA or SAP BW instead of the SAP BusinessObjects BI platform, you can choose to execute the application on either one of these platforms. You'll be asked to log in to SAP BW or SAP HANA, depending on which platform you're connected to.

Reload

The RELOAD command refreshes all components you're using in your current Design Studio application, which can be useful. For example, let's say you use an SAP BW BEx query as a data source in your application. Then, while you're working on your Design Studio application, you decide to make some changes to this BEx query. After you save the BEx query, the components that are assigned to this data source still show the initial data output. If you select the RELOAD command, the components are refreshed and the adjusted data output (as a result of the changes in the BEx query) is shown.

Open Repository Folder

The OPEN REPOSITORY FOLDER option is only available when starting up Design Studio in local mode. It opens Windows Explorer and goes to the *C:\<users>\Analysis-workspace\com.sap.ip.bi.zen\repository* directory where you can find the files of your locally stored applications.

Log Off and Restart, Exit

You can use the LOG OFF AND RESTART command if you want to log in to another SAP BusinessObjects BI platform or want to work locally without a connection to any platform. If you want to switch between a platform type—let's say you're working with an SAP BusinessObjects BI platform but want to log in to an SAP BW system—you first have to change the preferred startup mode in the application design preferences (see Section 5.1.7).

When you select the LOG OFF AND RESTART command, Design Studio quits and starts up again, and a logon window appears. Now you can log in to the platform you chose or click the SKIP button to start up in local mode.

5.1.2 Planning

The PLANNING menu contains two options: ADD PLANNING FUNCTION and ADD PLANNING SEQUENCE (see Figure 5.12). Planning functions and planning sequences are SAP BW objects that can be used in applications that use Integrated Planning (IP). Both of these objects are modeled in SAP BW.

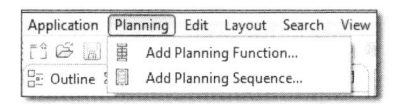

Figure 5.12 Planning Menu

With IP, users can enter plan values into an application that can be then saved back into the InfoCube in SAP BW. Entering plan values can sometimes be a lot of work. Instead of manually entering the values in every single data cell, the user can define some logic for this task. For instance, the logic for the plan values might be to use last year's actuals increased by 5%. A planning function is used to achieve this goal. Other planning functions might be to delete the data or to write to save the data. A planning sequence is just a series of planning functions executed one after the other. We'll discuss planning sequences in more detail in Chapter 9.

5.1.3 Edit

The EDIT menu (Figure 5.13) provides the basic productivity features that are common in desktop applications. You can quickly undo or redo a certain operation, or copy and paste an object.

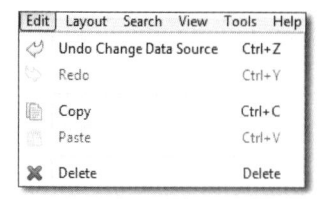

Figure 5.13 Edit Menu

Undo, Redo

You can use the UNDO option to reverse an action you performed. For example, if you deleted a BUTTON component from your application by accident, you can easily go back to the state of your application before you clicked the DELETE command. The keyboard shortcut for UNDO is [Ctrl]+[Z].

The UNDO option also shows what action will be undone. You can see in Figure 5.13 that the UNDO action will undo a change to the data source, whereas in Figure 5.14 a property for a BUTTON component will be undone.

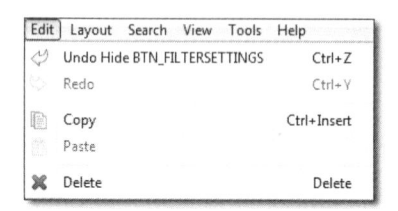

Figure 5.14 Undo the Hide Button

If you used the UNDO feature but still want to use the change, you can use REDO to reverse the undo action. The keyboard shortcut for REDO is [Ctrl]+[Y].

In Design Studio, you can go back and forth across multiple steps with these options.

Copy, Paste

Some other well-known features are COPY and PASTE. When you use the COPY option on a selected component, the component will be stored in your system's clipboard. You can use the PASTE option to paste it again in a desired location.

You can use these commands on multiple selected components at the same time. The keyboard shortcuts are [Ctrl]+[C] for COPY and [Ctrl]+[V] for PASTE.

Delete

The DELETE command erases the selected component or components from the application. The keyboard shortcut for this action is [Del].

5.1.4 Layout

The LAYOUT menu (Figure 5.15) is all about positioning components within a Design Studio application.

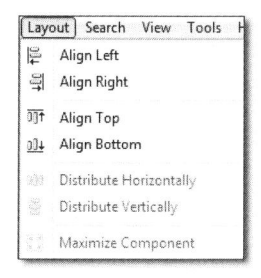

Figure 5.15 Layout Menu

Align

With the four ALIGN commands, you can position two or more components on the same left, right, top, or bottom edge. To do this, you have to select two or more components in the OUTLINE view (see Section 5.3.2) by using [Ctrl]+click or [Shift]+click. Next, select the ALIGN command for the alignment that you want to execute.

Design Studio uses the outermost component as the leading placeholder. Let's say you have three components in your application: component A positioned on the left of the application, component B in the middle, and component C on the right.

If you select these three components and choose the ALIGN LEFT command, components B and C will be aligned with the left side of component A because that component provides the outermost position for the ALIGN LEFT command. If you choose the ALIGN RIGHT command, components A and B will be aligned with the right side of component C.

Distribute

With the DISTRIBUTE HORIZONTALLY and DISTRIBUTE VERTICALLY options, a set of three or more selected components can be spaced evenly. The two outer components remain in position, but the components lying in between are arranged such that the distance between the center point of each component is the same.

Maximize Component

The MAXIMIZE COMPONENT command enlarges a component to its maximum size. When you use this option, the layout properties of the component will be set as shown in Figure 5.16, with zero for the margins and auto for the width and height.

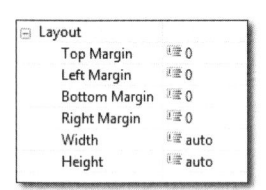

Figure 5.16 Layout Properties after Using the Maximize Component Command

5.1.5 Search

The SEARCH menu (Figure 5.17) brings some very powerful developer features to Design Studio—SEARCH APPLICATION and FIND REFERENCES—which come in handy when working with more complex applications.

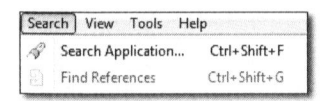

Figure 5.17 Search Menu

Search Application...

With the SEARCH APPLICATION option, you can search every text string that is used throughout the complete application—whether it's a part of code, a component name, or a property value. The result box displays the search results while you're typing. If you want the search to be case-sensitive, you can select this option after clicking the OPTIONS << button. You can also select that you want to search through the hidden components.

As you can see in Figure 5.18, 17 matches are available when searching for the string "false". The results are grouped by component, showing the corresponding component icon and its name. The items underneath the component show the properties, scripts, or Cascading Style Sheets (CSS) styles in which a match has been found.

You can double-click a component or property to select it. If you double-click a script or a CSS style, its editor opens instantly.

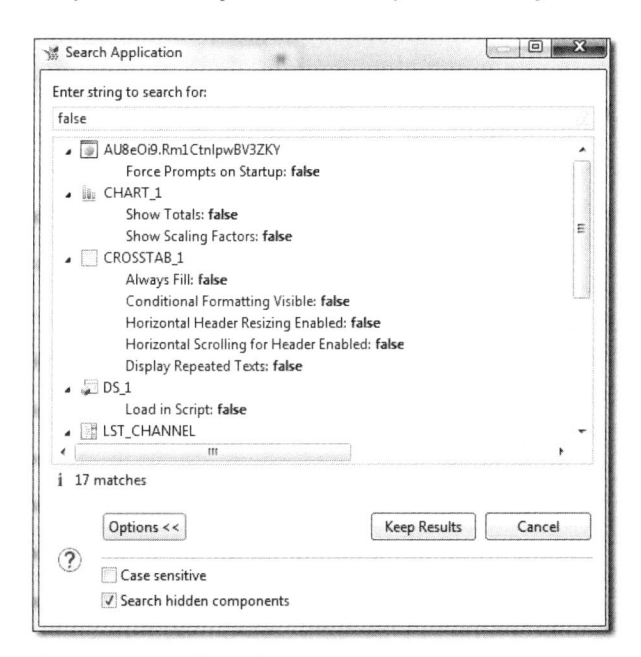

Figure 5.18 Search Application

Clicking the KEEP RESULTS button closes the SEARCH APPLICATION window, and the search results appear in the SEARCH RESULTS view (see Figure 5.19). You can also press `Enter` to do this.

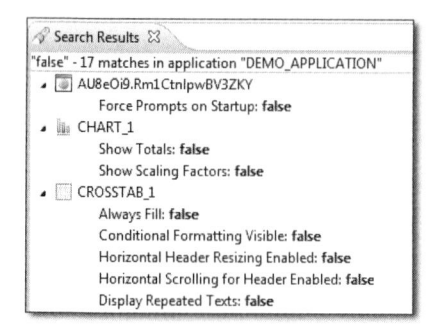

Figure 5.19 Search Results View

The keyboard shortcut for SEARCH APPLICATION is `Ctrl`+`Shift`+`F`.

Find References

The FIND REFERENCES option lets you easily find the components and their scripts that have a linkage to the currently selected component. The results are displayed in the SEARCH RESULTS view (Figure 5.20). The keyboard shortcut for this command is `Ctrl`+`Shift`+`F`.

Just as with the SEARCH APPLICATION results, you can double-click a component to select it. Double-clicking a script or a CSS style will open its editor.

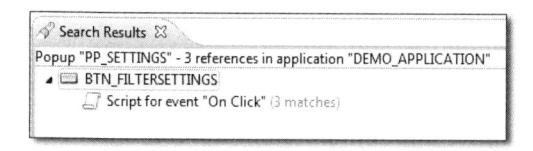

Figure 5.20 Find References

5.1.6 View

The VIEW menu enables you to show or hide the views that are present in Design Studio (Figure 5.21). We'll discuss these views in depth later on in this chapter, so here we'll only briefly mention the key purpose of each view.

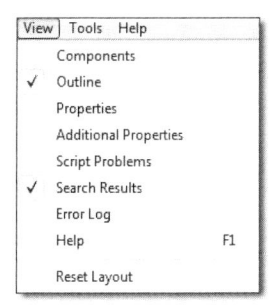

Figure 5.21 View Menu

Components

The COMPONENTS view lists all the components you can use to create a UI in the Layout Editor for your Design Studio application.

Outline

The OUTLINE view lists all the data sources, planning objects, layout components, and technical components that are currently used in the Layout Editor of the Design Studio application.

Properties

The PROPERTIES view shows the properties of the Design Studio application or one or more selected components.

Additional Properties

Some components such as charts and geo maps have additional properties that further configure the look and features of the component. The ADDITIONAL PROPERTIES view displays these settings.

Script Problems

The SCRIPT PROBLEMS view shows script errors if there are any in the application.

Search Results

The SEARCH RESULTS view lists the search results from the SEARCH APPLICATION command in the SEARCH menu.

Error Log

The ERROR LOG view lists general errors in the Design Studio application itself.

Reset Layout

The RESET LAYOUT command rearranges the views around the Layout Editor. All views are shown except the SEARCH RESULTS view and the ERROR LOG.

5.1.7 Tools

The TOOLS menu has four options: INSTALL EXTENSION TO DESIGN STUDIO, INSTALL CVOM CHART EXTENSION, PLATFORM EXTENSIONS, and PREFERENCES (Figure 5.22).

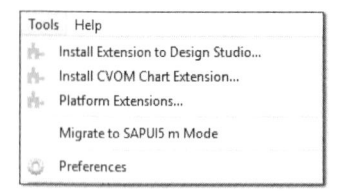

Figure 5.22 Tools Menu

Although a lot of standard components are available in Design Studio, you can also use components that are developed using the Design Studio software development kit (SDK). These components are installed using the INSTALL EXTENSION TO DESIGN STUDIO menu item. A window pops up asking for the path to the SDK (Figure 5.23). This can be a local path or a URL. When you click on the GET PARTNER EXTENSIONS link, you'll be guided to a catalogue of third-party extensions that you can use. Some are even free! The URL to the partner extension is *https://newportal-i050426trial.dispatcher.hanatrial.ondemand.com/biExtensions.html*.

Figure 5.23 Installing Extensions

The INSTALL CVOM CHART EXTENSION option also lets you install a third-party CHART component. The difference is that Design Studio treats CVOM chart extensions like regular CHART components. In the properties of any CHART component, there is an option to switch between chart types. When a third-party chart is installed as a CVOM chart extension, this chart will also be available in the list of selectable charts.

You can use the MIGRATE TO SAPUI5 M MODE option to migrate your application components to the new SAPUI5 m rendering mode. These components feel more like SAP Fiori, however, and not all components can be migrated. In Section 5.1.1, we've listed which components are available in which rendering mode.

In the PREFERENCES menu (Figure 5.24), you can review and change the settings for Design Studio. On the left side of the window, you can choose between the following menus:

- APPLICATION DESIGN
  - APPLICATION TEMPLATES
  - BACKEND CONNECTIONS
  - NETWORK CONNECTIONS
  - SUPPORT SETTINGS
- SCRIPTING
  - SYNTAX COLORING
  - TEMPLATES

163

The Integrated Development Environment

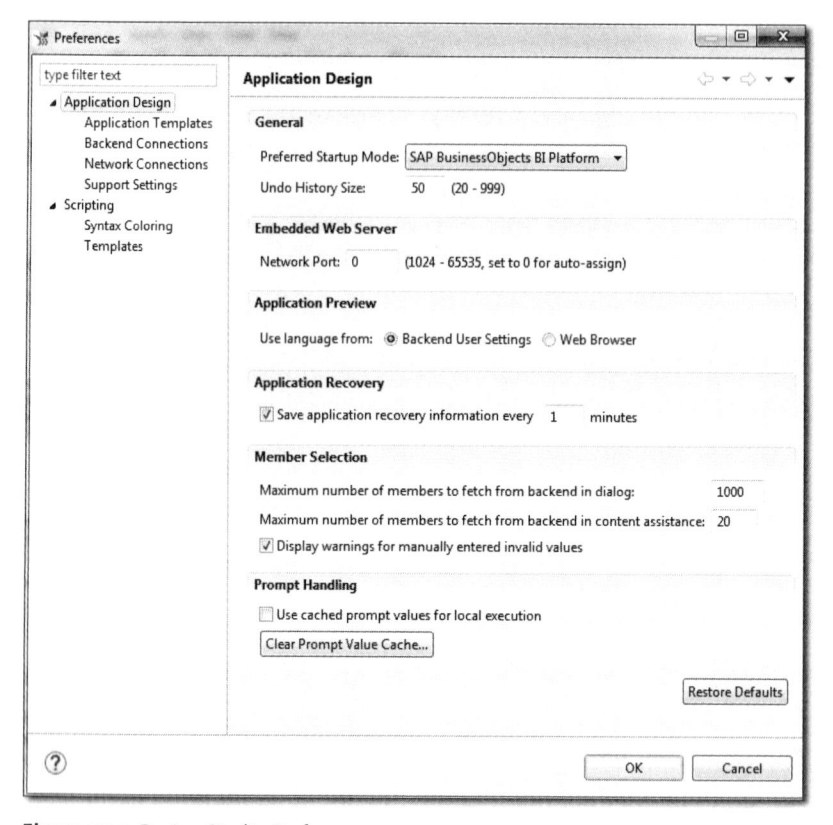

Figure 5.24 Design Studio Preferences

Because the bulk of the functionality in the TOOLS menu is within this PREFERENCES option, we'll devote some time to it here.

Application Design

First let's take a look at the APPLICATION DESIGN settings.

In the GENERAL area, you can change the preferred startup mode for Design Studio. You can choose between the following options:

- LOCAL MODE
- SAP BUSINESSOBJECTS BI PLATFORM
- SAP HANA
- SAP NETWEAVER (SAP BW)

The UNDO HISTORY SIZE setting determines how many changes can be undone by using the UNDO command from the EDIT menu.

In the EMBEDDED WEB SERVER area, the NETWORK PORT for the web server embedded in Design Studio to execute applications locally can be defined. If you use the default value of 0, Design Studio assigns a network port.

In the APPLICATION PREVIEW area, you define which language settings to use when executing an application: BACKEND USER SETTINGS, which are the language settings in the BI Launch Pad, or WEB BROWSER, which are the language settings that defined in the web browser. The selected language is used for message texts, tooltips, and determining the correct formatting of numbers, dates, and times.

The APPLICATION RECOVERY area gives you the option to have Design Studio create a recovery copy of your application. To enable this, select the checkbox and define the time interval between each copy.

The MEMBER SELECTION area allows you to define how many members of a dimension are shown when using the Script Editor. Figure 5.25 shows the Script Editor creating a script on a BUTTON component.

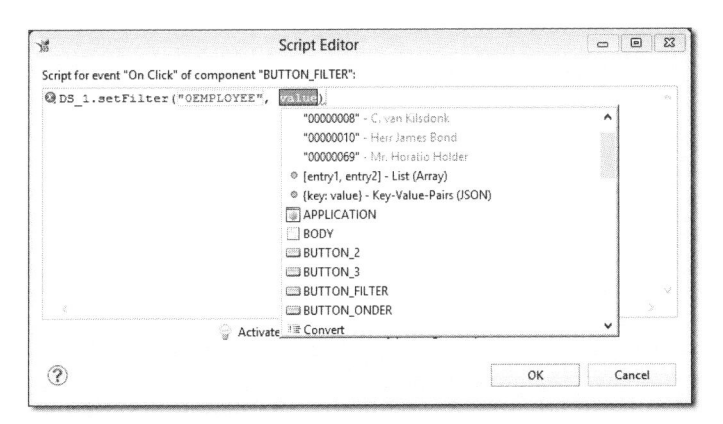

Figure 5.25 Script Editor Member Selection of Fewer Than 20 Members

As you can see, the CONTENT ASSISTANCE feature ([Ctrl]+[Space]) has been used to show a list of members for the OEMPLOYEE dimension. Because this list consists of fewer than 20 members, it's shown here. You can change this value by editing the MAXIMUM NUMBER OF MEMBERS TO FETCH FROM BACKEND IN CONTENT ASSISTANCE NUMBER setting.

The Integrated Development Environment

In the example in Figure 5.26, more than 20 members for the `0CALMONTH` dimension are available. In this case, the SELECT MEMBER option is shown instead of a list of members. When you select this option, the SELECT MEMBER window appears, giving a list of a maximum of 1,000 members, as shown in Figure 5.27. You can adjust this value by editing the MAXIMUM NUMBER OF MEMBERS TO FETCH FROM BACKEND IN DIALOG setting.

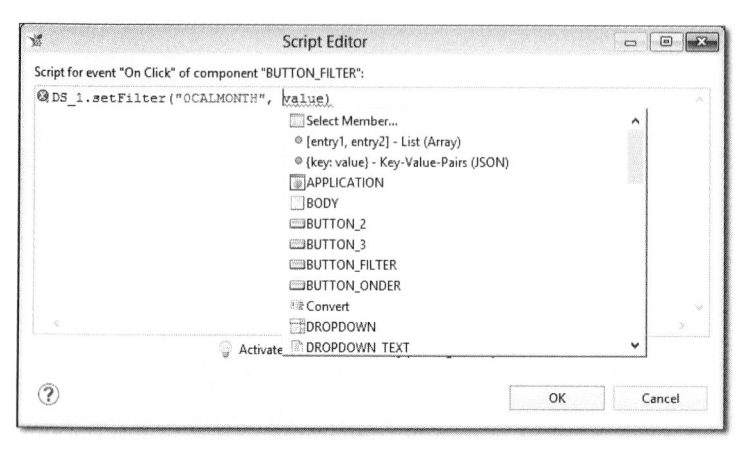

Figure 5.26 Script Editor Member Selection with More than 20 Members

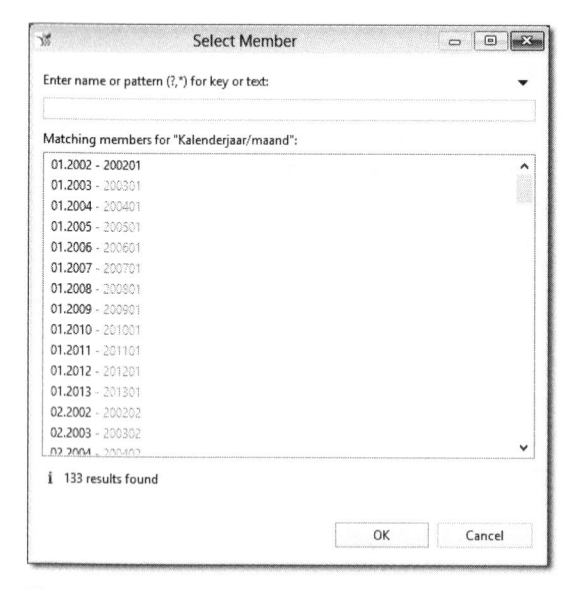

Figure 5.27 Select Member Window

Finally, you can select the DISPLAY WARNINGS FOR MANUALLY ENTERED INVALID VALUES setting to let Design Studio display warnings in the Script Editor when nonexistent values are entered.

If your application uses a BEx query with input variables as a data source, you can use the SHOW PROMPTS command from the APPLICATION menu to select the prompt values. If the USE CACHED PROMPT VALUES FOR LOCAL EXECUTION option is selected in the PROMPT HANDLING section of the APPLICATION DESIGN screen, the application will use the prompt values that are already set in Design Studio when executing the application locally.

You can clear these prompt values with the CLEAR PROMPT VALUE CACHE button. The dialog screen gives you the option to choose the applications for which the cache should be emptied (Figure 5.28).

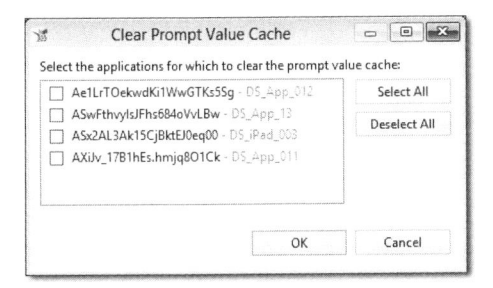

Figure 5.28 Clear Prompt Value Cache

The PATHS area is where you set the path to the application templates folder. These are templates you can choose from when creating a new application.

This brings us to the end of the options on the APPLICATION DESIGN screen.

Application Templates

You can create your own application templates and even share these with other developers. When you've developed an application that you want to use as template, select the EXPORT AS TEMPLATE option from the APPLICATION menu. Give the template a name and a description, and then save this template somewhere on your local or shared drive (Figure 5.29).

You'll notice that the next time you create a new application, the template will be available to choose in the NEW APPLICATION screen (Figure 5.30).

5 | The Integrated Development Environment

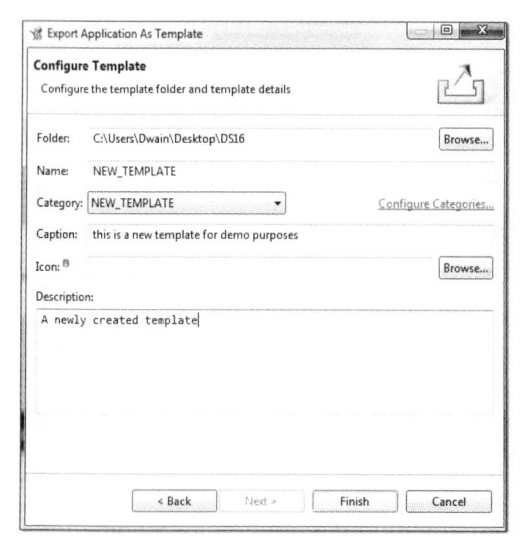

Figure 5.29 Creating and Exporting a Template

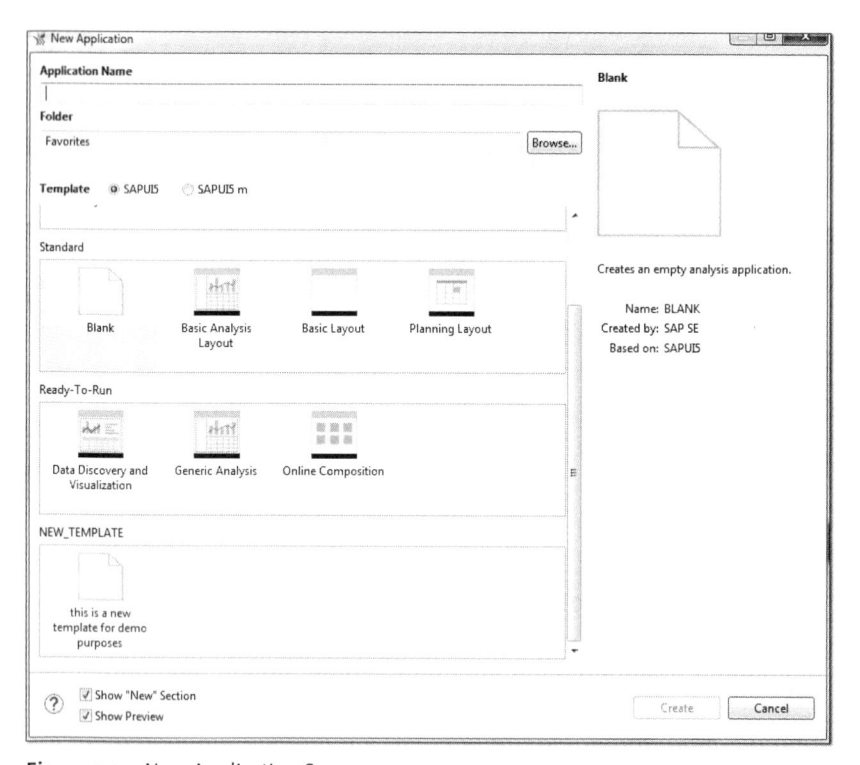

Figure 5.30 New Application Screen

168

In addition, when you look at the APPLICATION TEMPLATES option in the PREFERENCE menu, you'll see the name and path of the template (Figure 5.31).

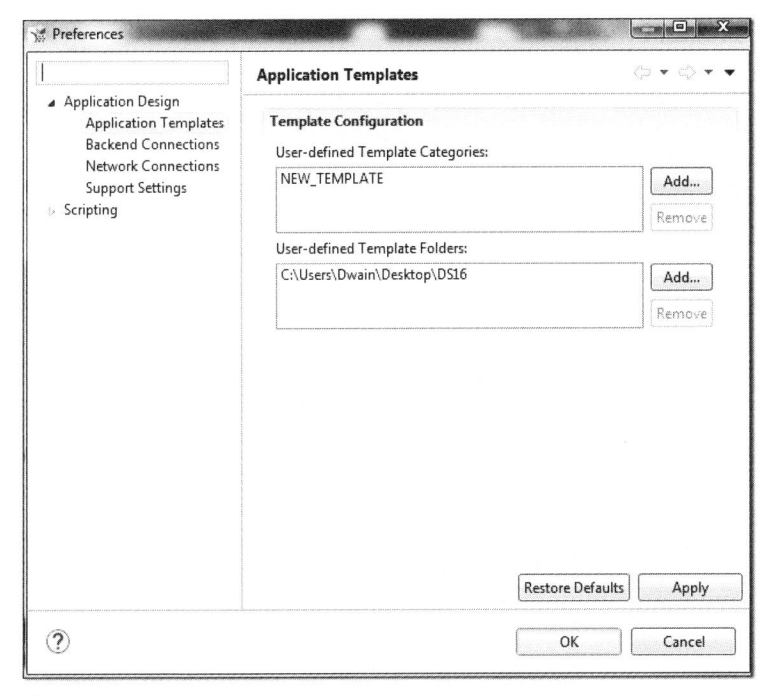

Figure 5.31 Application Template Settings

Backend Connections

Now refer back to the PREFERENCES screen shown in Figure 5.24. Click on BACKEND CONNECTIONS under APPLICATION TEMPLATES. This area displays the available backend connections, which you can use to create data sources. The contents of this area can differ depending on the startup mode you used. In Figure 5.32, the backend connections are shown when connecting to an SAP BusinessObjects BI platform. The connections can be edited in the SAP BusinessObjects BI Central Management Console (CMC).

The Integrated Development Environment

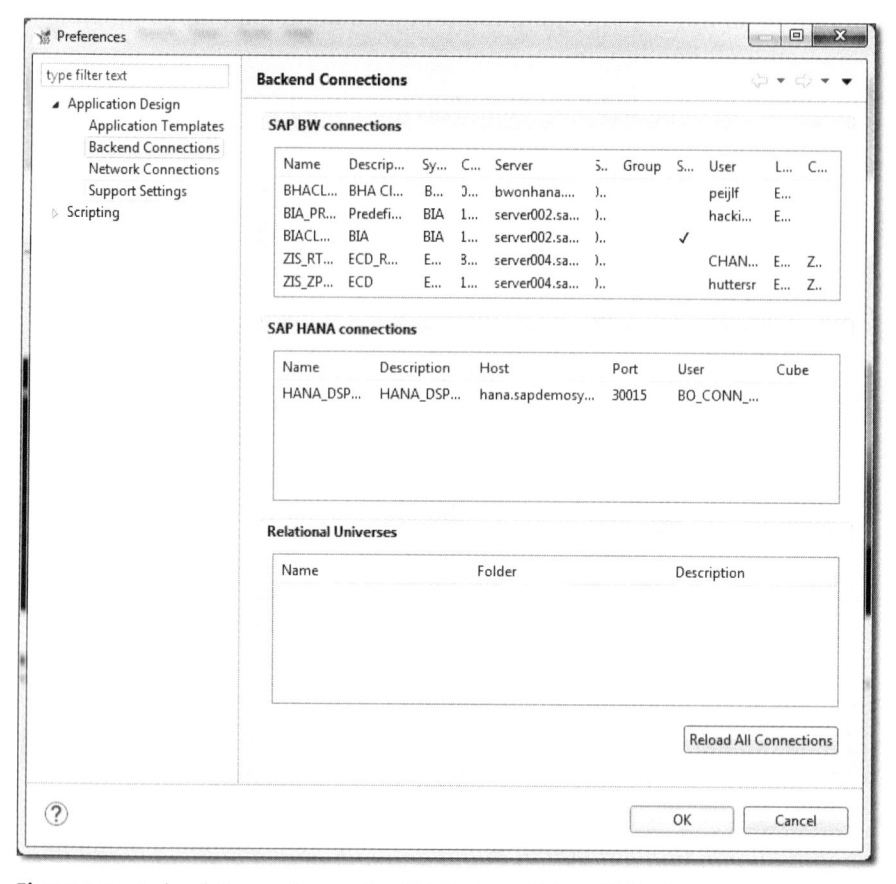

Figure 5.32 Backend Connections on the SAP BusinessObjects BI Platform

Figure 5.33 shows the connections that are defined in SAP Logon (SAP BW) and the ODBC Data Source Administrator (SAP HANA). You can go to these tools by clicking the icon with the gear wheels in the upper right. You can also add an SAP HANA connection by HTTP protocol by clicking the ADD button and defining the connection.

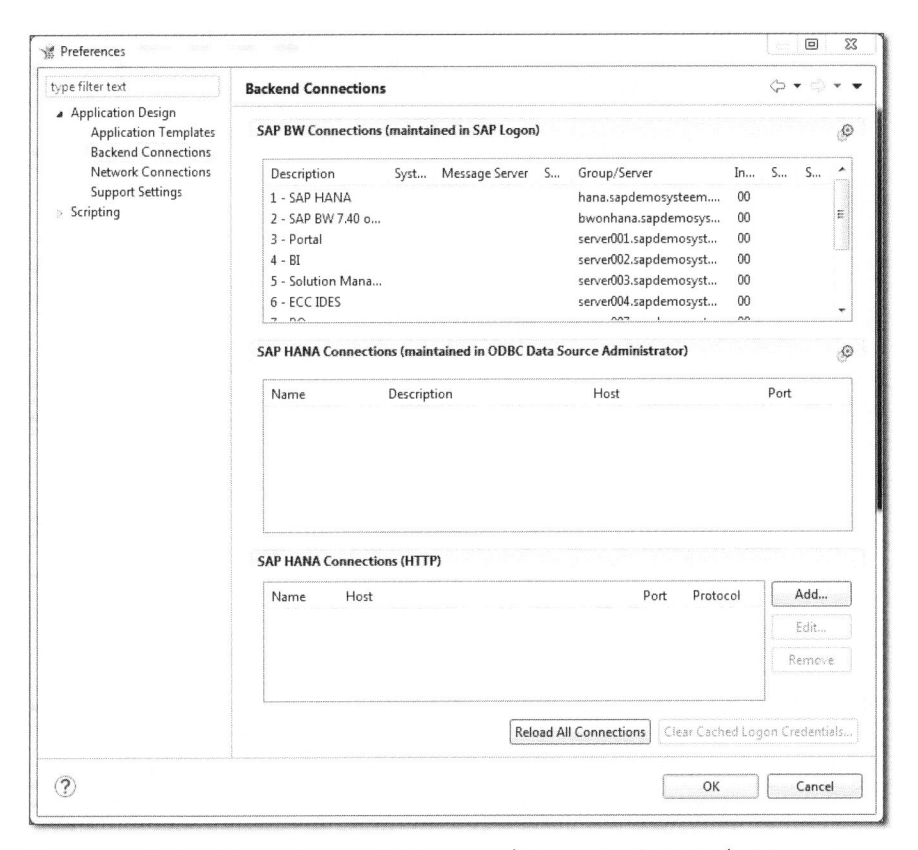

Figure 5.33 Backend Connections in SAP Logon and ODBC Data Source Administrator

Network Connections

On the Network Connections tab, you can configure the system to use a proxy server. Proxy servers serve as a connection between the client browser and application and can be used to increase the performance and security of an application.

In Figure 5.34, you see that the Active Provider is set on Native. This means that the proxy settings that are discovered from the operating system are used. When the Active Provider is set to Direct, all connections are opened without the use of a proxy server. When the Active Provider is set to Manual, the settings defined in Eclipse are used.

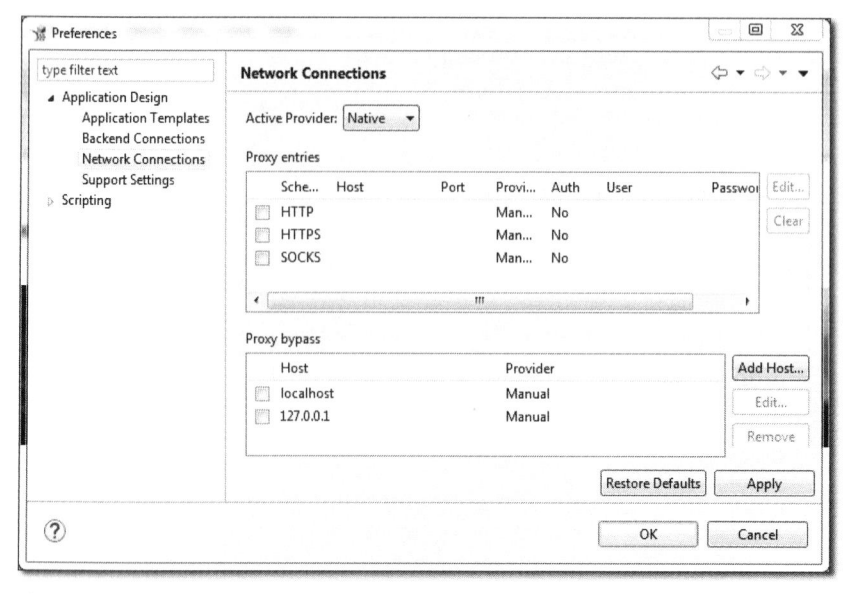

Figure 5.34 Network Connections

Support Settings

Now click the SUPPORT SETTINGS option. The options in SUPPORT SETTINGS can provide help in case of problems or errors (Figure 5.35).

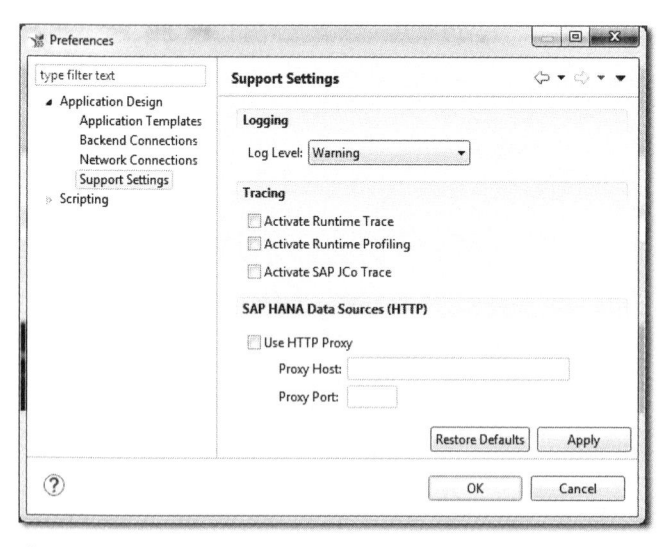

Figure 5.35 Support Settings

With the LOG LEVEL setting, you can define the level of detail in logs that are shown in the ERROR LOG view.

To generate a trace file that can be used for an in-depth analysis of the activities performed in Design Studio and in the executed application, you can select the ACTIVATE RUNTIME TRACE checkbox. The trace file is stored in the following location: *C:\<user>\Analysis-workspace\.metadata\.plugins\com.sap.ip.bi.zen\logs\RSTT*.

You can also record SAP Java Connector (SAP JCo) traces by checking the ACTIVATE SAP JCO TRACE setting. The trace level is set to 8, and the trace files can be collected with the COLLECT SUPPORT INFORMATION option (see Section 5.1.8).

> **SAP Java Connector (SAP JCo)**
>
> More information on SAP JCo and SAP JCo traces is available at *http://wiki.sdn.sap.com/wiki/display/SI/Java+Connectivity* .

Scripting

In the SCRIPTING section, you can adjust some settings that support coding activities.

Syntax Coloring

With SYNTAX COLORING (Figure 5.36), you can adjust the styling of scripts to make the code easier to read.

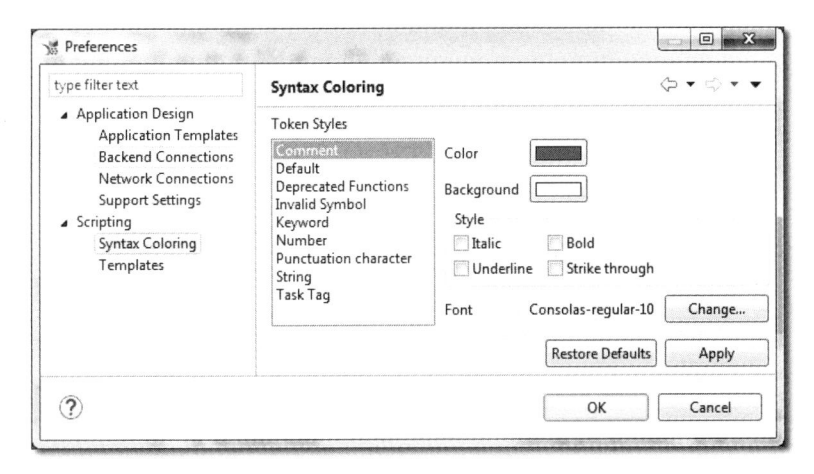

Figure 5.36 Syntax Coloring

The Integrated Development Environment

Templates

Templates for scripts (Figure 5.37) can be used in the Script Editor to generate a predefined code template, as shown in Figure 5.38.

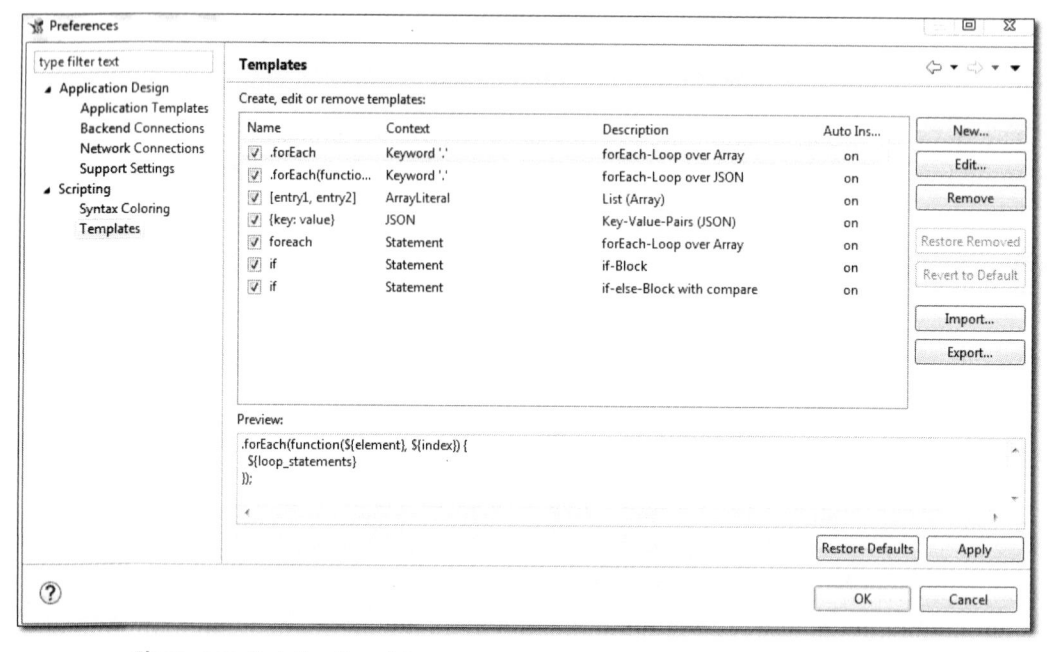

Figure 5.37 Scripting Templates

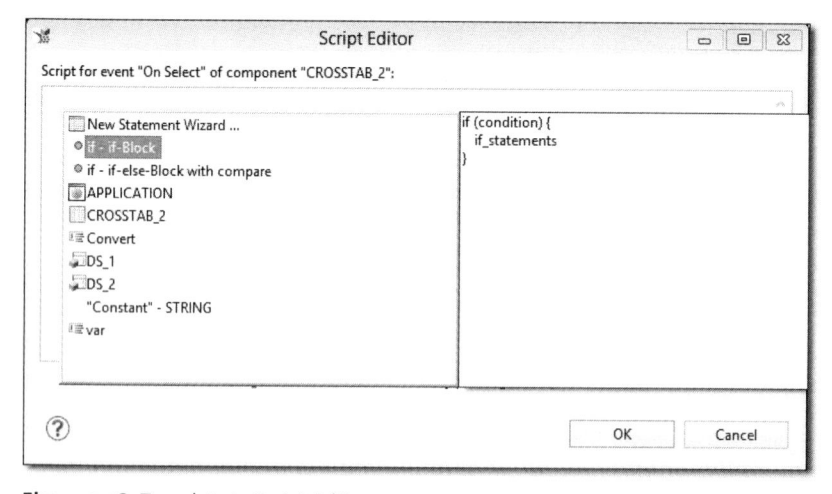

Figure 5.38 Template in Script Editor

5.1.8 Help

As the final item in the menu bar, the HELP menu (Figure 5.39) provides several support options for Design Studio, as well as some more detailed information about your current Design Studio installation.

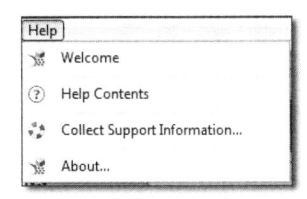

Figure 5.39 Help Menu

Welcome

The WELCOME option shows the WELCOME page that you also see when you start Design Studio (Figure 5.40). It consists of four sections:

- GETTING STARTED
  This area provides a number of links to introductory video tutorials. The MORE link redirects to SAP's official product tutorial website for Design Studio.

- CREATE NEW
  The button in this area closes the WELCOME page and creates a new Design Studio application.

- RECENTLY-USED ANALYSIS APPLICATIONS
  The five most recently used Design Studio applications are listed here.

- USEFUL LINKS
  Some links to the SAP website are listed here.

As you might have concluded for yourself already, this WELCOME page doesn't bring any real added value to Design Studio because most of its features are also available elsewhere. Luckily, in the bottom-left corner, you can deselect the checkbox to disable showing this page at each startup of Design Studio.

5 | The Integrated Development Environment

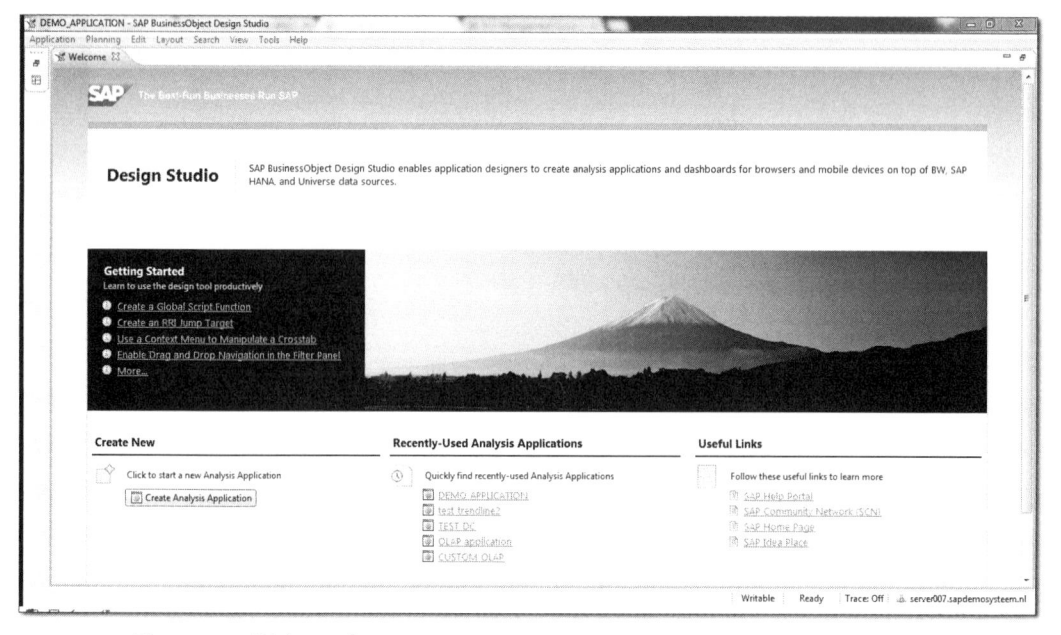

Figure 5.40 Welcome Page

Help Contents

The HELP CONTENTS option provides the default guide for Design Studio created by SAP.

Collect Support Information

When you select the COLLECT SUPPORT INFORMATION option, a ZIP file is created that includes several configuration settings and logs.

About

You can use the ABOUT option to check the installation and versioning details of your Design Studio setup (Figure 5.41). When you click on the INSTALLATION DETAILS button, a new window opens with some additional information about the installed components.

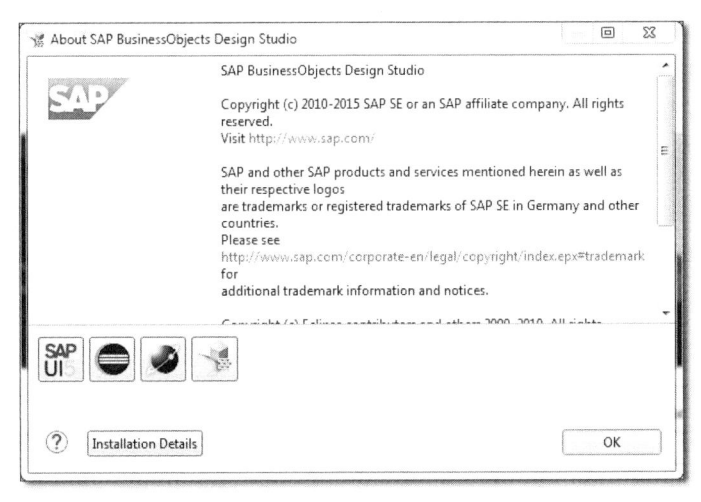

Figure 5.41 About Design Studio

5.2 Toolbar

Positioned just below the menu bar, the toolbar includes many commands that are also available in the menus; however, they are just a bit easier and faster to access from the toolbar (Figure 5.42).

Figure 5.42 Design Studio Toolbar

You can use a toolbar button by simply clicking it. Just as with the commands from the menus, depending on the component or components you've currently selected, some of the buttons are enabled, and some are disabled. For example, the ALIGNMENT buttons are only active when two or more components are selected.

The toolbar is divided into eight command groups. Each new group starts with a vertical line of dots. You can rearrange these command groups by selecting the vertical line of dots and dragging it to the desired position on the toolbar.

The only command that is listed in the toolbar but isn't available in one of the menus is the SEND TO MOBILE DEVICE (USING QR CODE®) command (see Figure 5.43). This function generates a QR code (quick response code) of the URL of the

5 | The Integrated Development Environment

Design Studio application (Figure 5.44). This QR code can be read by a QR code scanner application on a mobile device. Free applications with this functionality are widely available in app stores. After scanning the QR code, you can run the application URL in a browser on the mobile device to execute the Design Studio application.

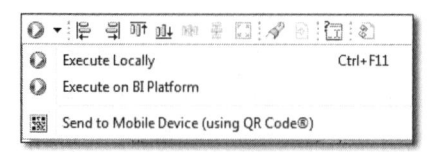

Figure 5.43 Send to Mobile Device Toolbar Command

Figure 5.44 Generated QR Code

Table 5.1 lists all the toolbar buttons with a short description of their commands.

Toolbar button	Command Description
	Create a new Design Studio application.
	Open an existing application.
	Save the current application.

Table 5.1 Toolbar Buttons and Their Commands

Toolbar button	Command Description
	Add a new data source to this application.
	Add a planning function to the application.
	Add a planning sequence to the application.
	Undo an operation.
	Redo an operation.
	Execute the application locally.
	Execute the application on the SAP BusinessObjects BI platform.
	Generate a QR code to send the application's URL to a mobile device.
	Left-align two or more selected components.
	Right-align two or more selected components.
	Top-align two or more selected components.
	Bottom-align two or more selected components.
	Distribute three or more selected components horizontally.
	Distribute three or more selected components vertically.
	Maximize the size of a selected component.
	Search the application.
	Find references to a selected component.
	Show prompts.
	Edit custom CSS.
	Reload the application.

Table 5.1 Toolbar Buttons and Their Commands (Cont.)

5.3 Layout Editor

The Layout Editor is the central area of Design Studio (refer to Figure 5.1). Because it functions as the visual representation of an application, this is the place to design your applications in a WYSIWYG format.

When you make changes to your application, an asterisk (*) is placed in front of the technical name that is shown on top of the Layout Editor. This indicates that the current version of the application hasn't been saved yet.

5 | The Integrated Development Environment

The Layout Editor is affected by what views you select in the VIEW menu, which we briefly introduced in Section 5.1.6. Now, we'll go into a lot more detail about what each of these views means for you.

5.3.1 Components View

The COMPONENTS view (Figure 5.45) houses all the visual building blocks to create an application, including an interactive UI. To add a component to an application, just drag and drop the component from the COMPONENTS view into the Layout Editor.

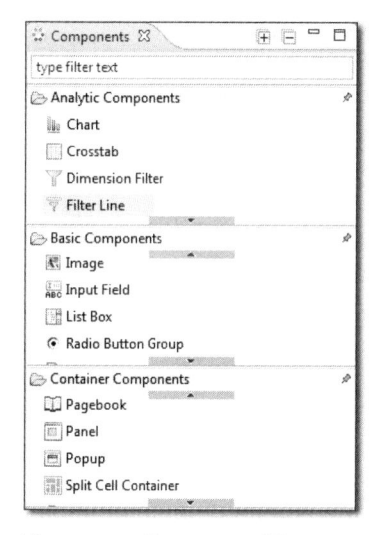

Figure 5.45 Components View

The components are grouped in three categories:

- ANALYTIC COMPONENTS
  These components present data through charts and tables and deliver standard filtering options.

- BASIC COMPONENTS
  These components are used to create more advanced filters and interactivity, as well as to display images and texts.

- CONTAINER COMPONENTS
  These components are used to define the framework of an application by grouping and structuring the other components.

5.3.2 Outline View

The OUTLINE view provides a structured overview of all the components and data sources used in the application. As shown in Figure 5.46, there are four folders under the top application level: DATA SOURCES, PLANNING OBJECTS, LAYOUT, and TECHNICAL COMPONENTS.

As the name indicates, all data sources are displayed in the DATA SOURCES folder. In the PLANNING OBJECTS folder, you can add planning functions and planning sequences to the application. Components that can be seen on screen are shown in the LAYOUT folder. As you can see, this happens in a structured way. The example in Figure 5.46 shows a TABSTRIP component with two tabs. Because this is a container component, other components can be placed within it. TAB 1 contains CROSSTAB, BUTTON, and FILTER PANEL components. TAB 2 contains CHART and FILTER PANEL components. In the TECHNICAL COMPONENTS folder, you can define technical objects such as BACKEND CONNECTIONS, CONTEXT MENUS, GLOBAL SCRIPT OBJECTS, PDF OBJECTS, and TEXT POOL OBJECTS (Figure 5.47).

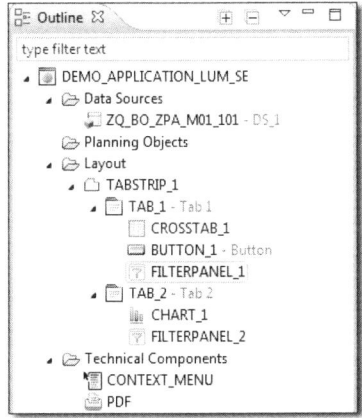

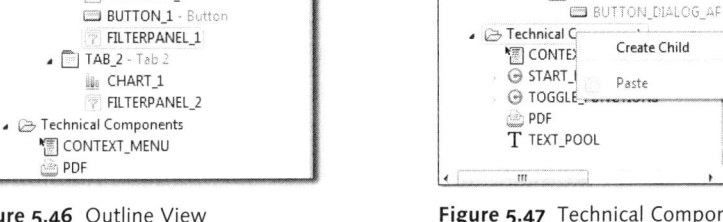

Figure 5.46 Outline View

Figure 5.47 Technical Components

Not only does the OUTLINE view give you a very clear overview of the application and its components and data sources, but it can also be used to select and rearrange these items. With [Ctrl]+click, you can select multiple items, and with [Shift]+click, you can select a range of items. With the search box on top of the OUTLINE view, you can quickly look for an item. The search results appear as soon as you start typing.

When you right-click an item, its context menu is shown, which provides a number of quick commands. These commands differ according to the type and number of items selected. The options for COPY, PASTE, RENAME, DELETE, and FIND REFERENCES are available for all items.

For the data source items here, the options EDIT INITIAL VIEW and RESET INITIAL VIEW are also available (Figure 5.48). The INITIAL view of a data source represents the formatting of the data source. The RESET INITIAL VIEW command sets the output of a data source back to its original state by eliminating all the changes you made using the EDIT INITIAL VIEW option.

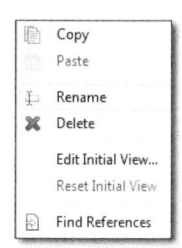

Figure 5.48 Context Menu for Data Sources

You can change the INITIAL view of a data source with the EDIT INITIAL VIEW option, which brings you to the screen shown in Figure 5.49. This screen is divided into the following four areas:

- The available dimensions and measures are placed on the left, including their attributes and hierarchies (when available). To add an attribute, right-click the attribute, and select ADD from the context menu. An attribute is only visible in the result set when its dimension is also added to the columns or rows. If a dimension has a hierarchy, you can go to the context menu of this hierarchy to activate it, deactivate it, and set its expansion level.

- At the bottom-left side of the screen, you see the GLOBAL DATA SOURCE SETTINGS. Here, the user can select how negative values (-X, X-, or X) and zero values (DEFAULT, WITH CURRENCY/UNIT, AS EMPTY CELL, or CUSTOM) should be displayed.

- The middle column is the area to place and arrange the dimensions and measures that should be shown in the columns and rows of the result set. In the BACKGROUND FILTER section, measures can be added that are being filtered but don't appear in the result set.

▶ On the right side of the window, a LIVE PREVIEW of the result set is given with the number of data cells. In the upper-right corner, a PAUSE REFRESH checkbox is available to suspend the automatic refreshing of the result set. This comes in handy when you need to make a lot of alterations to the INITIAL view, and there is no need for an updated preview of the result set after each change. When all changes are done, deselect the checkbox again to refresh the preview of the result set.

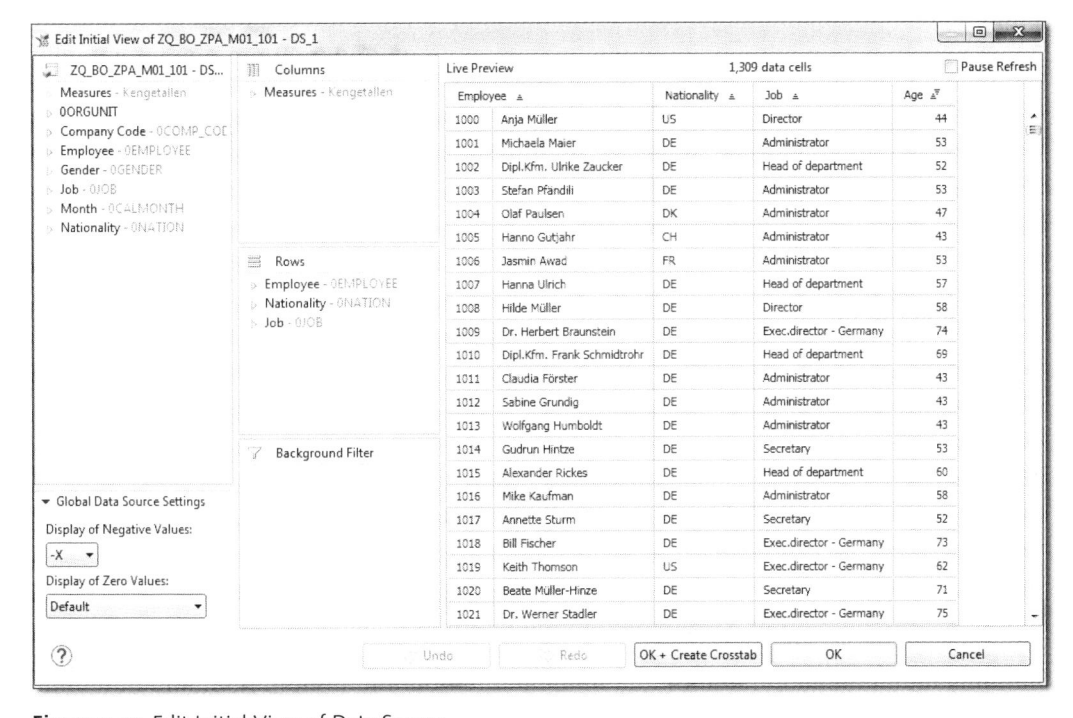

Figure 5.49 Edit Initial View of Data Source

For each measure, you can change the following by right-clicking the measure (Figure 5.50):

▶ Number of decimal places
▶ The scaling factor
▶ How the totals are calculated (e.g., SUM, MINIMUM, MAXIMUM, or AVERAGE)
▶ The sorting order

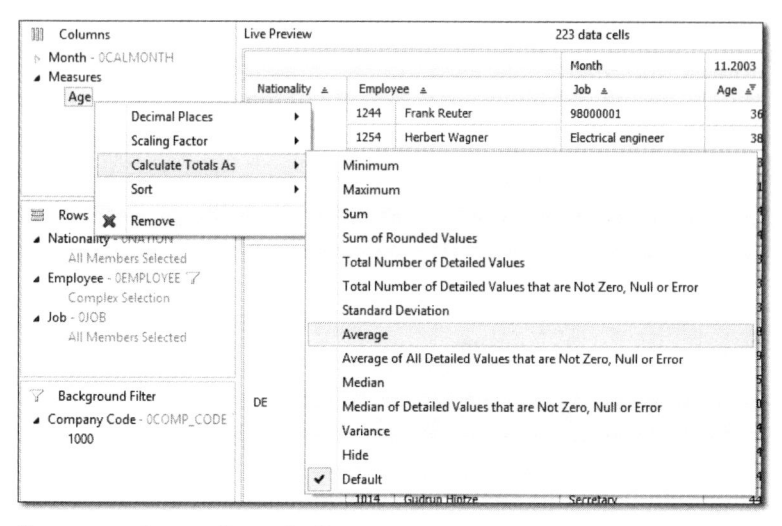

Figure 5.50 Context Menu of a Measure

You have serval options to change the presentation of the data. These options correspond to features that are known from SAP BEx. To change the presentation of a certain dimension, use the context menu (right-click). You have the following options to choose from (Figure 5.51):

- Additional attributes to be displayed.
- The active hierarchy and its initial expansion level.
- With the MEMBER FOR FILTERING option, you can set which members of a dimension are available in the filter. You can choose between the members with posted values, members that exist in the InfoProvider, or all members in the master data.
- A member to be filtered.
- The filter by input string.
- Member presentation (key, text, key + text, etc.).
- The totals display mode.

Use the MEMBER DISPLAY option to define whether the text and/or key value of a dimension should be shown, its order, and which text type should be used. You can also choose FILTER MEMBERS, which allows you to add filters from a list of values. If you want to make a complex filter, you can choose the FILTER BY INPUT-STRING option. An editor opens in which you can enter a filter expression. For example, if you want the product numbers 0001 through 0005, product number 0008, and all above 0010 in your selection, you can type this filter into the editor: "[0001;0005],0008,[>0010]". To remove all filters, use SELECT ALL MEMBERS.

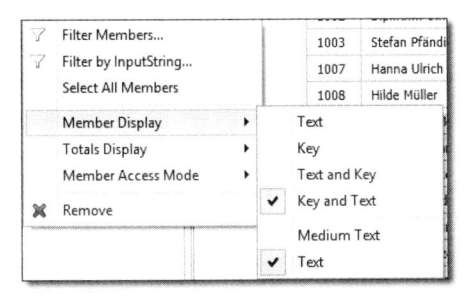

Figure 5.51 Context Menu of a Dimension

The TOTALS DISPLAY option determines whether a totals column or row should be shown for the dimension. Here you can choose among SHOW TOTALS, HIDE TOTALS, and HIDE TOTALS IF ONLY ONE MEMBER.

Finally, the MEMBERS IN RESULT SET option defines whether all available members in the master data should be shown or only those members for which values can be posted.

The context menu of a component has the option to hide a component (Figure 5.52). This is a very important feature for developers. Applications that consist of a large number of components, which are also nested within each other and form multiple interface layers, quickly lead to an overcrowded Layout Editor. This might make it hard for a developer to oversee the application. With the HIDE feature, the selected component or components can be hidden from the Layout Editor. When a component is hidden, the HIDE option is replaced with the SHOW option, which can be used to reveal the component again. The HIDE option has no effect on the application when executing it.

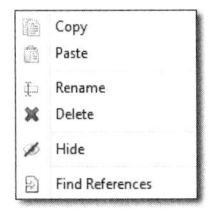

Figure 5.52 Context Menu for Components

When you select two or more components, the ARRANGE command is added to the context menu, providing the commands for alignment. When you select three or more components, the DISTRIBUTE commands are available (see Figure 5.53).

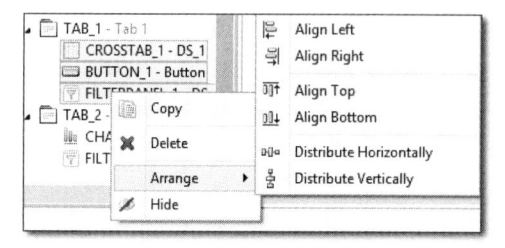

Figure 5.53 Arrange Commands in the Context Menu for Components

You can add new items to the application from the context menus of the DATA SOURCES, PLANNING OBJECTS, LAYOUT, and TECHNICAL COMPONENTS folders. Components from the first three folders can also be copied and pasted. In addition, the context menu for the LAYOUT folder has the option SHOW ALL HIDDEN COMPONENTS to undo all the HIDE settings on the hidden components in one click.

5.3.3 Properties View

The PROPERTIES view contains all the settings that can be edited for a selected item, such as a data source, a component (either layout components, planning objects, or technical components), or the application itself. When multiple items are selected, only those properties that are common to all selected items are shown.

In the remainder of this section, we'll give a short overview of the properties that are available in the various PROPERTIES views in Design Studio. In Chapter 7, we'll discuss in detail the item-specific properties for all available components.

The PROPERTIES view of a data source consists of four areas (Figure 5.54):

- GENERAL
  The data source name and type.

- DATA BINDING
  Loading settings, source information about the data source, and a PROCESSING GROUP that can be assigned to a data source.

▶ DISPLAY
Description of the data source shown when the application askes for a prompt value. When the text field isn't filled, the data source alias (NAME) is used instead.

▶ EVENTS
A script is triggered when the result set changes.

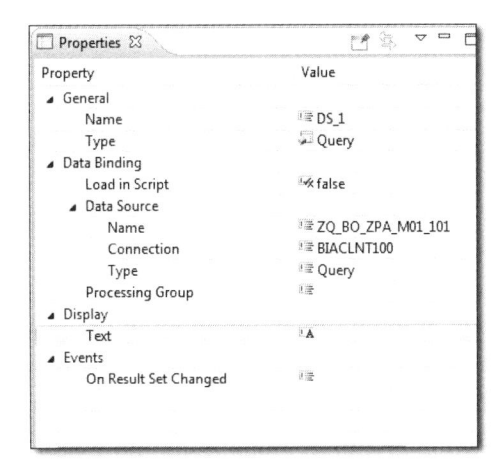

Figure 5.54 Properties View of the Data Source

The PROPERTIES view of a component can consist—depending on the type of selected component—of the following areas (Figure 5.55):

▶ GENERAL
Name and type of component, plus a visibility setting.

▶ DATA BINDING
The data source assigned for this component.

▶ OPTIMIZATION FOR LOW DATA VOLUME
Settings to improve usability.

▶ USER INTERACTIVITY
Various user interaction settings, such as single or multiple data selection and enabling or disabling the context menu.

▶ DISPLAY
Formatting and display features.

187

▶ EVENTS
Options to create interactivity on this component.

▶ LAYOUT
Size and positioning options.

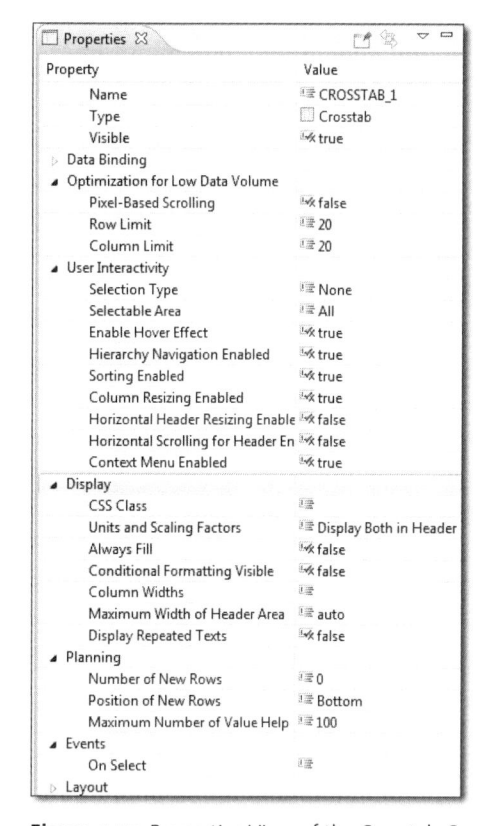

Figure 5.55 Properties View of the Crosstab Component

Finally, the PROPERTIES view for the application consists of the following sections (Figure 5.56):

▶ GENERAL
Name, location, and application file information.

▶ BEHAVIOR
The number of navigation steps the application needs to remember to allow the user to undo actions.

- **DISPLAY**
  Formatting and display options.

- **PROMPTS**
  Setting to display prompts when starting the application.

- **PLANNING**
  Settings related to IP connections and models.

- **SCRIPTING**
  Definition of global variables.

- **EVENTS**
  Scripts that have to run when the application starts.

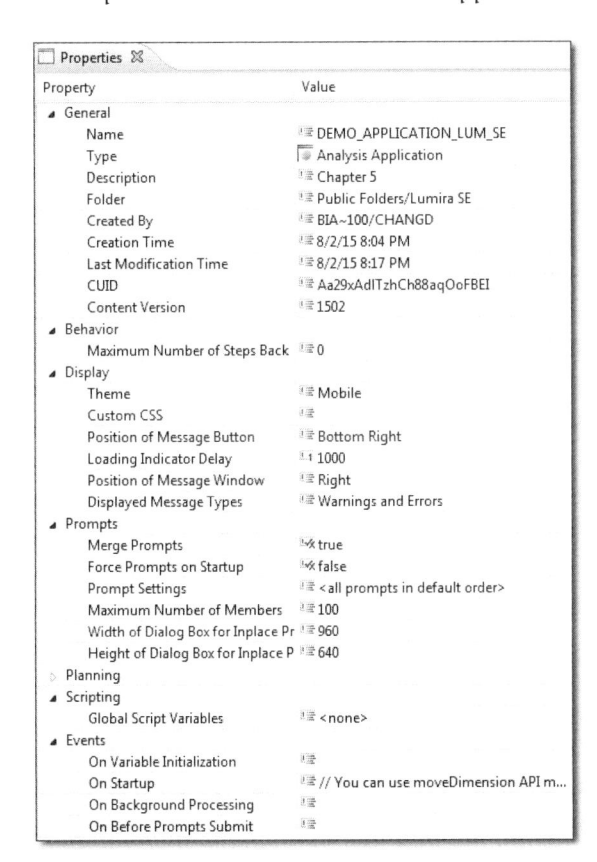

Figure 5.56 Properties View of the Application

5.3.4 Additional Properties View

The ADDITIONAL PROPERTIES view is an extension of the PROPERTIES view for charts and geo maps. These are the only two types of components for which the ADDITIONAL PROPERTIES view has a function.

The ADDITIONAL PROPERTIES view of a CHART component is divided into three panes: the CHART AREA pane (Figure 5.57), the DATA SERIES pane (Figure 5.58), and the CSS pane (Figure 5.59).

The CHART AREA pane (Figure 5.57) provides a lot of options to edit the way a chart looks and behaves. In the GENERAL area, you can set the padding of a chart. With this option, you can define how much space a CHART component should leave open before it reaches its border. In the TITLE area, you can give a chart a title, set whether the title is displayed or not, and align the title (left, right, or middle). You can also select a background color in the BACKGROUND area of the properties.

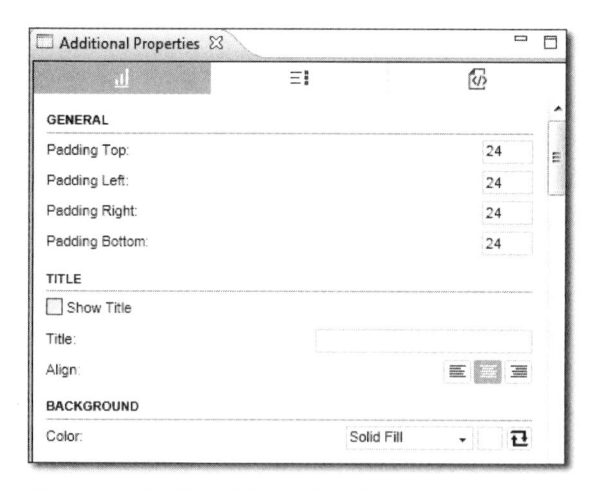

Figure 5.57 Additional Properties: Chart Area

In the X-AXIS section, you can show or hide the X-axis. You can do the same for the title for the X-axis. You can change the line size, show or hide the X-axis labels, show or hide the sublevels, and use the option to extend the label capacity, which means that the labels on the axis will always be shown, no matter how small the chart area is. In the Y-AXIS properties, you have the same properties as for the X-axis, along with the addition of setting up a gridline and using axis scaling to define minimum and maximum values for the Y-axis.

The LEGEND properties allow you to show or hide a legend, along with setting its position (top, bottom, left, or right). With the TOOLTIP properties, you can show or hide the tooltip and set how tooltips should be displayed in the chart. In the PLOT AREA properties, you can set whether or not animations should be used when data is loading, updating, or when the screen is resized. You can also set how a point in the chart should be displayed. In the INTERACTION part of the properties, you can set how the application interacts with a click in the chart. For instance, you can set whether a single value alone can be clicked or whether multiple values can be clicked.

The DATA SERIES panel (Figure 5.58) provides settings to adjust the presentation of the data. In the DISPLAYED SERIES FORMAT area, you can edit the color of each series by clicking the colored squares.

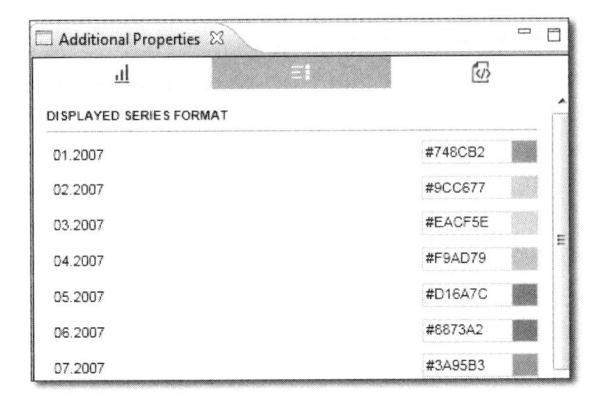

Figure 5.58 Additional Properties: Data Series

The combination charts have an additional DISPLAYED MEASURES area in which you can set a series to be displayed as a line or a bar/column.

Waterfall charts have an additional DATA SERIES SEQUENCE area. With this feature, you can switch between the options to display a dimension's value as a cumulative value (floating in the waterfall) or as a total value (starting at the X-axis).

In the additional chart properties on the CSS tab (Figure 5.59), you can edit the default style of different parts of the chart, such as the chart title, the X- and Y-axis title, values and labels, and the legend by editing the default CSS style. We'll discuss in more detail how you can use CSS in the application in Chapter 10, but, for now, let's look at the chart CSS properties.

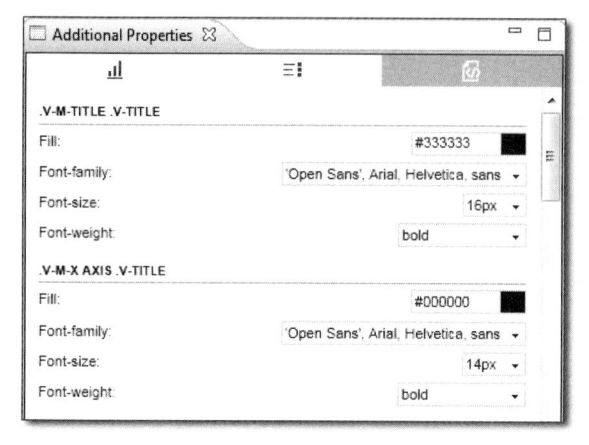

Figure 5.59 Additional Chart Properties: CSS

In the .V-M-TITLE. V-TITLE property, you edit the look of the chart title by setting a color of the title, specific font, size, and weight. Similarly, you can edit the properties for the X-axis title and label, for the Y-axis title and label, and for the legend title and label with the .V-M-X Axis .V-TITLE, .V-M-X AXIS .V-LABEL, .V-M-Y AXIS .V-TITLE, .V-M-Y AXIS .V-LABEL, .V-M-LEGEND .V-TITLE, and .V-M-LEGEND .V-LABEL, respectively. You can also edit the way the scrollbar looks for the chart legend in the .V-M-LEGEND .V-SCROLLBAR THUMB property. Data labels for CSS properties can be edited in the V-M-DATALABEL .V-DATALABEL property, and colors for hidden Y- and X-axis titles can be set in the .V-M-Y AXIS .V-HIDDEN-TITLE and .V-M-X AXIS .V-HIDDEN-TITLE properties.

5.3.5 Error Log View

All Design Studio system and application errors are displayed in the ERROR LOG view (Figure 5.60). In addition, messages are displayed when script validation methods are used in scripts. If you double-click an error, more details about the event are given in a popup window.

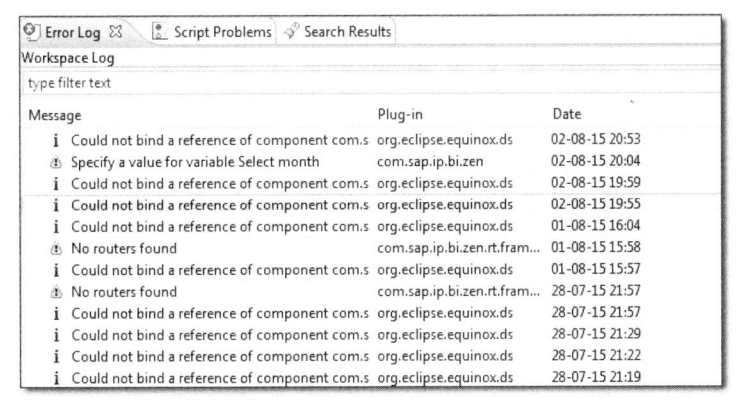

Figure 5.60 Error Log View

5.3.6 Script Problems View

The SCRIPT PROBLEMS view displays script errors encountered during script validation (Figure 5.61). This view is only updated when you open and save an application, so a problem can remain in the SCRIPT PROBLEMS view after it has been fixed. Double-clicking a problem opens the Script Editor of the component concerned.

Figure 5.61 Script Problems View

5.4 Summary

In this chapter, we took a detailed look at the Design Studio application, with the goal of getting more familiar with its IDE. We discussed all the available menu options in detail, from creating a new Design Studio application to checking the Design Studio software version in the ABOUT menu. You also learned that some of the most important commands are incorporated in the toolbar.

From there, we went through the Layout Editor and all the views in Design Studio: Components, Outline, Properties, Additional Properties, Error Log, Search Results, and Script Problems. We also discussed the menu items in the Help menu.

In the next chapter, you'll put this knowledge to use in the application design process.

Now that you've been introduced to the Design Studio development environment, it's time to get your hands dirty. In this chapter, we'll walk you through the basic steps in designing Design Studio applications.

6 The Application Design Process

At this point, you know what Design Studio is, what its abilities are, and how it compares to similar tools in the SAP BusinessObjects Business Intelligence (BI) portfolio. You've also been introduced to the Design Studio development environment. The next step is to learn about the general process of building a Design Studio application. This chapter serves as a tutorial to guide you through this process. Keep in mind that this is just a high-level overview to help you understand the process of building an application—all the specific details about the relevant components, properties, and methods will come in the next chapters.

Before you can build anything, you have to know what information the application should show and in what way it will be used.

In this example scenario, you'll create an application that can be used by department managers. With the application, managers have an overview of their personnel administration. For instance, they can see for any given month how many employees are active, what the full time equivalent (FTE) is, how many people joined and left the department, and what the employee mix is (average age, average years in service, and age range of employees).

The application in this scenario consists of three main sections:

- A main section that shows information (totals of the measures in the data source) in text form
- A section that shows information in charts
- A section in which some filters are applied

This example scenario uses several GRID LAYOUT components to align components on the screen. The screen is divided into eight blocks, as shown in Figure

6.1. A GRID LAYOUT of 2 × 1 (two rows and 1 column) is used to divide the screen into two for the main section (measure totals in the data source) and the second section (chart information). In the first cell of the GRID LAYOUT, another 2 × 3 GRID LAYOUT component is added to create six equal spaces to store the TEXT components that will display the measure values and their labels. In the second cell of the first GRID component, yet another GRID LAYOUT (1 × 2) is added to divide the bottom part of the screen into two equal spaces for the CHART components. The use of LIST BOX components is a great way to divide available screen space equally.

Finally, some LIST BOX components are used to add filters to the application.

Figure 6.1 Structure of the Application

Adding data to CHART components doesn't require any scripting. However, filtering and filling TEXT components with values does require minimal scripting. In Chapter 8, we'll explore what you can achieve using scripts in Design Studio in detail.

Now that you know the requirements of the example scenario, we'll use the rest of the chapter to walk you through the following major development steps:

1. Set up the user interface (UI) and visualizations.
2. Add the data.
3. Make it interactive.

4. Format and fine-tune it.
5. Execute the application.

Now, let's build an application!

6.1 Setting Up the User Interface and Visualizations

In this first step of building an application, you'll start by setting up the components for the UI and visualizations by following these steps:

1. Open Design Studio and log in to your system. This example uses the SAP BusinessObjects BI platform.
2. Select APPLICATION • NEW to create a new application.
3. Enter a unique APPLICATION NAME for your application (Figure 6.2).

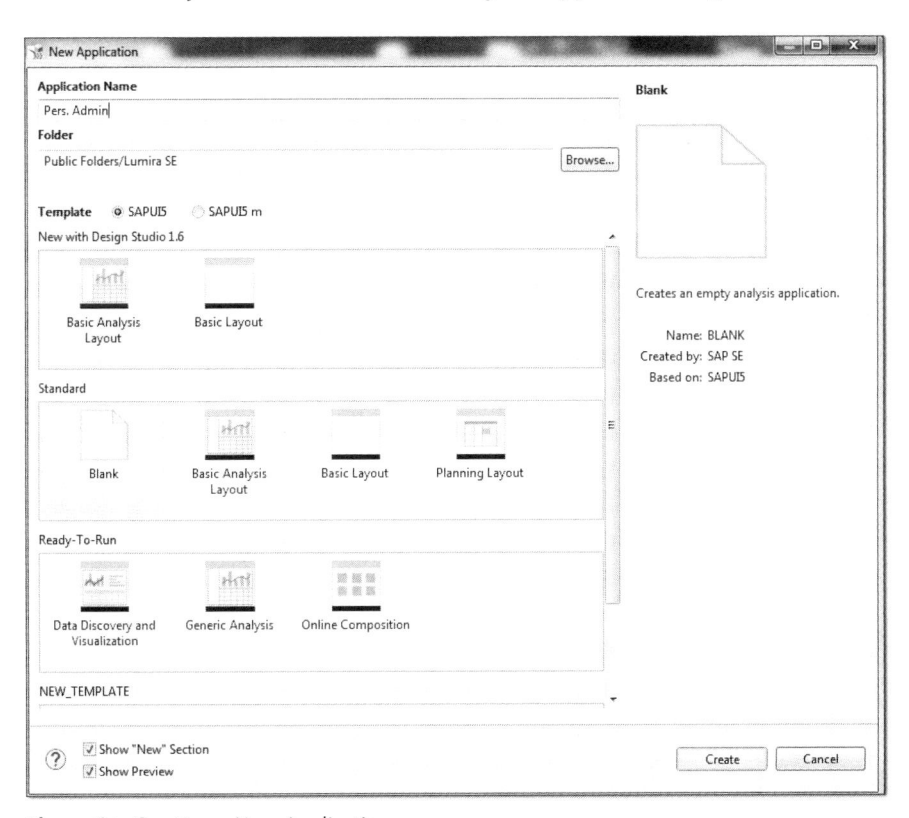

Figure 6.2 Creating a New Application

6 | The Application Design Process

4. You're going to create an application from scratch, so choose the BLANK template from the list of standard templates, and click CREATE. A clean Design Studio Layout Editor appears.

5. Now it's time to add some components to create the UI. First, add the GRID LAYOUT component. Select the GRID LAYOUT component from the CONTAINER COMPONENTS area in the COMPONENTS view. Drag and drop the component onto the Layout Editor. The component will appear in the Layout Editor and also in the OUTLINE view in the bottom-left corner of the screen (Figure 6.3). Keep the default names of the components. The first GRID LAYOUT component will be named GRID_LAYOUT_1, the second GRID_LAYOUT_2, and so on. This way, you can refer to the GRID LAYOUT components when needed.

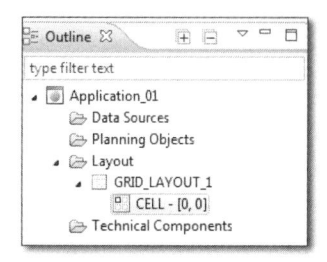

Figure 6.3 Outline View with the Grid Layout Component

6. Now to divide the first GRID LAYOUT component into two parts (two rows), you have to edit the properties of this component and set the NUMBER OF ROWS to 2 (Figure 6.4).

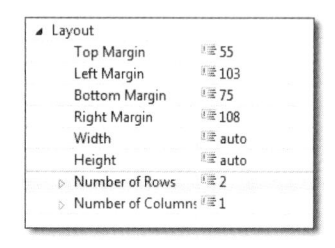

Figure 6.4 Grid Layout Properties

The GRID LAYOUT is now divided into two parts. These parts, called *cells*, are now also visible in the OUTLINE view (Figure 6.5).

198

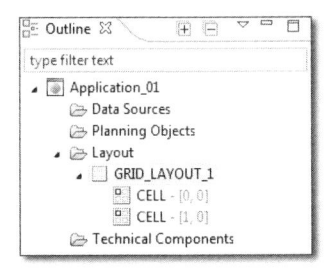

Figure 6.5 Grid Layout Divided into Cells

7. Next, add another GRID LAYOUT component in the top cell. This GRID LAYOUT component will contain two rows and three columns. Also, make sure that this component fills the available space by changing the default values for the BOTTOM MARGIN and TOP MARGIN to 0. Figure 6.6 shows the properties of the second GRID LAYOUT component.

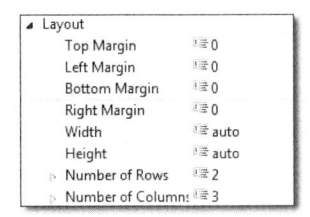

Figure 6.6 Second Grid Layout Properties

8. Remember, that in the first GRID LAYOUT component, you had two cells: a top cell, which you just divided into 6 blocks, and a bottom cell. Add another GRID LAYOUT component, this time to the bottom cell. Again, make sure it fills the entire available space, and set the NUMBER OF ROWS to 1 and the NUMBER OF COLUMNS to 2.

9. Add a CHART component by dragging it from the ANALYTICAL COMPONENTS view into each block (cell) that you created in the previous step.

10. You can edit the properties of both CHART components at the same time by holding down the Ctrl key and selecting both CHART components (either from the OUTLINE view or from the application canvas itself). Select both charts, and set the WIDTH and HEIGHT to AUTO. Set the TOP MARGIN, LEFT MARGIN, BOTTOM MARGIN, and RIGHT MARGIN to 0. This way, each CHART component will fill all the available space in its cell automatically.

11. Select the first chart, and set the CHART TYPE property to BAR. Then select the second chart, and set the CHART TYPE property to COLUMN.

12. Save your application. The layout of your application should look like Figure 6.7.

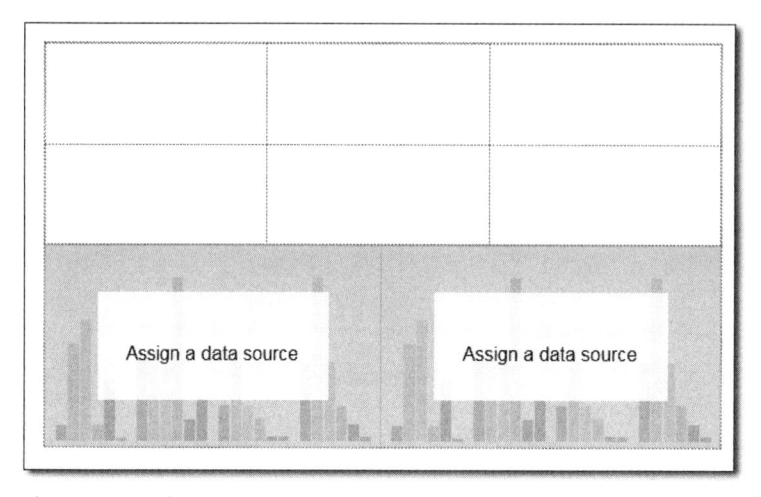

Figure 6.7 Application Layout

13. Now you'll add some TEXT components to GRID_LAYOUT_2 (the six blocks on top in Figure 6.7). Add two TEXT components in the first cell (CELL – [0,0]), and place them below each other. You'll use the first TEXT component to describe the measure that you'll display, and you'll use the second TEXT component to display the actual value.

14. Select and copy both TEXT components by using Ctrl+C. Now use Ctrl+V to paste these components into the other five cells of GRID_LAY-OUT_2. Your application should look like Figure 6.8. In Figure 6.9, you can see an example of how the OUTLINE view of the application should look.

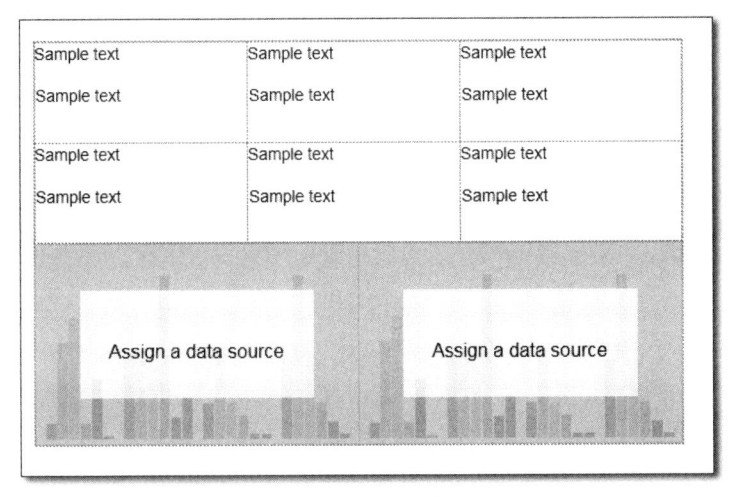

Setting Up the User Interface and Visualizations | **6.1**

Figure 6.8 Application with Grid Layout and Text Components

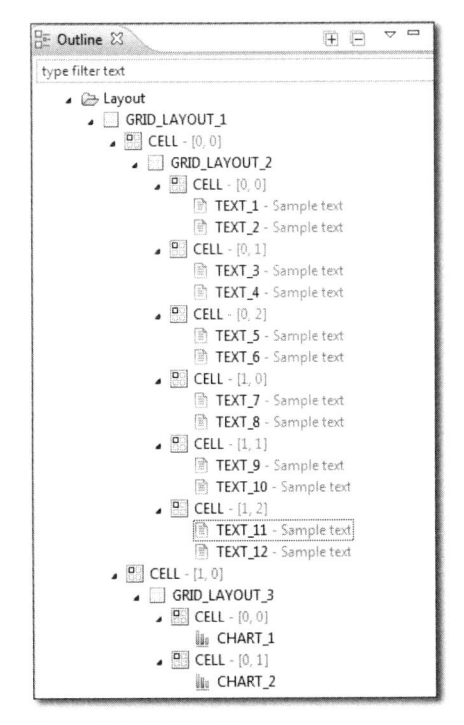

Figure 6.9 Outline View

201

Now let's continue to add some components for filtering. In this example, you'll add three LIST BOX components to the application.

15. Add three LIST BOX components below each other on the screen to the left of GRID_LAYOUT_1.

16. Select all three LIST BOX components, and use the ALIGN LEFT option to align them. Don't worry about the positioning of the other components, as you'll take care of that later.

17. After adding the last component to the application, your screen should look like Figure 6.10.

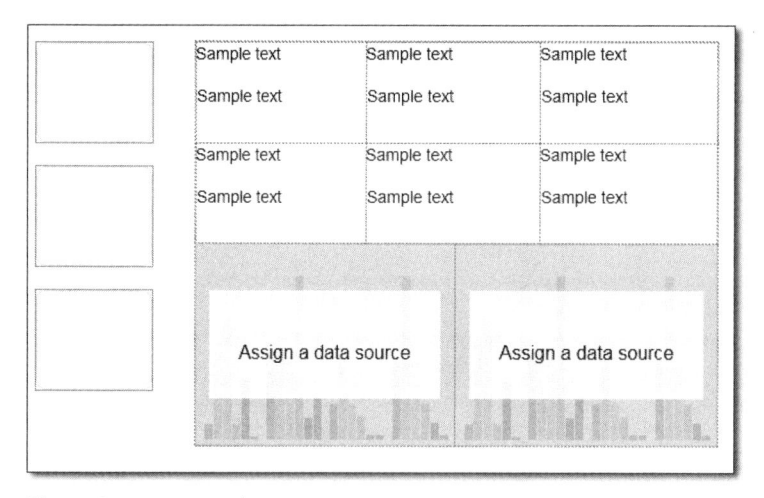

Figure 6.10 Layout with List Box Components

You're now ready to add some data to the application.

6.2 Adding the Data

To bring data into the application, you need to add some data sources. This example uses a BEx query as the data source. This BEx query (Figure 6.11) contains six measures that are located in the COLUMNS of the query and a lot of dimensions that are located in the FREE CHARACTERISTICS part of the query. This example application uses variants of this query as a data source. As you'll see next, you can alter the view of this one query in Design Studio by adding or removing measures and dimensions from the ROWS or COLUMNS areas.

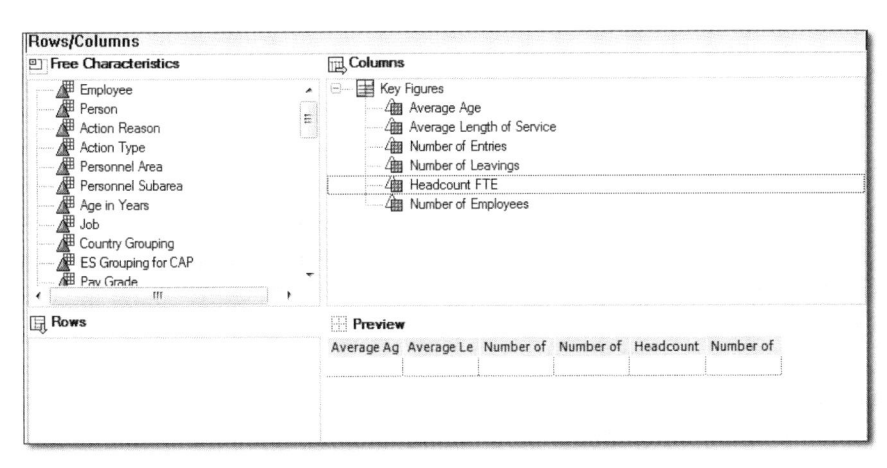

Figure 6.11 BEx Query Setup

Follow these steps to add the data:

1. In Design Studio, select APPLICATION • ADD DATA SOURCE, or right-click the DATA SOURCES folder in the OUTLINE view to add a new data source. Connect to SAP BusinessObjects BI by clicking the first BROWSE button.

2. Enter the technical name of the BEx query in the DATA SOURCE field. You can also use the second BROWSE button to search for the query (Figure 6.12). The data source gets the alias name DS_1 by default, and you can leave it that way.

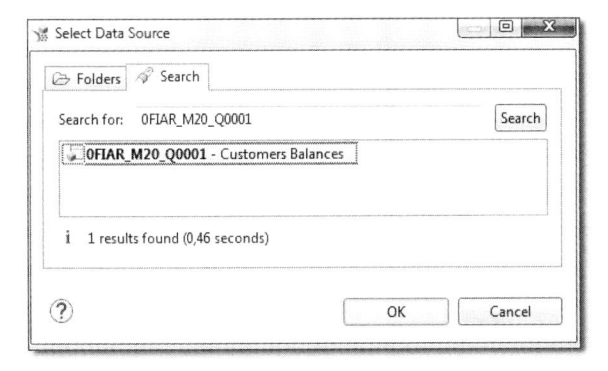

Figure 6.12 Adding a Data Source

3. Right-click on the data source, and select EDIT INITIAL VIEW. Notice that the structure of the view (Figure 6.13) is the same as in the BEx query (refer to Figure 6.11).

6 | The Application Design Process

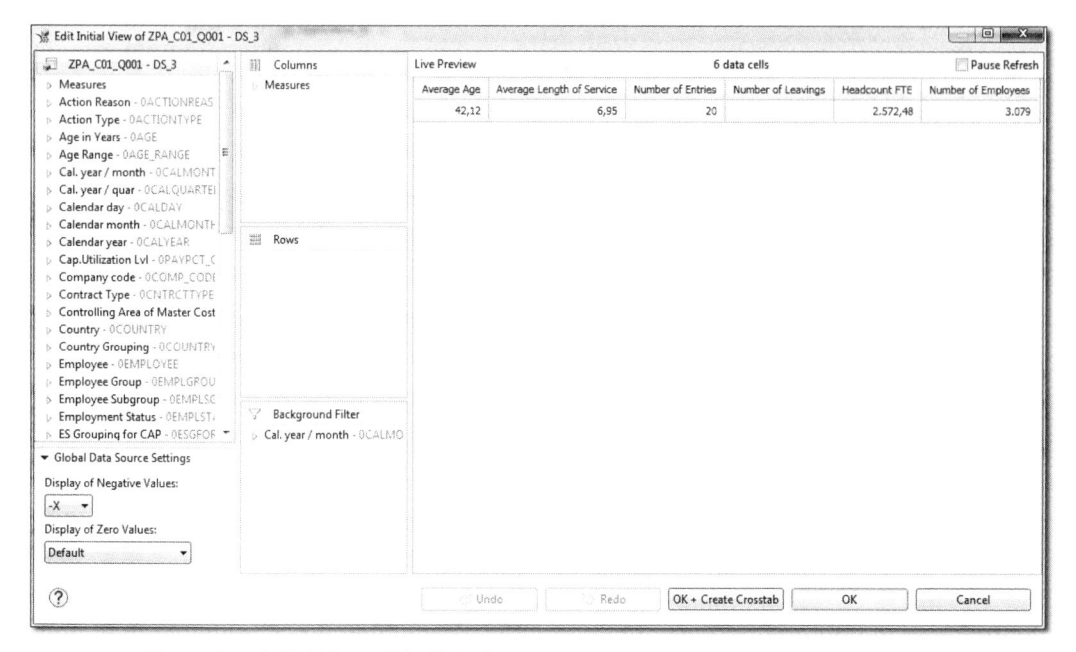

Figure 6.13 Initial View of the Data Source

4. Edit the data source by moving the AGE RANGE into the ROWS area. For this example, you're only interested in the NUMBER OF EMPLOYEES measure, so you can remove all other measures. Select OK, and drag the data source into the first chart (CHART_1).

5. The second chart needs to show the number of male and female employees, so copy DS_1, and use the default name (DS_2) for the new data source. Now edit DS_2 by removing the AGE RANGE dimension from the ROWS area and adding the GENDER dimension. Drag DS_2 into the second CHART component (CHART_2).

Let's move on to filling the six TEXT components with the values of the six measures and adding the filters to the LIST BOX components.

Follow these steps:

1. Copy one of the data sources. Right-click to open the context menu, and select RESET INITIAL VIEW. This resets the data source to its original setting as shown in Figure 6.13.

2. Start with TEXT_1 and TEXT_2 in cell [0,0]. Edit the text for TEXT_1. Set the text AGE IN YEARS instead of the default text: SAMPLE TEXT.

3. Next, fill TEXT_2 with the AVERAGE AGE IN YEARS measure in the data source by creating a script that fetches this value. This script will be called every time the application starts or when a filter is applied to the data source. Create a GLOBAL SCRIPT OBJECT by right-clicking on the TECHNICAL COMPONENTS folder in the OUTLINE, selecting CREATE CHILD, and then selecting GLOBAL SCRIPT OBJECT.

4. Create a GLOBAL SCRIPT FUNCTION by right-clicking the GLOBAL SCRIPT OBJECT that you've just created and selecting CREATE SCRIPT FUNCTION. Name this function `Calculate`. Add the following code to the CALCULATE SCRIPT FUNCTION:

```
var age = DS_
3.getData("20GPGXJS52B97QRI42FGOVGK8", {}).formattedValue;
TEXT_2.setText(age);
```

5. The `getData` method has two parameters. The first one is a measure, which you can select using the Ctrl + Space command in the Script Editor. The second is a selection; in this case, you want to select everything, so you use {}.

Enterprise ID

Notice the parameter in the `getData()` method. The parameter 20GPGXJS52B97QRI42FGOVGK8 corresponds to the Enterprise ID for the key figure that is referenced. In Design Studio, in any Script Editor, you can use Ctrl + Space to select from the available key figures (both the ID and name of the key figure will be displayed). In the BEx query, you can see this Enterprise ID by checking the properties of the key figure.

6. Now, you need to test this script. In the ON STARTUP script in the EVENT properties of the application, add the following line of code:

```
GLOBAL_SCRIPTS_1.Calculate();
```

7. SAVE AND RUN the application. You can see that TEXT_2 is now filled with the value from the data source (Figure 6.14).

Age in Years 42,12	Sample text	Sample text
	Sample text	Sample text
Sample text	Sample text	Sample text
Sample text	Sample text	Sample text

Figure 6.14 Text Component Filled with Values from the Data Source

6 | The Application Design Process

8. In the same way, set the text for TEXT_3, TEXT_5, TEXT_7, TEXT_9, and TEXT_11 with the following texts, respectively: Service years, Joiners, Number of Employees, FTE, and Leavers. Assign the appropriate values from the data source to TEXT_4, TEXT_6, TEXT_8, TEXT_10, and TEXT_12. You can do this by editing the script function you used earlier. The code will look something like this:

```
var age = DS_
3.getData("20GPGXJS52B97QRI42FGOVGK8", {}).formattedValue;
TEXT_2.setText(age);
var ser_years = DS_
3.getData("20GPGXJS52B97QRI42FGOVMVS", {}).formattedValue;
TEXT_4.setText(ser_years);
var joiners = DS_
3.getData("20GPGXJS52B97QRI42FGOVT7C", {}).formattedValue;
TEXT_6.setText(joiners);
var empl = DS_
3.getData("20GPGXJJRE0UK371U7PNLBGGD", {}).formattedValue;
TEXT_8.setText(empl);
var fte = DS_
3.getData("20GPGXJJRE0UK371U7PNLAXHP", {}).formattedValue;
TEXT_10.setText(fte);
var leavers = DS_
3.getData("20GPGXJS52B97QRI42FGOVZIW", {}).formattedValue;
TEXT_12.setText(leavers);
```

Listing 6.1 Setting the Text

9. Save and execute the application. As you can see in Figure 6.15, all text components will have a value assigned if there is a value present in the data source.

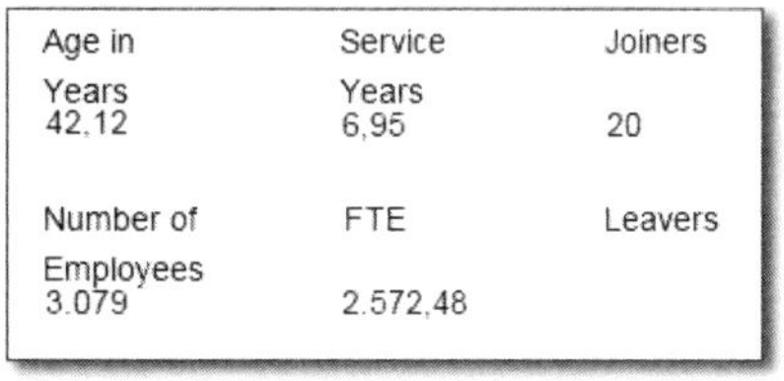

| Age in Years 42.12 | Service Years 6.95 | Joiners 20 |
| Number of Employees 3.079 | FTE 2.572,48 | Leavers |

Figure 6.15 All Text Components Assigned a Value

10. The last components that need to be filled are the three LIST BOX components. You'll fill the first LIST BOX manually and the second and third one dynamically. On the properties screen of LISTBOX_1, add the following three items (Figure 6.16):

- Item 1 with the VALUE set to 1000 and the TEXT set to COMPANY 1
- Item 2 with the VALUE set to 2000 and the TEXT set to COMPANY 2
- Item 3 with the VALUE set to 3000 and the TEXT set to COMPANY 3

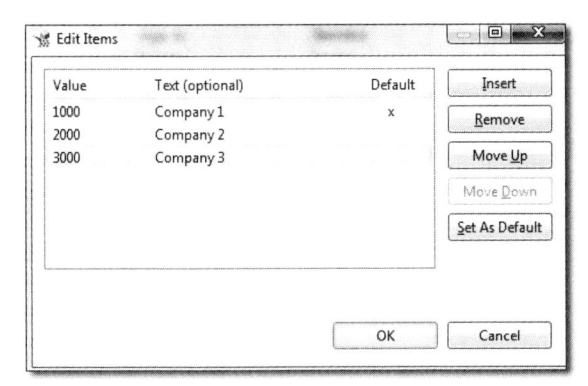

Figure 6.16 List Box Items

11. This example application is only using company code 1000, 2000, and 3000. The preferred way to filter this data is in a BEx query, but it's also possible to use a BACKGROUND FILTER in the data source. Add the BACKGROUND FILTER to all data sources by editing the INITIAL view of the data sources. You can use the FILTER BY INPUTSTRING (Figure 6.17) menu option to filter the company code dimension.

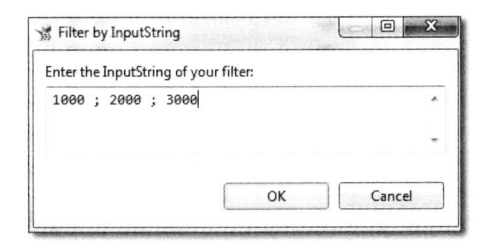

Figure 6.17 Filter by InputString

Now that you've added the data, next you can work on making the application interactive for the users.

6.3 Making It Interactive

You now have all the components set up in the Layout Editor, and the application is connected with a BEx query, delivering the data you want to show. You've also seen the scripting to set the TEXT component values. In this section, you'll use some scripts to add interactivity to the application and to set up the filters.

Don't worry if you're a bit overwhelmed by the coding we're going to discuss here. In Chapter 8, we'll explore scripting in a far more detailed way. For now, we're just giving you the big picture. The following things need to happen:

- When the application first starts up, the values of the two remaining LIST BOX components have to be populated with the values for the Employee groups and Employee subgroups.

- When someone selects a value from any one of the LIST BOX components, the data for that specific value needs to be shown.

- When a user clicks on a member in a chart, the data for that member needs to be shown (either data for a specific age group or data for a specific gender).

To provide these points of interactivity, follow these steps:

1. Select your application from the OUTLINE view. This is the top level.

2. In the PROPERTIES view, click on EVENTS • ON STARTUP to edit the script. This script will be executed when the application first starts up.

3. To populate the two LIST BOX components with the values from the Employee group and Employee subgroup, use the following script shown in Listing 6.2.

   ```
   LISTBOX_2.setItems(DS_3.getMemberList("0EMPLGROUP",
     MemberPresentation.INTERNAL_KEY, MemberDisplay.TEXT, 100,
     "Empl. Group"));
   ```

   ```
   LISTBOX_3.setItems(DS_3.getMemberList("0EMPLSGROUP",
     MemberPresentation.INTERNAL_KEY, MemberDisplay.TEXT, 100,
     "Empl. Sub Group"));
   ```

   Listing 6.2 Populating the List Box Components

4. Using a script to fill the LIST BOX components, dimension members gives you a lot of flexibility; for instance, you could add some extra logic into filling the LIST BOX components. However, in this case, you could also have used the DATA BINDING option in the properties of the LIST BOX components. You can activate

the Data Binding option by clicking on the two arrows at the top of the Properties screen and selecting Dimension Members Binding, as shown in Figure 6.18. When you do this, the Input Binding properties become available from which you can select which data source to use and what dimension to set.

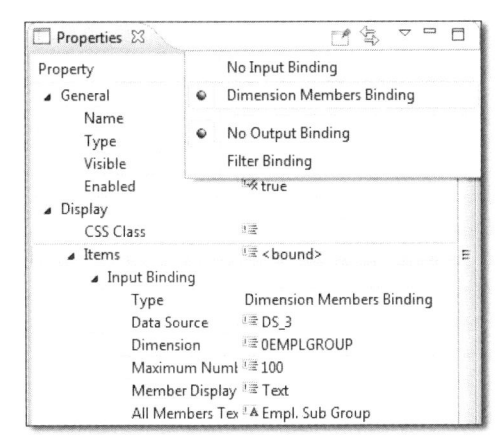

Figure 6.18 Data Binding Option

5. Save and execute the application. Notice that all the List Box components are also filled with members now (Figure 6.19).

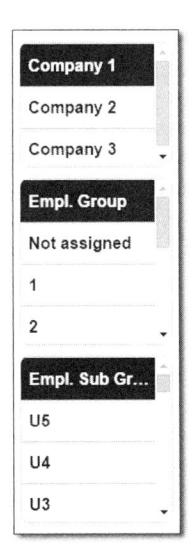

Figure 6.19 List Box Components Filled Manually and Dynamically

6. When a user clicks on a member in one of the List Box components, you have to make sure to filter all data sources. Start by selecting LISTBOX_1. In the On Select property, add the following script to filter all the data sources with the value in LISTBOX_1 that was selected by the user:

```
var filter = LISTBOX_1.getSelectedValue();
DS_1.setFilter("0COMP_CODE", filter);
DS_2.setFilter("0COMP_CODE", filter);
DS_3.setFilter("0COMP_CODE", filter);
```

7. Just like the input binding example, you can use the Filter Binding option instead of the code to filter on a specific company code. By choosing the Filter Binding option in Figure 6.20, an extra property called Output Binding is made available. Here, you can select the data sources on which the filter should apply and the dimension that should be used for filtering.

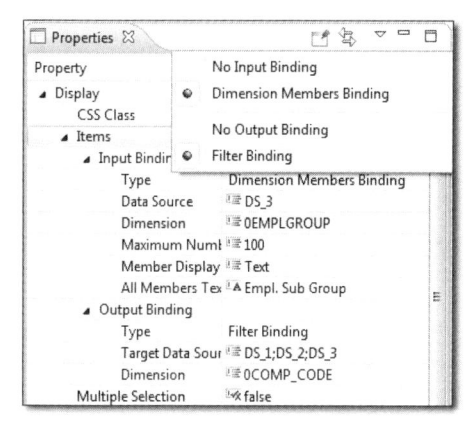

Figure 6.20 Output Binding Property

8. In the same way, add the following script to LISTBOX_2:

```
var filter = LISTBOX_2.getSelectedValue();
DS_1.setFilter("0EMPLGROUP", filter);
DS_2.setFilter("0EMPLGROUP", filter);
DS_3.setFilter("0EMPLGROUP", filter);
```

9. Add a similar looking script to LISTBOX_3:

```
var filter = LISTBOX_3.getSelectedValue();
DS_1.setFilter("0EMPLSGROUP", filter);
DS_2.setFilter("0EMPLSGROUP", filter);
DS_3.setFilter("0EMPLSGROUP", filter);
```

10. Now move on to the charts. The script for filtering the data sources based on what the user clicks is pretty much the same as you've seen before. For CHART_1, use the following script:

    ```
    var filter = CHART_1.getSelectedMember("0AGE_RANGE");
    DS_1.setFilter("0AGE_RANGE", filter);
    DS_2.setFilter("0AGE_RANGE", filter);
    DS_3.setFilter("0AGE_RANGE", filter);
    ```

11. For CHART_2, use the following script:

    ```
    var filter = CHART_2.getSelectedMember("0GENDER");
    DS_1.setFilter("0GENDER", filter);
    DS_2.setFilter("0GENDER", filter);
    DS_3.setFilter("0GENDER", filter);
    ```

12. At this point, you're almost finished with the scripting portion. After each filter is executed, you still need to update the TEXT components that contain the six different measure values. Add the following line of code to the three LIST BOX components and the two CHART components:

    ```
    GLOBAL_SCRIPTS_1.Calculate();
    ```

13. All the scripts that handle the interaction are now in place. Save and execute the application, and test the interactivity of your application.

Congratulations! Your Design Studio application is now fully operational. However, before you can start using it, you should take some time to focus on the application's appearance to create a superb user experience.

6.4 Formatting and Fine-Tuning

So far, in our example, we've provided only the main building blocks needed to make the application operational, without much time taken on formatting and fine-tuning the look and feel.

If an application meets all its functional requirements but is designed in such a way that the user doesn't understand what he is seeing or how things work (or comes off as visually unappealing), the application quickly loses its value. Frustrated users may tire of how cumbersome the application is and stop using it all together.

Luckily, Design Studio provides many options to customize and format the appearance of an application. In this section, we'll go through a few of the features that apply to the example application. We'll use the properties in the LIST BOX and

6 | The Application Design Process

CHART components that you've used to build the application to align these components nicely on the screen. You'll also add a title to both charts and format the values that are displayed in each chart.

Follow these steps:

1. First, make some room for the three LIST BOX components:
    ▸ For LISTBOX_1, set the TOP MARGIN to 60, the LEFT MARGIN to 20, the BOTTOM MARGIN and RIGHT MARGIN to AUTO, the WIDTH to 150, and the HEIGHT to 120.
    ▸ For LISTBOX_2, set the TOP MARGIN to 190, the LEFT MARGIN to 20, the BOTTOM MARGIN and RIGHT MARGIN to AUTO, the WIDTH to 150, and the HEIGHT to 160.
    ▸ For LISTBOX_3, set the TOP MARGIN to 360, the LEFT MARGIN to 20, the BOTTOM MARGIN and RIGHT MARGIN to AUTO, the WIDTH to 150, and the HEIGHT to 160.

2. Next, go to the properties of GRID_LAYOUT_1, and use the following settings: set the TOP MARGIN to 60, the LEFT MARGIN to 200, the BOTTOM MARGIN to 100, the RIGHT MARGIN to 100, the WIDTH to AUTO, and the HEIGHT to AUTO.

    The components should be positioned now so that they don't overlap each other on the screen (Figure 6.21).

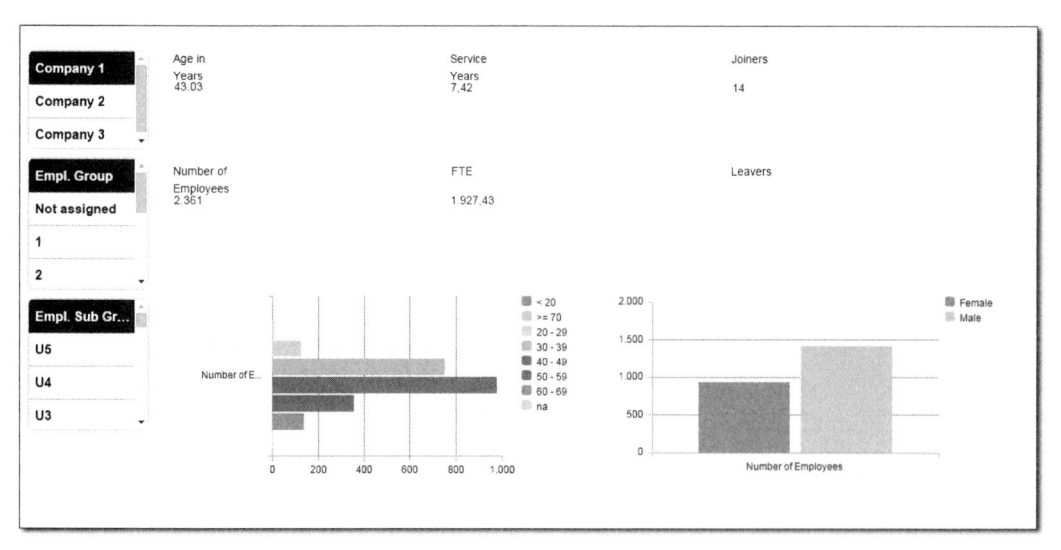

Figure 6.21 All Components Positioned

3. Now you need to edit the two charts so that they look a bit nicer. In Figure 6.21, you can see that the measures of both CHART components are positioned

212

on the X-axis. In addition, all the dimension members are given another color in the charts. Using a lot of colors usually makes your application look very crowded. An easy fix for this problem is to go to the properties of each CHART and set the SWAP AXES property to TRUE.

4. In the ADDITIONAL PROPERTIES of CHART_1, check the SHOW TITLE checkbox, and enter the title for this chart as "Age diversity". Because there is only one measure in this chart and the title of the charts gives you enough information, you can uncheck the SHOW LEGEND checkbox in the ADDITIONAL PROPERTIES.

5. Do the same for CHART_2, but give this chart the title "Gender".

Your charts should now look like those in Figure 6.22.

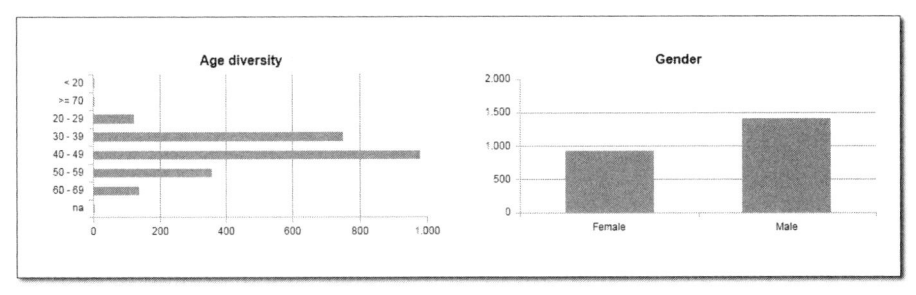

Figure 6.22 After Swapping the Chart Axis

6. Finally, you need to take care of the TEXT components:

   ▸ Select TEXT_1, TEXT_3, TEXT_5, TEXT_7, TEXT_9, and TEXT_11 while holding down the Ctrl key. Set the TOP MARGIN, LEFT MARGIN, and RIGHT MARGIN to 0; set the BOTTOM MARGIN and WIDTH to AUTO; and set the HEIGHT to 30.

   ▸ Now, select TEXT_2, TEXT_4, TEXT_6, TEXT_8, TEXT_10, and TEXT_12 while holding down the Ctrl key. Set the TOP MARGIN to 30; the LEFT MARGIN, BOTTOM MARGIN, and RIGHT MARGIN to 0; and set the WIDTH and HEIGHT to AUTO.

7. We'll discuss Cascading Style Sheets (CSS) in greater detail in Chapter 10, but for now, just make the TEXT components that you still have selected bold. To do this, open the CSS Style Editor in the properties of the TEXT components, and add the following CSS code:

   ```
   Font-weight: bold;
   ```

8. Save the final application.

6.5   Executing the Application

You have three options for executing an application, depending on how you're connected:

- Execute the application locally.
- Execute the application via the platform to which you're connected.
- Execute the application by sending it to a mobile device to test how it looks on SAP BusinessObjects Mobile.

To execute the application, follow these steps:

1. Select the EXECUTE LOCALLY option from the APPLICATION menu to check the application in a browser window. The result is shown in Figure 6.23.

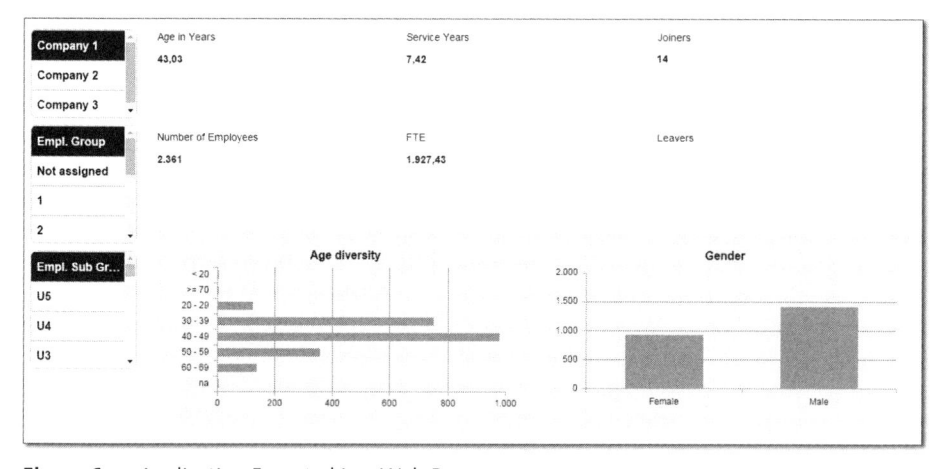

Figure 6.23 Application Executed in a Web Browser

Executing an Application on Other Platforms

You can use the EXECUTE LOCALLY option to quickly test developments you've made. There is no need to save your work first. If you're connected to an SAP BusinessObjects BI platform, you also have the option to execute the application from this platform. A new browser window will open, and you'll see the OpenDocument link that is provided by SAP BusinessObjects BI in the URL bar of the browser. There is no need to log in first.

When you're connected to the SAP BW portal or SAP HANA, you have the options EXECUTE ON SAP ENTERPRISE PORTAL and EXECUTE ON SAP HANA, respectively. In both cases, the application will be loaded in a new browser window, and you'll be prompted to log in to the respective system.

2. Apply some filters, and click on some member in the charts to see how the filters work in action.

3. Check the application on your mobile device by selecting the SEND TO MOBILE DEVICE (USING QR CODE®) command in the toolbar. A QR code will appear (Figure 6.24), which you can scan on your mobile device using a QR code reader. In Figure 6.25, you see the result on a mobile device.

Figure 6.24 QR code

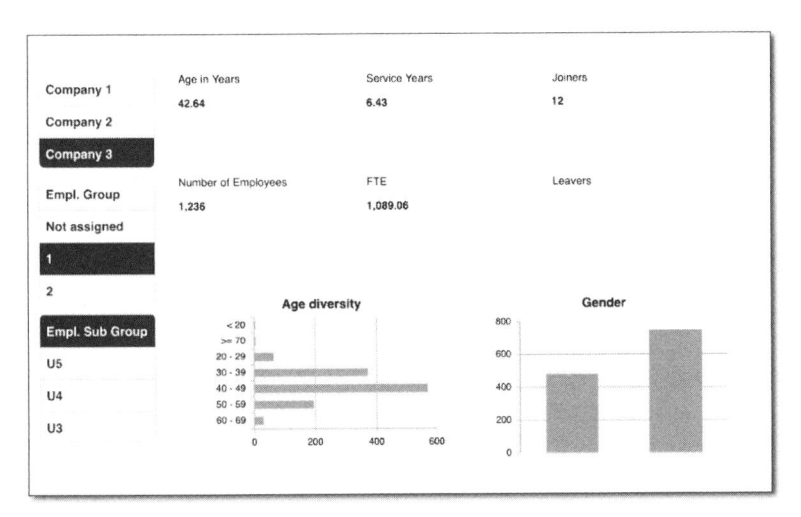

Figure 6.25 Application on a Mobile Browser

6.6 Summary

In this chapter, we provided a step-by-step tutorial of how to build a simple application with Design Studio. In the example application, you used CHART and TEXT components to visualize and display data from a BEx query data source.

To set up the overall layout of the application, you used GRID LAYOUT components to divide the available screen space. With the LIST BOX components and some associated event scripts, you created the interactive elements in this application to filter the data and select the measures to be presented in the CHART and TEXT components. Finally, you executed the application and checked its functionality, both on a regular browser and on a mobile browser.

By now, you've already seen and used some of the many components that are available in Design Studio. In Chapter 7, we'll explore all the components with their properties.

This chapter introduces the components and properties in Design Studio that serve as your basic tools for building applications.

7 Components and Properties

In this chapter, we'll look at all the building blocks—in other words, the components and their properties—of Design Studio. We'll start by discussing the properties of the APPLICATION component, and then we'll move on to the properties of the DATA SOURCE ALIAS component. In the heart of the chapter, we discuss the properties of all the visual components of Design Studio. To finish things off, we end the chapter with the technical components.

7.1 Application Component Properties

The APPLICATION component (Figure 7.1) is the main component in Design Studio because it's the application itself. APPLICATION is the top-level node in the OUTLINE view, and its PROPERTIES view contains settings that cover the entire application.

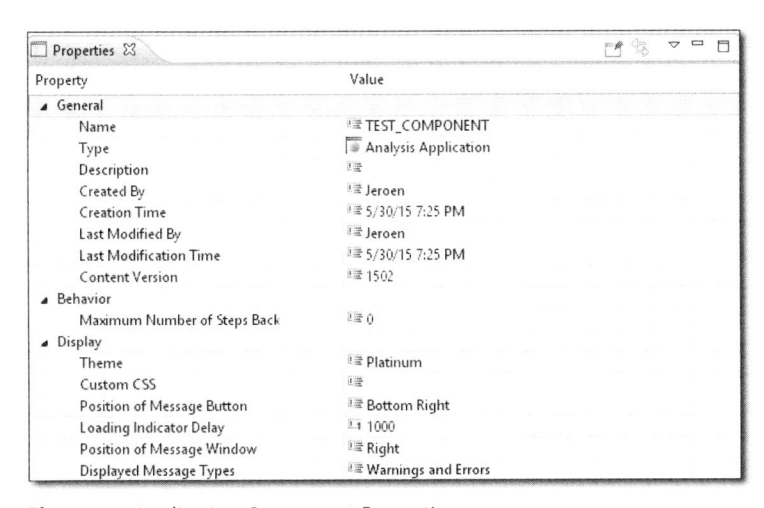

Figure 7.1 Application Component Properties

7 | Components and Properties

Global variables are maintained in this component, and scripts can be added that will start at different phases in the startup of the application. Furthermore, you can insert a central Cascading Style Sheets (CSS) file that will allow you to have a single source of layout classes that you can use for every component within the application.

Table 7.1 shows the changeable properties of the APPLICATION component.

Properties	Usage
DESCRIPTION	The description of the application is set when you create a new application, but it can be changed at design time.
NUMBER OF STEPS BACK	Set this number anywhere between 1 and 20 to enable the methods back one step and back to start. These methods allow you to let users undo their navigational steps in the application. This number represents the number of times a user can retrace his steps in the application.
THEME	This specifies the theme of the application. A theme is a set of layout choices that applies to all the components used in the application. SAP recommends using the SAP Platinum theme for desktop applications and using the SAP Mobile theme for iPad and iPhone applications.
CUSTOM CSS	You can upload a CSS file to the root folder of the application (local) or the SAP BusinessObjects Business Intelligence (BI) platform. In the CUSTOM CSS property, you can point to this CSS file. In this CSS file, CSS classes are defined that can be used by other components that have a CSS class property.
POSITION OF MESSAGE BUTTON	This sets the location of the button in a message. The button can be located on the top-left, top-right, bottom-left, or bottom-right area of the application screen. The message button informs the user about information, warnings, and errors at runtime.
POSITION OF MESSAGE WINDOW	This sets the location of a message on the application during runtime. This message can be positioned on the top-left, top-right, bottom-left, or bottom-right area of the application.

Table 7.1 Changeable Properties of the Application Component

Properties	Usage
LOADING INDICATOR DELAY	This is the delay in milliseconds until the loading indicator is shown.
DISPLAYED MESSAGE TYPES	This sets the kind of messages that will show up at runtime. Following are the available message types: ▸ NONE: No messages will be shown. ▸ ERRORS: Only errors will be shown. ▸ WARNINGS: Warnings and errors will be shown. ▸ ALL: All information messages will be shown.
MERGE PROMPTS	This enables the grouping of variables by technical name. When the property has the value TRUE, the application will keep one value for the variable and apply it to all queries that contain that variable.
FORCE PROMPTS ON STARTUP	When set to TRUE, this setting forces the application to prompt for new variable values at the start of the application when SAP Business Warehouse (BW) or SAP HANA variables are used in the application.
PROMPT SETTINGS	This defines which prompts should be visible and in what order they should appear.
MAXIMUM NUMBER OF MEMBERS	This specifies the maximum number of members displayed in the value help for prompts. If the actual number exceeds this number, the user has to limit the number of members by entering a search string that filters the possible members more strict.
WIDTH OF DIALOG BOX OF INPLACE PROMPTS	This setting is the width in pixels of the dialog box.
HEIGHT OF DIALOG BOX OF INPLACE PROMPTS	This setting is the height in pixels of the dialog box.
PLANNING CONNECTION	This specifies the backend connection that holds the planning model.
PLANNING MODEL	This setting reflects the planning model you want to use.
GLOBAL SCRIPT VARIABLES	You can define global variables that are available in all the scripts throughout the application. You can also define the variable as a URL parameter so parameter values can be read from other applications.

Table 7.1 Changeable Properties of the Application Component (Cont.)

7 | Components and Properties

Properties	Usage
ON VARIABLE INITIALIZATION	This event is triggered after the data sources are loaded and before the variables are submitted. This is the best place to submit initial values for variables.
ON BEFORE PROMPTS SUBMIT	This event is triggered when the OK button on the prompts variable dialog box is clicked, but before the variables are submitted. You can do some last-second modifications based on the input.
ON STARTUP	This script code is run when the application starts. Editing this property will start the Script Editor. In the startup phase of the application, you typically insert code to work with external parameters or use data sources to populate the items of basic components.
ON BACKGROUND PROCESSING	This event is triggered by the method `doBackgroundProcessing()`. The script is executed in the background and doesn't halt screen rendering.

Table 7.1 Changeable Properties of the Application Component (Cont.)

There are a number of scenarios where you work with the properties of the APPLICATION component. These properties have a bigger impact than those of other components because the APPLICATION component influences the behavior of scripting and layout of many other components. Let's look at some examples.

7.1.1 Custom CSS

The CUSTOM CSS property allows you to use the CSS classes defined in a CSS text file. Either you can use a CSS file that is already uploaded to the platform, or you can upload a CSS file to the platform.

For example, you can create your own CSS file on your local computer with the code in Listing 7.1.

```
.TextPanelOrange
{
background-color:#d0e4fe;
 color:orange;
 text-align:center;
}
```
Listing 7.1 CSS to Create an Orange Panel

Next, you upload the CSS file, and after the file is in place, you can select the file. The CUSTOM CSS property of the application is then set to this file, so the defined classes in the CSS file can be used by components in the application.

In each component, you can now assign TextpanelOrange to the CSS CLASS property of any component. Assigning this class to a component will result in a change of the component layout to an orange text with a blue background.

There are specific applications available that make editing CSS easier, for example, Notepad++. Insert the code as shown in Figure 7.2.

```
.TextPanelOrange {
    background-color:#d0e4fe;
    color:orange;
    text-align:center;
}
```

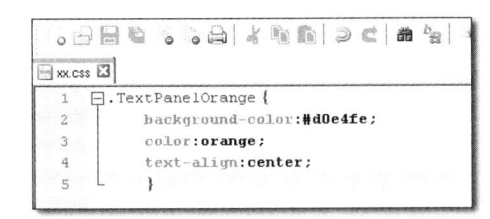

Figure 7.2 Creating a CSS File

Notepad++

To determine whether this program may be useful to you, download it free at *http://notepad-plus-plus.org/*.

Save the file as a .css file. In the SAVE AS SAVE dialog box, select all files, and name the file "mycssfile.css".

You'll now notice that one of the advantages of Notepad++ over Notepad is that it can recognize the CSS coding and performs code formatting, which makes editing and deciphering the code much easier. Additionally, if you forget one of the { or } symbols in the code, it's clear where that happened due to color coding.

As of version 1.6, a more advanced CSS editor is available in Design Studio (Figure 7.3).

The updated CSS editor provides syntax coloring and a feature that makes the classes you define in the CSS editor visible in the OUTLINE panel (Figure 7.4).

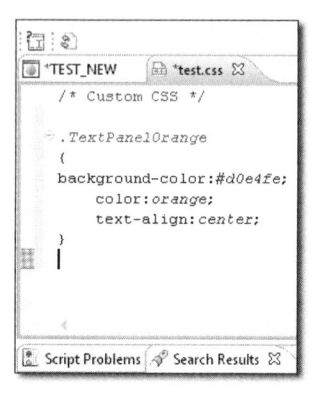

Figure 7.3 CSS Editor in Design Studio

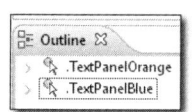

Figure 7.4 CSS Outline in Design Studio

You can open the individual classes in the OUTLINE panel and click on the available properties. The cursor in the CSS editor will move to the part of the CSS code that handles that particular property (Figure 7.5). You can highlight that selection by double-clicking on a property. Double-clicking the class highlights the entire class code in the CSS editor.

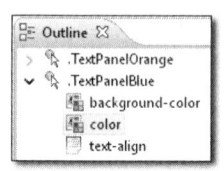

Figure 7.5 Selecting a CSS Property in Outline panel

Now, open the application in Design Studio, and go the properties of the APPLICATION component. Click the ... button on the right side of the CUSTOM CSS field (Figure 7.6).

Application Component Properties | 7.1

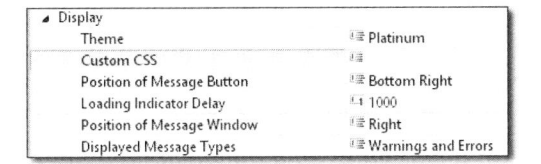

Figure 7.6 Custom CSS

You're now looking at the SAP BusinessObjects BI platform folders. We've selected a folder in the PUBLIC FOLDERS section, which means that other applications can access the CSS file. To upload, click the button with the upward arrow on the top left of the window (Figure 7.7).

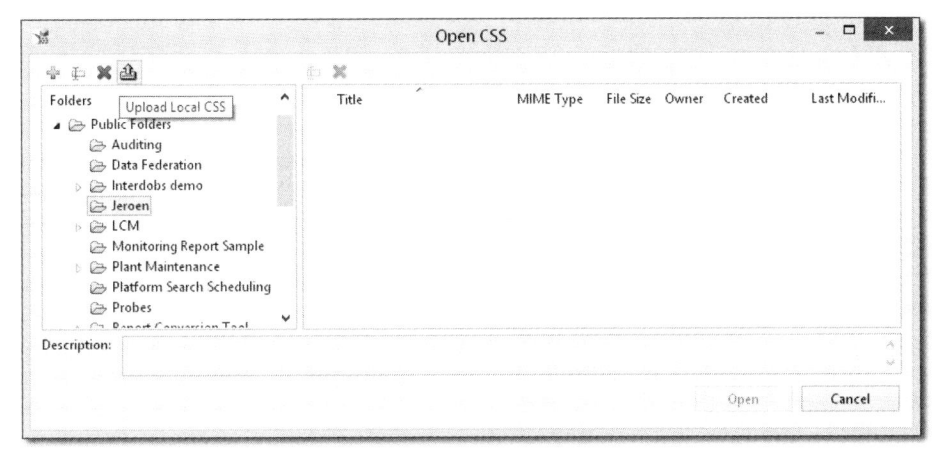

Figure 7.7 Public Folder on the SAP BusinessObjects BI Platform

You should now see a window where you can select your CSS file. Navigate to the location where you saved your file, and select the file by either double-clicking it or selecting the file and clicking OPEN. In SAP BusinessObjects BI, you'll see your CSS file next to the already present CSS file. Select MYCSSFILE.CSS, and click OPEN (Figure 7.8).

7 | Components and Properties

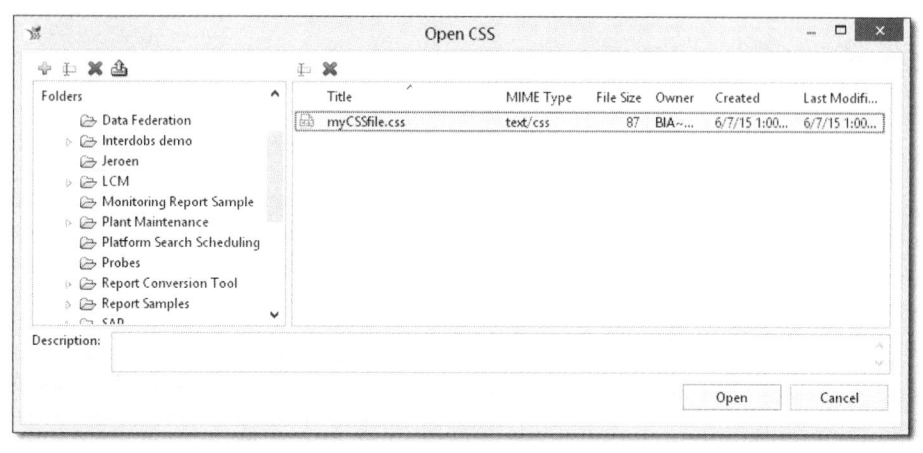

Figure 7.8 CSS File on the SAP BusinessObjects BI Platform

After you've selected the CSS file, return to the application. In the properties of the APPLICATION component, you'll notice that the CUSTOM CSS property points to the file on SAP BusinessObjects BI (Figure 7.9).

Figure 7.9 Custom CSS Property after Selection

As the final step, add a TEXT component to the application, and set the CSS CLASS property to `TextPanelOrange`. As you can now see in Figure 7.10, we changed the CSS class of the graph labels. These labels are all TEXT components with the CSS class assigned. You now see how the TEXT components holding the label values change the background color and the font color. If you change the contents of the CSS class in the custom CSS file, all the labels will change their formatting accordingly. This is a very powerful feature that works across applications.

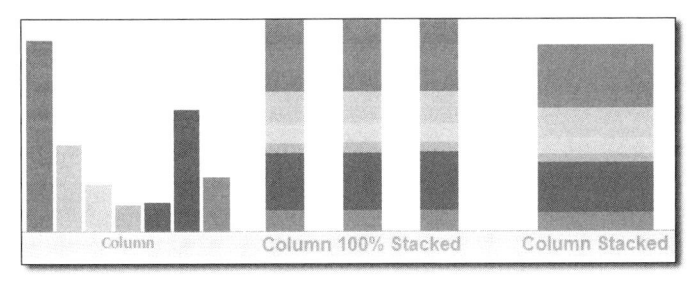

Figure 7.10 Applying the CSS Class

7.1.2 Global Script Variables and On Startup

Global script variables offer a way to store information and use it across component scripts in your application. Using the external parameter feature gives other applications a way to pass information to your application.

As the number of applications in the SAP BusinessObjects BI portfolio increases, you'll eventually need a way for the applications to communicate with each other. Instead of building large applications that have to offer many features, you can specialize applications and use hyperlinks with parameters to allow applications to link to each other and pass information. This is much easier to maintain than a few very big applications that have to handle a lot of functions.

Design Studio is able to open a website or another Design Studio application by using the `APPLICATION.openNewWindow` method. The URL of the application can include parameters for the other application. Using a global script variable, the other application will receive those parameters and use those values to set up the application accordingly. This setup will give outside applications a way to influence internal features of that application.

Now you can set up an external parameter by adding it as a variable to the VARI-ABLES property of the APPLICATION component (Figure 7.11). Any application can pass a value to the `XStore` variable now by adding the parameter in the URL, as we'll show shortly. After the application starts, it will automatically run the application's `On Startup` script. In this handler, you'll insert script code. When the external parameter value is any other value other than `none`, the application will filter the data source to reduce the dataset to only show this store that has been passed via the parameter.

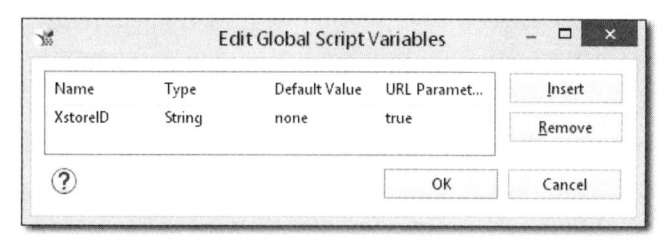

Figure 7.11 Editing the Global Script Variable

The `On Startup` script looks like this:

```
var currentStore = XstoreID;

if (currentStore != "none") {DS_1.setFilter("COUNTRY_
NAME", currentStore);}
```

> **Note**
>
> In Chapter 8, we'll provide more specific instructions about scripting. For now, we're just using this as an example to show you how the VARIABLES property of the APPLICATION component can be used.

The application is now set up to check whether parameter values are passed. If they are, it will filter the data source to reflect the store ID passed in the parameter.

If another Design Studio application wants to pass the parameter, it can do so by using the `APPLICATION.openNewWindow` method as shown in Listing 7.2.

```
APPLICATION.openNewWindow
("http://myBOserver.com:8080/BOE/OpenDocument/1302122240/OpenDocument/
opendoc/openDocument.jsp?sIDType=CUID&icdocID=
AR1LC4JJgDxDujA4IODZobk" + "& XstoreID =" + CHART_
1.getSelectedMember(ZSTORES).getSelectedValue());
```
Listing 7.2 Open Application with Parameters

In this method, you use a CHART component that visualizes the sales per store. When the user clicks on the graph, the script will use the `openNewWindow` method. The method will look at the CHART component and use the selected store value to pass it as a parameter to the detail application.

Because the URL with the CUID—the unique ID of a document—is quite complicated, the code in Listing 7.2 looks a bit messy and is hard to comprehend. To make the script code more readable, you can split up the URL and parameters into several variables. These variables hold the value of the URL of the application. The resulting script will be easier to read and maintain, especially when you want to link from several components and reuse the variables.

The code now looks like Listing 7.3.

```
var serverName = "http://myBOserver.com:8080" ;
var serverPath= "BOE/Open-Document/1302122240/OpenDocument/opendoc/";
var docName = "openDocument.jsp?";
var appID = 'sIDType=CUID&icdocID=AR1LC4JJgDxDujA4IODZobk"';
var parameters = "&XstoreID=" + CHART_1.getSelectedMember(ZSTORES);

APPLICATION.openNewWindow(serverName + serverPath + docName + appID + p
arameters);
```

Listing 7.3 Clean Code to Open Different Applications with Parameters

Typically, the variables for `serverName` and `serverPath` should be made global because these variables are needed for any link that has to be set up in the application and stay the same. This means you have to define them only once.

7.2 Data Source Alias Component Properties

The DATA SOURCE ALIAS component represents an instance of a data source. An APPLICATION component can contain many DATA SOURCE ALIAS components. Multiple DATA SOURCE ALIAS components can be linked to the same data source, for example, if you need different perspectives on the same data and to show them both at the same time. The component can be loaded either at startup or at a later point in the application using script code to trigger the load.

The DATA SOURCE ALIAS component properties are shown in Table 7.2.

Property	Description
NAME	This is the name of the DATA SOURCE ALIAS.
VISIBLE	This toggles the visibility of the component.
LOAD IN SCRIPT	This specifies whether the data source is loaded immediately when initializing the application or is loaded in the script later. The standard setting is FALSE, meaning the data source will load immediately.

Table 7.2 Data Source Alias Properties

Property	Description
TEXT	This text will be displayed in the prompts dialog box, which will help when you have unmerged variables. The descriptive text will help users identify for which query they are setting variable values.
PROCESSING GROUP	Currently, this property can only be used if the application runs on the SAP BusinessObjects BI platform or locally. This property specifies the processing group. When loading queries, all queries in the same processing group will load in parallel. Groups are loaded sequentially. If you don't specify a group, a default group is used.
DATA SOURCE NAME, CONNECTION, AND TYPE	These fields change the data source underneath the DATA SOURCE ALIAS. The ADD DATA SOURCE screen will open with the current settings.
ON RESULT SET CHANGED	This event triggers the script entered when the data source is initialized and when the result set of the data source has changed. This script will run after other scripts. If other scripts set multiple changes, this script will run only once at the end.

Table 7.2 Data Source Alias Properties (Cont.)

The LOAD IN SCRIPT property allows you to delay the moment when the data is loaded. This property tells the application whether the data will be immediately loaded at startup or will be triggered from a script at a later time. Reasons for delaying include minimizing the startup time of the application or applying filters before you load the data for performance reasons. To load the data, add this script line:

DS_MYDATA SOURCE.loadData source();

As long as the data source isn't loaded, the DATA SOURCE ALIAS won't have any impact on performance. Therefore, it's worthwhile to postpone loading data sources until you actually need them. If a user doesn't need them using the application, he'll have a performance advantage because fewer queries need to be loaded.

7.3 Visual Component Properties

In this section, we'll discuss the properties of all the visual components in Design Studio. Visual components are divided into three categories: analytic, basic, and container components. We'll discuss the properties for each category, but we'll begin by discussing the common properties.

7.3.1 Common Properties

The common properties are shared by all visual components. These involve the layout of the components—specifically, their sizes and margins. You can alter the layout and the relative positioning of a component by editing the numbers in the LAYOUT section of the properties. You can also use the mouse to drag the component or its borders to the desired size or position.

Table 7.3 provides a list of common properties in Design Studio.

Property	Description
NAME	Sets the unique name of the component. If you don't enter a name, the system will take a default name, for example, TEXT_32. For maintainability, it's important to use a naming convention.
TYPE	Displays the component type (CHECKBOX, LISTBOX, DROPBOX, etc.). You can't alter this property.
VISIBLE	Specifies whether a component is visible (TRUE) or not visible (FALSE).
ENABLED	Specifies whether a component is enabled (TRUE) or disabled (FALSE). Disabled means that the user can see the component, but can't interact with it.
CSS CLASS	Sets the CSS class from which the layout properties should be applied to the component. These CSS classes are defined in the CSS file attached to the APPLICATION component (see Section 7.1.1).
TOP MARGIN	Sets the distance between the top of the component and the top of the parent component. Either enter a number in pixels or choose AUTO.
LEFT MARGIN	Sets the distance between the left side of the component and the left side of the parent component. Either enter a number in pixels or choose AUTO.

Table 7.3 Common Properties

7 | Components and Properties

Property	Description
RIGHT MARGIN	Sets the distance between the right side of the component and the right side of the parent component. Either enter a number in pixels or choose AUTO.
BOTTOM MARGIN	Sets the distance between the bottom of the component and the bottom of the parent component. Either enter a number in pixels or choose AUTO.
HEIGHT	Sets the height of the component. Either enter a number in pixels or choose AUTO.
WIDTH	Sets the width of the component. Either enter a number in pixels or choose AUTO.

Table 7.3 Common Properties (Cont.)

By setting the layout properties to AUTO, you're allowing this property to shrink and grow along with the screen size. When a fixed number is entered for a property, then the value for that property remains constant.

For example, consider a component with the following layout parameters:

- TOP MARGIN: 10
- LEFT MARGIN: 10
- BOTTOM MARGIN: 10
- RIGHT MARGIN: 10
- WIDTH: AUTO
- HEIGHT: AUTO

The result of these settings is that the margins will remain equal in relation to the parent component, but the component itself will resize according to the parent component. The example is typical for when you want a background that covers nearly the whole screen with a little margin on the sides.

As another example, consider these parameters:

- TOP MARGIN: 10
- LEFT MARGIN: 10
- BOTTOM MARGIN: AUTO

- RIGHT MARGIN: AUTO
- WIDTH: 100
- HEIGHT: 100

The result of these settings is that the component size is fixed to 100 × 100 pixels with a margin of 10 pixels to the left and top. A bigger screen size will mean larger right and bottom margins. Typically, these settings are used when you want a logo to appear on the top-left area of the screen.

You can create more advanced settings by combining the settings of container panels. If you place the second example within the first, a LEFT MARGIN of 10 is relative to the left side of the first component.

> **Databound Component**
>
> The common property of the DATABOUND components, such as CHARTS and CROSSTABS, is expanded so you can change the data source of a DATABOUND component at runtime. You'll read more on this in Chapter 8.

7.3.2 Analytic Component Properties

Analytic components use data to show numbers in either table or graphical form. Additionally, components in this category enable users to work with the data and alter the way the data is filtered and shown. These components are tied to data by assigning a data source to a component and then using the component to visualize the data output that is defined in the INITIAL view of the data source.

We'll describe the different types of analytic components next.

Chart Component

CHART components can be added to an application to visualize data graphically. They can identify trends or outliers in data, and they also help users to focus on those data points. The CHART component appears as soon as you assign a data source to it. The default CHART TYPE is a column chart.

A CHART component is meant to communicate data in a clear, concise way. The example in Figure 7.12 shows the total population per region from 1990 to 1999. When you hover over a year, you see a tooltip with the exact data value.

7 | Components and Properties

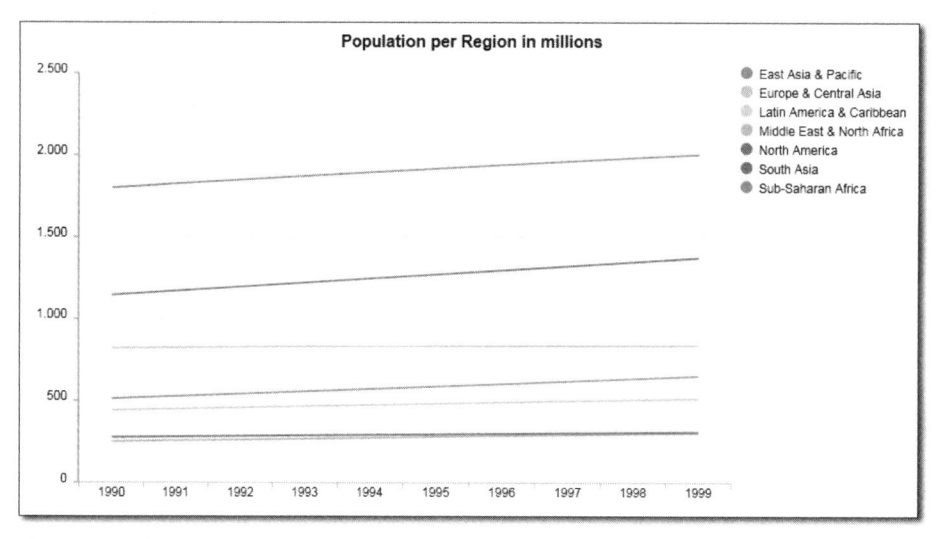

Figure 7.12 Chart Component Example

Table 7.4 lists the properties of the CHART component.

Property	Description
DATA SOURCE	This assigns data to the component for visualization. You can choose from the defined DATA SOURCE ALIAS components that are added to the application.
DATA SELECTION	This is a selection string in JavaScript Object Notation (JSON) format. A dialog box allows you to create a subset of the data in the data source to visualize in the CHART component.
CHART TYPE	A number of chart types are available, as outlined in more detail later in this section. In Figure 7.13, all the chart types are listed with a screenshot for reference.
CONDITIONAL FORMATTING	This is a selection string in JSON format. A dialog box allows you to apply conditional formatting rules to measures or dimension members in a chart.
SWAP AXES	This specifies whether to swap the horizontal and vertical axes of the data source before visualization.
SHOW TOTALS	When TRUE, the data source output totals will be visualized.

Table 7.4 Chart Component Properties

232

Property	Description
SHOW SCALING FACTORS	Select TRUE to show the scaling factors in the chart. The scaling factors are defined in the INITIAL VIEW of the DATA SOURCE ALIAS.
DIMENSION LABEL	This determines whether you want the dimension values shown as defined in the DATA SOURCE ALIAS or forced to either the texts or keys.
ON SELECT	This opens the Script Editor. The On Select handler is triggered when a value is selected or deselected.

Table 7.4 Chart Component Properties (Cont.)

The types of charts are as follows (see Figure 7.13):

- **Line**
  A line graph shows a trend by showing a line with the labels in the X-axis and the values in the Y-axis. In addition, there are line chart variations:
  - *Horizontal line*: A horizontal line chart shows the line going in a vertical direction with the labels horizontal.
  - *Dual line*: Two lines chart where each line has its own axis (one on the left and the other one on the right).

- **Bar**
  A bar chart shows a bar for each value in the data source. There are several bar chart variations:
  - *Stacked bar*: In a stacked bar chart, you can also show how different values add up to the total of the bar. The length of the stacked bar depends on the sum of the values.
  - *100% stacked bar*: This shows bars in which each value is a part of the bar. This type of chart will always show the total bar length at 100%.
  - *Bar combination*: This is a combination of a bar chart and a line chart.
  - *Bar dual axis*: This is a two bar series where each series has its own axis.

- **Column**
  A column chart shows each value in a column. There are several column chart variations:

- *Stacked column*: In a stacked column chart, you can also show how different values add up to the total of the column. The total length depends on the sum of the values.
- *100% stacked column*: This shows columns in which each value is part of the column.
- *Column combination*: This is a combination of a column chart and a line chart.
- *Column combination dual axis*: This is a combination of a column chart and a line chart where both have their own axis.

- **Area**
An area chart is like a line chart with the area under the line colored in. In addition, there is a variation of an area chart:
    - *Horizontal area*: This is an area chart where the line is vertical and the labels are horizontal.

- **Crosstab**
A crosstab is a table in which numbers are presented along rows and columns.

- **Bubble**
In a bubble chart, you can map three key figures: one on the X-axis, one on the Y-axis, and one that affects the size of the bubble.

- **Waterfall**
A waterfall chart is a bar chart where bars are shown in a cumulative way. The total value of bar 1 is the starting point of bar 2. There are two variations of a waterfall chart:
    - *Stacked waterfall*: This waterfall chart has the added ability to add up several values in each bar.
    - *Horizontal waterfall*: This waterfall chart shows the bars going from left to right and the labels are horizontal.

- **Pie**
A pie chart shows the relative size of entities compared to the whole. In addition, there is a variation of a pie chart:
    - *Multiple pie*: A multiple pie chart shows a different pie graph for each key figure and shows the relative sizes for each value on the graphs.

▶ **Radar**

A radar chart shows the relative size for each value. It's like a line graph with a round axis. In addition, there is a variation of a radar chart:

▷ *Multiple radar*: A multiple radar chart shows a radar graph for each key figure.

▶ **Scatter**

A scatter chart shows combinations of key figures, where one key figure is plotted along the X-axis, and the other along the Y-axis.

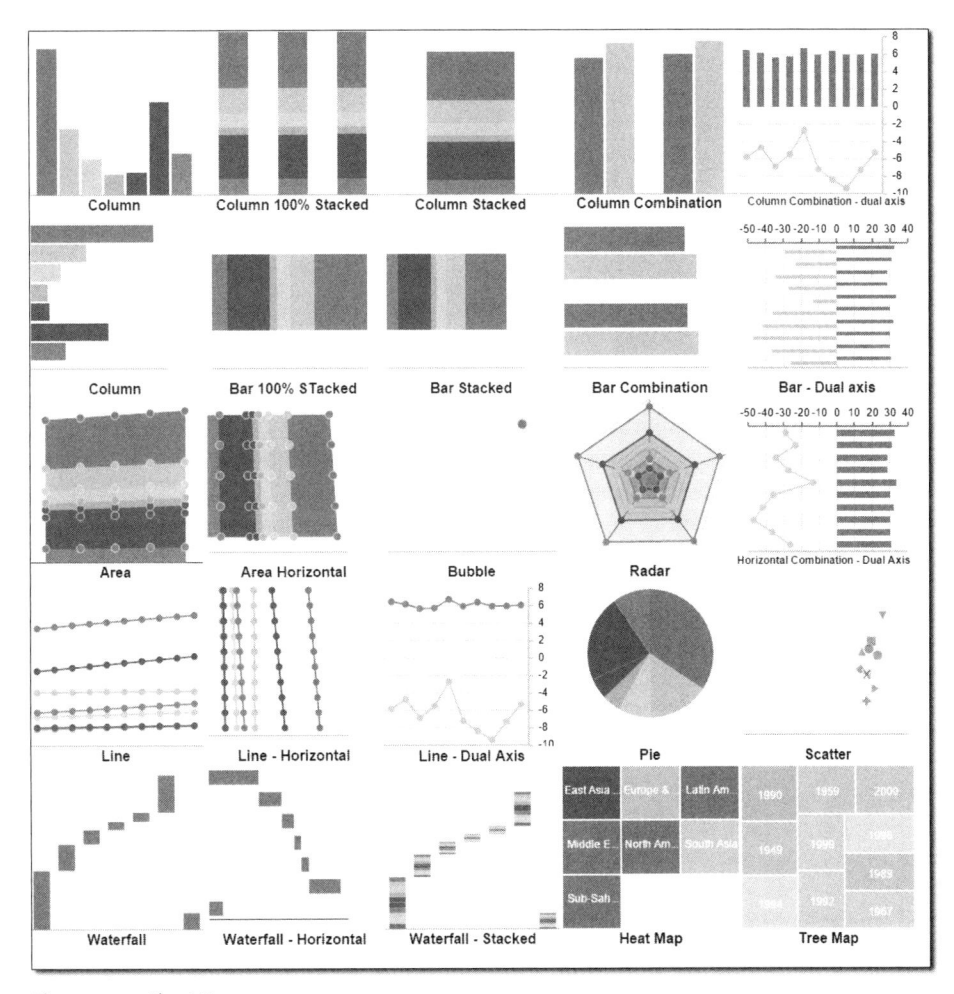

Figure 7.13 Chart Types

Additionally, you can pick one of the special chart types when you choose ADDITIONAL CHART TYPES. With this option, you have, by default, the option to choose from a trellis, heat map, tree map, and, if you installed the real-time package, the time-based line.

In graphs, you can set up conditional formatting, which enables you to highlight a particular item when a condition is met. For example, you can highlight all regions with red that missed their targets by at least 5%.

In the following steps, we'll walk through how to apply this format based on our example:

1. Select the GRAPH component for which you want to add conditional formatting.
2. In the GRAPH component's properties, click the CONDITIONAL FORMATTING button.
3. If you want to create a new rule, on the CONDITIONAL FORMATTING screen, click the NEW RULE button. The NEW RULE dialog box appears (Figure 7.14). If you click the EDIT RULE button, the EDIT RULE dialog box appears (Figure 7.15). Both the NEW RULE and the EDIT RULE screens are identical. Therefore, whether you're creating a new rule or editing an existing rule, enter or edit the name of your rule in the NAME field.
4. Under RULE DESCRIPTION, select either a MEASURE or a DIMENSION MEMBER from the dropdown list. When you select MEASURE, you'll be able to highlight based on the evaluation of a value. If you select DIMENSION MEMBER, you can highlight cells that belong to that member. If you choose MEASURE, the screen will look like Figure 7.14. If you choose DIMENSION MEMBER, the screen will look like Figure 7.15.
5. For the MEASURE, select the type of condition (EQUAL TO, IS GREATER THAN, IS LESS THAN). Select IS GREATER THAN, as shown in Figure 7.14.
6. Input the value threshold that the measure value is compared to, for example, "100,000." With this input, you've instructed the application to highlight every cell in the measure that has a value greater than 100,000.
7. In the PREVIEW area, click the FORMAT button to assign a color to your rule.
8. Click OK to finish customizing your rule.

Figure 7.14 Conditional Formatting Screen for a Measure Value

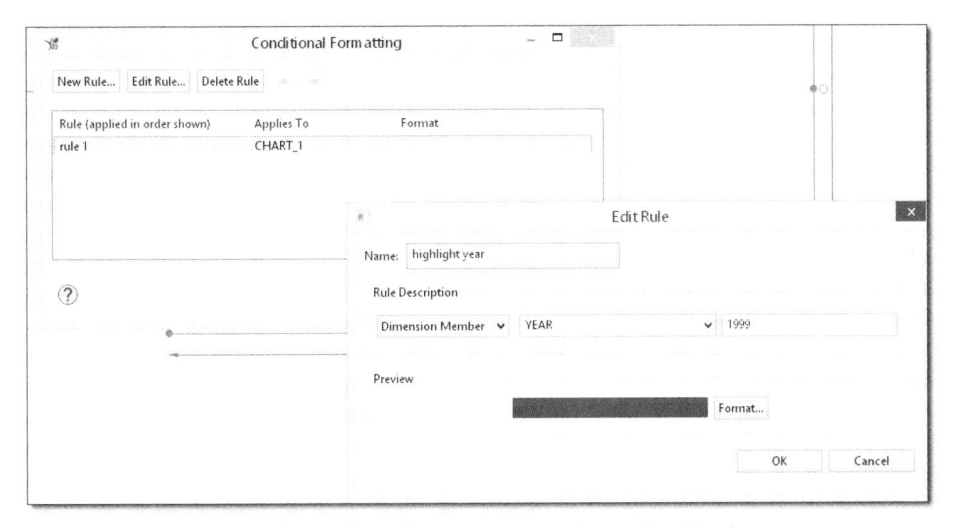

Figure 7.15 Screens to Apply Conditional Formatting on a Dimension Member

Your new formatting rule is now listed in the CONDITIONAL FORMATTING dialog box. As previously discussed, if you want to edit your rule, on the CONDITIONAL FORMATTING screen highlight, the rule you want to edit, and click EDIT RULE. Use the up and down arrows to change the order of the rules on the CONDITIONAL FORMATTING screen.

In the ADDITIONAL PROPERTIES tab (Figure 7.16) of a chart, you can alter the look of the CHART component. In the CHART AREA, you can choose which labels to make visible, whether you want a tooltip (a message that appears when the users hovers the mouse over the graph), and whether a chart animation should be shown at application startup. You can also choose the fill color of your background and how the dimension values are displayed in the chart.

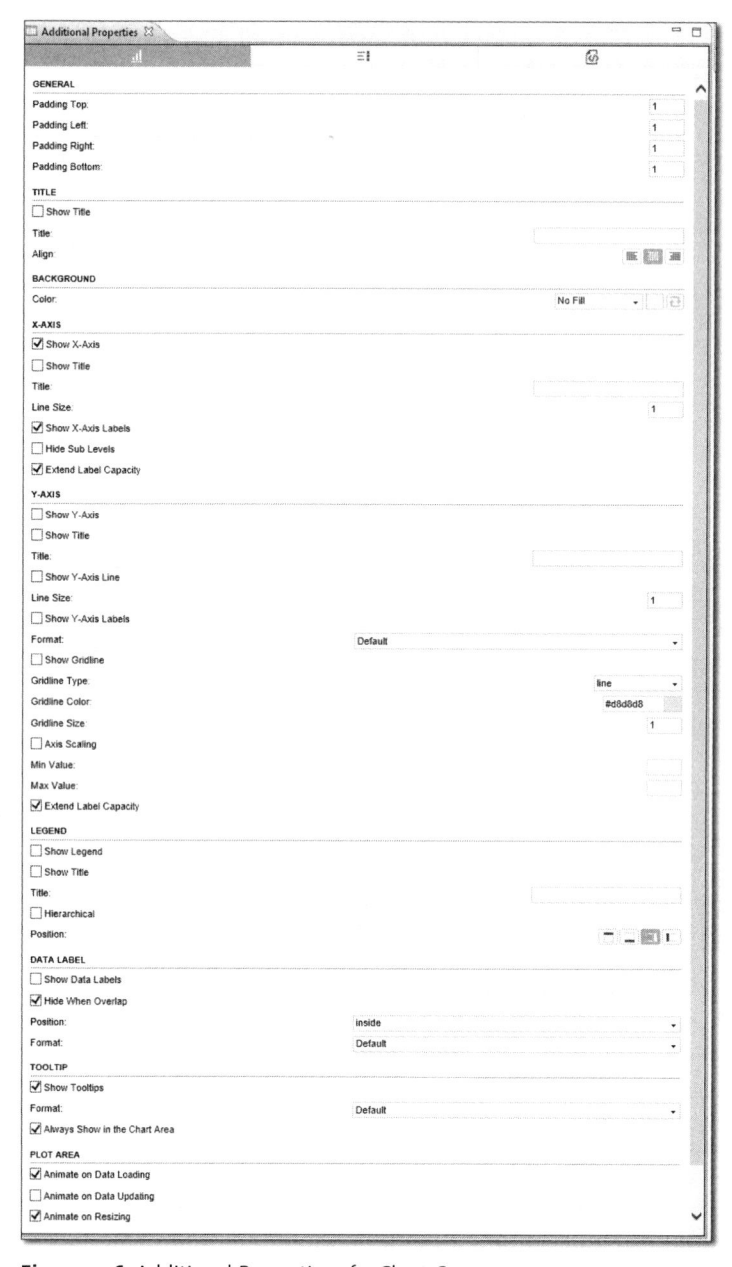

Figure 7.16 Additional Properties of a Chart Component

With the DATA SERIES FORMAT additional property of a chart (Figure 7.17), you can set the colors for all the data series. Keep in mind, however, that the colors are attached to the index number, not to the data series name. Therefore, if you change the order of the data series, the colors will change accordingly.

Figure 7.17 Data Series Properties

The CSS additional properties (Figure 7.18) allow you to format different parts of the chart, specifically the CSS settings. By changing fonts, sizes, and so on, you can control how labels and titles are formatted within your application. Be aware, however, that these settings only apply to the component you're editing. If you want the settings to apply to all charts, you have to work with custom CSS.

Figure 7.18 Subset of the CSS Additional Properties

7 | Components and Properties

Info Chart Component

New to Design Studio 1.6, the INFO CHART component (Figure 7.19) is the future replacement for the CHART component. One of the main differences between the INFO CHART component and the CHART component is the way you configure the chart. For the INFO CHART component, you can use the CHART CONFIGURATION property to open the CONFIGURE CHART screen for setting up your chart (Figure 7.19).

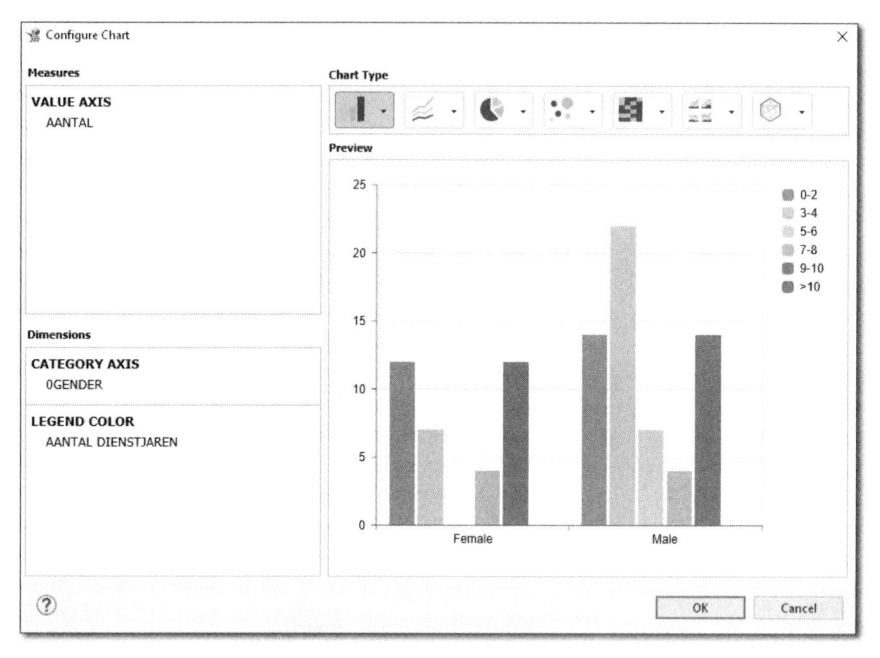

Figure 7.19 Info Chart Configuration

On the CONFIGURE CHART screen, you can choose the type of graph you want to you use under CHART TYPE. On the left side of the screen, you see the layout of the data source, where you can change the layout for this graph. Here, you can work with all the dimensions that have been added to the rows or columns in the data source.

Follow these steps to configure an INFO CHART component:

1. Assign a data source to your INFO CHART component.
2. Within the PROPERTIES tab, select the current value for the CHART CONFIGURATION property, which opens a screen for further configuration.

3. Select the CHART TYPE above the rendered chart. Under CHART TYPE are seven collections of charts that you can choose from. The selected graph will change the example graph below the picker.

4. Move the measures and dimensions up and down within their areas to configure the binding of data to the INFO CHART component. Changes influence the chart directly.

5. Select OK. The CHART TYPE and data binding are now applied to the INFO CHART component. The newly configured INFO CHART is displayed in the Layout Editor.

6. To display conditional formatting, set the CONDITIONAL FORMATTING VISIBLE property to TRUE.

7. To display the totals in your charts, set the SHOW TOTALS property to TRUE.

Info Chart Feeding Panel

The INFO CHART FEEDING PANEL (Figure 7.20) allows users to change the layout of the INFO CHART at runtime. Users can drag the dimensions that will influence the appearance of the chart. The INFO CHART component doesn't influence the data source, which means changes only will apply to the related graph.

In the PROPERTIES tab, you have to define which graph it should influence. Other graphs will remain unaffected.

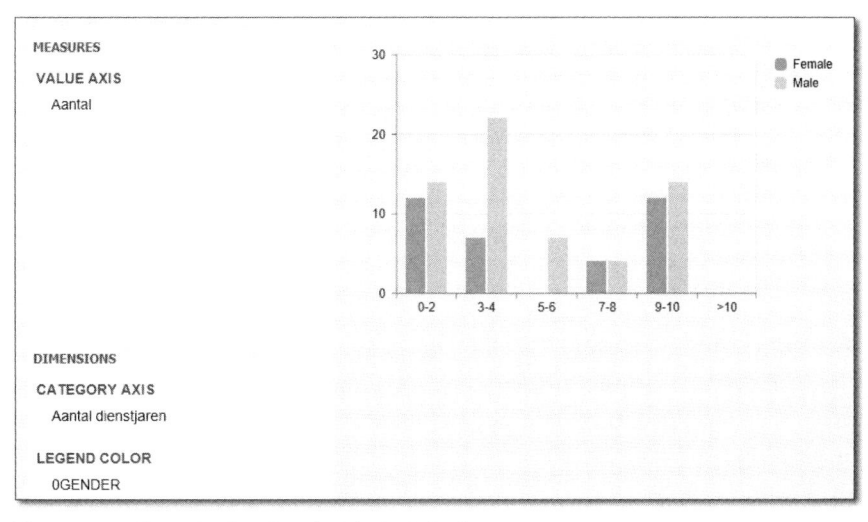

Figure 7.20 Chart Feeding Panel with the Info Chart

> **Flexibility**
>
> The INFO CHART FEEDING PANEL allows you to set the data source of an INFO CHART component and design an application for a single graph and change the dataset and layout at runtime. By doing this, you can create applications that allow users to explore and choose their own graph types. At startup, you can create a new application with the DATA DISCOVERY AND VISUALIZATION template.

Scorecard Component

The SCORECARD component (Figure 7.21) is used to create a table with numerous graph options. You can create tables with graphs in each row visualizing that particular dataset. This is similar to the trellis function in SAP Lumira.

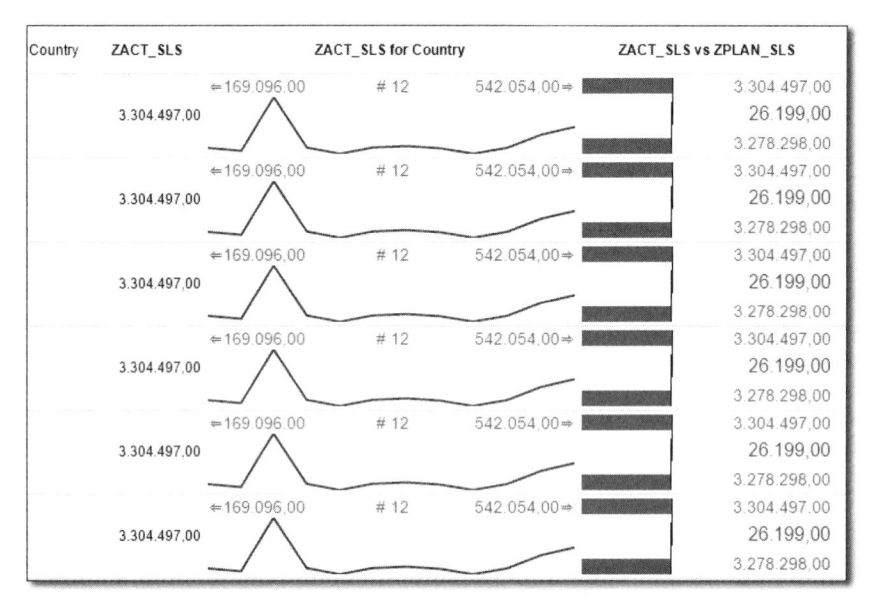

Figure 7.21 Scorecard Component

This is a complicated component to configure because you're able to determine each row and each cell content, the values, the graph types, and the grouping. Therefore, let's discuss the step-by-step approach to configure the SCORECARD component. Follow these steps:

1. Add a SCORECARD component to the application.
2. Add a data source to the application.

> **Warning!**
> Given the complexity of this component, make sure you have a separate data source for this component and that the INITIAL view is set properly. If you have to change either of these options later on, chances are you'll have to redo the configuration entirely.

3. Select the SCORECARD component, and go to the PROPERTIES tab.
4. Set the row and header heights.
5. Set the SELECTION TYPE (SINGLE or MULTI-TOGGLE).
6. Set the NAVIGATION MODE (NAVIGATOR or SCROLL).
7. Go to the ADDITIONAL PROPERTIES tab (Figure 7.22).

Figure 7.22 Scorecard Additional Properties

8. Select the DIMENSION FOR ROW SCOPE. This will determine which dimension will group the scorecard into rows.
9. Click the GENERATE INITIAL SCORECARD button. A first rendition of the SCORECARD is shown in Figure 7.23.

    When you click the button, the system generates the following columns:

    ▸ For every dimension included in the rows: One column with dimension members.

    ▸ For the first measure: One dimension displaying the measure sum of the row scope definition.

    ▸ For the first dimension, which is outside of the row scope: A column with a trend chart displaying the measure members for that dimension as a line or column chart.

    ▸ If the data source has more than one dimension: A column with a comparison chart displaying the delta between the first and second measure.

7 | Components and Properties

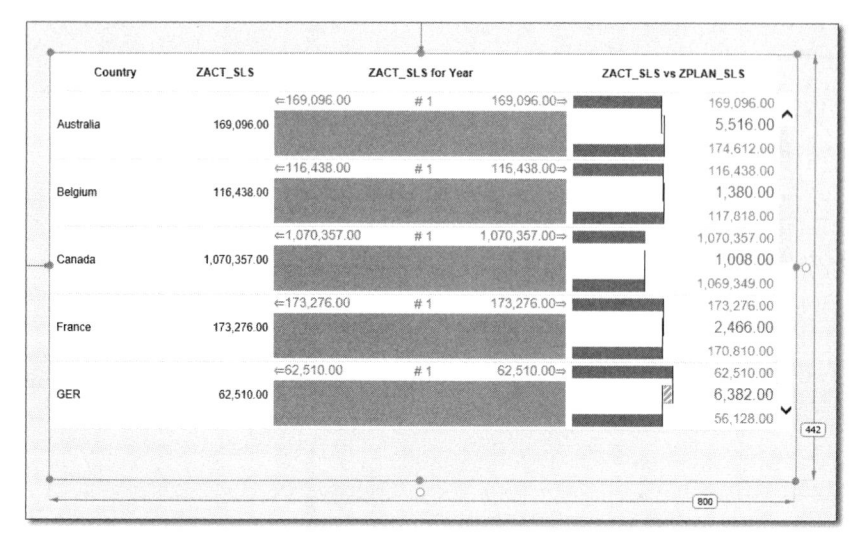

Figure 7.23 First Rendition of the Scorecard

10. Select the SCORECARD, and go back to the ADDITIONAL PROPERTIES tab. The ADDITIONAL PROPERTIES are now expanded to include columns (Figure 7.24). These columns relate to the columns you see in the initial rendering.

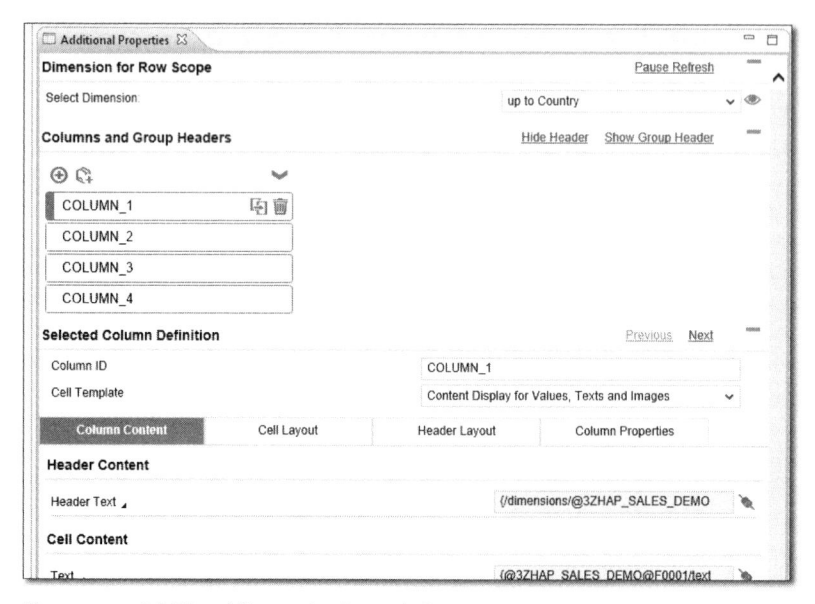

Figure 7.24 Additional Properties Expanded

244

11. In the ADDITIONAL PROPERTIES tab, you now can select columns. The selected column can be configured below the selection.

12. Select the CELL TEMPLATE (text or graph type). The other selections below will change based on the selection made for the CELL TEMPLATE.

For our example, you'll configure a text column and a graph column. In the two subsections that follow, we'll walk through each of these processes.

Text Column

Some properties are bound to data and some aren't. You can tell whether a property is bound to data by the icon on the right side of the property, as shown in Figure 7.25 and Figure 7.26. Bound implies that the value of the cell is dependent on the underlying data source. Unbound implies the cell values are independent values. Figure 7.25 shows an example of a bound property, and Figure 7.26 of an unbound property.

Figure 7.25 Bound Scorecard Property

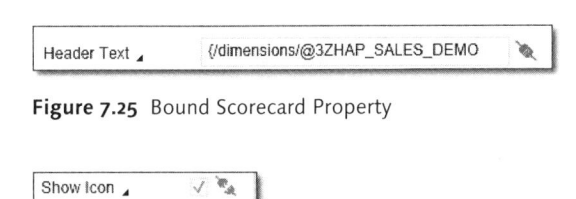

Figure 7.26 Unbound Scorecard Property

By clicking on the icon on the right side of the property, you can change the property. For unbound properties, you can insert manual entries. For bound properties, you can link to parts of the data source.

To edit a text column in a SCORECARD component, follow these steps:

1. Go to the HEADER TEXT section, and click on the BOUND property.

2. Open the BINDING TYPE dropdown menu to see the available options. Select DIMENSION METADATA CONTENT.

3. Select the DIMENSION.

4. Select VALUE TEXT or VALUE KEY for the DIMENSION DISPLAY. The first is the unique technical value of the dimension member, and the second is the text description. If you want to replace the value of the property with your own text:

- Change the Binding Type to Unbind, Manual Entry.
- Type your own text into the input box.

5. Go to Cell Content – Text.
6. Open the Binding Type dropdown menu to see the available options. Select Dimension Member Content.
7. Select the Dimension.
8. Select the way the value is presented in the Member display. Select either Value text or Value key for Dimension Display.
9. Select which part should be cut off if the member text is too long in the Member Presentation Part property. Options include Default, First Part, or Last Part.
10. In the other tabs, set the layout for both the colors and margins.
11. In the Column Properties tab, set the width of the column.

Graph Column

Now you're going to configure a graph column. First, you'll set up the graph type. Then, you'll bind the values and configure the labels. There are many more options, however, this will get you through the first steps. Follow these steps:

1. Select a column that contains a graph. Note the Cell Template; it states the type of chart used.
2. Go to the Chart Size property. Choose Chart with Data Labels if you want labels included.
3. For the Actual Values property, click the Bound icon.
4. In the Bound Type field, select Multiple Cell Count.
5. If you click the icon on the right side of the selected data cells, you'll see a pop-up where you can define the cell set you want to visualize (Figure 7.27).
6. Repeat the steps for each column. First, select a template, and from there, adjust the individual properties.

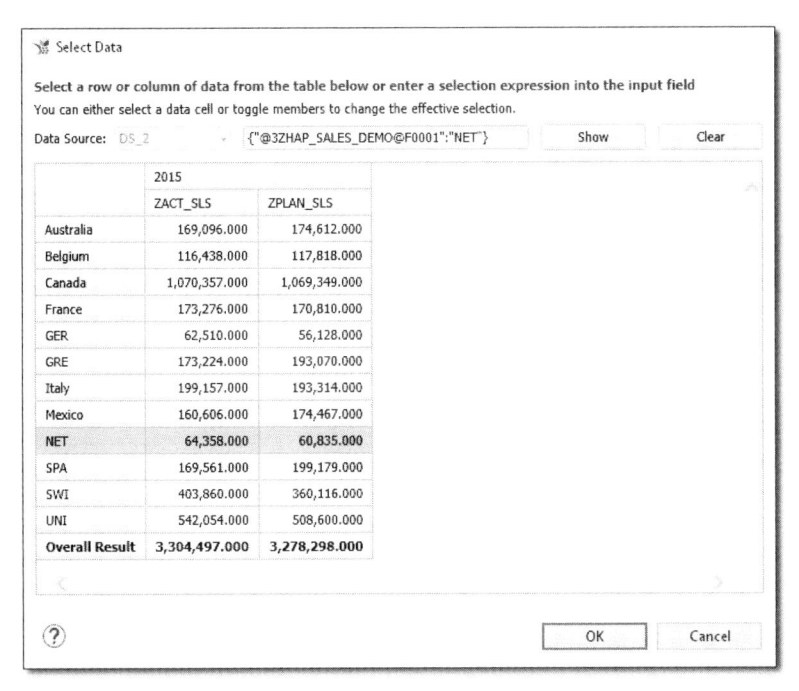

Figure 7.27 Data Selection for a Column in the Scorecard Component

Crosstab Component

The CROSSTAB component (Figure 7.28) is useful for displaying detailed multidimensional data for analytical purposes.

Figure 7.28 Crosstab Component

Used together with the DIMENSION FILTER component and the FILTER PANEL component, which will be described later in this chapter, a CROSSTAB component is a very flexible way to show and work with data. You can use the CROSSTAB component to sort and filter data, move or swap dimensions, and select cells that in turn can be scripted to add filters to data sources.

Table 7.5 shows the properties of the CROSSTAB component.

Property	Description
DATA SOURCE	Assigns data to the component to visualize it. You can choose from the defined DATA SOURCE ALIAS components you added to the application.
PIXEL-BASED SCROLLING	Enables a smooth scrolling experience. This property is recommended when building an application for mobile devices or applications with a low data volume.
ROW LIMIT	Sets the maximum number of rows for pixel-based scrolling.
COLUMN LIMIT	Sets the maximum number of columns for pixel-based scrolling.
SELECTION TYPE	Sets whether the user can select a row, a column, or single data cells.
SELECTABLE AREA	Sets the area of the CROSSTAB where selection is allowed.
ENABLE HOVER EFFECT	Enables a hover effect when selection is allowed.
HIERARCHY NAVIGATION ENABLED	Specifies whether the user can collapse or expand hierarchies in the CROSSTAB.
SORTING ENABLED	Specifies whether the user can sort columns in the CROSSTAB.
COLUMN RESIZING ENABLED	Specifies whether users can resize columns in the CROSSTAB.
HORIZONTAL HEADER RESIZING ENABLED	Enables or disables resizing of horizontal headers.
HORIZONTAL SCROLLING FOR HEADER ENABLED	Enables users to scroll horizontally for headers.
CONTEXT MENU ENABLED	Specifies whether the user can open a context menu in the CROSSTAB by right-clicking. You're also able to modify the menu items in the context menu.
CSS CLASS	Assigns a class when a custom CSS file is assigned to the APPLICATION component's properties.

Table 7.5 Crosstab Component Properties

Property	Description
UNITS AND SCALING FACTORS	Shows the unit and scaling factor in the header, in the data cells, or not at all.
ALWAYS FILL	If set to TRUE, sizes the CROSSTAB component as defined in the LAYOUT properties. This means if the number of cells isn't sufficient to fill the space that was set for the CROSSTAB component, the cells will increase in size until the entire frame (the width and height of the component) is filled.
CONDITIONAL FORMATTING VISIBLE	Specifies whether conditional formatting is visible in the CROSSTAB. Earlier in the chapter, we discussed how you can set up rules for conditional formatting.
COLUMN WIDTHS	Sets the column width per column. Clicking the button opens a dialog box with a table that allows you to enter widths for each column.
MAXIMUM WIDTHS OF HEADER AREA	Sets a fixed maximum width for the header area. The default setting is AUTO, which ensures that the header will use all the horizontal space it needs.
DISPLAY REPEATED TEXTS	Specifies if you want the texts to repeat when multiple rows have the same value or to group the rows in one larger cell.
NUMBER OF NEW ROWS	Specifies the number of new rows for planning applications.
POSITION OF NEW ROWS	Determines whether you want new rows for planning on top or at the bottom of the CROSSTAB.
ENABLE SELECTION	When set to TRUE, allows users to select cells in the CROSSTAB component by hovering over or clicking the inner members of the required dimension. This doesn't apply for result cells. Selecting a cell will result in an On Select handler where you can insert script to perform several actions based on the user's selection.
MAXIMUM NUMBER OF VALUE HELP MEMBERS	Specifies the maximum number of members displayed in a value help for dimension (non-hierarchical) selection.
ON SELECT	Opens the Script Editor. The On Select handler is triggered when the selected item has been changed.

Table 7.5 Crosstab Component Properties (Cont.)

As an example of when this component can come in handy, you can use the CROSSTAB component in combination with a CHART component. Users can click a value on the CHART component, and the CROSSTAB component will show detailed

7 | Components and Properties

information about the selected value. The selected value then can be used as a filter for a second component for a more detailed view.

For this example, let's assume that a second data source is being filtered based on the selection made in the CROSSTAB component. This results in an interactive screen that will pop up with additional information when a cell is being selected. Figure 7.29 shows an application where the user selected the decade 1950–1959 from below the graph, and a CROSSTAB component appeared to show each year in that decade.

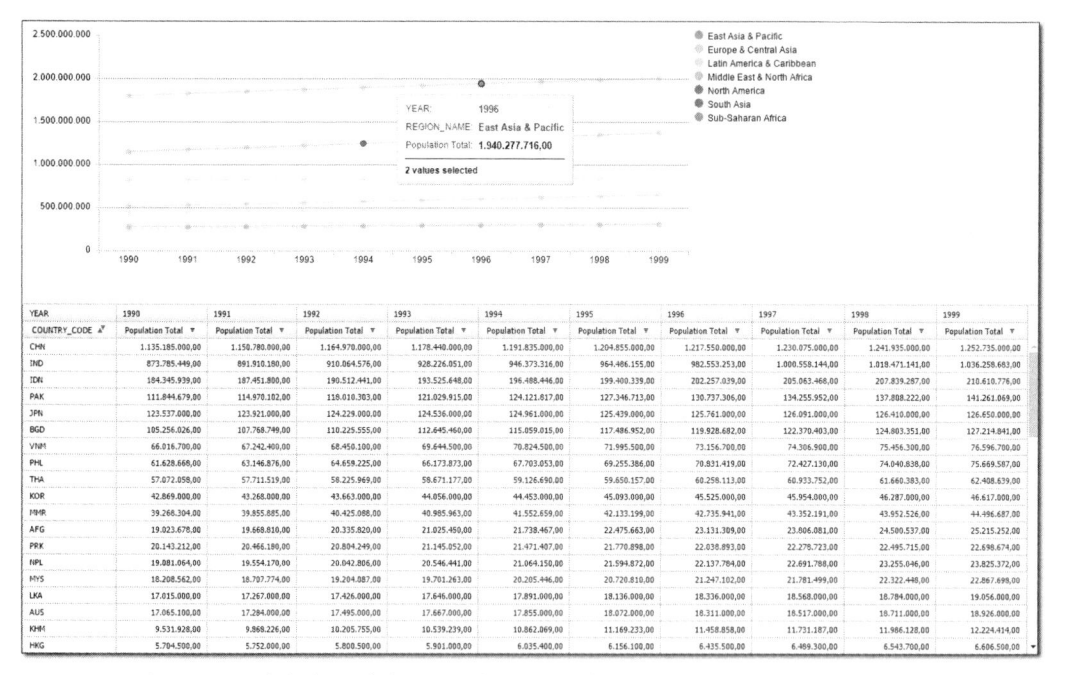

Figure 7.29 Click Through from Graph to Crosstab

The CROSSTAB component is placed inside a PANEL component that isn't visible at the start of the application. When the user clicks on a line in the chart, a filter is applied to the second data source, and the PANEL component is set to VISIBLE.

The code for this is shown in Listing 7.4.

```
var currentMembers = CHART_1.getSelectedMembers("REGION_NAME");

if (currentMembers.length > 0) {
    DS_2.setFilter("REGION_NAME", currentMembers);
```

```
    PNL_COUNTRIES.setVisible(true);
}
Else
{
    PNL_COUNTRIES.setVisible(false);
}
```
Listing 7.4 Script to Click Through for Detailed Information

Additionally, you see a conditional statement in the example script. In this statement, you check how many members are selected in the chart. If any are selected, the panel with the CROSSTAB is made visible, and the filter is applied. If no selection is made, the CROSSTAB disappears again.

Spreadsheet Component

The SPREADSHEET component displays data in a grid (Figure 7.30). The main advantage the SPREADSHEET component has over the CROSSTAB component is that it has easy-to-use copy and paste functions. These functions are useful in planning scenarios because employees can use data that they've gathered in their Excel spreadsheets and directly copy them to the SPREADSHEET component.

	A	B	C
1		Year	Measures
2		2015	
3	Country	ZACT_SLS	ZPLAN_SLS
4	Australia	169,096.000	174,612.000
5	Belgium	116,438.000	117,818.000
6	Canada	1,070,357.000	1,069,349.000
7	France	173,276.000	170,810.000
8	GER	62,510.000	56,128.000
9	GRE	173,224.000	193,070.000
10	Italy	199,157.000	193,314.000
11	Mexico	160,606.000	174,467.000
12	NET	64,358.000	60,835.000
13	SPA	169,561.000	199,179.000
14	SWI	403,860.000	360,116.000
15	UNI	542,054.000	508,600.000
16	Overall Result	3,304,497.000	3,278,298.000

Figure 7.30 Spreadsheet Component

When using the SPREADSHEET component, there are a few limitations:

- You can't use the universal display hierarchy of SAP BW data sources. Therefore, opening and closing nodes isn't possible.
- Only one hierarchy per axis is supported.
- The key and text of dimensions are only displayed in one cell/column.
- Attributes aren't supported.
- In SAPUI5 m rendering mode, the SPREADSHEET component is only supported in the COMPACT FORM FACTOR.
- The SPREADSHEET component can only be used with the Blue Crystal theme.
- The SPREADSHEET component doesn't allow any interaction in mobile applications.

When using the SPREADSHEET component in Design Studio on SAP HANA, there are more limitations:

- Bottom-up hierarchies aren't supported.
- New lines can't be inserted.
- Dynamic calculations and calculations based on the menu entry CALCULATE TOTALS AS aren't supported.

In most circumstances, the CROSSTAB component may be a better option due to these limitations. A SPREADSHEET component is only a good choice when you have a scenario where copying and pasting numbers for planning is required.

Filter Line Component

The FILTER LINE component (Figure 7.31) offers the user a list of filters that are applied to the assigned data source.

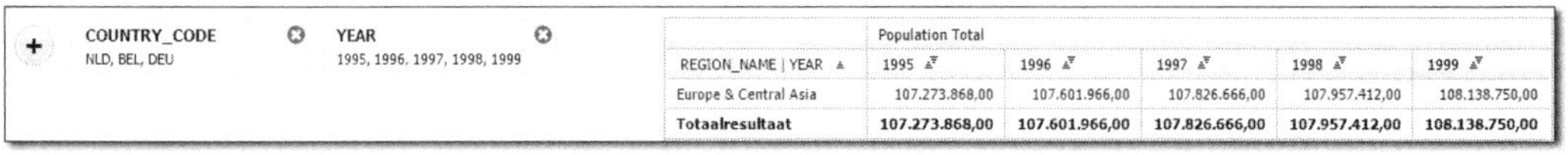

Figure 7.31 Filter Line Component in Combination with the Crosstab Component

The component behaves the same as a FILTER PANEL component, but with the FILTER LINE component, you can add, remove, edit, and view the dimensions and measures on which they can apply filters. When the user clicks on the + sign, all dimensions without filters appear (Figure 7.32).

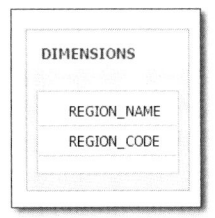

Figure 7.32 Selecting Dimensions for a New Filter

If a user clicks on one of the existing filters, the filter dialog (Figure 7.33) appears, and the user can edit or remove that filter.

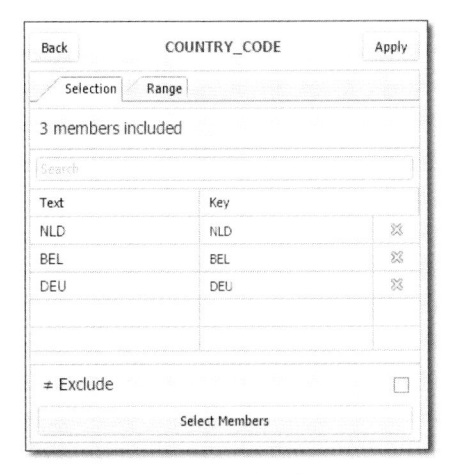

Figure 7.33 Filter Line Edit Filter

Table 7.6 lists properties for the FILTER LINE component.

Property	Description
CSS CLASS	When a custom CSS file is assigned to the APPLICATION component's properties, you can assign a class here.
MEASURES VISIBLE	You can specify whether the user is able to filter measures.

Table 7.6 Filter Line Properties

Dimension Filter Component

The DIMENSION FILTER component (Figure 7.34) is useful for adding a filter for one dimension. This filter can be applied to multiple data sources. When clicked at runtime, the component opens a popup in which the user is able to select a value or a range of values. In the SELECTION tab, you can choose filter values by selecting the members in the table, and you can limit the number of possible choices by entering a search string in the textbox. For example, if you want to choose from all the products starting with N, enter "N*" in the text box.

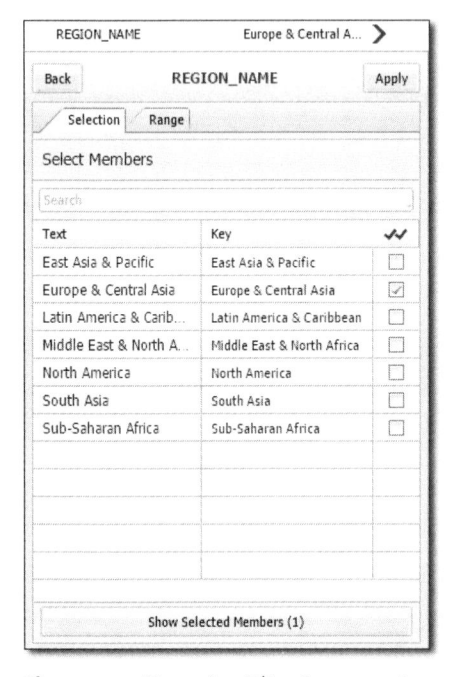

Figure 7.34 Dimension Filter Component

In the RANGE tab, you can build a range filter with a lowest and highest value. First, select the STARTS AT row, and then select the value. Then select the ENDS AT row, and select the highest value. Click the ADD TO LIST button on the bottom of the popup screen. Now you can make a new range filter and add it to the list. When you're finished, click the APPLY button at the top-right area of the screen. When you click BACK, the last filter you entered will be ignored.

When you want the user to be able to filter on more dimensions, you have to add a DIMENSION FILTER component for each dimension to which you want to allow filtering for. (Alternatively, you could use the FILTER PANEL component, which is discussed next.)

Table 7.7 shows the properties of the DIMENSION FILTER component.

Property	Description
DATA SOURCE	This assigns data to the DIMENSION FILTER component. This data source delivers the items for which you can set a DIMENSION FILTER on the target data sources defined in the next property.
TARGET DATA SOURCES	With this property, the DIMENSION FILTER component can be applied to other data sources. Data sources must have the same dimension and must be defined in the application. If you have an application that shows sales, purchases, the general ledger, and transport for regional offices, you have several data sources for each dataset. One DIMENSION FILTER component on a regional office dimension would set the correct filter on all these data sources.
DIMENSION	This is the dimension to be filtered.
DIMENSION NAME	This is the dimension name.
DISPLAY MODE	This property sets the way filters are displayed: ▶ FILTER LIST: Filter values are displayed as comma-separated values. ▶ FILTER COUNT: The number of applied items is displayed.
MEMBER DISPLAY	This specifies the way the dimension members are displayed.
POPUP WIDTH/HEIGHT/POSITION	This is the layout of the POPUP component that is used to define the DIMENSION FILTER component.
POPUP IS MODAL	If set to TRUE, the user can't interact with any other part of the application.
REMOVE REDUNDANT SELECTIONS	This is for hierarchical dimensions. If set to TRUE, the system will remove redundant selections, for example, a node and a subnode within.
AUTO APPLY	This specifies if the changes made by the user are applied automatically.
ON APPLY	This is the script that is executed when a filter is applied. A Script Editor opens for this property.

Table 7.7 Dimension Filter Properties

When you use multiple DIMENSION FILTER components, you can limit the usage by hiding the components that can't be used. For example, if the user already filtered on products, you could stop him from also filtering on customers by hiding the DIMENSION FILTER component that handles the customer filter by using the following code:

```
DIMENSIONFILTER_CUSTOMER.setVisible(false);
```

The best part about the DIMENSION FILTER component and the FILTER PANEL component is that filters can be applied to multiple data sources. This can be very useful if you need to keep multiple data sources in sync. The user performs only one filter action, and all data sources have the same filter.

Filter Panel Component

The FILTER PANEL component (Figure 7.35) allows you to apply filters on several dimensions to target data sources without having to resort to scripting. The DIMENSION FILTER component, discussed previously, can also be used to apply filters to target data sources, but the FILTER PANEL component can put filters on more than one dimension.

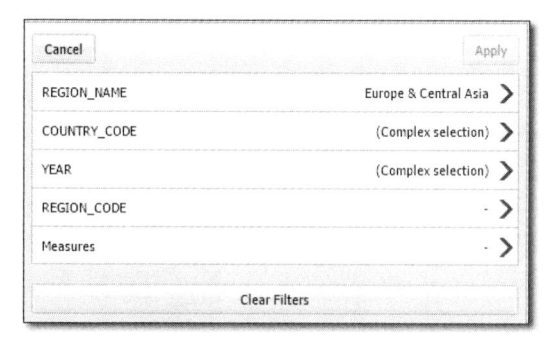

Figure 7.35 Filter Panel Component

The FILTER PANEL component shows all the dimensions of the data source to which it's assigned. The user can open an input box by clicking the name of the dimension. By clicking the - sign on the right, the user can open a selection screen to pick values.

Table 7.8 shows the properties of the FILTER PANEL component.

7.3 Visual Component Properties

Property	Description
Data Source	This assigns data to the component for filtering. You can choose from the defined Data Source Alias components added to the application.
Target Data Sources	With this property, the Filter Panel component can be applied to other data sources. Data sources must have the same dimension and must be defined in the application.
Mode	This enables you to set the way the component works: ▶ Filtering: Enables the user to filter data. ▶ Navigation: Allows the user to add or remove dimensions from rows or columns. ▶ Filtering and navigation: Enables both functions at once.
Dimensions	This selects and orders the dimensions that will be available for the user.
CSS Class	When a custom CSS file is assigned to the Application component, you can assign a class here.
Dimension Name	This shows the dimension name.
Display Mode	This shows the filters or the number of filters applied.
Member Display	This sets member display mode, for example, key + text.
Title	This sets a title for the Filter Panel component.
Remove Redundant Selections	This is for hierarchical dimensions. If set to True, the system will remove redundant selections, for example, a node and a subnode within.
drag & drop	This specifies whether the user can interact using drag and drop.
Direct Input for Filter	This specifies whether the user can use direct input for dimension or measure keys.
Auto Apply	This specifies whether all the changes made in the component are applied automatically.
Maximum Number of Members	This specifies the maximum amount of members in the value help. If the actual number exceeds the maximum, no members are displayed. Instead, the user has to limit the number of members by searching for more specific text or a key.

Table 7.8 Filter Panel Component Properties

Property	Description
ON APPLY	This script is executed when a FILTER PANEL component is applied. A Script Editor opens for this property.
ON CANCEL	This script is executed when the CANCEL button is clicked. A Script Editor opens for this property.

Table 7.8 Filter Panel Component Properties (Cont.)

One of the things you can do using the FILTER PANEL component is control which dimensions you display. Although you could put all the dimensions in one FILTER PANEL, it's easier for the user of the application when you put dimensions that belong together in one FILTER PANEL. For example, in an application that shows sales data, you can put all the customer dimensions in one FILTER PANEL, the product dimensions in the second, and the time dimensions in the third panel. You could also put a couple of FILTER PANEL components in one PANEL CONTAINER component and, for example, allow the user to toggle the visibility of these PANEL components. That way, you can create a dimension-like menu structure in which the user can navigate.

The FILTER PANEL component already has interactivity built into it because it interacts with the data source. You can, however, add something to the layout to highlight that this component has been used to add a filter. In the On Apply handler, set the following code:

FILTERPANEL_1.setCSSClass("Active");

This will assign a CSS class with, for example, a different font color to signal that this filter has been used.

Geo Map

The GEO MAP component allows you to display layers of information on top of a map and allows users to drill down through the different layers (Figure 7.36). You can create three types of layers: shapes, points, and bubble charts.

Visual Component Properties | **7.3**

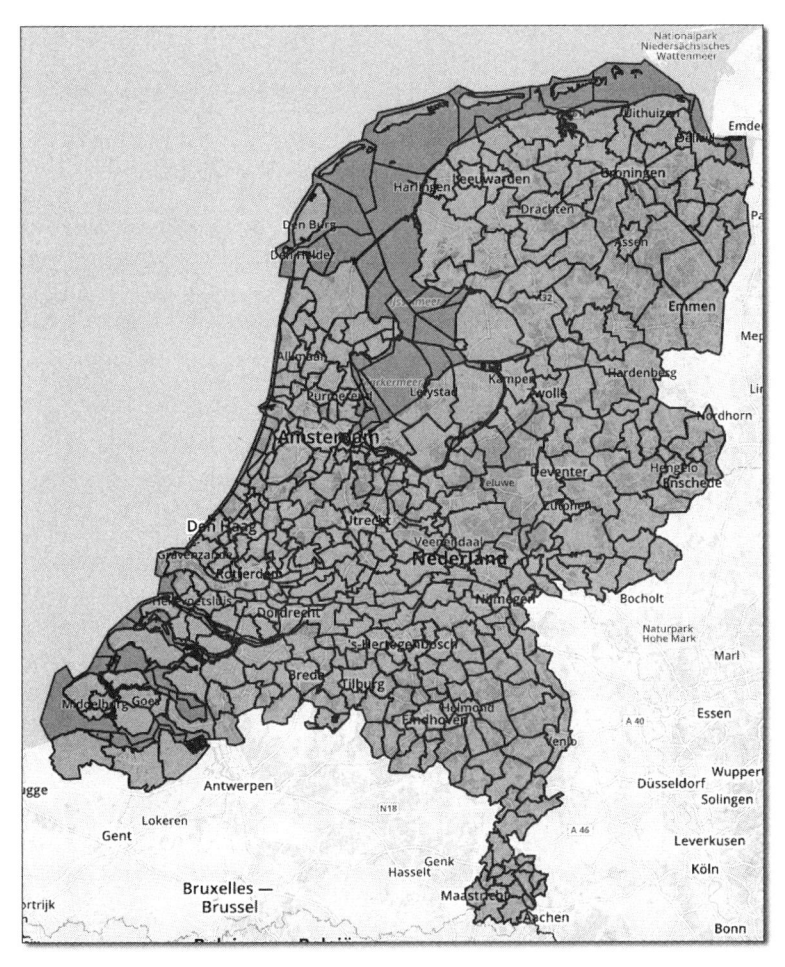

Figure 7.36 Example of Layers on Top of a Map

The GEO MAP component properties are described in Table 7.9.

Property	Description
BASEMAP URL	This is the URL to retrieve the basemap. The *basemap* is the map rendered underneath the graphical representation of the data.
BASEMAP COPYRIGHT	This is the copyright text for the basemap tiles.
MAP LEGEND VISIBLE	This specifies whether the map legend is visible.
ON SELECT	This is triggered when the selected item on the map is changed.

Table 7.9 Geo Map Component Standard Properties

7 | Components and Properties

The layers on top of the map are created in the ADDITIONAL PROPERTIES tab (Figure 7.37). In this tab, you can create multiple layers that will be placed on top of the map.

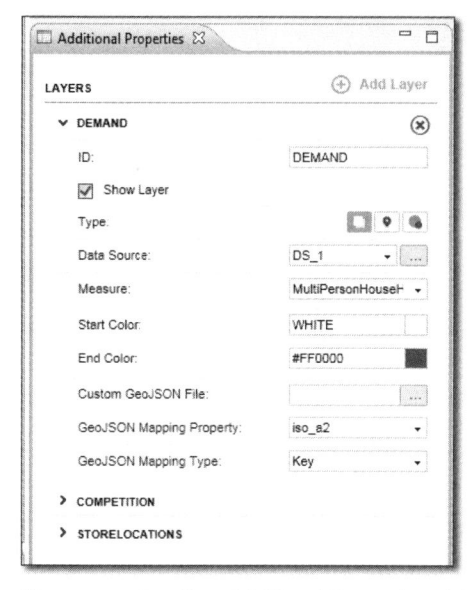

Figure 7.37 Geo Map Additional Properties with Layers for Demand, Competition, and Store Locations

For each layer, you can set a number of properties that will influence the way that the layer will appear on the map (see Table 7.10).

Property	Description
ID	This is the unique ID for a layer. This ID is also used for the `setLayerVisible()` method that will allow users to show/hide layers by interacting with the application.
SHOW LAYER	This is the initial setting to show or hide the layer on the map.
TYPE	This is the type of layer. There are three settings: ▶ SHAPES ▶ POINTS ▶ CHARTS

Table 7.10 Additional Properties for Geo Maps

Property	Description
DATA SOURCE	This is the data source that holds data to be assigned to the layer.
MEASURE	This is the measure used to set the visualization of the layer.
START COLOR	This is the color for the lowest value.
END COLOR	This is the color for the highest value. All other colors will be somewhere in between the START COLOR and END COLOR based on their value in relation to the minimum and maximum value.
CUSTOM GEOJSON FILE	Include your GeoJSON file to show shapes on the map. GeoJSON is a set of coordinates that can be translated to shapes in a map. You need your own GeoJSON file to be able to show shapes.
GEOJSON MAPPING PROPERTY	Select the property in the GeoJSON file just mentioned to determine which property should shape the layer.
GEOJSON MAPPING TYPE	This is used to determine if you want to map by key or by text.

Table 7.10 Additional Properties for Geo Maps (Cont.)

7.3.3 Basic Component Properties

In this section, we're going to look at the basic components, which are BUTTON components, TEXT components, and IMAGE components. They don't visualize the content of a data source or allow child components. There are some options to bind data sources to properties to set the properties automatically instead of via script.

Data Binding

Basic components' properties now have the ability to use a data binding function (Figure 7.38) to set the property value. This feature allows you to create applications with a lot less scripting because many properties are automatically updated if the underlying data source changes. Previously, you had to transfer those values using script.

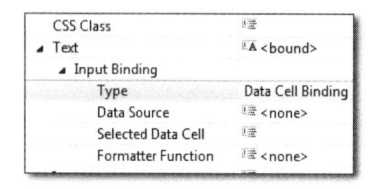

Figure 7.38 Data Binding Property

There are three types of binding:

- DATA CELL BINDING
  This allows you to retrieve the numerical value of a single cell from your data source.

- DIMENSION MEMBERS BINDING
  This allows you to retrieve a list of dimension members.

- FILTER BINDING
  This allows you to use the selected data and automatically create a filter on another data source.

The second and third options are typically used for components such as the LIST BOX component, DROPDOWN component, and the CHECKBOX GROUP component to get a list of options.

You can use DATA CELL BINDING for many properties. DATA CELL BINDING looks at a single cell value in the data source. In the binding, you first select the data source, then select the cell within the data source, and finally you create a formatter function that will take the cell as an input and enable you to change it with script. For item properties, you can use the DIMENSION MEMBERS BINDING where you can bind to a dimension so the property will get all the members of that dimension. Finally, FILTER BINDING is an automated task that you can create based on the selected value in the component. You can automatically set the FILTER BINDING to apply a filter to a data source.

Now let's look at a step-by-step example for a DROPDOWN component. Here, you want to have all the regions in the items and apply a filter when a region is selected. Follow these steps:

1. First, drag a radio button group onto the canvas (Figure 7.39).

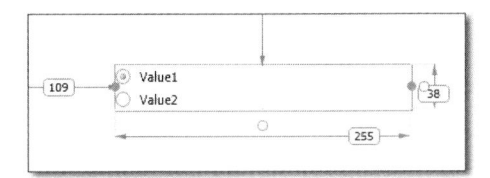

Figure 7.39 Radio Button Group for Data Binding

2. Select the ITEMS property, and click on the ARROWS icon on top of the PROPERTIES pane (Figure 7.40).

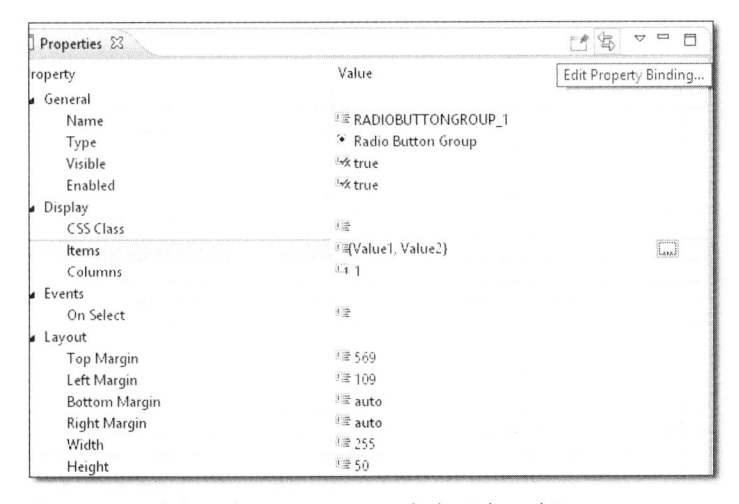

Figure 7.40 Clicking the Arrows Icon with the Selected Property

3. Select both the DIMENSION MEMBERS BINDING and the FILTER BINDING options (Figure 7.41).

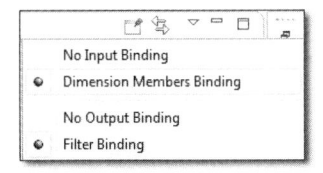

Figure 7.41 Options for Input Binding and Output Binding

4. In the PROPERTIES pane, you can now set the data binding options (Figure 7.42)

7 | Components and Properties

```
▲ Items                              <bound>
   ▲ Input Binding
      Type                           Dimension Members Binding
      Data Source                    <none>
      Dimension
      Maximum Number of Members      100
      Member Display                 Text and Key
      All Members Text               A
   ▲ Output Binding
      Type                           Filter Binding
      Target Data Sources
      Dimension
Columns                              1
```

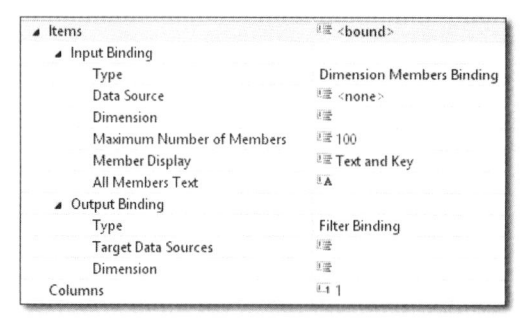

Figure 7.42 New Options Available for Data Binding

5. Provide values for the DATA SOURCE, DIMENSION, and MEMBER DISPLAY fields for the input binding (Figure 7.43).

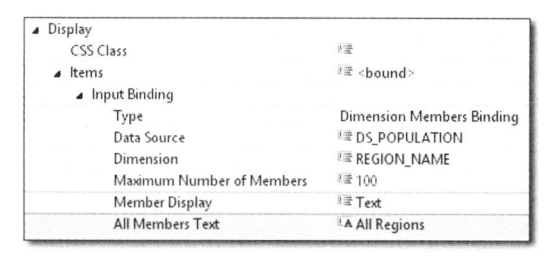

```
▲ Display
   CSS Class
   ▲ Items                           <bound>
      ▲ Input Binding
         Type                        Dimension Members Binding
         Data Source                 DS_POPULATION
         Dimension                   REGION_NAME
         Maximum Number of Members   100
         Member Display              Text
         All Members Text            A All Regions
```

Figure 7.43 Input Binding Properties Set

6. Now go to the OUTPUT FILTER BINDING properties, and set the DATA SOURCE that should be filtered. When clicking on the DATA SOURCE, the SELECT TARGET DATA SOURCES screen appears, where you can select multiple data sources (Figure 7.44).

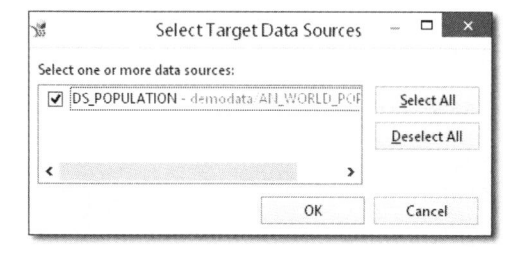

Figure 7.44 Data Source Selection for Output Binding

7. Finally, set the DIMENSION on which the filter must be applied. (Figure 7.45).

264

Figure 7.45 Setting Up Output Data Binding

With this feature, you can create an action in response to the selection of one or more of the items listed in the component. The action will change the other components based on your selection. This way, you don't have to write additional scripts.

The ability to add FILTER BINDING is available in any component that has an item property. With DATA CELL BINDING, there is an option to format the value before it's applied to the property using the FORMATTER FUNCTION (Figure 7.46). Besides formatting, this function can also perform any action on the value you like. For example, you might use the returned number value to look up a text.

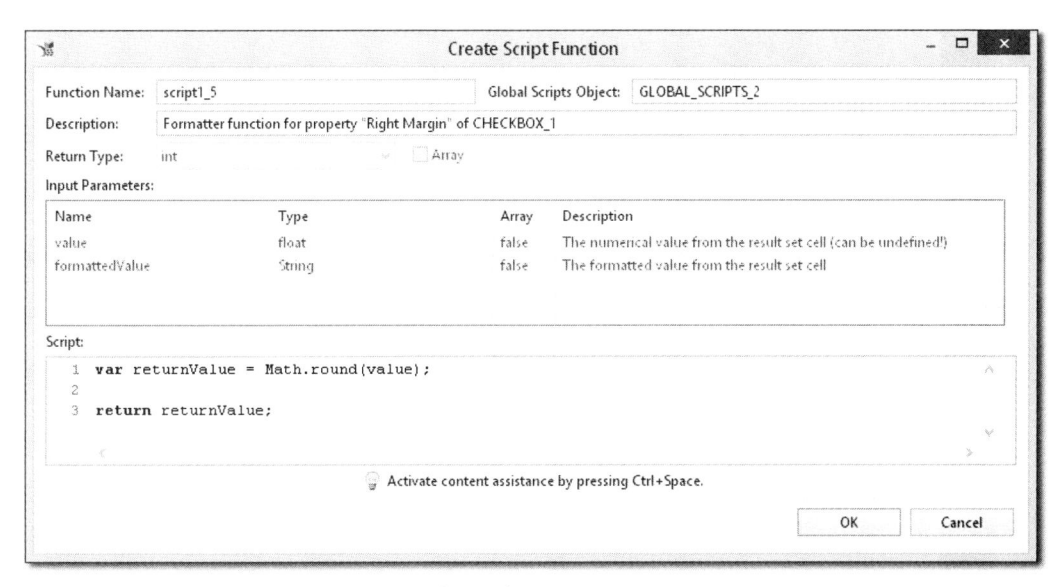

Figure 7.46 Script Function to Format a Binding Value

Button Component

Buttons allow the user to interact with the application (Figure 7.47). To build this interactivity, you add a script to the BUTTON component's `On Click` property.

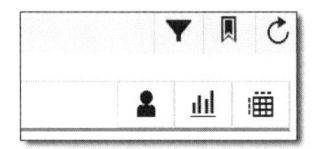

Figure 7.47 Button Components

Table 7.11 shows the properties of the BUTTON component.

Property	Description
TEXT	This specifies the text displayed on the BUTTON component. It's possible to display text, icons, or a combination of both.
ICON	This specifies the icon to be displayed on the BUTTON component. If the icon image is in the application directory, providing the file name is sufficient. When the file is located somewhere else, click the ... button to the right of the text box of the property to navigate to the image. If the image is located on the Internet or intranet, you can use a URL, for example, *http://www.imageserver.com/myimage.jpg*.
TOOLTIP	In this property, enter a message that will show up when a user hovers the mouse over the button.
CSS CLASS	When a custom CSS file is assigned to the APPLICATION component, you can assign a CSS class here.
ON CLICK	This pens the Script Editor to add user interaction.

Table 7.11 Button Component Properties

Having the appearance of the BUTTON component itself change when the user clicks the button helps the user to understand what is happening in the application. For example, if the user switches to another screen and comes back five minutes later, it's immediately apparent where he is in the application.

For a simple example, if you have a BUTTON component that, when clicked, excludes internal sales, it would be helpful if the BUTTON component showed that state. When you look at the examples in Figure 7.48, it's clear that INTERCOMPANY SALES and DELIVERED NOT INVOICED sales are included, but INTERNAL SALES and SOLD NON DELIVERED aren't.

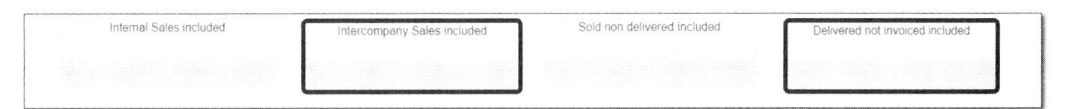

Figure 7.48 Button States

To make the switch between the enabled state and the disabled state possible, the script checks the BUTTON component's current state and switches to the other state. The script for our internal sales example is shown in Listing 7.5.

```
if (BUTTON_INTERNAL.getText() =="Include Internal Sales" ) {
 BUTTON_INTERNAL.setText("Internal Sales included");
 BUTTON_INTERNAL.setCSSClass("Included");
}
else
{
 BUTTON_INTERNAL.setText("Include Internal Sales");
 BUTTON_INTERNAL.setCSSClass("Included");
}
```
Listing 7.5 Script to Switch between States

To further emphasize the state, we've added a script line to set the CSS class of the text object depending on its current state, so the user can see the state based on the appearance of the button.

Chart Type Picker Component

The CHART TYPE PICKER component allows a user to choose a different graph type to visualize the data. An application designer is able to add additional visualization types to the existing palette (Figure 7.49).

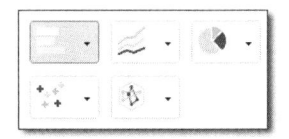

Figure 7.49 Chart Type Picker Component

In the CHART TYPE PICKER component, the properties shown in Table 7.12 are included.

Property	Description
CHART REFERENCE	This is the chart that will change based on the selection.
ADDITIONAL TYPES	You can add or remove additional visualization types for the CHART PICKER component.
ON SELECT	This script is triggered when the selection has been changed. In the script, it's possible to perform additional changes to the chart based on the selected CHART TYPE that you can find using the `getSelectedValue()` method.

Table 7.12 Properties of the Chart Type Picker

Checkbox Component

CHECKBOX components help the user interact with the application (Figure 7.50). CHECKBOX components can be used as on/off buttons to support other components. If you have multiple options, it's easier to use the CHECKBOX GROUP component (Figure 7.50). The CHECKBOX component is useful when you don't want to present all checkbox options as a single group.

Figure 7.50 Checkbox Component

Table 7.13 shows the properties for the CHECKBOX component.

Property	Description
TEXT	Specifies the text displayed on the CHECKBOX component.
SELECTED	Specifies whether the CHECKBOX component is initially selected.
TOOLTIP	Specifies the message that will be shown when the user hovers the mouse over the checkbox.
ON CLICK	Opens the Script Editor to add user interaction.

Table 7.13 Checkbox Component Properties

To understand how the CHECKBOX component can improve an application, look at Figure 7.51. In this example, you can see the CHECKBOX GROUP component on the bottom of the screen. You use the CHECKBOX component to manipulate the graph so that it only shows one of the three key figures based on the choice of CHECKBOX components. By using an `On Click` event for each CHECKBOX component, you can select and deselect key figures and see the graph change accordingly. The result is that the graph on top will only show those lines for which the checkbox on the bottom is selected.

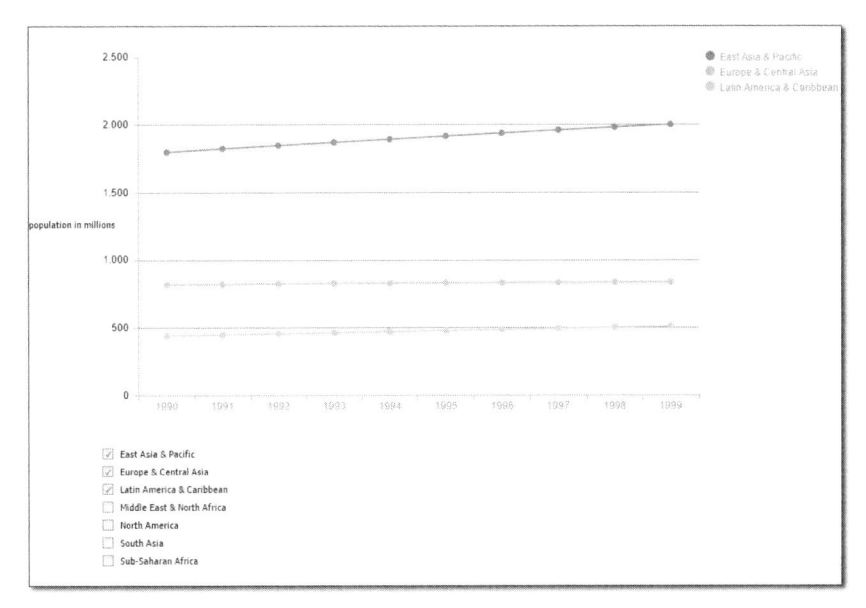

Figure 7.51 Example Checkbox Group for Region Selection

You might also imagine more complicated scenarios where some choices make other options unfeasible. An example is when a user has multiple CHECKBOX components to filter the data source. If you want to avoid a situation where the user applies a filter that results in zero records, you can disable all the components that will lead to this result. Using the enabled and selected property in the script, you can manage the CHECKBOX components to reflect those scenarios.

In the `On Click` property of `Checkbox_1`, the script would look like this:

```
CHECKBOX_1.setChecked(true);
CHECKBOX_2.setChecked(false);
CHECKBOX_3.setChecked(false);
```

Checkbox Group Component

The CHECKBOX GROUP component is an extension of the CHECKBOX component because it's able to show a list of checkboxes in one component (Figure 7.52).

Just as with other components, the CHECKBOX GROUP component can be populated using script or data binding. In script, you can get an array of selected values (all the checkboxes that have been selected).

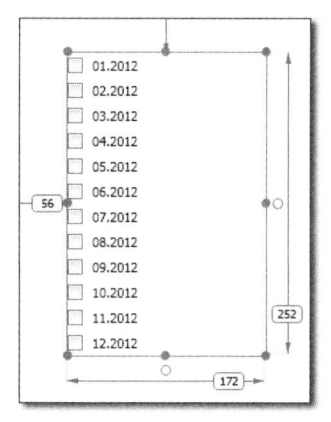

Figure 7.52 Checkbox Group Component

The properties of the CHECKBOX GROUP component are listed in Table 7.14.

Property	Description
ITEMS	List of items that can be completed by manual input, data binding, or script.
ON SELECT	The script that is run when the selection of items has been changed.

Table 7.14 Checkbox Group Properties

The CHECKBOX GROUP component can be used to apply filters to data sources. Using the group, it's very easy to select multiple members of a dimension and pass that list to the filter.

To use the selected items to create a filter, the following script will suffice in the On Select event of the CHECKBOX GROUP component:

```
var currentSelection = CHECKBOXGROUP_1.getSelectedValues();
DS_PRODUCTION_OUTPUT.setFilter("0CALMONTH", currentSelection);
```

The output in the `getSelectedValue()` method is an array of key values that are passed as filter values to the data source. For readability, it's split in two lines where the list is assigned to the variable `currentSelection`.

Instead of using the script, you also can use data binding to create an outbound bind to the ITEMS property. This will yield the same result as the preceding script.

Date Field Component

The DATE FIELD component enables the user to select a date (Figure 7.53). The entered date can be used in other parts of the application. To enable this interactivity, a script has to be added to the `On Select` handler.

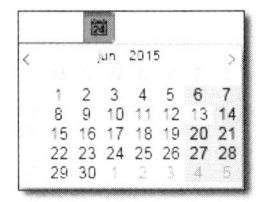

Figure 7.53 Date Field Component

Table 7.15 shows the properties of the DATE FIELD component.

Property	Description
CSS CLASS	When a custom CSS file is assigned to the APPLICATION component, you can assign a CSS class here.
DATE	This sets the initial date.
ON SELECT	This opens the Script Editor to add user interaction.

Table 7.15 Date Field Component Properties

The main use for the DATE FIELD component is to set a date, which is then used to filter a data source dimension that holds calendar day values. The statement to do this is as follows:

```
Var SelectedDate = DATEFIELD_SALESDATE.getDate()
DS_SALES.setFilter("0CALDAY", SelectedDate);
```

Dropdown Box Component

The DROPDOWN BOX component enables the user to select items from a list (Figure 7.54). A common use for this component is setting a filter.

Figure 7.54 Dropdown Box Component

Table 7.16 shows the properties of the DROPDOWN BOX component.

Property	Description
CSS CLASS	When a custom CSS file is assigned to the APPLICATION component, you can assign a CSS class here.
ITEMS	With this property, the items available in the DROPDOWN BOX component can be edited. A key has to be entered for each value. Providing a text label and setting a default item is optional. Items can be added manually at design time, via script, or via data binding.
ON SELECT	This opens the Script Editor to add user interaction.

Table 7.16 Dropdown Box Component Properties

A common way to set the items you can select in a DROPDOWN BOX component is to populate the items of the component at runtime. To do this, you can add a script to the APPLICATION component at the `On Startup` handler:

```
Var calendarMonths = DS_SALES.getMemberList("0CALMONTH",
 MemberPresentation.EXTERNAL_KEY, MemberDisplay.KEY_TEXT, 20
DROPDOWN_1.setItems(calendarMonths);
```

Script Readability

You may already have noticed that variables are used to store the values for use in the script. Although the script will work fine without using a variable, we still advise you to do this because it enhances the readability of the script, something you'll appreciate when you have to revisit the script later. Chapter 11 provides more details on design principles.

This script instructs the application to fill the items of `dropdown_1` with the `0CALMONTH` dimension of the data source `DS_1`.

Using the actual values in the data source ensure that the DROPDOWN BOX component only holds the values that are actually available in the data source. This avoids situations where a user applies a filter, and the result is an empty dataset. In this example, the current year might not have ended yet so not all months are available. In this situation, there will be fewer than 12 months to choose from.

Formatted Text Field Component

A FORMATTED TEXT FIELD component allows you to format the text (Figure 7.55). In the ADDITIONAL PROPERTIES panel, you'll find a simplified text editor with some extra options to add formatting. Additionally, you can assign HTML tags. In the custom CSS file, you can create classes that allow for some extra formatting.

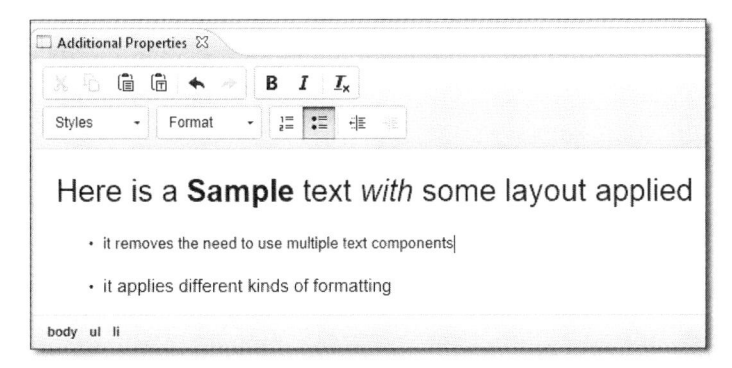

Figure 7.55 Formatted Text Additional Properties

The FORMATTED TEXT FIELD component is configured in the ADDITIONAL PROPERTIES, where you'll find the CSS CLASS property to assign a class if you want to apply extra formatting

Fragment Gallery Component

With the FRAGMENT GALLERY component, a user can see fragment bookmarks (Figure 7.56). The user can then drag bookmarks into a SPLIT CELL CONTAINER component to compose his dashboard.

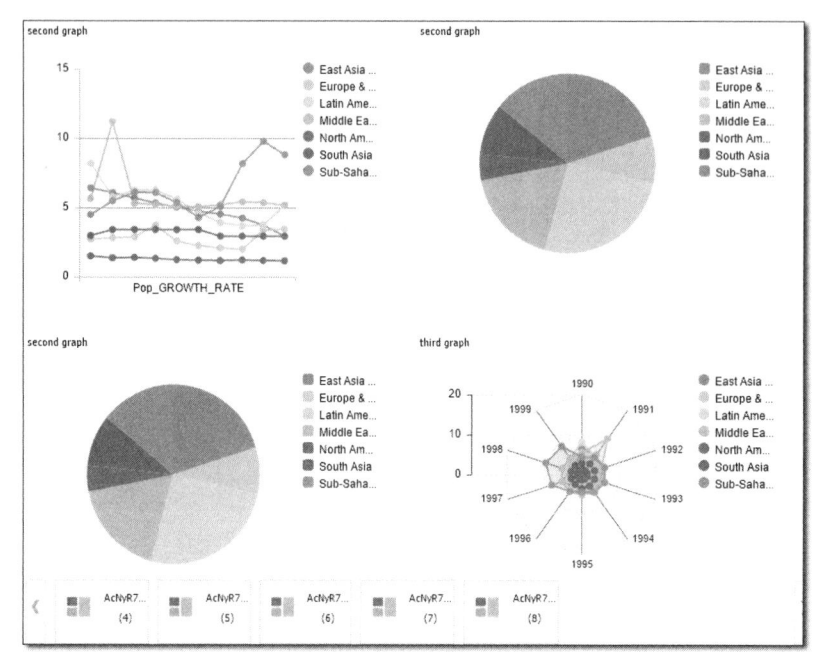

Figure 7.56 Fragment Gallery with the Split Cell Component

Table 7.17 lists the properties of the FRAGMENT GALLERY component.

Property	Description
ITEM DIMENSION	Specifies the value in pixels from which the width or height (depending on orientation) is calculated.
DISPLAY MODE	Specifies the display mode: ▶ TEXT ▶ IMAGE ▶ IMAGE/TEXT
ORIENTATION	Shows whether to display the fragments vertically or horizontally.

Table 7.17 Fragment Gallery Component Properties

Icon Component

The ICON component (Figure 7.57) is used to show icons based on a font file. The standard choices delivered by SAP already give you many options. You can add your own by adding a font file.

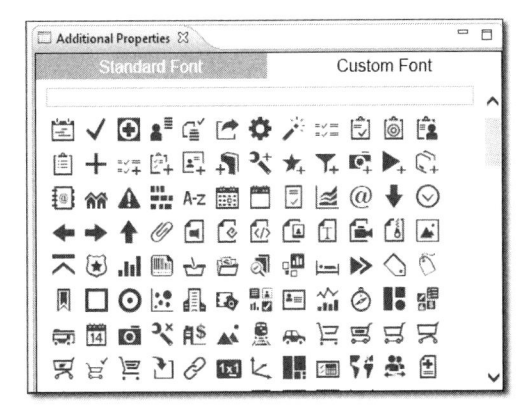

Figure 7.57 Choice of Icons in Additional Properties

In the component properties, you have a few options to set the front and background color and the relative size of the icon to the whole component. In the ADDITIONAL PROPERTIES, there is a tab to select an icon and a second tab to select a font file and then select an icon there.

The ICON component properties are listed in Table 7.18.

Property	Description
CUSTOM FONT	Name of the font file where you can add your own icons.
COLOR	Color of the image.
BACKGROUND COLOR	Color of the background.
SIZE FACTOR	Relative size of icon in relation to the background.
ICON URI	Selection of icon in the font.
TOOLTIP	Text shown when mouse cursor hovers over icon.

Table 7.18 Icon Component Properties

Image Component

With the IMAGE component, you can enhance the layout of the application (Figure 7.58). The IMAGE component also has a number of properties for interactivity purposes. One of the most useful properties is the ability to change the IMAGE component at runtime, which means you can change the look of the application based on the data values or as the result of specific user interactivity actions. IMAGE components can also respond to hovering and clicking.

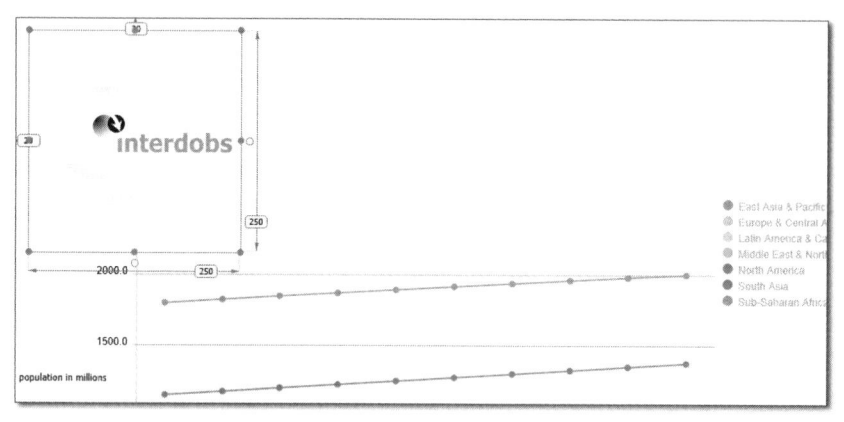

Figure 7.58 Image Component Useful for Logos

Table 7.19 shows the properties of the IMAGE component.

Property	Description
CSS CLASS	When a custom CSS file is assigned to the APPLICATION component, you can assign a CSS class here.
IMAGE	This is the location of the main image file.
HOVER IMAGE	This is the location of the image file that shows when the user hovers over the image.
CLICK IMAGE	This is the location of the image file that is shown when the user clicks the image.
OPACITY %	By controlling this property, you can establish how transparent the IMAGE component is. 0% opacity means that the IMAGE component isn't visible, and it becomes more opaque the closer to 100% you go. This property can be used for layout reasons; by setting the opacity of some IMAGE components a bit higher than others, you can send a subtle but clear message to the user. For example, if you have ON and OFF buttons, you can make the buttons that are in the ON position more opaque than those in the OFF position. This gives you the ability to convey a lot of information about the state of the buttons without using much room or color, thus keeping your design easy to grasp for the user.
TOOLTIP	This is the text message shown when the user hovers the mouse over the image.
ON CLICK	This opens the Script Editor to add user interaction.

Table 7.19 Image Component Properties

The IMAGE component can often come in handy, for example, when creating scorecards. For a scorecard, green, yellow, and red symbols are typically used. In Listing 7.6, the script evaluates the value of a key figure in the data source. If the value of the key figure is 1, then a green light image is used; if the value of the key figure is 2, then a yellow light will show; and for the value 3, a red light will show.

Instead of writing the location of the image in these statements, we've introduced three global variables holding the location of the images. The three variables are Greenlight, Yellowlight, and Redlight.

```
Var EvalData=DS_1.getDataAsString("ZBB_NMBR","ZBB_KPIID=00001")
if (EvalData == "1")
{IMG_FIN1_EVAL.setImage(Greenlight);}
else {
if (EvalData == "2")
{IMG_FIN1_EVAL.setImage(Yellowlight);}
else {
if (EvalData == "3")
{IMG_FIN1_EVAL.setImage(Redlight);}
}}
```

Listing 7.6 Script to Change Image Based on the Key Figure Value

Input Field Component

The INPUT FIELD component enables the user to type specific content into the application at runtime (Figure 7.59). For example, an INPUT FIELD component can be useful for filtering with wildcards (*). This kind of filtering is possible because the user is free to type anything he wants into the component's text box.

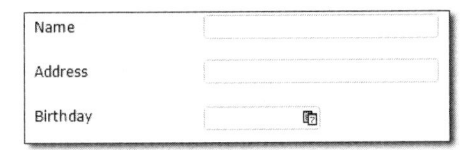

Figure 7.59 Input Field Component for Address Entry

Table 7.20 shows the properties for the INPUT FIELD component.

Property	Description
CSS CLASS	When a custom CSS file is assigned to the APPLICATION component, you can assign a CSS class here.
EDITABLE	This specifies whether the field is editable.
TOOLTIP	This is the text message that will be shown when a user hovers the mouse pointer over the component.
VALUE	This is the initial value of the INPUT FIELD component. The VALUE can be set initially manually, via script, or via data binding. The user can change the value at runtime.
ON CHANGE	This opens the Script Editor to add user interaction.

Table 7.20 Input Field Component Properties

The INPUT FIELD component can come in quite handy, for example, if you don't want to restrict a user in setting a filter value. For example, if a user wants to select all the years in the range 2001–2009, he can input "20*", and with that value, a filter can be set on the data source with this script:

```
Var selectedYear = INPUTFIELD_1.getValue();
DSSALESYEAR.setFilterExt("0CALYEAR", selectedYear);
```

As another example, if you want to filter on products and you have a lot of different kinds of product types in your product line (red sauce, green sauce, sweet sauce, etc.), a user can input "*sauce" and apply the filter to see which products come up.

This also could set up a cascading filter where a LIST BOX or DROPDOWN BOX component is filtered based on the input in the INPUT FIELD component.

List Box Component

The LIST BOX component enables users to select items (Figure 7.60). A selected item can be used to filter for or choose a particular functionality in the application. The LIST BOX component shows all the values in a list, so it's advisable to limit the number of items.

> **List Box Component versus Dropdown Box Component**
>
> If the number of items is large, a DROPDOWN BOX component is more advisable because the list of values is collapsed when the user isn't selecting a value.

Figure 7.60 List Box Component

Table 7.21 shows the properties of the LIST BOX component.

Property	Description
CSS CLASS	When a custom CSS file is assigned to the APPLICATION component, you can assign a CSS class here.
ITEMS	With this property, the items available in the LIST BOX component can be edited. A key has to be entered for each value. Having a text and a default item is optional. Click the ... button on the right side of the property to open an EDIT SCREEN dialog box where you can add, edit, or remove items. Additionally, you can populate the ITEMS list using either script or data binding.
MULTIPLE SELECTION	This specifies whether the user is allowed to select multiple items.
ON SELECT	This opens the Script Editor to add user interaction.

Table 7.21 Properties of the List Box Component

Consider a case where a user has to navigate through a lot of data. In this situation, you probably want a way to drill down instead of finding your way through a lot of choices. With the help of LIST BOX components, you can achieve this by creating one LIST BOX component that contains all the product categories and a second LIST BOX component that contains all the products. When you select a product category from the first LIST BOX component, the second LIST BOX component is populated with the products within that category. Using this technique, you can lead the user step-by-step through the possible choices.

Let's look at an example where you apply a category filter to the data source. The data source repopulates the items of the second LIST BOX component with the accompanying products and makes this second component visible, while the first LIST BOX component is set to invisible. Finally, when the user selects a product on the second LIST BOX component, the script in this component filters the data source on that product. Other components that use that same data source then only show the data for that one product.

7 | Components and Properties

The code is shown in Listing 7.7.

```
DS_1.setFilterExt("0PRODUCTGROUP", LISTBOX_
CATEGORY.getSelectedValue());
Var ProductItems = DS_
1.getMemberList("0PRODUCT", MemberPresentation.EXTERNAL_
KEY, MemberDisplay.TEXT, 20);
LISTBOX_PRODUCT.setItems(ProductItems);
LISTBOX_CATEGORY.setVisible(false);
LISTBOX_PRODUCT.setVisible(true);
```
Listing 7.7 Script to Create a Drill Through

Instead of using script to filter the data source and populate the second LIST BOX, you can use input and output binding on the ITEM property of the first LIST BOX. In that case, the only script lines you need are the `setVisible()` script lines.

Radio Button Group Component

The RADIO BUTTON GROUP component enables users to select a single item from a list (Figure 7.61). A selected item can be used to filter or to make a choice for a particular functionality in the application. Because the RADIO BUTTON GROUP component shows all the values in a list, we recommend limiting the number of items to not overwhelm the user with too many options.

Figure 7.61 Radio Button Group Component

Table 7.22 shows the properties of the RADIO BUTTON GROUP component.

Property	Description
CSS CLASS	When a custom CSS file is assigned to the APPLICATION component, you can assign a CSS class here.
COLUMNS	This is the number of columns used to display the RADIO BUTTON GROUP components.

Table 7.22 Radio Button Group Component Properties

Property	Description
ITEMS	With this property, the available items can be edited. A key has to be entered for each value. Having a text and a default item is optional.
ON SELECT	This opens the Script Editor to add user interaction.

Table 7.22 Radio Button Group Component Properties (Cont.)

The RADIO BUTTON GROUP component should be used when you need to give users different navigational choices. For example, if you allow your sales team to navigate through the customer base, there are many ways they might segment their customer base. For instance, they may want to look at married customers in their fifties who bought something in the past four weeks and show a pattern of purchases that puts them in the luxury buyers segment. Using four checkbox groups allows this kind of selection (Figure 7.62).

Marital Status	Age Group	Last Purchase	Buying Pattern
✓ Single	✓ 21 - 30	✓ this week	✓ budget
☐ Married	☐ 31 - 40	☐ last week	☐ standard
☐ Divorced	☐ 41 - 50	☐ last 4 weeks	☐ luxury
☐ Widowed	☐ 51 - 60	☐ last quarter	
	☐ 61 - 70		

Figure 7.62 Selection Options with Radio Button Groups

Two RADIO BUTTON GROUP components together with the five selection options give the user a variety of choices. Now imagine four RADIO BUTTON GROUP components, with each holding five options. This creates 625 different combinations for the user to choose from. In other words, this component offers a lot flexibility.

Text Component

The TEXT component is used to add text, such as labels or values, to an application (Figure 7.63). TEXT components can be formatted at runtime by reassigning the CSS class. With all the possibilities of CSS, the TEXT component is a very flexible tool to use in an application. With the DATA BINDING option, you can set texts at runtime without having to resort to the TEXT POOL component while still having all the flexibility and central management in place.

Figure 7.63 Text Component Using CSS for Layout

> **Note**
>
> You can even set the width of the TEXT component using CSS, although this is also possible via the common properties of components.

Table 7.23 shows the properties of the TEXT component.

Property	Description
CSS CLASS	When a custom CSS file is assigned to the APPLICATION component, you can assign a CSS class here.
STYLE	This is the style applied to the TEXT component. In the application, the text will get a CSS class with standard formatting. For Header 1, it's the class `.sapUiTvH2`, for Header 2, it's class `.sapUiTvH2`, and so on. If you want to enhance these stylings you can update these classes in the custom CSS.
TOOLTIP	This is a text message that will appear when the user hovers the mouse over the TEXT component.
CSS STYLE	You can insert CSS code to further enhance the layout of the component. The starting point for the CSS code inserted here is based on the theme of the application and the assigned CSS class, so keep this in mind when setting this property. If the theme sets the font size a little higher, the class sets the font size a little higher, and you set the font size in this property a little higher, your font size might turn out to be enormous.
ON CLICK	This opens the Script Editor to add user interaction when the user clicks on the TEXT component.

Table 7.23 Text Component Properties

> **CSS Tip**
>
> When applying formatting using CSS, try to use the CSS CLASS property as much as possible. When a class is altered in the central CSS file, all dependent components will automatically be updated. When using the CSS STYLE, however, you only influence the components where you have put the CSS code. This means when the same code is used in more than one component, any changes to the layout require that you manually change each component.

Tree Component

The TREE component can be bound to a hierarchical dimension in a data source (Figure 7.64). If there is no hierarchy, the TREE component shows a standard list. The TREE component shows the actual result set. Changes in the TREE component affect results in a CROSSTAB component tied to the same data source. Changes in a CROSSTAB component affect the TREE menu.

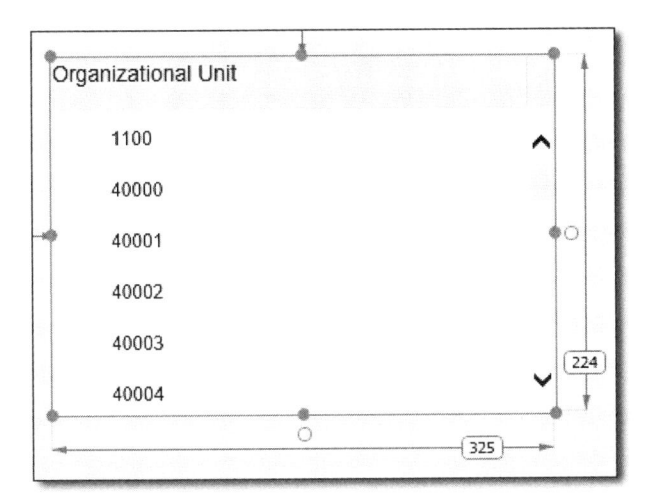

Figure 7.64 Tree Component

This component can be used as a navigational element. The component has methods to retrieve the selected elements, and you can work with that to add navigations.

Tree items are an important property in TREE components. You have to bind this property to a data source from where it collects the items to build the component.

7.3.4 Container Component Properties

Container components are used to group components into meaningful groups. These grouped components can be managed together by manipulating the container component (also known as the parent component) and therefore making maintenance easier. Components inside a container component are dependent on that container component; for example, if the container component's visibility is set to FALSE, then this setting will also apply to all the components inside the container component.

7 | Components and Properties

The margin properties are set in relation to the borders of their container component. For example, when the LEFT MARGIN of a container component is set to 100, and the LEFT MARGIN of a TEXT component within that container component is set to 10, this will set the text box at 110 pixels from the left side of the screen.

> **Using Panel Components**
>
> Use PANEL components in the application in the same way as you use folders on your computer. The OUTLINE view will look like Windows Explorer/Finder with a hierarchical view of the components. Additionally, if you use meaningful names, it will be a lot easier to find the component you're looking for in larger applications.

That being said, it's possible to place components outside their container component but still maintain dependency. For example, you can set the top-, bottom-, left-, or right margin to a negative value. If you move the container component, the component outside will move along with the container but remain outside. In this case, if the LEFT MARGIN is set to –50, the object will be placed to the left of the container component, but there will still be a dependency between them.

In the example in Figure 7.65, you see a main component with a LEFT MARGIN of 25, a container component with a LEFT MARGIN of 50, and another container component with a LEFT MARGIN of 100. The total LEFT MARGIN for the main component will then be 175.

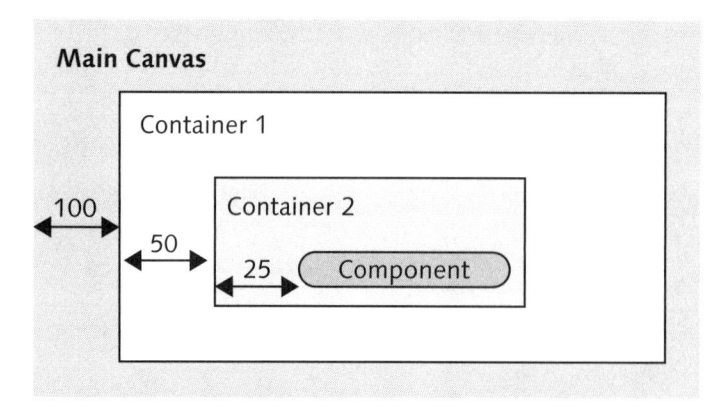

Figure 7.65 Layered Container Components with their Respective Left Margins

There are five types of container components, all of which we discuss next.

Grid Layout Component

The GRID LAYOUT component is used to group and order the components in a grid (Figure 7.66). (The grid itself isn't shown at runtime.) The GRID LAYOUT component is very useful for dividing the screen into rows and columns. The sizes of the rows and columns can be adjusted by setting the relative size of each column and row.

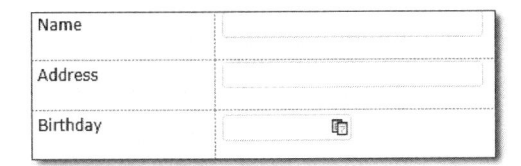

Figure 7.66 Grid Layout Component for Aligning Form Fields

Table 7.24 shows the properties of the GRID LAYOUT component.

Property	Description
NAME	The name of the component must be a unique name within the application.
CSS CLASS	Set the CSS class corresponding to a class defined in the custom CSS file to enhance the look of the grid. Because the component at runtime is an HTML table, you'll find <TR> and <TD> elements that you can format using a class with a child selector (more in-depth CSS information is available in Chapter 10).
NUMBER OF ROWS	This is the number of rows in the grid.
ROW HEIGHT	This is the relative height of the row in comparison to the other rows. Each row starts with the value 1. Setting the rows' heights then divides the height of the grid according to the ROW HEIGHT settings for each row.
NUMBER OF COLUMNS	This is the number of columns in the grid.
COLUMN WIDTH	This is the relative width of the column in comparison to the other columns. Each column starts with the value 1. Setting the columns' widths divides the width of the grid according to the COLUMN WIDTH setting for each column.

Table 7.24 Grid Layout Component Properties

7 | Components and Properties

You can create advanced layouts using several GRID LAYOUT components. For example, if you have a main GRID LAYOUT component with three rows, of which the middle row is the largest, you can divide the top and bottom row by adding a new GRID LAYOUT component in the top row and bottom row.

Let's consider a case where you choose to divide the top row into three columns and the bottom row into five. In Figure 7.67, you can see how this layout would look to the user. In Figure 7.68, you can see the outline as it would look in Design Studio at design time.

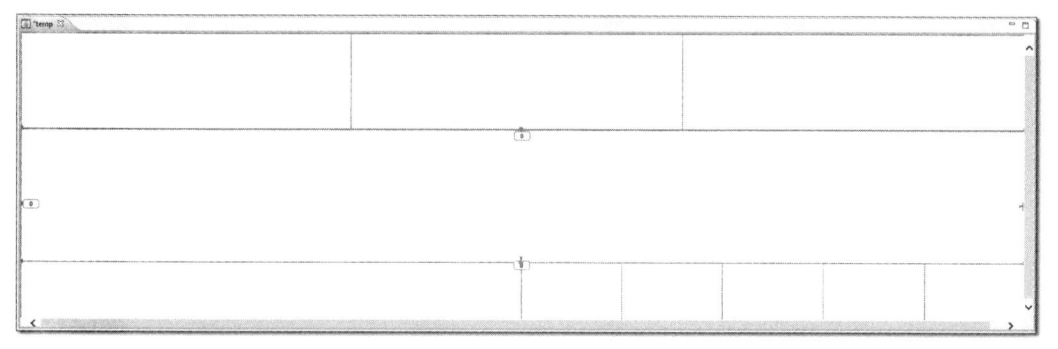

Figure 7.67 Grid Layout View with Three Rows and Several Columns

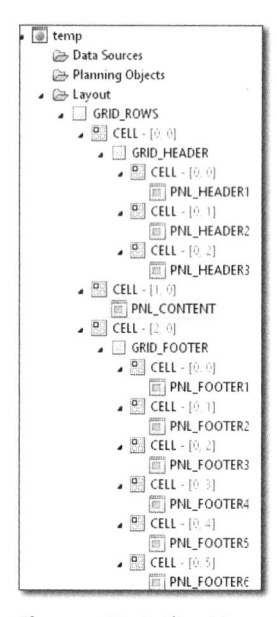

Figure 7.68 Outline View with Nested Grid Layout Components

Pagebook Component

The PAGEBOOK component shows one page at a time and enables the user to switch to other pages by either swiping (iPad or iPhone) or dragging (computer mouse) (Figure 7.69). It's also possible to switch pages by using the script language.

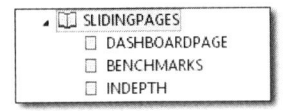

Figure 7.69 Pagebook Component in the Outline View

In Figure 7.69, you can see several pages connected to the PAGEBOOK component. In design mode, it's possible to add or remove pages from the component. Each page is an empty canvas. Only the canvas of the selected page is visible to the user.

Table 7.25 shows the properties of the PAGEBOOK component.

Property	Description
CSS CLASS	When a custom CSS file is assigned to the APPLICATION component, you can assign a CSS class here.
SELECTED PAGE INDEX	This sets the initial visible page of the PAGEBOOK component. Note: 0 represents the first page of the PAGEBOOK component, 1 represents the second page, and so on.
TRANSITION EFFECT	This specifies the transition effect when a user swipes between pages. The following options are available: ▸ SLIDE IN ▸ FADE ▸ FLIP ▸ CUBE
TRANSITION DIRECTION	This specifies the transition direction when a user switches between pages. Options are HORIZONTAL or VERTICAL.

Table 7.25 Pagebook Component Properties

Property	Description
PAGE CACHING	This specifies the caching behavior of the PAGEBOOK component. If set to ALL, every page of the component will be cached; if set to ADJACENT, the page before and after the current page will be cached.
	Caching leads to a smoother swipe, but as more components are loaded, it can lead to performance issues. Do test the different options before going to production because this will always be a compromise between startup time and navigation speed.
SHOW PAGE INDICATOR	This specifies whether an indicator is visible that shows the page you're on.
ENABLE SWIPING	This specifies whether the user will be able to swipe pages of the PAGEBOOK.
ON SELECT	This opens the Script Editor.

Table 7.25 Pagebook Component Properties (Cont.)

The PAGEBOOK component is useful when you're designing menus and want an extra effect when changing pages. In Figure 7.70, you can see three menu items on the left and the data that corresponds to the second menu item on the right. The application is made in such a way that when you tap one of the menu items, the content on the right side will fade away, and new content relating to the menu choice will fade in. The fading effect is achieved by using the TRANSITION EFFECT property, which you can set to FADE. The script in the text box contains the following line for the second menu:

`PAGEBOOK_1.setSelectedPageIndex(1);`

This will result in the current screen fading away and being replaced with another screen.

An alternative way to do the same is addressing the page by name. The advantage is an improved readability of the script. In this example, we add an external parameter. If this isn't set, the application will start with `Page Main`; otherwise, it uses the parameter that was passed to the application:

```
var selectedPage = XPage;
if(selectedPage == "none"){selectedPage ="MAIN";}
PAGEBOOK_DASHBOARDS.setSelectedPageByName(selectedPage);
```

> **Numbering for Pagebook Pages**
>
> Although we mentioned it in Table 7.25, we want to emphasize this fact as it sometimes creates confusion: The numbering of PAGEBOOK pages starts at 0, and the second page is actually listed as page 1.

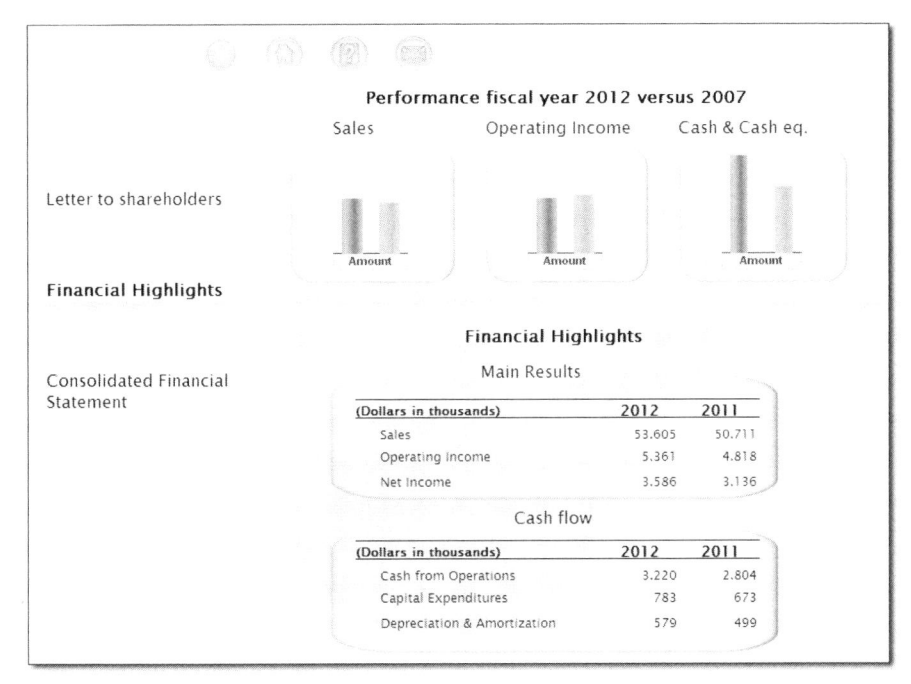

Figure 7.70 Example of Using a Pagebook Component

Panel Component

A PANEL component is used to group components together. By using the methods of the PANEL component, including .setCssClass, it's possible to build interactivity into the application. As the number of components tends to grow quickly in an application, it's advisable to use these PANEL components often to group components that belong together, even if no interactivity is planned. Grouping allows you, for example, to hide a group of components at design time so your screen isn't cluttered when you're working on another part of the application.

Table 7.26 shows the properties of the PANEL component.

Property	Description
CSS Class	When a custom CSS file is assigned to the Application component, you can assign a CSS class here.
CSS Style	In this setting, enter the CSS code to change the layout of the Panel component.
On Click	This opens the Script Editor.

Table 7.26 Panel Component Properties

Popup Component

The Popup component can be used to let a screen appear in the application, on top of all the other components, where users can make quick entries or configurations, see important messages, or make selections (Figure 7.71). Popup components can also be quite helpful for help messages and for providing further information about elements. The main reason to use a Popup component is to allow the user to perform a particular task and freeze the rest of the application until that task is done. You can ensure this by using the Modal property of the component.

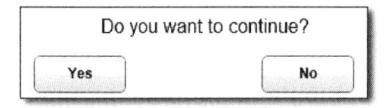

Figure 7.71 Example Usage for a Popup Component

There are two restrictions you should consider when using a Popup component:

- The Popup component can only be located in the root layout and not within another container element.
- The Popup component can only be positioned in relation to the root layout.

Table 7.27 shows the properties of the Popup component.

Property	Description
Name	The name of the component must be a unique name within the application.

Table 7.27 Popup Component Properties

Property	Description
MODAL	If the POPUP component is set to MODAL, the user can only navigate within the popup screen. If the MODAL property is set to FALSE, the user can also interact with other elements of the application.
AUTOCLOSE	This specifies whether the popup screen automatically closes when the user interacts outside of the popup in the application.
ANIMATION	This specifies the animation effect when the popup is opened or closed: ▸ NO ANIMATION ▸ FLIP ANIMATION ▸ POP ANIMATION ▸ HORIZONTAL SLIDE ANIMATION ▸ VERTICAL SLIDE ANIMATION

Table 7.27 Popup Component Properties (Cont.)

A useful way to work with a POPUP component is to set up a BUTTON component in the application and have the POPUP component appear near the button. For example, if you want to show a POPUP component with some application settings, a BUTTON component to the top right of the screen can be combined with a POPUP component. The setting for animation can be set to VERTICAL SLIDE ANIMATION. When you use the POPUP component this way, it will look like the popup appears directly out of the button and immediately grabs the user's attention, as the user was already clicking that button.

To show the POPUP component, add this code in the first BUTTON component:

`POPUP_CONFIGSCREEN.show();`

You add a second BUTTON component in the POPUP component itself and set the following code in the second button component to hide the component again:

`POPUP_CONFIGSCREEN.hide();`

Tabstrip Component

A TABSTRIP component allows you to group your application into tabs (Figure 7.72). It's an easy way to divide your application in multiple screens. By clicking a tab, the user can move to a different screen in the application. The TABSTRIP component works much the same way as the PAGEBOOK component, creating several tabs, only one of which is visible at a time. The difference with a PAGEBOOK component is the way it allows you to navigate. With the TABSTRIP component, you automatically have a direct way to go from one tab to any of the other tabs. With a PAGEBOOK component, you can only go to the previous or next page, or you have to write scripts and add BUTTON components to create this same functionality.

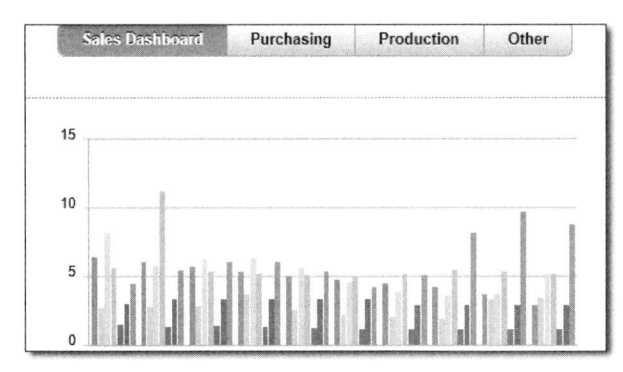

Figure 7.72 Tabstrip Component

Table 7.28 shows the properties of the TABSTRIP component.

Property	Description
CSS CLASS	When a custom CSS file is assigned to the APPLICATION component, you can assign a CSS class here.
SELECTED TAB INDEX	This specifies the tab that will initially be shown at the start. Index 0 opens the first tab of the component, index 1 the second, and so on.
ON SELECT	This opens the Script Editor. ON SELECT triggers each time a user selects a tab.

Table 7.28 Tabstrip Component Properties

If you want to go through the tabs step-by-step, you can add a BUTTON component outside the TABSTRIP. Each time the BUTTON component is clicked, the user goes to the next page until reaching the last (Listing 7.8). Then the TABSTRIP component jumps back to the starting tab.

```
var tabnumber = TABSTRIP_1.getSelectedTabIndex();

if (tabnumber == 4)
{
 TABSTRIP_1.setSelectedTabIndex(0);
} else {
 TABSTRIP_1.setSelectedTabIndex(tabnumber + 1);
}
```
Listing 7.8 Loop Through Tabs Using a Button Component

You could use this for a wizard-like navigation through several steps, and if the final step is done, return to the starting page. A wizard-like solution is handy for when you want to enable users to do complicated tasks and guide them through the process.

Split Cell Container Component

The SPLIT CELL CONTAINER is an area where a user can drag and arrange portable fragments. The fragments are shown in a tabular format. The area is similar to a placeholder area where the user has his own room to arrange fragments.

Table 7.29 lists the properties of the SPLIT CELL CONTAINER component.

Property	Description
ON DROP	The event script for when a user adds a new fragment to the SPLIT CELL CONTAINER.
ON DELETE	The event script for when a user removes a fragment from the SPLIT CELL CONTAINER.

Table 7.29 Split Cell Container Properties

7.4 Technical Component Properties

In this section, we'll discuss the properties of all the technical components. You won't find these in the COMPONENTS pane, but you can add them directly in the OUTLINE pane in the TECHNICAL COMPONENTS folder. These kinds of components play a central role in the application and are used in relation with other components.

7　Components and Properties

7.4.1　Backend Connection Component

The BACKEND CONNECTION component (Figure 7.73) is a dialog box that allows you to navigate through a backend system and select a data source. After the user selects a data source, the application can run a script to assign it to a DATA SOURCE ALIAS component and show the contents to the user.

Figure 7.73 Backend Connection Component

Table 7.30 lists the properties of the BACKEND CONNECTION component.

Property	Description
SYSTEM ID	The initial ID of the backend system connection.
DEFAULT TAB	The tab that will be shown initially when the browser is visible.
VISIBLE TABS	The tabs that are visible in the browser when applicable. For example, with an SAP HANA connection, you'll only see the SEARCH and FOLDERS tabs, even if you selected more.

Table 7.30 Backend Connection Properties

Property	Description
ON DATA SOURCE BROWSER CONFIRMED	The event when a data source is chosen and the OK button is clicked.
ON DATA SOURCE BROWSER CANCELLED	The event that occurs when the CANCEL button is clicked.

Table 7.30 Backend Connection Properties (Cont.)

This popup is very useful when you create a generic Online Analytical Processing (OLAP) application, which allows you to open any query that is available in the backend systems.

This application can either be opened directly by the user or via a link from another application. An example of an application that links to an OLAP application is a dashboard application that is used to analyze a particular subject more in-depth. The dashboard application then includes a link to the OLAP application with an external parameter to define the query to be explored. The OLAP application then automatically opens with the configured query.

In the first example, where the user opens the application, the user must have the option to select the query. When another application refers to the OLAP application and provides a query to explore, the OLAP application should immediately load the right query.

Using the BACKEND CONNECTION component in combination with external parameters achieves this goal. You can define external parameters that allow other applications to pass information on the query and system (Figure 7.74).

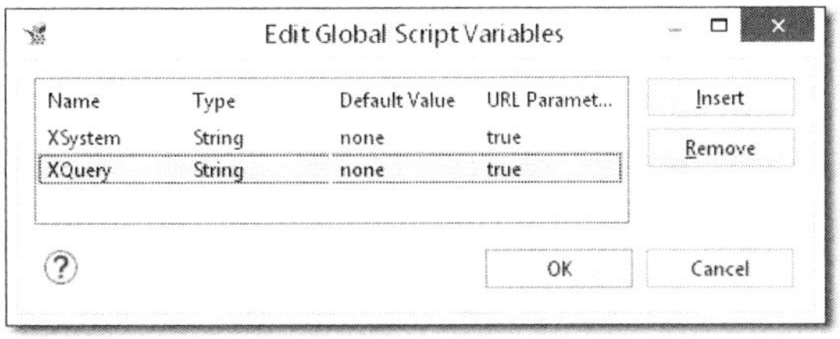

Figure 7.74 External Parameters to Set Up the Query and System

In the startup event of the application, you insert the script shown in Listing 7.9. This script will check if a query was provided, and, if so, that query will be loaded. If not, then a popup will appear that allows the user to select a query.

```
    System = XSystem;
    Query = XQuery;
    if (Query!= "none" && System != "none")
    {
        DS_1.assignDataSource(System, DataSourceType.QUERY, Query;
    }
    else
    if (Query== "none" && System != "none")
    {
        CONNECTION_OLAP.setSystem(System);
    }
        CONNECTION_OLAP.showDataSourceBrowser();
    )
```
Listing 7.9 Startup Script to Load the Query of the Show Query Choice Popup

If a query and system are provided, the application will load the given system and query; if only a system name was provided, then that system will be opened in the BACKEND CONNECTION component. If no values were passed to the application, the BACKEND CONNECTION component will fall back to a default system.

In the ON DATA SOURCE BROWSER CONFIRMED event in the BACKEND CONNECTION component, add the following script:

```
var ds = CONNECTION_1.getSelectedDataSource();
DS_1.assignDataSource(ds.connection, ds.type, ds.name, true);
```

This particular script can be copied from the tooltip provided by Design Studio.

You can then make it so that when the user clicks the CANCEL button, a notice informs the user that a query selection is necessary. You can add a popup panel with an OK button and some explanatory text.

To do this, in the ON DATA SOURCE BROWSER CANCELLED event, add the following script to show a popup panel:

```
POPUP_WARNINGMESSAGES.show();
```

7.4.2 Context Menu Component

A CONTEXT MENU component enables the user to right-click on a CROSSTAB component and have additional options for navigation and analysis (Figure 7.75). In the CONTEXT MENU component, you'll find a number of standard context-related items, and you can add a number of items yourself. Although a CONTEXT MENU component is immediately added when you create a new application, this component isn't compulsory, and you can remove it if you don't need one.

Technical Component Properties | **7.4**

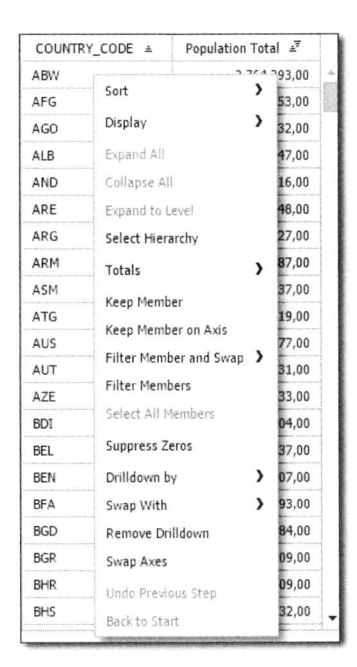

Figure 7.75 Context Menu Component at Runtime

Table 7.31 lists the properties of the CONTEXT MENU component.

Property	Description
CSS CLASS	Class referencing a class in the custom CSS to provide additional formatting component.
CUSTOM MENU OPTIONS	Opens a dialog box to add other items to the CONTEXT MENU component.

Table 7.31 Context Menu Component Properties

If you click on the EDIT MENU ENTRIES on the right side of the CUSTOM MENU OPTIONS property (Figure 7.76), you'll open a new dialog box to add new entries (Figure 7.77).

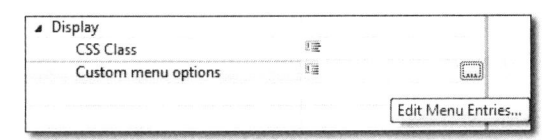

Figure 7.76 Edit Menu Options

297

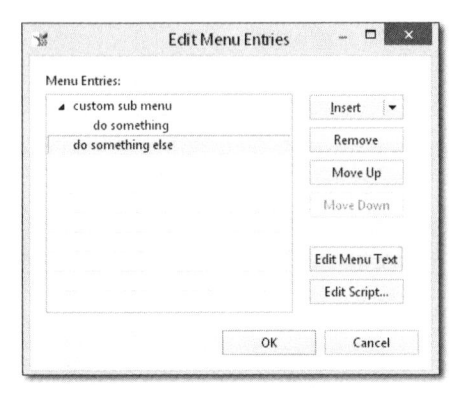

Figure 7.77 Dialog Box to Add New Entries to the Context Menu

In the dialog box, you can insert menus, items, and submenus that in turn can hold menu items. For each menu item, you can create a script. If you want to work with the area where the user right-clicked, you can use the `.getClickArea()` method.

7.4.3 Global Scripts Object Component

The GLOBAL SCRIPTS OBJECT components allow you to create central subroutines or functions (SCRIPT FUNCTIONS) that can be called to perform tasks and/or return values (Figure 7.78). In earlier versions that didn't include this component, designers used buttons as script containers to avoid having to repeat code over and over.

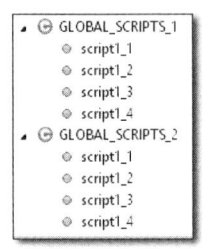

Figure 7.78 Global Scripts in the Outline View

A GLOBAL SCRIPT OBJECT (Figure 7.79) is a container object where you can store multiple script functions. You can specify input and output parameters for the script function. To understand the role this component can fulfill, we'll show you an example where a script function is useful. In the earlier example with the message warning in the popup, we created a warning message in case the user canceled the data source selection. However, in an application, you can have a lot of different messages to inform users, so you need to make the messages flexible.

In the script, you can make a simplified function where you store all the texts and return one text based on a number provided.

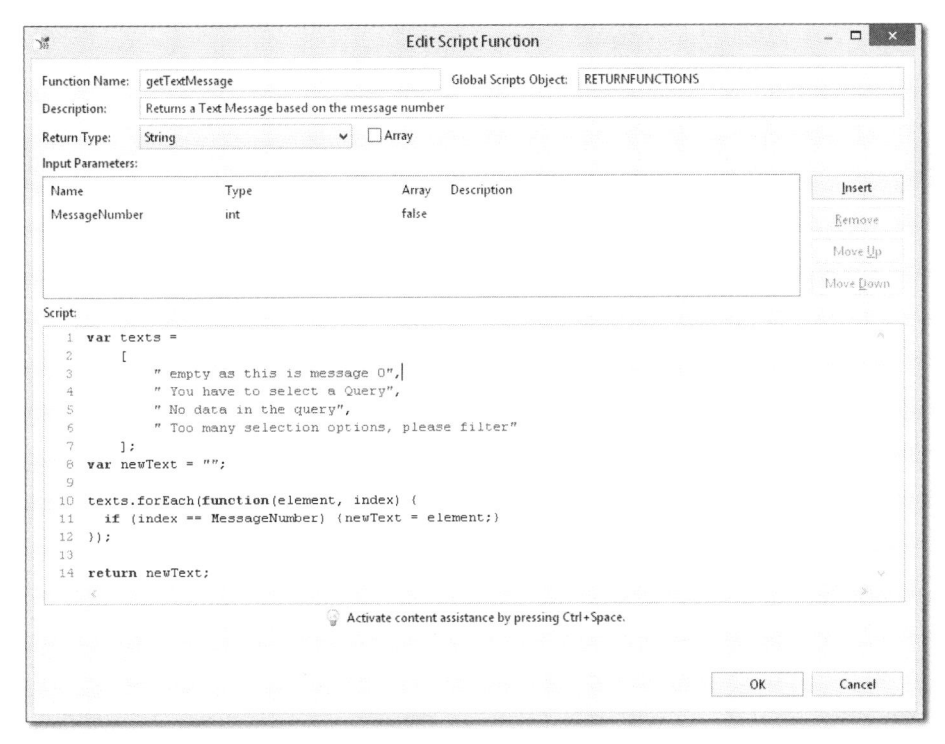

Figure 7.79 Script to Return a Text Message

To set the text of the warning to the right setting, you can add the following script:

```
var WarningMessage = RETURNFUNCTIONS.getTextMessage(1);
TXT_WARNING.setText(WarningMessage);
```

This way, you can keep all your warning texts centralized. You can take it a step further. Instead of an array of texts, as shown in Figure 7.79, you can use the key to filter a data source. The input parameter is the text key. The function will use that key to look in a data source to retrieve the corresponding text and return the text:

```
DS_1.getFilterText(dimension)
```

7.4.4 PDF Component

A PDF component allows you to export the application as a PDF document. If you add this component, you get an option to add script lines to export (parts of) the application as PDF.

There are a couple of ways that you can use the component to create documents. You choose the option by using the script methods. The following options are available:

- **Export application as PDF**
  The PDF looks like a report where the application screens are formatted into different pages.

- **Export screen as PDF**
  The PDF document looks like a screenshot (i.e., a one-to-one copy of what you see on screen).

- **Export panel as PDF**
  The resulting PDF document looks like a screenshot.

When the script to export to PDF is run, the user will see a dialog box (Figure 7.80) in which the user can configure the resulting PDF. After clicking PRINT, the PDF will be exported.

Figure 7.80 Dialog Box PDF Export

7.4.5 Text Pool Component

The TEXT POOL component is a placeholder component for texts. Using this component, you can store all kinds of text and refer to them in components.

This feature is very useful when you have, for example, a lot of help texts in your application. Instead of having to go through your application to update them, you now can maintain them from the TEXT POOL component. You can use this for the dynamic application of texts or translations.

When you run Design Studio on an SAP BW platform, you can add a dynamic translation. When you add items to the TEXT POOL component at design time, you need to enter the texts in English (Figure 7.81).

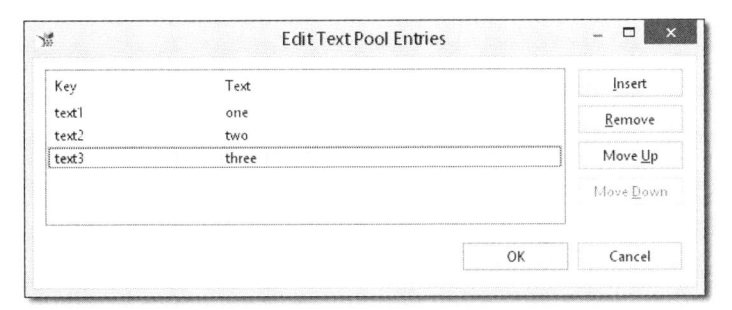

Figure 7.81 Editing the Entries for the Text Pool Component

The design tool automatically saves the texts with language key EN (English) in the `TLOGO` object in table `RSAO_T_TEXT`. The texts are stored separately for each analysis application. You can translate the texts with standard translation tools, for example, Transaction SE63.

7.4.6 Action Sheet Component

The ACTION SHEET component (Figure 7.82) is a way to add a list of actions related to a component. On interaction, for example, right-clicking a button on a component, you can let the component popup next to a component. In the method to do this, you set the related component as a parameter. This allows you to hand a number of options to the user based on the component the user is interacting with.

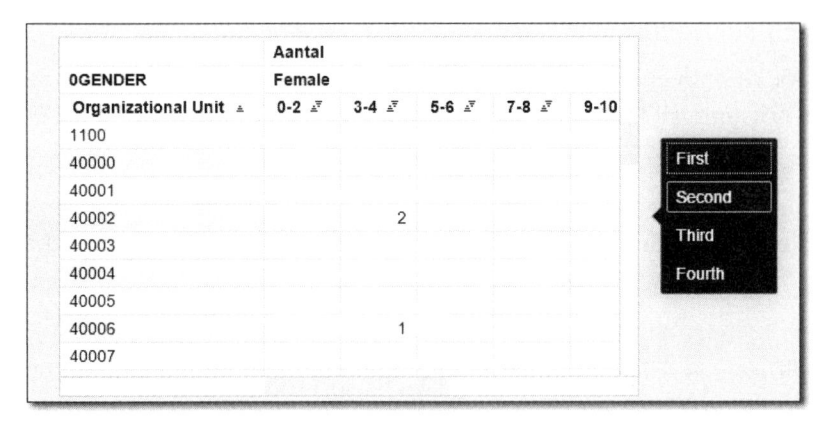

Figure 7.82 Action Sheet

Because you can also add/remove items and set texts and icons, you can create a flexible way of adding possible actions to components in your application.

7.5 Summary

In this chapter, we looked at all the components of Design Studio, from the APPLICATION component down to each individual visual component. You've seen all their properties, what the components look like, and a number of examples of how you can use them in an application.

In the next chapter, we discuss scripting. We'll look at the syntax and options you have with each component, and provide some examples.

PART III
Advanced Concepts

Interactivity is the key to Design Studio applications. In this chapter, we'll show you how it's done.

8   Scripting for Interactivity

Design Studio is a tool used to create interactive applications. To support this interactivity, Design Studio uses a script language that is executed when the user performs an action in the application. In this chapter, we'll take a closer look at Design Studio's script language and show examples of how to use the script in your applications.

In Section 8.1, we'll introduce you to the script language, including its elements and what you need to know to build your first script. In Section 8.2, we'll explain the basics of script writing, including some Design Studio tools that will come in handy for this purpose. In Section 8.3, we'll provide a comprehensive description of all the script methods and properties of the components in Design Studio. Finally, we'll devote the entire second half of this chapter (Section 8.4, Section 8.5, Section 8.6, and Section 8.7) to showing you examples of how to build interactivity in applications.

> **Tips for CSS**
>
> This chapter uses Cascading Style Sheets (CSS). For some additional tips about CSS, see Chapter 10.

8.1   BI Action Language

The script language in Design Studio is called *BI Action Language (BIAL)*. BIAL is a true subset of JavaScript, but unlike JavaScript, which is executed in a web browser, BIAL scripts are executed on an Analysis Application Design Service. It's also present on the client computer to run the Design Studio tool locally. An example of BIAL on the web can be found at *www.ecma-international.org/publications/standards/Ecma-262.htm*.

BIAL script consists of individual statements in lines and is written inside event handlers. (As you'll recall from Chapter 7, all components have event handlers.) These event handlers are triggered by user interaction with Design Studio, such as clicking a button, navigating to another part of the application, or starting the application.

In this section, we'll dive into the script language itself. We'll look at the syntax and the general way BIAL is built, including expressions, script variables, and event handlers.

8.1.1 Syntax

The official syntax of BIAL is based on three types of statements: *call statements*, *conditional statements*, and *assignment statements*. In the following subsections, we'll look at each of these pieces.

> **Note**
>
> Although this section is a bit theoretical, it provides very useful background information that will help you more easily understand what is happening in the script.

Call Statements

Call statements call component methods by stating the name of the component followed by a method that the component has. *Component methods* are predefined reactions of the component, and they control one of two things: Either the component method performs an action, or the component method returns a property value of the component. In the first case, call statements play a central role in writing scripts because the call statement is what makes the components behave as you want them to. In the second case, call statements are essential because they return information about the state of the component.

An example of this second type of method is `.getselectedvalue`. This method returns the currently selected value of the component, which you can then use in your further script. You can, for example, use the value you got back from the `.getselected` method to present it to the user or use it to add a filter to a data source.

The call statement has the following format:

`<Component>.<Method><Arguments>;`

Each element of this format is described in Table 8.1.

Format	Description
`<Component>`	This is the name of the component in the application you want to script with. This component can be the application itself, a data source, or a component that you've added to the application. When you add components, be sure to name them properly. Later on, when scripting, it makes a lot more sense if the name of the component suggests what functionality it delivers. For example, `LISTBOX_1` doesn't provide the same information as `LISTBOX_PRODUCTFILTER`, although you can work with both names. You can always change these names later; references in scripts will change accordingly.
`<Method >`	This is the operation that you want the component to do. Each component type has its own set of operations. Some operations, such as `setVisible`, are quite common and are available in numerous components. Others, such as `setFilter`, are limited to a specific type of component.
`<Arguments >`	This is a comma-listed set of *expressions*. These expressions must match the requirement of the method. You can use functions or other call statements as an argument for another component.
`;`	Each statement has to end with a semicolon.

Table 8.1 Format of a Call Statement

Conditional Statements

Conditional statements can have two formats. The first is as follows:

```
If (<condition>)
{
<Statements when the condition is met>
}
```

The second is as follows:

```
If (<condition>)
{
<Statements when the condition is met>
}
```

```
else
{
<Statements when the condition is not met>
}
```

In both of these formats, `<condition>` is a Boolean expression, meaning it must have a value of either `true` or `false`. The Boolean expression can be a constant, but it also can be a combination of expressions that together result in a `true` or `false` value.

There are a lot of possible constructions to build a Boolean expression resulting in a `true` or `false` value, as shown in Table 8.2. You're not limited to these constructions. You can combine them with other constructions as long as the end result is `true` or `false`.

Construction Type	Construction Example
Constant	`true`
Call statement	`Button_1.isEnabled;`
Comparison	`Button_1.isEnabled ==` `Button_2.isEnabled`

Multiple comparisons where all the values must be `true`
(AND logic)
	`Button_1.isEnabled ==`
	`Button_2.isEnabled`
	`&&`
	`Button_3.isEnabled`

Multiple comparisons where any of the values must be `true`
(OR logic)
	`Button_1.isEnabled ==`
	`Button_2.isEnabled`
	`||`
	`Button_3.isEnabled`

Table 8.2 Constructions That Result in a Boolean Value

Assignment Statements

Assignment statements assign values to variables. There are two formats to assign a value variable, as described in Table 8.3: a format for a global variable and another format for a local variable. For local variables, you need to define the variable first with the VAR statement. For the global variable, this isn't necessary because you already defined the global variable in the APPLICATION component. In Section 8.1.3, we explain variables in more detail.

Context	Format
Variable isn't yet defined.	VAR <variable_name> = <Expression>;
Variable is defined.	<variable_name> = <Expression>;

Table 8.3 Assigning a Value to a Variable

Assigning values to variables in an application is very useful for storing values that you can reuse later. Variables can also be used extensively when calculations have to take place in the application. For example, you can pull the numbers from the components, store them in variables, perform the calculation, and, finally, store the result in another variable and assign the value back to another component.

Doing it like this, step-by-step, helps you keep an overview of the code, making it easy to read by reducing the complexity of each line.

8.1.2 Expressions

An *expression* is a combination of variables, component values, and subexpressions that together result in a value. Value results of an expression have a type, which indicates the format of the result (e.g., string or integer). If an expression is used to produce a result that is used in another statement, that result type must match the requirement of that statement.

With operators, you can combine several arguments into one result value. Table 8.4 describes all the operators that are supported in BIAL.

Operator	Description	Result Type	Example
+	Concatenates	String	"foo" + "bar"
+	Adds two values	Integer, float	45 + 12
-	Subtracts two values	Integer, float	45 – 12
*	Multiplies two values	Integer, float	5*7
/	Divides one value by another	Integer, float	8 / 2
==	Checks if both values are equal	Any	"A" == "A"

Table 8.4 Supported Operators in BIAL

309

Operator	Description	Result Type	Example
!=	Checks if both values aren't equal; this gives the opposite result of ==.	Any	"A" != "A"
&&	Results in true when the expression to the left and right both result in true.	Boolean	"A" == "A" && "B" == "B"
||	Results in True when either the expression to the left *or* to the right results in true.	Boolean	"A" == "B" || "B" == "B"
!	Turns the Boolean result around; if the result is true, it will be set to false; if the result is false, it will be set to true.	Boolean	! "A" == "B"

Table 8.4 Supported Operators in BIAL (Cont.)

If an expression is to be used as an argument for a component method, the type of expression must match the required expression for the component method.

Table 8.5 describes the expression types.

Expression Type	Description
Primitive types	These are the basic types, such as the following: ▶ Boolean: true, false ▶ String: "foobar" ▶ Float: 123.45 ▶ Integer: 123 Primitive types are also arrays. The following values are stored in a variable: ▶ String array: ["foo","bar"] ▶ Integer array: [14,15] ▶ JSON: {"key"; "value"}
SAP Business-Objects BI types	These are special types such as data source alias, dimension, and measure, which are often combinations of primitive types to help you enter the appropriate input in the component methods.

Table 8.5 Expression Types

Expression Type	Description
Component types	These are components, for example, BUTTON, PAGEBOOK, LIST BOX, and IMAGE.

Enum	Enum or enumeration is a set of predefined values. Enums are SAP BusinessObjects BI types. A value is written as:
	`<EnumType>.<EnumValue>`
	Examples are the components themselves, which in a sense are expression types. For example, the APPLICATION component has methods, and if you want to address them, you write:
	`Application.getinfo`

Table 8.5 Expression Types (Cont.)

8.1.3 Script Variables

Script variables are used to store values for later use. Variables can be used in a number of ways, for example, storing results for calculation, keeping tab on the current state of the application, and holding values that are used at several points in the application.

Like expressions, script variables are of a certain type depending on the assigned value. These types are the same as the types for expressions, which were described in Table 8.5. If you want to use a variable as a parameter for a method, the variable type must match the parameter type.

There are two kinds of script variables:

- **Local variables**
  These are variables that are defined in a local script and can't be used in other places. These kinds of variables are useful if you want to compute a result and need a place to store a temporary value. A local variable is defined by adding the following line:

  `var <variable> = <expression>;`

  The variable type is determined by the result of the expression. Local variables can be preferred over global variables if you want to perform only a local action. Using a local variable ensures that you don't alter something that will hurt another part of the application because the local variable value disappears when the script in that component has ended. Using the same local variable name in another component doesn't result in an overlap.

▸ **Global script variables**
Global variables can be used in every script in your application. Global variables are used for storing values that will be used in multiple parts of your application. Constant values can be held in global variables; the maintenance of these values is less time-consuming. Additionally, a global variable can be defined as a URL parameter. If you set a global variable as a URL parameter, it's possible to add this variable as a parameter in the URL when someone calls the application. The value in the parameter will be stored in the variable. When you run Design Studio on the SAP BusinessObjects BI platform, you can use OpenDocument links (URLs) to call an application. In the URL of such an application, you can incorporate variables and values for these variables. For example, you can add a filter value for a specific plant in the URL of the application.

8.1.4 Calling the Event Handler

Event handlers are placeholders for scripting and are defined for each component; for example, for a BUTTON component, the handler event is `On Click`, and for the APPLICATION component, it's `On Startup`. When the handler is triggered, the application will run the script that has been entered.

Event handlers are triggered by user interaction. For example, when a user changes a selected value in a component, the `On Change` handler will be triggered. Note, however, that when a script line performs the same action, the `On Change` handler *won't* be triggered.

If you do need to trigger an event handler using code, you can use the handler method for that component. For example, the PAGEBOOK component has an `On Select` handler. With the code `Pagebook_1.onSelect();`, you can trigger the handler and run the code that is in the `On Select` handler of the PAGEBOOK component.

8.1.5 Global Scripts

Sometimes when a piece of code is repeated in several components, it can be useful to use global scripts instead of writing the same code for all the components separately. The global script object acts as a grouping of various script functions. These global scripts and script functions can be called from any event handler.

Each script function has a configurable return type and any number of typed input parameters. The following types can be used for return values and input parameters:

- Primitive types
- Data source alias
- All user interface component types such as BUTTONS and TABSTRIPS, as well as software development kit (SDK) extension components.

8.2 Creating a Script

Now that you understand the basics of the scripting language, you can build your first script. To dive right into writing statements, let's start by going to the properties of a component (Figure 8.1). Follow these steps:

1. Navigate to the ON CLICK, ON SELECT, or — for the APPLICATION component — the ON STARTUP section in the PROPERTIES view. Click the EDIT THE SCRIPT button next to the property.

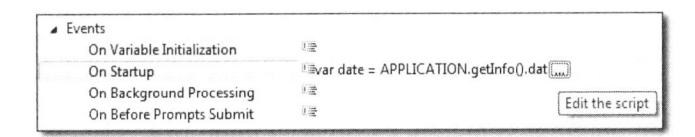

Figure 8.1 Edit the Script Button

2. The Script Editor opens. On the top of the screen, you can see the component and method handler you're editing (Figure 8.2).

3. In this screen, you can type statements as described in Section 8.1.1. When you're done typing, click OK. If you don't want to save the script, click CANCEL.

In this section, we'll describe some essential functionalities of the Script Editor. Understanding these functionalities will be instrumental when you write your own script.

8 | Scripting for Interactivity

Figure 8.2 Script Editor Screen

8.2.1 Using the Content Assistance Screen

When you're entering script lines, you can use the Ctrl+Space shortcut at any time. The CONTENT ASSISTANCE screen will give you suggestions on how to continue writing code—it knows which continuations make sense. For example, if you've already entered a data source alias name, the context-sensitive help will know this and propose specific data source methods (Figure 8.3). More detailed information is available for each method, including input parameters and method outputs.

Figure 8.3 Content Assistance Offering Available Methods for the Data Source

If, in this case, you select the .getData method, you can press Ctrl+Space again, and you'll see that the CONTENT ASSISTANCE screen gives you new options

(Figure 8.4). Because the value in this example can be derived in multiple ways now, all the components show up in the CONTENT ASSISTANCE screen.

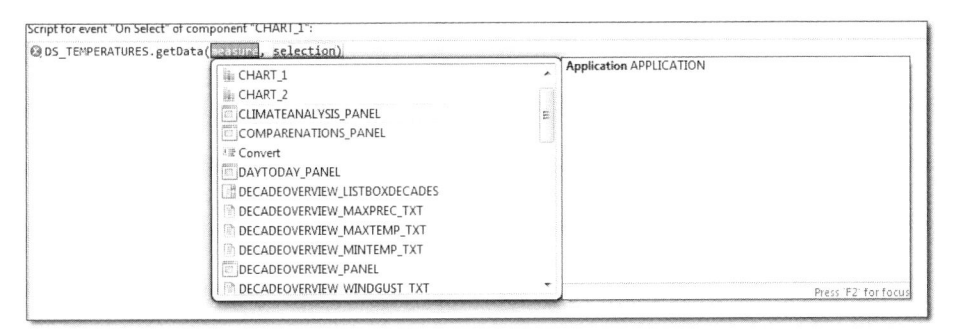

Figure 8.4 Content Assistance on Selecting the Measure

Within the CONTENT ASSISTANCE screen, there are a number of helpful options that you should know about. Let's discuss these next.

For each – for each – loop over array Predefined Statement

Besides the NEW STATEMENT WIZARD in the CONTENT ASSISTANCE screen, you can also use three other predefined statements, as shown in Figure 8.5. The first one is the `for each - for each - loop over array` statement. When you select this option, the following piece of code is inserted in the editor:

```
array.forEach(function(element, index) {
  loop_statements
});
```

This code can be used to loop through an array of data and execute some statements. Listing 8.1 calculates the total sum of the members in the array.

```
var sum = 0;
var array = [1, 2, 3];
array.forEach(function(element, index) {
sum = sum + element;
});
```
Listing 8.1 Using Loops and Arrays

8 | Scripting for Interactivity

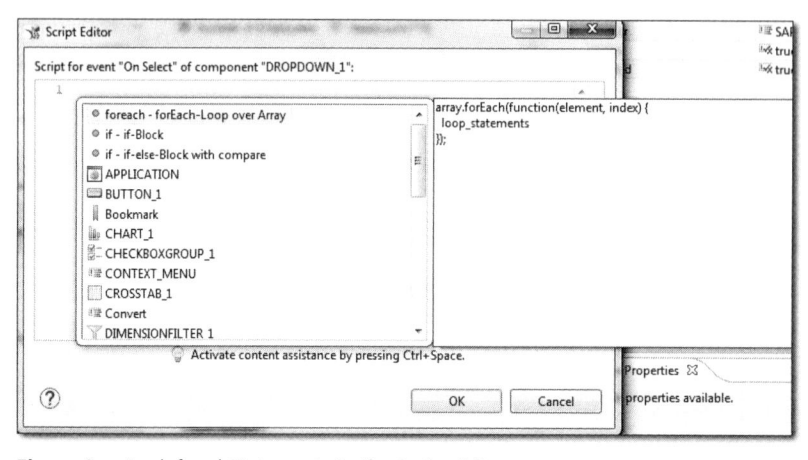

Figure 8.5 Predefined Statements in the Script Editor

if – if Predefined Statement

Another helpful option in the CONTENT ASSISTANCE screen is the `if - if block`, which you can find just below `for each - for each - loop over array` (refer to Figure 8.5). When you select this option, the following code is automatically inserted in the editor:

```
if (condition) {
    if_statements
}
```

Using this predefined statement puts the structure of the `IF - IF` statement in place. By double-clicking either `condition` or `if_statements`, you select that variable, and you can fill it with script code by using the Ctrl+Space shortcut (Figure 8.6).

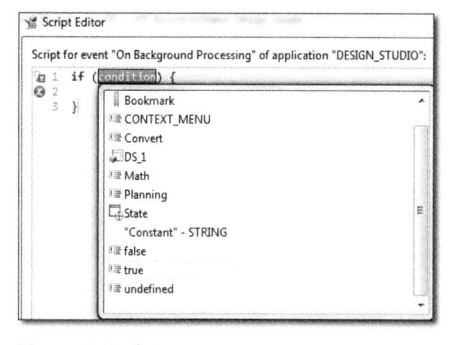

Figure 8.6 If Statement

316

if – if –else block with compare

When the `if-if-else block with compare` option is selected, the piece of code in Listing 8.2 is added in the editor.

```
if ((expression1 == value1) || (expression2 == value2)) {
    if_statements
} else {
    else_statements
}
```
Listing 8.2 if – else Statement

This code can be used when multiple `if` statements are needed in the evaluation. The first line of code will return the value `true` when either one of the expressions is true. When this happens, the first `if` statement will be executed. When both the expressions in the first line are `false`, the statements in the `else` part of the code will be executed.

8.2.2 Creating Predefined Statement Templates

Besides the predefined statement templates that are available in Design Studio, you can create your own in the SCRIPTING TEMPLATES menu.

Adding new predefined statements can increase your scripting speed, especially for those statements you use often. To achieve this, follow these steps:

1. Go to PREFERENCES in TOOLS.
2. Open the SCRIPTING segment, and click TEMPLATES. In the screen (Figure 8.7), you see the current predefined statements.

Name	Context	Description	Auto Ins...
.forEach	Keyword '.'	forEach-Loop over Array	on
.forEach(functio...	Keyword '.'	forEach-Loop over JSON	on
[entry1, entry2]	ArrayLiteral	List (Array)	on
{key: value}	JSON	Key-Value-Pairs (JSON)	on
foreach	Statement	forEach-Loop over Array	on
if	Statement	if-Block	on
if	Statement	if-else-Block with compare	on

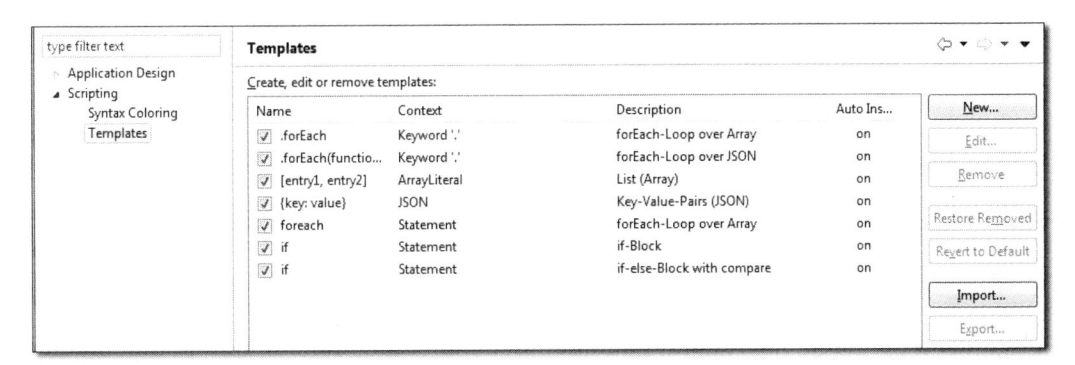

Figure 8.7 Predefined Statements Screen

3. In Figure 8.7, you see three templates that have the word STATEMENT in the CONTEXT column. When you look at the DESCRIPTION column belonging to these templates, you'll see that they correspond to the templates we discussed earlier.

The JavaScript Object Notation (JSON) template is only visible when you use the Ctrl+Space shortcut within the code where a `json` argument is needed (Figure 8.8).

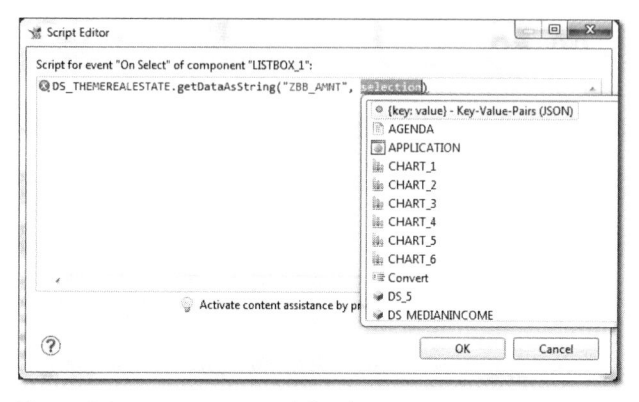

Figure 8.8 Using a JSON Predefined Statement Template

4. For this example, you want to create a predefined JSON list of US states so you don't have to type them all. Click NEW.
5. Fill in the fields as shown in Figure 8.9.

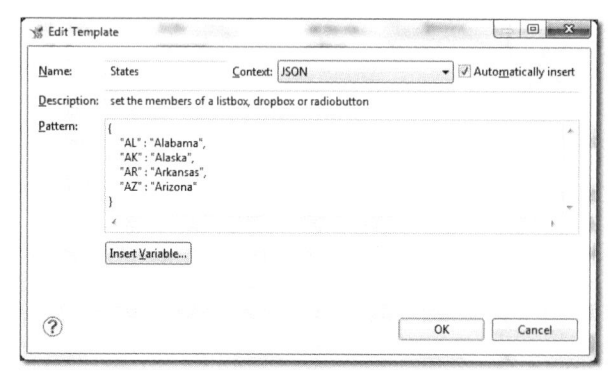

Figure 8.9 Template Code Using the Context JSON

6. Click OK.

Creating a Script | **8.2**

You now see the states in the predefined statement templates (Figure 8.10).

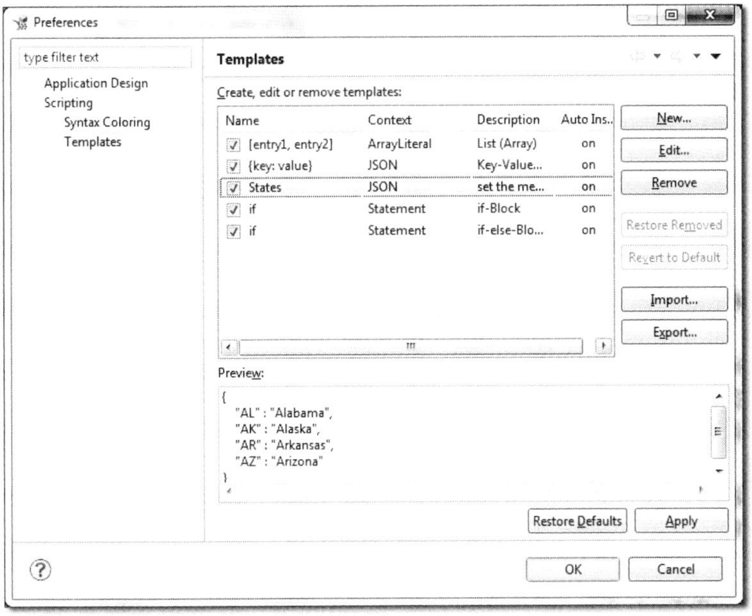

Figure 8.10 New Predefined Statement Ready

Now when you go to the Script Editor, you can type in sample code to get data from a data source (Figure 8.11).

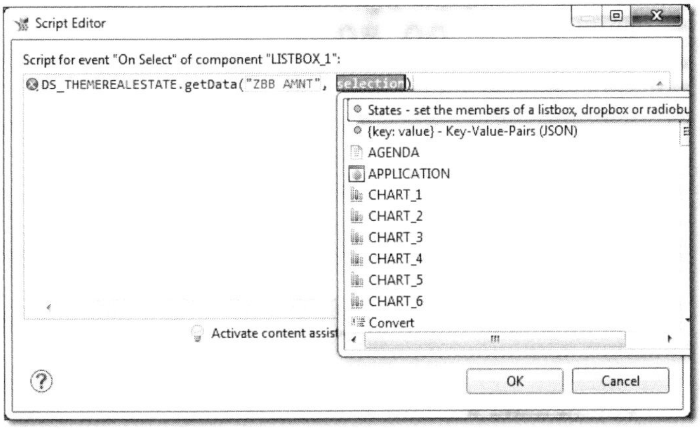

Figure 8.11 Using the New Predefined Statement

319

The end result is that the code from the predefined statement template is inserted into the script and looks like Figure 8.12.

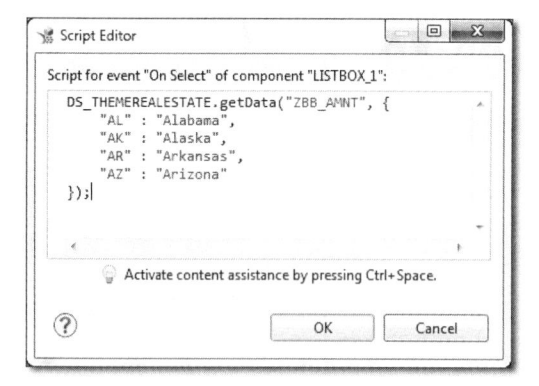

Figure 8.12 Script Editor after Inserting Predefined Code from the Template

> **JSON**
>
> JSON is a subset of the JavaScript programming language. A JSON statement consists of a name and a value and is used to process data between applications or parts of an application.

8.2.3 Finding Script Errors

Even after you've built your script, the Script Editor can still be put to good use. The Script Editor helps identify errors in your script by putting a marker at the beginning of the line (Figure 8.13). It also underlines the error with a red squiggle line.

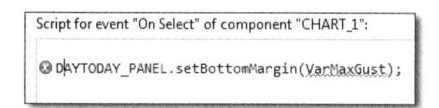

Figure 8.13 A Line with a Syntax Error

When you hover your mouse over the marker, the Script Editor gives more information about the error. In Figure 8.14, you can see how the application delivers more information about the error. Even when there are multiple errors in the line, the Script Editor gives details about all the errors.

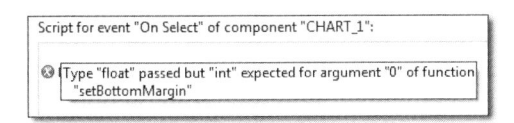

Figure 8.14 Syntax Error Explained

In this example, you can see that the variable `VarMaxGust` is of type `float`, but the Application Programming Interface (API) for the method `.setBottomMargin` requires a value of type `int`. You could repair this issue by either altering the variable or replacing the parameter in the line with an `integer` value.

The Script Editor also distinguishes between errors (red crosses) and warnings (yellow exclamation marks). In the example shown in Figure 8.15, you see a script with a warning. When you hover the mouse over the warning, the Script Editor says that the value "`2015.01`" probably isn't valid.

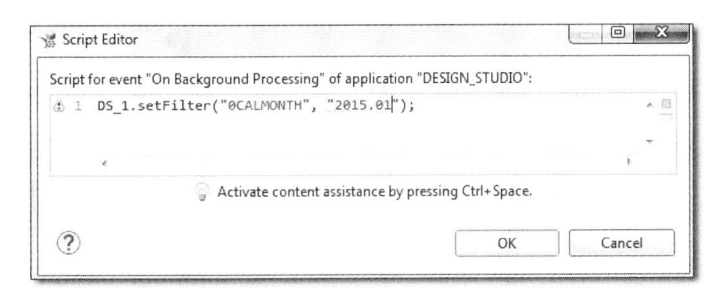

Figure 8.15 Script with Warnings

8.2.4 Creating a Global Script

A *global script object* is a predefined script in Design Studio that can be executed multiple times when needed. A global script object can be created in the OUTLINE view by right-clicking on the TECHNICAL COMPONENTS folder and selecting CREATE CHILD • GLOBAL SCRIPTS OBJECT (Figure 8.16).

To create a global script function, right-click on the global script object that you created first (Figure 8.17), and then select CREATE SCRIPT FUNCTION. Enter the FUNCTION NAME in the following dialog box, and click OK. The CREATE SCRIPT FUNCTION dialog box will appear in which you can specify a description for the function and write your code. A global script function is a child of a global script object (Figure 8.17). A global script object can contain multiple script functions that can be called individually from any script event handler.

8 | Scripting for Interactivity

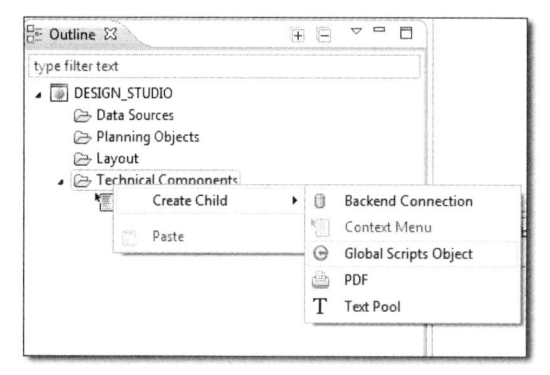

Figure 8.16 Creating a Global Script Object

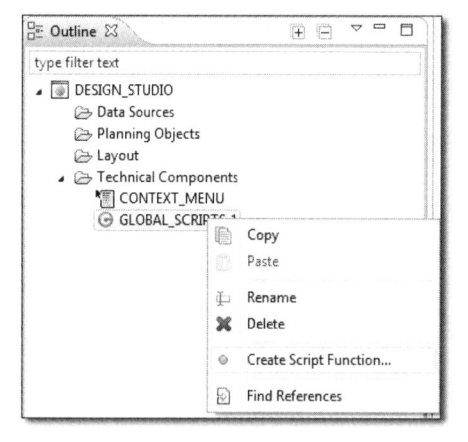

Figure 8.17 Creating a Script Function

8.3 Methods

Now that you understand the basics of BIAL and using the Script Editor to write scripts, let's take a close look at the scripting options in Design Studio. The scripting options in Design Studio are controlled using *methods*. We'll discuss many methods in the following sections as noted here:

- Section 8.3.1: Methods for the CONVERT component, which is used to convert the value of an expression into another type
- Section 8.3.2: Methods for the DATA SOURCE ALIAS component

322

- Section 8.3.3: Methods for the APPLICATION component
- Section 8.3.4: Methods for the APPLICATIONINFO component, which provide some extra information about the application itself
- Section 8.3.5: Methods for the BOOKMARK component
- Section 8.3.6: Methods for the MATH component
- Section 8.3.7: Methods for the PLANNING component
- Section 8.3.8: Methods for the CONTEXT MENU component
- Section 8.3.9: Methods and associated functions of all the visual components, starting with the common methods

8.3.1 Convert Component

The CONVERT component (Table 8.6) isn't a visual component, but a global object that provides functions for data conversion. This is useful, for example, when you want to show a number in a text box and want to apply formatting.

> **Note**
>
> As you may have noticed, the CONVERT component wasn't mentioned in Chapter 7 because you can't see it or set any properties at design time. You can only use this component in script by referring to it using call statements.

You can use the CONVERT component to format a number so the number becomes more readable for users. If you have a number value 12345678, you can use the convert method `floatToString`, which could result in a string value of 123,456.78 EUR. When you set the text of a TEXT component using this resulting value, you present the user with an easy-to-comprehend value.

The script line would look like this:

`Convert.floatToString(123456.78, "###,###,##0.00 EUR");`

In addition, if you have variables or parameters of different types, you can use the CONVERT component to change them so they will align. You can view this object as a toolkit to handle all kinds of values. Table 8.6 lists all the CONVERT methods.

8 | Scripting for Interactivity

Method	Description
`floatToString`	Converts a float number type value to a string and applies a formatting pattern. English local is standard, but you can apply your own formatting in a parameter.
`floatToStringUsingLocale`	Converts a float number type to a string and applies the local formatting pattern. You can set the number of decimals.
`indexOf(string, searchFor, startIndex?)`	Returns the index or position of a keyword (`searchString` parameter) in another string (`string` parameter). You can also supply a start index to indicate where the search should start.
`replaceAll(string, searchFor, replaceWith)`	Searches for a given string and replaces it with another.
`stringLength`	Returns the length of the string type value given in the parameter.
`stringToFloat`	Converts a string type to a float number.
`stringToFloatUsingLocale`	Converts a string type to a float number using the local formatting pattern.
`stringToInt`	Converts a string type to an integer.
`Substring`	Returns a substring of the original string based on the start and end positions set in the parameters.
`urlEncode(string)`	Encodes a string to a format that is readable in HTML format. This is useful, for instance, when a string needs to be passed as a URL variable in an external application.

Table 8.6 Convert Methods

8.3.2 Data Source Alias Component

The DATA SOURCE ALIAS component has numerous methods to navigate and filter data (Table 8.7). In addition, you can assign a data source to the alias at runtime, meaning you can switch between the queries or views the data source is referring to, based on the interaction with the user.

Method	Description
`activateHierarchy`	Takes a dimension as a parameter and activates that dimension hierarchy is available.
`assignDataSource`	Defines and loads new data sources (e.g., a new BEx query) to an existing DATA SOURCE ALIAS.
`assignHierarchy`	Activates a specified hierarchy for a specified dimension.
`clearAllFilters`	Removes all applied filters, if any.
`clearFilter`	Removes all filters for a specified dimension.
`collapseNode`	If a specified node for a specified dimension is shown, this method will collapse that node.
`configureInputReadiness`	Indicates that the data source will be used for planning. If a parameter is set to `true`, the data source is input-ready. If the parameter is `false`, the data source is set to display data.
`copyFilters`	Copies the applied filters from a specified data source. You can also copy the filters on measures by adding `true` as the second parameter.
`deactivateHierarchy`	When there is an active hierarchy on a specified dimension, this hierarchy will be deactivated.
`expandNode`	Expands a specified node of a specified dimension. You can also indicate to which level the node should be expanded.
`export`	Exports the `resultSet` of the data source.
`getAssignedHierarchy`	If a hierarchy is assigned to a certain dimension, the hierarchy will be returned.
`getConditionalFormats`	If multiple conditional formats are defined, an array of the conditional format names will be returned.
`getConditionalFormatName`	If a conditional format is defined, the name of the conditional format will be returned.
`getConditionalFormatValue`	Returns a number between 0 and 9. A value of 0 indicates that no conditional format is applied. A value between 1 and 9 indicates the priority level of the conditional format. Priority levels indicate the order in which a condition should be applied. Higher levels get applied first.

Table 8.7 Data Source Alias Methods

Method	Description
getConditionalFormat-ValueExt	Returns a number between 0 and 9 using external member keys. A value of 0 indicates that no conditional format is applied. A value between 1 and 9 indicates the priority level of the conditional format.
getData	Returns a single data cell in the resultSet.
getDataAsString	Returns a single data cell in the resultSet as a string.
getDataAsStringExt	Returns a single data cell in the resultSet as a string based on the user's local settings, scaling factors, and unit of measurement.
getDecimalPlaces	Returns the number of decimals displayed for a specified measure.
getDimensionText	Returns the text value of a specified dimension.
getDimensions	Returns an array of available dimensions. You can also specify from which dimension you want to get the dimensions if needed.
getFilterExt	Returns the filter value of a dimension in a data source in an external key format.
getFilterText	Returns the filter value of a dimension as a String.
getHierarchies	Returns an array of available hierarchies for a given dimension.
getInfo	This method can be used to return more information regarding the data source.
getMeasuresDimension	Returns an array of all the measures in the data source.
getMeasureFilters	Returns an array of applied filters on the measures in the data source.
getMeasureFilterName	Returns the name of a filter that is applied on a specified measure.
getMembers	Returns an array of members of a specified dimension. You can also set a max number of members to be fetched, along with the desired attributes.
getMemberDisplay	Retrieves the member display of a specified dimension.
getMemberList	Returns a list of dimension members for a specified dimension.
getNegativeNumberDisplay	Returns the display format of negative values.

Table 8.7 Data Source Alias Methods (Cont.)

Method	Description
getScalingFacto r	Returns the defined scaling factor for a specified measure.
getStaticFilterExt	Returns the static filter value of a specified dimension.
getStaticFilterText	Returns the static filter value of a specified dimension as string.
getText	Returns a string with the description of the data source set by the application designer.
getTotalsDisplay	Returns how the totals of a specified dimension are displayed.
getTotalsPosition	Returns the position of the totals of a specified dimension.
getVariables	Returns an array of variables that are available in the data source.
getVariableValue	Returns the values that were set for a specified variable in an internal key format.
getVariableValueExt	Returns the values that were set for a specified variable in external key format.
getVariableValueText	Returns the values that were set for a specified variable as string.
getZeroDisplay	Returns the format for zero values.
getZeroDisplayCustomText	Returns a string with a custom text for zero values, if this is defined.
isConditionalFormatActive	Returns `true` if a specified conditional format is active; otherwise, `false` is retuned.
isHierarchyActive	Returns `true` if a specified hierarchy is active; otherwise, `false` is returned.
isInitialized	Returns `true` if a specified data source is assigned and loaded; otherwise, `false` is returned.
isInputReady	Returns whether a specified data source is input-ready or not.
isMeasureFilterActive	Returns `true` if a specified measure's filter is active and `false` if not.
isResultSetEmpty	Returns `true` if a specified data source isn't initialized or the result set is empty or too large.

Table 8.7 Data Source Alias Methods (Cont.)

8 | Scripting for Interactivity

Method	Description
`loadDataSource`	Triggers the loading of a data source.
`moveDimensionAfter`	This method has two parameters, `dimension` and `otherDimension`. When `otherDimension` is already present in the `resultSet`, this method will place `dimension` after it.
`moveDimensionBefore`	This method has two parameters, `dimension` and `otherDimension`. When `otherDimension` is already present in the `resultSet`, this method will place `dimension` before it.
`moveDimensionToColumns`	Moves a specified dimension to the columns of a data source.
`moveDimensionToRows`	Moves a specified dimension to the rows of a data source.
`openPromptDialog`	Opens a prompt dialog window.
`reloadData`	Reloads the data in a data source. This can be used, for instance, in a semi-real-time application, where the user can indicate that he wants to refresh the data.
`removeDimension`	Removes a specified dimension from the rows or columns in a data source.
`setConditionalFormatActive`	Activates or deactivates a specified conditional format based on a parameter of `true` or `false`.
`setDrillLevel`	Sets the level of a hierarchy to where drilling down is possible for a certain dimension.
`setFilter`	Sets a filter for a specified dimension in an internal key format. Previously applied filters will be removed for that dimension.
`setFilterExt`	Sets a filter for a specified dimension in an external key format. Previously applied filters will be removed for that dimension.
`setMeasureFilterActive`	Activates or deactivates a specified measures filter.
`setMemberDisplay`	Changes the member display for a data source dimension. Options are KEY, TEXT, KEY + TEXT, or TEXT + KEY.
`setNegativeNumberDisplay`	Sets the way negative numbers should be displayed.

Table 8.7 Data Source Alias Methods (Cont.)

Method	Description
setScalingFactor	Sets the scaling factor for a specified measure.
setTotalsDisplay	Sets how totals should be displayed for specified dimensions.
setTotalsPosition	Sets the position for the totals on either the X- or Y-axis for a specified dimension.
setVariableValue	Sets a value for a variable in an internal key format and then executes the data source again.
setVariableValueExt	Sets a value for a variable in an external key format and then executes the data source again.
setZeroDisplay	Specifies how zero values are displayed. You can set your own text here, for instance.
sortByAttribute	Sorts the result set in an ascending or descending order based on a specified attribute.
sortByHierarchy	Sorts the result set in the order defined in a specified dimension's hierarchy.
sortByMeasure	Sorts the result set in an ascending or descending order based on a specified measure.
sortByMember	Sorts the result in an ascending or descending order based on the members of a specified dimension.
swapDimensions	Swaps dimensions in the rows and columns if at least one dimension exists in either the rows or columns.
unassignHierarchy	Unassigns a specified hierarchy from the dimension.

Table 8.7 Data Source Alias Methods (Cont.)

8.3.3 Application Component

As you'll recall from Chapter 7, the APPLICATION component is the main component, and its methods are therefore meant for the main application functions. Some methods are used for debugging purposes when creating messages. There are also methods for setting query variables. Other methods in the APPLICATION component enable applications to open new URLs, including URLs to other Design Studio applications. All the APPLICATION component methods are listed in Table 8.8.

8 | Scripting for Interactivity

Methods	Descriptions
`Alert`	Opens a message box where a text message can be displayed.
`export`	Exports the data in the application to either a CSV, XLS, or XLSX file.
`createErrorMessage`	Creates a custom error message that is visible in the MESSAGE view.
`createInfoMessage`	Creates a custom info message that is displayed in the MESSAGE view.
`createWarningMessage`	Creates a custom warning message that is displayed in the MESSAGE view.
`doBackgroundProcessing`	Triggers the `BackgroundProcessing` script. This script is defined on the ON BACKGROUND PROCESSING property of the application. Background scripts are executed after rendering the screen.
`getInfo`	Returns extra information about the application.
`getResourceString`	Returns a resource string based on its ID.
`getTickCount`	Used for performance measurement and returns a point in time in milliseconds.
`getUserAgent`	Returns information about the browser that is used to execute the application.
`loadDataSources`	Loads an array of specified data sources. This can be used to load data sources in parallel. Each data source must be assigned to an individual group. This method doesn't allow for the merging of variables.
`log`	Used for debugging purposes. When this method is triggered, a specified message is written to the error log of the application.
`openNewWindow`	Opens a specified URL in a new browser window.
`openPromptDialog`	Opens a dialog box.
`setVariableValue`	Sets query variable values in the internal key format and executes the data source query again.
`setVariableValueExt`	Sets query variable values in the external key format, and then executes the data source query again.
`print`	Opens the browser's PRINT dialog box.
`searchDataSources`	Searches for data sources in the application.

Table 8.8 Application Component Methods

8.3.4 ApplicationInfo Object Component

The methods in Table 8.9 can be used to provide more information about the application itself. It's used in combination with the `APPLICATION.getInfo()` method that is explained in Table 8.8 to retrieve some extra information.

Method	Description
dateNow	Returns the current date in the user's own regional format.
dateNowInternalFormat	Returns the current date in the following format: "YYYYMMDD".
IsRightToLeft	Returns whether or not the application is in right-to-left mode.
name	Returns the name of the application.

Table 8.9 ApplicationInfo Object Methods

8.3.5 Bookmark Component

The BOOKMARK component can be used to create personalized applications. You can store the navigation state of an application with bookmarks. Table 8.10 shows the methods that can be used with the BOOKMARK component.

Method	Description
assignToFolder	Saves a bookmark in a specific folder.
bookmarkWithTitleExists	Checks whether a bookmark with a specific title exists.
deleteAllBookmarks	Deletes all previously saved standard bookmarks in an application.
deleteBookmark	Deletes a specific standard bookmark.
getAllBookmarks	Retrieves all standard bookmarks that exist in the current application.
getAllBookmarksByFolder	Retrieves all standard bookmarks that exist in a specific folder in the current application.
getBookmarkFolders	Returns all the folders that are used for bookmarking.
getBookmarkInfo	Returns a standard bookmark based on a specific ID.

Table 8.10 Bookmark Component Methods

8 | Scripting for Interactivity

Method	Description
getBookmarkUrl	Returns the URL of a standard bookmark.
loadBookmark	Loads the navigation state of an application the bookmark was saved in.
saveBookmark	Saves the navigation state of an application to a specified bookmark.
shareBookmark	Shares a URL to a saved bookmark.

Table 8.10 Bookmark Component Methods (Cont.)

8.3.6 Math Component

You can use the MATH component for various mathematical calculations. These calculations range from simple calculations, such as finding the maximum or minimum value in a list of values, to more complex calculations, such as calculating the square root or using mathematical values (Table 8.11).

Method	Description
E	Returns the constant number that is the base of the natural logarithms, approximately 2.7182818284590452354.
LN10	Returns the natural logarithm of 10, approximately 2.302585092994046.
LN2	Returns the natural logarithm of 2, approximately 0.6931471805599453.
LOG10E	Returns the base-10 logarithm of E, the base of the natural logarithms, approximately 0.4342944819032518.
LOG2E	Returns the base-2 logarithm of E, the base of the natural logarithms, approximately 1.4426950408889634.
PI	Returns the value for pi, approximately 3.1415926535897932.
SQRT1_2	Returns the square root of 1/2, approximately 0.7071067811865476.
SQRT2	Returns the square root of 2, approximately 1.4142135623730951.
abs	Returns an absolute value of a specified value.
acos	Returns the arc cosine of a specified value.

Table 8.11 Math Component Methods

Method	Description
asin	Returns the arcsine of a specified value.
atan	Returns the arc tangent of a specified value.
atan2	Returns the arc tangent of the quotient y/x.
ceil	Returns the smallest integer number that isn't less than x.
cos	Returns the cosine of a specified value.
exp	Returns the result of e raised to the power of x.
floor	Returns the greatest integer number that isn't greater than x.
log	Returns the natural logarithm of a specified value.
max	Takes a list of values as input and returns the largest value present in that list.
min	Returns the smallest values given a specified list.
pow	Returns the result of raising x to the power of y.
random	Returns a random number.
round	Returns a rounded number.
sin	Returns the sine of a specified value.
sqrt	Returns the square root of a specified value.
tan	Returns the tangent of a specified value.

Table 8.11 Math Component Methods (Cont.)

8.3.7 Planning Component and Planning Function Component

In Chapter 16, we'll show you how to set up an application that uses the PLANNING component and the PLANNING FUNCTION component. In this section, we describe the methods belonging to these components. In Table 8.12, we list the methods belonging to the PLANNING component, and in Table 8.13, we list the methods belonging to the PLANNING FUNCTION component. Apart from the PLANNING component and PLANNING FUNCTION component, we also have the PLANNING SEQUENCE object, which can be used to execute a series of planning functions (Table 8.14).

Method	Description
clientReset	Resets the application to the last successfully calculated state.
hasClientChanges	Returns true if there is any unsaved planning data on the client.

Table 8.12 Planning Component Methods

8 | Scripting for Interactivity

Method	Description
hasUnsavedChanges	Returns true if there is any unsaved planning data.
recalculate	Recalculates changed planning data and returns a status indicating whether the recalculation was successful or not.
reset	Resets the application to the last saved server state.
save	Saves changed planning data to the server and returns a status indicating whether or not the save executed successfully.

Table 8.12 Planning Component Methods (Cont.)

Method	Description
clearAllFilters	Removes all the applied dimension filters.
clearFilter	Removes the filter for a specific dimension.
copyFilters	Copies dimension filters from a data source.
execute	Executes the planning function and returns a status indicating whether the execution was successful.
getDimensionText	Returns the dimension text.
getDimensions	Returns all dimensions of an axis in an array.
getFilterExt	Returns the dimension filter value in an external key format.
getFilterText	Returns the dimension filter value in a text format.
getMemberList	Retrieves a list of dimension members.
setFilter	Sets a dimension filter.
setFilterExt	Sets a dimension filter in an external key format.

Table 8.13 Planning Function Component Methods

Method	Description
Execute	Executes the planning function and returns a status indicating whether or not the execution was successful.
setVariableValue	Sets query variable values in the internal key format and executes the data source query again.
setVariableValue-Ext	Sets query variable values in the external key format, then executes the data source query again.

Table 8.14 Planning Sequence Methods

Method	Description
getVariableValue-Ext	Get the current value of the variable in the external key format.
getVariableValue-Text	Get the text of the current variable value.
getVariables	Get a list of all the variables that are in this planning sequence.

Table 8.14 Planning Sequence Methods (Cont.)

8.3.8 Context Menu Component

The CONTEXT MENU component will be shown during runtime when a user right-clicks on certain components such as a CROSSTAB or NAVIGATION PANEL. In the context menu, the user can set various options such as scaling factor, decimal spaces, and sorting, among others. The context menu has six methods, which are listed in Table 8.15.

Method	Description
getClickArea	Retrieves the name of the area that was clicked on by the user.
getComponent	Retrieves the component that was clicked on.
getContext	Retrieves the data context of what was clicked.
getDataSource	Retrieves the data source that is bound to the component that was clicked on.
isItemVisible	Returns true if the item is set to visible.
setItemToVisible	Sets an item to visible or invisible.

Table 8.15 Context Menu Component Methods

8.3.9 Visual Components

Visual components are all the components used to present data in your application, such as CHART components, CROSSTAB components, TEXT components, and FILTER components.

Common Methods

Just as all visual components have common properties, they also all have common methods. These methods are part of the component class (described in Table

8.16). As a parent class of all the visual components, these components inherit the methods of this class.

The methods in this class are useful for changing the size, the location, and the layout of the objects at runtime.

Method	Description
`getBottomMargin`	Gives the bottom margin of the component as long as BOTTOM MARGIN is set to a number (not AUTO).
`getCSSClass`	Returns the CSS class that is assigned to the component.
`getHeight`	Returns the height of the component as long as HEIGHT is set to a number (not AUTO).
`getLeftMargin`	Returns the left margin of the component as long as LEFT MARGIN is set to a number (not AUTO).
`getRightMargin`	Returns the right margin of the component as long as RIGHT MARGIN is set to a number (not AUTO).
`getTopMargin`	Returns the top margin of the component as long as TOP MARGIN is set to a number (not AUTO).
`getWidth`	Returns the width of the component as long as WIDTH is set to a number (not AUTO).
`hideLoadingState`	Hides the loading state indicator.
`isVisible`	Returns whether the component is visible (`true`) or not (`false`).
`setBottomMargin`	Sets the bottom margin as long as BOTTOM MARGIN is set to a number (not AUTO).
`setCSSClass`	Sets the CSS class of the component.
`setHeight`	Sets the height of the component as long as HEIGHT is set to a number (not AUTO).
`setLeftMargin`	Sets the left margin of the component as long as LEFT MARGIN is set to a number (not AUTO).
`setRightMargin`	Sets the right margin of the component as long as RIGHT MARGIN is set to a number (not AUTO).
`setTopMargin`	Sets the top margin of the component as long as TOP MARGIN is set to a number (not AUTO).
`setVisible`	Sets the visibility of the component based on the parameter value (`true` or `false`).

Table 8.16 Component Methods

Method	Description
setWidth	Sets the width of the component as long as WIDTH is set to a number (not AUTO).
showLoadingState	Show the loading state indicator.

Table 8.16 Component Methods (Cont.)

When you use visual components, you'll see that they all have these methods.

Button Component

The methods of the BUTTON component (Table 8.17) allow you to get information about the BUTTON component and change its state. Using a combination of .getEnabled and .setEnabled, for example, allows you to construct an if then else statement that allows the user to toggle the status of a BUTTON component.

Method	Description
getText	Gives the text that is displayed on the BUTTON component.
getTooltip	Returns the tooltip of the component.
isEnabled	Returns true when this component is enabled.
On Click	Executes the On Click script when the user clicks the BUTTON.
setEnabled	Sets the BUTTON to enabled when the value true is passed as a parameter, or sets it to disabled when false is passed as a parameter.
setText	Sets the text that is shown on the BUTTON component.
setTooltip	Sets the tooltip of the component.

Table 8.17 Button Component Methods

Chart Component

The CHART component methods (Table 8.18) allow you to manipulate the CHART component. You can set the kind of CHART component, the totals, and the swapping axis, as well as perform all kinds of other manipulations. One particularly interesting method is the .getSelectedMember method with which you can use a data point on the CHART component clicked by a user. For example, when a user clicks on a value in a graph, you can use this interaction to set a filter in a data

8 | Scripting for Interactivity

source. This is helpful when you want to present details about the selected value in a CROSSTAB component.

The script line to do this is the following:

```
DS_DETAIL.setFilter("0CALYEAR",
   GRAPH.getSelectedMembers("0CALYEAR"));
```

Method	Description
getChartType	Gives the name of the CHART component.
clearSelection	Removes the data selection from the CHART.
getAxisScalingMax	Return the highest value on an axis.
getAxisScalingMin	Return the lowest value on an axis.
getLegendPosition	Returns the position of the legend.
getSelectedMember	Gives you information about the selected data point. With the parameter dimension, you define the dimension value you want to see.
getSelected-Members	Gives you information about the selected data points. With the parameter dimension, you define the dimension values you want to see.
getStyle	Returns the chart style name.
isVisible	Shows the CHART component's visibility status.
On Select	Executes the On Select script that is defined in the properties of the CHART.
removeAxisScaling	Removes axis scaling if this was defined in the CHART properties.
setAxisScaling	Sets axis minimum and maximum values.
setChartType	Changes the CHART component type.
setDataSelection	Selects a subset of data to be shown in the CHART.
setLegendPosition	Specifies where the legend should be placed.
setStyle	Changes the CHART component style.
setVisible	Sets the CHART component's visibility.
showDataLabels	Turns data labels on or off.
showScaling-Factors	Shows the scaling factors on the axis and tooltip.

Table 8.18 Chart Component Methods

Method	Description
showTotals	Shows or hides totals and subtotals.
swapAxes	Swaps the axes as they appear in the data source for a different chart perspective.

Table 8.18 Chart Component Methods (Cont.)

Info Chart Component

The INFO CHART component is a new component that allows you to configure a chart in a more user-friendly way. Configuration is performed via the graphical modeler. The methods that you can use for scripting are the same as for the regular charts.

Geo Map Component

The GEO MAP component allows you to display different layers of geographical information on a map and allows users to drill down through these different layers to reveal data in a variety of ways. You can apply three different types of layers to your GEO MAP: shapes (polygons and multipolygons), points, and bubble charts.

You can use the methods described in Table 8.19 with the GEO MAP component.

Method	Description
centerMap	Positions the map in the center of a layer.
getCopyrightText	Returns copyright text of the basemap.
getSelectedLayer	Returns the layer of a map that is selected.
isLayerVisible	Turns the visibility on or off for the layer map.
setCopyrightText	Sets copyright text for the basemap.
setLayerVisible	Shows or hides a map layer.
setMapUrl	Specifies the basemap URL.
getSelectedMember	Returns the selected member.

Table 8.19 Geo Map Component Methods

Spreadsheet Component

This component is a spreadsheet in which data can be shown in tabular form. The user can also copy and paste data in this SPREADSHEET component. The common methods are the only methods that can be used for scripting.

Scorecard Component

A SCORECARD component can be used to plot different information using different visualizations in one component. This component can be useful, for instance, to create a visual overview of plan and actual values. The methods that can be used for this component are the common methods previously discussed.

Checkbox Component

The methods for the CHECKBOX component (Table 8.20) return information about the current status of the component as well as the value of the CHECKBOX (selected `true` or `false`). The CHECKBOX component script can also be useful to set the value of the CHECKBOX component based on the state of the application.

Method	Description
getText	Returns the text with the CHECKBOX component.
getTooltip	Returns the associated tooltip.
isChecked	Returns `true` if the CHECKBOX component is selected or `false` if the CHECKBOX component isn't selected.
isEnabled	Returns `true` if the CHECKBOX component is enabled.
isVisible	Returns `true` if the CHECKBOX component is visible.
On Click	Executes the `On Click` script that is defined in the properties of this component.
setChecked	Selects the CHECKBOX component when the parameter is set to `true`; otherwise, the CHECKBOX component isn't selected.
setEnabled	Sets the CHECKBOX component to enabled when the parameter is `true`; otherwise, it's disabled.
setText	Sets the CHECKBOX component text.

Table 8.20 Checkbox Component Methods

Method	Description
setTooltip	Configures a tooltip for this component.
setVisible	Shows the component when the parameter is true, but not when it's false.

Table 8.20 Checkbox Component Methods (Cont.)

Let's consider an example where you want to let the user know that the data (read from the InfoProvider) is up to date. In this case, you can insert a CHECKBOX component that is selected if the data was refreshed the previous night. You use the data source key date, which is set to today, and compare it to the last refresh date. If the dates are the same, then the CHECKBOX is selected, informing the user that everything is up to date. Additionally, you can use a CSS class assignment to create an alert when things aren't up to date. This logic can be setup by using the script in Listing 8.3 in the On Startup script of the application.

```
if (DS_THEMEREALESTATE.getInfo().lastDataUpdateMaximum == DS_
PRICEHISTORY.getInfo().keyDate) {
    CHECKBOX_1.setChecked(true);
    CHECKBOX_1.setCSSClass("NoAlert");
} else {
    CHECKBOX_1.setChecked(false);
    CHECKBOX_1.setCSSClass("Alert");
}
```

Listing 8.3 Using an if-else Statement to Check Values of a Checkbox

Checkbox Group Component

The CHECKBOX GROUP component serves as a group of checkboxes. Its methods (Table 8.21) can be used to create interaction for all checkboxes combined. For instance, when you want to dynamically create checkboxes for all values of a certain dimension in the data source, you can use the CHECKBOX GROUP component instead of individual checkboxes. The following piece of code creates a CHECKBOX GROUP with a checkbox for each individual month value in the data source (DS_1):

```
CHECKBOXGROUP_1.setItems(
    DS_1.getMemberList("0CALMONTH", MemberPresentation.INTERNAL_
KEY, MemberDisplay.TEXT, 24)
);
```

8 | Scripting for Interactivity

Method	Description
addItem	Adds a checkbox that can be checked/unchecked by the user.
getSelectedTexts	Returns the text of the items that is selected.
getSelectedValues	Returns the values of the selected checkbox items.
isEnabled	Return true when the specified component is enabled; otherwise, returns false.
removeAllItems	Removes all checkbox items.
removeItem	Removes a specific checkbox item.
setEnabled	Enables or disables the CHECKBOX GROUP component.
setItems	Creates a list of checkbox items.
setSelectedValues	Selects a specified set of items.
sort	Sorts items in alphabetical order.

Table 8.21 Checkbox Group Component Methods

Crosstab Component

As with the CHART component, the CROSSTAB component also has a .getSelectedMember method that returns information about the selected value in the CROSSTAB component (Table 8.22). The parameter of this method is the dimension about which you want to receive information. For example, if your CROSSTAB component has a dimension Month, and, based on the selected cell, you want to filter a data source, you use the following code:

```
DS_1.setFilter("Month",
  CROSSTAB_1.getSelectedMembers("Month"));
```

Method	Description
removeSelection	Removes the selection if a cell is selected.
getSelectedMember	Returns information about the selected members of a dimension.
getSelectedMembers	Returns information about the selected member of a dimension.
getSelection	Returns the selection that was made by the user.
isColumnResizingEnabled	Returns true if column resizing is enabled.

Table 8.22 Crosstab Component Methods

Method	Description
isConditional-FormattingVisible	Returns true if conditional formatting is activated.
isHierarchy-NavigationEnabled	Returns true if navigation among hierarchies is enabled.
isSortingEnabled	Returns true when sorting along the columns is enabled.
On Select	Executes the On Select script that is defined in the CROSSTAB component's properties.
removeSelection	Removes the current selection.
resetAllColumn-Widths	Sets the column sizing to AUTO for all columns.
resetColumnWidth	Sets the column sizing to AUTO for a specified column.
setColumn-ResizingEnabled	Enables column resizing.
setColumnWidth	Resizes a specific column to a specified width.
setConditional-FormattingVisible	Enables or disables conditional formatting in the CROSSTAB.
setDefaultColumn-Width	Specifies a default width for all the columns.
setHierarchy-NavigationEnabled	Enables the collapsing/expanding of hierarchies.
setSortingEnabled	Enables the sorting of columns.
setUnitsAndScal-ingFactorsDisplay	Specifies the display of units and scaling factors.

Table 8.22 Crosstab Component Methods (Cont.)

Date Field Component

The DATE FIELD component allows the user to select a date. Methods for this component deliver or set the date (Table 8.23).

Method	Description
getDate	Returns the date.
isEnabled	Returns true if the component is enabled.

Table 8.23 Date Field Component Methods

8 | Scripting for Interactivity

Method	Description
On Select	Executes the On Select script that is defined in the properties of this component.
setDate	Sets the date on the component.
setEnabled	Allows you to enable or disable the component.

Table 8.23 Date Field Component Methods (Cont.)

Dimension Filter, Filter Panel, and Filter Line Components

The methods in the DIMENSION FILTER and FILTER PANEL components (Table 8.24) retrieve information about the dimension and the filter. You can use this information to apply filters. Because the DIMENSION FILTER is a more generic component, it has a method, getDimensionName, to determine the dimension you're working in. This method isn't present in the FILTER PANEL component.

Method	Description
Cancel	Removes entered filters that haven't been submitted yet.
getDimensionKey	Gets the technical dimension key.
getDimensionName	Returns the name of the dimension (only with the DIMENSION FILTER component).
setDimension	Sets a specific dimension as a filter.
showFilterDialog	Opens a dialog window where filters can be applied.
Submit	Applies the filter values that have been entered.

Table 8.24 Dimension and Filter Panel Component Methods

Besides the FILTER PANEL and DIMENSION FILTER, there is a third component that can be used for filtering: the FILTER LINE component.

The FILTER LINE component offers the user a list of filters that are applied to the assigned data source. It behaves similarly to the FILTER PANEL component. With the FILTER LINE, the user can add, remove, view, and edit the dimensions and measures to which they can apply filters. When the user selects to add or edit a filter, the DIMENSION FILTER will appear. The filter on the selected dimension and member(s) is added to the row of filters in the FILTER LINE, and the filter is applied to your data source.

The FILTER LINE component has a method called `setTargetDataSources`. This method is used to specify a list of data sources on which this component should filter data. The FILTER LINE component also uses the common methods that are described earlier in this section.

Navigation Panel Component

Using the NAVIGATION PANEL component, you can easily change the drilldown of the data and see at a glance the navigation state of the data source at runtime. To change the drilldown, the user can drag and drop the dimensions from the list into the rows or columns area. The user can also rearrange the drilldown by dragging and moving dimensions from the rows into the columns area or vice versa. To remove dimensions from the drilldown, the user can drag a dimension and drop it anywhere in the application. The NAVIGATION PANEL component has one specific method: `setDimensions`. With this method, you can select which dimensions to include in the NAVIGATION PANEL.

Selection Components

The following selection components are used to select a value from a list of members:

- LIST BOX
- RADIO BUTTON GROUP
- DROPDOWN BOX

You may recall from Chapter 7 that these components are all part of the *basic components* category. *Selection components* (Table 8.25) are a subset of this category and are grouped together based on the fact that their methods allow you to pick a value from a set of values. In other words, the methods available with these components allow you to determine a number of possible selections and select a value from those selections. One of the main uses for this is to collect the selected value with the `.getSelectedValue` method and use this value as a parameter for other actions.

8 | Scripting for Interactivity

Method	Description
addItem	Adds an item as a selection option to this component.
getSelectedText	Returns the text of the item that was selected by the user.
getSelectedTexts	Returns the texts of multiple items that are selected by the user.
getSelectedValue	Returns the value of the item that was selected by the user.
getSelectedValues	Returns the values of multiple items that are selected by the user.
getTooltip	Returns the tooltip that was defined for this component.
isEnabled	Returns whether or not this component is enabled.
On Select	Executes the On Select script that was defined in the properties of this component.
removeAllItems	Removes all items from the item list that was defined for this component.
removeItem	Removes a specified item.
setEnabled	Enables or disables this component.
setItems	Adds a list of items to this component. Items that where manually defined before will be removed.
setSelectedValue	Selects a specific item from this component.
setSelectedValues	Selects multiple items from this component.
setTooltip	Sets the tooltip for this component.
Sort	Sorts the items in the list in alphabetical order.

Table 8.25 Selection Component Methods

Image Component

With the methods for the IMAGE component (Table 8.26), you can retrieve the file path of the images linked to the IMAGE component and set new images to the component. You can also view or set opacity.

Method	Description
getClickImage	Returns the path of the image file that is shown when clicked.
getHoverImage	Returns the path of the image file that is visible when the mouse hovers over the IMAGE component.

Table 8.26 Image Component Methods

Method	Description
getImage	Returns the path of the image file that is initially visible.
getOpacity	Returns the opacity value. 0 is fully transparent; 100 is fully visible.
getTooltip	Returns the tooltip for this component.
On Click	Executes the On Click script that was defined in the properties of this component.
setClickImage	Sets the image file to show when the IMAGE component is clicked.
setHoverImage	Sets the image file to show when the mouse hovers over the IMAGE component.
setImage	Sets the main image.
setOpacity	Sets the opacity of the image. 0 is fully transparent; 100 is fully visible.
setTooltip	Sets the tooltip of the component.

Table 8.26 Image Component Methods (Cont.)

Input Field Component

In the INPUT FIELD component methods (Table 8.27), the user can freely write a text. The INPUT FIELD methods can be used to set and retrieve the value and enable or disable the component.

Method	Description
getValue	Returns the value that is entered in the INPUT FIELD component.
getTooltip	Returns this components tooltip.
isEditable	Specifies whether or not this component can be edited.
isEnabled	Returns true if the component is enabled or, otherwise, false.
setEditable	Enables user input.
setEnabled	Sets the component to enabled or disabled.
setTooltip	Sets this components tooltip.
setValue	Sets the value of the INPUT FIELD component.

Table 8.27 Input Field Component Methods

Pagebook Component

The PAGEBOOK component is a container component that allows you to swipe or drag between pages. The methods in this component (Table 8.28) allow you to retrieve the current page or move to another page based on the name or index number of the page.

Methods	Description
getPageCount	Returns the number of pages this component has.
getSelectedPage	Returns the name of the currently selected page.
getSelected-PageIndex	Returns the index value of the selected page. If the first page is currently selected, then the index is 0.
setSelectedPage-ByName	Selects the page by passing the name of the page in the parameter.
On Select	Executes the On Select script that is defined in the properties of this component.
setSelected-PageIndex	Selects a specific page based on the input parameter specified.
setSelectedPage-ByName	Selects a specific page based on the name that is passed in a parameter.

Table 8.28 Pagebook Component Methods

Panel Component

The PANEL component is a basic container that helps you organize other components. The PANEL component has only the On Click method. A handler method allows you to run the script in a component from another component.

Popup Component

The POPUP component is a screen that shows at the top of the application. The methods (Table 8.29) are used for checking if it's visible and showing or hiding the component.

Methods	Description
hide	The POPUP component isn't visible anymore.
isShowing	Returns true if the POPUP component is currently visible.
show	The POPUP component is visible.

Table 8.29 Popup Component Methods

Tabstrip Component

The TABSTRIP component is a container component that allows you to navigate between pages. The methods (Table 8.30) allow you to retrieve the current page and go to another page.

Method	Description
getSelectedTab	Returns the name of the currently selected tab.
getSelectedTab-Index	Returns the index value of the selected tab. If the first page is currently selected, then the index is 0.
getTab	Returns the name or number of a specified tab.
On Select	Executes the On Select script that is defined in the properties of this component.
setSelectedTab	Selects a specific tab based on the input parameter.
setSelectedTab-Index	Selects a specific tab based on the index value that is passed a parameter.

Table 8.30 Tabstrip Component Methods

Text Component

The TEXT component shows text that is visible for the user. The methods (Table 8.31) can set the current text or look at the current text. Combined with the common layout methods described earlier in this section, the TEXT component is very useful for applying layout changes to an application based on interaction with the user.

Method	Description
getText	Returns the text currently in the TEXT component.
getTooltip	Return the tooltip that is defined for this component.
setText	Sets a string as text for this component.
setTooltip	Enables this components tooltip.

Table 8.31 Text Component Methods

We've now gone through the different methods that are used for the Design Studio components. The next four sections provide scripting examples for specific scenarios.

8.4 Example: Building Navigation Items

In this section, we'll set up navigation items so the user can move through the application. We'll be using different components in combination with scripts and CSS to reflect the choices the user makes in the application.

8.4.1 Menu Navigation

In the first example, we'll build a menu navigation. We'll use TEXT components in combination with CSS classes to build navigation buttons to navigate through the screens of a PAGEBOOK component in the application. Additionally, we'll highlight the last selected button so the user can see where he is in the application.

As you can see in Figure 8.18, BUTTON 3 is selected, and the third screen of the PAGEBOOK component is selected.

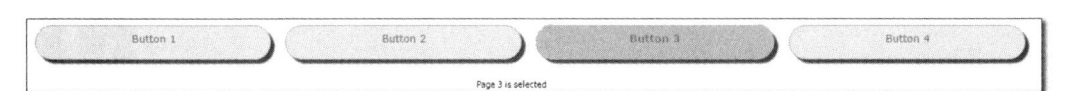

Figure 8.18 Menu with Four Buttons

To create such a menu structure, you first define two CSS classes. For this purpose, we made a CSS file that we've attached to the application's CUSTOM CSS property. In this file, we've defined two CSS classes: one for the selected button and one for the standard, unselected button.

In *Notepad.exe*, create a file with the extension *.css,* and insert the following lines as shown in Listing 8.4.

```
.button
{
border:1px solid #a1a1a1;
padding:5px 20px;
background:#dddddd;
border-radius:25px;
font-family:"Verdana", Arial, serif;
color:rgb(128,128,128);
box-shadow: 5px 5px 2px #666666;
font-size:120%;
font-weight:500;
text-align: center;
}

.buttonselected
{
border:1px solid #a1a1a1;
padding:5px 20px;
background:#cccccc;
border-radius:25px;
font-family:"Verdana", Arial, serif;
color:rgb(128,128,128);
box-shadow: 5px 5px 2px #666666;
font-size:120%;
font-weight:700;
text-align: center;
}
```
Listing 8.4 Buttons Created in CSS using Text Components

You can create a CSS file and use this file in your application. In the properties of the application, you can create a link to the file. After you've linked the application to the CSS file, you can use the classes that are defined in the CSS file on most of the components in Design Studio. In Figure 8.19, a TEXT component uses a CSS CLASS named `button` (you can see the definition of this class in the preceding code).

8 | Scripting for Interactivity

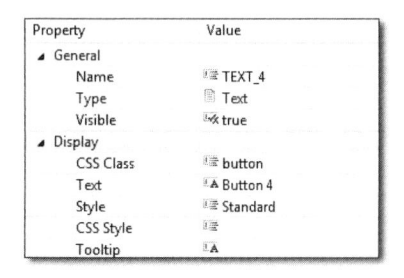

Figure 8.19 Properties of a Text Component

In Figure 8.18, shown earlier, you can see that with this CSS code, we've created rounded buttons with shadows.

We'll create a GLOBAL SCRIPT component that will do two things when a button is clicked:

- Set all the buttons to the CSS class `button`, and apply the CSS class `buttonselected` to the appropriate button (the one selected).
- Select the correct PAGE to be shown.

As shown in Figure 8.20, the script uses input parameters; the first one is an INTEGER, and the second one is a TEXT component.

```
1  // First set the CSS class button to all the buttons (TEXT components)
2  TEXT_1.setCSSClass("button");
3  TEXT_2.setCSSClass("button");
4  TEXT_3.setCSSClass("button");
5  TEXT_4.setCSSClass("button");
6
7  // Set the buttonselected CSS class for the button that is selected
8  button_num.setCSSClass("buttonselected");
9
10 // Select the correct page
11 PAGEBOOK_1.setSelectedPageIndex(index);
```

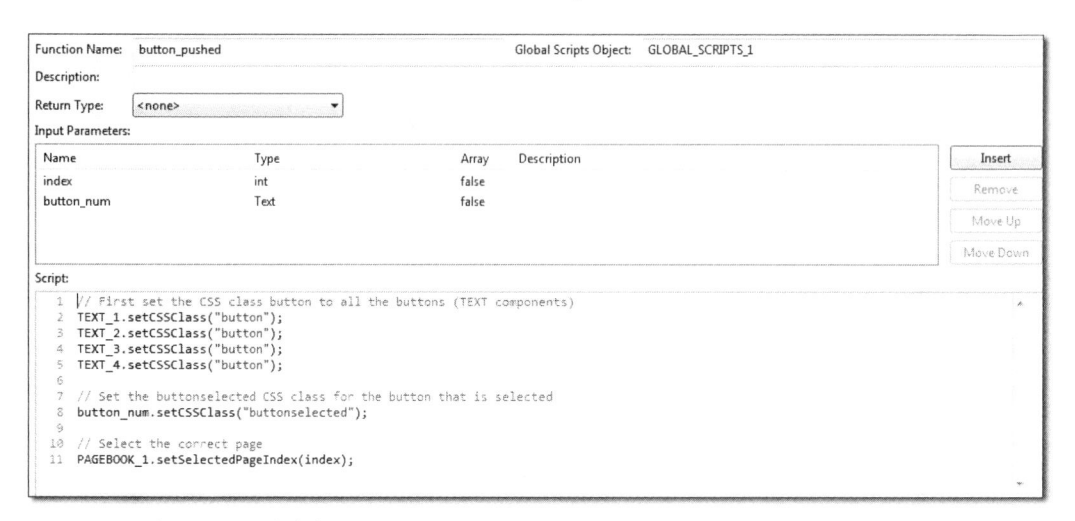

Figure 8.20 Global Script with Input Parameters

Add the code shown in Listing 8.5 to the script.

```
// First set the CSS class button to all the buttons (TEXT components)
TEXT_1.setCSSClass("button");
TEXT_2.setCSSClass("button");
TEXT_3.setCSSClass("button");
TEXT_4.setCSSClass("button");

// Set the buttonselected CSS class for the button that is selected
button_num.setCSSClass("buttonselected");

// Select the correct page
PAGEBOOK_1.setSelectedPageIndex(index);
```
Listing 8.5 Use of Script to Apply a CSS Class to a Component

When using a GLOBAL SCRIPT component, you can reuse scripts that are (almost) similar. Without the GLOBAL SCRIPT, you would have to add this code to all the buttons, replacing the selected button and the PAGEBOOKINDEX.

The advantage of using a GLOBAL SCRIPT is that when you want to edit the code, you don't have to edit the code in all the buttons but simply in the GLOBAL SCRIPT alone.

Now, all you have to do is add the following code to each button to execute the GLOBAL SCRIPT:

`GLOBAL_SCRIPTS_1.button_pushed(0, TEXT_1);`

The number 0 indicates that PAGEINDEX 0, which is the first page, must be selected. For BUTTON 2, change the index to 1; for BUTTON 3, change the index to 2; and for the last button, change the index to 3.

The TEXT_1 component in the script is the second parameter that is passed to the GLOBAL SCRIPT. The parameter that is passed to the GLOBAL SCRIPT will be assigned CSS class buttonselected.

Because you want to pass the TEXT component from where the GLOBAL SCRIPT component is called, you can use the term this instead of the name of the TEXT component. The code will look like this:

`GLOBAL_SCRIPTS_1.button_pushed(0, this);`

8.4.2 Popup Navigation

In this section, we'll build a popup menu where a user can change the behavior of the application. In the popup menu, the user will be able to select the currency, the unit of measure, and the color settings of the application. In the script, we'll use BEx variables to enforce the currency and unit of measure settings for the data sources. For the color settings, we'll use CSS classes that we assign based on the user's choice. As an additional technique, we'll use an extra component as a placeholder for the script to assign a new CSS class to all the components. Other components will then call this extra component by using the event handler method.

As you see in Figure 8.21, the popup screen allows you to set the currency, the measurement unit, and a color scheme for the application. Because resetting all the CSS classes is a lot of work, we put all the scripting in a GLOBAL SCRIPT component that is added only for holding the script. Additionally, we used a global variable to store the value of the currently selected color scheme so we can reuse that value for any color scheme selected.

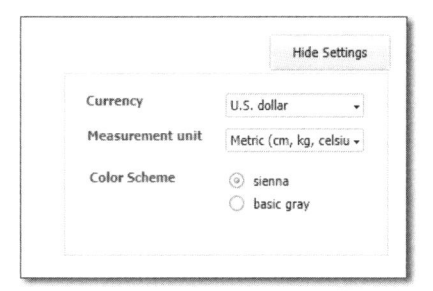

Figure 8.21 Popup Screen

First, we want to use a BUTTON component to toggle the POPUP component. If the POPUP is hidden, the BUTTON component should make it visible, and when the POPUP is visible, clicking the BUTTON component should hide the POPUP.

In the script for the BUTTON component, add the code shown in Listing 8.6.

```
if (POPUP_1.isShowing()) {
    BUTTON_1.setText("Show Settings");
    POPUP_1.hide();
} else {
    BUTTON_1.setText("Hide Settings");
    POPUP_1.show();
}
```

Listing 8.6 if-else Script to Show or Hide the Popup Screen

This code looks at the POPUP component and performs an action based on its current state.

For the currency and unit of measure setting, we're going to use BEx variables that we'll set based on the user's choice. You have the option to merge BEx variables. This means that when two or more data sources require the same variable to filled, when merging is enabled, the user will only have to fill the variable value once. When this is done, setting a value for a BEx variable will automatically lead to a reload of all the BEx queries that use that variable. When BEx variables aren't merged, you can choose to reload specific data sources instead of all.

In the first DROPDOWN BOX component, we put the following code in the `On Select` handler. When the user changes the selected value, the new selected value will be used to change the BEx variable `ZCURVAL`, which is used for selecting the currency.

```
APPLICATION.setVariableValue("ZCURRVAL", DROPDOWN_1.getSelectedValue());
```

When we want to reload a specific data source instead of all the data sources that use the variable `ZCURVAL`, we can use the following script, where `DS_1` is the data source that we want to reload:

```
DS_1.setVariableValue("ZCURVAL", DROPDOWN_1.getSelectedValue());
```

In the second DROPDOWN BOX component, a similar script code will change the BEx variable `ZMEASVAL`. This will change the unit of measure.

```
APPLICATION.setVariableValue("ZMEASVAL", DROPDOWN_2.getSelectedValue());
```

In the RADIO BUTTON GROUP component, we can select a color scheme for the application. In this example, we have two settings: sienna and basic gray.

In the CSS file we've attached to the application property CUSTOM CSS, two classes are defined as shown in Listing 8.7 and Listing 8.8.

```
.sienna
{
background-color:#A0522D;
border:4px solid #a1a1a1;
border-radius:25px;
}
```

Listing 8.7 Class 1

```
.basicgray
{
background-color:#D3D3D3;
```

```
border:4px solid #a1a1a1;
border-radius:25px;
}
```
Listing 8.8 Class 2

In the APPLICATION component, we've defined a global variable, `ColorScheme`, as a string with the initial value `sienna`.

When the application starts, the CSS classes of all components should be set to the initial setting. When the user alters the value of the color scheme in the POPUP component, the CSS classes should be set to reflect that choice.

Because setting the CSS class for all components calls for a lot of code, we don't want to write and maintain all those lines in two places. In the application's `On Startup` handler, we see only this code:

`GLOBAL_SCRIPT.setScheme();`

When the RADIO BUTTON GROUP component value changes, we only see two lines of code: the first resets the value of the global variable, and the second addresses the `colorscheme` setter:

```
colorscheme = RADIOBUTTONGROUP_1.getSelectedValue();
GLOBAL_SCRIPT.setScheme();
```

The component with the name `GLOBAL_SCRIPT.setScheme` is a GLOBAL SCRIPT component that is used to hold the script for changing the CSS script. It will use the variable value to set all the CSS values.

Because there are different CSS classes for buttons, texts, and so on, concatenation is used to address the different types of classes (Listing 8.9).

```
// Sets all the components' CSS classes to the desired
// color scheme
//Buttons
BUTTON_1.setCSSClass(ColorScheme + "_button");
BUTTON_2.setCSSClass(ColorScheme + "_button");
BUTTON_3.setCSSClass(ColorScheme + "_button");
BUTTON_4.setCSSClass(ColorScheme + "_button");
BUTTON_5.setCSSClass(ColorScheme + "_button");

//Text boxes
BUTTON_1.setCSSClass(ColorScheme + "_text");
BUTTON_2.setCSSClass(ColorScheme + "_text");
BUTTON_3.setCSSClass(ColorScheme + "_text");
```

```
BUTTON_4.setCSSClass(ColorScheme + "_text");
BUTTON_5.setCSSClass(ColorScheme + "_text");
```
Listing 8.9 Script to Select Specific CSS Classes

By using the variable, we ensure that we only have to put this code in one place. In addition, if there should be a third color scheme choice, this can be easily implemented by adding classes to the CSS file and adding another selection option to the RADIO BUTTON GROUP component.

8.4.3 Navigating between Applications

In this third navigation example, we'll move outside the application. Additionally, we'll make it possible to pass parameter values from outside the application. These parameters will influence the settings we've chosen in the settings screen in Figure 8.22. We'll also look at how to use global variables to make things easier for ourselves.

When you want an application to accept the parameter values from outside the application, you first have to define global variables. As you can see in Figure 8.22, we now have three additional variables in our example, but these are set as URL parameters.

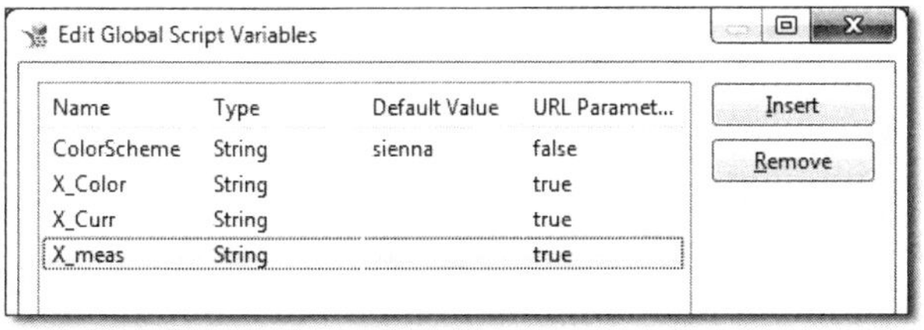

Figure 8.22 Global Script Variables

In our On Startup code, we'll use these global variables to set the color scheme and our two query variables (Listing 8.10).

```
APPLICATION.setVariableValue("ZCURRVAL", X_Curr);
APPLICATION.setVariableValue("Z_MEASVAL", X_meas);
ColorScheme = X_Color;

GLOBAL_SCRIPT.setScheme();
```
Listing 8.10 Populate Variables

As you can see, the code uses the parameter values to set the variable values on the application itself. The CSS classes will then be set with the value passed in the parameter. Our application is now able to use the parameters to change the initial settings.

We'll now look at what you need to do in another application—let's refer to it as App2—to open our initial application (App1) and pass the parameter values. We'll assume that App2 has the same popup screen to specify the setting values.

To start App1, App2 has to open a new window with the URL of App1. This URL consists of three parts: the general server address, the unique CUID of the application, and the parameters.

For easier maintenance, we'll first set up variables for the server name and for the application CUID in App2. In Figure 8.23, you can see that we store every value in a global variable for flexibility purposes and ease of maintenance. Based on selections in the application, we now can link to several other applications. As you'll see later, the code to open the application is easily readable with the use of these global variables.

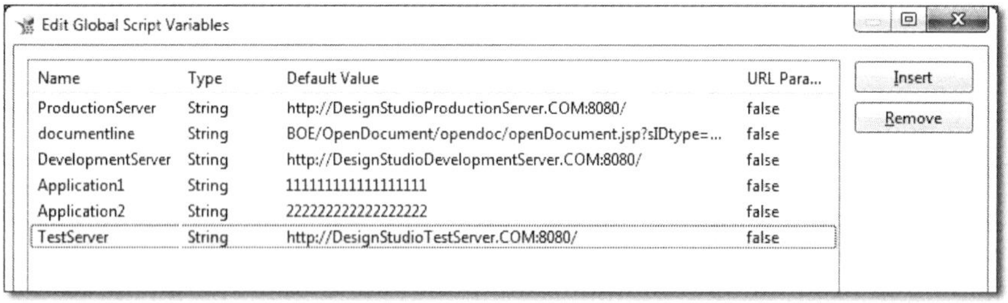

Figure 8.23 URL Values Stored in Global Variables

Again, we can use a GLOBAL SCRIPT component in App2 with the script in Listing 8.11.

```
APPLICATION.openNewWindow(ProductionServer + documentline
  + Application1 +
    "&X_Curr=" + DROPDOWN_1.getSelectedValue() +
    "&X_meas=" + DROPDOWN_2.getSelectedValue() +
    "&X_color=" + RADIOBUTTONGROUP_1.getSelectedValue()
);
```

Listing 8.11 Open a New Document URL Defined in the Script

This code will result in opening App1 with the settings passed in the parameters.

8.5 Example: Manipulating Data Output

In this section, we'll demonstrate the use of some scripts that relate to manipulating the output of data in Design Studio—ranging from simple scripts to present data, to more complex scripts such as looping through arrays and using `if` statements. We'll also take a look at how some data binding features work by using a script.

8.5.1 Presenting Data in Text Components

In this example, we'll loop through the data in a data source to find the oldest and the youngest employee. We'll also calculate the average age of all employees.

Figure 8.24 shows a live preview of the data in our data source. The data consists of six employees, along with his or her age. The idea is that we'll use a `loop` statement to loop through the data along with some `if` and `else` statements to find the minimum and maximum age.

Live Preview	
Employee	Average Age
Antonio Carlos Jobim	64.00
Maria Rita	39.00
Alexandre Casarini	40.00
Beth Carvalho	50.00
Elis Regina	46.00
Caetano Veloso	65.00

Figure 8.24 Data Source

For this simple application, we use one SPREADSHEET component to display the data in the data source and three TEXT components to display information such as the oldest employee, the youngest employee, and the average employee age. The code will be executed when the application starts up (`On Startup` script). Take a look at the script in Listing 8.12.

```
// First, an array is defined containing the members in the
// Employee dimension. The "100" is a maximum number that is a
// requirement for this method.
var array = DS_1.getMembers("0EMPLOYEE", 100);
// Next we define some local variables, like the minimum and
// maximum age, the total of all the ages, and the average.
// Initially, all these values are set to 0.0 (the decimal indicates
// that this variable is of type float).
```

8 | Scripting for Interactivity

```
// We also define variables for the oldest and youngest employee.
// These are of type String, which you can see by the "";.
// We also define a counter, which is actually the same as the
// size of the array. The counter is used to calculate the average
// value (total/counter).
var total = 0.0;
var min_age = 0.0;
var max_age = 0.0;
var min_empl = "";
var max_empl = "";
var average = 0.0;
var counter = 0;

// Loop through the array and calculate the
// total, min, max, and average

array.forEach(function(element, index) {
// Store the employee name in a variable called var employee
  var employee = element.text;
  var employee_number = element.internalKey;
// Use a variable called age to store the value that is found using
// the getDataAsString method. This method selects a data cell in
// the data source based on the input parameters (GUID of the key
// figure and employee number).
  var age = DS_1.getDataAsString("20GPGXFW7KZGU0HEG1WGGNFGM", {
      "0EMPLOYEE": employee_number
  });
// Convert the age string to a float
  var age_Int = Convert.stringToFloatUsingLocale(age);
// The previously defined variables get the value of the first
// employee in the list
  if (index == 0)
  {
      min_age = age_Int;
      min_empl = employee;
      max_age = age_Int;
      max_empl = employee;
  }
  Else
// In the if statement, the minimum and maximum age values are
  {
      if (age_Int <= min_age)
      {
          min_age = age_Int;
          min_empl = employee;
      }
      if (age_Int >= max_age)
      {
          max_age = age_Int;
          max_empl = employee;
```

```
      }
   }
// Calculate the sum of all employee ages, and increase the counter
// each time the loop passes through a line
   total = total + age_Int;
   counter = counter + 1;
});

// Calculate the average age
average = total/counter;
// Convert the float number to a string with 2 decimal places,
// indicated by the 0.00
var av_text = Convert.floatToString(average,"0.00");

// Set the text components
TEXT_1.setText("Oldest employee: "+max_empl+" - "+ max_age + " years");
TEXT_2.setText("Youngest employee: "+min_empl+" - "+ min_age +
               " years");
TEXT_3.setText("Average age: "+av_text+" years");
```
Listing 8.12 Start Up Script to Calculate Values and Apply These Values to Text Components

The results of this script are shown in Figure 8.25.

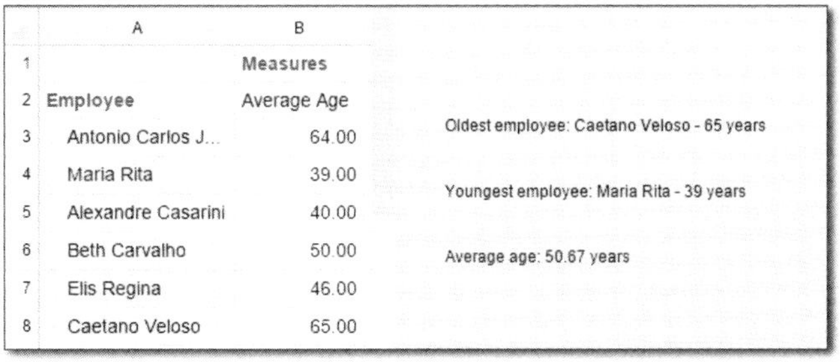

Figure 8.25 Application Output

8.5.2 Preparing Data for Variable Input

In some cases, you may need to fill a variable value dynamically during the execution of an application. Consider the following example where we have a BEx query that contains a data variable. The data in our application must always be filtered with the previous period. This period must be calculated when the application is executed and will be passed to the BEx query.

In Figure 8.26, you see that the dataset contains data about the number of male and female employees for multiple years. The source of this data is a BEx query containing a variable called VAR_0CALMONTH that is used to filter the data when the application starts up.

		Measures
Cal. year / month	Gender	Number of Employ...
01.2000	Fem...	6
	Male	28
02.2000	Fem...	6
	Male	28
03.2000	Fem...	6
	Male	29
04.2000	Fem...	6
	Male	30
05.2000	Fem...	7
	Male	30
06.2000	Fem...	7
	Male	32

Figure 8.26 Initial View of the Data

In the On Startup script of the application, we apply the simple script shown in Listing 8.13. First, today's date is obtained, and then the year and the month are extracted from this date. We want to filter on the previous month, so we extract one month from today's date, keeping in mind that when you're in January, you have to go back to December in the previous year.

```
// Store today's date in a variable called today
// By using the dateNowInternalFormat method, we make sure the date is
// stored in format: YYYYMMDD
var today = APPLICATION.getInfo().dateNowInternalFormat;

// Based on the variable today, create 2 new variables, month and year
// year is a substring of today: starting at position 0 to 4
var year = Convert.subString(today, 0,4);

// month is also a substring of today, starting at position 4 to 6
var month = Convert.subString(today, 4,6);

// Convert month and year from String to Integers so that they
// can be used in calculations
var year_Int = Convert.stringToInt(year);
var month_Int = Convert.stringToInt(month);
```

```
// Calculate the previous period: month = month - 1
// If that leads to month being 0, then set month to 12 and year
// to year - 1
month_Int = month_Int - 1;
if (month_Int == 0)
{
    month_Int = 12;
    year_Int = year_Int - 1;
}
// When month is less than 10, place a 0 before it
if (month_Int < 10)
{
    month = "0"+month_Int;
}
else
{
    //Use "" + an integer to convert an Integer into a String
    month = ""+month_Int;
}
year = ""+year_Int;

// Give the BEx variable called "VAR_
OCALMONTH" the value that you just calculated
DS_1.setVariableValueExt("VAR_OCALMONTH", month+"."+year);
```

Listing 8.13 Fill a BEx Variable Using Calculations Done in Script

As displayed in Figure 8.27, only one period is selected and shown in the output of this application.

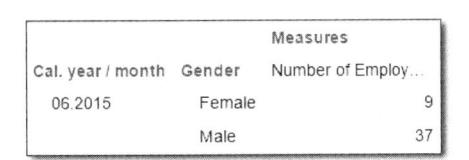

		Measures
Cal. year / month	Gender	Number of Employ...
06.2015	Female	9
	Male	37

Figure 8.27 Data after Applying the BEx Variable Filter

8.5.3 Data Binding

You can use the data binding option in the properties of components such as the DROPDOWN BOX or LIST BOX to bind dimension members of a data source to that specific component. Sometimes, however, it's useful to use a script to bind the dimension members instead of the data binding option. Let's look at an example where we'll use both the data binding option and the data binding script in an application.

In this example application, we'll use two large BEx queries as data sources in Design Studio. We'll use the default names, DS_1 and DS_2. For performance reasons, we'll only execute DS_1 when the application starts up. The application will show a LIST BOX on the screen, where the user can make a period selection. When the user makes a period selection, the second data source (DS_2) will be loaded, and a BEx variable will be used to filter the data. After this is done, a new LIST BOX component will be filled with the active employees in the selected period.

Let's start by filling the first LIST BOX by using the data binding option. In the properties of the first LIST BOX, select the + sign in the BINDING column, as shown in Figure 8.28.

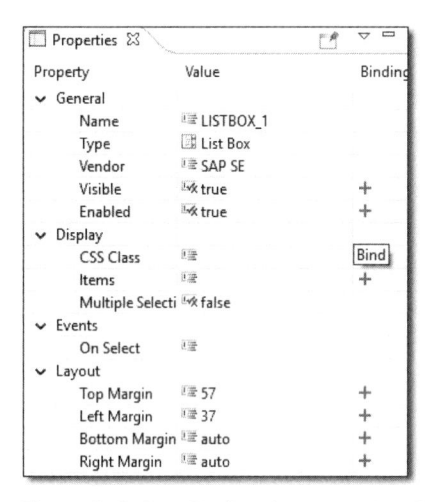

Figure 8.28 Data Binding Option in a List Box Component

New options will become available in the properties of this component. In the DATA SOURCE field, specify that DS_1 needs to be used. Also, select 0CALMONTH as a dimension, and choose to display the key of this dimension. The properties should look like Figure 8.29.

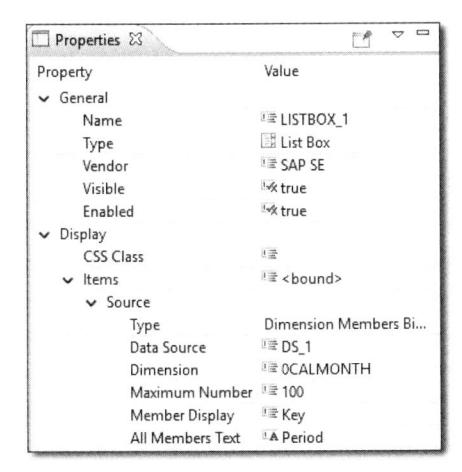

Figure 8.29 Data Bound to the 0CALMONTH Dimension in Data Source DS_1

The next step is to specify that DS_2 can only be loaded in a script. In Figure 8.30, you can see that the LOAD IN SCRIPT property of the DS_2 is set to TRUE.

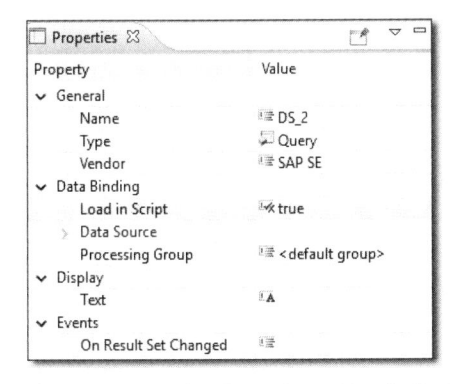

Figure 8.30 Load in Script Set to True in the Data Source

Now, add a second LIST BOX component on the screen. This time we won't use the data binding option in the properties. Instead, we'll use the `On Select` script in the first LIST BOX to populate the second LIST BOX.

Figure 8.31 shows what the application looks like at this point. You can see that the first LIST BOX is filled with some period values from DS_1.

Figure 8.31 Output When Application Starts Up

When the user selects a value from the first LIST BOX, the script shown in Listing 8.14 will be executed (the On Select script in the first LIST BOX) to load and filter DS_2 and populate the second LIST BOX component with the employee dimension from DS_2:

```
// Get user selection
var value = LISTBOX_1.getSelectedValue();
// Load new query. If the filter is applied again, the query
// doesn't have to be loaded again.
if (DS_2.isInitialized()==false)
{
    DS_2.loadDataSource();
}
//Set BEx variable
DS_2.setVariableValue("VAR_0CALMONTH", value);
// Fill the new dropdownbox with employees
LISTBOX_2.setItems(DS_2.getMemberList("0EMPLOYEE",
  MemberPresentation.INTERNAL_KEY, MemberDisplay.TEXT, 250,
  "Employee"));
```
Listing 8.14 Populating a List Box Based on the Value Selected by the User in Another List Box

The output after a period selection has been made should look like Figure 8.32.

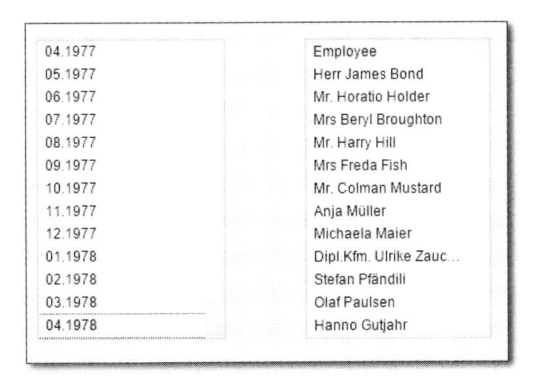

04.1977	Employee
05.1977	Herr James Bond
06.1977	Mr. Horatio Holder
07.1977	Mrs Beryl Broughton
08.1977	Mr. Harry Hill
09.1977	Mrs Freda Fish
10.1977	Mr. Colman Mustard
11.1977	Anja Müller
12.1977	Michaela Maier
01.1978	Dipl.Kfm. Ulrike Zauc…
02.1978	Stefan Pfändili
03.1978	Olaf Paulsen
04.1978	Hanno Gutjahr

Figure 8.32 Output after a Filter Value Is Selected

8.5.4 Changing the Chart View

In the following examples, we'll take a look at how you can use scripting in Design Studio to change the view of data that is presented in a chart.

Let's start with an application that shows a group of checkboxes and a CHART component. To populate the checkbox with all available measure in the data source, you use the data binding option in the properties of this component, as shown in Figure 8.33.

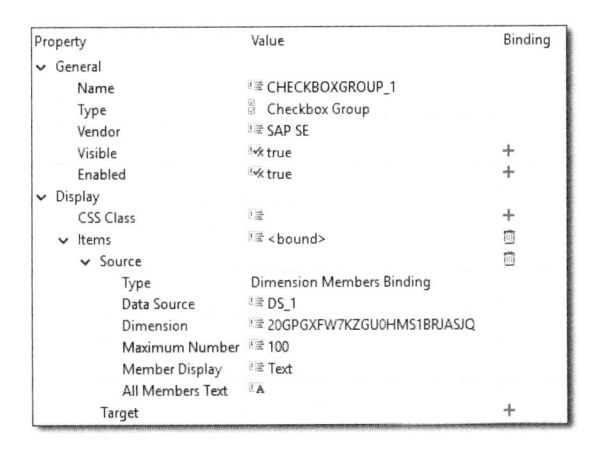

Property	Value	Binding
∨ General		
Name	CHECKBOXGROUP_1	
Type	Checkbox Group	
Vendor	SAP SE	
Visible	true	+
Enabled	true	+
∨ Display		
CSS Class		+
∨ Items	\<bound\>	🗓
∨ Source		🗓
Type	Dimension Members Binding	
Data Source	DS_1	
Dimension	20GPGXFW7KZGU0HMS1BRJASJQ	
Maximum Number	100	
Member Display	Text	
All Members Text	A	
Target		+

Figure 8.33 Checkbox Group Properties

After you've set up data binding, the CHECKBOX GROUP component is automatically populated with all the available measures in the data source. Next, when a user selects one or more measures in the CHECKBOX GROUP component, the corresponding measure is shown in the chart. To achieve this, the code in Listing 8.15 can be used in the ON SELECT property of the CHECKBOX GROUP component.

```
// Store all the selected values (keys) in an array
var array = CHECKBOXGROUP_1.getSelectedValues();
// Use the array as input parameter for the setDataSelection
// method on the chart
CHART_1.setDataSelection({
    "(MEASURES_DIMENSION)": array
});
```
Listing 8.15 Using the Data Selection Method

Each time a checkbox is selected or removed, the chart will be updated (Figure 8.34).

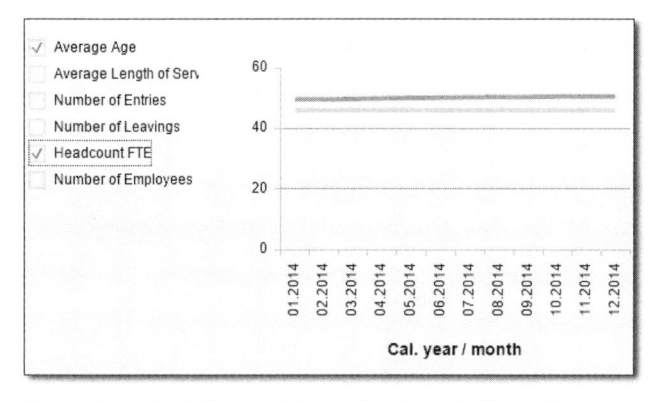

Figure 8.34 Chart Changes When a Checkbox Is Checked

Now let's extend this example a bit by adding a button to the application. Initially, the chart shows the month of the year on the X-axis. This is defined in the data source, where the dimension `0CALMONTH` is used in the rows of the data source.

The button in the application initially gets the text "Quarter view" (Figure 8.35) to indicate that the user can click this button to change the view to quarterly instead of monthly.

Example: Manipulating Data Output | 8.5

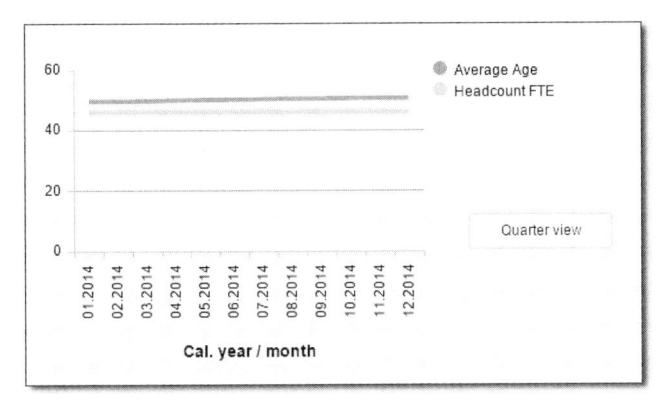

Figure 8.35 Monthly View of the Data

When the user clicks on the QUARTER VIEW button, a couple of things happen. First, the X-axis changes from showing months to showing quarters. Second, the chart changes from a line chart to a bar chart. And last, the text in the button changes from "Quarter view" to "Month view". The result is shown in Figure 8.36. When the user clicks on the button again, the chart changes back to its original state. To achieve all these tasks, use the script shown in Listing 8.16.

```
// Check what the text in the button is to determine what to do
// If "Quarter view" is pressed, switch from months to quarters,
// use a Bar chart, and change the text in the button to "Month view"
if (BUTTON_1.getText()== "Quarter view")
{
    DS_1.removeDimension("0CALMONTH");
    DS_1.moveDimensionToRows("0CALQUARTER");
    CHART_1.setChartType(ChartType.VERTICAL_BAR);
    BUTTON_1.setText("Month view");
}
// When "Month view" is pressed, restore the chart to its
// original state
else
{
    DS_1.removeDimension("0CALQUARTER");
    DS_1.moveDimensionToRows("0CALMONTH");
    CHART_1.setChartType(ChartType.LINE);
    BUTTON_1.setText("Quarter view");
}
```
Listing 8.16 Changing the View of a Data Source Using Scripts

8 | Scripting for Interactivity

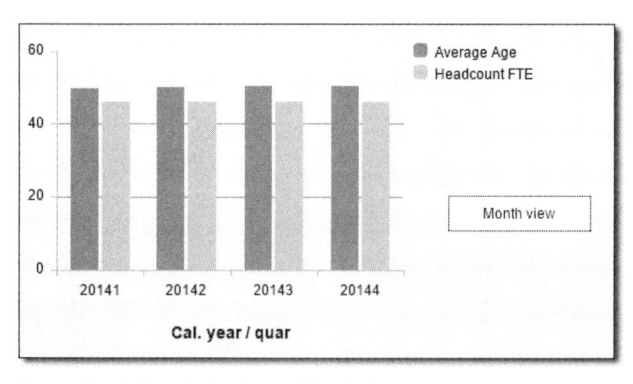

Figure 8.36 Quarterly View of the Data

8.6 Example: Building a Scorecard

In this section, we'll build a scorecard. In a scorecard, a graphical element indicates whether the value is satisfactory, good, or needs improvement. In Figure 8.37, a weather scorecard has been built with five levels of alerts. In the table, the precipitation amount per day is shown for a week. Based on the amount of rain during the day, an alert level is set and shown in the form of a circle. Black means no rain, while white means a lot of rain, with varying shades of gray in between.

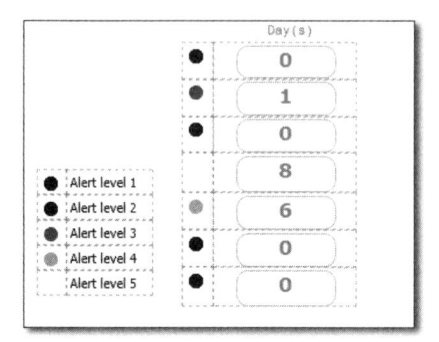

Figure 8.37 Scorecard Application

For this setup, we need a query that has exceptions defined as a data source. In an SAP BW BEx query, you can assign exception values and thus categorize the results. In Figure 8.38, you see the exceptions that have been defined in this example. These are the rules that determine which result leads to which indicator.

The layout that is applied based on this outcome is defined in the Design Studio application.

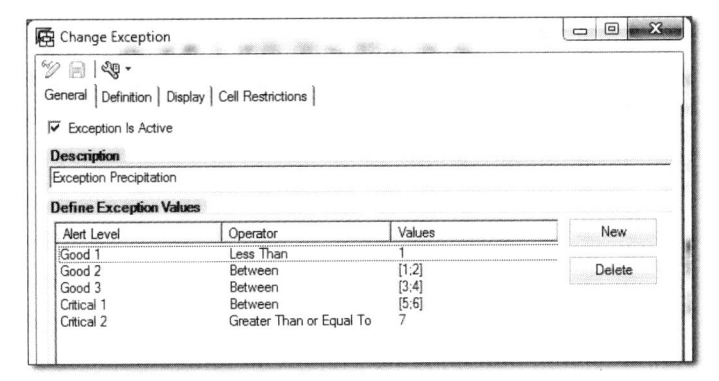

Figure 8.38 BEx Query Exception

In the application's `On Startup` handler, we'll define the code to set the values on the right side of the table in Figure 8.37, and use the exception values that we receive from the data source to apply the appropriate layout to the indicators.

First, we set the layout. We've uploaded a CSS file and assigned this to the application's CUSTOM CSS property with five CSS classes. The classes are named `alert1` through `alert5`.

We use the CSS code in Listing 8.17.

```
.alert1
{
 border:1px solid;
 border-color:#000000;
 border-radius:25px;
 background-color:#000000;
}
.alert2
{
 border:1px solid;
 border-color:#333333;
 border-radius:25px;
 background-color:#333333;
}
.alert3
{
 border:1px solid;
 border-color:#666666;
```

```
  border-radius:25px;
  background-color:#666666;
}

.alert4
{
  border:1px solid;
  border-color:#999999;
  border-radius:25px;
  background-color:#999999;
}
.alert5
{
  border:1px solid;
  border-color:#E6E6E6;
  border-radius:25px;
  background-color:#E6E6E6;
}
.alert5
{
  border:1px solid;
  border-color:#E6E6E6;
  border-radius:25px;
  background-color:#FFFFFF;
}
```

Listing 8.17 CSS Code to Define Different Alert Levels

We use five Text Box components in the application layout, which we'll apply to each one of the CSS classes. The size of the Text components is set to 10 × 10 in the Properties view. Combined with the `border-radius` property, this transforms the Text components into circles. Each class has a different background color, going from white through several shades of gray to black.

In the application's `On Startup` handler, we set the value of the Text component and then set the layout of the indicator. We have seven indicators and seven values. For each set of indicators and values, we apply the same steps.

First, we set the value of the Text component using the `.getdata` method from the data source. In this example, we take the precipitation amount of one day. The measure in the code is displayed as a CUID. Use Ctrl+Space on the measure parameter, and you'll see a list of available measures:

```
VALUE_1.setText(DS_PRECIPITATION.getDataAsString("4SXP85F39
  VXDKO4D5EMHYMBPF", {"0CALDAY": "19910316" }));
```

Then we set the CSS class of the indicator TEXT component using the `get Conditional FormatValueExt` method. We use a global variable `AlertCSS` to set the first part of the class. The global variable is a string and is assigned the value `alert`. We then concatenate this value with the value returned from the data source.

```
AlertValue = DS_PRECIPITATION.getConditionalFormatValueExt("4S
    XP85F39VXDKO4D5EMHYMBPF", {"0CALDAY": "19910316"});
INDICATOR_1.setCSSClass(AlertCSS + AlertValue);
```

Using the global variable gives us a little bit of extra flexibility. In one of our other examples, we showed a way to change a color scheme based on user choices. Using a global variable allows us to offer a similar choice. For example, by adding `alertcolor` classes to the CSS file and setting the global variable to `alertcolor`, you can switch to a different set of alerts.

> **Variable Usage for Flexibility**
>
> By having one variable for the name and another for the number, you can set up lots of layouts that can be applied dynamically. If the variable `LayoutClass` has the value `Class1_`, and the variable `LayoutLevel` has the value 1, you can concatenate these to assign the CSS class `Class1_1` to a component in the application. By altering `LayoutClass` and `LayoutLevel`, you can have as many classes and levels as you like.

8.7 Example: Building an OLAP Application

In this section, we'll create an Online Analytical Processing (OLAP) application just like SAP BusinessObjects Analysis, edition for OLAP that we know from the SAP BusinessObjects BI 4.x platform. The user will be able to perform tasks such as changing the drilldown of the data by dragging and dropping dimensions and measures into rows and columns, showing a graphical representation of the data as well as a tabular representation, choosing which data source to use in the application, and saving a view of the navigation state as a bookmark.

8.7.1 Initial Setup

Although it might sound like a lot of work to set up all the features mentioned in the introduction of this section, the NAVIGATION PANEL actually does most of the work for you. First, you'll use a BEx query as a data source and use the default

8 | Scripting for Interactivity

name (DS_1) as reference. Then, you'll remove the connection to the BEx query and give users the option to select their own query.

Let's start by adding a CROSSTAB component and NAVIGATION PANEL so that you can see the output on screen (Figure 8.39).

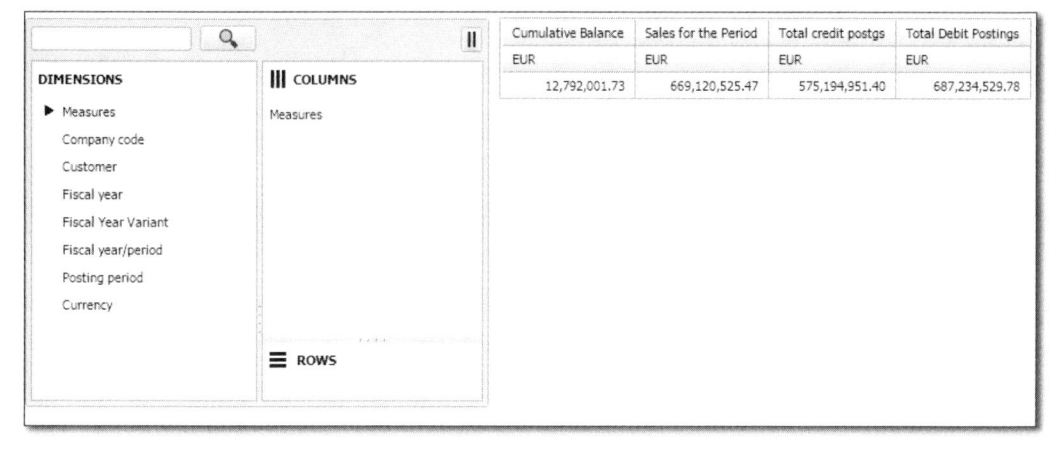

Figure 8.39 Crosstab and Navigation Panels

Follow these steps:

1. Add a NAVIGATION PANEL to the canvas.
2. Set the TOP MARGIN to 120.
3. Set the LEFT MARGIN to 10.
4. Set the BOTTOM and RIGHT MARGIN to AUTO.
5. Set the WIDTH to 400.
6. Set the HEIGHT to 500.
7. Add DS_1 as DATA SOURCE in the DATA BINDING part of the properties.
8. Set the PAUSE REFRESH setting to FALSE. This ensures that the data is automatically refreshed when the user alters the view of the rows or columns.
9. Add a PAGEBOOK component next to the NAVIGATION PANEL.
10. Add a PAGEBOOK component with two pages. PAGE_1 will be used to display data in a CROSSTAB, and PAGE_2 will be used to display data graphically.

11. Set the TOP MARGIN to 120.
12. Set the LEFT MARGIN to 420.
13. Set the BOTTOM and RIGHT MARGIN to AUTO.
14. Set the WIDTH to 700.
15. Set the HEIGHT to 500.
16. Add a CROSSTAB component on PAGE_1 of the PAGEBOOK.
17. Set the TOP MARGIN, LEFT MARGIN, BOTTOM MARGIN, and RIGHT MARGIN to 0.
18. Set the width and height to AUTO.
19. Use DS_1 as DATA SOURCE.
20. The first part of the application is now done. Figure 8.40 shows the output of the application when a dimension is dragged into the rows.

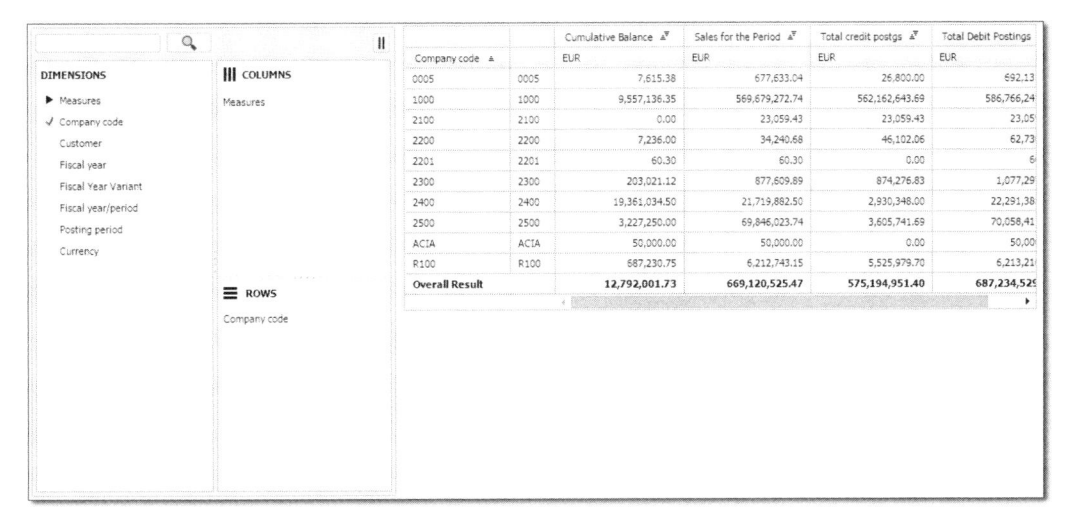

Figure 8.40 Application with Dimension in the Rows

You can filter measures and dimensions during runtime by right-clicking on the appropriate object and selecting the FILTER MEMBERS option. Right-clicking on an object also gives you some other options to change the presentation of the output, such as displaying the dimension text or key (or both), showing or hiding totals, and adding attributes to your table (Figure 8.41).

When FILTER MEMBERS is chosen, a FILTER PANEL component opens with all the possible filter values (Figure 8.42).

8 | Scripting for Interactivity

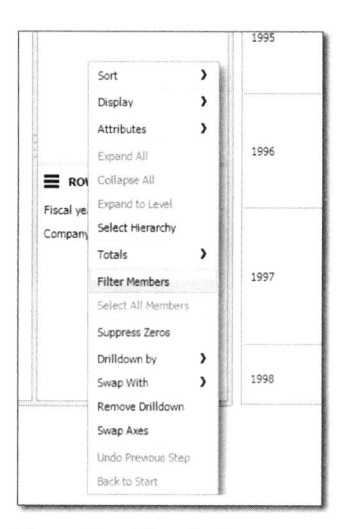

Figure 8.41 Filter Options

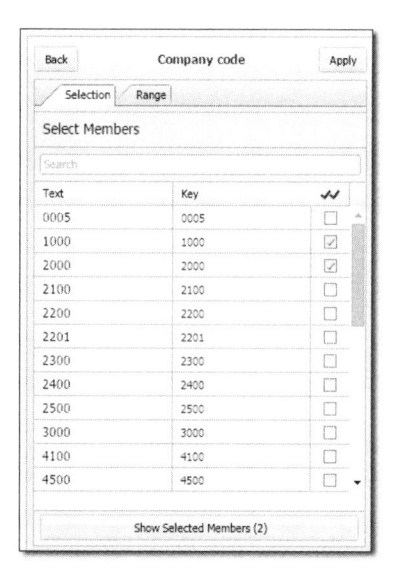

Figure 8.42 Selecting the Filter Values

8.7.2 Adding Charts

Next, you'll add a button to the application to switch to PAGE_2 of the PAGEBOOK component. On PAGE_2, you'll allow the user to browse through some available charts to use.

Let's start by adding a BUTTON to the application to switch back and forward between pages in the PAGEBOOK component:

1. Add a BUTTON to the canvas.
2. Set the TOP MARGIN to 80.
3. Set the LEFT MARGIN to 10.
4. Set the BOTTOM MARGIN and RIGHT MARGIN to AUTO.
5. Set the WIDTH to 80.
6. Set the HEIGHT to 30.
7. Set the TEXT to CHARTS.
8. In the On Click event, use Listing 8.18.

```
if (PAGEBOOK_1.getSelectedPageIndex()==0)
{
    PAGEBOOK_1.setSelectedPageIndex(1);
    this.setText("Table");
}
else
{
    PAGEBOOK_1.setSelectedPageIndex(0);
    this.setText("Charts");
}
```

Listing 8.18 Changing Text Based on the Selected Page

Now when a user clicks the button, the script will evaluate which page is currently shown. When PAGE_1 is shown, and then the BUTTON is clicked, PAGE_2 will be shown, and the text of the button will change to TABLE because the next time the user clicks the button, the user will go back to the tabular overview (PAGE_1).

Next, you'll add a CHART component and a CHART TYPE PICKER component to the canvas.

Let's start with the chart:

1. Add a CHART component on PAGE_2 of the PAGEBOOK component.
2. Set the TOP MARGIN to 100.
3. Set the LEFT MARGIN, BOTTOM MARGIN, and RIGHT MARGIN to 0.
4. Set the WIDTH and the HEIGHT to AUTO.

8 | Scripting for Interactivity

5. Use DS_1 as DATA SOURCE.
6. Use the default NAME of the chart: CHART_1.
7. Add a CHART TYPE PICKER component on the canvas in PAGE_1 of the PAGEBOOK, and place it above the chart.
8. Set the TOP MARGIN to 0.
9. Set the LEFT MARGIN to 0.
10. Set the BOTTOM MARGIN to AUTO.
11. Set the RIGHT MARGIN to 0.
12. Set the WIDTH to AUTO.
13. Set the HEIGHT to AUTO.
14. Set the CHART REFERENCE to CHART_1.

The second part of our application is now completed. You can use the NAVIGATION PANEL to change the view of the data. You can also toggle between PAGE_1 of the PAGEBOOK component where the data is shown in a CROSSTAB and PAGE_2 of the PAGEBOOK where the data is shown graphically. On PAGE_2, you also have the option to use different chart types. In Figure 8.43, you see an example of a LINE CHART chosen from the chart picker.

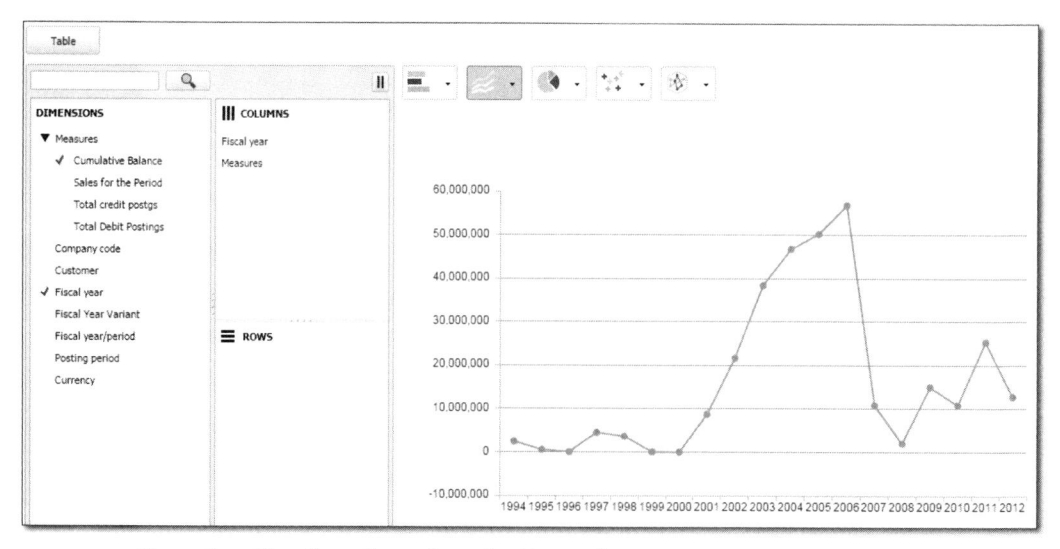

Figure 8.43 Line Chart Chosen from the Chart Picker

8.7.3 Selecting a Data Source

In this section, you'll add a BUTTON component to the application that will open a dialog box where you can choose a BEx query that will be used in the application as a data source.

First, set the LOAD IN SCRIPT property of DS_1 to `true`. This way, the data source won't be loaded at startup.

Add a new BACKEND CONNECTION component in the TECHNICAL COMPONENTS folder of the OUTLINE view in Design Studio (Figure 8.44).

Figure 8.44 Defining a New Backend Connection Component

Follow these steps:

1. Use the default name: CONNECTION_1.
2. Choose the SAP BW system that is defined as an OLAP connection on the SAP BusinessObjects BI platform.
3. On the DEFAULT tab, choose FOLDERS/INFOAREAS.
4. On the VISIBLE tab, select only SEARCH TAB AND FOLDERS/INFO AREAS TAB.

Now, add a BUTTON to the canvas. When this BUTTON is clicked, a dialog window will open where you can select available BEx queries. Follow these steps:

1. Add a BUTTON component to the canvas, and use the following settings to define its width, height, position, and text.
2. Set TEXT to BEX QUERY.
3. Set the TOP MARGIN to 80.
4. Set the LEFT MARGIN to 100.
5. Set the BOTTOM MARGIN and the RIGHT MARGIN to AUTO.
6. Set the WIDTH to 80.
7. Set the HEIGHT to 30.
8. In the `On Click` event property, use the following script to open the data source browser dialog window:
   ```
   CONNECTION_1.showDataSourceBrowser();
   ```

This script will open a new window where you can browse through InfoAreas and search for available BEx queries (Figure 8.45).

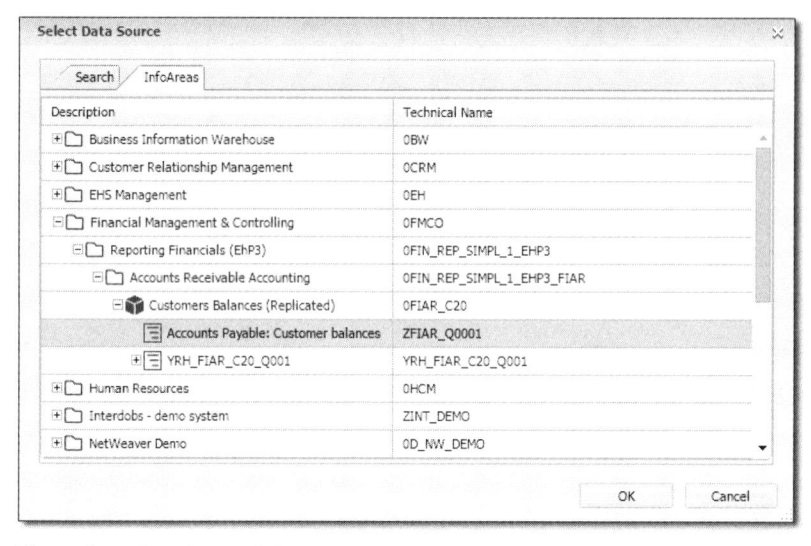

Figure 8.45 Data Source Selection

The next thing you need to do is make sure that DS_1 is assigned with the selected query by adding a script in the `On Data Source Browser Confirmation` property in `CONNECTION_1`:

```
var ds = CONNECTION_1.getSelectedDataSource();
DS_1.assignDataSource(ds.connection, ds.type, ds.name);
```

In the first line, the BEx query object is stored in a variable called `ds`.

In the second line, DS_1 gets assigned with the new properties of the BEx query. Remember that DS_1 is initially not loaded. When this script is called, DS_1 will be loaded automatically.

8.7.4 Bookmarking

When you use the application and want to save your navigational state, you can use bookmarks. You'll add a BUTTON component to the application to save the bookmark and a DROPDOWN BOX to select a previously saved bookmark. You'll also add an INPUT_FIELD to the application so that you can give the bookmark a meaningful name.

Let's start by adding the INPUT_FIELD component to the canvas:

1. Add the INPUT_FIELD component.
2. Set the TOP MARGIN to 80.
3. Set the LEFT MARGIN to 280.
4. Set the BOTTOM MARGIN and RIGHT MARGIN to AUTO.
5. Set the WIDTH to 100.
6. Set the HEIGHT to 50.
7. Use the default name: INPUTFIELD_1.

Now add a BUTTON component to the canvas next to the BEX QUERY button. This BUTTON will be used to save the current state of the application as a bookmark with the name that is entered into INPUTFIELD_1. Proceed with the following steps:

1. Add a BUTTON component to the canvas.
2. Set the TOP MARGIN to 80.
3. Set the LEFT MARGIN to 190.
4. Set the BOTTOM MARGIN and RIGHT MARGIN to AUTO.
5. Set the WIDTH to 80.
6. Set the HEIGHT to 30.
7. In the On Click event, add the following script:
   ```
   var bmName = INPUTFIELD_1.getValue();
   Bookmark.saveBookmark(bmName);
   ```

The first line of the script saves the name that is entered into the INPUT_FIELD component.

The second line of the script saves the current navigation state as a bookmark with the name of the value that is entered in INPUTFIELD_1.

Now add a DROPDOWN BOX component to the canvas to select a saved bookmark by following these steps:

1. Add a DROPDOWN BOX component.
2. Set the TOP MARGIN to 80.
3. Set the LEFT MARGIN to 390.
4. Set the BOTTOM MARGIN and the RIGHT MARGIN to AUTO.

8 | Scripting for Interactivity

5. Set the WIDTH to 120.
6. Set the HEIGHT to AUTO.
7. Use the default name: DROPDOWNBOX_1.
8. In the `On Select` event, enter the following script:

   ```
   var selection = this.getSelectedValue();
   Bookmark.loadBookmark(selection);
   ```

The first line of the script saves the value of the selected bookmark in a variable. The second line of the script loads the bookmark with the name that is equal to the value stored in the variable.

The last thing that you need to do is populate DROPDOWNBOX_1 with all the saved bookmarks. In the `On Startup` event in the application's properties, enter the code shown in Listing 8.19.

```
// Get all the bookmarks
var bm = Bookmark.getAllBookmarks();

bm.forEach(function(element, index) {
  DROPDOWN_1.addItem(element.id, element.text,index);
});
```
Listing 8.19 Adding Bookmarks to a Dropdown Box

This script will populate DROPDOWNBOX_1 with all the saved bookmarks.

Figure 8.46 shows what the application looks like when it initially starts. In this case, two bookmarks where previously saved. When a bookmark is chosen from the DROPDOWN BOX component, the application will be loaded to the state that it was in when it was saved.

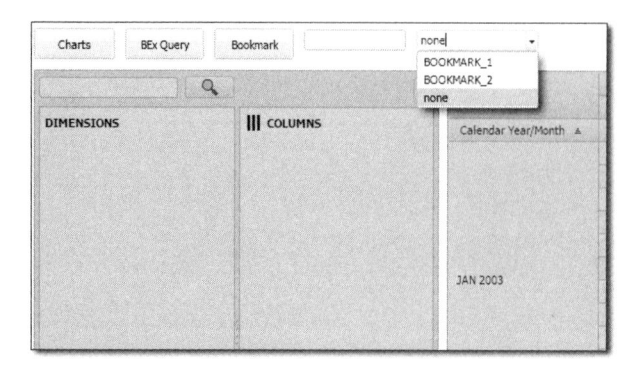

Figure 8.46 Working with Bookmarks

382

In Figure 8.47, you see the navigation state that BOOKMARK_1 was saved in.

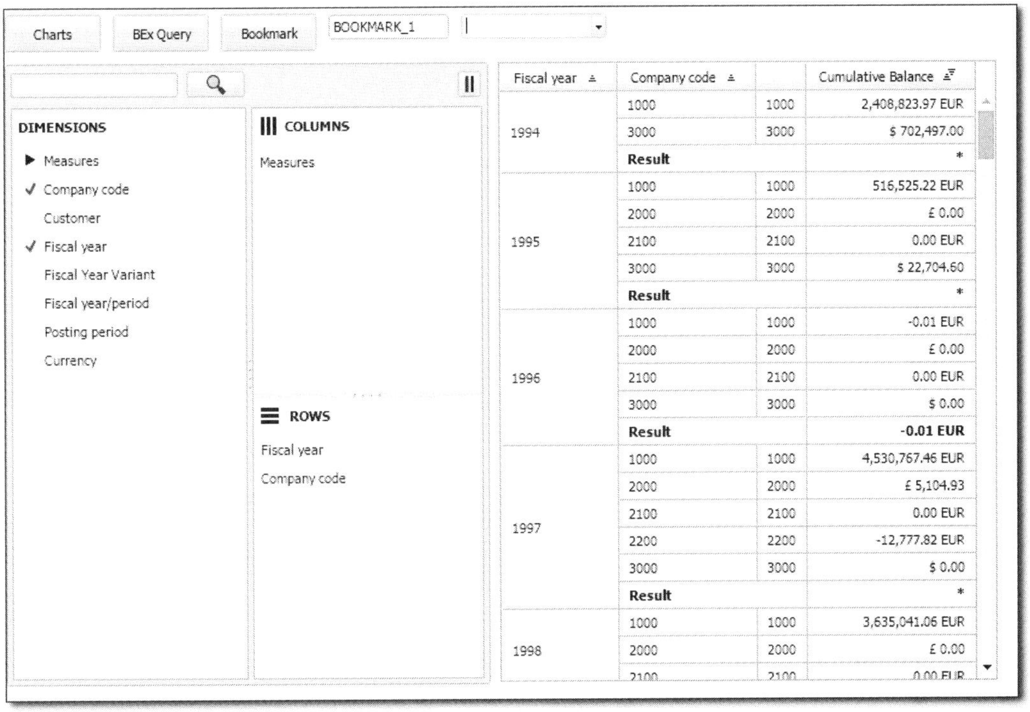

Figure 8.47 Application after Bookmark Is Selected

8.8 Summary

In this chapter, we looked at several ways to add interactivity to a Design Studio application using scripting. In the first half of the chapter, we described the basic information you need to know to script: information about the language syntax, how to use tools such as the Script Editor, and the predefined script templates. In the second half of the chapter, we walked you through some examples of adding interactivity to Design Studio applications. Most notably, we talked about data binding, filtering, and how to use calculations in scripts to populate variables. You've also seen how you can use scripts to populate a TEXT component and how you can apply CSS code to components based on some logic.

In the next chapter, we'll move on to further enhancements that can be made to Design Studio applications using CSS.

Planning models allow you to create applications that enable manual and automatic planning for business data. In this chapter, we'll show you how.

9 Planning Applications

Design Studio applications aren't limited to just visualizing data. In Design Studio, you also can create *planning applications* in which users can plan business data. Planning applications support the manual entry of data and the use of planning functions, sequences, and objects that reside in SAP Business Warehouse Integrated Planning (SAP BW-IP), for automated data entry.

Actually, you can regard the application that you create as a frontend screen for your planning model that uses all of the layout and interactivity options at your disposal to create a user-friendly environment to plan numbers. In this chapter, we'll begin by looking at the prerequisites for planning. Then, we'll discuss how to add a planning connection and the differences between manual and automated planning. We'll then look at the script of a planning application before moving on to building an example planning application.

9.1 Prerequisites for Planning

Before you can create a planning application with Design Studio, a number of conditions must be met. The following prerequisites must be in place to create planning applications in Design Studio:

- **A Design Studio deployment scenario with SAP BusinessObjects BI platform or SAP NetWeaver as the platform**
  This is necessary for the SAP BW backend system (see the next bullet point). Only the SAP BusinessObjects BI platform and the SAP NetWeaver platform can enable you to connect to an SAP BW backend system.

- **An SAP BW backend system as the planning system**
  You're connecting to SAP BW-IP, which resides in SAP BW systems.
- **An SAP BW BEx query or BEx query view as a data source, which is defined as a planning query in the BEx Query Designer**
  Defining a query as a planning query tells the SAP BW source system that this query is supposed to be a two-way street where SAP BW will allow data entry and store information using the planning model.
- **A Design Studio desktop browser application as the planning application**
  This is necessary given that there is no official CROSSTAB component support for planning on mobile devices yet, and the SPREADSHEET component is only for a desktop browser.

Planning in the Backend Systems

When creating planning applications, we assume you already have a planning model in place in the backend system. If you need to configure the SAP BW system, there is documentation available:

Planning Business Data with BW Integrated Planning: *http://help.sap.com/saphelp_nw74/helpdata/en/4c/bb4ebeed80606be10000000a42189e/frameset.htm*

If you work with planning models in SAP Business Planning and Consolidation, version for SAP NetWeaver, then you can find more information here:

SAP Business Planning and Consolidation, version for SAP NetWeaver: *http://help.sap.com/saphelp_bopacnw101/helpdata/en/82/f51cf12cfc48c58975b9b5e6fba9aa/frameset.htm*

In addition, before you start creating planning applications, you should set up some kind of *cell locking* mechanism so that when one user opens a set of data, another user can't change that dataset until the first user releases the set of data. This avoids potential problems when multiple users make changes in the same set and at the same time.

SAP BW administrators manage cell locks in the backend system for one individual input-ready BEx query or all input-ready BEx queries of the planning application. By locking a cell in all queries of a planning application, a cell locked in one query will display as locked in other queries, and users won't be able to change the value of the locked cell. These backend cell locks are global cell locks in a planning application.

To activate the global cell lock in the backend, you need to set a parameter in table `RSADMIN`. You can use the program `SAP_RSADMIN_MAINTAIN` to do this. Set the following parameter:

```
OBJECT = RSPLS_PQ_BACKEND_CELL_LOCKING
VALUE = X
```

These cross-query cell locks can be particularly useful if a planning application contains multiple tabs or pages with closely linked queries that are used for different aspects of the planning application. This will avoid potential overlaps where the user might change something in page 1 and change the same number in page 3.

Now that we've covered planning application prerequisites, let's move on to adding the planning connection.

9.2 Adding a Planning Connection

A *planning connection* sets up a link between the Design Studio application and the backend system that contains the planning applications. After you've established a planning connection, you'll be able to add planning functions, planning sequences, and input-ready queries to the application to build a frontend for the planning application. These items are developed in the backend system. In Design Studio, you can configure these pieces and use them.

Planning functions perform a task on the data, for example, copying it, increasing the amount, or moving it. A *planning sequence* is a series of planning functions that are performed sequentially. You can configure these to add a filter, for example. The filter will limit the data that is being used and changed. For instance, if you add the filter "South" to the `Region` dimension and start a planning function to increase targets, only the South regions will get a higher target.

Adding a planning function is nearly identical to adding a planning sequence. There are two ways to add a planning function or a planning sequence: The first way is via the top menu (Figure 9.1). When you click the PLANNING menu option, you can choose either ADD PLANNING FUNCTION or ADD PLANNING SEQUENCE. After selecting one of these options, you'll see a screen that asks you to identify the function or sequence that you want to add.

9 | Planning Applications

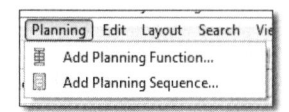

Figure 9.1 Add Planning via the Top Menu

The second way is by right-clicking on the PLANNING OBJECTS folder in the OUTLINE view (Figure 9.2). Here again, you see the options ADD PLANNING FUNCTION and ADD PLANNING SEQUENCE. Selecting one of the options will lead you to the screen to identify the function or sequence.

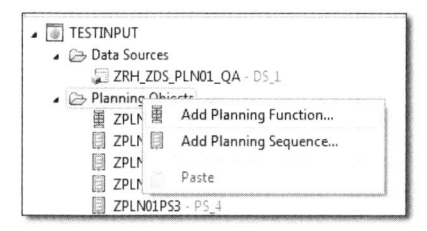

Figure 9.2 Add Planning Function via the Outline View

After selecting either ADD PLANNING FUNCTION or ADD PLANNING SEQUENCE, a screen pops up where you can select the planning function or planning sequence you want to add. As these processes are identical, we'll show you how to add a planning function. You can apply what you've learned to adding a planning sequence as well.

Follow these steps to add a planning function:

1. In the first screen, select the planning function from the planning system, and set the name of the planning function in Design Studio (Figure 9.3). You can type in the technical name for the PLANNING FUNCTION field, if you know it. If you need to search for the technical name, click the BROWSE button next to the field. The SCRIPT ALIAS field sets the name that is used in Design Studio. When you create scripts referencing the planning function, you'll be using this name.

2. If you choose to search via the BROWSE button, a new screen appears where you can search and select one of the functions that is returned (Figure 9.4). Although this example used an asterisk (*), which is a wildcard for all values, if there were many functions in the source system, it would be better to refine the selection more to reduce the results.

Adding a Planning Connection | **9.2**

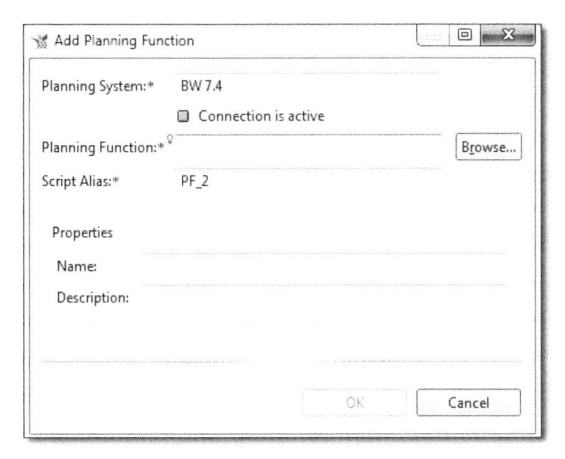

Figure 9.3 Add Planning Function Screen

Planning Functions and Planning Sequences

A planning function is a single function to do something to the plan data. This can be a copy, a move, or a calculation. A sequence is a series of steps that runs functions sequentially.

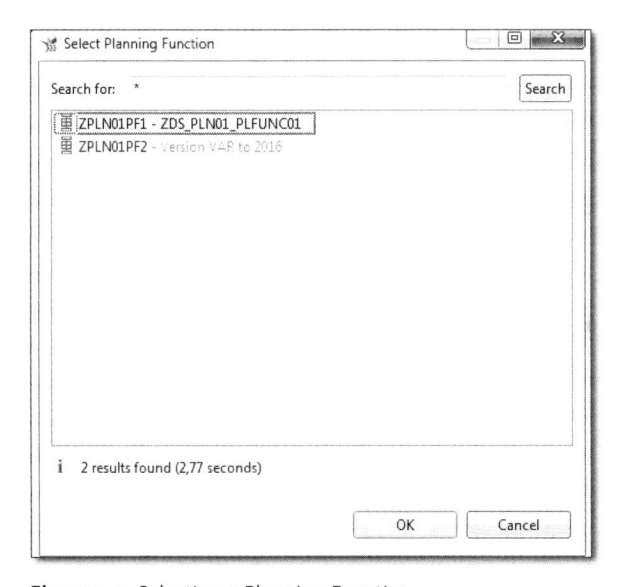

Figure 9.4 Selecting a Planning Function

3. You'll return to the previous screen, but now with a planning function name in the upper input box. Click OK to add the planning function to the OUTLINE view (Figure 9.5).

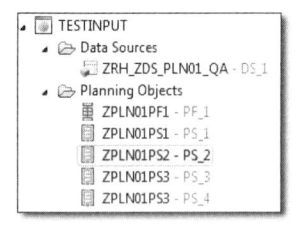

Figure 9.5 Planning Functions and Sequences Added to the Outline View

These planning functions and sequences are now available for scripting. We'll discuss the available options for these in Section 9.4. In the next two sections, we'll look at manual and automated planning.

9.3 Manual Planning: Crosstab and Spreadsheet Components

In this section, we'll look at the methods for *manual planning* in Design Studio. To allow users to manually input data, you need an input-ready BEx query. There are two ways to input data manually in a planning application: via the CROSSTAB component or via the SPREADSHEET component.

When you bind a data source to a CROSSTAB component, it shows the numbers just like any other query (Figure 9.6).

Figure 9.6 Crosstab with Input-Ready BEx Query Set to False

There are script lines that allow you to see the status of input readiness for a data source in Design Studio and change the input readiness to TRUE or FALSE. If a data source is set to input-ready (TRUE), this means that a user can now manually input data. If it's set to FALSE, the user won't be able to change numbers, independent of the capabilities of the backend query.

When you use the following script for the data source, the input readiness will toggle between TRUE and FALSE:

```
var current = DS_1.isInputReady();
DS_1.configureInputReadiness(!current);
```

When the input readiness is set to TRUE, the CROSSTAB component will look like Figure 9.7.

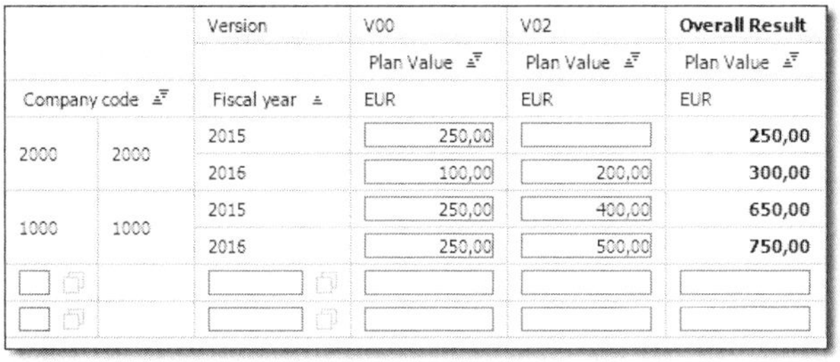

		Version	V00	V02	Overall Result
			Plan Value	Plan Value	Plan Value
Company code		Fiscal year	EUR	EUR	EUR
2000	2000	2015	250,00		250,00
		2016	100,00	200,00	300,00
1000	1000	2015	250,00	400,00	650,00
		2016	250,00	500,00	750,00

Figure 9.7 Input Readyness Set to True

In this input-ready state, you're able to manually add or change numbers.

Besides the CROSSTAB component, you can also use the SPREADSHEET component. With the SPREADSHEET component, the user has some more freedom to copy and paste data (Figure 9.8).

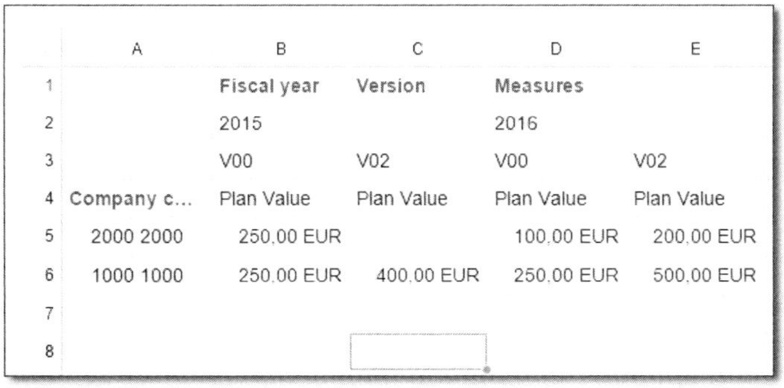

	A	B	C	D	E
1		Fiscal year	Version	Measures	
2		2015		2016	
3		V00	V02	V00	V02
4	Company c...	Plan Value	Plan Value	Plan Value	Plan Value
5	2000 2000	250.00 EUR		100.00 EUR	200.00 EUR
6	1000 1000	250.00 EUR	400.00 EUR	250.00 EUR	500.00 EUR
7					
8					

Figure 9.8 Spreadsheet Component

9.4 Automated Planning: Planning Functions and Sequences

Planning objects are the main building blocks of a planning application, defined in the backend application. As previously discussed, a planning function will perform one task on a set of data. This task can be a copy, movement, change in amount, or a more complex task. A planning sequence is a series of planning functions that are performed sequentially.

In Design Studio, you can configure these using filters and variables. The filters limit the data that is touched by the function or sequence. Variables are defined by the planning function or planning sequence builder and offer a wide range of possibilities.

These planning objects allow you to do mass updates on planning data. Using manual input (see Section 9.3), you're forced to change the cell values one by one. The beauty of these planning objects is that they can change many records at one click of a button. This is *automated planning*.

Instead of manually inputting numbers, you can start functions and sequences that are defined in the backend system.

In Section 9.2, we discussed how to add links to these functions and sequences in Design Studio. Now we're going to show how you can use them in an application.

9.4.1 Planning Functions

Planning functions allow you to enable users to input data in the backend systems. Typically, the numbers they input are planning numbers, that is, forecasts for the coming periods. In Design Studio, you can create a frontend screen for those planning functions that includes selections, filters, and manual input options. You can use the frontend to make an intuitive layout so that users can easily work with these functions.

Planning functions have, in comparison to planning sequences, a larger number of methods to work with. Table 9.1 describes these different methods.

Automated Planning: Planning Functions and Sequences | 9.4

Method	Description
clearAllFilters	Removes filters for all dimensions. Filters limit the impact of a planning function on the planning data because only the filtered records are affected by the planning function.
clearFilter	Removes the filter from a dimension.
copyFilter	Copies a filter from another data source to the planning function.
getDimensionText	Retrieves the description of the dimension.
getDimensions	Retrieves the dimensions that are used in the planning function.
getFilterExt	Retrieves the current filter in the external key format.
getFilterText	Retrieves the current filter text.
setFilter	Sets the filter value.
setFilterExt	Sets the filter value using the external format. An external format is easier to use because it's more compact, and it's easier if you want to make a more complex filter using greater than or less than symbols. However, the internal key is more complete because it keeps applications language-independent to ensure that they can work for multilingual user groups.
copyVariableValue	Copies the variable value from a data source.
Execute	Starts the planning sequence.
GetVariableValueExt	Provides the value of a variable in the external key format.
GetVariableValueText	Provides the description of the currently set variable value
getVariables	Provides the list of variables associated with the planning sequence.
setVariableValue	Sets the variable value.
setVariableValueExt	Sets the variable value in an external format.

Table 9.1 Methods for Planning Functions

9.4.2 Planning Sequences

Planning sequences are used in SAP BW-IP to group planning functions. They allow you to save groups of planning functions in a sorted sequence and execute groups of planning functions sequentially. Sequences can be very powerful because you can add many functions to one sequence.

9 | Planning Applications

Planning sequences in Design Studio have a number of methods to work with, as described in Table 9.2.

Method	Description
copyVariableValue	Copies the variable value from a data source.
Execute	Starts the planning sequence.
GetVariableValueExt	Provides the variable value.
GetVariableValueText	Provides the description of the currently set variable value.
getVariables	Provides the list of variable associated with the planning sequence.
setVariableValue	Sets the variable value.
setVariableValueExt	Sets the variable value in an external format.

Table 9.2 Methods for Planning Sequences

These functions help you set up the sequences and execute them. Planning sequence variables are similar to application parameters in that you can influence the way the planning sequence works with the data. If all the variables are set, you can run the sequence using the Execute method.

9.5 Planning Functionality Options

When you create a planning application, you have script methods at your disposal to do general functions on the data. The PLANNING component is found in the Script Editor and offers a number of methods. These methods allow you to reset, save, and recalculate the data after the user either executed a planning function/planning sequence or performed a manual entry.

> **.save**
>
> The .save method is important because without it, all the changes made by the user would have no effect at all.

In Table 9.3, you see a list of methods that are available to you for planning in the script.

394

Method	Description
clientReset	Makes the application reset to the last successful state after recalculation. This means that all the steps taken by the user after the last calculation are rolled back, and the data is back to the state that it had after the last recalculation was done.
hasClientChanges	Tells you if there is still unsaved data. This is important to check before you let the user close the screen. This method specifically determines whether the user entered manual data into either a CROSSTAB or SPREADSHEET component and didn't save those entries yet.
hasUnsavedChanges	Tells you whether there is unsaved planning data. This can be either from an executed function or from a manual input.
Recalculate	Recalculates the planning application based on the changed planning data.
Reset	Resets the application back to the last state on the server.
Save	Saves the last changes to the server.

Table 9.3 Planning Object Methods

9.6 Building a Planning Application

Having walked through the different prerequisites, terms, planning approaches, and planning functions, sequences, and object methods, we'll now walk you through building a very basic planning application.

In many organizations, you'll see an elaborate system where sales managers have to forecast their sales for the coming year. As such, you'll build a planning application that supports this forecasting. The application will allow an individual to create a copy of the data as a basis for planning, create functions to enable the managers to make changes to groups of records, and allow the manual input of data to fine-tune the forecast. The result is that the manager will be able to create a forecast using the most recent end-of-year expectations.

The first step in building this type of planning application is to look at the predicted end-of-year results as a baseline for the coming year. Figure 9.9 supplies some mock data to use as part of this example.

9 | Planning Applications

	Jan	Feb	Mar	Apr	May	Jun	Jul	Aug	Sept	Oct	Nov	Dec	YTD	Estimate
Product Group 1	527	483	525	520	507	469	478	470	482	501			4,962	5,954
Product Group 2	251	246	269	267	265	256	274	273	249	229			2,579	3,095
Product Group 3	792	703	766	741	773	680	698	813	743	804			7,513	9,016
Product Group 4	1,245	1,200	1,138	1,303	1,233	1,322	1,168	1,317	1,208	1,188			12,322	14,786
Product Group 5	130	135	126	117	126	119	133	124	115	131			1,256	1,507
	2,945	2,767	2,824	2,948	2,904	2,846	2,751	2,997	2,797	2,853	-	-	28,632	34,358

Figure 9.9 YTD Sales Report

Next, you need to copy the estimated end-of-year number data to the next year and add a percentage (which is the new goal set by management) (Figure 9.10).

		senior management increase +5%
	Estimate	Goal next year
Product Group 1	5,954	6,252
Product Group 2	3,095	3,250
Product Group 3	9,016	9,467
Product Group 4	14,786	15,525
Product Group 5	1,507	1,582
	34,358	36,076

Figure 9.10 Higher Estimate Set by Management

After the rough goal is set by management, the sales manager looks at his own product groups. Some newly introduced product groups will likely have a steep growth in sales and will carry more of the growth while other, more mature product groups, may be in a different phase of their product life cycle and probably will lag in terms of growth. The sales manager wants to adjust those product groups accordingly.

In Figure 9.11, you see an example where the sales manager estimated per group how each group would do. The total goal is now reduced by 1.6% in comparison with the general goal set by senior management earlier.

	Estimate	Goal next year	delta	Sales Manager estimate
Product Group 1	5,954	6,252	-2%	6,127
Product Group 2	3,095	3,250	3%	3,348
Product Group 3	9,016	9,467	2%	9,656
Product Group 4	14,786	15,525	-5%	14,749
Product Group 5	1,507	1,582	2%	1,614
	34,358	36,076	-1.6%	35,494

Figure 9.11 Sales Manager Estimates

The sales manager will end up with a grand total that differs from the goal set by higher management. That difference then should be discussed between the manager and higher management.

The application that you'll create supports the role of the sales manager in this scenario. The sales manager should be able to prepare data using a planning sequence. Following the first step, the sales manager can make adjustments using a planning function. This allows him to adjust all products within a product group without addressing each product.

The following tasks will be performed:

1. Add the CROSSTAB component for reviewing the data.
2. Add buttons to invoke the planning functions and sequences to make the scenario described possible.
3. Add a SAVE option to store the data.
4. Create an input-ready state button to make manual adjustments possible.

The application you'll build will be a simplified version of a real-life scenario forecast application. This will show you how to perform the functions necessary.

Follow these steps:

1. Add the button to the application that will reference the planning sequence created to prepare the data. Clicking this button will copy the end-of-year estimate to the first version of the forecast data. This will be done via a sequence of multiple steps that is already defined in the backend system. The only thing you need to do in the application now is start it and wait.

   The script for the button is given here:

   ```
   PS_1.execute();
   ```

   The script is easy because variables, such as who is actually logged in, are automatically handled in the backend system. If you need to set some variable values before you can execute the planning sequence, you add this. In this example, let's assume you need to tell the system which user is starting the planning sequence:

   ```
   PS_1.setVariableValue("ZUSER", DS_1.getInfo().user);
   PS_1.execute();
   ```

2. The second part is to increase the value based on a percentage and a product group selection. To enable this function, you allow the user to select a part of the CROSSTAB component. You collect the selected row's product group value and use it to apply a filter to the planning function. Furthermore, you can manually enter a number into an input component:

```
PF_1.setFilter("PRODUCTGROUP", filter)
PF_1.setVariableValue("INCREASE", INPUTFIELD_1.getValue())
PF_1.execute();
```

3. The third part is to divide it over the months. As an additional step, you can add the option to manually include seasonal effects. Normally, you could let the analysts figure this out and include it in the calculation. However, for the sake of the example, let the sales manager manually set a seasonal effect (Figure 9.12).

Figure 9.12 Setting Seasonal Effect by Value per Month

4. The calculation is done in the planning function. In Design Studio, you pass on the values per script (Listing 9.1).

```
PF_2.setVariableValue("Jan", INPUT_JAN.getValue());
PF_2.setVariableValue("Feb", INPUT_FEB.getValue());
PF_2.setVariableValue("Mar", INPUT_MAR.getValue());
PF_2.setVariableValue("Apr", INPUT_APR.getValue());
PF_2.setVariableValue("May", INPUT_MAY.getValue());
PF_2.setVariableValue("Jun", INPUT_JUN.getValue());
PF_2.setVariableValue("Jul", INPUT_JUL.getValue());
PF_2.setVariableValue("Aug", INPUT_AUG.getValue());
PF_2.setVariableValue("Sept", INPUT_SEP.getValue());
PF_2.setVariableValue("Oct", INPUT_OCT.getValue());
PF_2.setVariableValue("Nov", INPUT_NOV.getValue());
PF_2.setVariableValue("Dec", INPUT_DEC.getValue());
PF_2.execute()
```

Listing 9.1 Set Seasonal Effect

As you can see, many variable values are passed to the planning function. Inside the planning function, the relative size is determined, and the relative total is calculated.

5. After the automated steps, it's now time to allow the sales manager to manually change the numbers. Earlier, we showed you how to toggle the input readiness. The script to allow users to enter data is given here:

```
var current = DS_1.isInputReady();
DS_1.configureInputReadiness(!current);
```

6. You need to add one last button that saves the data that has been changed:

```
Planning.save();
```

7. Additionally, you might want to inform the user if there are still unsaved changes. In the buttons, you can set a script that points to a central function, as shown in Listing 9.2.

```
var saved = Planning.hasUnsavedChanges
if (saved == true)
{
    TXT_STATUS.setText("Not Saved")
}
Else
{
    TXT_STATUS.setText("saved")
}
```

Listing 9.2 Script to Inform Users about the Save State of the Planning Object

8. Finally, save the changes you've made.

9.7 Summary

In this chapter, we looked at the planning functionality. Design Studio serves as the frontend to the planning application that has been made in the backend. In this chapter, we discussed planning prerequisites and how to add a planning connection. We then explained manual and automated planning and planning functionality options before diving into steps for building your own planning application in which a sales manager uses the planning functionality to create a forecast.

In the next chapter, we'll look at methods to enhance Design Studio applications further with Cascading Style Sheets (CSS).

The way your application looks has a great influence on users' perceptions of an application. You can fully customize the way your application looks and standardize the look of all your applications according to your company's style using CSS.

10   Enhancing Applications with CSS

Cascading Style Sheets (CSS) play a very important role in the layout settings of a Design Studio application. All colors, sizes, and other stylings of the components in your application are defined in a CSS file. The great thing about using CSS in combination with Design Studio is that you can use your own CSS code to modify the way existing components look.

When building an application in Design Studio, you have to start with one of the predefined standard themes, which we'll discuss next in Section 10.1. CSS is first applied by the standard theme; then by the custom CSS class, which you can add to the application; and—finally—by editing the CSS style of individual components. For faster development, it's very important to have a standard set of classes available. The developer then only has to assign classes to components to use the predefined style.

Throughout this chapter, we'll explain how CSS works by guiding you through some examples. Specifically, we'll discuss the different CSS themes, classes, and styles; how to create responsive applications; and how to modify standard components. Before you start using your own CSS, let's explore the standard CSS themes that are already available in Design Studio.

10.1   CSS Themes

There are four different themes in Design Studio:

- HIGH CONTRAST BLACK
- BLUE CRYSTAL

10 | Enhancing Applications with CSS

- MOBILE
- PLATINUM (the default theme when you create a new blank application)

> **Figures in This Book**
>
> The size and colors of most components in your application will change when you select a different theme. This book is printed in black and white, so the color changes might not always be clear in the printed version. In the e-book, however, the examples will be in full color.

A theme can be set in the DISPLAY properties of the application (Figure 10.1).

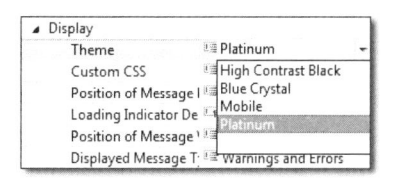

Figure 10.1 Themes

To demonstrate how CSS themes can enhance your applications, we've created an application containing various components in Design Studio (CROSSTAB, CHART, DROPDOWN BOX, FILTER PANEL, DIMENSION FILTER, BUTTON, CHECKBOX GROUP, and LIST BOX). You can see the results in Figure 10.2. Remember, the PLATINUM theme is selected by default.

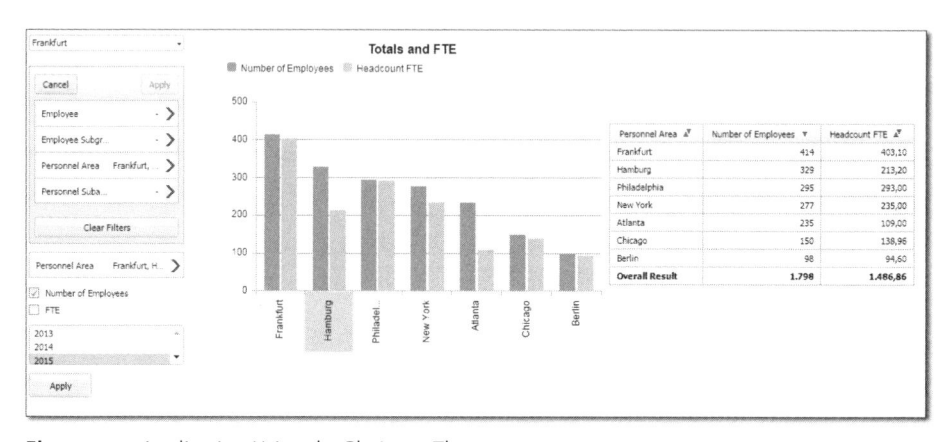

Figure 10.2 Application Using the Platinum Theme

Applying other themes to your application properties will change the CSS classes assigned to the components of your application. For instance, when you select the HIGH CONTRAST BLACK theme, your application will get a black background by default, and the font colors in all components will be white (Figure 10.3). Keep in mind that the component properties in your application don't change when you set another theme; only the CSS code changes that is used by default for your application. The HIGH CONTRAST BLACK theme gives your application a more modern look.

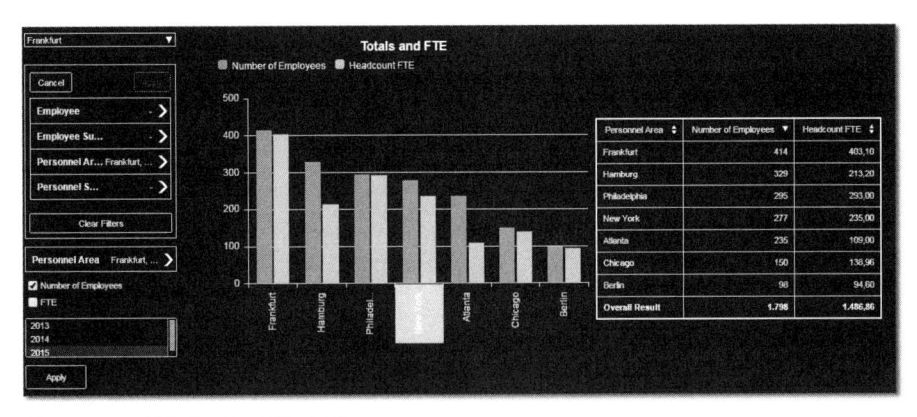

Figure 10.3 High Contrast Black Theme

The BLUE CRYSTAL theme looks a bit like the PLATINUM theme but has a light blue background color by default (Figure 10.4). In addition, the light gray colors for most of the components are replaced by white. This theme uses softer colors and is a great theme to use for applications with a white background.

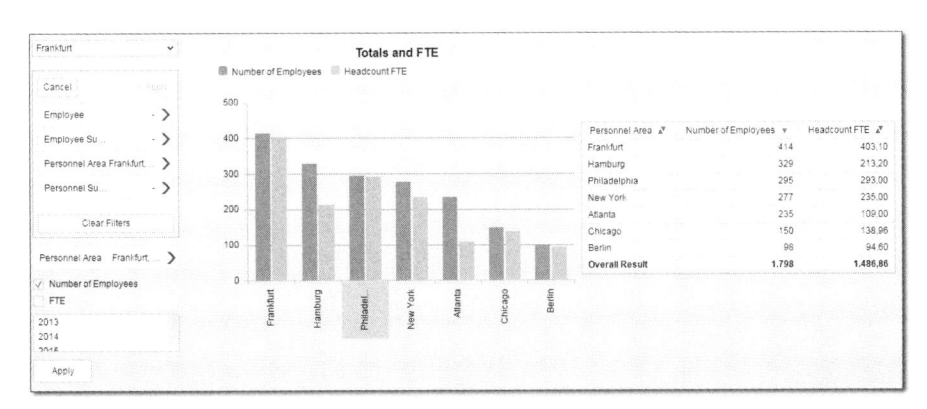

Figure 10.4 Blue Crystal Theme

You might notice that the application looks a bit more crowded when the MOBILE theme is used (Figure 10.5) because most of the components are a little bigger by default. The components are bigger because the interaction on a mobile device usually happens with a finger instead of a mouse, which leads to less precise component selection.

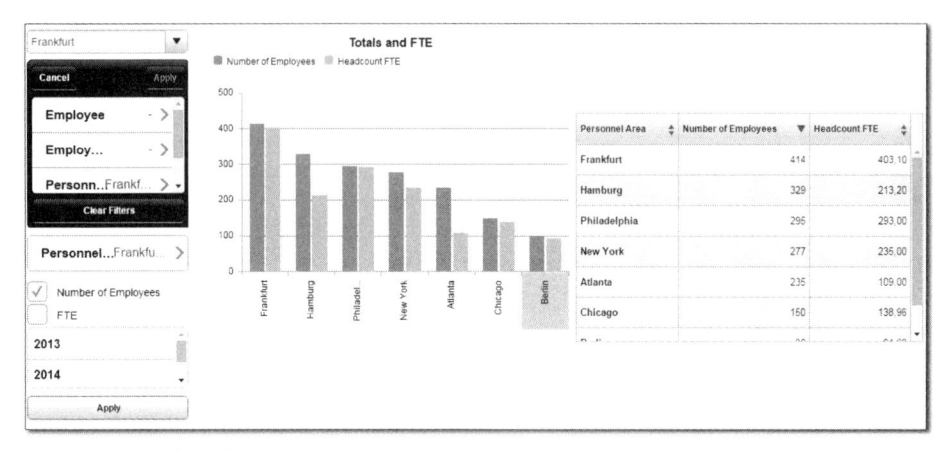

Figure 10.5 Mobile Theme

Now that we've looked at the different themes available in Design Studio, we'll discuss the CSS classes and styles that provide further customization capabilities.

10.2 Using CSS Classes and Styles

Using the standard themes provided by Design Studio is a good starting point for designing your application. However, you can customize the look of your application even more by using your own CSS code.

For some components such as TEXT components and PANEL components, it's possible to use the CSS STYLE property to apply CSS code directly on the selected component. Let's take a look at a TEXT component that we'll use for the title of the application in Figure 10.6. We see that the text is aligned left by default, and the font size is too small.

For this example, we need to use a bigger font size for the APPLICATION TITLE, center the title in the middle of the page, and make the font bold and green. To achieve this goal, we add some CSS code to the CSS STYLE property of this TEXT component.

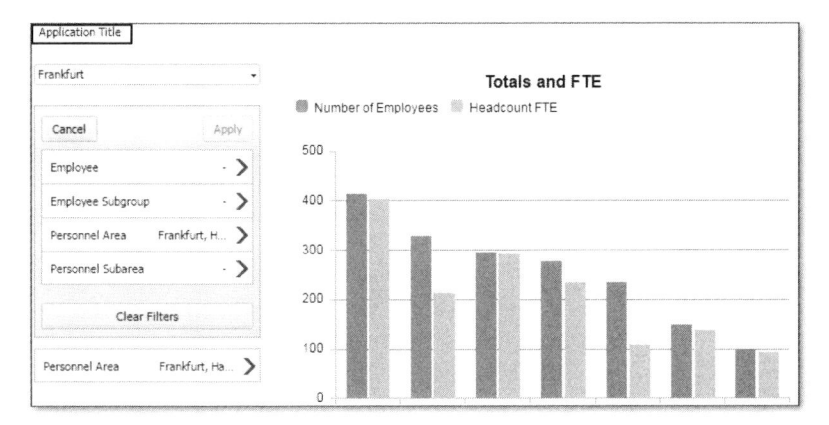

Figure 10.6 Standard Text Component without Custom CSS

CSS code statements are composed of properties and values. Many properties can be used with CSS. There are various resources available online on this subject, such as the W3schools website (*www.w3schools.com/css*).

In this section, we'll show you how to add some basic CSS code to the components in your application. First, you open the CSS Style Editor by clicking on the CSS STYLE property (Figure 10.7). By adding the following CSS code in the CSS Style Editor (Figure 10.8), the look of the text will change to Figure 10.9. You can see that in all four lines of the code, a property is called, and a value for that property is set. *Properties* and *values* are separated by colons (:), and each line of code ends with a semicolon (;).

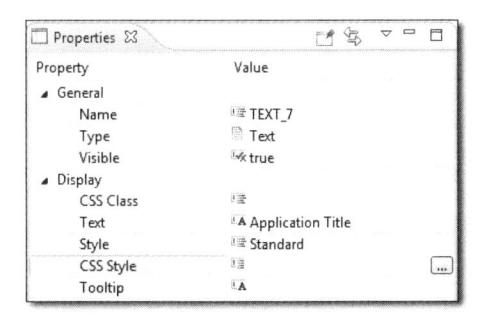

Figure 10.7 Text Component Properties

Figure 10.8 CSS Style Editor

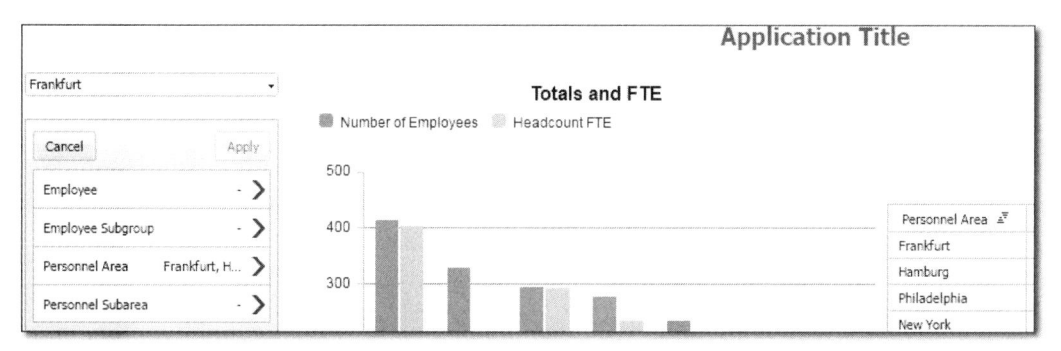

Figure 10.9 Application Title with Custom CSS Code

Let's take a look at another example in which you'll apply some CSS code to a PANEL component instead of a TEXT component. Figure 10.10 shows a PANEL component that has a height of 100px. At the bottom of the PANEL component, the following CSS code defines a bottom border for this PANEL component:

```
border-bottom-style: double;
border-bottom-width: 10px;
```

Figure 10.10 Header Panel with Bottom Border

The border has the style property `double`, indicating that two lines should be used for the bottom border with a width of `10px`.

In the following example, we set some CSS styles for the background of our application. All of the components are grouped inside a PANEL component. This PANEL component resizes automatically to fit the entire screen. A background color can be added to the application by applying some CSS code to this component. For example, the following line of code adds a blue background color to the PANEL component:

```
background-color: #b0c4de;
```

Instead of using the `background-color` property, you can also use the `background-image` property to set an image as background for the application.

> **CSS Color Codes**
>
> Each color in CSS is a combination of the colors red, green, and blue. There are three ways of defining a color for a component in your CSS code. As we've seen in the preceding example, #b0c4de is a hexadecimal value that represents a soft blue color. This color is built out of the combination 69% red, 77% green, and 87% blue.
>
> Another way of defining this color is to use the code `rgb(69,77,87)`. For less complex colors, you can also use the name of the color. For instance, when using the statement `background-color: blue;` to define a blue color, you can instead use the hexadecimal value #000FF or the RGB value `rgb(0,0,255)`.
>
> There are a lot of great online resources (such as *www.w3schools.com/tags/ref_color-picker.asp*) where you can pick a color and obtain the color code for your CSS.

Now let's consider another example in which you'll not only add CSS to change the font size and color, but you'll also edit the background of a TEXT component. You can use TEXT components in your application to act as buttons. The advantage here is that you can easily modify the CSS of this component in its properties. The normal BUTTON component doesn't have a CSS STYLE property, so if you want to modify the look of a BUTTON component, you have to use a CSS file. Using the CSS code shown in Listing 10.1, your TEXT component will look like Figure 10.11.

```
background-color:#768d87;
border-radius:15px;
border:2px solid #566963;
text-align: center;
font-weight: bold;
```

Listing 10.1 Background Color

The background color is set to gray in the `background-color` property. With the `border-radius` property, you can make the edges of the component round. With the `border` property, you can assign a thickness for the border and also a color, in this case, a darker shade of gray. With the `text-align` property, you can align the text in the center of the component, and with the `font-weight` property, the font for the text is set to bold.

Figure 10.11 Text Component Acting as a Button

In the next sections, we'll show how you can create and add your own CSS classes as opposed to using the CSS Style Editor to enhance the look of your application. The advantage with using a CSS file is the maintainability. When you have several applications with many components, you'll have to spend a lot of time when you want to change a certain piece of the CSS code. If you've defined the CSS code in a class and linked that class to the objects in your application, all you have to do is change the code one time in the CSS file!

10.3 Adding Custom CSS Classes

A CSS class is a group of CSS statements that can be applied on many objects in your application. A CSS class is always defined in a CSS file, which can be accessed by the application.

Before you create applications, it's advisable to think about how you want to deal with custom CSS files. You can apply three strategies:

- **Centralized**
  In this scenario, there is a single CSS file on the platform that you're connected to that will be used by every application. The advantage is that every application will have the same look and feel because they all will be using the same CSS file and thus the same colors and fonts. The disadvantage is that there is only limited freedom for applications to apply their own format. The only way is to use the CSS STYLE property in components.

- **Federated**
  In this scenario, you have a central CSS file—but when you start the development of an application, you copy the central CSS file to the repository of the

application. You can then alter the CSS of this copied file. The advantage here is that everyone has the same starting point and still has some flexibility. The disadvantage is that when the central CSS file changes, you have a rollout scenario to deal with.

- **Local**

    In this scenario, every Design Studio developer can build his own CSS file. The advantages and disadvantages are exactly the opposite of the centralized scenario. Now there is a lot of freedom, but every application will look different, and different standards will be applied.

If you already have a CSS file available, then CSS code will be grouped in classes that can be used instead of the CSS STYLE property. When you want to use a CSS class, you first have to link the CSS class to the application in the application properties (Figure 10.12), and then make a reference to a CSS class in the properties of the component (Figure 10.13) where you want to apply the CSS code.

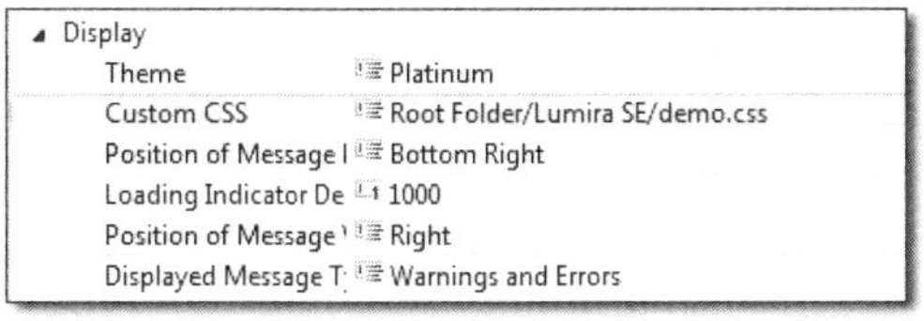

Figure 10.12 Application Properties

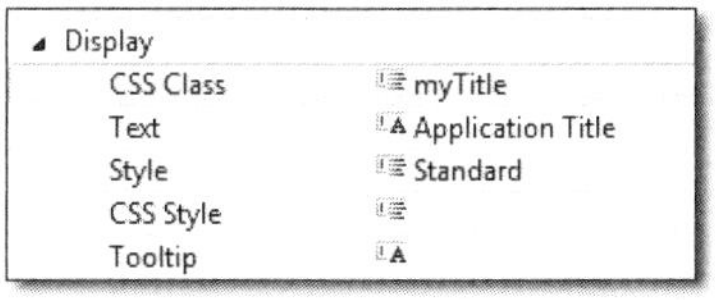

Figure 10.13 Reference to CSS Class in the Text Component Property

You've seen in the previous section that you can use a CSS file in your Design Studio application. The advantage here is that you define the look of your components in this file, instead of in each component individually. You still have to link the CSS class to each component, but when you want to edit the look of a component, you simply edit the CSS file instead of all the components in your application.

The CSS code statements used to create the application title in the previous section (refer to Figure 10.8) can be grouped into a class. A group of CSS code statements is called a *class*, and classes can be defined in CSS files. A CSS class consists of a *class name*, which always starts with a dot, and then a *logical name*, followed by a curly left bracket ({) and ending with a curly right bracket (}).

In the CSS file, the class for the title will look like Listing 10.2.

```
.myTitle {
font-size: 20px;
text-align: center;
font-weight: bold;
color: green;
}
```
Listing 10.2 Application Title Class

You can create and edit CSS files using a simple text editor such as Notepad++. CSS files are text files stored with the extension *.css*. In Figure 10.14, you can see how Notepad++ gives you suggestions on how to edit your code.

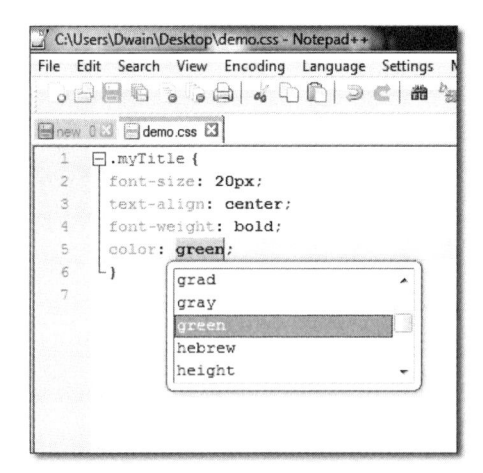

Figure 10.14 Notepad++ Code Editor

You can also use the built-in CSS Style Editor in Design Studio. This option can be found in the PROPERTIES tab of the application (Figure 10.15). A new tab in Design Studio will open where you can edit your CSS file (Figure 10.16). The advantage of using this built-in CSS editor is that changes are directly applied to the document, whereas when you use a local CSS editor, such as Notepad++, you have to upload the CSS file to a platform to apply your changes.

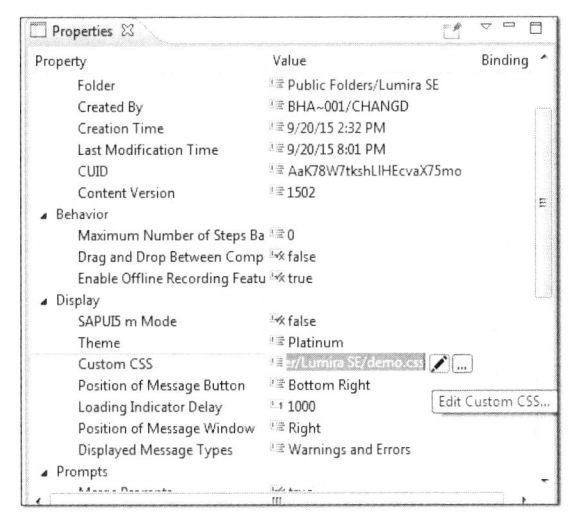

Figure 10.15 Editing Custom CSS Properties

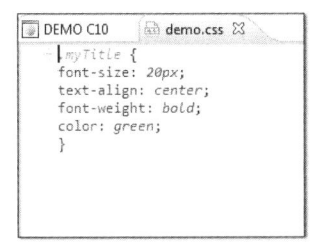

Figure 10.16 Design Studio CSS Editor

After you've finished creating your CSS file, you have to upload this file to the platform with which you're connected. Depending on the platform you use, you should consider the following:

▸ **SAP BusinessObjects BI platform**
In Design Studio, upload the CSS file by using the CUSTOM CSS option in the application properties, and select UPLOAD LOCAL CSS (Figure 10.17). The CSS file will be stored on the SAP BusinessObjects BI platform. You can transport this file through your systems using Promotion Management.

▸ **SAP Business Warehouse (SAP BW)**
If you're connected to the SAP BW platform, you can upload the CSS file to the MIME repository in SAP BW. You can access the MIME repository in SAP BW via Transaction SE80. Here, you can create a folder (Figure 10.18) where you

want to save the CSS files (and other files such as images). You can transport the CSS file just like other objects using Transaction STMS.

If you're connected to SAP HANA, you can upload the CSS file to the SAP HANA repository. You can transport these files using the SAP HANA delivery units.

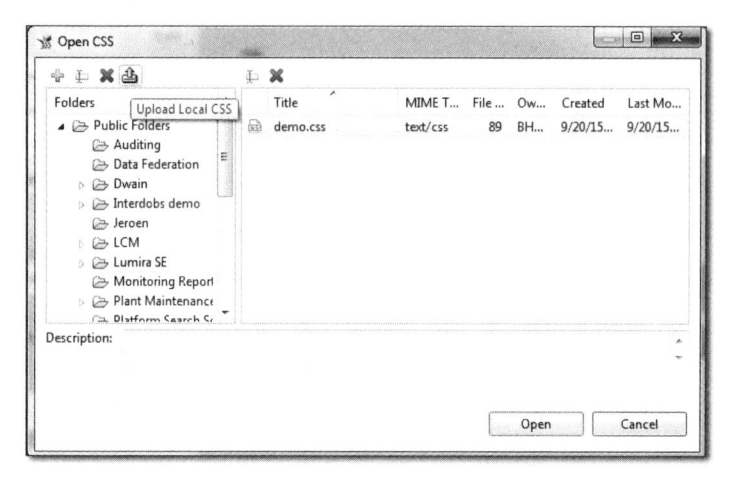

Figure 10.17 Upload CSS in the SAP BusinessObjects BI Platform

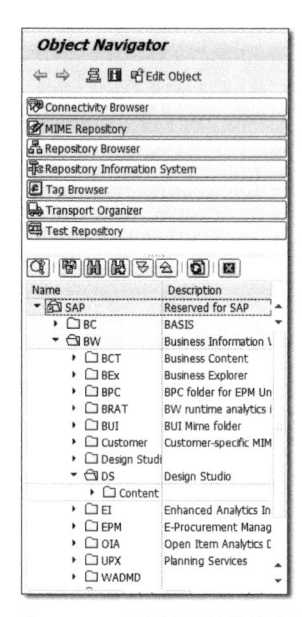

Figure 10.18 SAP BW MIME Repository

Before moving on to more advanced CSS topics, consider the following guidelines. These guidelines will help you in building and maintaining custom CSS files. It's especially important to follow these rules when you build a master CSS file used by many applications:

- **Give the classes appropriate names**
  Don't name a class for the style it performs; name it for its function. For example,
  ```
  .redmessage { background-color: yellow }
  ```
  could also be named
  ```
  .alertmessage { background-color: yellow }
  ```
  In addition, when assigning a class to a TEXT component that is supposed to give an alert message, the latter naming method is much more logical and easier to understand.

- **Try to keep the declarations in one line**
  Although keeping your code on multiple lines may look nicer, it doesn't help you find the class you're looking for. If you know that each line starts with a new class, you only have to scan the first word of each line.

- **Use shorthand code**
  Shorthand code is a lot easier to write than the full code. Furthermore, having fewer characters in the CSS file increases the speed of the application (although, admittedly, not very much).

  For example, the following is the full code to set the background settings with CSS:
  ```
  .mycustomclass
  {
  background-image:url('img_tree.tif');
  background-repeat:no-repeat;
  background-position:right top;
  }
  ```
  In shorthand, the code is the following:
  ```
  .myclass {background:#ffffff url('img_tree.tif') no-repeat right top;}
  ```

> **Shorthand Guide**
>
> For those who want to learn about shorthand code, we recommend this site:
> *www.dustindiaz.com/css-shorthand/*

> It's an old site, but one of the few that gives an overview of all the shorthand codes. All the shorthand codes are also mentioned at W3Schools:
>
> *www.w3schools.com/*

- **Know the browsers**
  If you build CSS code, you'll want to know which browsers are being used and if your application will be run on an iPhone or iPad. Don't try to build in support for all the browser versions—just maintain it for the browser types that are actually being used.

- **Group your classes**
  If you have more classes with the same properties, group them. This will save you a lot of double entries. If you want to define more classes, but those classes will have the same layout for the time being, it saves a lot of time.

  Without grouping:

  ```
  .class1
  { font-family:Arial,Helvetica,Lucida,Sans-Serif; color:#
  000; margin:1em 0;}
  .class2
  { font-family:Arial,Helvetica,Lucida,Sans-Serif; color:#
  000; margin:1em 0;}
  .class3
  { font-family:Arial,Helvetica,Lucida,Sans-Serif; color:#
  000; margin:1em 0;}
  ```

  With grouping:

  ```
  .class1 .class2 .class3
  { font-family:Arial,Helvetica,Lucida,Sans-Serif; color:#
  000; margin:1em 0;}
  ```

In the next section, you'll create custom CSS files.

10.4 Making Applications Responsive

One cool thing about CSS is that you can use it to make your application even more responsive. This means that you can define the way the components in your application look based on the device that you're using or based on the screen size of the client device. For instance, you can shrink the text size of the title of your application or hide parts of the application if the user opens it on a device with a small screen size.

Let's start with a simple example in which you have an application with a TEXT component that contains the title of the application. You can create a CSS file along with the CSS code in Listing 10.3 that you link to this TEXT component.

```
.mytitle
{
font-size: 36px;
font-weight: bold;
}
```

Listing 10.3 Code Linked to the Text Component

In this code, .mytitle is the name of the class that you link to the TEXT component. This simple piece of code sets the size of the text to 36px and makes the text bold as you can see in Figure 10.19.

SAP BusinessObjects Design Studio

Figure 10.19 Title for Large Screens

Now, let's reduce the size of the text to 20px and underline the text when the screen is less than 750px wide. To do this, you have to add the code shown in Listing 10.4 to the CSS file to make the application responsive to the users' screen size:

```
@media screen and (max-width:750px)
{
.mytitle{
font-size: 20px;
text-decoration: underline;
}
}
```

Listing 10.4 Text Size

By using the @media part of the code, you can define different style options and specific rules. In this code, when the screen size is smaller than 750px wide, the .mytitle class will change. In Figure 10.20, you see the result on a screen that is less than 750px wide.

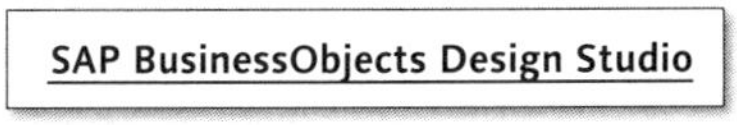

SAP BusinessObjects Design Studio

Figure 10.20 Title for Smaller Screens

10.4.1 Hiding Panels Based on Screen Size

The following example is based on the same principle as shown in the previous section but is a bit more complex (see Figure 10.21). You see a typical application with a header, a body, and a footer section. With CSS, it's possible to check the screen size of the device that is running the application and adjust what the user sees on their screen. In this example, you'll hide the footer if the screen is too small.

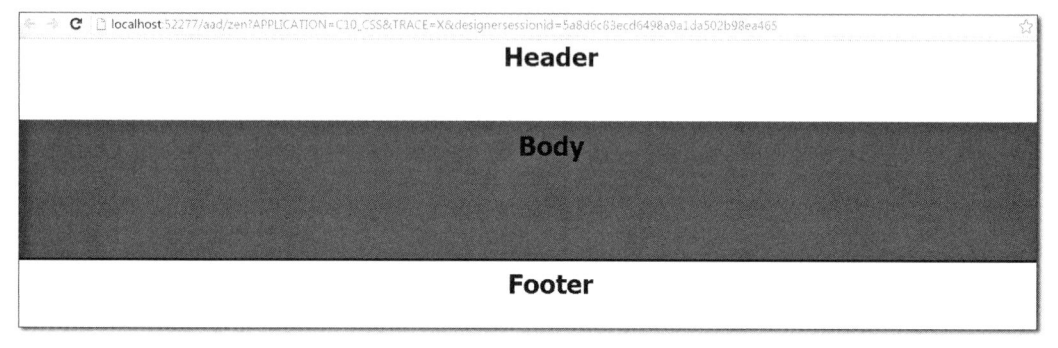

Figure 10.21 Application Consisting of a Header, Body, and Footer

This application contains three panels:

- **Header panel**
  This component has a HEIGHT of 100 set in its properties. No action will be performed on this component.

- **Body panel**
  In the properties of this component, you set the TOP MARGIN to 200 (this may seem strange because the header has a HEIGHT of 100, but we'll address this in a moment); set the BOTTOM MARGIN, LEFT MARGIN, and RIGHT MARGIN to 0; and set the WIDTH and HEIGHT to AUTO.

- **Foot panel**
  This component has the following properties: TOP MARGIN and WIDTH are set to AUTO; LEFT MARGIN, RIGHT MARGIN, and BOTTOM MARGIN are set to 0; and HEIGHT is set to 100.

The CSS file contains two classes, `myBodyPanel`, which is assigned to the body panel, and `myFooterPanel`, which is assigned to the footer panel. Take a look at Listing 10.5.

```
.myBodyPanel
{
position: absolute;
bottom: 100px;
}
.myFooterPanel
{
}
@media screen and (max-height: 610px)
{
.myFooterPanel {display:none }
.myBodyPanel{
position: fixed;
top: 100px;
}
```
Listing 10.5 Body and Footer Panel

The CSS class `myFooterPanel` gets assigned to the footer panel in Design Studio. As you can see in the code, this class is empty. All formatting (height and margins) is done in the properties of the component itself.

Notice that in the CSS file is a `@media screen` call. In the `@media` part of the code, you can define special style rules. For instance, you can apply CSS code if your screen is smaller or larger than a specified height, or if the device is used in landscape or portrait mode.

In the CSS file, a check is made on the screen size, and if the screen size is less than `610px`, the CSS code in this block is executed. If you look at the `myFooterPanel` part in the `@media` block, you see that the `display` is set to `none`, which means the footer will be hidden.

Now let's take a look at the `myBodyPanel` class. The height of the body should always remain on AUTO. Remember, that you set the TOP MARGIN of this component to `200`, instead of `100`, as you might expect. In the CSS class, the bottom margin is set to `100px`, creating space for the footer. This statement moves the whole body panel up 100px, so that the header, body, and footer now exactly align on the screen.

In the `@media` block of the code (so when the screen is smaller than 610px), the position changes from absolute (position is relative to its nearest positioned ancestor) to fixed and now starts at 100px from the top. The footer will now disappear, and the body will consume the remaining screen space (Figure 10.22).

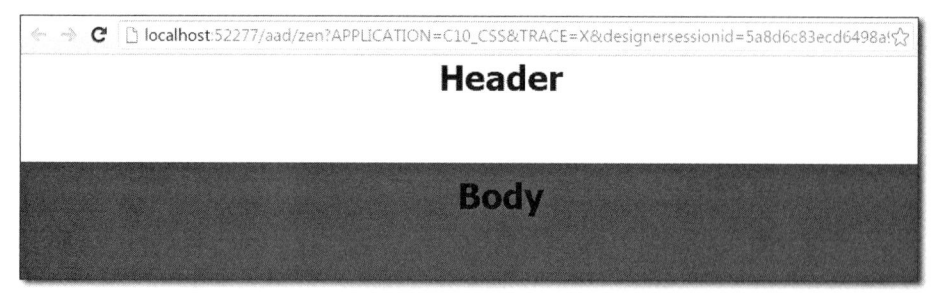

Figure 10.22 Automatic Removal of the Footer

10.4.2 Rearranging Blocks

The next example is a bit more common in web design but also a bit more complex to implement. In Figure 10.23, you see an application with six PANEL components, each containing a TEXT component and a number. When the screen size becomes too small (less than 750px), the PANELS are rearranged, and the application looks like Figure 10.24.

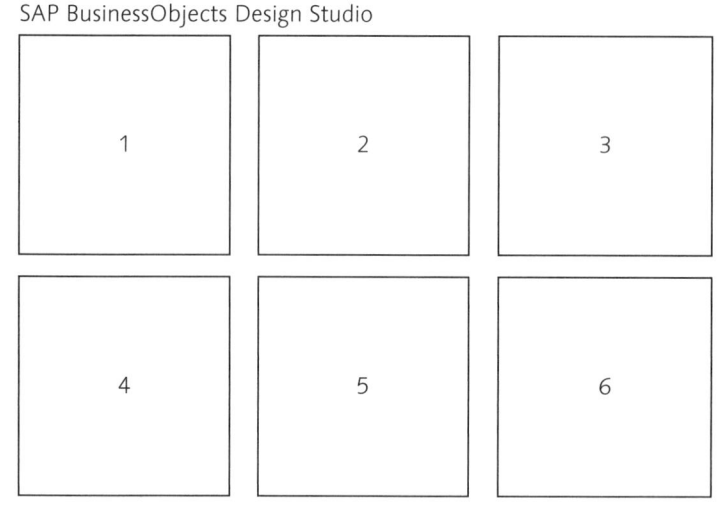

SAP BusinessObjects Design Studio

Figure 10.23 Application with Wider Screen

SAP BusinessObjects Design Studio

```
┌─────────┐  ┌─────────┐
│         │  │         │
│    1    │  │    2    │
│         │  │         │
└─────────┘  └─────────┘

┌─────────┐  ┌─────────┐
│         │  │         │
│    3    │  │    4    │
│         │  │         │
└─────────┘  └─────────┘

┌─────────┐  ┌─────────┐
│         │  │         │
│    5    │  │    6    │
│         │  │         │
└─────────┘  └─────────┘
```

Figure 10.24 Application with Smaller Screen

The trick here is to know exactly where to positon each PANEL on the screen in both situations (when the screen size is smaller than 750px and when the screen size is larger than 750px).

Follow these steps to set up the CSS of the application:

1. Place the six PANEL components on the screen. In this example, we placed TEXT components inside the PANEL components, but you can do this with any component as long as the width and height of this component is set to AUTO. Give all of the six PANEL components the same width and height. Don't worry about the position of the PANEL components, as you'll arrange this in the CSS file.

2. Now execute the application. When the application is rendered on the screen, you have to look at the source code. Some browsers such as Google Chrome have built-in tools to check out source code and preview what the application looks like when you adjust the code.

10 | Enhancing Applications with CSS

> **Inspecting the Source Code in the Browser**
>
> In most web browsers, you can inspect the source code of web pages. To do this in Google Chrome, Internet Explorer, Microsoft Edge, or Mozilla Firefox, simply press [F12].

3. Inspect the source code of the application. When you click on the magnifying glass (Figure 10.25) and then on one of the PANELS on the screen, you'll jump to a part of the code belonging to that PANEL. In Design Studio, we named the PANEL PANEL_2. You're looking for the ID of the container that PANEL_2 is wrapped in. In this example, it's __container1.

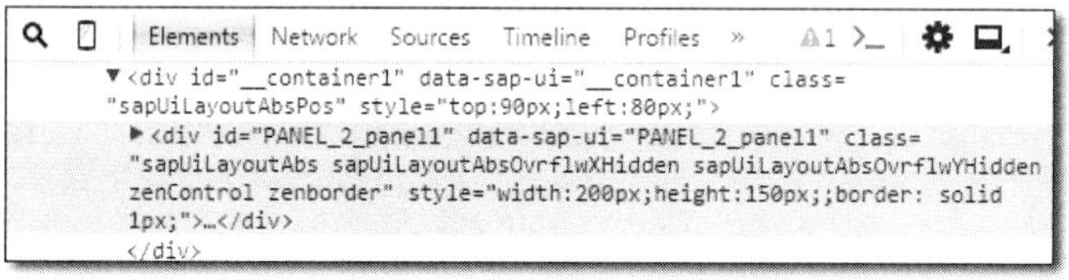

Figure 10.25 Source Code of the Application in Google Chrome

4. Identify the IDs of all six containers and remember to which PANEL they are mapped.

5. Now add the following lines of code as shown in Listing 10.6 to the CSS file, and link the CSS file to your application. You don't have to assign any class to the PANEL components:

```
/* Screen width < 750px*/
@media screen and (max-width: 750px) {
    #__container1  { top:90px!important;  left:80px!important  }
    #__container3  { top:90px!important;  left:300px!important }
    #__container5  { top:250px!important; left:80px!important  }
    #__container7  { top:250px!important; left:300px!important }
    #__container9  { top:410px!important; left:80px!important  }
    #__container11 { top:410px!important; left:300px!important }
}
/* Screen width > 750px*/
@media screen and (min-width: 750px) {
    #__container1  { top:90px!important;  left:80px!important  }
    #__container3  { top:90px!important;  left:300px!important }
    #__container5  { top:90px!important;  left:520px!important }
    #__container7  { top:250px!important; left:80px!important  }
```

420

```
#__container9 { top:250px!important; left:300px!important }
#__container11 { top:250px!important; left:520px!important }
}
```

Listing 10.6 Screen Size

In the first part of the code, a check is made to see if the screen width is 750px or less. When this is true, the containers (with PANEL components inside) are arranged in three rows and two columns. When the screen has a minimum width of 750px or larger, the containers will be arranged in two rows and three columns.

Let's highlight one line of the code to see how the positions get assigned:

```
#__container1 { top:90px!important; left:80px!important }
```

Here, `__container1` will be positioned at 90px from the top of the application. The `!important` statement indicates that all other position options (like the one defined in Design Studio) must be overruled with this one. In addition, `__container1` will be positioned 80px from the left margin of the application, as defined in the last part of this line of code.

In this method, you don't need to assign any class to any component in Design Studio. The drawback of this method is that container IDs as we identified them in the example can change when you add or remove components in your application. So, be sure to check the IDs again when you do this.

10.5 Modifying Standard Components

You've seen that some components such as TEXT components and PANEL components have a property called CSS STYLES that can be used to add CSS code directly, without a CSS file. You can modify other standard components by adding CSS to a class in a CSS file and linking this class to these components.

Let's examine how this is done. In the following example, you'll start with a CHECKBOX GROUP component. In Figure 10.26, you can see what this component looks like by default.

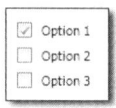

Figure 10.26 Default Checkbox Group

Now, unlike the TEXT and PANEL components, this component doesn't have the CSS STYLE property, so you can't edit the CSS properties directly. You need to define a CSS class with the CSS properties and values in a CSS file and link the class to the CHECKBOX GROUP component. Follow these steps to change the font style and color of this component:

1. Create a CSS file, and link it to your application.
2. In this CSS file, use the code in Listing 10.7 to define a CSS class called `.myCheckBox`:

```
.myCheckBox
{
font-style: italic;
color: red;
}
```

Listing 10.7 myCheckbox CSS Class

3. Link this class to the CHECKBOX GROUP component, as shown in Figure 10.27.
4. Reload the application, and view the results. Your component should look like Figure 10.28.

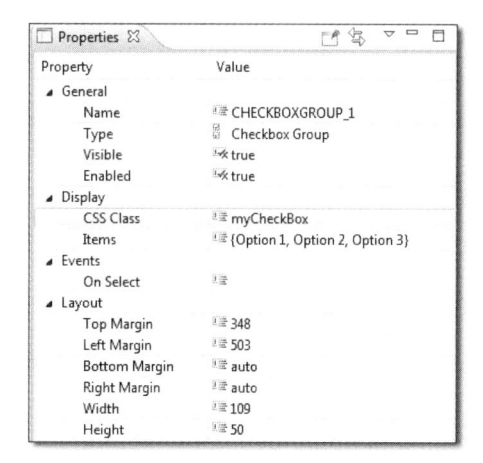

Figure 10.27 Checkbox Group Properties

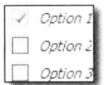

Figure 10.28 Checkbox Group Component with Custom CSS

By now, you might also want to change the blue checkmark. To do this, you'll have to know the name of the default CSS class where the properties of this checkmark are defined.

By inspecting the source code that is generated by the web browser, you can identify the CSS class that is used by the CHECKBOX GROUP. This component uses an image with 12 different checkboxes below each other, 26px apart (Figure 10.29).

Figure 10.29 Checkbox Images

You can use one of these checkboxes or create your own image with your custom checkboxes. By default (for this theme), when a checkbox is selected, the second checkbox in the image is selected. To select the red box that is checked, you need to move the selection nine steps downwards ($9 * -26px = -234px$). The code in Listing 10.8 does just that.

```
.sapUiCbChk>label
{
  background-position: left -234px;
  background-position-x: 0%;
  background-position-y: -234px;
}
```
Listing 10.8 Selecting a Checkbox

Looking at this code, you see that we edited a standard SAP CSS class called `.sapUiCbChk>label`. You can find the names of the standard SAP CSS classes by following these steps:

1. Run the application.

2. Inspect the code by pressing F12.

3. Use the element selector (first icon in Figure 10.30), and select the element for which you want to know the CSS class on the page.

4. The CSS class name and properties will appear in the STYLES part of the console (Figure 10.31).

Figure 10.30 Google Chrome Console

Figure 10.31 CSS Properties

Copy this code into the CSS file used in your application, and reload the application to view the result.

You can edit the default CSS class of other components as well, such as the LIST BOX component. Again, let's begin with an example. Figure 10.32 shows a LIST BOX component filled with employee names. The first employee is selected here, which is indicated by the blue selection line.

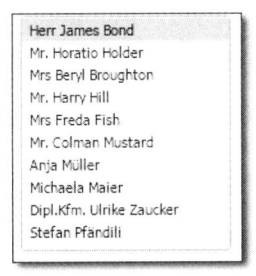

Figure 10.32 List Box Component

You can edit this color to any color you like by following these steps:

1. Execute the application (preferably in Google Chrome).
2. The application will be run in a browser. Check out the source code that is generated by the browser (usually right-click on the page, and select INSPECT ELEMENT or press F12).
3. Find the CSS class that sets the color for this component (use the magnifying glass in chrome). When you found the CSS class, you can play around with the values and see how changing the value affects your application. The CSS class and properties in Listing 10.9 are linked to the LIST BOX component:

```
.sapUiLbxStd>ul>.sapUiLbxISel>span,
.sapUiLbxStd>ul>.sapUiLbxISel {
  color: #000000;
  background-color: #7ac3e9;
}
```

Listing 10.9 CSS for List Box Component

4. Copy the CSS class to your own CSS file.
5. Change the value for the background property. For instance, change the `background-color` property from #7ac3e9 to white.
6. Save the CSS file, and reload the application.

Your LIST BOX component should look like Figure 10.33 now.

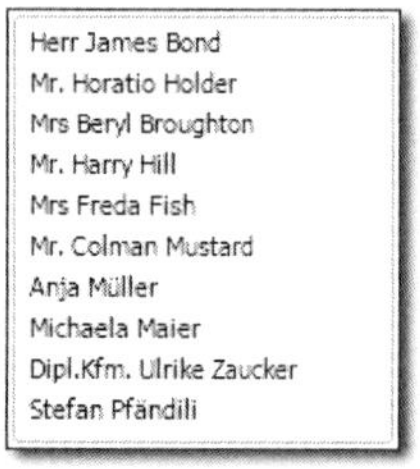

Figure 10.33 List Box Component without Colored Selection

By now, you have all the tools to identify standard CSS classes and know how to edit these classes to suit your own needs. Let's take a look at one last example. In this example, you'll edit the default style of a CROSSTAB component (Figure 10.34) by changing the color of the header background and text.

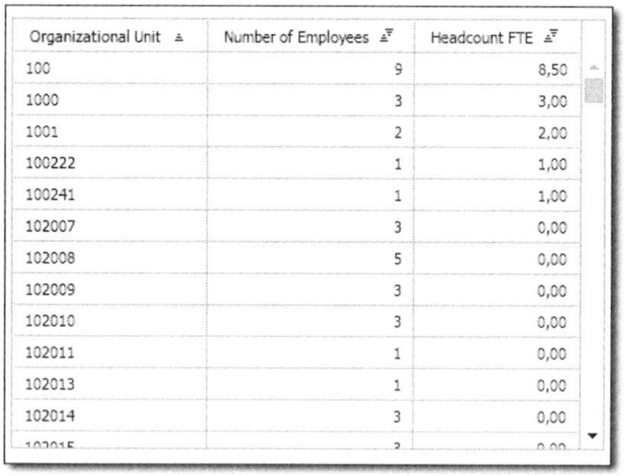

Organizational Unit	Number of Employees	Headcount FTE
100	9	8,50
1000	3	3,00
1001	2	2,00
100222	1	1,00
100241	1	1,00
102007	3	0,00
102008	5	0,00
102009	3	0,00
102010	3	0,00
102011	1	0,00
102013	1	0,00
102014	3	0,00

Figure 10.34 Default Crosstab Component

As explained in the preceding steps, execute the application in a web browser (preferably Google Chrome), and inspect the source code of the output. The colors in the table header are defined in two classes as shown in the source code:

- `.sapzencrosstab-DimensionHeaderArea.sapzencrosstab-HeaderCellDefault`
- `.sapzencrosstab-ColumnHeaderArea.sapzencrosstab-HeaderCellDefault`

Use these classes in your CSS file, and add the CSS properties and values shown in Listing 10.10.

```
.sapzencrosstab-ColumnHeaderArea.sapzencrosstab-HeaderCellDefault,
.sapzencrosstab-DimensionHeaderArea.sapzencrosstab-HeaderCellDefault
```

```
{
   color: white;
     font-weight: bold;
   background-image: none !important;
   background-color: blue !important;
}
```

Listing 10.10 CSS Link to the Crosstab Component

The text color will be set to white, and the font will be made bold. The default CROSSTAB component uses a background image that you don't want, so in the third line of the CSS code, specify that no image should be used. In the last line of the code, the background is set to blue. Figure 10.35 shows the result.

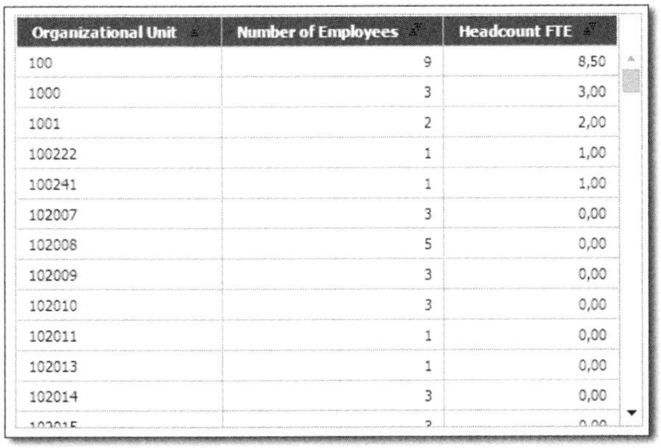

Organizational Unit	Number of Employees	Headcount FTE
100	9	8,50
1000	3	3,00
1001	2	2,00
100222	1	1,00
100241	1	1,00
102007	3	0,00
102008	5	0,00
102009	3	0,00
102010	3	0,00
102011	1	0,00
102013	1	0,00
102014	3	0,00

Figure 10.35 Crosstab Component with Custom CSS

10.6 Summary

In this chapter, you've seen how you can add CSS code to enhance your Design Studio application. You can add CSS code directly to components such as PANEL components and TEXT components. You've also seen how you can create and use your own custom CSS file, where you can edit the default style of each component you put on the screen, as well as make the application more responsive.

In the next chapter, we'll talk about design principles. We'll discuss certain principles to keep in mind when designing complex Design Studio applications.

You've now seen how to combine components to create applications. When designing applications, you need to consider some standard guidelines that help users work with your application and help you maintain it.

11 Design Principles and Visualization Options

Building an application using Design Studio is about more than knowing how all the pieces and parts work—it's also about understanding how to put them together in a way that makes sense to users. Additionally, it's also something that you need to maintain after it's in use. In this chapter, we'll walk you through some design principles to guide you in this process. We'll then describe all the possible visualization options that Design Studio provides and offer some hints about when an option might be the right visualization method for you.

Furthermore, we'll look at design principles for building complex applications. We'll then look at some performance considerations that you should calculate into your designs.

11.1 General Design Principles

When you build an application, it's important to do so with the user in mind, meaning that you need to think about how this application is going to help the user. Try to look at your application through the eyes of someone who is looking at the screen for the first time. In this section, we'll describe some principles that will help you build a user-centric application. Some of these may seem intuitive; however, you might be surprised how often basic, intuitive principles are violated at design time.

11.1.1 Don't Make Users Think

An application should be as obvious and self-explanatory as possible. It's your job as a developer to limit the number of question marks for the user and make the application navigation as intuitive as possible. If this goal isn't accomplished, users won't understand how to use the application to find the information they are looking for. Eventually, they will stop looking.

For example, if a manager asks for a report so he can see how every region performed the day before, you can show him all kinds of comparisons. In the first example in Figure 11.1, you see a table with comparisons to the budget in the month, cumulative year values, last year values, and so on. In the second example, shown in the same figure, you see only a percentage. The second one is much easier to grasp because it doesn't require much thinking. Now imagine that this report was about 50 stores instead of just four regions—this has the potential to make a huge difference in user comprehension.

	ACT	BUD	Delta	LYR	Cum	cum Bud	Cum Lyr	Delta
Region A	100	103	-3	101	402	421	413	-19
Region B	96	99	-3	97	391	393	385	-2
Region C	92	94	-2	92	389	430	421	-41
Region D	107	103	4	101	374	371	364	3

Region A	-3%
Region B	-3%
Region C	-2%
Region D	4%

Figure 11.1 Don't Make Users Think

11.1.2 Don't Make Users Wait

When you build an application, always keep performance in mind. How long do users have to wait at the start? How long does it take when they go to page 3 of the PAGEBOOK component? When an application contains many data sources, think of a scenario where some basic information is already visible at startup, and the rest will be loaded when needed. Then the user has some instant gratification because he already sees some results.

It has been found that if a website takes longer than seven seconds to show anything, half the users give up. After another seven seconds, the remaining half gives up too.

11.1.3 Managing User Focus

The human eye immediately recognizes edges, patterns, and motions. Think of how often you've reacted to a movement you saw out of the corner of your eye. Use those elements for the most important information, and avoid using them for the rest.

In this example, we again show the table with the sales of four regions. In the bottom table, we highlighted one number that we think is the most important (Figure 11.2). Note that finding this number on the top table is much more difficult.

	ACT	BUD	Delta	LYR	Cum	cum Bud	Cum Lyr	Delta
Region A	100	103	-3	101	402	421	413	-19
Region B	96	99	-3	97	391	393	385	-2
Region C	92	94	-2	92	389	430	421	-41
Region D	107	103	4	101	374	371	364	3

	ACT	BUD	Delta	LYR	Cum	cum Bud	Cum Lyr	Delta
Region A	100	103	-3	101	402	421	413	-19
Region B	96	99	-3	97	391	393	385	-2
Region C	92	94	-2	92	389	430	421	**-41**
Region D	107	103	4	101	374	371	364	3

Figure 11.2 Focus the Eye

11.1.4 Emphasizing Features

Another key principle is to emphasize clearly the important features in your application. Design a clear structure, and create buttons that are obvious for the user. At first glance, the user should immediately know where he can click and what he can expect after clicking. Letting the user know what is available is one of the fundamental principles of design.

In the example in Figure 11.3, there are three buttons with the same function. The left one is the most obvious. The right one, on the other hand, would give you pause because it doesn't look like a button.

Figure 11.3 Emphasizing Features

11.1.5 Keeping It Simple

Users go to an application to get information or to perform a particular task. Although they might be amused at the first look of a fancy design, in the end, they want to get their information or perform their task as easily as possible.

As you saw in Figure 11.1, the second example was much easier to grasp. One of the reasons for this is that the second table is much simpler and is dedicated to the question, "How did we do?" Sometimes, more isn't always better.

> **Simple Is Difficult**
>
> Experience shows that keeping applications simple is hard to do. People will always ask for more features, and if you keep adding them, at some point your application needs a large manual to understand how to use it. Be mindful of this from the beginning, and try to say "no" more often to keep the application focused.

11.1.6 Using Conventions

Although it's fun to think of new ways to show information, often the basic conventions are the best choice. Users are accustomed to these conventions and therefore don't need much time to get started with a new application. Only deviate from conventions when you have a clear reason why you think that the new option will be an improvement over the convention.

A commonly used convention is the *International Business Communication Standards (IBCS)*. The IBCS are proposals for the conceptual, perceptual, and semantic design of comprehensible business reports and presentations. We'll discuss this convention in more depth in Section 11.2.13.

As you saw in Figure 11.3, the left button is the easiest to recognize. This button is easier to grasp than the second one because we're used to this kind of button. Over the years, we've clicked thousands of buttons like this. Now when we see a visualization like that, we immediately assume it's a button, without even looking at the text on it.

11.1.7 Getting the Most Out of Screen Room

The most challenging aspect of application design in this mobile age is that you have to put a lot of information, often very different in theme, into a small amount of real estate: the computer screen, tablet screen, or even a mobile phone screen. Inserting all this information mustn't jeopardize the clarity of the application.

The following principles apply:

- Summarize the information, and show the exceptions.
- Try to avoid elements that don't present data.
- If you can't avoid non-data elements, try to make them blend in as much as possible.
- Highlight the most important information because it needs to be seen first.
- Keep the most important part of the screen for the most important information. The top left and middle are the most important parts.

To help you do more with less, let's briefly discuss the *data-to-pixel ratio*. The data-to-pixel ratio is derived from the data-ink ratio, which was introduced by Edward R. Tufte. When information is displayed on the screen, some of the pixels show the data, and the other pixels show visual elements that don't represent data. To build a lean dashboard that uses the screen well and avoids overloading the user with too many elements, you should try to maximize the ratio. This creates room to put more information in the same amount of space without overwhelming the user with all kinds of signals.

In the example in Figure 11.4, two tables show the exact same information. However, notice how the second table provides a lot less distraction and allows you to focus on the numbers.

2016 to date				2016 to date (1000$)		
Product Line	Sales	Leads		Product Line	Sales	Leads
Product A	13,660.91	818.00		Product A	14	818
Product B	68,579.27	776.00		Product B	69	776
Product C	55,598.57	212.00		Product C	56	212
Product D	51,615.03	552.00		Product D	52	552
Total	189,453.77	2,358.00		Total	189	2358

Figure 11.4 Tables Redesigned with the Data-to-Pixel Ratio in Mind

Another advantage of reducing the number of elements is that you don't have to shout if you want to highlight a particular number. Just emphasizing it slightly is enough, as you can see in Figure 11.5.

11 | Design Principles and Visualization Options

Sales per product in ($ 1000)						
Product	2008	2009	2010	2011	2012	Total
Product 1	66	64	95	91	43	359
Product 2	18	88	91	77	51	325
Product 3	60	63	73	35	97	328
Product 4	10	36	67	8	51	172
Product 5	30	25	53	36	27	171
Product 6	33	86	89	78	89	375
Product 7	65	44	32	39	27	207
Product 8	93	63	20	24	24	224
Product 9	86	73	84	**22**	81	346
Product 10	62	81	26	99	89	357
Product 11	8	71	80	73	89	321
Product 12	11	16	44	5	65	141
Product 13	72	95	39	14	99	319
Product 14	5	19	37	50	56	167
Product 15	72	17	9	62	76	236
Product 16	26	32	33	17	39	147
Total	717	873	872	730	1.003	4.195

Figure 11.5 Emphasizing the Data

Design Studio has numerous visualization options, which we'll introduce next. When choosing your method, make sure to keep the previously mentioned principles in mind.

11.2 Choosing a Visualization Method

In this section, we'll discuss data visualization and how to choose the best visualization method for your application. First, we'll look at why visualization is so important. From there, we'll walk through all kinds of graph types offered in Design Studio and think of situations where they may be useful. Finally, we'll look at the IBCS. These standards will give you a setup plan for how to use visualizations to get a data message across clearly.

Visualizations help users understand data. Often the data in a data warehouse consists of millions of rows that users have only a limited time to make sense of. That is where data visualization comes in.

Good visualizations expose information, revealing underlying patterns and trends, and highlighting the important messages hidden in the data.

Look at the example in Table 11.1. This is a well-known example called Anscombe's quartet, which was created by Frank Anscombe in 1973.

Property	Value
Mean of x	9
Sample variance of x	11
Mean of y	7.50
Sample variance of y	4.122 or 4.127
Correlation between x and y	0.816
Linear regression line	Y = 3.00 + 0.500x

Table 11.1 Anscombe's Quartet: Values Are Equal among Datasets

In Table 11.1, you see a list of properties that apply to four different datasets. This means that this table will give a user no way to tell the difference between these four datasets.

However, if you look at the charts in Figure 11.6, it's immediately clear that the data is very different.

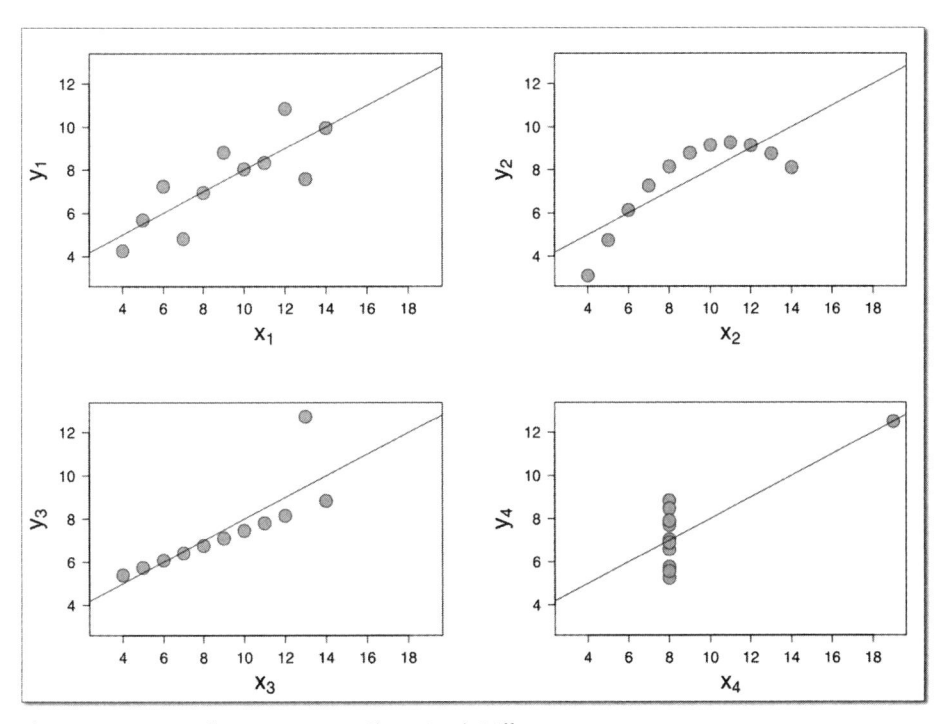

Figure 11.6 Anscombe's Datasets in Charts Look Different

11 | Design Principles and Visualization Options

When choosing from among the visualization methods that Design Studio offers, it's essential to think about how the user wants to look at the data. Remember to start by always asking yourself these questions:

- What is important? Specifically, which dimensions and key figures are important?
- What is the message that you need to communicate? Do you want to know the trend? The exception? Do you want to compare numbers?
- What options do you have in Design Studio to present the data?
- Which of the options is best to present the data?

The following subsections discuss the visualization options in Design Studio.

11.2.1 Single Number

A single number is a very effective way to present data (Figure 11.7). If the most important metric of the organization is sales, then just one number can be enough to provide the user with critical information. Use this kind of visualization when you want to emphasize that this is an important number and when you want the user to know the exact number.

397.724 sales

718   leads

Figure 11.7 Single Number

11.2.2 Line Chart

A line chart is a chart where a line flows from left to right (Figure 11.8). It usually involves time, plotted along the X-axis. Because of its format, a line chart is very useful to show trends in data. If you want to emphasize a comparison between values, then you should think about a column or bar chart instead of a line chart.

There is one variation on a line chart, which we discuss next.

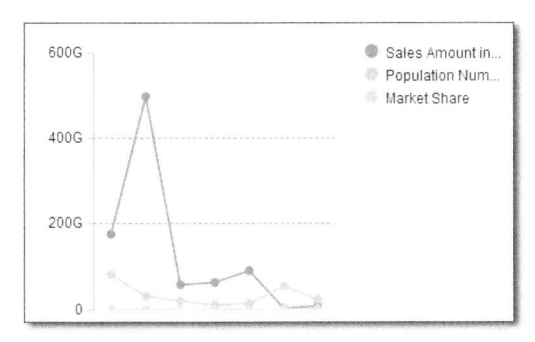

Figure 11.8 Line Chart

Horizontal Line Chart

A horizontal line chart is similar to a line chart, but instead of showing the data from left to right, this chart goes from top to bottom (Figure 11.9). If you have a specific need to display labels horizontally, this chart may be useful, but, in general, we don't recommend it. It's easier to read trends going from left to right, so the traditional line chart is usually best (and again, if you want to compare values, we recommend the bar chart).

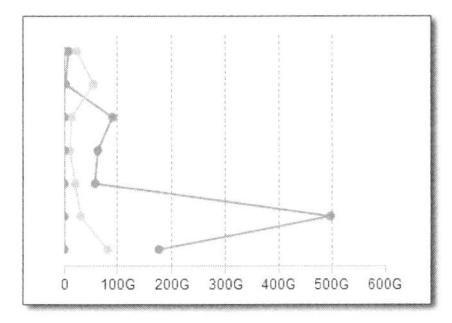

Figure 11.9 Horizontal Line Chart

11.2.3 Bar Chart

A bar chart compares the values of several entities with each other across dimension values that are set below each other. As you can see in Figure 11.10, it's very easy to see which region has the highest values. An advantage of the bar chart over the column chart is that the labels are horizontal, which makes them easier to read. A bar chart is used to compare values. For trends or exact numbers, you're better off using a line graph or crosstab.

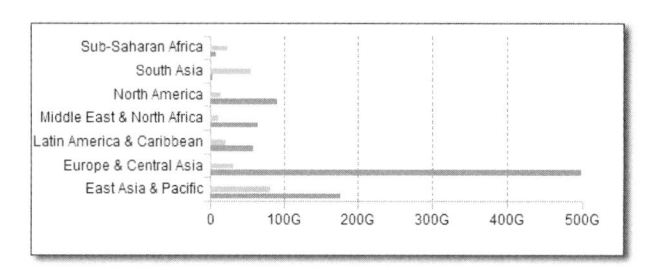

11 | Design Principles and Visualization Options

Figure 11.10 Bar Chart

There are several variations of bar charts.

Stacked Bar Chart

In a stacked bar chart, the bar itself is divided into colors based in the part-to-whole relationship of the underlying entities (Figure 11.11). The chart shows the part-to-whole relationship in the bar, and the bars themselves can be compared to each other. If you have only one bar, a standard bar chart with a bar for each entity is more useful. A stacked bar chart can be used when you have multiple whole values (e.g., sales per month) and the whole is divided by region.

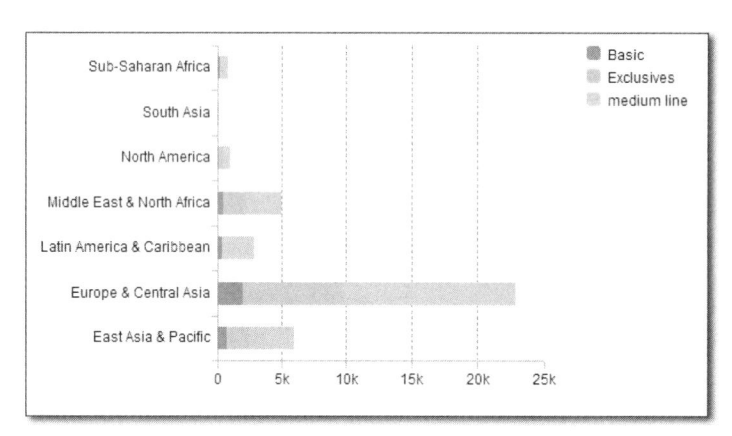

Figure 11.11 Stacked Bar Chart

Keep in mind, however, that comparing the colored parts across bars is difficult because the starting points are dependent on values of the entities, so you don't have a base value to compare. This type of chart is most useful when you want to compare a value across entities and also want to see something of the part-to-whole relationship with that entity. This chart doesn't show trends, outliers, or exact values well.

100% Stacked Bar Chart

A 100% stacked bar chart is a stack of horizontal bars where you show the part-to-whole data (Figure 11.12). This visualization allows you to show part-to-whole relations across a dimension. The disadvantage is that you can't compare the dimension itself because everything is added to 100%. An alternative that paints a part-to-whole relation more clearly is the bar or column chart, as it's easier to make comparisons with them.

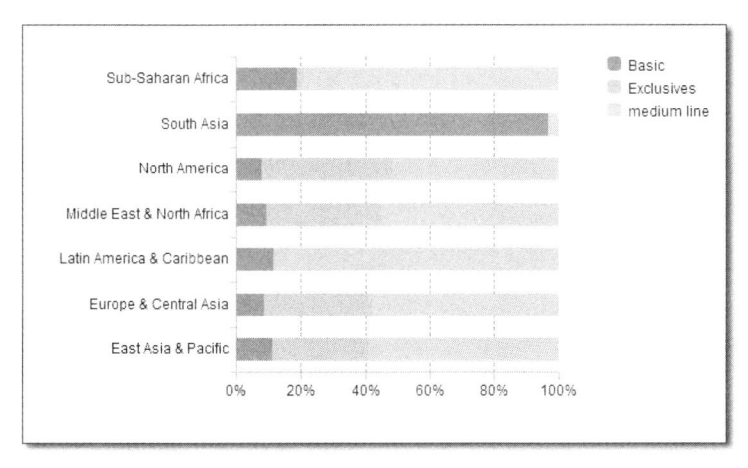

Figure 11.12 100% Stacked Bar Chart

Bar Combination Chart

A bar combination chart is a bar chart with a vertical line chart added, allowing you to show two key figures across the dimensions (Figure 11.13). A bar combination chart is useful for comparing data, like the bar chart, but you can also show a trend, as you also have a line graph at your disposal. For example, if you want to show the profitability per region and the cumulative value as well, a combination chart would be very useful.

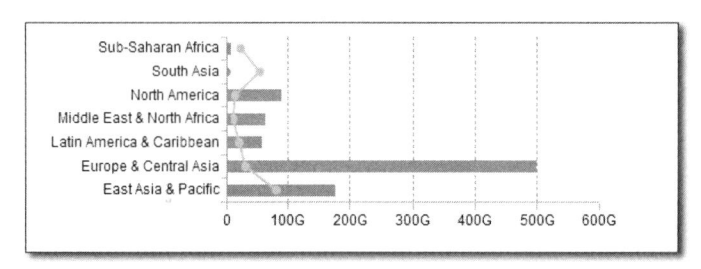

Figure 11.13 Bar Combination Chart

11.2.4 Column Chart

A column chart shows columns from left to right, where the height of the column conveys the value for a particular entity (Figure 11.14). A column chart is used for comparing entities with each other. The size of the bars allows you to compare the values in the chart to each other.

We like the bar chart a bit more than the column chart because the column chart makes it more difficult to place labels—they go beneath the X-axis. A column chart is best suited for comparing values, while it's less useful for showing trends or exact values.

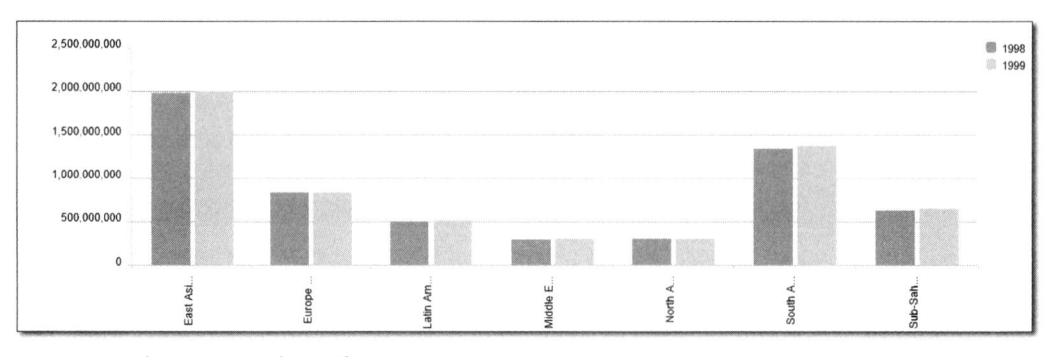

Figure 11.14 Column Chart

As with the line and bar charts, there are several variations of column charts.

Stacked Column Chart

The stacked column chart has the same advantages and disadvantages as the stacked bar chart, but the labels are in vertical alignment (Figure 11.15).

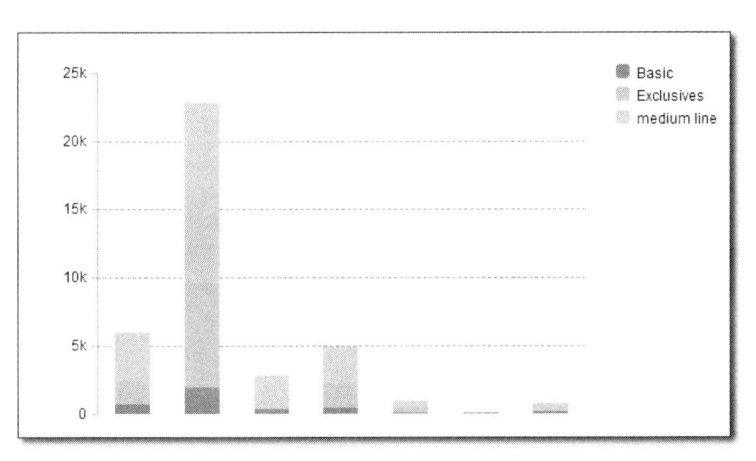

Figure 11.15 Stacked Column Chart

100% Stacked Column Chart

The 100% stacked column chart does the same thing as the 100% stacked bar chart, but it has vertical columns instead of bars (Figure 11.16). Again, for comparisons of part-to-whole, you're better off with standard bar or column charts.

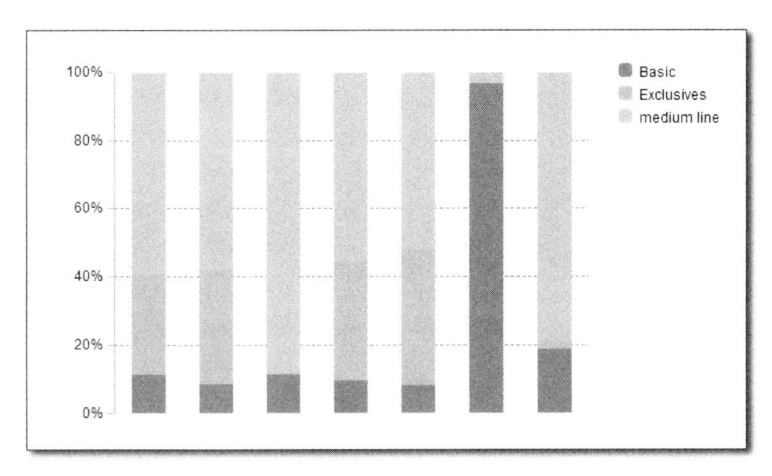

Figure 11.16 100% Stacked Column Chart

Column Combination Chart

A column combination chart is like a column chart, but with a line chart added so that you can show a second value across the dimension (Figure 11.17). The

11 | Design Principles and Visualization Options

column combination chart is best used when data needs to be compared and when you want to show the aggregated part-to-whole relationship. This type of chart is less suitable for exact values and for trend analysis.

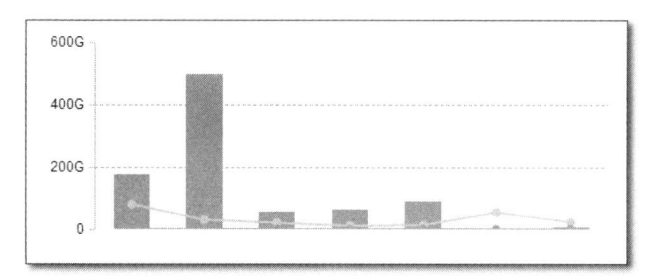

Figure 11.17 Column Combination Chart

11.2.5 Area Chart

An area chart emphasizes trends of data and allows you to compare the trends of several entities with each other (Figure 11.18). This visualization type is good for when you need a little bit of both. If you want to emphasize the comparison more, a bar or column chart is better; for the trend, a line chart is preferable.

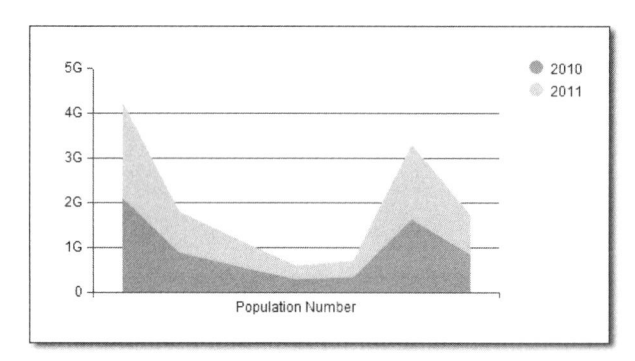

Figure 11.18 Area Chart

There is also one variation of the area chart.

Horizontal Area Chart

A horizontal area chart is a horizontal chart that goes from top to bottom (Figure 11.19). As with the area chart, it does a bit of comparing and a bit of trending, but it doesn't show exact values.

We find horizontal area charts to be somewhat less effective than standard area charts because the trending function is hampered by the fact that you have to read from top to bottom instead of left to right. As it's quite difficult to compare data using this type of chart, you might want to consider a bar combination chart instead.

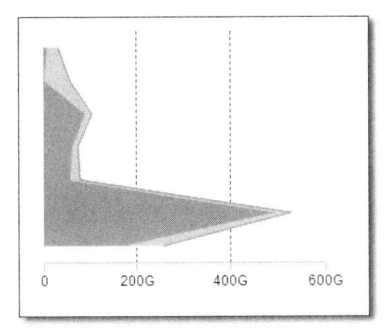

Figure 11.19 Horizontal Area Chart

11.2.6 Crosstab

You may recall from earlier chapters that we often use CROSSTAB components. In a CROSSTAB table, numbers are presented along rows and columns, which is very useful for displaying exact information (Figure 11.20). You can show a lot of data in an efficient way. However, CROSSTABS aren't very useful for identifying trends and other relations between data points. You can highlight outliers by changing the layout of numbers that are outside of the main trend, but you can't show how much or how good or bad something is.

Figure 11.20 Crosstab Visualization

11.2.7 Bubble Chart

A bubble chart shows data in three dimensions (Figure 11.21). You use three values: one shown on the X-axis, one shown on the Y-axis, and one shown via the size of the bubble. A well-known example of this is the Boston Consultancy Matrix, where market share and market growth are on the axes, and there are four quadrants for the product life cycle. The size of the bubble is the relative amount of sales.

This type of chart is designed for comparison. The position of each bubble allows you to compare the values to each other. The sizes of the bubbles can also be used for comparison, but this is a less exact way of comparing because you can only tell if a bubble is large or not. You can't show exact numbers or trends with this chart.

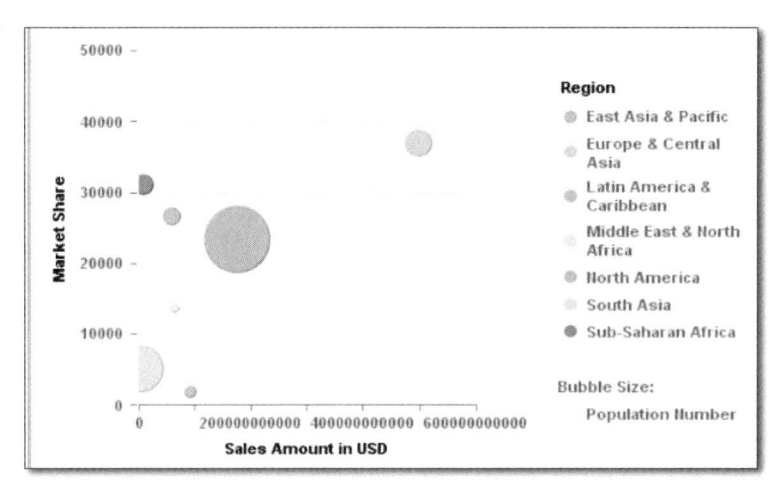

Figure 11.21 Bubble Chart

11.2.8 Waterfall Chart

A waterfall chart emphasizes the cumulative addition to the end result with positive and negative values (Figure 11.22). A stacked bar chart would have difficulties presenting the negative values, so that is where the waterfall chart comes in handy. If you want to emphasize the comparison between values, a standard bar chart is a better choice.

There are several variations on the standard waterfall chart.

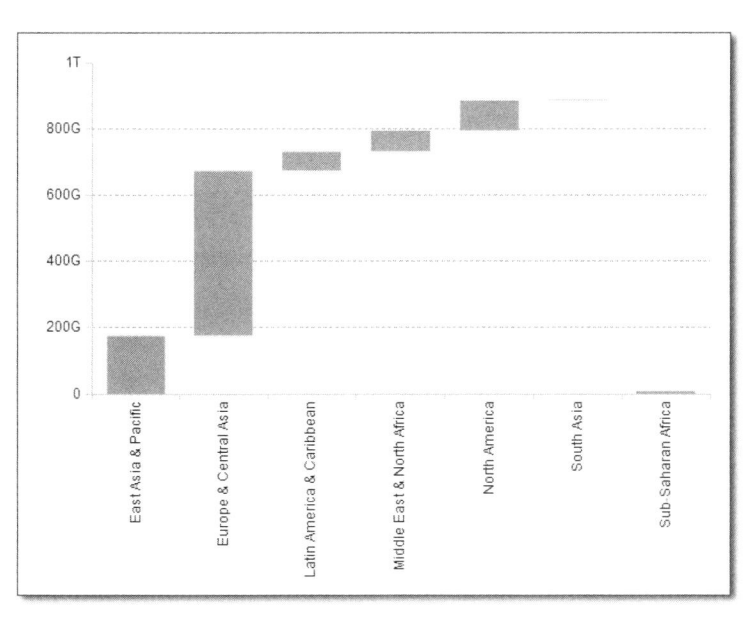

Figure 11.22 Waterfall Chart

Horizontal Waterfall Chart

A horizontal waterfall chart (Figure 11.23) shows data in a cumulative way, where the starting point of one bar is based on the endpoint of the previous bar. The endpoint of the final bar is the cumulative result over all the entities. This helps you to see every entity's part of the whole value.

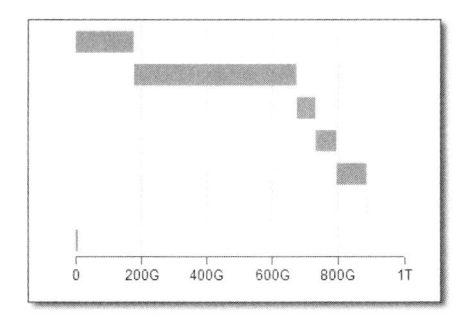

Figure 11.23 Horizontal Waterfall Chart

The advantage of a waterfall chart over a stacked bar chart is that here you're able to see negative values clearly. This is why this chart is often used to show budget overruns and underruns across departments. To make comparisons across entities easier, the entities are often sorted by their value, so the order of entities enables you to compare the contribution of each entity to the whole. This chart is best used when you want to compare results that contain negative values; otherwise, a bar chart will do the job. This chart isn't suitable for showing trends or exact values.

Stacked Waterfall Chart

A stacked waterfall chart can put multiple values in each part of the waterfall chart (Figure 11.24). This makes creating more advanced versions of a waterfall possible. However, these charts are a bit harder to understand—the user has to concentrate on the chart before he can make sense of all the values, especially when one part of a bar is positive, and one is negative.

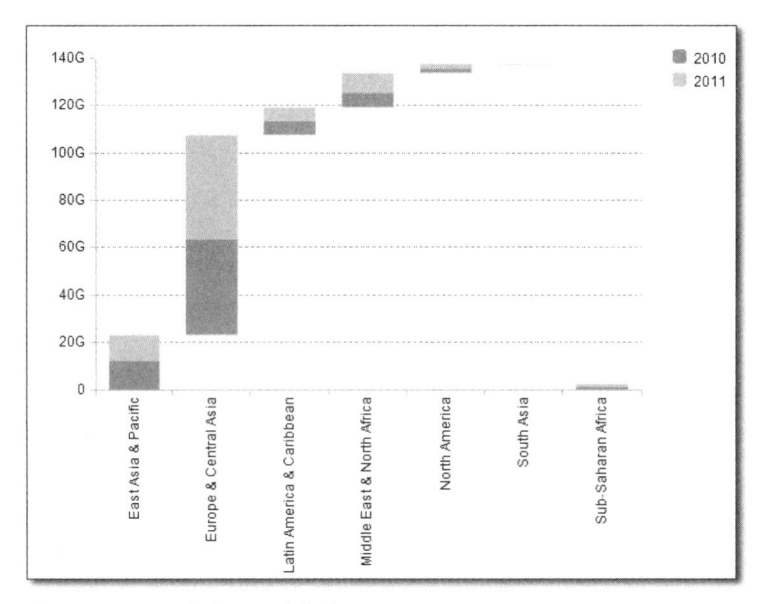

Figure 11.24 Stacked Waterfall Chart

11.2.9 Pie Chart

In a pie chart, values are shown as slices of a circle (Figure 11.25). A pie chart's strength is that it shows the part-to-whole relation in an easy to understand way.

However, as the number of slices grows, it's more difficult to see which entity holds what part, so comparing values gets more difficult. Trends and exact values don't work with this chart.

We generally recommend bar or column charts over pie charts, but they may be effective when you only need to compare two or three values.

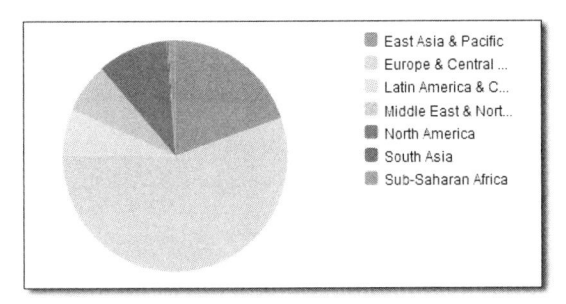

Figure 11.25 Pie Chart

Multiple Pie Chart

A multiple pie chart shows the same pie chart for several key figures, which allows you to show the relative sizes of the entities (Figure 11.26). However, you could also place three identical bar charts next to each other to accomplish the same goal. The problems we already mentioned for a single pie chart are also valid for this type of chart. We don't recommend using this type of chart.

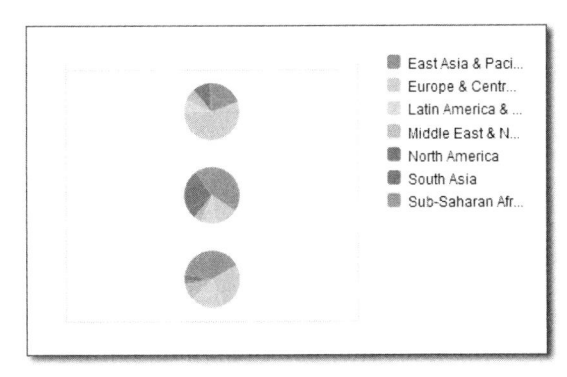

Figure 11.26 Multiple Pie Charts

11.2.10 Radar Chart

A radar chart is basically a line chart in which the X-axis is a circle instead of a line (Figure 11.27). The result is a circle where a data point's distance from the center shows the value of the key figure. A radar chart can be useful for comparing the shape of properties for several entities in a multiple radar chart or when you want to show data that is naturally ordered in a circular way, such as hours on a clock.

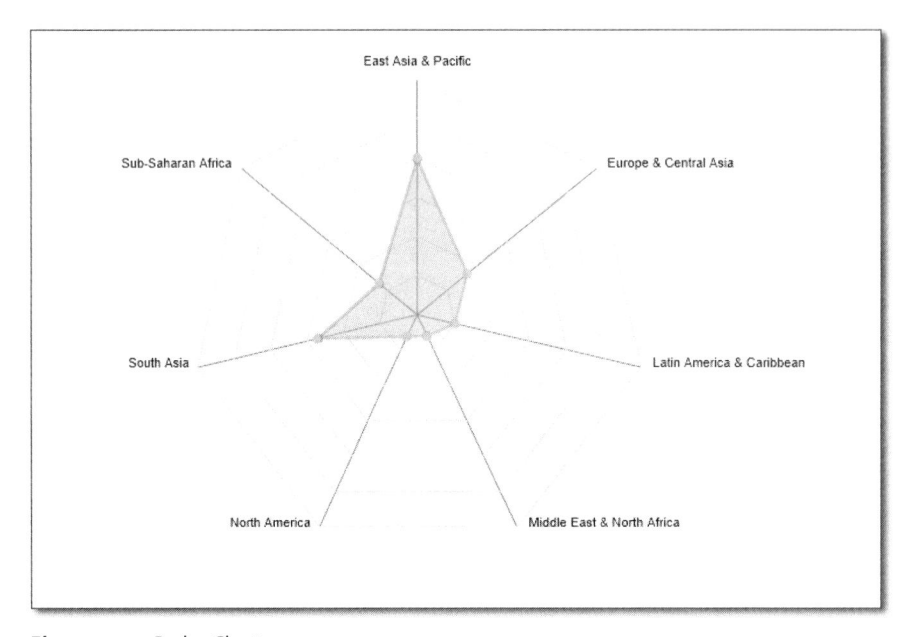

Figure 11.27 Radar Chart

The radar chart has one variation.

Multiple Radar Chart

A multiple radar chart is a multiple version of the radar chart that is useful for comparing several entities with each other for a number of values (Figure 11.28). Compared to the multiple pie chart, this type of chart emphasizes the change in value more than actually comparing the absolute values. This graph is useful when you want to give a rough impression of the properties but not an exact comparison.

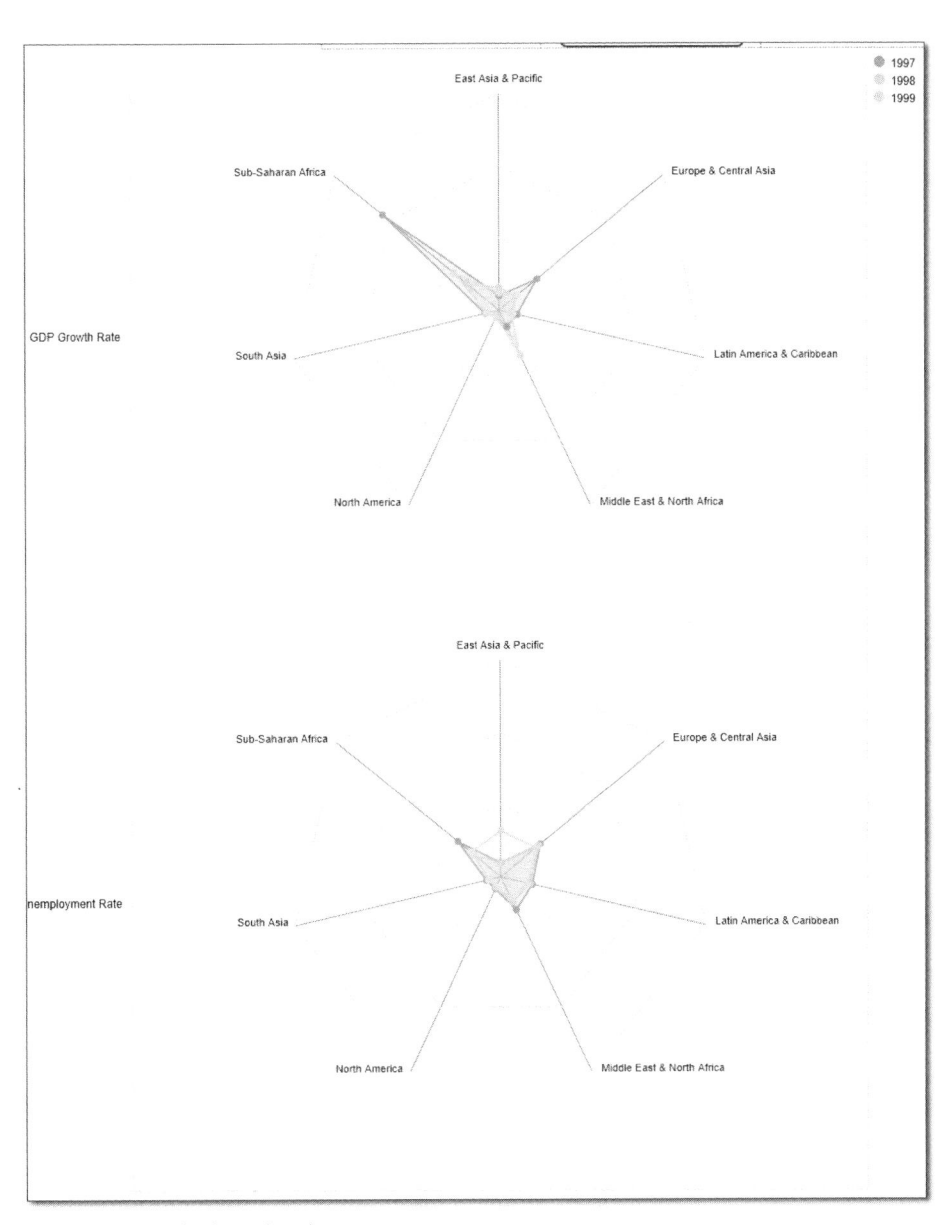

Figure 11.28 Multiple Radar Chart

11 | Design Principles and Visualization Options

11.2.11 Scatter Chart

A scatter chart is used to show the relationship between two key figures (Figure 11.29). It's great at showing trends of a relationship as well as highlighting outliers—often you add trend lines to the scatter cloud to identify a trend that you can use for future predictions. Compared to the bubble chart, it lacks one dimension, but, in return, you get more clarity and can plot much more data into the chart. This kind of chart isn't suitable for showing part-to-whole relationships.

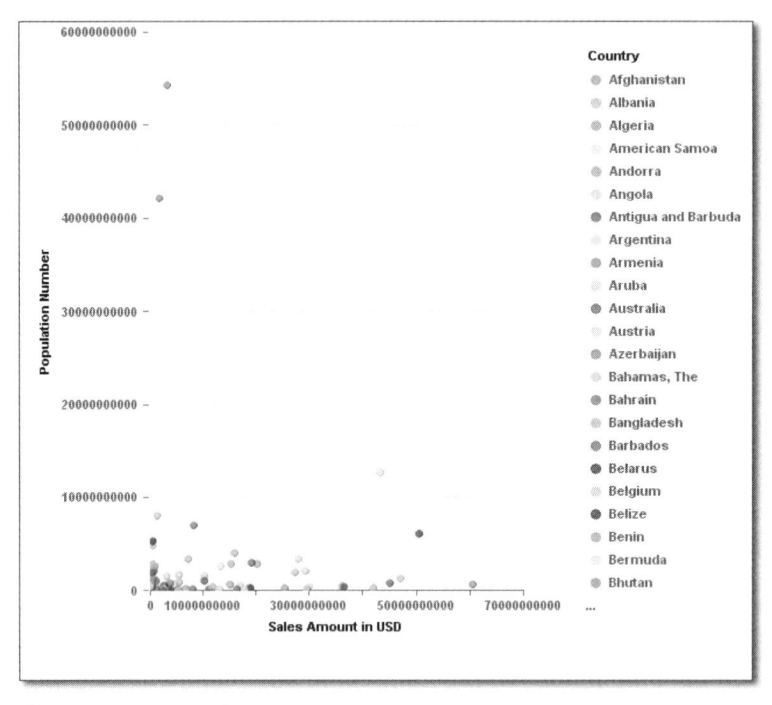

Figure 11.29 Scatter Chart

11.2.12 Chart Comparison

We've covered a lot of charts. For an overview of all the charts and their strengths and weaknesses, see Figure 11.30. A ++ means that it a major strength in comparison with other tools, a –, a major weakness.

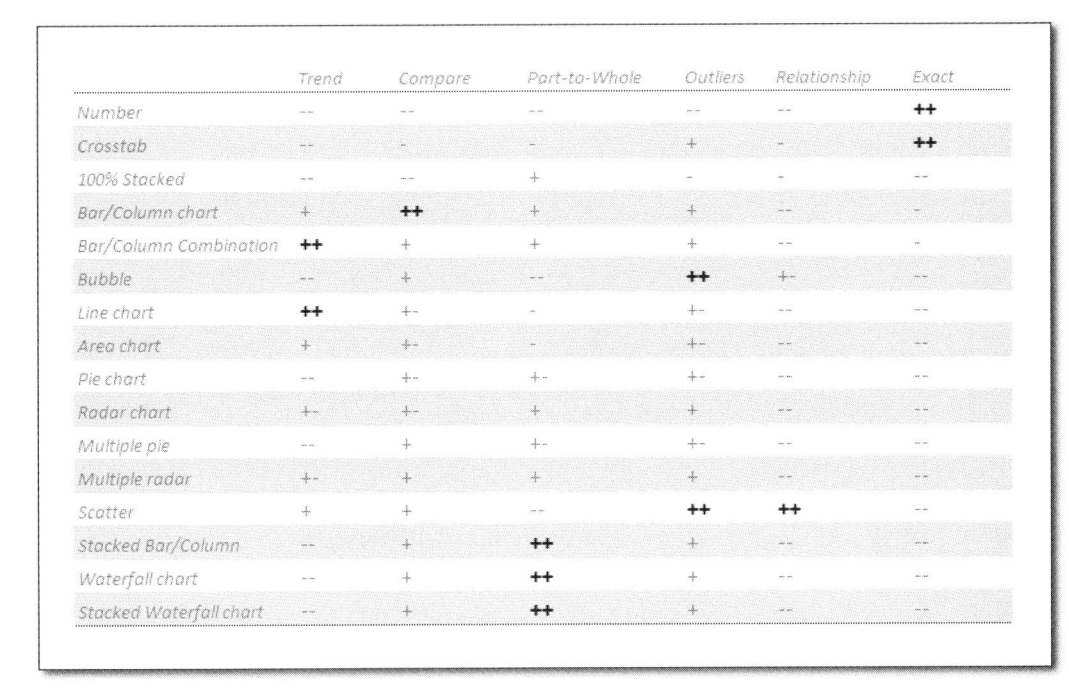

	Trend	Compare	Part-to-Whole	Outliers	Relationship	Exact
Number	--	--	--	--	--	++
Crosstab	--	-	-	+	-	++
100% Stacked	--	--	+	-	-	--
Bar/Column chart	+	++	+	+	--	-
Bar/Column Combination	++	+	+	+	--	-
Bubble	--	+	--	++	+-	--
Line chart	++	+-	-	+-	--	--
Area chart	+	+-	-	+-	--	--
Pie chart	--	+-	+-	+-	--	--
Radar chart	+-	+-	+	+	--	--
Multiple pie	--	+	+-	+-	--	--
Multiple radar	+-	+	+	+	--	--
Scatter	+	+	--	++	++	--
Stacked Bar/Column	--	+	++	+	--	--
Waterfall chart	--	+	++	+	--	--
Stacked Waterfall chart	--	+	++	+	--	--

Figure 11.30 Chart Comparison

11.2.13 International Business Communication Standards

If you're looking for a good way to visualize data and get messages to users, it's a good idea to consider the *International Business Communication Standards (IBCS)*. IBCS includes proposals for the design of comprehensible business reports and presentations.

IBCS is a wide methodology that covers topics such as data visualization, key performance indicator (KPI) selection, message delivery, structuring reports, and many more. In this section, we'll give a very high-level overview of the methodology.

The IBCS is set up in three rule groups that are the pillars of IBCS:

- **Conceptual rules**
  These rules are in place to get the message across by using the appropriate storyline. These rules look at the conveyance of the message (*say*) and organization of the content (*structure*).

11 | Design Principles and Visualization Options

- **Perceptual rules**
  Perceptual rules are there to use appropriate visual design. They correspond with the rule sets for the following:
  - *Express*: Choose the right visualization to convey the message and the underlying facts.
  - *Simplify*: Avoid clutter.
  - *Condense*: Increase information density.
  - *Check*: Present information in the most truthful and the most easily understood way possible.
- **Semantic rules**
  Semantic rules help to relay content clearly by using a uniform notation (IBCS notation).

In Figure 11.31, you see a small part of the express rule set. This is a list of charts organized by use based on the type of analysis. For example, you see that a column chart is reserved for time series and that bar charts are used for structural data such as regions, countries, products, and so on.

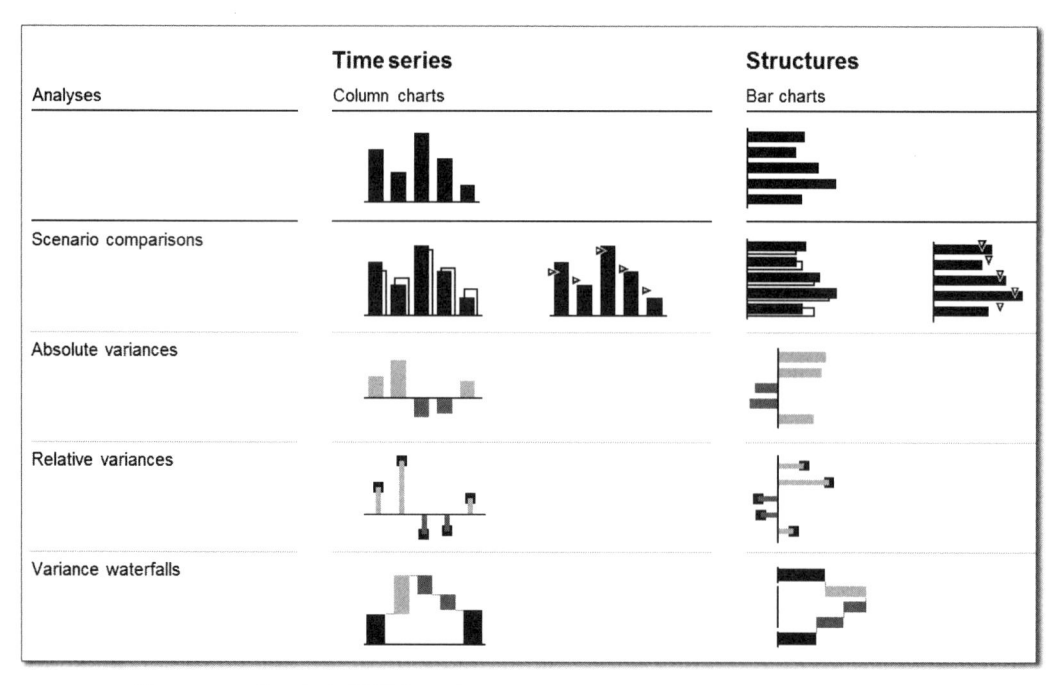

Figure 11.31 Graphs in IBCS Format

452

> **More information on IBCS**
>
> For more information on IBCS, visit *http://www.ibcs-a.org/*. There you'll find not only a set of rules but also a community that is actively reviewing and updating the visualization rules based on their experiences in organizations applying those rules. In Part IV we'll show a software development kit (SDK) that allows you to invoke Hichert charts into your application.

11.3 Building Complex Applications

As applications grow, you'll notice that they become harder to maintain. In this section, we'll show you some guidelines to keep the complexity in check and enable you to create well-performing, maintainable, and robust applications.

In this section, we'll first establish a number of general guidelines in the form of building principles. Then, we'll go into tips for building applications. Following this, we'll look into scripting before discussing using CSS.

11.3.1 Building Principles

Before we go into the specifics of Design Studio building principles, we want to look at some common principles. Often, you'll witness situations where guidelines are set up, but things don't work that easily when the guidelines are enforced. As developers try to create their solutions on time and within a certain budget, guidelines can feel like a burden. It's very tempting to skip them, even when you know in your heart that it will come back and hurt you in the long run.

Make Guidelines Easy to Follow

When you have the guidelines in place, be sure to create a template application that is already formatted according to those guidelines. Using this template will give projects a head start when developing.

Additionally, when creating CSS classes for designers, ensure that the class names are logical and easy to remember. On the same note, it's important to ensure that the information on which classes are available and what they do is easily accessible.

Follow Up on Projects That Can't Follow the Guidelines

Some projects may not follow the guidelines when there is too much time pressure or a project works differently from the established guidelines. If that is the case, allow it. However, be sure that there is enough budget available to fix this after go-live.

Change Slow, But Follow Up

It's important that after guidelines are in place, changes are made with a very low frequency. Designers and users should be able to get used to the guidelines; too many changes would hurt that.

Additionally, be aware that after a guideline changes, it must be applied to all applications. In some cases, these implement easily. A change in a SDK element or in a CSS class automatically results in a change in all depending applications. However, changes in an application's layout have to be made in all applications one by one.

11.3.2 Application Building Tips

Before we go into some tips for improving your application-making skills, let's discuss why this is necessary. Basically, you'll find that the application building process is very much like the phone game Snake. The beginning is easy enough, and then you start to notice that every move you make is more and more difficult because your tail keeps growing and getting in your way.

This is very much like what happens in a lot of applications, especially when they are poorly structured. Keep these tips in mind to spare yourself a lot of headaches later on.

> **Snake**
>
> For those of you that have no idea what the game snake is all about, here is a link: *http://playsnake.org/*. Notice how the difficulty increases as your snake body grows. Just as the application building process gets more complex as the application grows.

Creating a Portfolio of Smaller Applications Instead of a Large One

Creating dedicated small applications that focus on a particular job can be a better idea than building a larger application designed for multiple tasks. As you limit the data sources and components in one application, you'll get better performance. To make applications work together, you define a number of external parameters in your guidelines, which every application must adhere to. This way, a designer creating a new application can use these guidelines to know how to link to another application. By expanding the URL of the other application with parameters, you're able to pass information that is contained in the first application to the newly opened application

> **Scripting**
>
> We'll discuss scripting with external parameters in greater detail in Chapter 8.

As an example, let's assume that you created an application that lets the user choose a query and freely discover the detailed information by using filters, adding drill downs, and so on. Other applications that want to offer such additional detailed information functionality can then link to your application. All they have to do is use the link and pass the information regarding the query and the system the query resides in.

You application needs some external parameters, as shown in Figure 11.32.

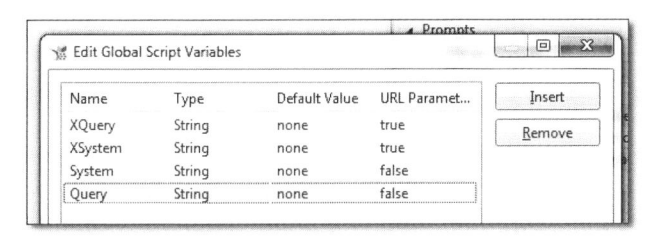

Figure 11.32 External Parameters

If an application wants to open a query using the navigation application, all it has to do is open the URL with added parameters:

http://myServer/APPLICATION=MY_APPLICATION&Xquery=ZSALES&XSystem=BWP

This example will open the application and tell it to open the query ZSALE in system BWP.

Variables

In your script, you can use local variables as a placeholder for almost any type of value. Use this to your advantage. Before you apply any logic, assign the values to variables, and work with the variables from that point on. The additional advantage is that if you need to change the value itself, for example, take it from another component, you only have to change this once at the beginning of the script. This avoids having to walk through the entire script looking for references.

In the following example, you see two scripts that do the exact same thing. The first one is built with a minimum amount of coding without doing anything extra for readability. The second script uses variables as placeholders.

Script without placeholder variables:

```
DS_FIN_DRILLDOWN.setFilter("ZVEST__ZBUSUNIT", CHRT_FIN_
TREND.getSelectedMember("ZVEST__ZBUSUNIT"));
```

Script with placeholder variables:

```
DS_FIN_DRILLDOWN.setFilter(storeDimension, selectedStore);
```

Without knowing much about Design Studio, this script, or anything else about the application, you can know by looking at the second script that you use the selected store to apply a filter to the data source.

> **Naming Revisited**
>
> We already discussed the importance of naming your components consistently in Section 11.3.2. In scripting, when you activate the content assistant by pressing [Ctrl] + [Space] to find a component, you'll really find out how much this consistent naming helps because you can find components much easier.

Global Variables

If local variables are great, global variables are ideal! Global variables are the best way to ensure that you have a place to store central values. For example, what about that selected store in the previous example? What if you have 10 or maybe 20 scripts that need the selected store? The global variable can be used everywhere and only set once.

Typically, you have to look for all the references if for some reason you have to assign a new value to a global variable. You need to check where your application is using the global variable to ensure that the change doesn't break anything in the application.

The drawback, however, is that there is no easy way to find out where a global variable is used. For components, you can use your right mouse button to find the REFERENCES feature, but not with global variables. Within a large application, it can be worse than finding a needle in a haystack because with this needle, you know how many needles you have to find.

Because those global variables are so valuable, it's worthwhile to use a workaround to avoid this drawback. To work around this issue, you can create global functions to represent the global variable. The idea is that in script, you always refer to the global script instead of referring to the global variable directly. The advantage here is that this global script does have a FIND REFERENCES feature (Figure 11.34).

Figure 11.34 Find References for Global Script

You create the function with one parameter, `newStore`, which when filled with a value, sets the new value for the global parameter. In the script itself, you can add additional functions for layout, logic, and so on. In this example, there is some logic included to ensure that if there is no value, and no new value is set, the script falls back to a BEx variable to get the value of the selected store (Figure 11.35).

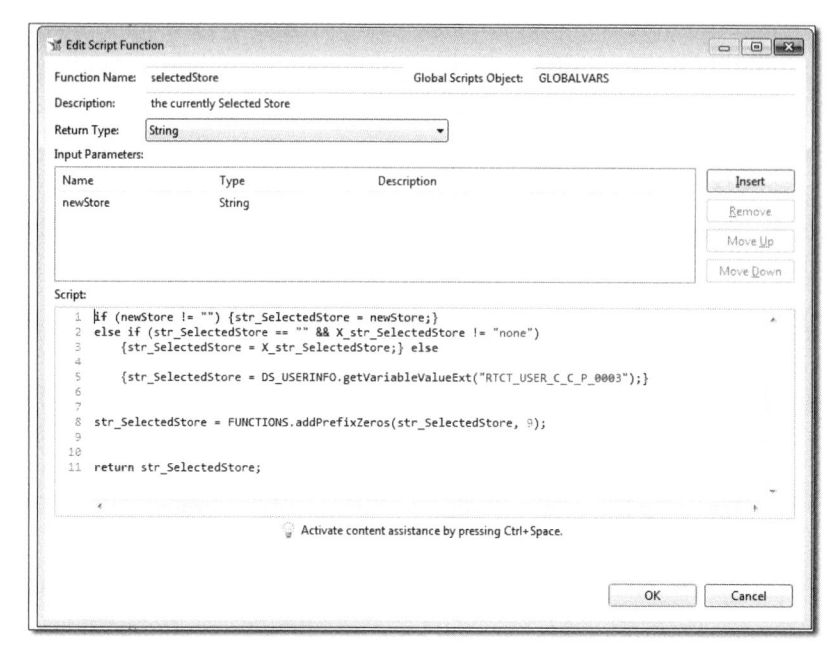

11 | Design Principles and Visualization Options

Figure 11.35 Global Variable Function

Additionally, there is a function called `addprefixzeros`. This function looks at the length of the value and the new value. It will reformat the value with prefix zeros to fill out the entire length.

Anywhere in the application, you can get the selected store value using the script line:

`var selectedStore = GLOBALVARS.selectedStore("");`

If you want to assign a new value to the global variable, use the line:

`var selectedStore = GLOBALVARS.selectedStore("9");`

People with experience in JavaScript will recognize the setup just shown as a typical `getter/setter` function.

> **More on Readability**
>
> If you want a more in-depth look into readability best practices, we recommend the following blog:
>
> *http://code.tutsplus.com/tutorials/top-15-best-practices-for-writing-super-readable-code--net-8118*

460

Centralize Your Code

Use global functions to centralize your script code. Avoid repetition as much as possible. In the previous section, you saw an example where you don't have to do all that testing and formatting to get a value for the selected store. However, there are many more examples.

If you notice that you have to perform the same actions again and again to a number of components, you can put that into a global function. You can pass the component as a parameter, and apply all the actions to the component in the function.

This is a big code saver. If, for example, you perform 7 actions on 20 components, you need 140 lines of script. With the global function, the number is reduced to 27.

11.3.4 Managing the CSS Layout

As an application grows, the CSS layout is used to format applications. The increased size and number of applications does provide a risk that it will be more and more complex for designers to add new formatting to applications. The result is often that designers just add local formatting everywhere. This will lead to increased difficulty when maintaining layouts. In this section, we'll show you how to avoid such scenarios.

First, we'll look at ways to make CSS classes accessible. We'll then examine CSS in regards to reusability. Finally, we'll provide recommendations for formatting standard components with internal classes.

Logical Naming, Template, and Documentation

Use logical class names and make sure that documentation, templates, and applications are available so that designers can easily see what classes they can use and how to apply them. A template is an obvious choice to list all the CSS classes (Figure 11.36). The designer can see the effect of the classes immediately. When he wants to apply one of these layouts, he just copies the relevant components.

11 | Design Principles and Visualization Options

Figure 11.36 Template Layout to Showcase CSS Classes

Avoid CSS Style Properties

The problem with the CSS style property is that it only applies to a single component, so making a change means finding and changing every component with that CSS style property one by one. If you have to change a certain look of an application, you have to revisit each component with that particular formatting; finding the CSS style properties in an application isn't easy. The best way to find all CSS style properties in an application is to download the application and use Notepad++ or a similar tool to search for CSS formatting.

Change Internal Formatting of Components

If you know the default CSS classes used in the components, you can change those settings. When doing this, embed the CSS class within your own class name.

Using only the internal class name as in the following code will result in changing all the components of that type in your application:

```
sapzencrosstab-Crosstab {color: #4c4a37;}
```

However, when you do it as shown in the following, it will only change those components of that type to which you assigned the class `MyC1`:

```
myC1.sapzencrosstab-Crosstab {color: #4c4a37;}.
```

11.4 Designing for Performance

In this section, we'll look at some guidelines on using data sources for performance purposes. Using data sources correctly ensures better performance.

11.4.1 Creating Row-Based Data Models

With row-based data models, you create flexible queries that allow a lot of freedom for navigation. In doing this, you provide all the necessary dimensions and allow Design Studio as much freedom as possible to put these dimensions in rows and columns as needed. Creating a fixed structure in a query robs Design Studio of all the options it has to manipulate the data source and may put you in a spot where you've created a complex workaround in the application to do something that would have been easy to do if the query was more flexible.

11.4.2 Ensuring Calculations Are Done in the Backend

Currently, it's possible for users to add their own calculations in CROSSTABS. However, designers can't add these in data sources in Design Studio. Create these calculations in the backend. Putting them in the Design Studio application means that you have to repeat that calculation in every application that needs it. Better to create one calculation in the query to service all the applications.

11.4.3 Avoiding Variable Usage in Queries

Using variables in queries causes a number of problems. First, you have to think about merging/unmerging them. Second, variables aren't easy to find in the code where you manipulated them. There are only two good reasons to use variables:

▶ **Authorization purposes**
If a user is only allowed to see a subset of the data, it's much easier to have one central variable in place than to filter a number of queries. The latter always has

a risk that you might forget to filter one of the queries, resulting in unauthorized data access.

- **Synchronization**
  You can ensure that all queries are synchronized. If you have multiple data sources that all need the same store filter, it's easier to force them to align if they all have the same variable. One variable change ensures that all data sources are showing data from the same store.

You can argue that it's necessary in situations where you need some functionality that isn't offered yet in Design Studio. For example, if you want to show the top customer, but the user is allowed to choose how many he wants to see, you're forced to use a variable to pass that information to the backend query. In the current version (1.6), we now see the ability for users to add these calculations themselves using the CROSSTAB component. The next step is to add them to the data sources. When this is available, you should remove the variable and use the in-application features.

11.4.4 Be Thoughtful When Loading Data Sources

Timing the moment to load data sources right goes a long way in increasing the perceived performance of an application. Use background processing to load those data sources that you don't show on the first screen, and use the load in script feature. As long you don't load the data source, the data source will have no impact at all on performance.

You can also create parallel groups that run in parallel to each other. Data sources in the same group run sequentially. Therefore, it makes sense to create a separate group for your query with the longest duration, so that when this query is done, the others are done as well.

The combination of loading in a script, background processing, and processing groups in parallel gives you a lot of options to work with. Take your time, and map things out.

Using the parameter `&PROFILING=X` when starting the application provides a detailed overview of the performance. Use this to improve the loading of your data sources.

11.4.5 How to Navigate

The best option to script navigation in applications by far is the use of `setDataSelection` within components. Using this method avoids roundtrips to the backend system altogether, and performance isn't measured in seconds, but in milliseconds.

To give yourself room to use this method, use data sources to deliver larger datasets where the graphs use subsets of the available data. For example, if you have five regions, load all of them. Group them by that dimension, and use the `setDataSelection` to pick one of the regions.

11.5 Summary

In this chapter, we looked at design principles and visualizations. We began by discussing some general user-friendly design principles. In the next section, we continued by discussing the graphs in Design Studio and the situations they can best be used. We then dove further into design standards and looked at the IBCS.

In Section 11.3, we looked at a number of building principles regarding some common principles, and moved on to application building, scripting, CSS, and data sources. In the final section, we discussed the importance of designing for performance and the methods that can enable you to do so.

For "just" a report design tool, this seems like a lot of rules. These guidelines are important because you can build large complex data visualization applications that can grow over time and must be maintained and supported. Using these rules makes life much easier after the first version of the application is added to the list of applications and you need to maintain them all.

In the next part of this book, we will focus on Design Studio's SDK.

PART IV
The Software Development Kit

In this chapter, we'll show you how to install and deploy ready-made SDK extensions in a landscape, as well as how to test new versions. We'll also describe an example of a third-party SDK extension that is available.

12 Using SDK Extensions in SAP BusinessObjects Design Studio

Design Studio has a software development kit (SDK) that allows for the design of custom extensions to enhance standard functionality. In this chapter, we'll take premade SDK extensions and walk through the steps to install an SDK component and make it available throughout the full SAP landscape (development, test, production, etc.).

In Section 12.1, we'll describe what extensions are and how they work. In Section 12.2, we'll look at the steps to install SDK components on your local application. In Section 12.3, we'll look at moving SDK components from your local installation to a platform. In Section 12.4, we'll then take the SDK and move it through the system landscape from the development to the production environment. Finally, in Section 12.5, we'll focus on some third-party providers of SDK extensions.

To begin, let's answer the big questions first: What are extensions, and how do they work?

12.1 Extensions: What They Are and How They Work

In this section, we'll describe what extensions are and how they interact with Design Studio. When talking about SDKs, we're referring to either *SDK extensions* or *SDK components*:

469

- **SDK extension**

    An SDK extension is an installed package that contains one or more SDK components.

- **SDK component**

    An SDK component is an element that you'll find in the COMPONENTS panel in Design Studio after the extension is installed.

When installed, the SDK extension is a separate package that is loaded into Design Studio when needed. The need only arises when one or more SDK components are used in an application.

If you open the application in a text editor, you'll find in the first line, the call from the application to load an SDK extension when one or more SDK components are present in the application:

```
xmlns:sdk1="com.sap.ip.bi" sdk1:version="15.0" xmlns:sdk2=
"org.scn.community.databound" sdk2:version="2.0" xmlns:sdk3=
"org.scn.community.datasource" sdk3:version="2.0">
```

SDK extensions are loosely coupled to applications, and the internal functions are a black box, which means that you only see what it does and not how it works. The application tells the SDK extension which component it wants to render and the property values that are set for that component. In reply, the SDK extension executes the appropriate JavaScript code and provides the resulting visualization back to the application. The application places the visualization in the predetermined location, which means that if the internal code of the SDK extension changes, all applications that use the extension will change with the extension.

For example, if you change the extension component code that until now renders a chart into a table, from then on, all applications will show tables. Changes will only be required in the applications when the property list changes because the applications and the extension need to interact on that level.

Extensions are separate objects, meaning they are independent of each other and not included in Design Studio. You have to install them on your local Design Studio software and on any platform where you want to run applications with SDK components.

Now that we've gone through the "what" and "how," let's being looking at the steps necessary to install, remove, and updated premade SDK extensions.

12.2 Installing, Updating, and Removing SDK Extensions

In this section, we discuss how to install a premade SDK into your Design Studio application, how to update an existing SDK extension, and how to uninstall an SDK extension.

12.2.1 Installing

This section walks through the steps for setting up a new installation and provides platform-specific installation instructions for SAP BusinessObjects Business Intelligence (BI), SAP Business Warehouse (BW), and SAP HANA.

New Install

To install a premade SDK extension to your application, follow these steps:

1. Go to the menu bar, and select TOOLS • INSTALL EXTENSION TO DESIGN STUDIO (Figure 12.1).

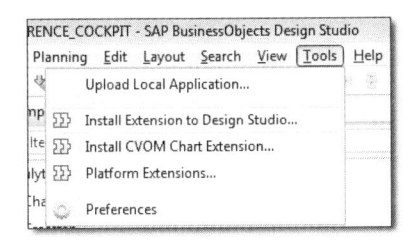

Figure 12.1 Install Options from the Tools Menu

2. A dialog box opens where you can insert either a URL or a file location on your local drive (Figure 12.2) to select the installation file for the SDK. For the latter choice, you can click the ARCHIVE button.

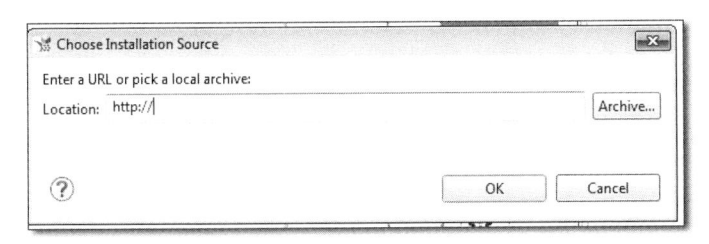

Figure 12.2 Choosing the Installation Source

3. A new dialog box appears with all the SDK extensions that the application found on either the URL or the file (Figure 12.3). Select all the extensions that you want to install, and click FINISH.

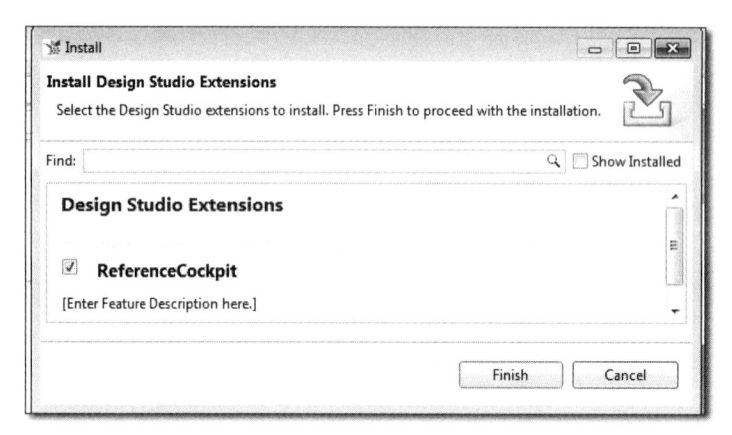

Figure 12.3 SDK Extensions That You Can Install

4. A dialog box appears that asks you to confirm the Design Studio extensions that you want to install (Figure 12.4). Keep the items to install selected, and click NEXT.

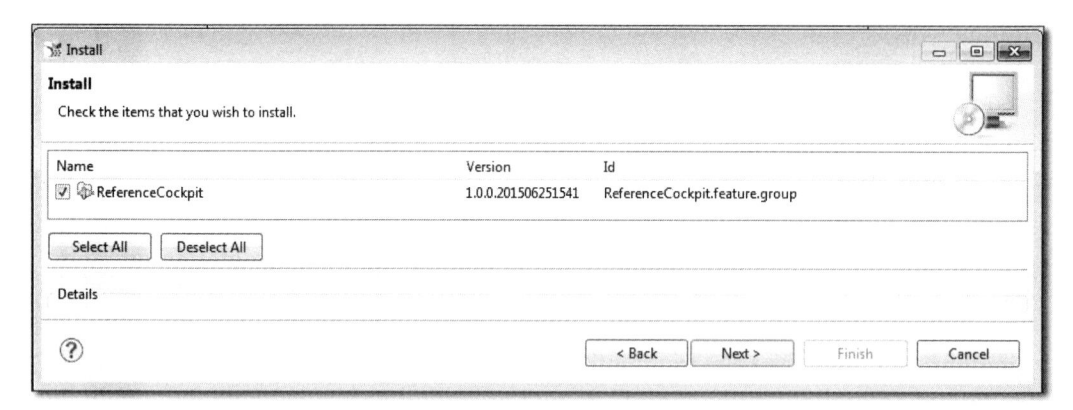

Figure 12.4 Confirmation of Item Install

5. A new dialog box appears and shows the install details of the items that are about to be installed (Figure 12.5). Click NEXT.

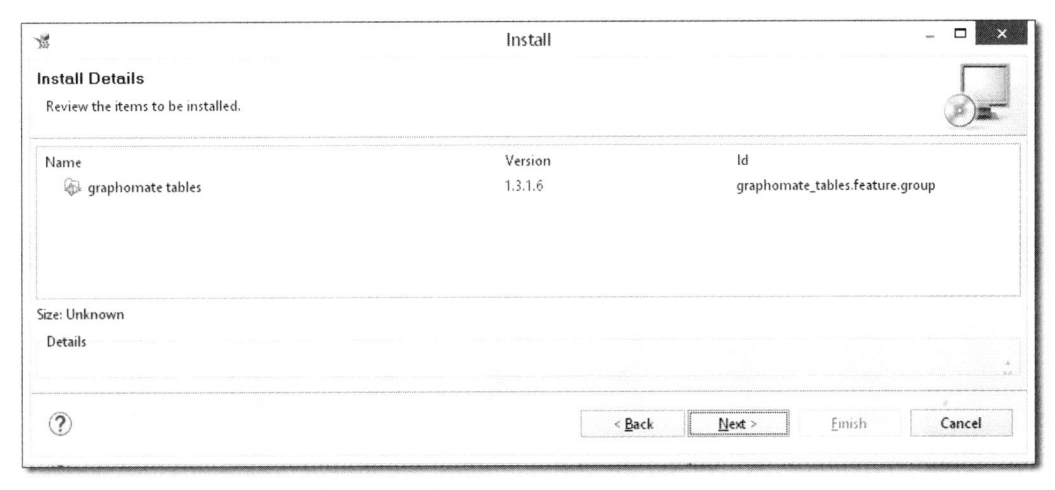

Figure 12.5 Reviewing the Installation Details

6. After selecting the items, you arrive at the license screen. Read the user license and select the radio button to accept if you agree with the license. Click the FINISH button to continue with the installation (Figure 12.6).

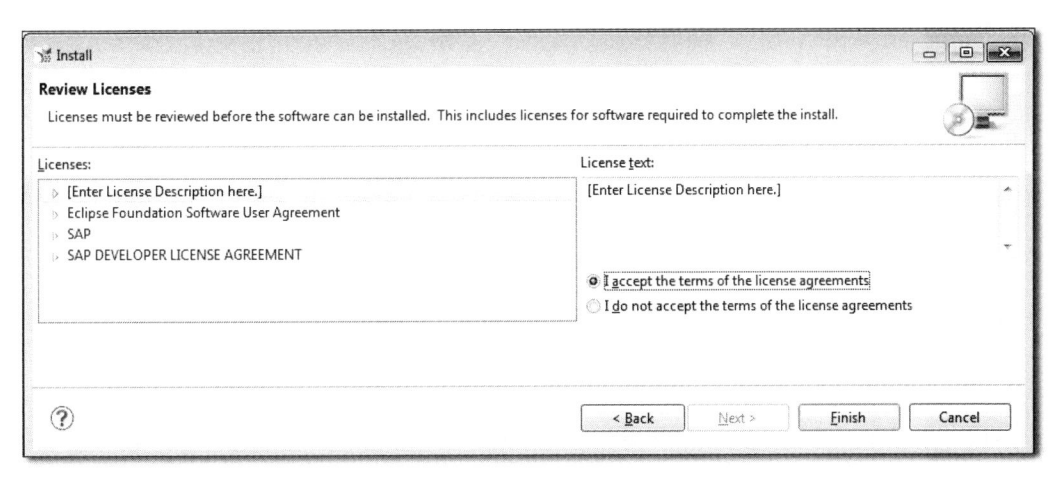

Figure 12.6 Reviewing Licenses

7. The next dialog screen asks if you trust the certificates of the installation file (Figure 12.7). Click the DETAILS button to obtain additional information on the certificates (Figure 12.8). Select the certificates that you trust, and click OK.

Figure 12.7 Trust Certificates

Figure 12.8 Certificate Details

No Certificate

When development is done in the organization, you'll find that instead of trusting a certificate as we just described, the installation will warn you that there is no certificate attached. You can still install, but make sure there is a secure environment in your organization from where you can download the SDK components.

8. The installer will continue. At the end, it will ask you to restart your application (Figure 12.9). Click YES.

Installing, Updating, and Removing SDK Extensions | **12.2**

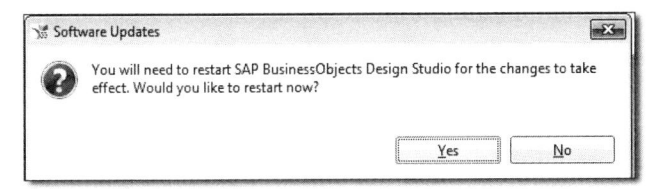

Figure 12.9 Restart Dialog Box

After restarting, you'll find the new SDK components in the COMPONENTS view (Figure 12.10), and you'll be able to use them pretty much in the same way as you would use standard components (Figure 12.11). Of course, this depends on how these components were designed.

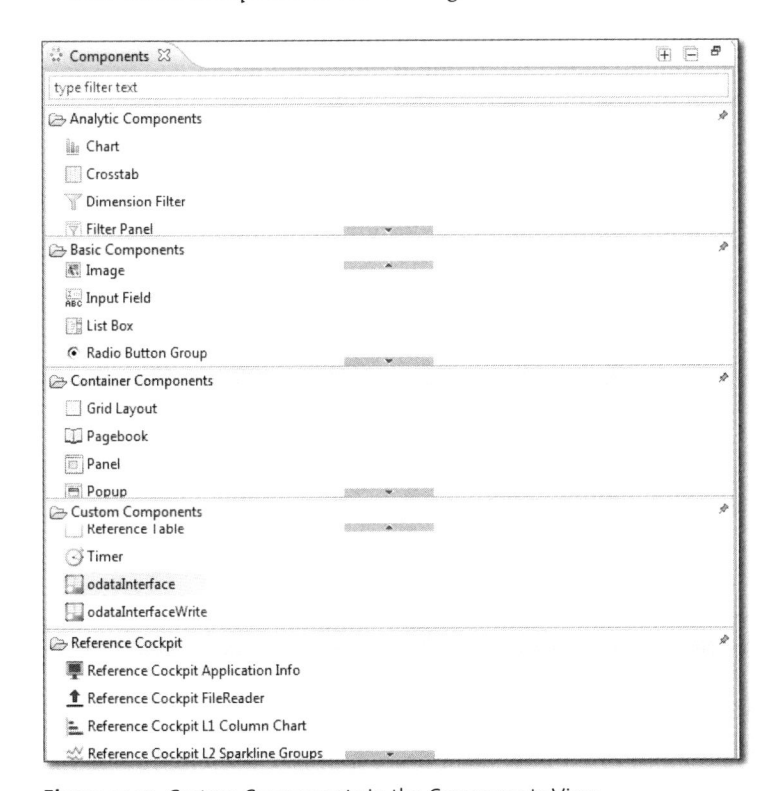

Figure 12.10 Custom Components in the Components View

475

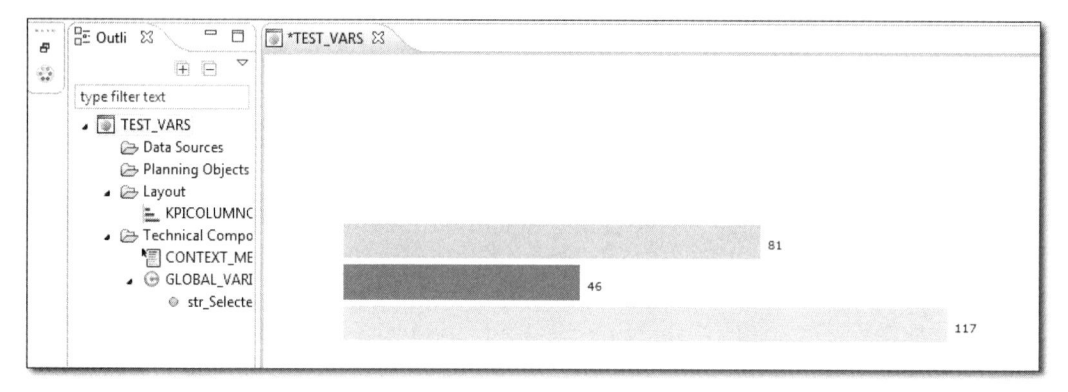

Figure 12.11 Using SDK Components Just Like Standard Components

Installing SDK Extensions to Other Platforms

If you save applications with SDK components on the SAP BusinessObjects BI platform, SAP BW, or SAP HANA, you'll also need to have the SDKs installed on the same platform. In this section, we'll show you how to move the SDK from the local installation to each of the three platforms.

If you're logged in to a platform, open the TOOLS menu and choose PLATFORM EXTENSIONS to install SDK extensions to the platform (refer to Figure 12.1). A dialog box opens showing all the locally installed SDK extensions on the left-hand side and the platform-installed extensions on the right-hand side (Figure 12.12).

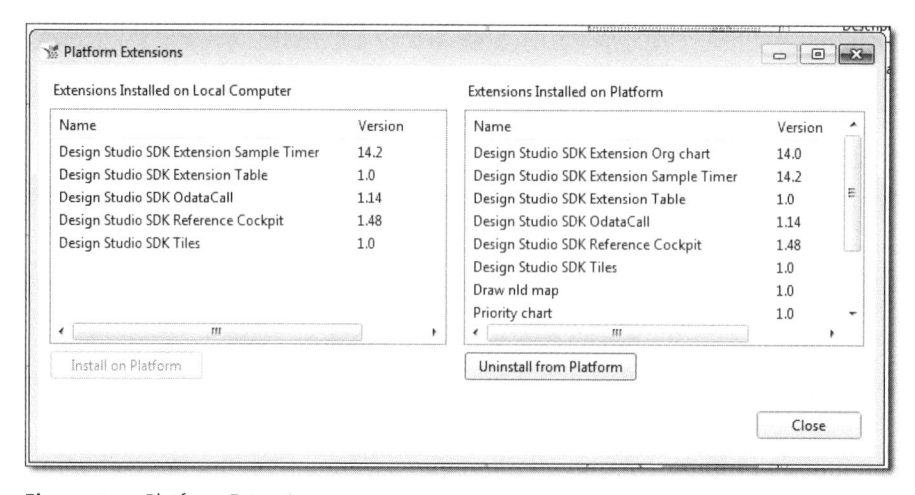

Figure 12.12 Platform Extensions

You can install an SDK extension by selecting it on the left-hand side and clicking INSTALL ON PLATFORM. You also can uninstall SDK components by selecting them on the right-hand side and clicking UNINSTALL FROM PLATFORM.

After reviewing these basic steps, next we need to look at the platform-specific steps to enable the use of the SDK extension on a platform. These steps are necessary to allow the application to run on the platform and use the SDK.

SAP BusinessObjects BI

For the SAP BusinessObjects BI platform, you need the SAP BusinessObjects BI administrator rights, or your administrator must add you to the Design Studio administrators group.

Before the changes on the platform take effect, restart the SAP BusinessObjects BI platform's Adaptive Processing Servers that host the Analysis Application Service. If you have access, you can do the restart of the processing servers from the Central Management Console (CMC), or you have to ask an administrator to do the restart for you (Figure 12.13).

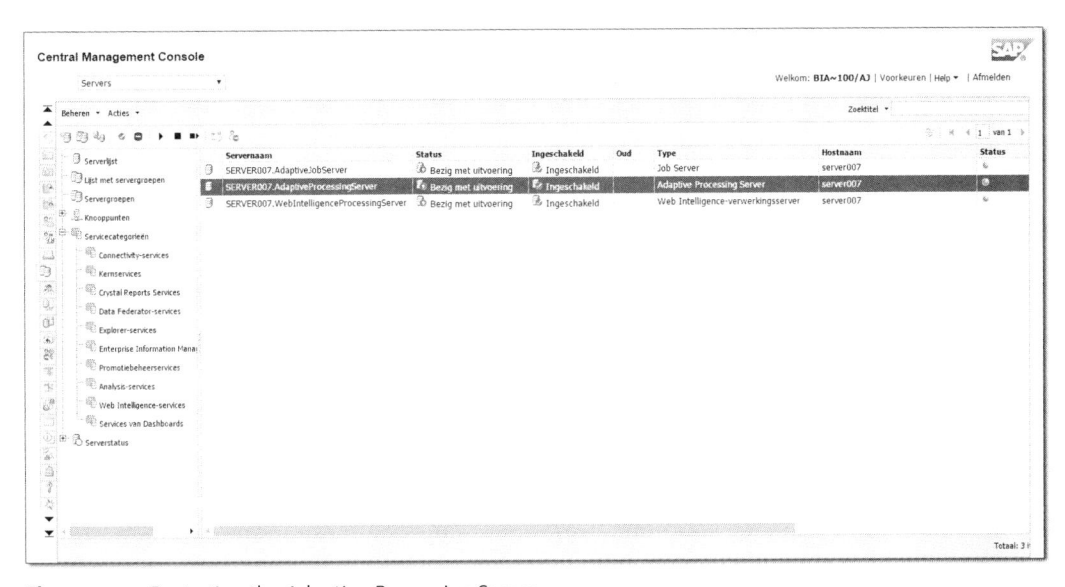

Figure 12.13 Restarting the Adaptive Processing Server

SAP Business Warehouse

Restart the SAP Enterprise Portal component com.sap.ip.bi.designstudio.nw.portal (Figure 12.14).

Figure 12.14 Stop and Start Screen

After restarting, the Design Studio archives, which have been deployed to the SAP Enterprise Portal, will be available. Ask an administrator to restart the component.

The SDK extensions are available in the SAP BW system and on the SAP Enterprise Portal. Application users can now launch the Design Studio applications containing these SDK extensions from SAP Enterprise Portal.

SAP HANA

Before users can launch applications containing SDK extensions from the SAP HANA platform, you need to deploy the SDK extensions to SAP HANA. The SDK extensions appear in the `designstudio_extensions` package. To do this, you need privileges for the `designstudio_extensions` package.

Contrary to the other two platforms, no restart is necessary in SAP HANA.

12.2.2 Updating

When a new version of an SDK component is available, you'll probably want to update your installed SDK extension. The procedure for this depends on whether you installed the extension from a local file or through a URL. In this section, we'll look at both of these possibilities.

Update from a Local File Installation

If your installation was via a local file, when you want to update, you first have to uninstall the old version (see Section 12.2.3). After the uninstallation, you have to remove remnants of the SDK install to avoid problems when you reinstall the SDK extension. Let's go through these steps now:

1. Go to the ANALYSIS-CONFIG folder in your user folder. Typically, the folder name is *C:\Users\myUser\Analysis-config* (Figure 12.15).

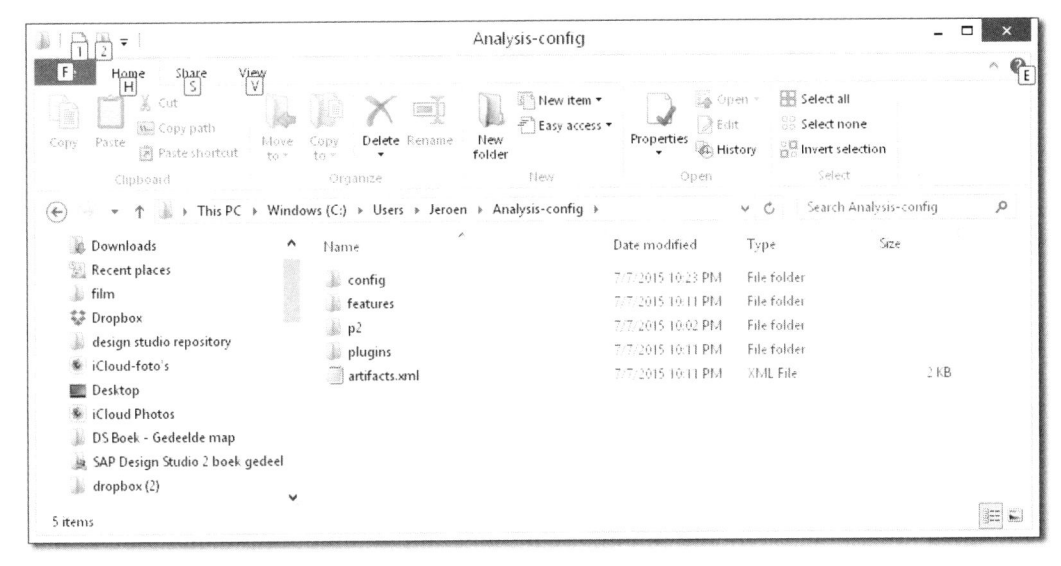

Figure 12.15 Analysis-Config Folder

2. Delete everything in this folder.

3. When you restart, Design Studio rebuilds all the items that you see in this folder with the exception of the SDK installation files, resulting in a rapid and complete uninstall of the SDK extensions.

4. After this, you can redo the installation steps, as we discussed in Section 12.2.1.

Update from a URL Installation

If you used a URL to install the SDK extension earlier, you have the option to use the update procedure instead of uninstalling and reinstalling the SDK extension. Follow these steps to perform an update:

1. In the menu bar, choose HELP • ABOUT.

2. In the ABOUT SAP BUSINESSOBJECTS DESIGN STUDIO dialog box that opens, select the INSTALLATION DETAILS button to open an installation details dialog box.

3. Select the INSTALLED SOFTWARE tab, and then select the SDK component that you want to update.

4. Click the UPDATE button.

12.2.3 Uninstalling the SDK

Follow these steps to uninstall SDK extensions:

1. In the menu bar, choose HELP • ABOUT (Figure 12.16).

Figure 12.16 Choosing About from the Help Menu

2. In the ABOUT SAP BUSINESSOBJECTS DESIGN STUDIO dialog box that appears (Figure 12.17), click the INSTALLATION DETAILS button. An installation details dialog box opens (Figure 12.18).

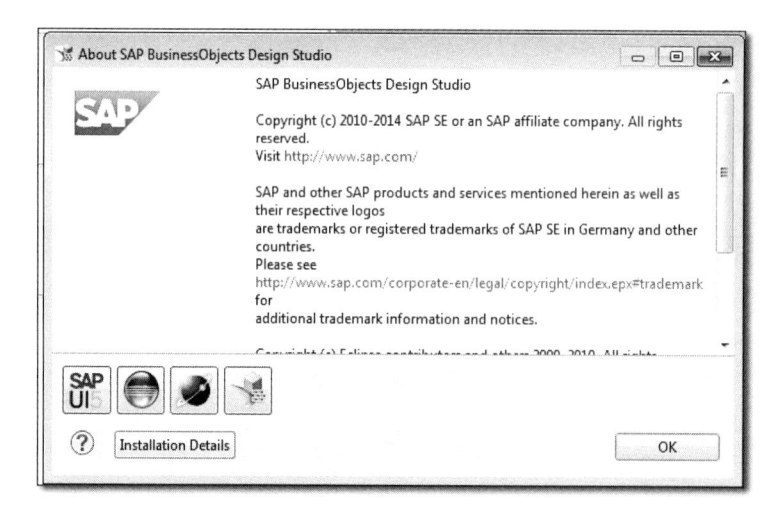

Figure 12.17 About Design Studio

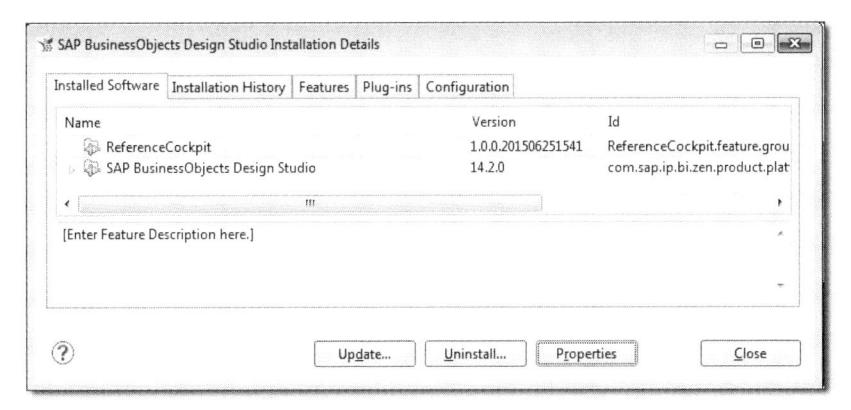

Installing, Updating, and Removing SDK Extensions | **12.2**

Figure 12.18 Installation Details

3. Select the INSTALLED SOFTWARE tab, and choose the SDK component that you want to uninstall.

4. Click the UNINSTALL button.

5. To finish of the uninstallation, you need to restart Design Studio for the changes to take effect (Figure 12.19).

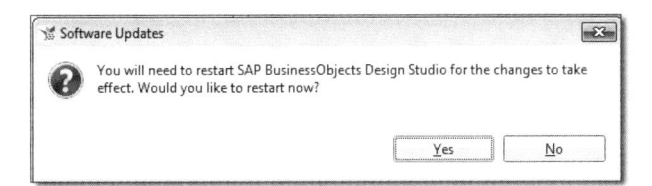

Figure 12.19 Restarting for Changes to Take Effect

> **Shortcut for Uninstall**
>
> If you just want to remove all SDK extensions, there is a shorter way to go about the uninstall process. In Section 12.2.2, we mentioned the ANALYSIS-CONFIG folder on *C:\Users\myUser\Analysis-confi* (refer to Figure 12.15). If you remove all contents and then restart Design Studio, you'll see that all SDK extensions are uninstalled as well.

12.2.4 Falling Back to a Lower SDK Version

When using a new version of an SDK extension, you might find that it has some bugs that are interfering with your work. However, just uninstalling and installing the older version doesn't solve the problem. There are some extra steps to

481

make your applications work again with the older version of the SDK extension components. The problem is that applications store the version number of the used SDK extension in the application save file and refuse to open with an older version of the same SDK extension.

To fix this, you have to download the application from the platform with which you saved the application to your hard drive. In the download location of the application you chose, you'll find the *content.biapp* file. This file contains the application. Open the application with a text editor, and find the SDK version number in the top row (Figure 12.20).

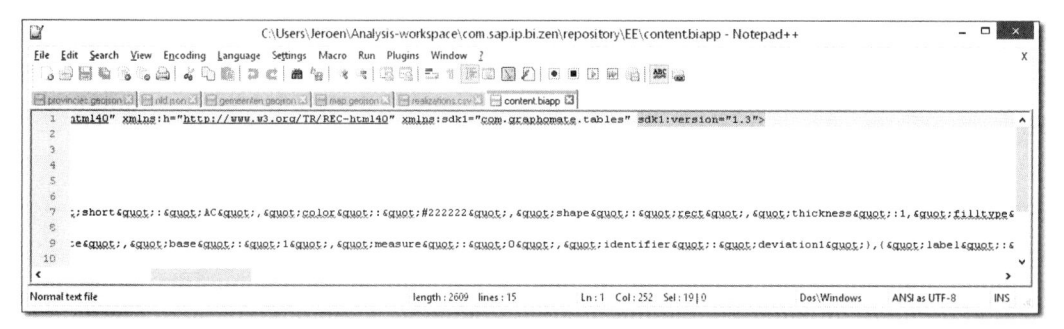

Figure 12.20 Edit Application in Text Editor

Lower the version number to the previous version number you installed. Then, upload the application to the platform, and run the application again.

This is only necessary on the development environment because this problem only shows up when you open the application in the design tool. Running the application is no problem, as long as the application doesn't depend on some functionality that was added in the newer version.

12.3 Moving an SDK through the System Landscape

In this section, we'll provide an overview of how to move an SDK extension through the SAP system landscape. Typically, most organizations have separate development, testing, and production systems. After moving the SDK extension to the platform your organization uses, the SDK will be only available on the development system; however, at some point, it has to move to production.

In this section, we'll look at how to move your installed SDK to each of the three platforms: SAP BusinessObjects BI, SAP BW, and SAP HANA.

12.3.1 Promoting in SAP BusinessObjects BI

Unfortunately, for the SAP BusinessObjects BI platform, there is no option to promote the SDK installation. You need to install the extensions on each platform separately.

12.3.2 Transporting with SAP Business Warehouse

Design Studio applications are stored as TLOGO objects of type AZAP in the SAP BW system. If your applications contain SDK extensions, these extensions are stored as TLOGO objects of type AZEX.

When you collect Design Studio applications that contain SDK components in the DATA WAREHOUSING WORKBENCH: TRANSPORT CONNECTION screen, you can automatically collect those SDK components as well for transport (Figure 12.21). In addition, you'll be able to collect other objects on which the application depends.

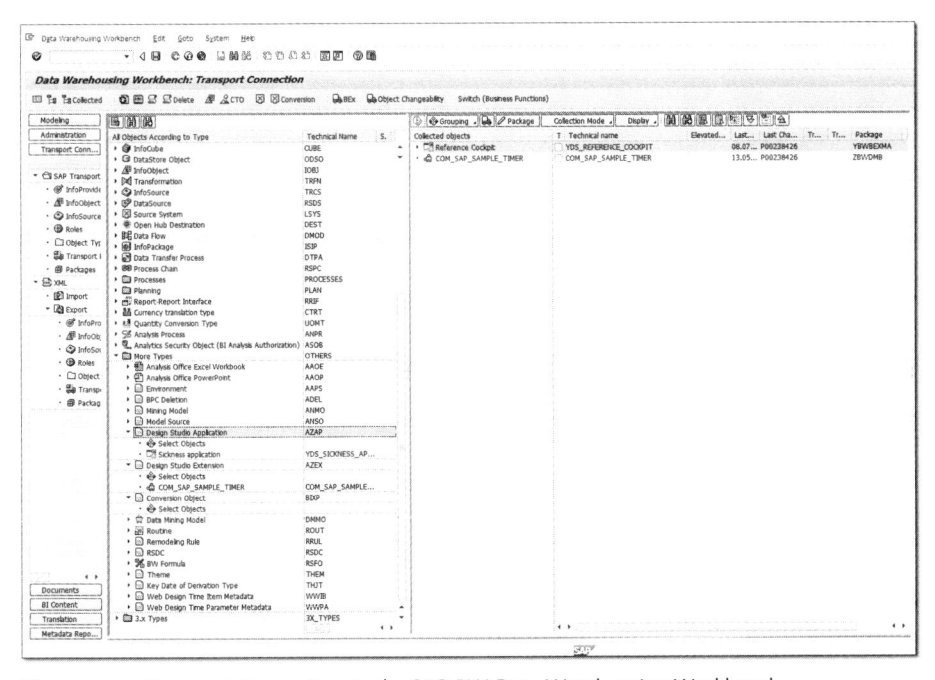

Figure 12.21 Transport Connection in the SAP BW Data Warehousing Workbench

Alternatively, you can collect the SDK extensions separately for transport to the other SAP BW systems. Remember that you need to do the restart as described in Section 12.2.1 for the target SAP BW system.

12.3.3 Transporting with SAP HANA

With SAP HANA, you use delivery units to transport SDK extensions between SAP HANA systems. Follow these steps:

1. Install the Design Studio for the HANA Delivery Unit (*HCOBIAAS.tgz*) on the target SAP HANA system.
2. In SAP HANA Studio, create a delivery unit, and add the SDK extensions you want to transport from the `designstudio_extensions` package.
3. Select the SELECT ALL SUB-PACKAGES UNDER SELECTED NODES checkbox.
4. Export the delivery unit to the target SAP HANA system as described under IMPLEMENTING LIFECYCLE MANAGEMENT in the *SAP HANA Developer Guide* on the SAP Help Portal at *http://help.sap.com/hana_appliance*.

12.4 Testing Changes to an SDK Extension

Even when working with a third-party SDK extension, testing is a good idea. In this section, we'll briefly discuss the steps to test an SDK extension.

When you install a new version of an SDK extension, all applications that use the extension are impacted. Before you install the SDK extension on the platform, you need to first check locally because bugs can have a large impact depending on the number of applications that use the SDK extension.

First, you need to create a test application (Figure 12.22). The goal of this application is to test all the aspects of the SDK components that are included in the extension. You set them up and surround them with buttons. Each button uses a method that is associated with the component.

After you've built the test application, you can keep it and use it every time a new version of the SDK extension arrives to retest the extension. Try all these buttons, and see what results it provides. If you get information from the component, don't only check whether it works but also check whether the output format has changed from the original version.

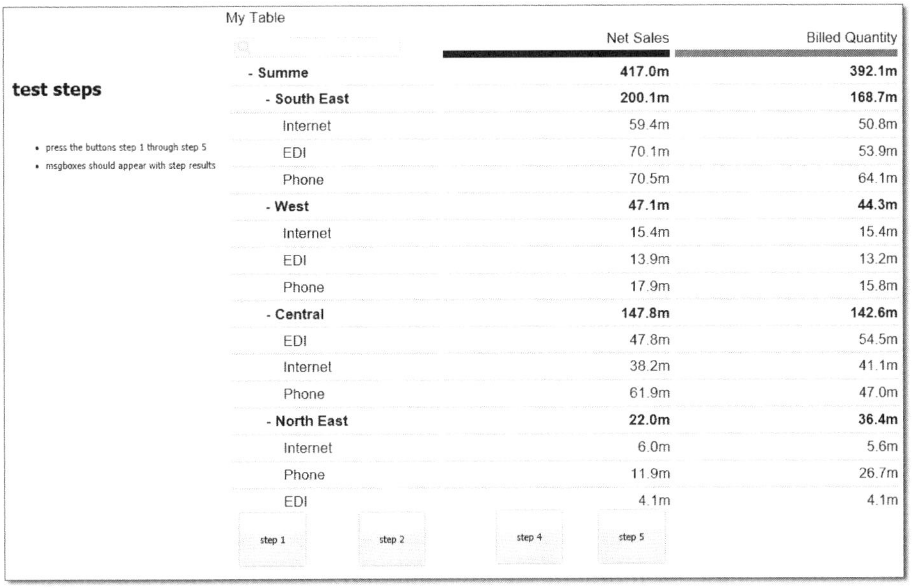

Figure 12.22 Test Application

The second step is to do a *regression test* on the existing applications. There is a chance that the new version creates errors because it's not backward compatible. The only way to know for sure is to open and run the existing applications and test all the interactions with the SDK components in the extension.

You can log in to the platform and open an application in local mode so that you don't have to install the SDK on the platform. Don't save the application, however. If you do this, the application will remember the version number of the SDK extension. You can't edit the application anymore when you have the old version installed.

12.5   Third-Party SDK Extensions

The usage of an SDK extension depends on how it's built. However, it's largely identical to how would you use standard components. As with standard components, you add SDK components to the canvas and maintain properties in the PROPERTIES panel.

12 | Using SDK Extensions in SAP BusinessObjects Design Studio

In the PROPERTIES panel, you'll see that there are properties listed and available for editing just like with standard component properties (Figure 12.23).

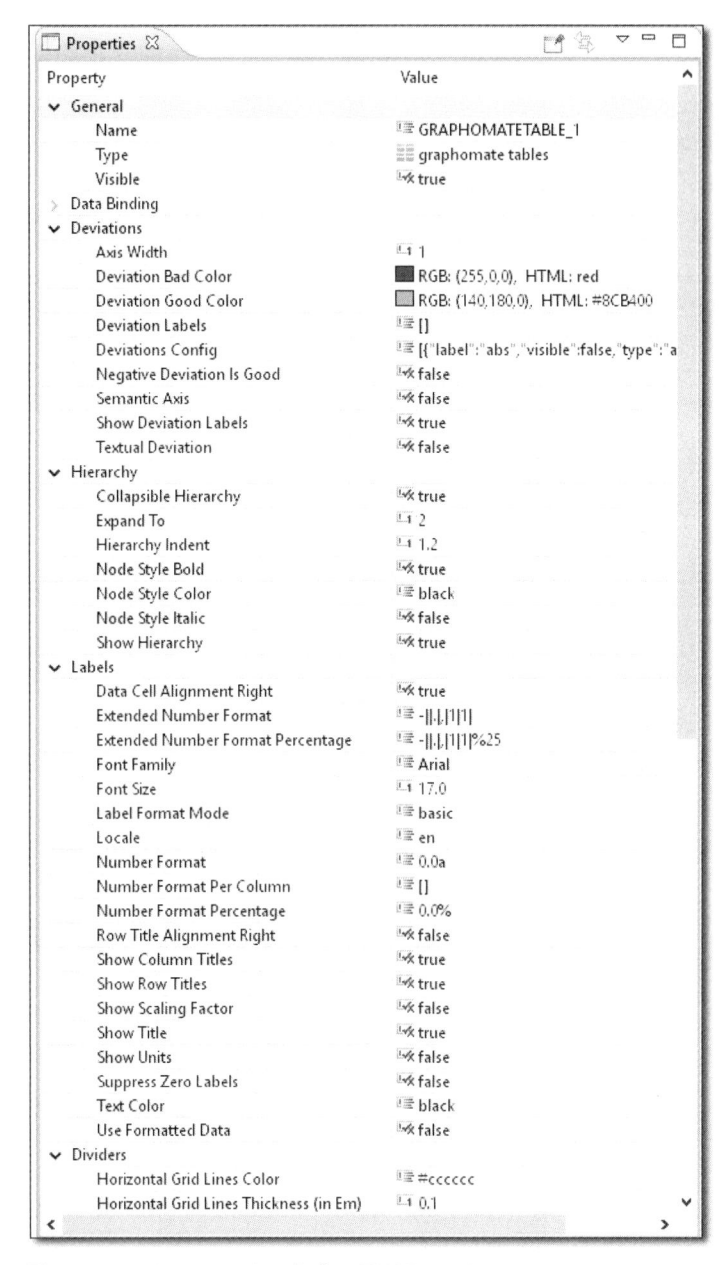

Property	Value
∨ General	
Name	GRAPHOMATETABLE_1
Type	graphomate tables
Visible	true
> Data Binding	
∨ Deviations	
Axis Width	1
Deviation Bad Color	RGB: (255,0,0), HTML: red
Deviation Good Color	RGB: (140,180,0), HTML: #8CB400
Deviation Labels	[]
Deviations Config	[{"label":"abs","visible":false,"type":"a
Negative Deviation Is Good	false
Semantic Axis	false
Show Deviation Labels	true
Textual Deviation	false
∨ Hierarchy	
Collapsible Hierarchy	true
Expand To	2
Hierarchy Indent	1.2
Node Style Bold	true
Node Style Color	black
Node Style Italic	false
Show Hierarchy	true
∨ Labels	
Data Cell Alignment Right	true
Extended Number Format	-|.|,|1|1|
Extended Number Format Percentage	-|.|,|1|1|%25
Font Family	Arial
Font Size	17.0
Label Format Mode	basic
Locale	en
Number Format	0.0a
Number Format Per Column	[]
Number Format Percentage	0.0%
Row Title Alignment Right	false
Show Column Titles	true
Show Row Titles	true
Show Scaling Factor	false
Show Title	true
Show Units	false
Suppress Zero Labels	false
Text Color	black
Use Formatted Data	false
∨ Dividers	
Horizontal Grid Lines Color	#cccccc
Horizontal Grid Lines Thickness (in Em)	0.1

Figure 12.23 Properties Panel of an SDK Extension

There are already quite a few suppliers of SDK extensions. Many look to fill the functional gaps that are found in the standard Design Studio application. In Table 12.1, we describe a few of the third-party extensions available and what they offer.

Vendor	Description
Graphomate	Provides Hichert charts and table formatting
BI Excellence	Exports to PDF and PTT
SAP Consulting	Provides a commentary solution
Archius	Provides additional chart types
Galigeo	Adds location analytics to applications

Table 12.1 Examples of Vendors and their SDK Extension Offerings

Vendors

A larger list of vendors and SDK extensions can be found at *http://scn.sap.com/community/businessobjects-design-studio/blog/2014/12/10/scn-design-studio-sdk-development-community*.

One example mentioned in the table is Graphomate, which offers a number of extensions that include graph types currently not available in the standard Design Studio offering (Figure 12.24).

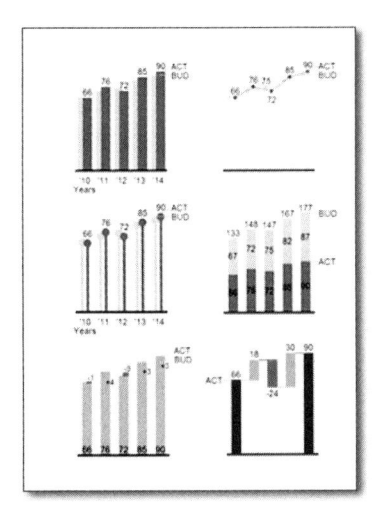

Figure 12.24 Graphomate Charts

After they are installed, the way you work with these extensions is nearly identical to the standard components: dragging elements onto the canvas that you need, editing properties, and adding scripts to events.

SDK programmers have the option to create their own user interface in Graphomate charts to set up the component they added to the application. Graphomate is used to create all the components in its SDK extension with an ADDITIONAL PROPERTIES panel to set up tables, as shown in Figure 12.25.

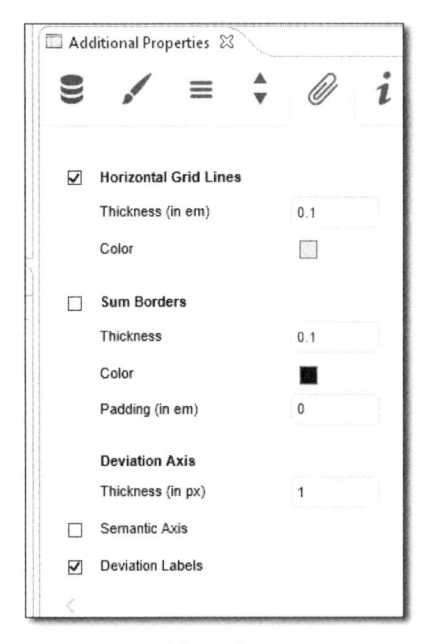

Figure 12.25 Additional Properties

On the SCN community website, you can locate a large number of available SDK components bundled in a couple of extensions that are offered in the SDK Community. These components are open source. You can find the SDK extensions at *http://scn.sap.com/community/businessobjects-design-studio/blog/2014/12/10/scn-design-studio-sdk-development-community*.

> **Additional Third-Party Extensions**
>
> SAP lists the third-party extensions by partners at *https://newportal-i050426trial.dispatcher.hanatrial.ondemand.com/biExtensions.html*. There are many extensions available on the market covering a wide range of subjects.

12.6 Summary

In this chapter, we walked through the installation, updating, and removal of SDK extensions. We installed the SDK components locally and then moved them to SAP BusinessObjects BI, SAP HANA, and SAP BW. We briefly looked at the actions that need to take place on the platform side and how lifecycle management is handled for each platform. In the last section, we looked at third-party vendors and how they can add functionality to Design Studio. We used Graphomate as an example to show how they offer graphs that aren't available in the standard Design Studio.

In the next chapter, you'll install the tools necessary to build your own SDK extension.

Before you can make your own SDK components, you first have to install the Eclipse tool and configure it to work with Design Studio.

13   SDK Installation and Deployment

In this chapter, we'll go through each step to install Eclipse and make it ready so you can create your own software development kit (SDK) components for Design Studio. In Section 13.1, we'll walk through the installation of Eclipse and Java. In Section 13.2, we'll configure the XML, and then import your first project in Section 13.3. In Section 13.4, we'll show you how to configure the platform so you can run Design Studio directly from Eclipse and test your creations.

13.1   Installing Eclipse

Eclipse is an open source community with a focus on building extensible development platforms, runtimes, and application frameworks for building. Most people start by downloading one of the different download packages. You can add plug-ins to Eclipse to expand its functionality. Perhaps you already work with SAP Business Warehouse (BW) or SAP HANA. In that case, you might already have installed different packages into Eclipse. However, before you can install the Eclipse software, you first have to install Java Development Kit (JDK) 7 or higher for Windows 64-bit. The JDK is a prerequisite that you need to have installed before you can work with Eclipse.

13.1.1   Java Development Kit

To install the JDK, go to the Java website to get the right download (Figure 13.1).

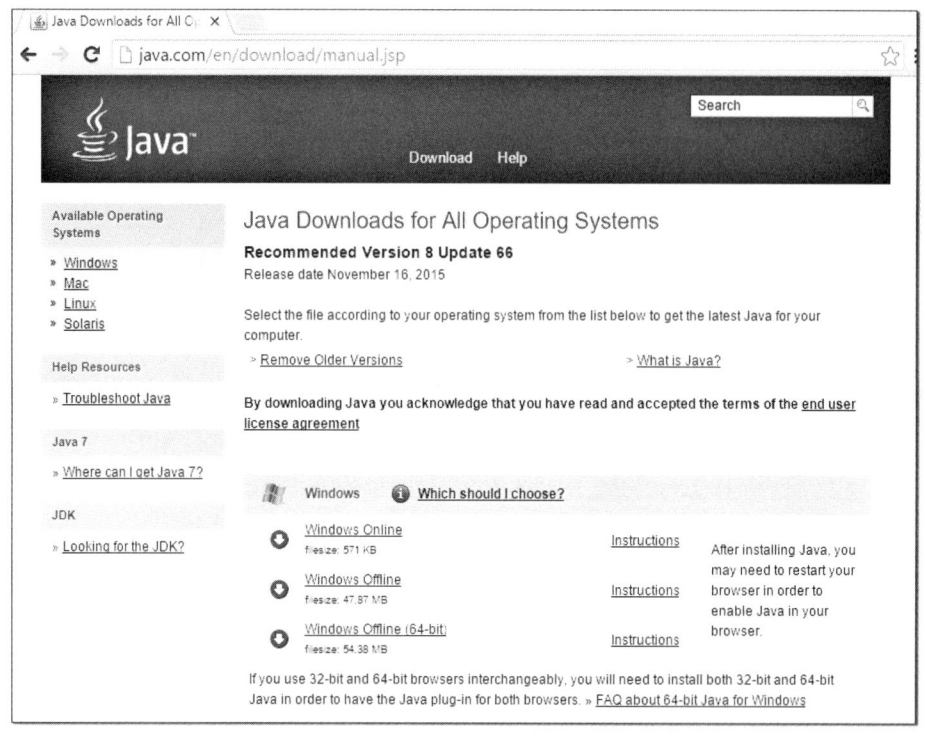

Figure 13.1 Java Download Site

Now, proceed with the following steps:

1. Go to *http://www.java.com/en/download/manual.jsp*, and choose the WINDOWS OFFLINE (64-BIT) version. At the time of writing (February 2016), version 8 update 66 was the most recent Java version. Download the most recent version.

2. Double-click on the downloaded application. A popup screen will welcome you to the installation process (Figure 13.2).

3. On this screen, click INSTALL. You can change the location of the installation here as well, however, we recommend keeping it as is. Changing the installation location means that you have to change other settings such as Windows variables for Eclipse to work.

If you already have an older Java installation on your computer, you may find that the installation stops, and the screen appears as shown in Figure 13.3.

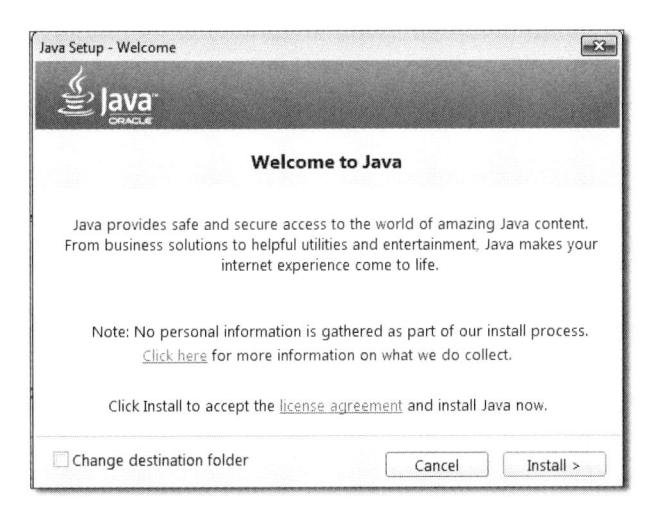

Figure 13.2 Welcome to Java Screen

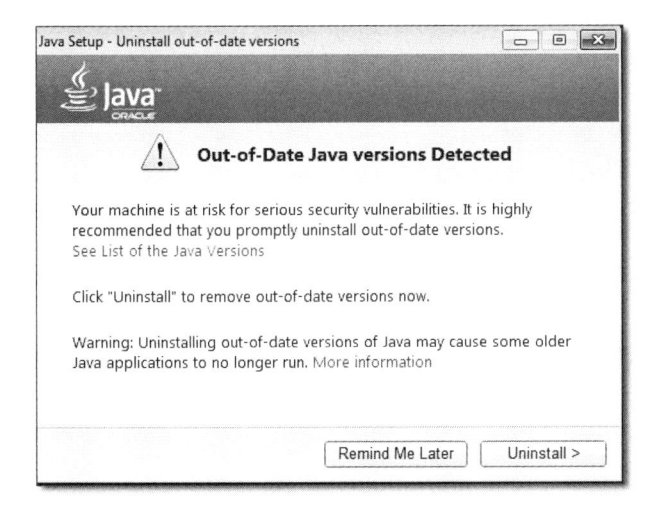

Figure 13.3 Out-of-Date Java Versions Detected

4. Use the UNINSTALL button to remove the older versions of Java. An exception to this applies when you have software on your computer that relies on that older version of Java. In that case, don't remove the older Java versions so that the other programs keep working.

5. When the installation process is complete, you'll see a finish screen as shown in Figure 13.4, which you can close by clicking CLOSE.

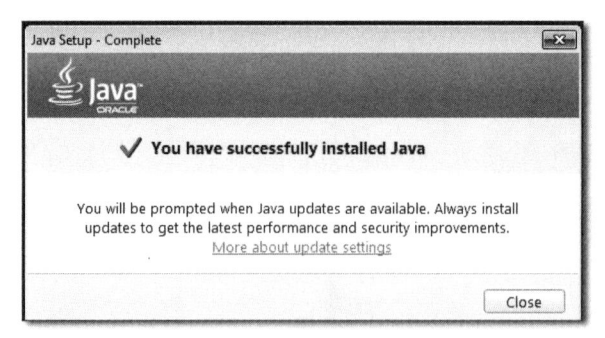

Figure 13.4 Successful Java Install

This completes the Java installation, and you can continue with the Eclipse installation.

13.1.2 Eclipse

Now you're ready to install Eclipse. For starters, you need to download the right version of Eclipse, as there are many versions available. Proceed with the following steps:

1. Go to *http://download.eclipse.org/* (Figure 13.5).

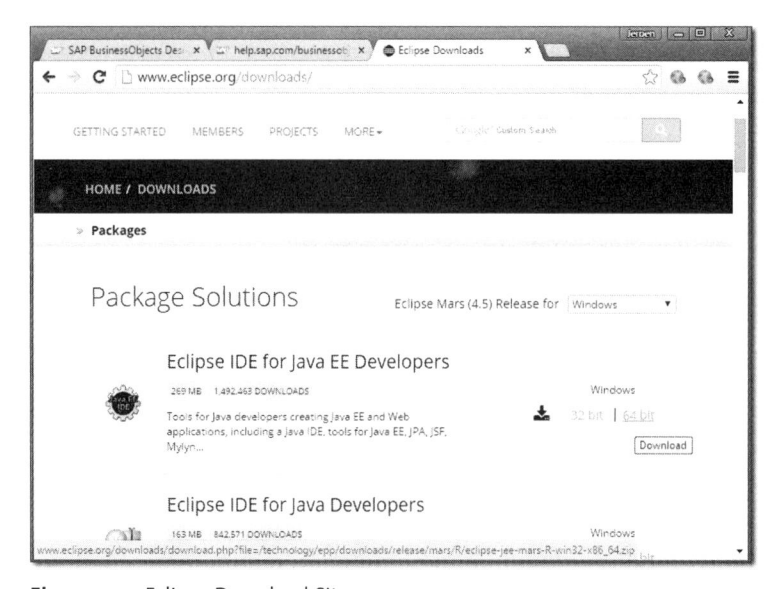

Figure 13.5 Eclipse Download Site

2. Choose the Eclipse IDE for Java EE Developers (64 bit) download. When you click the Download button, a second window will open that asks you for the location where you want to download the program files (Figure 13.6).

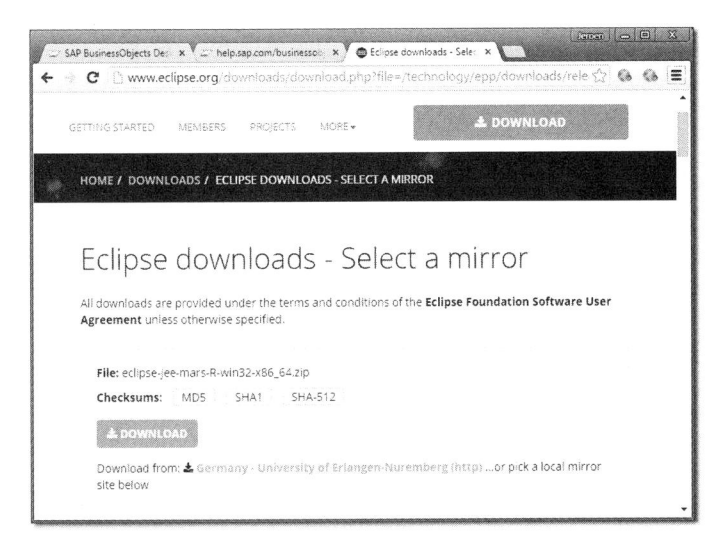

Figure 13.6 Mirror Choice

3. Choose a location, and the download will commence (Figure 13.7). In the downloading screen, it will ask you for a contribution.

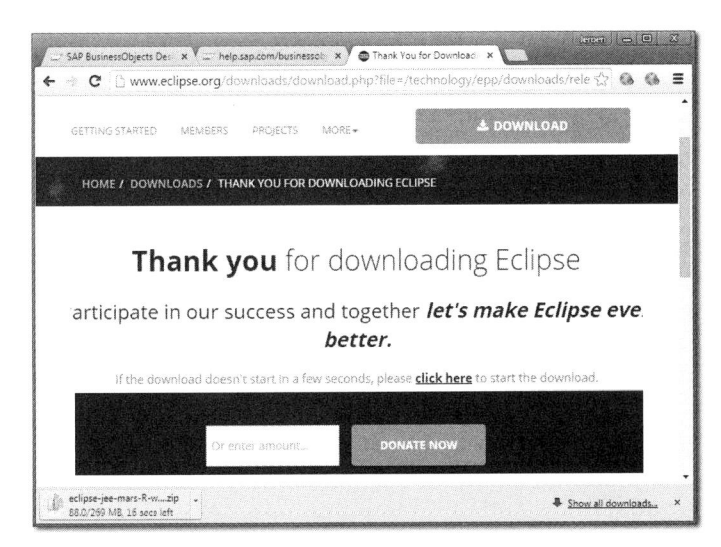

Figure 13.7 Downloading the Installation Files

4. After the zip file is downloaded, copy the file to a location on your hard drive, and extract the programming files. The files will be extracted into an ECLIPSE folder within the chosen location (Figure 13.8).

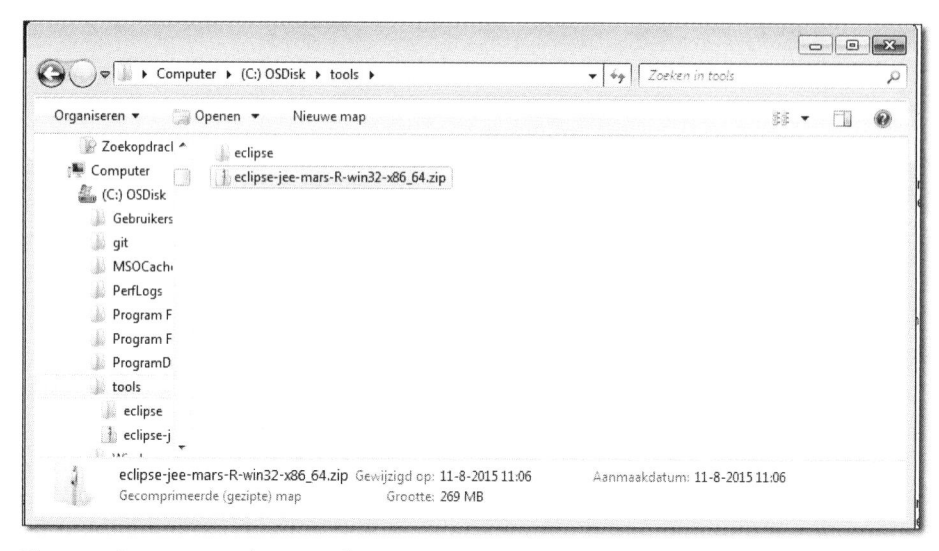

Figure 13.8 Location and Extract of Program Files

5. Go into the ECLIPSE folder, and run the file ECLIPSE.EXE. For later use, you can create a shortcut that you copy to your desktop or START menu. For now, you can just continue with the installation.

The first question you'll see when you start up Eclipse for the first time is where you want to set the workspace location. This is an important question because it dictates where all of your projects and settings will be stored. Make sure that you have a shortcut to the location.

> **Backup**
> You can choose a location in a Dropbox folder or another synced folder so that the backup is automatic.

The Eclipse environment opens with a welcome screen (Figure 13.9). You can close this screen by clicking the X next to the WELCOME tab. Now the full layout of the Eclipse environment appears (Figure 13.10).

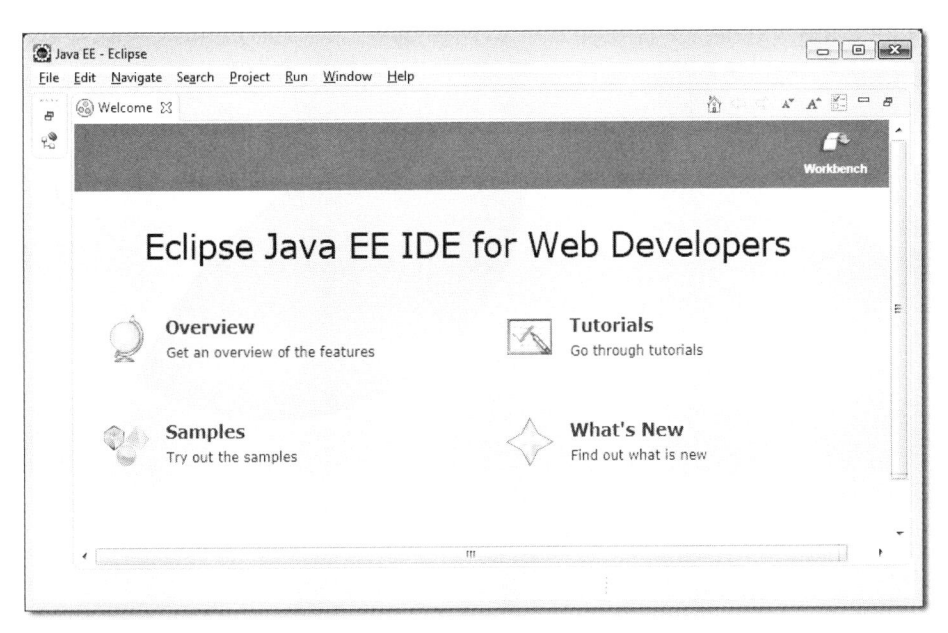

Figure 13.9 Eclipse Welcome Screen

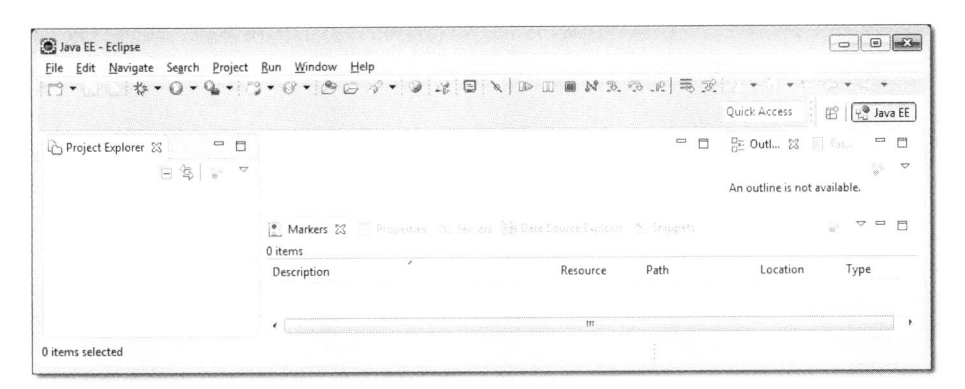

Figure 13.10 Eclipse Environment

As you get more familiar with this layout, you'll notice things that work similar to the design environment in the Design Studio application.

13.2 Registering the XML Definition

In this section, you'll set up the XML standards. This XML will help you later because it will inform Eclipse what values are allowed and how the *contribution.xml* file needs to be structured.

After you've set up the XML, you'll import your first project into the Eclipse environment.

13.2.1 Downloading SAP Templates

Before you can set up everything, you need to download the template files from *http://help.sap.com/boad* (Figure 13.11).

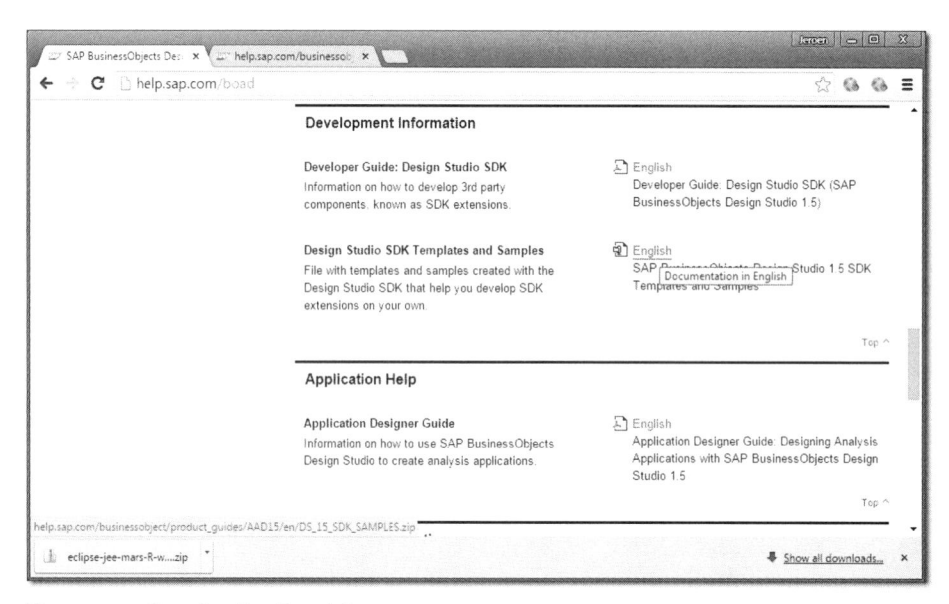

Figure 13.11 Downloading Templates

Download the DESIGN STUDIO SDK TEMPLATES AND SAMPLES. You can extract this zip file to a folder. The contents of the folder look like Figure 13.12.

In the folder, you'll find many projects and one XML file. You'll refer to this folder when you set up the XML and import your first project.

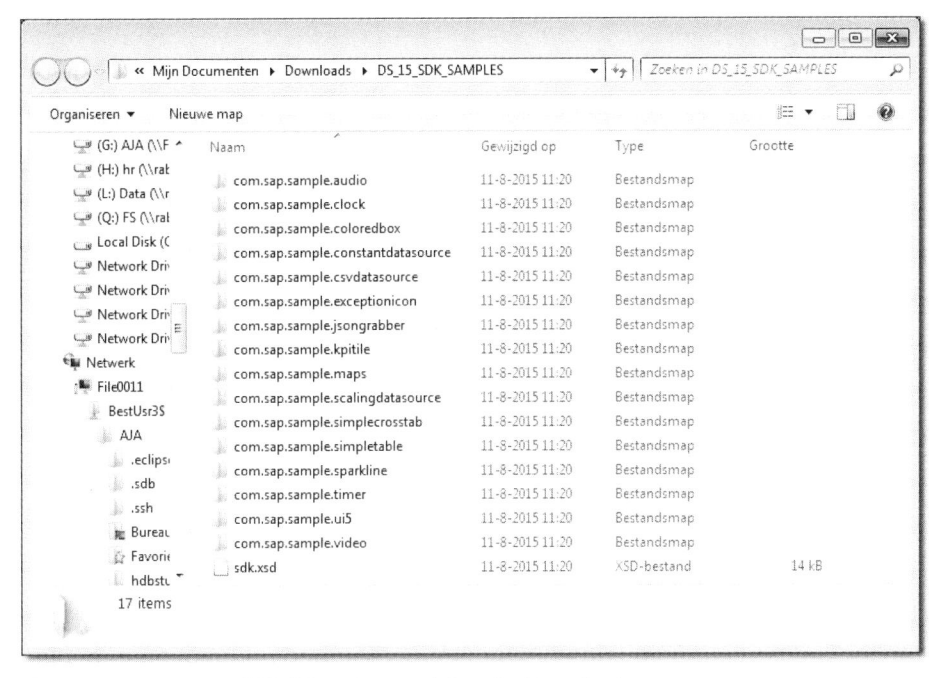

Figure 13.12 Contents of SDK Templates and Samples Download

13.2.2 Setting Up XML

Now that you have the proper files and template, proceed with the XML setup steps:

1. Open Eclipse, and choose WINDOW • PREFERENCES. In the dialog window that opens (Figure 13.13), navigate to XML • XML CATALOG.

2. Click the ADD button. This will open a new screen (Figure 13.14) where you can locate the XML file and add it to the XML catalog entries.

3. Click the FILE SYSTEM button, and locate the folder where you extracted the SDK template and sample files. Select the SDK.XSD file. Click OK to close the screen, and click OK again to close the PREFERENCES dialog box.

This concludes registering the Design Studio SDK XML schema definition. In the next section, you'll import a project from the templates and sample folder.

13 | SDK Installation and Deployment

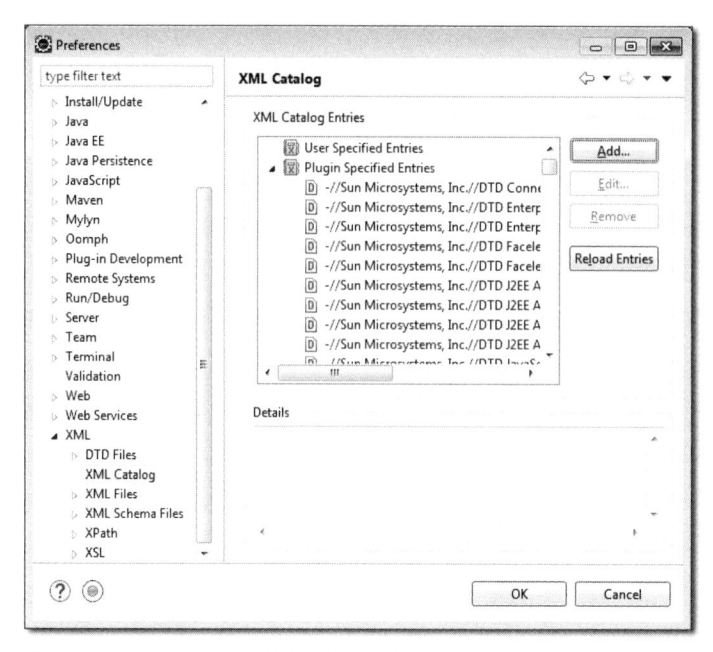

Figure 13.13 Preferences Dialog Box with XML Catalog Selected

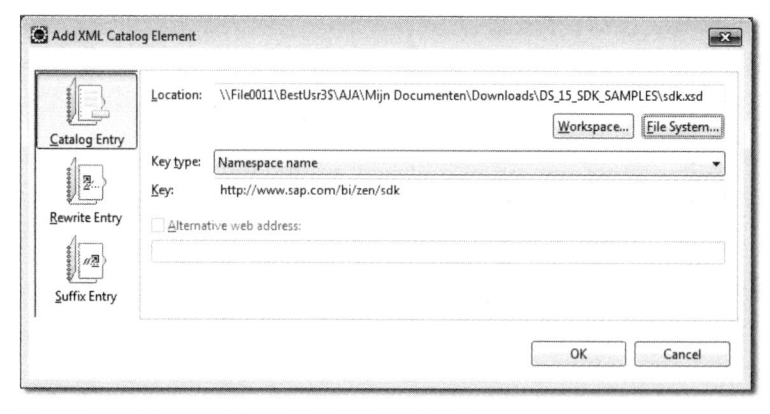

Figure 13.14 Add XML Catalog Element Dialog Screen

13.3 Importing the Project

Your next step is to import a project from the sample folder by following these steps:

1. Choose FILE • IMPORT. A dialog box will open (Figure 13.15).

500

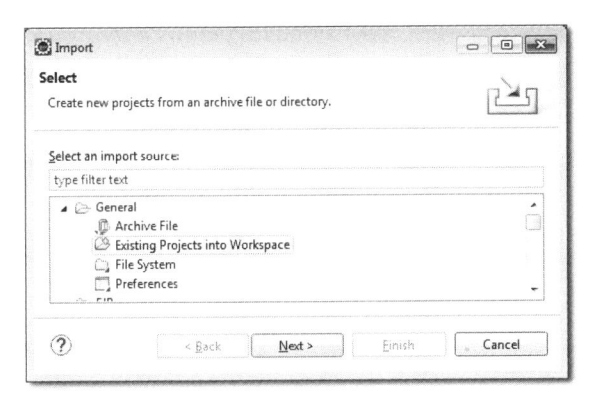

Figure 13.15 Import Dialog Screen

2. On this screen, select EXISTING PROJECTS INTO WORKSPACE within the GENERAL folder, and click NEXT.

3. On the next screen, select the root directory by using the BROWSE button (Figure 13.16).

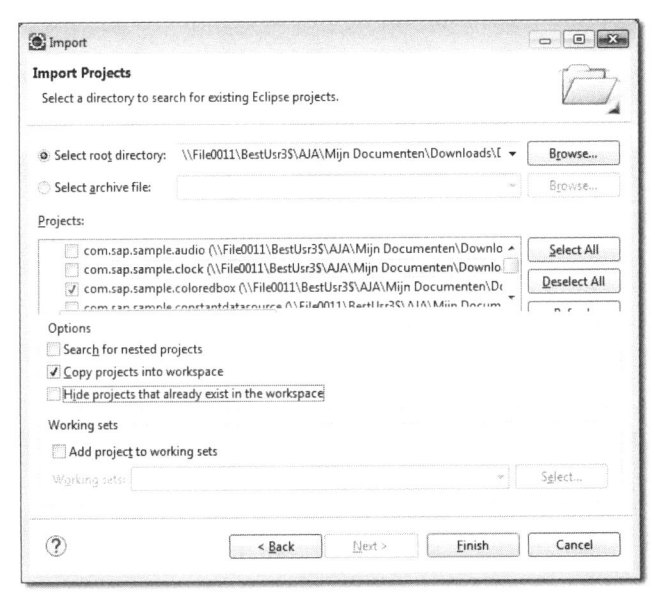

Figure 13.16 Import Projects Dialog Box

4. After you've located the directory, a list of projects will appear. Select the COM.SAP.SAMPLE.COLOREDBOX project. Additionally, select the COPY PROJECTS

INTO WORKSPACE checkbox. This means that the files belonging to the project will be copied to the workspace, and you'll be working from that copy. If you don't, you'll be working directly from the import directory.

5. Click FINISH to conclude the import. If you now look in the PROJECT EXPLORER panel, you'll find the imported project (Figure 13.17).

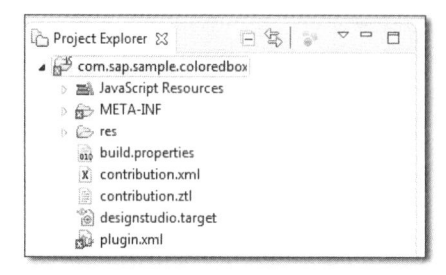

Figure 13.17 Result of Import

Notice that there are some red markers in the project. Those markers will be resolved after you've set the platform in the next section.

13.4 Setting the Target Platform

In this section, you'll set the target platform in Eclipse. This will allow you to run Design Studio directly from Eclipse and debug your work.

Follow these steps:

1. Choose the WINDOW • PREFERENCES. The same dialog box appears as in the previous section, but now you choose PLUG-IN ENVIRONMENT • TARGET PLATFORM (Figure 13.18).

2. Select the DESIGNSTUDIO entry checkbox. This is assuming that you installed Design Studio in the default directory. If not, you have to click EDIT and change the directory. Click APPLY, and then click OK.

3. Apply the changes to all the projects. Currently, you only have one project, but for later, you want to know this step after you have multiple projects in the Eclipse environment.

4. Choose PROJECT • CLEAN. A dialog box opens (Figure 13.19).

Figure 13.18 Target Platform in Preferences Dialog Box

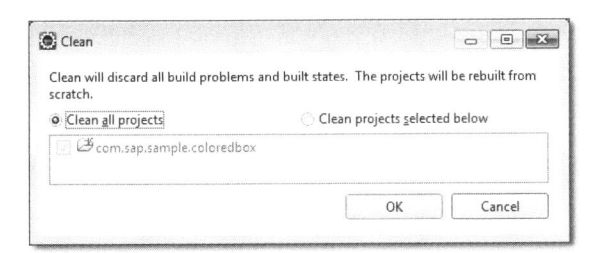

Figure 13.19 Clean Dialog Box

5. Keep the selection on CLEAN ALL PROJECTS, and click OK. This will synchronize the setting to the new platform for all selected projects.

6. After all these steps, there is one step left to do: testing the sample SDK extension in Design Studio. In Eclipse, choose RUN • PROFILE CONFIGURATIONS. A dialog screen will open. Double-click the ECLIPSE APPLICATION item to create a new configuration (Figure 13.20).

13 | SDK Installation and Deployment

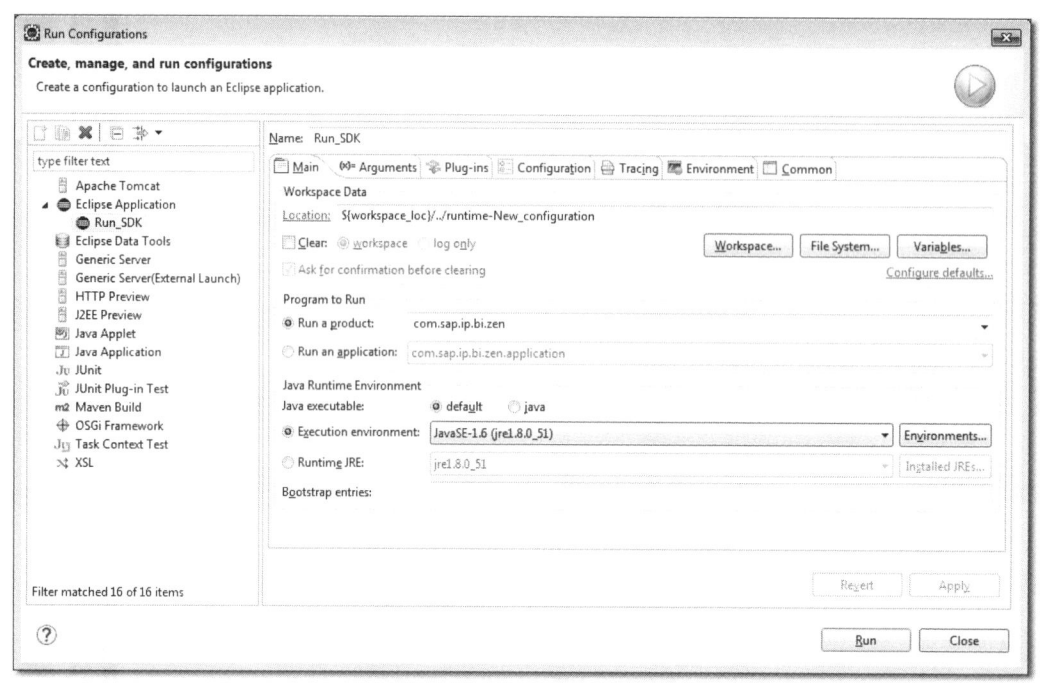

Figure 13.20 Run Configurations Dialog Box

7. Rename the configuration if you want to. In the PROGRAM TO RUN section, look at RUN A PRODUCT and see if the text in the input field reads COM.SAP.IP.BI.ZEN. Add this to the field if this value is missing. Then, click the ARGUMENTS tab (Figure 13.21).

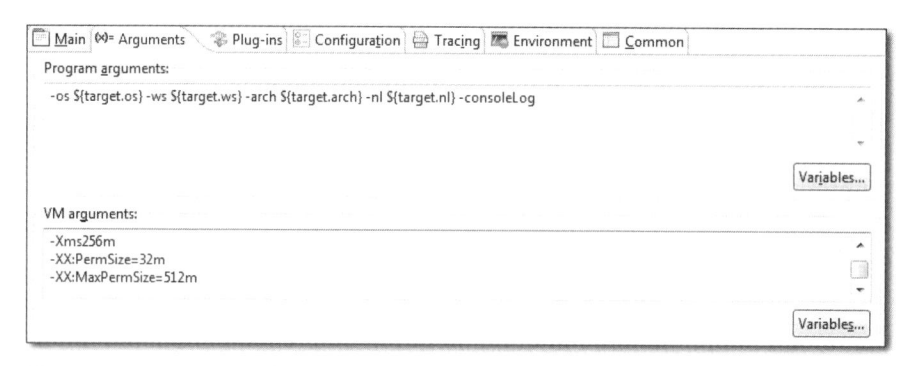

Figure 13.21 Arguments Tab

8. Add the following arguments to the VM ARGUMENTS input box:
   - `-Xmx1024m`
   - `-Xms256m`
   - `-XX:PermSize=32m`
   - `-XX:MaxPermSize=512m`

   Click APPLY, and then click CLOSE.

9. Now choose the ORGANIZE FAVORITES option in the RUN menu item. You can find it by clicking the triangle to the right of the green play button (Figure 13.22).

Figure 13.22 Organize Favorites Menu Item

10. A dialog box opens where you can select favorites that will show up in the PLAY menu. Choose the configuration you just made by clicking the ADD button and selecting the configuration. The result is visible in Figure 13.23.

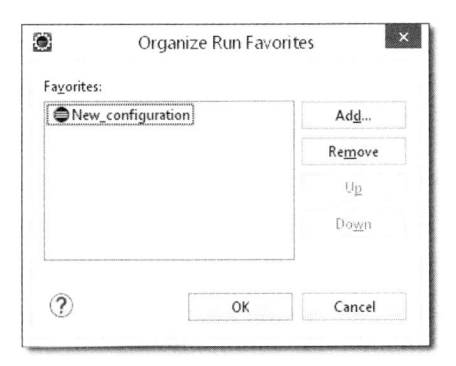

Figure 13.23 Organize Run Favorites Menu

11. Click OK.

You can now run Design Studio from Eclipse by clicking the PLAY button. If you want to pick the configuration, you can also use the triangle next to the button.

You'll find the favorite configuration at the top of the screen, as shown in Figure 13.24. When you click the PLAY button, Design Studio will start with that configuration, and your SDK components are included.

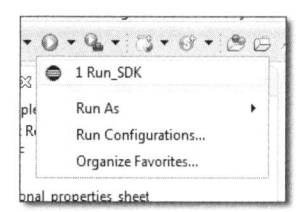

Figure 13.24 Run SDK on Design Studio

13.5 Summary

In this chapter, we walked through the steps to install Eclipse. First, we installed the software, and then we attached the XML and imported a sample project. Finally, we set up the target platform so you can run Design Studio directly from Eclipse.

In the next chapter, we'll walk through the steps for creating your own SDK component.

After installing and deploying the SDK, you can build components with it. In this chapter, we'll discuss how to use an SDK to build a custom extension in Design Studio.

14 Building Components Using the SDK

Chapter 12 introduced SDK extensions and explained how to work with them. Chapter 13 looked at the installation and deployment steps for developing your own SDK. In this chapter, you'll build an SDK extension, and we'll describe the main techniques used during the process.

We'll begin by explaining the SDK framework in Section 14.1, before looking at the different languages used to build an SDK in Section 14.2. From there, in Section 14.3, we'll move on to the basic building blocks that make up the composition of an SDK. After we've covered the basics, we'll discuss the steps for configuring an SDK extension in Section 14.4. This will include configuring both the extension and component levels in addition to creating the necessary data bound properties. We move to implementing internal functionality using JavaScript in Section 14.5, before discussing the steps to create methods in Section 14.6. In Section 14.7, you'll learn about three JavaScript libraries: jQuery, D3, and SAPUI5. As a demonstration, we'll end the chapter by looking at how to build a BULLET GRAPH SDK extension in Section 14.8.

14.1 Understanding the SDK Framework

This section looks at how an SDK extension is organized internally. We'll address all the main parts briefly, discuss their function in the SDK, and explain how they relate to each other. After discussing all the parts of an SDK extension, you'll begin building the skeleton of the project.

14 | Building Components Using the SDK

SDK extension components, just like standard components, use a client-server architecture. The JavaScript code you develop in the SDK runs in the browser (client). In the backend server, there is a generic implementation for extension components. As shown in Figure 14.1, the different parts of an SDK extension interact with each other. The Design Studio script at runtime can only see the property values that are stored on the server. As a developer, you have to make sure that new property values in the browser are moved to the server so that other parts of Design Studio can interact with those new values.

For example, if you have a graph with four regions, and the user clicks one, you want to use that clicked value to show more on that selected region. The internal JavaScript mechanics know what was clicked; however, if you want to use Design Studio script to further work with that information, the internal JavaScript of the SDK has to inform the platform server of the property's value change. JavaScript is then sent back to the server. In Section 14.5, we'll show you how to send values back to the server.

Furthermore, at design time, you can also use additional properties. Here, too, you have to invoke a mechanism to exchange information with the central server.

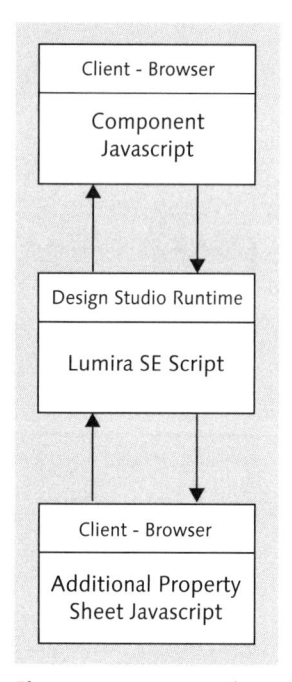

Figure 14.1 Interaction between Parts of the SDK Extension

Before building SDK extensions in Design Studio, you should be aware of the following limitations:

- They can't act as container components.
- They can't use all available property types; they are restricted to a subset of property types.
- They can't use large result sets. The standard maximum is 10,000 cells; however, this can be expanded.
- They can't extend standard components because standard components are built in Java not JavaScript.

Before we look at the various building blocks of an SDK extension, next we'll provide overviews for the different programming languages you'll encounter when building an SDK extension.

14.2 Languages Used in an SDK

In this section, we'll look first at JavaScript, which is used for creating the functionality within an SDK. Then, we'll provide an overview of *Extensible Markup Language (XML)*. XML is used to set up the structure of an SDK in the *contribution.xml* file. We'll then look at basic HTML and CSS principles in the last two subsections.

14.2.1 JavaScript Overview

JavaScript is an open, lightweight, interpreted programming language designed to create network-centric applications. JavaScript is also cross-platform, and it complements and integrates with Java and HTML5 languages. JavaScript is the main language used to build the frontend functionality and the additional properties for HTML (see Section 14.3.3).

JavaScript can change *Document Object Model (DOM)* elements where each HTML element in a document, including the document itself, is a node. This means that you can add, delete, change, copy, clone, or otherwise work with HTML elements. Additionally, you can change HTML attributes.

Because JavaScript is a programming language, you can invoke logic and checks, as well as add a wide variety of functionality that you can't with a static web page.

For example, in the following colored box example, you'll see where a function is defined in the `init()` function (see Section 14.5.2) when someone clicks on a component:

```
this.$().click(function() {
    that.fireEvent("onclick");
});
```

This example uses the jQuery library, but the point is that a function can be assigned to a click. This function doesn't have to be directly in the `click` parameter. You can also do something like this:

```
Var myFunction = function() {
    that.fireEvent("onclick");
}
this.$().click(myFunction);
```

Or, you can do this:

```
this.$().click(theFunction);
```

Later on in the component subclass, you define the actual function to which the previous statements are pointing:

```
function theFunction() {that.fireEvent("onclick");};
```

There are also a variety of options to do the same thing within JavaScript. The advantage of the last two is that you can reuse them for other elements. In the subsections that follow, we'll discuss some important elements of JavaScript that you should keep in mind when building your own SDK extension.

Variables

JavaScript has five types of primitive values:

- Numbers (e.g., 45, 3.14159)
- Boolean (e.g., true or false)
- Strings (e.g., "Hello World")
- Undefined (e.g., no value assigned)

You can assign values to a new variable without declaring the variable. In the following statement, we assigned a value to `myVar` without defining the variable first:

```
myVar = 3.14
```

JavaScript just assumes that it must be a global variable and moves on.

If you want a variable to be local, you have to declare it yourself. For example:

```
var myVar = 3.14
```

When you declare a variable outside of any function, it's also a *global variable*, which is available to any other code in the current document. When you declare a variable within a function, it's a *local variable* because it's only available within that function and the functions called from there.

You can test global versus local for yourself in a component. Just create a variable in the `init()`, and read the variable in the `afterUpdate()` function. You'll notice that using the first line will cause an error because `myVar` is unknown in `afterUpdate()`. If you put the declaration outside the `init()` function, the value will be readable in the `afterupdate()` function.

There are advantages to local variables. The most important one is that they disappear after the function closes. Imagine you want to use the same variable name in another place. If it was globally declared elsewhere, you could run into all sorts of trouble because the variable can hold all kinds of values that you don't expect. If you declare a variable without adding a value (`var myVar;`), the variable holds the value `undefined`. You can check for this value and act accordingly:

```
var myVar;
if(myVar === undefined)
{ doSomething();} Else { doSomethingElse();}
```

In this code, we check the value of `myVar`. Based on whether it has a value, we continue with one or the other function. When we look at the Component JavaScript, we see something similar in the `getter/setter` function in Listing 14.1.

```
    this.color = function(value) {
        if (value === undefined) {
            return this.$().CSS("background-color");
        } else {
            this.$().CSS("background-color", value);
            return this;
        }};
```

Listing 14.1 Checking for Undefined in Getter/Setter Function

A `getter/setter` function updates the value when a parameter is passed and returns the current value when no value is passed. A `getter/setter` function checks using an `if` statement if a parameter value is passed to the function. If there isn't a parameter value, it returns the current value. If there is a parameter value, it changes the current value to the new value passed in the parameter. In Section 14.5.2, you'll find an example of a `getter/setter` function.

The following sections discuss different types of variables you may encounter.

Array

A variable that holds a list of values is called an *array*. If you want to create an array, you use an *array object*. This object contains not only a list of values but also methods and properties that you can use as well.

To declare a new array, use the following syntax:

```
var myArray = new Array;
```

There are some other ways to initialize an array, such as the following:

- `var myArray = new Array (element1, element2, element3)`
- `var myArray = Array (element1, element2, element3)`
- `var myArray = [element1, element2, element3]`

If you want to initialize an array with a length without values, you can do the following:

```
var arraylength = 10;
var arr = new Array(arrayLength);
var arr = Array(arrayLength);
```

If you want to get a specific element, use `myArray[0]` to get the first element from the array. Because an array is an object, there are useful methods attached that you can use (Table 14.1).

Method	Description
.concat	Joins two arrays into one new array, for example: newArray = myArray.concat(otherarray)
.Join	Creates one string with all elements, for example: strList = myArray.join()
.push	Adds elements to the end of an array and returns the new lengths of the array.

Table 14.1 Array Methods

Method	Description
pop()	Removes the last element and returns that element value to the function that called the pop method.
shift()	Removes the first element of the array and returns that element.
.unshift()	Adds elements to the front of the array and returns new lengths.
.slice	Takes a section of the array and returns it to that section.
.splice	Removes an element and (optional) replaces them with other elements.
.reverse()	Reverses the order of the elements in an array.
.sort()	Sorts the elements of an array.

Table 14.1 Array Methods (Cont.)

Arrays can be nested to create *multidimensional arrays*. Each individual element of the main array is an array itself, which holds multiple values. If you want to get the first element of the array, within the fifth element of the main array, you collect it by using Array[5][1]. You do the nesting by assigning an array to an individual element of the main array. Listing 14.2 shows how you can generate a multidimensional array.

```
var mainArray = new Array(6);
for (i = 0; i < mainArray.length; i++) {
  mainArray[i] = new Array(4);
  for (j = 0; j < mainArray[i].length; j++) {
    mainArray[i][j] = "[" + i + "," + j + "]";
  }
}
```

Listing 14.2 Nested Arrays

The code declares an array with a length of 6 and loops through this until it reaches the last member. The last member is derived by mainArray.length. The index number of the last member is one number lower than the length of the array because index numbering starts at 0. This is why the loop iterates as long i<mainArray.length and not <=. The last member of this array has a length of 6 and an index number of 5. Within the loop, we assign a new array of length 4 to each element of mainArray. The elements of the subarray are strings that show the array addresses of all the elements.

JSON Variables

JavaScript Object Notation (JSON) is an easy way to create and store data structures in JavaScript. As the name suggests, a JSON variable is an object (just like an array). When creating a data bound SDK, you'll work with a JSON object that contains the data from the data source.

When you look at a JSON object (Listing 14.3), you'll find that, at a first glance, it's difficult to read.

```
var person     = {
  "firstname": "John",
  "lastname": "Doe",
  "Age": 41,
  "Country": "U.S.A."
}
```
Listing 14.3 JSON Object

If you want the first name of the variable `person`, you'll use `person.firstname`. You can combine elements to fill other variables or write something that shows up in your component Let's expand the JSON example further. Suppose you don't want to have just one person but a group of people in the JSON. In this case, you need to make an array that contains JSON objects. You can easily do this by adding brackets (`[]`) around the JSON, as shown in Listing 14.4. Each JSON is separated by a comma (,).

```
var data = {
  "person": [
    {
      "firstname": "Mike",
      "lastname": "Smith",
      "Age": 23,
      "Country": "U.K."
    },
    {
      "firstname": "John",
      "lastname": "Doe",
      "Age": 41,
      "Country": "U.S.A."
    }
  ]}
```
Listing 14.4 Array of JSON Objects

In this example, there are two people in the JSON object. To get the first name of John Doe, you use `data.persons[1].firstname`, which results in "John."

As you can see in the example code, the [and] signs have been added around the two persons in the JSON object. The JSON object has one main element, `persons`, that holds an array of persons. You can combine these at will, making very complex structures possible.

By Reference and By Value

You may want to change the value of a variable or create a copy of a value to work from. It's important to note that if you assign the value of a variable to another variable, you're not creating a copy but a reference to the same data. This is similar to asking two different booking sites if there is a seat available on the next flight to Amsterdam in exactly the same plane. You have two paths (the booking sites) to exactly the same information (whether there is an available seat). If you book via one of these booking sites, you'll find it has also influenced the information on the other site.

As another example, let's look at the following JavaScript code:

```
var bob = 1000;
var alice = bob;
alice = alice - 100;
console.log(bob) // result 900 as Alice deducted 100
```

In the above example we have two variables: Alice and Bob. Alice has access to the same value (1000) as Bob. When Alice deducts 100 from the value, this also impacts Bob because they have access to the same data. If you want a copy of the value so that Alice and Bob can work independently, then you have to make a shallow or deep copy of the value.

A *shallow copy* creates a new top-level object containing references to the same properties as the original object. If your object contains only primitive types such as numbers and strings, a deep copy and shallow copy will do exactly the same thing. However, if your object contains other objects or arrays nested inside it, then a shallow copy doesn't copy those nested objects; it merely creates references to them. A *deep copy* returns different lists of different data items.

The code for a shallow copy is as follows:

```
alice = $.extend( {}, bob );
```

While the code for a deep copy is as follows:

```
alice = $.extend( true, {}, bob );
```

14 | Building Components Using the SDK

Object-Oriented

JavaScript is object-oriented, which means that you can use, create, define, or reference objects that each have their own properties and methods. Understanding object-oriented JavaScript can help you build better components, grasp what is happening inside the functions, and know why and how all these things work together.

JavaScript uses functions as *classes*. Defining a class is defining a function. The following example defines a new class called Person. This kind of function is also called an *object constructor* or *constructor*.

```
Function Person() { };
```

If you want to create a new person in the code, you have to create a new *instance*:

```
Function Person() { };
var Hank = new Person();
var John = new Person();
```

The constructor function is called when a new object instance is created. In JavaScript, the function is the constructor. Every action in the constructor is executed when a new instance is created (Listing 14.5).

```
Function Person () {
    alert ('new person created');
}
var Hank = new Person();
var John = new Person();
```
Listing 14.5 Creating a Person Object

In the example in Listing 14.6, you'll get two popup messages stating that a person is created. *Properties* are variables that are held in the class. Every instance of the class has these properties. Properties should be set in the prototype property of the class (function) so that inheritance works correctly. If you want to work with properties from within a class, you use the keyword this. From the outside, you use InstanceName.Property.

```
function Person(firstName) {
    this.firstname = firstName;
}
Person.prototype.firstname = '';
var firstperson = new Person('Hank');
var secondperson = new Person('John');
```

516

```
alert('the firstname of person 1 is' + firstperson.firstname);
alert('the firstname of person 2 is' + secondperson.firstname);
```
Listing 14.6 Example Function for Objects

Methods follow the same logic as properties. The difference is that methods are functions. You call methods the same way you call properties, but at the end of the line, you add (). For example, if there was a function `tellAge`, you could call this by using the following statement:

`person.tellAge();`

Methods are normal functions that are bound to a class/object as a property, which means that they can be invoked out of context. In other words, you can create functions to call the method without mentioning the object. This allows you to postpone adding the context object until you know from which object you want to get the information (Listing 14.7).

```
function Person(firstName) {
    this.firstname = firstName;
}
Person.prototype.firstname = '';
Person.prototype.sayName = function () {
 alert(this.firstname);}
var firstperson = new Person('Hank');
var nameCaller = firstperson.sayName;
```
Listing 14.7 Using Methods Invoked Out of Context

If you call `firstperson.nameCaller`, you'll get `Hank` as an answer; however, `nameCaller` is undefined because the variable points to the function and not to the function within the context of `firstperson`. The following is defined with `var nameCaller`:

`var nameCaller = function () { alert(this.firstname);};`

If you want to use `nameCaller` this way, you have to give the function context, which results in the following:

`nameCaller.call(firstperson);`

Inheritance is a way to make a more specialized version of one or more classes. A specialized class is called a *child,* and the other one is the *parent*. In JavaScript, you assign an instance of the parent class to the child class and then specialize the child class (Listing 14.8).

14 | Building Components Using the SDK

```
function Person(firstName) {
    this.firstname = firstName;
}
Person.prototype.firstname = '';
Person.prototype.sayName = function () {
 alert(this.firstname);}
function employee(yearsinservice) {
this.yearsinservice = yearsinservice
Person.call(this);
 }
Employee.prototype = new Person();
employee.prototype.constructor = employee;

employee.prototype.yearsInService =
 function () { alert(this.yeasrsinservice) };
```
Listing 14.8 Inheritance in JavaScript

In this example, the class `employee` has been added. With the `Person.call` statement, you call the parent constructor. Using the `prototype.constructor`, you correct the constructor so that it points to `employee`. When you add an employee function, the end result is an object that has the first name function inherited from person and the method `yearsinservice`.

Method Chaining

Method chaining is often used in JavaScript, especially in the jQuery and D3 libraries (see Section 14.7). The method chaining technique keeps your code simple by allowing you to call several methods of the same object. To demonstrate, we'll show you an example with and without method chaining (Listing 14.9). The first three lines are standard lines. Then we'll compress it into one line with chaining and finally do some altering for readability.

```
this.$() .CSS('background', 'black');
this.$() .height(225);
this.$() .width(200);
// The same can be done with
this.$() .CSS('background', 'black') .height(225) .width(200);
You can also break it in several lines for easier readability:
this.$() .CSS('background', 'black')
    .height(225)
  .width(200);
```
Listing 14.9 Assigning Property Values With and Without Chaining

As shown, method chaining cleans the code as it refers to the object only once. First, let's define a class with a few methods (Listing 14.10).

```
var employee = function {
    this.name = 'John Doe;
    this.title= 'BI consultant';
    this.years='2';
};
employee.prototype.setName = function (name) { this.name =
 name ; return this; };
employee.prototype.setTitle = function(name) {this.title =
 title; return this; };
employee.prototype.setYears = function(years) {this.years =
 years; return this; };
```
Listing 14.10 Defining a Class with Methods

Notice that `return this;` is added at the end of each function. In method chaining, each method will work with the value that is returned from the previous value. If you omit `return.this`, you'll get an error message. Next, you use the class and assign values through chaining (Listing 14.11).

```
var John = new employee();
John
    .setName("John Doe")
    .setTitle("BI Consultant")
    .setYears(2);
```
Listing 14.11 Using a Class and Assigning Values

Conditionals

As with any other programming language, JavaScript uses conditional `if then` statements. The basic syntax of this statement is the following:

```
if (expression) { Statement(s) to be executed if expression is true; }
```

Expression **must be either** `true` **or** `false`. The statement can be expanded with `else`:

```
if (expression)
 { Statement(s) to be executed if expression is true; }
else
{ Statement(s) to be executed if expression is false; }
```

The previous code can be expanded again to an `if then else if` statement (Listing 14.12).

```
if (expression 1)
{Statement(s) to be executed if expression 1 is true}
else if (expression 2)
{ Statement(s) to be executed if expression 2 is true}
else if (expression 3)
{ Statement(s) to be executed if expression 3 is true}
else
{ Statement(s) to be executed if no expression is true }
```
Listing 14.12 Using if then else

You can also use `switch` instead of the `if then else if` statement, as shown in Listing 14.13.

```
switch(expression) {
case n:
 code block
 break;
case n:
 code block
 break;
default:
 default code block
}
```
Listing 14.13 Using switch

You'll notice the keywords `switch`, `case`, `break`, and `default`. The expression is compared to each `n` in the `case` blocks. If `n` matches the expression, then that block is executed. When the code comes across a `break` statement, it breaks out of the `switch` statement (omitting other `case` statements). If no value matches the expression, then it goes to the default: `block`.

The ternary conditional is actually the same as a standard `if then else` statement, but it's written in shorthand. In D3 sites, many examples use this kind of shorthand, so you'll want to understand the structure to reduce confusion. This is an example from some code in D3:

```
td.style("color", function(d, i) { return i ? null: "red"; });
```

Here you see that the function has the code `i ? null: "red";`. This code evaluates the variable `i`. If this variable evaluates to `true`, the value `null` is returned; if `i` evaluates to `false`, "red" is returned. The same can also be done with `if then else`; however, this code is often used because you need to type fewer characters. For many JavaScript developers, this is an important difference.

Loops

Looping occurs when the same block of code is run repeatedly until a certain condition is met. We'll discuss two loop statements: the `for` loop and the `while` loop. The `for` loop is used if you want to repeat the code for a determined number of times. The `while` loop is used for an undetermined number of times until a result is achieved. The following is an example of a `for` loop:

```
for (initialization; condition; increment)
{ // statements }
```

In this loop, you see the following keywords:

- `initialization`
  This is where the counter gets its initial value.

- `condition`
  The condition is evaluated; if it's true, the loop statements will be executers.

- `increment`
  The update expression of increment executes.

Let's look at an example where you want to loop through a list of elements inside an array:

```
for(var i = 0; i < a.length; i++) {
  Document.write ("<TR><TD>" + a[i] + "</TD></TR>");
}
```

Here, you write a table row for each element that is in array `a`. You continue to loop until `a` is smaller than the length of the array. The index `i` is incremented with 1 each round with `i++`. You see that `a[i]` is included in the body of the code. As you run each time with `i` holding a different value, you get new table lines with new values for each loop.

A `while` loop will continue as long as a condition is met. The following is an example of a `while` loop:

```
var i=0;
while (i<=10) //Output the values from 0 to 10
{
 document.write(i + "<br>")
 i++;
}
```

This particular example does the same thing as a `for` loop; however, because the evaluation is updated in the code block, this gives you the option to control when the `while` loop needs to continue or stop.

Closures

A *closure* is an inner function that has access to the outer function variables. The inner function has access to the variables and the parameters of the outer function that have been defined because the inner chain is defined within the context of the outer chain. The result is that the inner function has access to three scope chains: its own local variables, the outer function's variables, and the global variables.

Creating a closure is simple. You create a function inside another function. The following is an example of a closure:

```
for ( var i = 0; i < 5; i++ )
 {
   setTimeout( function() {alert( i );}, i * 100 );
 }
```

If you run this code, you'll notice that it doesn't behave as expected. The `alert` function inside the loop will return the value 5 five times, instead of the expected values 1, 2, 3, 4, 5. This is because functions have access to changing variable values. This also applies to functions defined in loops. The functions "see" that the variable value is changed after the function is created and will work with the latest value in the variable `i`.

Closures can create a scope for each iteration and store each unique variable within its scope (Listing 14.14).

```
var createFunction = function( i ) {
  return function() {
    alert( i );
  };
};
for ( var i = 0; i < 5; i++ ) {
  setTimeout( createFunction( i ), i * 100 );
}
```
Listing 14.14 Using Closures

In `createFunction(i)`, a function is returned. Because the inner function uses the outer function scope as a private scope, you have a place where each unique value is stored. Consider the example in Listing 14.15.

```
var makeCounter = (function() {
 var privateCounter = 0;
 function changeBy(val) {
 privateCounter += val;
 }
 return {
 increment: function() {
  changeBy(1);
 },
 decrement: function() {
  changeBy(-1);
 },
 value: function() {
  return privateCounter;
 }
 };
})();
```
Listing 14.15 Counter Object

You now have a *counter object* that can function as a constructor for new variables:

```
var myCounter = makeCounter();
var myCounter2 = makeCounter();
```

The current value of the counter is stored in the variable `privateCounter`. By using closures, that variable is available for the functions `changeBy`, `increment`, and `decrement`. You also can create several independent counters. The variables `myCounter` and `myCounter2` will behave independent of each other.

> **Additional Information**
>
> You can find more in-depth information on closures at *http://javascriptissexy.com/understand-javascript-closures-with-ease/*.

This

In JavaScript, the keyword `this` refers to the context where the current code lines are executed. When you execute a method of an object, `this` will refer to that object. The keyword `this` works similar to the way you use a pronoun to take the place of a noun when speaking. For example, "When does our train arrive? Oh wait, I can see it!" The pronoun "it" refers back to the noun "train"; the JavaScript `this` works pretty much the same way, as shown in Listing 14.16.

14 | Building Components Using the SDK

```
var employee = {
    firstname: "John"
    lastname: "Doe"
    fullname: function () { return this.firstname + " " + this.lastname;
  }
}
```
Listing 14.16 this Statement

In the example, `this.firstname` and `this.lastname` point to the variable `employee`. You also could use `author.firstname` and `author.lastname`, but then the code becomes ambiguous. In JavaScript, `this` is bound to the object that the function is bound to, just like "it" was bound to "train."

In many of the first lines in SDK code, you'll find `var that = this` because at the beginning of the SDK code, right after the function definition, the keyword `this` refers to the root element. If you're working within a function where the keyword `this` has another value, you can now refer to `that`.

14.2.2 XML Overview

Before we explain the different parts of the *contribution.xml* file, we want to introduce XML briefly. The most recognizable feature of XML is its tags, or elements (to be more accurate). The elements you create in XML are similar to the elements created in HTML documents. However, XML allows you to define your own set of tags. In XML, you use elements, tags, and nodes, as described here:

- **Elements**
  An element consists of an opening tag, its attributes, any content, and a closing tag. So everything between `<SDK extension>` and `</SDK extension>` is an element.

- **Tags**
  A tag—either opening or closing—is used to mark the start or end of an element.

- **Nodes**
  A node is a part of the hierarchical structure that makes up an XML document. Node is a generic term that applies to any type of XML document object.

`<SDK extension>` is an opening tag to an element. You can add an attribute to the element by adding it to the opening tag like this: `<SDK extension id= "my.sdk.exentsion">`.

14.2.3 HTML Overview

As you know, *Hypertext Markup Language (HTML)* is the language used to render websites. Essentially, everything shown in Design Studio applications are in HTML5.

> **Additional Resources**
>
> If you want some hands on experience with HTML5, go to *www.codecademy.com*. You'll find online tutorials and courses on how to build a professional website, which starts out with the basic HTML5 elements.

The following are some terms that you should be aware of when using HTML5:

- **Tags**

    Tags can be wrapped around different types of content to structure a layout. For example, the following tags are used for a header:

    `<H1>Header text</H1>`

- **Classes and IDs**

    Classes and IDs are assigned to tags to identify and change each element using JavaScript. A class is an identifier that can be used multiple times. An ID should only be used once. The following is an example of using classes and IDs in HTML5:

    `<div id = "myID" class = "myClass">`

- **`<div>`**

    The `<div>` element in HTML5 defines generic containers within the content of a page.

- **Scalable Vector Graphics (SVG)**

    SVG is a language for creating graphics. SVG drawings can be interactive and dynamic, and you can define and trigger animations. The main element tag is `<SVG>`. With these tags, you can set up attributes to define the size (view port) and a coordinate system for your SVG element. This setup allows you to resize components in Design Studio. Additionally, the coordinate system will translate the coordinates to the new size.

14 | Building Components Using the SDK

> **Additional Resources**
>
> You can find additional information on SVG elements at *http://tutorials.jenkov.com/svg/index.html*.

14.2.4 CSS Overview

In Chapter 10, we discussed CSS in great depth. This section aims to define terms that haven't yet been discussed. The following are terms that you should be aware of when using CSS to build an SDK extension:

- **Basic selectors**

  If you want to apply CSS, the first thing you need to do is select those elements to which you want to apply a certain formatting. Enter *selectors*. Selectors pinpoint the place where the CSS needs to be applied. The basics are the tags, classes, and IDs. You can also expand this into siblings, children, exceptions, and so on. *Basic selectors* are based on IDs, classes, and types. The following are used with this type of selector:

  - ***: Using this selector will target every element on the page. This is great to apply some common properties without having to repeat them. For example: `* { margin: 0; padding: 0; }`.
  - *Tags*: If you want to format a specific tag, you use the tag you want to format and then apply the formatting, for example, `a { color: red; }`. You can use pseudo classes in tags if you want, for example, a link that already has been clicked to look different, for example, `a:visited { color: purple; }`.
  - *Classes*: These are used to stylize a group of elements. Every element that contains a class (`myclass`) will be stylized when you input the following CSS, for example, `.myclass { color: red; }`.
  - *IDs*: This kind of selection allows you to pinpoint a single element within the document. The ID name must be unique within the document, for example, `#myid {width: 240px; height: 240px; margin: auto;}`.

- **Attribute selectors**

  This is by far the most flexible way of selecting elements. Using this selector allows you to work with any attribute within an element. You can look for all the elements that have a particular attribute, for example, `a [title] { layout options}` or `.myclass[title] {layout options}`. Additionally, you can select only those elements that have an attribute with a specific value, for example, a[href="http://www.myspecialurl.com"], or part of a specific value, for example, a[href*="productionsystem"].

> **Additional Resources**
>
> If you want more information on CSS, *www.w3schools.com/css/* provides a step-by-step CSS tutorial.

Now that we've walked through the SDK programming languages you'll encounter, next we'll look at the building blocks of an SDK extension.

14.3 Building Blocks of an SDK Extension

An SDK extension is a collection of files of which the central file is *contribution.xml*. Within this file, there are references to all the other files. There are more technical files in an SDK file, but many of these don't add extra functionality. Regardless, you need to be aware of some of them, so we'll discuss some of these other technical files in Section 14.8. In this section, we'll walk through the different building blocks of an SDK extension.

> **Getting Started with a New Extension**
>
> To get started, copy one of the SAP sample extensions, and rename all the elements to your own project. This gives you a starting point to work from. In Chapter 13, we show how to import SAP's sample SDKs.

14.3.1 Contribution.xml

The *contribution.xml* file houses the extension definition, as well as the definition of the components and their properties. This is where Design Studio receives all the information on how to deal with the SDK extension. Components defined in the XML file show up in the COMPONENT panel, where you can drag them onto the canvas. Properties defined here show up in the PROPERTIES panel of Design Studio when you select the component.

The *contribution.xml* file also informs Design Studio where other files are located so that they can be used for the functionality, methods, or additional properties. When an SDK extension is installed in Design Studio, the application looks at the contribution.xml file to see which components are available and what their respective properties are. In addition, it also finds the references to all the other files because they are defined per component.

14.3.2 Component JavaScript

This Component JavaScript file houses an SDK component's functional behavior. It also creates the visualization that you see when you run the application with the SDK component. For each component that you defined in the *contribution.xml* file, you have to define a JavaScript class with the same name in a separate file. The location and name of the file is defined in the *contribution.xml* file. Design Studio uses the reference defined in the *contribution.xml* file to find the accompanying class name.

Let's look at an example of an SDK to better understand this and see the connections in the code. We'll use a simplified *contribution.xml*, where one SDK extension is holding one component (Listing 14.17).

```
<sdkExtension xmlns="http://www.sap.com/bi/zen/sdk"
    title="SAP Design StudioDesign Studio Analytic charts"
    version="1.3"
    vendor="Interdobs"
    id="com.interdobs.analyticcharts">
    <group id="analytics" title="Analytic Charts"/>
    <component
        id="ScatterPlot"
        title="Scatterplot chart">
        <jsInclude>res/js/boxplot.js</jsInclude>
    </component>
</sdkExtension>
```
Listing 14.17 Main Structure of the SDK Extension

The name of the extension is `com.interdobs.analyticcharts`, and the name of the component is `Scatterplot`. In the line with the tag `jsInclude`, you see the location and name of the JavaScript file that holds the Component JavaScript.

In the JavaScript file *boxplot.js*, we create a class `com.interdobs.analyticscharts` that holds a function (Listing 14.18). You can see in the first line where the class and functions are defined as two parameters within the subclass method. When the defined class is called, the function runs. Design Studio knows the name of the component and the location of the JavaScript file from the *contribution.xml* file. Therefore, the JavaScript file looks for the class and runs the function inside the class (Listing 14.18).

```
sap.designstudio.sdk.Component.subclass("com.interdobs.analyticcharts.
ScatterPlot", function() {
// JavaScript code for functionality
}
});
```

Listing 14.18 Main Structure of the Component JavaScript

To organize your JavaScript classes, you can either hold them all in one file or use a separate file for each class. We like to use a separate file for each class because multiple classes in one file tend to create large documents that are difficult to navigate. Regardless, you can still use one file, as it makes no difference. Each component will then have a <JsInclude> with the same file name.

14.3.3 Additional Properties

Using additional properties is a designer-friendly way for the application designer to work with the SDK extension. Not all properties have to be visible in the PROPERTIES panel. You can hide properties in the standard panel and have a specific layout. The standard GEO MAP component, for example, has an ADDITIONAL PROPERTIES panel where properties are shown that aren't visible in the PROPERTIES panel (Figure 14.2).

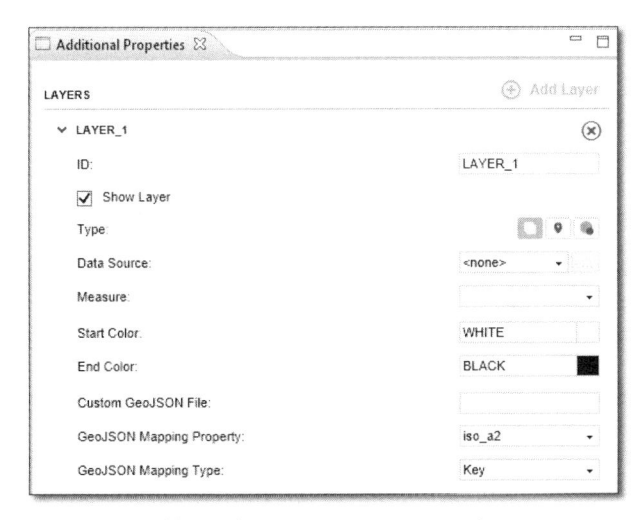

Figure 14.2 Additional Properties Screen Example

529

14 | Building Components Using the SDK

The ADDITIONAL PROPERTIES panel consists of an HTML file and a JavaScript file. The HTML file is necessary to define the layout of the ADDITIONAL PROPERTIES panel. The JavaScript file is used for the functionality. In the header of the component definition in the *contribution.xml* file (Listing 14.19), you state the location of the additional properties file.

```
<component
        id="LineTrendGraph"
        title="Line Graph with trend option"
        icon="res/icons/scatterplot.png"
        handlerType="div"
        propertySheetPath="res/ap_sheets/ap_linetrend.html"
>
```

Listing 14.19 Component Definition in Contribution.xml

As you can see, the `propertySheetPath` attribute defines the location of the HTML file. In the *ap_linetrend.html* file, you'll find a link that connects to the JavaScript functionality. First, you'll find a script tag with the location of the JavaScript file:

```
<script src="/aad/zen.rt.components.sdk/resources/js/sdk_
propertysheets_handler.js"></script>
```

Then, you'll find a line where a new instance of the JavaScript class is created:

```
<script>
new com.interdobs.analyticcharts.LineTrendGraphPropertyPage();
</script>
```

When you look into the JavaScript file, you'll find the definition of the class:

```
sap.designstudio.sdk.PropertyPage.subclass("com.interdobs.analyticchart
s.LineTrendGraphPropertyPage", function() {
});
```

Notice that the name of the class is the extension name plus the component name with the prefix `PropertyPage`.

14.3.4 Script Contributions

Script contributions define the methods accessed by the Design Studio script. Methods can change properties, collect property values, or trigger actions. In Design Studio, you can access the properties of an SDK extension by creating *script methods*. These methods allow you to interact with the SDK extension components at runtime. This means that adding methods will improve the usability of the component.

Script contribution methods allow application designers to create scripts that changes properties at runtime and retrieve information from the component at runtime. You create script contributions by adding a script contribution file named *contribution.ztl* to the same folder (Listing 14.20). The syntax is a little different from JavaScript.

```
class com.interdobs.analyticcharts.ScatterPlot extends Component
{
 /* Shows or hides trendline */
void setTrendline(/* Show trendline */ boolean showTrendline)
    {*
     this.trendline = showTrendline;
    *}
 /* returns the current visibility of the trendline */
 boolean getTrendLine () {*
 return this.trendline;
 *}
}
```

Listing 14.20 Script Contribution

Notice that the enclosures for the `setTrendline` methods are `{*` and `*}` instead of the `{}` that you find in JavaScript. Another important aspect to note is that the `this.trendline` variable gets a new value in the `setTrendline` method. This property was defined in the *contribution.xml* file, whose value is passed from the server to the Component JavaScript.

It also works the other way around, as shown in the second method. The second method returns a Boolean value about the current status of a trend line. Using these two methods, you can check the current value of the trend line and switch it to the opposite value. An example Design Studio script to toggle the status of the trend line might look like this:

```
SCATTERPLOT_1.setTrendline(!SCATTERPLOT_1.getTrendLine());
```

In Design Studio scripting, the Content Assistance (Ctrl+Space) works in the same way, allowing you to look up all the defined methods.

14.3.5 Component CSS

The Component CSS file contains CSS classes (Listing 14.21) that you use in the Component JavaScript. You first define the location of the CSS file in the *contribution.xml* file by using the tag `jsInclude`. In the XML script sample shown in Listing 14.21, this tag is included in the definition of the component.

14 | Building Components Using the SDK

```
<component
    id="LineTrendGraph"
    title="Line Graph with trend option"
    icon="res/icons/scatterplot.png">
    <jsInclude>res/js/linetrendgraph.js</jsInclude>
    <CSSInclude>res/CSS/linetrendgraph.CSS</CSSInclude>
```

Listing 14.21 CSS File with Classes for Use in the Component JavaScript

In the Component CSS file, you can create CSS classes, which hold layout styles that can be applied to the Component JavaScript. For example, you can define a CSS class for a tooltip that pops up in your graph (Listing 14.22).

```
.tooltip {
 position: absolute;
 width: 200px;
 height: 28px;
 pointer-events: none;
 background-color: #FFFFFF;
}
```

Listing 14.22 Component CSS File

The width and height are determined, and the background is set to white. When you create elements in the Component JavaScript you also assign the CSS class `tooltip` when creating the tooltip:

```
tooltip = d3.select(container).append("div")
  .attr("class", "tooltip")
  .style("opacity", 0);
```

The JavaScript code includes a `div` element that gets the `tooltip` class. The formatting defined in the CSS class is applied to the `div` element.

14.3.6 Icon

Icons (16 × 16 pixels) are shown in the COMPONENTS panel next to the name of the component on the left-hand side (Figure 14.3). You can add an image file to the extension and attach the image to a component.

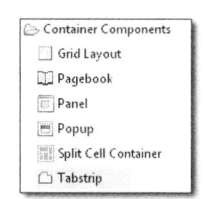

Figure 14.3 Icons in the Components Panel

The image needs to be sized at 16 × 16 pixels. You define the location of the icon file in the *contribution.xml* file (see Listing 14.23).

```
</component>
    <component
    id="LineTrendGraph"
    title="Line Graph with trend option"
    icon="res/icons/scatterplot.png"
```
Listing 14.23 Icon Definition in Contribution.xml

14.4 Configuring the SDK Extension

Configuring an SDK extension means changing the *contribution.xml* file. The XML file is based on an XML Document Type Definition (DTD) scheme definition that SAP provides during the install procedure. In this section, we'll describe the options available to define an SDK extension and its components, and we'll look at the steps involved in setting up the *contribution.xml* file.

14.4.1 Extension Level

The main level of an SDK is the extension level. An extension can hold one or more component elements to define the components that are part of the extension. In Table 14.2, you see the attributes on an extension level.

Attribute	Required	Description
id	Y	The unique ID for the SDK extension. It's combined with the unique IDs of the components to identify each individual component within the extension. Use a name for the extension such as `com.mycompany.myextension` with lowercase letters and a dot (.) as a delimiter.
title	Y	The title of a component that is visible in the installation details during install.
version	Y	The version number in major/minor, such as 1.3.
vendor	Y	The vendor name.
eula	N	The end user license agreement text. The designer must accept this text before he can install the extension.

Table 14.2 SDK Extension Attributes

14 | Building Components Using the SDK

The syntax in Listing 14.24 is used for the extension level attributes.

```
<sdkExtension
    id="mycompany.myextension"
    title="My Extension with some nice things"
    xmlns="http://www.sap.com/bi/zen/sdk"
    version="1.0"
    vendor="SCN SAP Design StudioDesign Studio Community"
    eula="Be Nice">
```
Listing 14.24 Extension Level Attributes

Within the SDK extension, you can define custom groups. Components and component properties can be assigned to groups. When a component is assigned to a group, it shows up in that group in the COMPONENTS panel (Figure 14.4).

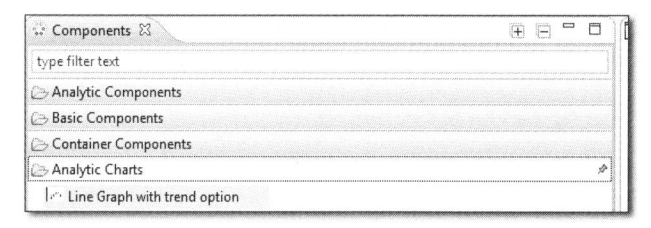

Figure 14.4 Components Assigned to a Group in the Components Panel

Grouping properties works in the same way. The PROPERTIES panel shows each property in its defined group (Figure 14.5).

Figure 14.5 Properties Grouped in the Properties Panel

You create these groups by first adding a group element to the extension. You then refer to the group in the component element or properties element, depending on what you want to group (Listing 14.25).

```
<SDKextension>
<group id="analytic" Title="Analytic Charts" >
<component id="scatterplot" group="analytic">
<property id"showtrendline" group = "analytic">
</SDKextension>
```
Listing 14.25 Setting Up Groups in Contribution.xml

In Table 14.3, you'll find all the properties of a group element.

Attribute	Required	Description
id	Y	Unique ID used in components and their properties as an attribute to assign them to this group using `group = "Id"`.
title	Y	Title of the custom group that is visible in Design Studio in either the COMPONENT panel or the PROPERTIES panel.
tooltip	N	Tooltip that appears when the cursor hovers over the group title (COMPONENT panel).
visible	N	If set to `true`, group is visible (default is `true`).

Table 14.3 Properties of the Group Element

14.4.2 Component Level

An extension can hold multiple component elements. Each component element defines a separate component within the extension. For an extension with four components, the basic XML will look like Listing 14.26.

```
<sdkExtension
    id="mycompany.myextension"
    title="My Extension"
    xmlns="http://www.sap.com/bi/zen/sdk"version="1.0" vendor=
" mycompany ">
<component id="comp1" title="comp1"> </component>
<component id="comp2" title="comp2"> </component>
<component id="comp2" title="comp3"> </component>
</sdkExtension>
```
Listing 14.26 Components in Contribution.xml

Each component can have a number of attributes, as shown in Table 14.4.

14 | Building Components Using the SDK

Attribute	Required	Description
id	Y	Unique component ID within the extension of the component.
title	Y	Title of the component.
tooltip	N	The text you'll see when you hover over the component in Design Studio COMPONENTS panel.
visible	N	If set to true, the component is visible in Design Studio.
group	N	Assign to group as defined in elements on extension level.
propertySheetPath	N	Location of the HTML file of the additional properties sheet.
data-bound	N	Indicates whether the component uses a data source.
newInstancePrefix	N	Prefix for the name of a newly created instance of an extension component. If this attribute isn't set, then a name in the form of "extension component type + number" is used.
handlerType	N	Specifies the technology that implements this extension component. Options include: ► div ► SAPUI5 ► Data source The standard option is div. if you work with SAPUI5, choose that option. If you create a data source SDK, choose data source.
icon	N	Location of an image file to be used as an icon.
modes	N	Sets the SAPUI5 libraries the SDK extension component supports. The component will only show up on the component view when the application is made in an SAPUI5 library that the SDK component supports. This attribute is important for extension components with a handlerType of SAPUI5. This attribute is ignored for extension components with a handlerType of data source (SDK data sources) or extension components with the TECHNICAL_COMPONENT group. Specify one or more of the following values separated by a space: commons or m (default setting: commons).

Table 14.4 Component Attributes

Each component can contain a number of elements. In the XML, you'll find them embedded in a component element as in Listing 14.27.

```
<component>
<property
    id="data"
    title="Data"
    type="ResultCellSet"
    group="DataBinding"/>
<stdInclude kind="d3"/>
<jsInclude>res/js/linetrendgraph.js</jsInclude>
<CSSInclude>res/CSS/linetrendgraph.CSS</CSSInclude>
<initialization>
    <defaultValue property="WIDTH">400</defaultValue>
</initialization>
<supportedBackend>BIPLATFORM</ supportedBackend>
</component>
```
Listing 14.27 Elements within Components

Each element has its own properties. As shown in Table 14.5, some elements can be inserted multiple times, and others only once.

Element	Frequency	Description
property	0 – *	Holds the properties of the component.
stdInclude	0 – *	JavaScript framework to include. These are JavaScript libraries that you can use in your own code. Specify either D3 or cvom.
jsInclude	0 – *	References a JavaScript file to be included. This is a relative path or a fully qualified URL. One of the files should hold your JavaScript SDK coding. You also can insert external JavaScript libraries using this.
CSSInclude	0 – *	References to a CSS file to include with this extension component at runtime. It's either a relative path to the root folder of the SDK extension or a fully qualified URL.

Table 14.5 Elements in Each Component

Element	Frequency	Description
`requireJS`	0 – *	References a resource file to be loaded with this extension component at runtime. It's either a relative path to the root folder of the SDK extension or a fully qualified URL. `requireJS` is the best way to include files. If you have old SDK extensions with `CSSInclude` and `JSInclude`, it's worthwhile to switch to `requireJS` elements because it has several advantages.
`initialization`	Once	Sets up the initial values for the properties you define. When a designer adds the component where the related property is a part of, it will look here for an initial value to start with.
`supportedBackend`	Once	Specifies which platforms are supported by the extension component. Specify one of the following values: `LOCAL`, `BIPLATFORM`, `HANA`, or `NETWEAVER`. If this element isn't specified, then all platforms are supported by this extension component.

Table 14.5 Elements in Each Component (Cont.)

The element you'll use most often is `property`. This element allows you to set up everything that a designer can change at design time to modify the behavior of the component. Properties show up in the PROPERTIES panel when the designer selects the component. Properties can be anything from the dataset that you want to visualize to the background color. Often, you start with a baseline of properties and expand them as you continue developing the SDK extension. Property values that designers set are used in the Component JavaScript. You can also set the properties using the `additional properties` function. Both the Component JavaScript and the JavaScript `additional properties` function will take care of the interaction.

You can set a number of attributes for each property, as shown in Table 14.6.

Attribute	Required	Description
id	Y	Unique ID of the property within the component. Use lowercase letters at the beginning of the ID. Make sure that you use a consistent method of capitalization. In other files, you'll reference this ID, and consistency ensures that you don't waste much time going back and forth because you mixed up lowercase/uppercase.
title	Y	Title of the property as you'll see it in the PROPERTIES panel in Design Studio.
tooltip	N	Tooltip of the property.
visible	N	If true, then the property is visible. You may want to set it to false if you want the designer to change the property in the additional properties or when it's used to set up a return value that the designer can collect using a Design Studio script.
type	Y	This property can have one of the following types: INT, FLOAT, BOOLEAN, STRING, TEXT, SCRIPTTEXT, COLOR, URL, RESULTCELL, RESULTCELLLIST, RESULTCELLSET, RESULTSET, MULTILINETEXT, and ARRAY OBJECT. Some of the property types offer a dialog box in the PROPERTIES panel in Design Studio.
group	Y	Using a group ID will create a group that designers can collapse in the PROPERTIES panel.
bindable	N	If this is set to true, then the property can be bound in the PROPERTIES panel using Design Studio binding.
mode	N	Indicates which SAPUI5 libraries this property supports. It won't be visible in the PROPERTIES panel if the library used in the application isn't supported.

Table 14.6 Attributes of Property Elements

To set up an array, you need to set up a property for the array itself and set up the values within the array:

```
<property id="SelectedMembers" type="Array" title="Selected Members">
    <property id="member" type="String" title="Member" />
</property>
```

The `type` object allows you to create a nested structure of values. You can create child properties and even objects themselves. This allows you to create complex properties like those shown in Listing 14.28.

```
<property id="Employee" type="Object" title="Employee">
 <property id="firstname" type="String" title="FirstName"/>
 <property id="Function" type="String" title="Function"/>
 <property id="color" type="Color" title="Color"/>
</property>
```
Listing 14.28 Object Properties

With the object in Listing 14.28, you can invoke the property value {"Ramya","Tester"} into the component.

> **Examples**
>
> In the sample projects from SAP, you'll find the extension UI5List sample component. In Chapter 12, we tell you how to import these extensions.

Property elements have two child elements: `possiblevalue` and `option`. `<possiblevalue>` can be used to limit the possible values that the property will accept (Listing 14.29).

```
<component>
    <possiblevalue>show no axis</possiblevalue>
    <possiblevalue>show x axis</possiblevalue>
    <possiblevalue>show y axis</possiblevalue>
    <possiblevalue>show both axes</possiblevalue>
</component>
```
Listing 14.29 Possible Value Elements

When you want to update this property, choose one of the four values shown in Listing 14.29. The `option` child element is used for additional options for data binding, which we'll discuss next.

14.4.3 Creating Data Bound Properties

In Table 14.6, we already glossed over the `type` attribute. You may not have noticed that there are some possible values such as `ResultCell`, `ResultCellList`, `ResultCellSet`, and `ResultSet`. If you select one of these, you'll create a data bound property. Before you can use this property type, you first have to declare that you're creating a data bound component. You declare this by setting the component attribute `databound` to `true`.

When you need data to be bound to a component, you can use the syntax shown in Listing 14.30.

```
<component
        id="LineTrendGraph"
        title="Line Graph with trend option"
        icon="res/icons/trendgraph.png"
        handlerType="div"
        databound="true"
        group="analytics"
```
Listing 14.30 Setting Up Data Binding in XML

After you've set the attributes, you can add the data bound property types. You can add multiple data bound properties and determine the shape of the data based on the data bound type you choose (Table 14.7). Additionally, with the child element <options>, you can add or remove properties of the data bound type.

Property Type	Data Values
ResultCell	A single value.
ResultCellList	A single row or column of data values.
ResultCellSet	A complex selection of data values from rows and columns. This means you can create a subset based on fields on rows and columns.
ResultSet	The entire dataset.

Table 14.7 Data Bound Property Types

After you've selected one of the types, you must also set the values for the child element options. You can change these values by adding a child element yourself to the property. The initial settings are shown in Table 14.8, and the description is given in Table 14.9.

Options	ResultCell	ResultCellList	ResultCellSet	ResultSet
includeAxesTuples	False	False	False	True
includeTuples	True	True	True	True
includeResults	True	True	True	True
presentationDelimiter							
selectionShape	0	1	2	2

Table 14.8 Default Values of Each Child Element Option Based on the Data Bound Property Type

14 | Building Components Using the SDK

Options	ResultCell	ResultCellList	ResultCellSet	ResultSet
swapAxes	False	False	False	False
includeData	True	True	True	True
includeFormattedData	False	False	False	False
includeMetadata	False	False	False	True
fillMetadataProperty	True	True	True	True
includeAttributes	False	False	False	False
includeConditionalFormats	False	False	False	False
allDataOnEmptySelection	True	True	True	True
maxCells	10.000	10.000	10.000	10.000

Table 14.8 Default Values of Each Child Element Option Based on the Data Bound Property Type (Cont.)

Options	Description
includeAxesTuples	If set to true, then the properties axis_rows and axis_columns are included in the Data Runtime JSON.
includeTuples	If set to true, then the property tuples is included in the Data Runtime JSON.
includeResults	If set to true, then the result values, for example, totals, are included in the Data Runtime JSON.
presentationDelimiter	This string separates the presentation of dimension member values in the text property of dimension members in the Metadata Runtime JSON.
selectionShape	This integer value indicates the geometry of the data in the Data Runtime JSON. Possible values include the following: ▶ 0 (ResultCell) ▶ 1 (ResultCellList) ▶ 2 (ResultCellSet or ResultSet)
swapAxes	If set to true, then the axes (and the relevant data) are swapped in the Data Runtime JSON and the Metadata Runtime JSON.

Table 14.9 Description of Data Bound Options

Options	Description
includeData	If set to true, then the property data is included in the Data Runtime JSON. It contains the data values.
includeFormattedData	If set to true, then the property FormattedData is included in the Data Runtime JSON. It contains the formatted data values as a string.
includeMetadata	If set to true, then the Metadata Runtime JSON is included as a part of the Data Runtime JSON.
fillMetadataProperty	If set to true, then the SDK component's implicit property metadata contains the Metadata Runtime JSON.
includeAttributes	If set to true, then the JSON properties attributes and attributeMembers are added to the Metadata Runtime JSON. They contain information about the display attributes of a result set. If the ResultSet doesn't contain attributes, then these JSON properties aren't added, regardless of the value of includeAttributes.
includeConditionalFormats	If set to true, then the JSON property ConditionalFormats is added to the Metadata Runtime JSON, and the JSON property conditionalFormatValues is added to the Data Runtime JSON if the ResultSet contains conditional format information.
allDataOnEmptySelection	If set to true, an empty selection string ("" or {}) set to the data-bound property returns the entire ResultSet in the Metadata Runtime JSON and Data Runtime JSONs. If false, then an empty selection string ("" or {}) set to this data-bound property returns a Metadata Runtime JSON with no dimension information and an empty Data Runtime JSON ("").
maxCells	This is the maximum number of selected ResultSet cells that are sent to this data-bound property. If the number of selected ResultSet cells is greater than the maximum number, then no ResultSet cells are sent to this data-bound property.

Table 14.9 Description of Data Bound Options (Cont.)

These options allow you to optimize performance as you remove everything that you don't need in your component. For example, if you want to create something based on the master data only, you can set the option `includeData` to `false`, removing a lot of the data traffic and memory consumption.

When you want to increase the maximum amount of cells, be aware of the impact this has on network traffic, CPU, and memory consumption. When you notice a performance degradation, lower the amount again.

14.5 Building Internal Functionality

The functionality of an SDK extension component is created using JavaScript classes. Everything you see in the component and each interaction is created in here. The location of the file is referenced in the *contribution.xml* file. Within this file, a JavaScript class is defined. The JavaScript class name is the same as the extension name and the component name.

In this section, we'll look at the different functions and interactions that can be made. First, we'll discuss function calls, as they are the entrance point for Design Studio to trigger the component. We'll then discuss the different functions for each phase in the component lifetime where you can add logic. Finally, we explain how the data from a data source is presented in the Component JavaScript so you know how to access the data.

14.5.1 Function Calls

You implement a Component JavaScript class for each extension component. In this section, you'll see the empty function that represents the component. At runtime, the SDK framework provides a `<div>` element, which acts as the main or root element. With the root element at base level, you can create all kinds of visualizations by creating HTML elements with a CSS layout. The name of the JavaScript class is a combination of the SDK extension namespace and the extension component ID:

```
sap.designstudio.sdk.Component.subclass(
    "com.rheinwerk.example.BulletGraph", function() {});
```

This example is an empty shell of a JavaScript class. Everything you create in JavaScript is within this class. You can access this root element as a jQuery object with `this.$()`. We addressed the keyword `this` before in Section 14.2.1. The `$()` part is the main jQuery function and gives you access to the methods and properties of this library.

The Component JavaScript follows a particular flow after it's created (Figure 14.6).

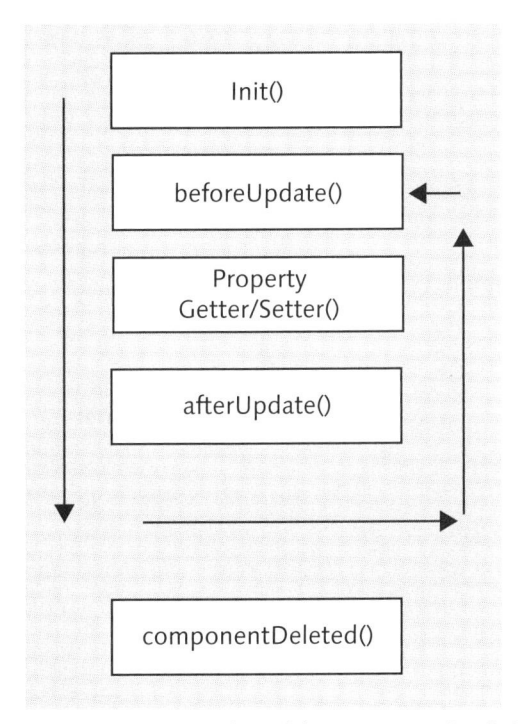

Figure 14.6 Process Flow of the Component JavaScript

As shown in Figure 14.6, the component starts off with the `init()` function, which it will run only once when the component is rendered at the start. The component then cycles through the `beforeUpdate()`, all the `getter/setter()` functions, and the `afterUpdate()` function each time one or more properties changes values. Finally, if a component is removed from the application, the `componentDeleted()` function is triggered.

If you add these functions to the empty shell code, the function will look similar to Listing 14.31.

14 | Building Components Using the SDK

```
sap.designstudio.sdk.Component.subclass(
    "com.rheinwerk.example.BulletGraph", function() {
    this.init = function() {};
    this.beforeUpdate = function() {};
    this.property = function() {};
    this.afterUpdate = function() {};
});
```
Listing 14.31 Adding Functions to the Component JavaScript

14.5.2 Functions

Now that you've added the functions, let's take a closer look at them. A parameter passed to a function stays local. In the following subsections, we'll address the `init()`, `beforeUpdate()`, `getter/setter`, and `afterUpdate()` functions, as these are the main functions used in the Component JavaScript for the SDK.

init()

The `init()` function is called when a new instance of a component is initialized. This function will start immediately after the root `<div>` element is created. This is the place where you can set up the basic parts of the JavaScript code that don't rely on the property values. An example of this is setting up the basic structure of a graph. If you build a line graph, the graph will have a number of parts that it always needs; therefore, you'll need the graph lines, a place to put the graph lines, and the X-axis/Y-axis. The first setup of these elements can be done in the `init()` stage (Listing 14.32).

```
this.init = function() {
        var container = this.$()[0];
        var graph =
 d3.select(container).append("svg:svg").attr("width", "100%").attr("hei
ght", "100%");
        //appending an svg:path element
        path = graph.append("svg:path");
    };
```
Listing 14.32 init() Function

As shown in Listing 14.32, the only thing the code does in the `init()` function is provide the basic setup. An SVG element is created, and a `path element` is set up within the SVG. You can use the `init()` function to introduce these elements because you'll need these in the graph, independent of the property values that you receive later on.

Notice the first line of code assigning the root element to the container variable. If you want to use that variable in other functions, you need to declare that variable outside the `init()` function, but within the JavaScript class. Almost every component you'll make will start with that line in the `init()` function.

beforeUpdate()

The `beforeUpdate()` function is called each time a property is updated. It runs before the properties are updated, thus it works only with old values. The big difference between the `init()` function and `beforeUpdate()` is that the `beforeUpdate()` function is called every time something changes and thus is run more frequently. This function is a good place to clean up things before you re-create your visualization with the new property values.

The following syntax removes all elements within the `div` element so that the `afterUpdate()` function can work with a clean slate. You can perform this function if you want to remove everything and start the graph from scratch.

```
This.beforeUpdate = function() {
    innerChart.selectAll("svg").remove();
};
```

The `beforeUpdate()` function creates multiple graphs, where each separate graph has its own SVG element. By using this statement, all SVG elements and the graphs that have been drawn inside the SVG elements are removed. `innerChart` is a variable that contains the parent element that was defined in the `init()` function.

Getter/setters

`Getter/setter` isn't a single function, but a collection of functions. For each property element you created in *contribution.xml*, you need the `getter/setter` function in the Component JavaScript to ensure that the values are passed from and to the Component JavaScript. The `getter/setter` function has a structure to exchange information on the property value with the server. A typical `getter/setter` function looks like Listing 14.33.

14 | Building Components Using the SDK

```
this.data = function(value) {
    if (value === undefined) {
        return properties.data;
    } else {
        properties.data = value;
        return this;
        }
    };
```
Listing 14.33 Getter/Setter Function

The `getter/setter` function has one parameter (`value`). If this parameter is empty, the function will return the current value of the property. Internally in JavaScript, the `value` parameter is stored in the local variable `properties.data`. This `getter` returns the current value. If the parameter contains a new value, the function will replace the current value in `properties.data` with the new value that it receives. This is the `setter` part. The `setter` finishes with the line `return this();`. This last line allows the function to be chained. We discussed method chaining in Section 14.2.1.

You'll find that as you create more properties, there will be more functions. A good way to keep track of the variable values that are stored in all the `getter/setter` functions is to declare a JSON object. You use this to store all the values, as shown in Listing 14.34.

```
sap.designstudio.sdk.Component.subclass(
    "com.company.extension", function() {
var chartProperties = {};
this.prop1 = function(e) { if (e ===
 undefined) {return chartProperties. prop1;}else{chartProperties. prop1
 = e;return this;}};
this.prop2 = function(e) { if (e ===
 undefined) {return chartProperties. prop1;}else{chartProperties. Prop2
 = e;return this;}};
});
```
Listing 14.34 JSON Object Usage for Property Values

Having one JSON object as a property repository helps you easily find the property value. The syntax is `chartProperties.yourproperty`. Keeping the property name consistent across *contribution.xml* and the JavaScript functions will minimize the complexity by being able to refer to the same name.

Afterupdate()

The `afterupdate()` function is called after all properties have their new value assigned. The `afterupdate()` function is where you'll most likely build the biggest part of your component. In this example, the `afterUpdate()` function immediately refers to another function:

```
this.afterUpdate = function() {
    drawKPIBarChart();
};
```

To complete the example, we'll show a few lines of the `drawKPIBarChart` function (Listing 14.35). The function starts out by setting the margins based on property values followed by collecting information from the data bound properties.

```
function drawKPIBarChart(){
        var width = that.$().outerWidth(true) - margin.left - margin.right;
        var height = that.$().outerHeight(true) - margin.top - margin.bottom;
        var barPadding = 5;
        dataset = returnDataSet();
```

Listing 14.35 drawKPIBarChart Function

The dataset collection is performed via the `returnDataSet();` function.

componentDeleted()

The `componentDeleted()` function is triggered when a component is deleted from the application. Typically, this function is used to clean up anything that stays in memory if you don't explicitly remove it. For example, if you created something outside the scope of a `div` frame, where your component should reside, you should make sure to clean the elements outside the scope using this function.

14.5.3 Data Runtime JSON

In this section, we'll look at how data is structured in the SDK extension when it arrives in the Component JavaScript. When you bind a data source to an SDK component, the data source will deliver data to the SDK component. This data arrives in the form of *DATA JSON*. There are many variations of the DATA JSON based on the choices you make in *contribution.xml*. Typically, you receive metadata (data about the master data) and fact data (the actual numbers plus references to the master data). This section will give an overview of how the metadata is structured in the Data Runtime JSON, and it will help you understand the data as it arrives in Component JavaScript as these elements come back in every variation.

Metadata is information about the fact data. It gives context by adding dimensions and layout information. You need the metadata to group the numbers. The next two sections discuss both metadata runtime and fact data runtime.

Metadata Runtime JSON

The metadata object is a JSON with an array of dimensions. In Figure 14.7, you see the main layout. After the dimensions, there is a final entry on the main level that holds the locale setting.

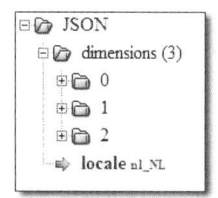

Figure 14.7 Main Level Metadata

If you look at the code of this JSON at a high level, it will appear as shown in Listing 14.36.

```
{ "dimensions":
    [{dimension},
     {dimension},
     {dimension}],
    "locale":"nl_NL"
}
```
Listing 14.36 High-Level JSON Code

The key dimension holds an array of dimensions. Each dimension in the array is a JSON object. Finally, there is a property for the locale. The layout of the JSON object is shown in Figure 14.8.

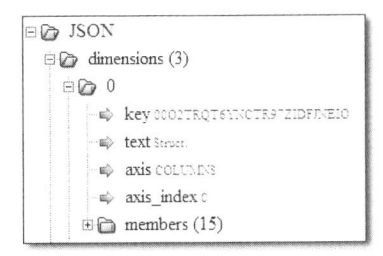

```
□ 🗁 JSON
  □ 🗁 dimensions (3)
    □ 🗁 0
      ⇒ key 0002TRQT6YNCTR9"ZIDFJNEIO
      ⇒ text Struct
      ⇒ axis COLUMNS
      ⇒ axis_index 0
      ⊞ 🗁 members (15)
```

Figure 14.8 Metadata Dimension Level

On this level, you'll find some of the dimension properties: the key or technical name, the text (description) of the dimension, and the location of the dimension in the data source view. In this example, you see that the dimension with index number 0 was placed in the column axis and that it's the first dimension (axis_index = 0).

The JSON dimension is a member of the dimension arrays. The following is the JSON dimension syntax:

```
{"key":"UniqueKey","text":"Name of dimension","axis":"COLUMNS","axis_index": 0,"members": [ {Member1}, {Member2}, {Member3}]}
```

This dimension holds 15 values. A detailed overview of one of those values is shown in Figure 14.9.

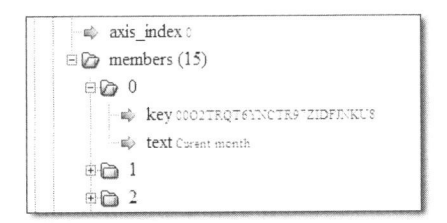

```
    ⇒ axis_index 0
  □ 🗁 members (15)
    □ 🗁 0
      ⇒ key 0002TRQT6YNCTR9"ZIDFJNKU8
      ⇒ text Curent month
    ⊞ 🗀 1
    ⊞ 🗀 2
```

Figure 14.9 Metadata Member Level

At the member level of this dimension, there is a unique key and text. A *member* is another type of JSON object, which appears as the following:

```
{"key":"Unique Key","text":"Description"}
```

Having looked at the different levels, we'll show you how to get this description out of the metadata JSON object. The following code will return the first member of the first dimension from the metadata:

```
var dimension_text = metadata.dimensions[0].members[0].text
```

This dimension is an example of a *characteristic*. You also have dimensions that hold *key figures*. These dimensions hold information about the numbers in the data (Figure 14.10).

```
⇒ containsMeasures true
⊟ members (45)
  ⊟ 0
     ⇒ key HIERARCHY_NODE 0002TRQT6YNCTR97ZIDFJFSFK 0002TRQT6YNCTR97ZIDFJFBR4
     ⇒ text Standard
     ⇒ type HIERARCHY_NODE
     ⇒ scalingFactor 0
     ⇒ formatString = ==0; = ==0
     ⇒ nodeState EXPANDED
```

Figure 14.10 Key Dimension

Again, this is also a dimension with members, which contain the following attributes: `scalingFactor`, `formatString`, and `nodeState`. At the dimension level, you can recognize this kind of dimension by the attribute `containsMeasures`. This attribute is set to `true` here, but it's omitted on other dimensions. The attribute `type`, also shown here, tells you if the value is an aggregate or a hierarchy node.

Fact Data Runtime

Fact data is divided into three sections (Figure 14.11).

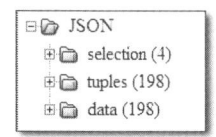

```
⊟ JSON
   ⊞ selection (4)
   ⊞ tuples (198)
   ⊞ data (198)
```

Figure 14.11 Main Level Fact Data

The SELECTION section tells you which selections have been made to build the dataset. In Figure 14.12, you see that each dimension has a –1 value. This means no selections have been made; the application returns to –1 to show that no selections have been made.

```
⊟ 🗁 JSON
  ⊟ 🗁 selection (4)
      ⇨ 0 :
      ⇨ 1 :
      ⇨ 2 :
      ⇨ 3 :
  ⊞ 🗀 tuples (198)
  ⊞ 🗀 data (198)
```

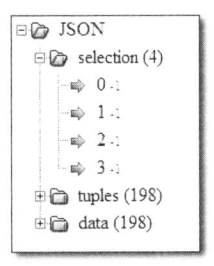

Figure 14.12 Fact Data Selection

For example, if you had a `ResultCellList` selection and selected one column, one of these values would be 0, pointing to the index 0 of the members in the metadata dimension array.

> **Differences in JSON Based on Your Selection**
>
> In Section 14.3.1, we discussed the available data binding options. These different options have an impact on the way the Data Runtime JSON is created. If you choose `ResultSet`, you won't get separate metadata and fact data JSON objects, but a single JSON object holding both. There are many variations based on the choices you make, but here we discuss the main variation.

The next section contain TUPLES (Figure 14.13). For each data line, there is an accompanying tuple. You can view the tuples as address lines for each number in the data section. Each tuple contains a list of numbers for each dimension that is in the dataset. The first number refers to the first dimension. The number itself tells you which member of that dimension relates to the fact number. Therefore, in Figure 14.13, you see TUPLE 198 with four numbers. The first 0 means that the fact relates to the first member of the first dimension.

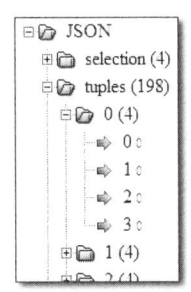

```
⊟ 🗁 JSON
  ⊞ 🗀 selection (4)
  ⊟ 🗁 tuples (198)
      ⊟ 🗁 0 (4)
          ⇨ 0 :
          ⇨ 1 :
          ⇨ 2 :
          ⇨ 3 :
      ⊞ 🗀 1 (4)
      ⊞ 🗀 2 (4)
```

Figure 14.13 JSON Tuples

In each tuple, you'll find a new array. For each dimension, there will be an item in the array. The value of the item depicts the index number of the member in that dimension. If you want to get all the metadata for this tuple, use the following syntax:

```
var dim1_text = metadata.dimensions[0].members[0];
var dim2_text = metadata.dimensions[1].members[0];
var dim3_text = metadata.dimensions[2].members[0];
var dim4_text = metadata.dimensions[3].members[0];
```

Tuples align with the data, which means that `data.tuple[0]` is the corresponding dimension line to `data.data[0]`. Therefore, if you want to find the corresponding metadata for each dimension, you look at the index number of the number. If you look up the same index number in the tuples, you'll get a list of index numbers. The first index number corresponds to the member in the first dimension in the metadata, the second to the second dimension, and so forth.

The final section of the data is DATA (Figure 14.14). This section consists of an array of dimensions holding all the actual numbers of the data. You can see that the first number with index 0 is 285.49.

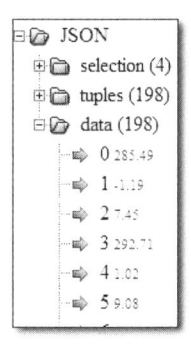

Figure 14.14 JSON Data Numbers

Together with the tuples, the DATA section delivers all the data from the data source. Typically, you want to use your data to create a visualization. The first step is then to remodel the data into something that is usable for the visualization you have in mind. In this section, we'll show you how you can create a simple table variable that can be used for bar charts or similar graphs. When you create a visualization, working directly on the JSON shown earlier is extremely complex. It's easier to modify the data to a structure that is readily usable for the visualization that you have in mind. In the following steps, you'll set up properties and then add JavaScript code to hold the data in the variables that you use for visualizations.

As you already know, you first have to make the component databound. The *contribution.xml* file contains the databound=true attribute. Next, create a property that will provide a single row or column of data from the data source:

```
<property id="data" title="Data Series"
type="ResultCellList" group="DataBinding"/>
```

Now that you've defined the data property in the Component JavaScript, you'll need the getter/setter functions for the data and metadata. All the coding for data manipulation can be invoked in the afterUpdate() function or the getter/setter function so you can rerun the code each time the data property has changed.

Follow these steps:

1. Define the parts of the DATA JSON that you want to use:
    ```
    var numbers = data.data
    var tuples = data.tuples
    var dimensions = metadata.dimensions
    ```

2. Loop through each number in the data variable, and, via the tuples, find the accompanying dimension values. For each row, combine the dimensions and numbers in a JSON object, and then add them to an array. In Listing 14.37, the numbers and tuples are collected and added to the table.
    ```
    for (var i=0,len=numbers.length; i<len; i++)
    {
    newjson = {};
    newjson.value = numbers[i];
    newjson.tuple = tuples[i];
    dataset.push(newjson);
    }
    ```
    Listing 14.37 Collecting and Adding Numbers to the Table

3. Use a loop that runs from 0 to the length of the numbers array to address each number in the number array. Note that looping stops when i is equal to the length (because the loop starts with index 0, the max index is the length of the array −1).

4. Create a temporary empty JSON `newjson`, and use the JSON object as a placeholder for the values before adding them to a new array dataset. This new array of JSON objects will have the same structure as `newjson`. Each time, you add the current number and tuple to the JSON. Because the index numbers are in sync, you know that `numbers[0]` and `tuples[0]` belong together.

5. Finally, push the resulting JSON to the dataset array. For each loop, a new row is added to the array until you've looped through all the number rows.

That was part one. Now you need to add the dimensions to the JSON. You'll use the same code as before and add some additional lines to invoke the dimensions.

This can be done several ways, such as creating a `dim_name` and a `dim_value` attribute for each dimension. However, in this example, you'll create a dimension array in the JSON. When you use this JSON for visualization, you can easily check the number of dimensions in a row by using `dataset[0].dimensions.length`.

Follow these steps:

1. Add the line:

   ```
   newjson.dimensionjson = getDimensions(newsjon.tuple)
   to the code just before the dataset.push command. We use a new
   function here: getDimensions
   ```

2. Create the function `getDimensions` using Listing 14.38.

   ```
   }function getDimensions(tuple) {
   var dimension = new array;
   for (var i=0,len=tuple.length; i<len; i++)

   {
   newjsondimension = {};
   newjsondimension.dimension = metadata.dimensions[i].key
   newjsondimension.dimensionname = metadata.dimensions[i].text
   newjsondimension.dimensionmemberkey = metadata.dimensions[i].
      member[].key
   newjsondimension.dimensionmembertext = metadata.dimensions[i].
      member[].text

   dimension.push(newjsondimension);
   }
   return dimension
   }
   ```

   Listing 14.38 Adding Dimension Members to JSON

The initial code includes a reference to a function that collects the dimension values for each row. This keeps the code organized. Additionally, when you have other places for which you want to invoke dimension information, you can refer to the same function.

The `getDimensions` function works in a similar way as the initial code. It loops through all the tuples for each row and adds a dimension row. Finally, the dimension is returned to the calling function.

You now have a new dataset created based on the original data and metadata information. Each row is a number, and you can use the dimension information by using `dataset.dimension[0].dimensionmembertext`. For other dimensions, you change the index number. If you want to know how many dimensions you have, call `dataset.dimension.length`. Instead of making an elaborate array of dimensions, you can also pick just one dimension and place it as a single attribute for each row. For this example, we went a little further to explore the possibilities of working with the metadata and data properties.

> **Create an Overview**
>
> If you want to look into the DATA JSON object that your own data source provides, you can use the example JSON GRABBER component. This component shows you the JSON provided at runtime when you assign a data source. You can create the overview you saw in this section by copying and pasting the JSON into *http://jsonviewer.stack.hu/*.

14.6   Creating Methods

Methods are predefined actions that an application designer can trigger using Design Studio scripting. By defining methods, you introduce a way to create applications that allow users to interact with the component at runtime. In each extension, there is one *contribution.ztl* file. In this file, you can define methods for each component.

> **Opening the ZTL File in Eclipse**
>
> The best way to open the file in Eclipse is to right-click on *contribution.ztl*, and select OPEN WITH OTHER. In the EDITOR SELECTION dialog box, choose the Java editor.

14 Building Components Using the SDK

The *contribution.ztl* includes the Java syntax that can be found in the script method signatures and the JavaScript syntax that is used in the script method bodies. This means that you use very little Java to define the methods and rely mostly on JavaScript (similar to the Component JavaScript). The JavaScript is executed on the script engine server, which means you work with "sand-boxed" JavaScript. The script engine ensures that any error within your code remains within this body and doesn't break anything else. You also don't have any HTML DOM elements to work with.

The first step to add methods is to define the class using the following statement:

```
class com.sap.sample.coloredbox.ColoredBox extends Component {
```

As shown in Listing 14.39, the first step in creating script contributions is to define the class name of the methods. The class name is the name of the extension plus the name of the component.

```
class com.sap.sample.coloredbox.ColoredBox extends Component {
  /* Returns the current color of the box */
  String getColor() {*
  return this.color;
  *}
  /* Sets the current color of the box */
  void setColor(/* the new color */ String newColor) {*
  this.color = newColor;
  *}
}
```

Listing 14.39 Example Script Methods

You'll then use `extends Component`. This will give the component some standard methods such as `isVisible()`, `getHeight()`, and `setHeight()` script contributions that come with any visible standard component.

The next method, `String getColor`, doesn't have any parameters and returns the current color as a string value. It uses `this.color` to retrieve the property value. The JavaScript is enclosed between `{*` and the `*}`. The second method doesn't return a value and is defined as `void setColor`. Based on the parameter `newColor`, the second method will change the `color` property value. The parameter that is defined for the method is set between the parentheses after the method name. The comment is shown in the script help. In the JavaScript, the value of `newColor` is assigned to the property `this.color`.

14.7 Using the JavaScript Libraries

In this section, we'll discuss three JavaScript libraries: jQuery, D3, and SAPUI5.

14.7.1 jQuery

jQuery is a fast, small, and feature-rich JavaScript library. It makes things such as HTML document traversal and manipulation, event handling, animation, and AJAX much simpler with an easy-to-use Application Programming Interface (API) that works across a multitude of browsers. In this section, we'll discuss the use of elements within the jQuery library. *Elements* are part of the HTML document on the browser, but, in our case, they are the parts within the SDK component. We'll begin with a basic example of selecting elements.

Selecting Elements with jQuery

In jQuery, you can select elements and perform actions on those elements. As shown in Table 14.10, you can select elements by ID, call name, attribute, CSS compound class rules, or pseudo selectors.

Selection Statements	Description
$("#ID")	Selects a unique ID.
$(".classname")	Selects all elements with the class `classname`.
$("input[name='first_name']");	Selects all input elements with the attribute name `first name`.
$(".class1.class2")	Selects all elements that are both `.class1` and `.class2`.
$("div:animated");	Selects all currently animated `div` objects.

Table 14.10 Selection Statements

Working with Selections

Now that we've selected our elements, the next step is to use them. jQuery methods function as a `getter/setter`. In other words, if you pass a parameter, the method will update the selection. If you don't, the method will return the current value. If you want to set the HTML of a `div` element within the example component, use the following syntax:

559

```
this.$("#myDiv").html("<h1>Hello World<h1>");
```

To see what the current HTML is of a `div` ID, you can assign the method to a variable. Because the method will act like a `getter`, it will return the current HTML of the element, as shown:

```
var currentHTML = this.$("#myDiv").html);
```

jQuery is built to support method chaining. If you add a method that returns a jQuery object, you'll be able to chain another method to the statement, as shown:

```
$( "#content" )
.find( "p" )
.eq( 4 )
.html( "<H2>We add new html for the 5th element</H2>" );
```

In this code, three methods have been chained to the selection: `.find`, `.eq`, and `.html`. Additionally, you can refine your selection within the chain and step back the original selection. In the previous example, the fifth element was changed. You can write the code in the chain to change several elements (Listing 14.40).

```
$( "#content" )
.find( "p" )
.eq( 4 )
  .html( "<H2>We add new html for the 5th element</H2>" )
  .end()
.eq( 5 )
  .html( "<H2>We add new html for the 6th element</H2>" );
```
Listing 14.40 Chaining Multiple Elements

In this chain, the `.end()` method is used to go back to the original selection at the start of the chain.

Manipulating Elements

There are many ways to manipulate selected elements. You can change the HTML, text, CSS, attributes, and so no. Table 14.11 highlights a few of the methods. However, if you want to see the entire list of options, go to *http://api.jquery.com/category/manipulation/*.

Method	Description
`.html()`	Gets or sets the HTML context.
`.text()`	Gets or sets the text (HTML will be stripped).

Table 14.11 Some jQuery Manipulation Methods

Method	Description
.attr()	Gets or sets the provided attribute.
addClass()	Adds the specified class or classes.
CSS()	Gets the value of a style property or set one or more CSS properties.
empty()	Removes all child nodes from the selection.

Table 14.11 Some jQuery Manipulation Methods (Cont.)

14.7.2 D3

The D3 library allows you to bind arbitrary data to a DOM, and then apply data-driven transformations to the document. For example, you can use D3 to generate an HTML table from an array of numbers or use the same data to create an interactive SVG bar chart with smooth transitions and interaction. In this section, we'll look at how you can use the D3 library to build a component.

Adding Elements

To create any kind of component, you need to add HTML elements. The following is the basic command to add an element with D3:

`d3.select(this.$()[0]).append("p").text("Hello World");`

This code selects the main root `div` with the syntax `d3.select(this)`. A p (paragraph) element was added to the end of the selection (just before the closure of the `div` element). The text of this new paragraph was set to "Hello World". When you put this code in the `init()` function, your component will show "Hello World".

As previously discussed, combining commands with dots is called method chaining. Table 14.12 shows how this applies to D3.

Method Chain	Description
D3	Provides action to the methods in the D3 library.
Select(this.$()[0])	Provides a reference to the first element in the DOM that is a match. This points to the one unique `div` element in the application, that is, the current instance of the component. As this is within the D3, you still have all the methods available.

Table 14.12 Breakdown of Chained Command

Method Chain	Description
.append("p")	Appends a p element to the selected element from the previous row.
.text("hello world")	Gets a string and inserts it between the tags of the previously appended p element.

Table 14.12 Breakdown of Chained Command (Cont.)

The goal in this example is to select an element and apply a number of methods to it to change the appearance. You'll add a paragraph element to the main element and then change the text of the paragraph element. First, call D3 to get access to the methods that D3 contains. Many of the D3 methods return a reference to the selection of what they just did. That's why the chaining works. The .text returns a text to the <p> element that was the returned value of the .append("p"), and this in turn relates back the select statement. In this example, the select statement relates back to a jQuery function that is chained to this, the keyword for the current instance of the component.

As you can imagine, if you have a lot of things to do, the chain gets longer and longer until it's not very manageable. If this happens, you can break these chains up. For example, you could break up the line shown in Table 14.12 like this:

```
var container = this.$()[0];
chart = d3.select(this.$()[0]).append("p")
chart.text ("hello world!");
```

Additionally, because you're working in the Component JavaScript with its lifecycle, you should think about where to put the lines. For example, if you place the .append("p") method in the afterUpdate() function, a new paragraph will be added for each updated property. Therefore, you should put that part into the init() before you create a plague of paragraphs running all over the application! Instead of just selecting one element, you can select all the DOM elements. The only difference is that you'll be using D3.selectAll() instead of select(). For example, if you already have five <p> elements in your component and want to update all the texts, you can do this with the following code:

```
chart = d3.select(this.$()[0]).append("p")
chart.selectAll("P").attr("class", "mybox");
```

The `selectAll` line will select all p elements within the chart. The chart is defined in the previous line. As the `d3.select` statement points to `this.$()[0]`, the second line points to all the p elements within `this.$()[0]`.

Now let's build a table using appends and variables. First, you create a table. This line is identical to the append p element except that you now insert a `table` element:

```
var container = this.$()[0];
table = d3.select(this.$()[0]).append("table")
```

Second, you add four rows to the table (Listing 14.41).

```
table.append("TR")
table.append("TR")
table.append("TR")
table.append("TR")
rows = table.selectAll("TR");
rows.append("TD")
rows.append("TD")
rows.append("TD")
and finally
var columns = rows.selectAll("TD").text("hello world");
```

Listing 14.41 Adding Rows and Columns

As shown, this is quite repetitive, so next we'll look at a way to remedy this with data binding.

Data Binding

Each individual statement in Listing 14.41 was repeated for every necessary element. You need an automated method of creating an additional element for each row in the dataset.

You still need one table that is independent of the data, so keep the following:

```
var container = this.$()[0];
table = d3.select(this.$()[0]).append("table")
```

Start the `afterUpdate()` function with some hard-coded data:

```
var myData = ["first row", "second row", "third row", "fourth row"];
```

Now set up a variable for each row in the table, and attach the data to this selection:

```
Var tableRows = table.selectAll("TR")
.data(myData);
```

You see that in the `afterUpdate`, the `table` variable is used again. It was already defined on the class level and didn't need a `var` in the `init()` phase. However, we need to address the fact that there are no rows in the component to select! How can you work with elements that don't exist? The answer is that D3 has methods to deal with these situations.

In the data that you defined, there are four data items. In the DOM, you still have nothing. Currently, all the data is in the data collection and outside the collection DOM elements. You also have data that has a DOM element attached and finally a DOM element, but the data was deleted. For the first situation (data no DOM), you can use the `enter()`method. This method looks at the DOM and at the data. For each data item that doesn't have a DOM element, it creates a placeholder to work with. These two lines will append a new row with a column for each data item that has no equivalent in the DOM:

```
tableRows.enter()
    .append("TR").append("TD").text("Hello World!");
```

You may notice that method chaining is used to add a column (`TD`) to each row and each column is filled with the text "Hello World!". Of course, we want to do a little more with the data, but let's wait for the final part where we handle the data that already has a DOM element. Before continuing with the code, you need the data to be a little more flexible to be able to test updates and deletions of data. You can create a property in the *contribution.xml* of type `string`. The standard value is the first value, second value, third value, and fourth value. You can also create the `getter/setter` for the new property. The first line in the `afterUpdate()` where you defined `myData` changes to the following:

```
var myData = _datastring.split(",");
```

When you start Design Studio, you'll now be able to set the `datastring` property. You'll notice that when you increase the number of elements, the number of "Hello Worlds!" also increases. However, when you remove items, the number stays the same. That's where the second part comes in. We'll now address the DOM elements that don't have data attached anymore. Again, only two lines are needed here:

```
tableRows.exit()
.remove();
```

The `exit()` method selects each DOM element that has no equivalent data item. On this collection, you can perform actions. Note that this action doesn't have to be a removal; it can be anything you want.

Last on our list is the collection that has both a DOM element and a data item. Because you already did the `enter()` and `exit()` methods, the entire dataset and each data item has its own DOM element. What we want to do is replace "Hello World" with the text that has been set into the elements. For this, you use *anonymous functions* that refer back to the data. An anonymous function doesn't have a name defined as you can see in the example in Listing 14.42.

```
tableRows.select("TD")
    .text(function (d) {return d;})
    .attr("class", "tableformat")
    .style("background-color", function(d, i) { return i % 2 ? "#fff": "#eee";});
```

Listing 14.42 Anonymous Function

This code example used two functions to make the properties dynamic. The first function for the text simply returned the current data item with return D. You can do this within a `D3.select` object and thus are always able to refer to the data that has been attached to the selection.

The second function is a bit more complicated. The `i` parameter stands for index. It passes the row number of the data, starting with 0. In the function, a modulus (a division remainder) is used to alternate the background colors. If the remainder is 0, then you get a white background; if not, then you get a light gray background. You'll notice that a function was used to fill the text. Style, attributes, and texts can be applied as data functions in D3 instead of simple fixed values.

The most common way to store information with D3 is a JSON array. We discussed this type of variable in Section 14.2.1. In Section 14.5.3, we discussed data binding in greater depth and also looked at how you can translate the data you receive from the data source into something useful to work with in D3. For example, the following is an array of JSON elements:

```
var myJSON = [{ "key": "NLD", "Descr": "Netherlands",
  "AmountSales": 104003},{ "key": "USA", "Descr": "United States",
  "AmountSales": 1804483}, "key": "DEU", "Descr": "Germany",
  "AmountSales": 9847220}];
```

565

If you used this dataset in the D3 selection, you could refer to these data elements respectively with `d.key, d.descr,` or `d.AmountSales`.

> **Data Binding with D3**
>
> If you want to walk through a good tutorial on data binding with D3, have a look at the Three Little Circles tutorial at *http://bost.ocks.org/mike/circles/*.

Transitions

Creating an animation or transition is easier than you might think. You specify a transformation by using the `.transition()` method within `D3.select` and then chain the properties that describe the end result. This can apply to position, height, width, color, or other properties of the DOM element.

Table 14.13 shows the basic layout of a transition method.

Method	Description
`.transition()`	Indicates that you want a transition between the old property values and the new property values.
`delay()`	How long before you start.
`.duration`	How long the transition should take.
`.ease()`	The way the tempo changes in the transition.
`.properties`	The end result.

Table 14.13 Methods Used for Transitions

If you want an element to be red, you use this statement:

`d3.select("body").style("color", "red");`

However, if you want a transition over time instead, you use a transition for the same style:

`d3.select("body").transition().style("color", "red");`

If you want to combine transitions with `enter()`, `exit()`, and `update()` patterns, you have to realize that a DOM element must exist before you can do a transition. Additionally, you can't make a transition of the creation or deletion of an element. Transitions are per element and exclusive, which means that when you create a transition, you create a set of transitions for each element. Different elements can have different delays and durations.

If you want to show transitions sequentially, you can chain transitions methods to do this:

```
.transition().attr("color","red").transition().attr("color", "blue")
```

In the code example, D3 will first transition the color to red and then from red to blue. A typical example of chaining in a chart is that you want to do some kind of transition when an object is removed from the DOM. Then you first want to do the transition and remove the element after the transition is ready (Listing 14.43).

```
Exit()
 .transition()
 .attr('opacity', 0);
 .each("end",function() {
 d3.select(this).
  remove();
 });
```
Listing 14.43 Chaining Exit Function

In this `exit` method, first the opacity is set to `0`, and then the element is removed. By changing the transition with `.delay`, `.duration`, and `.ease`, you can customize the transition.

Drawing Graphs with SVG

When you want to draw something, you use SVG elements. Graphics are rendered by an SVG viewer based on the specifications in XML. Because this is vector-based, the drawing is stored as numbers and not as pixels, which means that the element is scalable, without a loss in quality.

Creating an SVG Element

Creating an SVG element in your SDK is typically done in the `init()` stage. The only dependent properties are `width` and `height`, and a component is reinitialized when you resize it (Listing 14.44).

```
chart = d3.select(container).append("svg:svg")
.attr("width", "100%")
.attr("height", "100%")
.attr("viewbox", "0 0 100 100")
```

```
.append("g")
.attr("transform", "translate(" + margin.left + "," +
   margin.top + ")");
```
Listing 14.44 Creating an SVG Element

Within the SVG element, you typically create *groups*. These groups allow you to keep elements together and work with them as a whole instead of each single item. Notice that in the example in Listing 14.44, a variable is used instead of numbers to define the top margin and left margin. As a constant, use this JSON variable that holds the standard margins:

```
var margin = {top: 30, right: 30, bottom: 30, left: 40};
```

This central group is only used to set up the margins. Within the graph, you can use more groups for the different parts in the graph:

```
xAxisGroup = chart.append("g").attr("class", "x axis");
yAxisGroup = chart.append("g").attr("class", "y axis");
barsContainer = chart.append('g').attr("class", "barscontainer");
```

Because you assigned the first D3.select to a variable, you can now just go on from there using the chart variable. Then, you use the selectAll statement:

```
var bars = barsContainer.selectAll("rect") .data(dataset);
```

Next, go to the enter(), update(), exit() part. For purposes of demonstration, we'll show the update() part. The point is to show how almost every property is made dynamic using the data that was attached (Listing 14.45).

```
bars
.attr("x", function(d, i){return i * (width/dataset.length);})
        .attr("y", function(d) { return y(d.value); })
          .attr("height", function(d)
{ return height - y(d.value); })
        .attr("width", width / dataset.length - barPadding)
        .style("opacity", 0)
        .transition()
            .delay(function (d,i){ return i * 50;})
            .duration(750)
            .ease("elastic")
            .style("opacity", 1);
```
Listing 14.45 Dynamic Properties

Note that dataset.length is used to determine the number of bars, and that function y is used to determine the attribute height and y.

Scales

When you build a graph, you have to translate your numbers into pixels at some point. That is the only way to get the graph on the screen. Without this, you don't have a visualization, which is the most important part of all your work! Luckily, D3 provides *scales* to help you to do the calculations needed to map the data.

> **Scales in D3**
>
> To learn more about scales in D3, visit *https://github.com/mbostock/d3/wiki/Scales*.

In this section, we'll show two common scales so that you'll get the idea of how they work. With the principles given here, you'll be able to build any scale you want.

Linear scales are the most common type of scales and probably the ones you'll be using the most. Setting up this scale is a two-step process: First, you define the minimum and maximum value you want to map in the domain. Then, you give the maximum and minimum of the output in pixels (or coordinates) in the range.

The code for setting up a linear scale looks like this:

```
var y = d3.scale.linear()
.domain([0, d3.max(dataset, function(d)
{ return d.value * 1.2; })])
        .range([200, 0]);
```

The data range is set up from 0 to 120% of the maximum value in the dataset. The range is set from 200 to 0. Actually, this setup will return a function with a lower mapping result for higher numbers. The reason is specific for drawing bar charts.

If you look at the place where the rectangles are defined, you come across two lines of code that define the `height` and x value of the rectangle:

```
.attr("y", function(d) { return y(d.value); })
.attr("height", function(d) { return height - y(d.value); })
```

The reason we use an inverse scale is that when you draw a bar chart, the highest values should have the highest bars. In other words, when drawing them, your x value must be low because the starting point of your bar is higher than the other bars. In Figure 14.15, the attribute values translate to a graph. Additionally, the height of all the bars should be set up so that they all align vertically on the bottom.

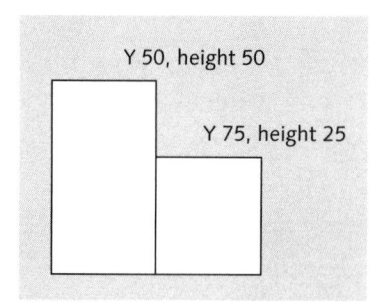

Figure 14.15 Template Bar Chart with Properties Visible

In the template bar chart in Figure 14.15, the y attribute of the higher bar is lower than the lower bar. The height of the bars must be adjusted so that they align at the bottom.

In the first attribute function, you see that the number is passed to the y function defined earlier as a scale function with the range and domain. Subsequently, the `height` attribute is defined as the height of the graph minus the same function as before.

The second type of scale you need in a bar chart is an *ordinal scale*. Ordinal scales have a discrete domain, such as a set of names or categories. From the D3 reference, here is an example of an ordinal scale (Listing 14.46).

```
var o = d3.scale.ordinal().domain([1, 2, 3, 4])
.rangeBands([0, 100]);
o.rangeBand(); // returns 25
o.range(); // returns [0, 25, 50, 75]
o.rangeExtent(); // returns [0, 100]
```
Listing 14.46 Example of an Ordinal Scale

In Figure 14.16, you see all the options you can set up for an ordinal scale.

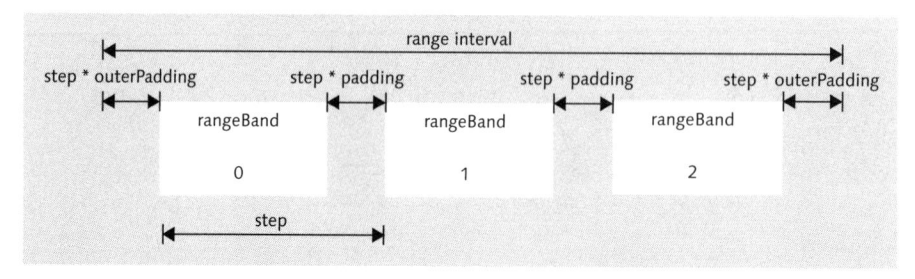

Figure 14.16 Range Interval

14.7.3 SAPUI5

SAPUI5 is a JavaScript library created by SAP. In Design Studio, you can select components that are available in that library and configure them. The library will take care of building and interaction. In the configuration, you can determine how the component looks and interacts. An SDK component will inherit all the properties of the SAPUI5 component.

> **SAPUI5 Components**
>
> You can go to *https://sapui5.hana.ondemand.com/* to see all the available components. In the API tab, you'll also find all the properties and methods available to each component.

To use an SAPUI5 component, you first have to set the `handlerType` property of the component to SAPUI5 (Listing 14.47).

```
<?xml version="1.0"encoding="UTF-8"?>
<sdkExtension ...
  id="com.example.extension">
<component ...
  id="myButton"
  handlerType="sapui5">
```

Listing 14.47 Contribution.xml SAPUI5 Setup

In the Component JavaScript, the syntax is different. Instead of creating a class, you extend the SAPUI5 component to include SDK functions. The code in Listing 14.48 first calls the SAPUI5 component `sap.ui.commons.ColorPicker` and extends it to include functions for the SDK extensions. The SDK extension inherits everything from the SAPUI5 component and adds additional functions.

```
sap.ui.commons.ColorPicker.extend("com.example.extension", {
    initDesignStudio: function() {
        this.attachChange(function() {
            this.fireDesignStudioPropertiesChanged(["colorString"]);
            this.fireDesignStudioEvent("onColorChange");
        });
    },
    renderer: {}
});
```

Listing 14.48 Using the SAPUI5 Component in the Component JavaScript

In Listing 14.48, you can see the `attachChange` property that included a function to inform Design Studio when something changed and to start an `onChange` script.

SAPUI5 components have a lifecycle with functions where you can add functionality:

- **initDesignStudio()**

  This function is triggered when the SAPUI5 component is rendered for the first time. You can compare it to the `init()` function. In this example, the function is used to create an event listener to inform Design Studio when the properties have changed.

- **beforeDesignStudioUpdate()**

  Insert this function when you need to execute JavaScript code before the properties are updated.

- **afterDesignStudioUpdate()**

  Use this function to insert JavaScript code that is executed after the properties have been updated. This is much like the `afterUpdate()` function.

- **renderer()**

  Usually, you leave this function empty. This will leave the rendering of the component to SAPUI5. (If you really need to change the rendering, you can read more on this at *https://sapui5.hana.ondemand.com/sdk/#docs/guide/OnTheFlyControlDefinition.html*.)

- **getter/setter**

  All the properties that are in the SAPUI5 component have their own `getter/setter` function that you don't need to add. If you add a new property, you still need to create a `getter/setter` function. The `getter/setter` function is still the same principle as earlier but with a slightly different syntax (Listing 14.49). You'll find that the SAPUI5 component has many properties, so you often don't need to add your own.

```
getMyProperty: function() {
 return this. MyProperty;
},
setCopyrightText: function(newPropertyValue) {
 this. MyProperty= newPropertyValue;}
```

Listing 14.49 Getter/Setter Function with SAPUI5

14.8   Example: Building a Bullet Graph SDK Extension

In this section, you'll build a BULLET GRAPH component using everything you've learned so far. We'll address all the parts mentioned in the previous sections and go through the building process step-by-step.

14.8.1   Overview

Before we go through the steps to build an example SDK extension, we want you to see the end result first. As shown in Figure 14.17, in this example, you'll build a BULLET GRAPH component with a trellis option. This component allows you to show multiple BULLET GRAPHS in a single component and divide them into rows and columns. There are also options to set the width and height of the BULLET GRAPH by setting a minimum and maximum height. Within that bandwidth, the graph can grow and shrink depending on the size of the component and the number of bullet graphs that it has to show.

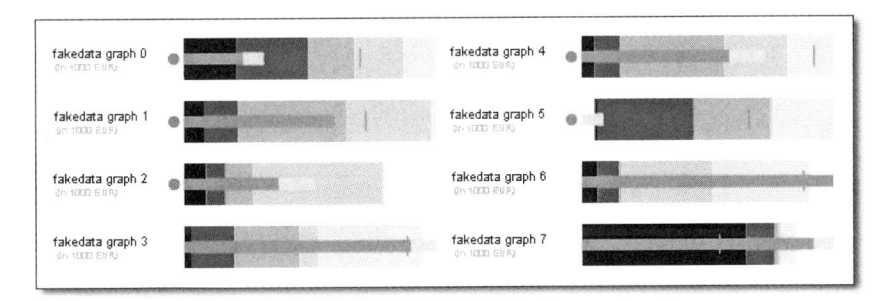

Figure 14.17 Example Bullet Graph

In the example component, we've rendered fake data. The graph falls back to this fake data if no data source is available. This will help you see how the graph looks in an application before any data is available. Each graph shows the performance of a single key performance indicator (KPI). The bars changing from black to light gray are performance areas depicting the performance level. The vertical line is a comparison value. On the left side, you see a red circle that is shown when the performance is worse than a chosen threshold. In some cases, the blue bar is lighter at the end. This is the extrapolation bar. The extrapolate option adds a number that shows the expected end-of-month result. Although this isn't calculated in the component, the component can visualize the result.

14 | Building Components Using the SDK

Now that you have an idea of what the goal is, the following subsections walk through the necessary steps to build the component.

14.8.2 Setting Up the Project and Structure

To begin, you need to access the sample project from SAP. In Chapter 13, you already imported these projects when installing the SDK development environment. You can create a copy by right-clicking on COM.SAP.SAMPLE.COLOREDBOX and pasting it in the PROJECT EXPLORER panel. After that, rename the project folder to "com.rheinwerk.example."

You now need to set up all the files for the project. You got most of them from the sample project, but some still need to be added. Follow these steps to create the structure (Figure 14.18):

1. You can create a copy by right-clicking on com.sap.sample.coloredbox and pasting it in the PROJECT EXPLORER panel. After that, rename the project folder to "com.rheinwerk.example."

2. Open the new folder in the PROJECT EXPLORER.

3. Open the RES folder inside the new folder. Inside the RES folder, you'll find a couple of folders.

4. Rename the ADDITIONAL_PROPERTIES_SHEET folder to "ap_sheets." Start the rename by selecting the folder and pressing [F2].

5. Go into the AP_SHEETS folder.

6. Rename ADDITIONAL_PROPERTIES_SHEET.HTML to "ap_bulletgraph.html."

7. Rename ADDITIONAL_PROPERTIES_SHEET.JS to "ap_bulletgraph.js."

8. Add a new CSS file with the name "ap_bulletgraph.css." Select the APP_SHEETS folder.

9. Right-click the AP_SHEETS folder, and select NEW • OTHER.

10. A popup screen opens. In the popup screen at for the ITEM TYPE, FILTER TEXT, type CSS. The number of options decreases, and you see the option CSS FILE.

11. Select CSS FILE, and click NEXT. Set the file name to "ap_bulletgraph.css," and click FINISH.

12. Rename the CSS file in the CSS folder to "bulletgraph.css."

13. Rename the JS file in the JS folder to "bulletgraph.js."

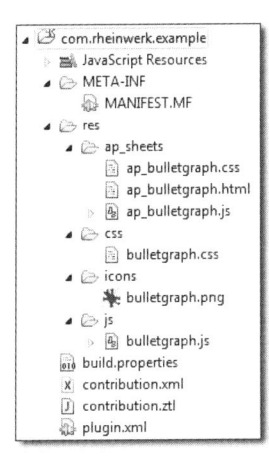

Figure 14.18 Structure of the Project

If you need to create an extra file, you can right-click the folder where you want to add the file, and choose NEW • FILE. With the same context menu, you can also add folders if necessary. Give the file the appropriate name, including the extension. Later, we'll look at the contents.

14.8.3 Setting Up the Base Folder Structure

As previously discussed in Section 14.3, SDK extensions have a basic structure. In this section, we'll again look at the different building blocks within our project and structure them to get the desired results.

Contribution.xml

Open *contribution.xml,* and insert the following code (Listing 14.50).

```
<?xml version="1.0" encoding="UTF-8"?>
<sdkExtension xmlns="http://www.sap.com/bi/zen/sdk"
    title="SDK Bulletgraph"
    version="1.0"
    vendor="example"
    id="com.rheinwerk.example">
    <component id="BulletGraph"
        title="Bullet Graph"
        propertySheetPath="res/ap_sheets/ap_linetrend.html"
        icon="res/icons/bulletgraph.png">
        <jsInclude>res/js/bulletgraph.js</jsInclude>
        <CSSInclude>res/CSS/bulletgraph.CSS</CSSInclude>
```

```
        </component>
</sdkExtension>
```
Listing 14.50 Contribution.xml

The highlighted parts in the code are the ones where you need to fill in the appropriate values. If you want to use a different project name, change it to the values that you chose yourself. Be aware that you need to use those values everywhere else as well.

MANIFEST.MF

You need to fill in a few values in the *MANIFEST.MF* file as well. Go to the META_INF folder in the project directory, and then follow these steps:

1. Double-click the *MANIFEST.MF* file.
2. Go to the BUILD tab. You'll see the screen shown in Figure 14.19.
3. Check all the folders within the RES folder by clicking on the checkbox to the left of the file name.

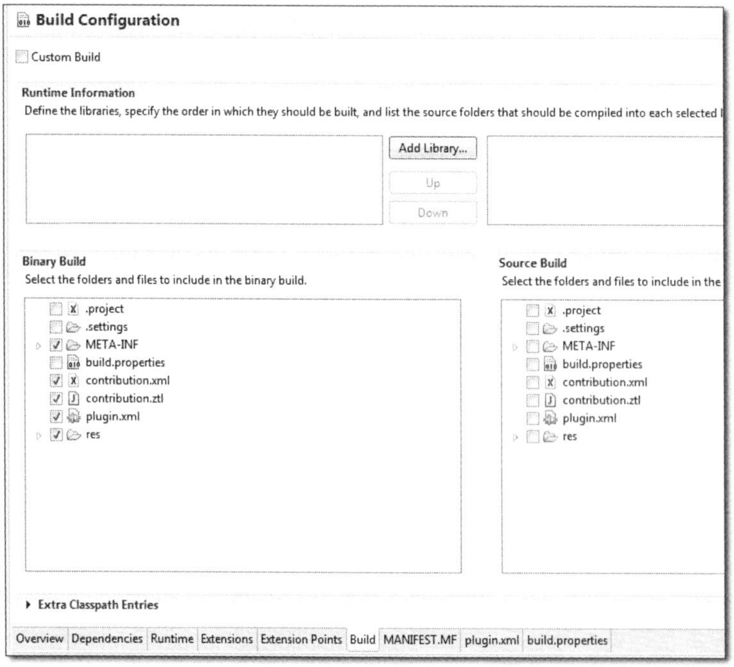

Figure 14.19 MANIFEST.MF Build Tab

4. Go to the MANIFEST.MF tab. You'll find the following lines with values of the project you copied from. Change the values so they are equal to the values in Listing 14.51.

```
Manifest-Version: 1.0
Bundle-ManifestVersion: 2
Bundle-Name: SDK Bulletchart
Bundle-SymbolicName: com.rheinwerk.example;singleton:=true
Bundle-Version: 1.0
Require-Bundle: com.sap.ip.bi.zen.rt.components.sdk.eclipse
Bundle-Vendor: example
```

Listing 14.51 MANIFEST.MF Lines

The highlighted values must be identical to values in the *contribution.xml* file. If you forgot one, then you won't find the extension when you start up Design Studio from Eclipse. You can retrace what went wrong in the console, if necessary. For example, here you see an error message when you raise the version in *MANIFEST.MF* to 1.1 and maintain it in the *contribution.xml* at version 1.0 (Figure 14.20).

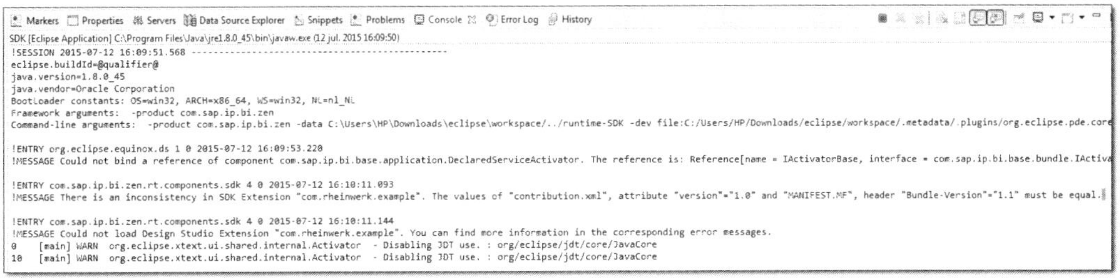

Figure 14.20 Error Message Due to Mismatching Version Numbers

Component JavaScript

In the Component JavaScript, we initially will set up a skeleton function that contains the definition of the function and the basic methods such as init(), beforeUpdate(), afterUpdate(), and a getter/setter function as we discussed in Section 14.3. In Section 14.8.5, we'll expand this skeleton with the actual functionality (Listing 14.52).

Before you can insert the JavaScript code, you need a new file to insert it. The next step is to create the file and then insert the JavaScript code. The *contribution.xml* file refers to this file and will run the function in the JavaScript class com.rheinwerk.example.BulletGraph.

14 Building Components Using the SDK

Follow these steps:

1. Go to the JS folder, and open BULLETGRAPH.JS.
2. Remove all the current code.
3. Add the code shown in Listing 14.52 to the file.
4. Save and close the file.

```
sap.designstudio.sdk.Component.subclass
("com.rheinwerk.example.BulletGraph", function() {
  "use strict";
  var that = this;
  var chartComponents = {};
  var chartProperties = {};
  this.init = function(){ };
  this.beforeUpdate = function() {};
  this.firstgettersetter = function(e) { if (e ===
  undefined) {return chartProperties.columnmargin;}else{chartProperti
es.columnmargin = e;return this;}};
  this.afterUpdate = function() { };
});
```

Listing 14.52 Component JavaScript

If you look at the highlighted parts of the code, the first part you see is the name of the class. This name is a combination of the extension name and the component name. Design Studio will find this class using that name. The second highlighted part is the "use strict" directive. The purpose of this directive is to force you to declare all variables that you use inside the function. Normally, JavaScript accepts undeclared variables and turns them into global variables. An unwanted side effect is that when you use multiple instances of the same component, these global variables will influence each other because they share the same variable names.

You also see the var that = this; line. As discussed in Section 14.2.1, this is a keyword in JavaScript that refers to the context of the function that you're executing, or rather, to the object the function is a method of. At this point, this refers to the main function. When you're inside a function, this refers to the caller of that function. If you still want to perform a change on the main level of the code, you must use the that keyword instead of this because that still refers to the main function.

You can find more in-depth JavaScript explanations in Section 14.2.1.

14.8 Example: Building a Bullet Graph SDK Extension

Additional Properties

For the ADDITIONAL PROPERTIES panel of the BULLET GRAPH component, you'll set up a basic HTML structure and the base function to communicate with the server. You'll begin with the initial setup. The end result should look like Figure 14.21.

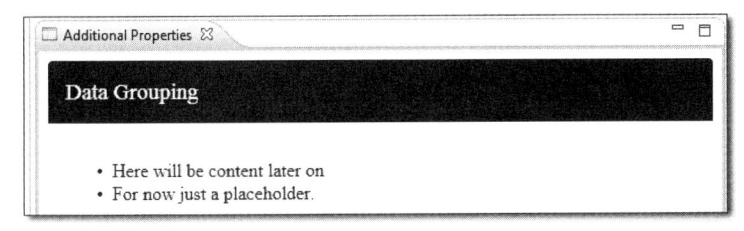

Figure 14.21 Additional Properties View Initial Setup

The HTML code of the ADDITIONAL PROPERTIES panel is the largest initial code as you can see in Listing 14.53. The HTML code provides the structure and layout of the ADDITIONAL PROPERTIES panel in the Design Studio tool. Additionally, the HTML file calls the JavaScript for the functionality to change property values.

Follow these steps to set up the ADDITIONAL PROPERTIES panel:

1. Go to the AP_SHEETS folder.
2. Open AP_BULLETGRAPH.HTML.
3. Remove all the current HTML code. Add the code in Listing 14.53 to the file.
4. Save and close the file.

```
<!DOCTYPE html>
<html>
<head>
 <title>BulletGraph Properties</title>
 <meta content="text/html; charset=utf-8" http-equiv="Content-Type">
 <script src="/aad/zen.rt.components.sdk/resources/js/sdk_property-sheets_handler.js"></script>
 <script src="ap_bulletgraph.js"></script>
 <link href="ap_bulletgraph.css" rel="stylesheet" type="text/css">
 <script>
        new com.rheinwerk.example.BulletGraphPropertyPage();
 </script>
</head>
<body>
 <div class="accordion">
   <div class="accordion-section">
    <a class="accordion-section-title" href="#accordion-
```

14 | Building Components Using the SDK

```
1">Data Grouping</a>
   <div class="accordion-section-content" id="accordion-1">
   <ul><li>here will be content later on</li>
          <li>for now just a place holder </li>
     </ul>
   </div><!--end .accordion-section-content-->
  </div><!--end .accordion-section-->
 </div><!--end .accordion-->
</body>
</html>
```

Listing 14.53 Base Setup for Additional Properties HTML

In this HTML file, you find links to the *ap_bulletgraph.css* file and the JavaScript file. You also see a link to the JavaScript class that will do the functionality part of the panel. In Design Studio, when you select the component, this HTML will be rendered in the ADDITIONAL PROPERTIES panel. The CSS will provide an additional layout. The JavaScript file will take care of all the selected values and collect possible values. When values are selected, the functions in the JavaScript file will update the central properties.

In the HTML file itself, you create a structure for an accordion menu. In the first version of the *ap_bulletgraph.js* file, you use the class name and set up functionality to enable the accordion menu to open and close (Listing 14.54). Later, you'll revisit this JavaScript to add code for each property that you want to maintain in the ADDITIONAL PROPERTIES panel.

First, you must set up a base by following these steps:

1. Go to the AP_SHEETS folder.
2. Open AP_BULLETGRAPH.JS.
3. Remove all the current JavaScript code.
4. Add the code in Listing 14.54 to the file.
5. Save and close the file.

```
sap.designstudio.sdk.PropertyPage.subclass("com.rheinwerk.example.Bu
lletGraphPropertyPage", function() {
    var that = this;
    this.init = function() {
        fillDropDown("#mainlabeldimension");fillDropDown("#subla-
beldimension");fillDropDown("#keydimension")

   $('.accordion .accordion-section-title').removeClass('active');
   $('.accordion .accordion-section-content').slideUp(300).remove-
```

```
  Class('open');

    $('.accordion-section-title').click(function(e) {
    // Grab current anchor value
    var currentAttrValue = $(this).attr('href');

    if($(e.target).is('.active')) {
    close_accordion_section();
    }else {
    close_accordion_section();

    // Add active class to section title
    $(this).addClass('active');
    // Open up the hidden content panel
      $('.accordion ' + currentAttrValue).slideDown(300).addClass('open
');
    }

    e.preventDefault();
   });
     function close_accordion_section() {
    $('.accordion .accordion-section-title').removeClass('active');
    $('.accordion .accordion-section-content').slideUp(300).remove-
  Class('open');
   }
  });
```

Listing 14.54 JavaScript Setup of Additional Properties

Finally, you'll update the *ap_bulletgraph.css* file. For this file, you immediately implement the final version of the file so that it doesn't have as much coding as the other two files. In the CSS file, you'll use class names and the :hover selector for when the cursor is moved over an element. In the following steps, you'll create a CSS file that contains the layout instructions for the additional properties HTML file. The HTML files already refer to this file. Using this CSS file, you can change colors, fonts, and many other layout features:

1. Open the *ap_bulletgraph.css* file.
2. Remove all the current CSS content, if there is any.
3. Add the CSS code in Listing 14.55 to the file.
4. Save and close the file.

```
  /*----- Accordion -----*/
  .accordion, .accordion * {
   -webkit-box-sizing:border-box;
   -moz-box-sizing:border-box;
```

14 | Building Components Using the SDK

```css
box-sizing:border-box;
}

.accordion {
 overflow:hidden;
 box-shadow:0px 1px 3px rgba(0,0,0,0.25);
 border-radius:3px;
 background:#f7f7f7;
}

/*----- Section Titles -----*/
.accordion-section-title {
 width:100%;
 padding:15px;
 display:inline-block;
 border-bottom:1px solid #1a1a1a;
 background:#333;
 transition:all linear 0.15s;
 /* Type */
 font-size:1.200em;
 text-shadow:0px 1px 0px #1a1a1a;
 color:#fff;
}

.accordion-section-title.active, .accordion-section-title:hover {
 background:#4c4c4c;
 /* Type */
 text-decoration:none;
}

.accordion-section:last-child .accordion-section-title {
 border-bottom:none;
}

/*----- Section Content -----*/
.accordion-section-content {
 padding:15px;
 display:none;
}

.myButton {
    -moz-box-shadow:inset 0px 1px 0px 0px #ffffff;
    -webkit-box-shadow:inset 0px 1px 0px 0px #ffffff;
    box-shadow:inset 0px 1px 0px 0px #ffffff;
    background:-webkit-gradient(linear, left top, left bottom, color-stop(0.05, #ededed), color-stop(1, #dfdfdf));
    background:-moz-linear-gradient(top, #ededed 5%, #dfdfdf 100%);
    background:-webkit-linear-gradient(top, #ededed 5%, #dfdfdf 100%);
```

```
        background:-o-linear-gradient(top, #ededed 5%, #dfdfdf 100%);
        background:-ms-linear-gradient(top, #ededed 5%, #dfdfdf 100%);
        background:linear-gradient(to bottom, #ededed 5%, #dfdfdf 100%);
        filter:progid:DXImageTransform.Microsoft.gradient(startColorstr=
'#ededed', endColorstr='#dfdfdf',GradientType=0);
        background-color:#ededed;
        -moz-border-radius:6px;
        -webkit-border-radius:6px;
        border-radius:6px;
        border:1px solid #dcdcdc;
        display:inline-block;
        cursor:pointer;
        color:#777777;
        font-family:Arial;
        font-size:15px;
        font-weight:bold;
        padding:8px 49px;
        text-decoration:none;
        text-shadow:0px 1px 0px #ffffff;
}
.myButton:hover {
        background:-webkit-
gradient(linear, left top, left bottom, color-stop(0.05, #
dfdfdf), color-stop(1, #ededed));
        background:-moz-linear-gradient(top, #dfdfdf 5%, #ededed 100%);
        background:-webkit-linear-gradient(top, #dfdfdf 5%, #
ededed 100%);
        background:-o-linear-gradient(top, #dfdfdf 5%, #ededed 100%);
        background:-ms-linear-gradient(top, #dfdfdf 5%, #ededed 100%);
        background:linear-gradient(to bottom, #dfdfdf 5%, #ededed 100%);
        filter:progid:DXImageTransform.Microsoft.gradient(startColorstr=
'#dfdfdf', endColorstr='#ededed',GradientType=0);
        background-color:#dfdfdf;
}
.myButton:active {
        position:relative;
        top:1px;
}
```

Listing 14.55 CSS Code for Additional Properties

As a result of these steps, when you add the component to Design Studio, you'll see a menu in the ADDITIONAL PROPERTIES panel that you can open and close. In Section 14.8.6, we'll expand the code to enable designers to set up the properties using the ADDITIONAL PROPERTIES panel.

14 | Building Components Using the SDK

Script Contributions

In the script contributions (*contribution.ztl* file), you start out by putting a placeholder line to define the method class (you don't add methods yet):

```
class com.rheinwerk.example.BulletGraph extends Component {}
```

Adding only this line is enough to enable some standard methods such as `getWidth`, `getHeight`, `setHeight`, and so on.

Component CSS

Now you can set up the CSS file that is used for rendering the component itself. The other CSS file was for the layout of the ADDITIONAL PROPERTIES panel and the icon that will show in the COMPONENTS panel next to the name of the component.

In the BULLET GRAPH CSS file, you'll set up a couple of classes to get started:

1. Open the *bulletchart.css* file in the CSS folder.
2. Remove any CSS code present in the file.
3. Add the code in Listing 14.56 to the file.
4. Save and close the file.

```
.bulletgraph { font: 9px sans-serif; }
.headerlabel { font-size: 12px; font-weight: bold; }
.subheaderlabel { fill: #999; }

.axis path,
.axis line {
 fill: none;
 stroke: black;
 shape-rendering: crispEdges;
}
.axis text {
 font-family: sans-serif;
 font-size: 9px;
}
.axis line.tick {
 stroke: #ccc;
 stroke-dasharray: 6 2;
}

.trendlinegraphdiv {
 position: absolute;
```

```
  background-color: #FFFFFF;
}

.thresh5 {fill: #e6e6e6; }
.thresh4 {fill: #cccccc; }
.thresh3 {fill: #b3b3b3; }
.thresh2 {fill: #999999; }
.thresh1 {fill: #666666; }
.real {fill: #4682b4; }
.compare {fill: #4682b4; }
.extrapol{fill: #a2c0d9;}

.alertgood {
 fill: #AACB4F;
 stroke: none;
}
.alertbad {
 fill: #D96663;
 stroke: none;
}
.alertnone {
 fill: #fff;
 stroke: none;
 fill-opacity:0 ;
 stroke-opacity:0;
}
.bulletgraphdiv {
 position: absolute;
 background-color: #FFFFFF;
}
```

Listing 14.56 First CSS Classes

Icon

For the icon, you already defined the location in the *contribution.xml* earlier this section with the line:

```
icon="res/icons/bulletgraph.png"
```

To download the icon for this example, go to this book's product page at *https://www.sap-press.com/3951*, and scroll down to the PRODUCT SUPPLEMENTS section. Alternatively, you can use an icon of your own, as long as it's 16 × 16 pixels.

14.8.4 Expanding the Bullet Graph Component

After the basic setup, where you created the bare minimum for a *contribution.xml* file, it's now time to create the full list. In this section, you'll add all the properties for the component and describe what they are supposed to do.

First, you need to add properties to the component that you'll use for the full graph. Follow these steps:

1. Open the *contribution.xml* file.
2. Remove any XML present.
3. Add the code from Listing 14.57 to the file.
4. Save and close the file.

```xml
<?xml version="1.0" encoding="UTF-8"?>
<sdkExtension xmlns="http://www.sap.com/bi/zen/sdk"
    title="SDK Bulletchart"
    version="1.1"
    vendor="example"
    id="com.rheinwerk.example">
    <group id="analytics" title="Analytic Charts"/><component id=
"BulletGraph"
        title="Bullet Graph"
        icon="res/icons/bulletgraph.png"
        propertySheetPath="res/ap_sheets/ap_bulletgraph.html"
        newInstancePrefix="BulletChartComponent"
        handlerType="div"
        databound="true"
        group="analytics">
</component>
</sdkExtension>
```

Listing 14.57 Component XML

Make sure you have the files that are referenced in *contribution.xml* in place on the locations that you stated in *contribution.xml*. You start with a separate element on the extension level to assign the component to the group `analytics`. This will make the component appear on a separate group in the COMPONENTS panel.

As you can see in the component attributes, the component is data bound. We discussed this in depth in Section 14.4.3.

In the second part, we look at the `includes` (Listing 14.58).

```xml
<jsInclude>res/js/common_basics.js</jsInclude>
<jsInclude>res/js/common_databound.js</jsInclude>
```

```
<jsInclude>res/js/BulletChart.js</jsInclude>
<CSSInclude>res/BulletChart/BulletChart.CSS</CSSInclude>
```
Listing 14.58 Includes in Contribution

You'll be using the D3 JavaScript library, which is already included in the SAP Design Studio framework.

Follow these steps to make sure that the SDK extension knows which files to include:

1. Open the *contribution.xml* file.
2. Insert the lines of Listing 14.58 in the XML code within the COMPONENT node.
3. Save and close the file.

The CSS file and three JavaScript files should point to the files you created earlier. The two common JavaScript files are functions from the SCN Design Studio SDK community. These reusable functions are included in the download.

The first property is used to create the option to add a script for when a user clicks on one of the BULLET GRAPHS:

```
<property id="onclick" type="ScriptText" title="On Click" group=
"Events" /><property id="clickedgraphkey" title="clickedgraphkey" type=
"String" visible="false"/>group="Events" />
```

In the On Click property, a dialog box will open, and the designer can add code to allow the application to respond to the click.

The second property will hold the unique key of the clicked dimension. Later, you'll create a method that allows the designer to work with that property. The designer can use this property to know on which BULLET GRAPH the user clicked. The unique ID provided will enable the designer to perform actions in other parts of the application.

Next, we will look at the data bound properties of our components. First let's revisit the component being created in this example one more time. A more detailed view of the design is shown in Figure 14.22. As you can see, several numbers are being visualized in a single chart. For each number that is visualized in each graph, you define a property in *contribution.xml*.

14 | Building Components Using the SDK

Each property will hold values that are visualized in the graph. You'll have one property for the actual value, one for the previous period value, and properties for each threshold.

You need to assign parts of the data source to a property to visualize the graph. Using the `getter/setter` functions in the Component JavaScript, this data will be used in the functions to build the graph. If you omit parts (e.g., some of the thresholds), those parts will be excluded from the graph.

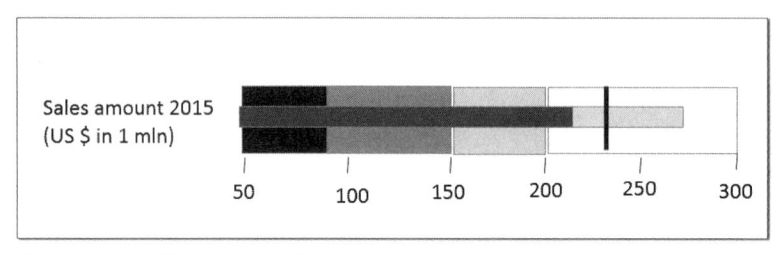

Figure 14.22 Bullet Graph Design

In the design on your screen, you should see a horizontal blue bar that depicts the current `realization` value. A lighter blue extension of the bar includes the estimated value until the end of the period. These values can be compared to a previous period. This previous period is visualized using a vertical black line, which is between the 200 and 250 mark. In the graph, you also see a black, dark gray, medium gray and light area. These areas depict poor performance, average, or good. Our performance indicator is in the light gray area, therefore, it states that this `realization` value is good. You can also add a red circle to the left-hand side of the graph when an alert is needed.

> **Bullet Graph Detailed Design**
>
> You can get more information on the detailed design of the BULLET GRAPH component at *www.perceptualedge.com/articles/misc/Bullet_Graph_Design_Spec.pdf*.

For all the numbers you need to visualize, you'll create six properties. In the following steps, you'll define these properties in *contribution.xml* so that you can see them in Design Studio and work with them in the Component JavaScript. Follow these steps:

1. Open the *contribution.xml* file.

2. Insert the lines of Listing 14.59 in the XML code within the COMPONENT node.

3. Save and close the file.

```xml
<property id="data" title="Dataset"
    type="ResultSet" group="DataBinding" visible="false"/>
<property id="realization" title="realization column"
    type="String"/>
<property id="extrapolation" title="expected realization outcome
    end of period column" type="String"/>
<property id="threshold1" title="first threshold column"
    type="String"/>
<property id="threshold2" title="second threshold column"
    type="String"/>
<property id="threshold3" title="third threshold column"
    type="String"/>
<property id="threshold4" title="fourth threshold column"
    type="String"/>
<property id="threshold5" title="fifth threshold column"
    type="String"/>
```

Listing 14.59 Properties for a Bullet Graph

The extrapolation is in an extra column so that you can compare the expected end of a period number to the goal and not the realization. The realization can be compared on a full period only as the target is also for a full period.

Now you can create some properties that should inform you on how to fill in the labels on the left-hand side of the bullet graph, and what to return when a user clicks on a part of the graph (Listing 14.60).

```xml
        <property id="labeldimension" title=
"Row Dimension holding main label" type="String"/>
        <property id="sublabeldimension" title=
"Row Dimension holding sub label" type="String"/>
        <property id="keydimension" title=
"Row Dimension holding unique key for clicking through" type="String"/>
```

Listing 14.60 Properties for Labels and Returned Values

You enter the dimension names in these properties. In JavaScript, you'll collect the information from the data source to populate the label, sublabel, and the key. For the rest, you have many properties that allow you to turn parts of the BULLET GRAPH component on or off (Listing 14.61).

```xml
        <property id="comparison" title="Comparison column" type=
"String"/>
        <property id="showaxis" title="Show X axis numbers" type=
"boolean"/>
```

```xml
        <property id="tooltip" title="Show tooltip" type="boolean"/>
        <property id="showalert" title= "show alert" type="String">
        <possibleValue>never</possibleValue>
        <possibleValue>worse than comparison</possibleValue>
        <possibleValue>worse than threshold 5</possibleValue>
        <possibleValue>worse than threshold 4</possibleValue>
        <possibleValue>worse than threshold 3</possibleValue>
        <possibleValue>worse than threshold 2</possibleValue>
        <possibleValue>worse than threshold 1</possibleValue>
        </property>
        <property id="showrealization" title=
 "show realization value" type="boolean"/>
        <property id="maxgraphheight" title=
 "maximum height of single graph" type="int"/>
        <property id="mingraphheight" title=
 "minimum height of single graph" type="int"/>
        <property id="numberofticks" title=
 "number of ticks in the graph" type="int"/>
        <property id="columnmargin" title=
 "horizontal margin between graphs" type="int"/>
        <property id="numberofcolumns" title="number of columns" type=
 "int"/>
        <property id="rowmargin" title=
 "vertical margin between graphs" type="int"/>
        <property id="charttopmargin" title="Bullet Top Margin" type=
 "int"/>
        <property id="chartbottommargin" title=
 "Bullet Bottom Margin" type="int"/>
        <property id="chartleftmargin" title="Bullet Left Margin" type=
 "int"/>
        <property id="chartrightmargin" title=
 "Bullet Right Margin" type="int"/>
        <property id="higherisbetter" title=
 "realization higher than target is better" type="boolean"/>
```
Listing 14.61 Entire Property Set

You now add a new set of properties into the *contribution.xml* file. These properties are layout properties, such as margins, and behaviors such as when to show an alert. Next, add these new properties to the *contribution.xml* file by following these steps:

1. Open the *contribution.xml* file.
2. Insert the lines of Listing 14.60 and Listing 14.61 in the XML code within the COMPONENT node.
3. Save and close the file.

These options help to configure the graph. Note that `possiblevalue` is used for the trigger for an alert. There are five possible options, so this limits those choices in the properties.

The `numberofcolumns` property is for the designer to divide the BULLET GRAPHS into multiple columns. You can have one row of graphs or multiple rows, based on how you want to lay out the application. The property `higherisbetter` allows the user to configure whether a realization higher than the target is either good or bad; for costs, obviously higher isn't necessarily an improvement.

The other properties are defined for layout purposes. These properties allow for the refinement of the BULLET GRAPH where the JavaScript code checks the value of the property and fine-tunes the layout based on that value.

Finally, you set a number of initial values, so that the component is visualized when it's dragged onto the canvas (Listing 14.62).

```
<initialization>
        <defaultValue property="numberofcolumns">1</defaultValue>
        <defaultValue property="maxgraphheight">70</defaultValue>
        <defaultValue property="mingraphheight">50</defaultValue>
        <defaultValue property="higherisbetter">true</defaultValue>
        <defaultValue property="showaxis">true</defaultValue>
        <defaultValue property="tooltip">false</defaultValue>
        <defaultValue property="showalert">true</defaultValue>
        <defaultValue property="numberofticks">4</defaultValue>
        <defaultValue property="showalert">worse than comparison
        </defaultValue>
        <defaultValue property="TOP_MARGIN">0</defaultValue>
        <defaultValue property="LEFT_MARGIN">0</defaultValue>
        <defaultValue property="RIGHT_MARGIN">auto</defaultValue>
        <defaultValue property="BOTTOM_MARGIN">auto</defaultValue>
        <defaultValue property="WIDTH">600</defaultValue>
        <defaultValue property="HEIGHT">500</defaultValue>
</initialization>
```

Listing 14.62 Initial Values

In the following steps, you'll include the initial values into *contribution.xml*. Once added, the component will start with these initial values when it's included in the Design Studio application.

1. Open the *contribution.xml* file.
2. Go to the last property node.

3. Insert the code from Listing 14.62 between the last property node and the closure of the component node.

4. Save and close *contribution.xml*.

14.8.5 Creating the Component JavaScript

In this section, you'll continue working on the BULLET GRAPH component. As in the previous section, we'll go through each event and describe what we're doing. You'll start out with an outline. The steps involved use the downloadable material to copy the code in *bulletgraph.js* to your own version. If you have different property names or a different project name, you have to change the code accordingly.

In this section, we'll zoom into parts of the JavaScript and explain how they work.

Outline

The first step is to create an outline version of the code. This enables you to keep an overview of the code that you're invoking. The code isn't actual JavaScript but a simplified fake code that just functions as a map for your usage (see Listing 14.63).

```
JavaScript Class
    Initialize main variables
    Init() : set up the main container div and the initial tooltip
    Getter/Setters() Set up functions for properties
    AfterUpdate()
        Collect the data from the data source
        Set up rows and columns to place all the bullet charts
        Call the bullet chart function for each row in the data
Separate Functions
DrawBulletChart() : function to draw the bullet chart
returnData(): function to collect data and can fall back to random data
returnRandomData(): returns random data to function returndData
returnBoundData(): returns data from data source to returnData
showAlert(): Evaluate conditions if we should show alert
createRandomArray(): Returns a list of random numbers to returnRandomData()
getRandomInt(): returns a random number between a minimum and maximum to returnRandomArray
formatNumber(): formats a number based on parameters and returns result
numberWithCommas: Change formatting from US to European format
```

Listing 14.63 Outline Coding of the SDK

We'll address each part of the outline code (Listing 14.63) to introduce the functions we will be using.

Set Up Class Variables

The first step is to declare variables and objects on the main class level. All variables declared here will be available in each subfunction. So any value you set in the init() function is also available in the afterUpdate() function (Listing 14.64).

```
var that = this;
 var chartIndex = {};
 var chartComponents = {};
 var chartProperties = {};
 var componentDimensions = {};
 var tooltip = undefined;
 var sourcedata = {};
 var data = undefined;
 var clicked = {};
 var oldscrollval = 0;
 var numberOfGraphs = 0;
 var tooltip = undefined;
```

Listing 14.64 Variable Declaration

Follow these steps:

1. Open the *bulletgraph.js* file.
2. Insert the code of Listing 14.64 between "use strict"; and this.init. The variables are available within all the functions such as init() and afterupdate() because they have been declared on the main class level.
3. Save and close the file.

The chartProperties object is where you'll store all the property values received in the getter/setter functions. chartComponents is where you put all the parts of the graph that you render, and tooltip is where you store the HTML to show a tooltip. You use a separate JSON object source data to store all the data that you receive for the data bound properties.

14 | Building Components Using the SDK

init() Function

In the `init()` function, you set up the main parts of our component (Listing 14.65).

```
this.init = function(){
    chartComponents.container = this.$()[0];
    chartComponents.chart=d3.select(chartComponents.container);
tooltip=d3.select(chartComponents.container)
.append("div")
.attr("class","tooltip")
.style("opacity", 0);
};
```
Listing 14.65 Main Parts Setup in init() Function

Follow these steps to invoke code that creates the main parts of the component:

1. Open the *bulletgraph.js* file.
2. Replace the current `init()` function with the contents of Listing 14.65.
3. Save and close the file.

The root `div` is now assigned to `chartComponents.container`. From now on, you can refer to this JSON attribute when you want to work with the root element. The second line is used to initialize the D3 library on the root element. `D3.select` and `D3.selectAll` are two top-level methods for selecting elements. In Section 14.7.2, you'll use D3 further but always within the `chartComponents.chart` variable. Each graph will be placed within the main component as a separate element.

Next, you need to create a separate variable for the tooltip. This will also result in a new `div` element within the root. If you open the development tools in Google Chrome by pressing the [F12] key, you can view the elements in the application. You'll see the structure you just created (Figure 14.23).

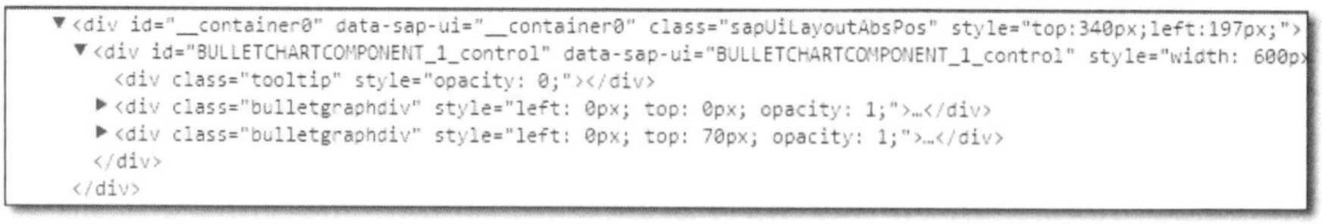

Figure 14.23 Main Structure in the Application

594

In this example, you see that two graphs were created within `chartComponents.chart`. Note also that each `div` has a class attribute. That attribute is used in the CSS file to apply formatting.

Getter/Setter()

The `getter/setter` functions are straightforward. The structure is always the same, and the `chartProperties` or `sourcedata` variable is used in each function to store the information. You'll create `getter/setter` functions for each of the properties you defined. Follow the example of either `chartproperties` (Listing 14.66) or `sourcedata` (Listing 14.67).

```
this.columnmargin = function(e)
{if(e===undefined)
    {return chartProperties.columnmargin;}
else
    {chartProperties.columnmargin = e;
    return this;}
};
```
Listing 14.66 Getter/Setter for Chart Properties

`Columnmargin` was defined earlier in *contribution.xml*.

For the data bound example, you'll see that it's identical to the standard property function.

```
this.data = function(e)
{
if (e === undefined)
    {return sourcedata.factdata;}
else
{sourcedata.factdata=e;
return this;}
};
```
Listing 14.67 Getter/Setter for Sourcedata

Follow these steps to define the `getter/setter` functions:

1. For each property, you have to define a function. This can be done directly, as shown in the previous code examples, for every property in *contribution.xml* except for the `On Click` property.

2. Use the template code:

14 | Building Components Using the SDK

```
this.columnmargin = function(e) { if (e ===
 undefined) {return chartProperties.columnmargin;}else{chartProperti
es.columnmargin = e;return this;}};
```

Each `getter/setter` function has the same structure. Using this template, we have a starter that we can copy for each property that we have.

3. Replace `columnmargin` with the name of the property you're currently invoking.
4. Copy the resulting template code with the new property name.
5. Paste the new `getter/setter` function in the Component JavaScript.

afterUpdate()

Next you'll create the `afterUpdate()` function, where most of the work will be done. You'll insert code that will create a table structure. The cells in the table are where we will place the graphs. The structure allows us to divide the graphs into rows and columns. To call the graph, you'll insert a call to a different function that you'll create later in the next section.

Set up the variables so that you can create the rows and columns needed for each BULLET GRAPH component, using the code in Listing 14.68.

```
data = returnData(sourcedata);
componentDimensions.numberOfGraphs = data.length;
componentDimensions.width = that.$().outerWidth() -
 chartProperties.rightmargin - chartProperties.leftmargin;
componentDimensions.height = that.$().outerHeight() -
 chartProperties.topmargin - chartProperties.bottommargin;
componentDimensions.columnCutOff =
 Math.floor(componentDimensions.numberOfGraphs /
 chartProperties.numberofcolumns);
componentDimensions.modulusgraphs =
 componentDimensions.numberOfGraphs % chartProperties.numberofcolumns ;
componentDimensions.graphWidth = componentDimensions.width /
 chartProperties.numberofcolumns - chartProperties.columnmargin;
componentDimensions.maxRows =
 Math.ceil(componentDimensions.numberOfGraphs /
 chartProperties.numberofcolumns);
componentDimensions.graphHeight = componentDimensions.height /
 componentDimensions.maxRows - chartProperties.rowmargin;
if (chartProperties.maxgraphheight>0){componentDimensions.graphHeight =
Math.min(componentDimensions.graphHeight,
chartProperties.maxgraphheight)}
```

```
    if (chartProperties.mingraphheight>0){componentDimensions.graphHeight =
    Math.max(componentDimensions.graphHeight, chartProperties.mingraphheigh
    t)}
    chartProperties.positions = [];
    componentDimensions.position = $(that.$()[0].parentElement).position();
          componentDimensions.titlelength =
     Math.max.apply(this,$.map(data, function(o){
     var returnval = Math.max(o.subtitle.length* 4, o.title.length* 6);
     return returnval; }));
          if (chartProperties.showalert!=
    "none"){componentDimensions.titlelength+=30};

       var i=0, j=0;
       for (i = 0; i < chartProperties.numberofcolumns; i++){
           for (j = 0; j < componentDimensions.maxRows; j++)
               {chartProperties.positions.push({"x":i, "y":j});
               }
           }
```
Listing 14.68 Setting up Calculations for the Graphs

The first line collects the data using `returnData()`. You then calculate all the dimensions based on the properties. The width for the graphs is the width of the component minus the margins. The `columnCutoff`, `maxRows`, and `modulusgraphs` are used to set up the graphs into rows and columns. The `titlelength` is calculated by looking at all the rows in the data. The longest title or subtitle determines the room that is needed for the titles.

The function looks quite complicated, so let's break it down into parts. On the outside, you see `Math.max.apply`. `Math.max` calculates the maximum, and `.apply` is a predefined JavaScript function method. You use `apply` to invoke a function that returns a list of values for `Math.Max`. The `.apply` function that you invoke uses `$.map` to create a function that returns the maximum length needed for the subtitle and title from each row. The length is calculated by multiplying the number of characters by a fixed amount of pixels.

The `for next` loop at the end creates a cell address in the variable `chartProperties.positions` based on the number of rows and columns needed.

In the second part (Listing 14.69), you're going to focus on `chartComponent.chart`.

```
chartComponents.chart.style("overflow-y","auto")
.style("position","relative")
.style("top",function(){return chartProperties.topmargin+"px"})
.style("height",function(){return componentDimensions.height+"px"})
.on("scroll",function(){vart=
(chartComponents.chart.property ("scrollHeight"),chartComponents.chart.
property("scrollTop"));
chartComponents.graphs.transition().duration(500).delay(function(o,n){r
eturn oldscrollval<t?30*(componentDimensions.numberOfGraphs-n):30*n})
.style("opacity",function(o,n){var e=
parseInt(d3.select(this).style("top").slice(0,-2));e-=t;var r=
1;return(0>e||e>componentDimensions.height-
componentDimensions.graphHeight)&&(r=0),r}),oldscrollval=t});
```

Listing 14.69 afterUpdate Function with a Focus on the Chart Component Chart Object

The `chartProperties.positions` variable was already defined in the `init()` function. However, now that we have all the property values, we need to configure `chartProperties.positions`.

The style attributes are set directly from the property settings. The `overflow-y` attribute ensures that if you have more graphs than can fit into the component, a scroll bar will appear allowing the user to scroll to the other components on the screen.

In the `.on("scroll`) function, the opacity of the graphs is recalculated. The `.on` function allows you to react to an event, in this case, a user that scrolls up or down in the component. Notice that you're working with the `chartComponents.graphs` variable, which is a collection of all the BULLET GRAPHS.

Using the `Scrolltop` attribute, which gets the current vertical position of the scroll bar, you know how far down the user scrolled. Based on that information, you compare that to the y position of each graph, and if it's within the component frame, it will be visible.

You may have noticed that the BULLET GRAPHS fade in and out when scrolling. The `.transition()` functions responsible for this. You can set how long the change has to take and how much delay is needed. The duration is fixed to 500 milliseconds, and the delay depends on the place of the graph in the list of graphs. The graphs lower in the list will have a smaller delay than the graphs that are higher up in the list. Notice that the `.style` attribute that is calculated is chained to the `.transition()` method. Any property that is chained to this function will get the same delay and duration.

In the final part of the `afterUpdate()` function, you'll use the D3 library to create a new graph element for each row in the data (Listing 14.70). You then hand the element over to a separate function that is responsible for drawing the component.

```
chartComponents.graphs =
  chartComponents.chart.selectAll("div.bulletgraphdiv").data(data);
chartComponents.graphs .enter()
    .append("div")
    .attr("class", "bulletgraphdiv");
chartComponents.graphs .exit()
    .transition()
    .delay(0)
    .duration(375)
    .style("opacity", 0)
    .remove();
chartComponents.graphs
    .style("left", function(d, i) { return chartProperties.positions[
i].x * ( componentDimensions.graphWidth + chartProperties.columnmargin)
 + "px";})
    .style("top", function(d, i) { return chartProperties.positions[
i].y * ( componentDimensions.graphHeight + chartProperties.rowmargin) +
 "px";})
    .style("opacity", function(d,i)
    {
    var calcpos = parseInt(d3.select(this).style("top").slice(0,-2));
    var result = 1;
    if (calcpos > componentDimensions.height - 50 ) { result = 0;}
       return result;})
       .each(function(d,i) { d3.select(this).call(bulletGraph);});
    };
```
Listing 14.70 D3 Function to Create a Graph

The main part is the `.selectAll` function. This is where you select all the available `div.bulletgraphdiv` components within the `chartComponents.chart` and compare them to the available data. In the `enter()` function, you do the append, and the only attribute you set is the class.

In the `exit` function, you remove the graph with a `.transition()` that lets the graph fade out first before removing it.

In the final part of the code, you work with all the elements that remain. The `left`, `top`, and `opacity` attributes are set for the `div` element holding the graph. In the `.each` function, you refer to the `bulletGraph` function. This function is chained to the `d3.select(this)` with the `.call` function, which means that inside the `bulletGraph` function, the outside `div` and the current data line can be referred to.

You finish the `afterUpdate` function with a simple statement: `drawBulletGraph`. We'll discuss this function in greater detail next.

drawBulletgraph()

The `drawBulletGraph` function is responsible for drawing all the required elements of the BULLET GRAPH in the structure. This function is fairly complex compared to the structure you created in the `afterUpdate` function. In this section, we'll show the steps required to create the structure in Figure 14.24.

```
▼<div class="bulletgraphdiv" style="left: 0px; top: 0px; opacity: 1;">
  ▼<svg class="bulletgraph" width="600" height="61.25">
    ▼<g class="x axis" transform="translate(126,61.25)">
      ▶<g class="tick" transform="translate(0,0)" style="opacity: 1;">…</g>
      ▶<g class="tick" transform="translate(172.992700729927,0)" style="opacity: 1;">…</g>
      ▶<g class="tick" transform="translate(345.985401459854,0)" style="opacity: 1;">…</g>
    </g>
    ▼<g class="label" transform="translate(0,10)">
      <text class="headerlabel" x="3" y="23.0625">fakedata graph 0</text>
      <text class="subheaderlabel" x="8" y="38.4375">(in 1000 EUR)</text>
    </g>
    ▼<g class="grapharea" transform="translate(126,10)">
      ▼<g class="threshholds">
        <rect class="thresh thresh0" width="141.85401459854015" x="0" y="0" height="46.125"></rect>
        <rect class="thresh thresh1" width="10.379562043795621" x="141.85401459854015" y="0" height="46.125"></rect>
        <rect class="thresh thresh2" width="3.45985401459854" x="152.23357664233578" y="0" height="46.125"></rect>
        <rect class="thresh thresh3" width="44.97810218978102" x="155.6934306569343" y="0" height="46.125"></rect>
        <rect class="thresh thresh4" width="138.39416058394158" x="200.6715328467153" y="0" height="46.125"></rect>
      </g>
      ▼<g class="actuals">
        <rect class="act real" width="432.48175182481754" x="0" y="17.9375" height="15.375"></rect>
        <rect class="act extrapol" width="41.518248175182485" x="432.48175182481754" y="17.9375" height="15.375"></rect>
      </g>
      ▼<g class="compare">
        <rect class="act compare" width="2" x="273.32846715328463" y="12.8125" height="25.625"></rect>
      </g>
    </g>
  </svg>
</div>
```

Figure 14.24 Structure of a Single Bullet Graph

In the first part of the `drawBulletGraph` function (Listing 14.71), you start by collecting the information from the parent element.

```
function bulletGraph(selection) {
    selection.each(function(d, i)
    {
    var currentDiv = d3.select(this);
    var data = [];data.push(d);
    var thisGraph =
```

```
currentDiv.selectAll("svg.bulletgraph").data(data);
    var barheight = componentDimensions.graphHeight -
chartProperties.bottommargin - chartProperties.topmargin
    var maxBarWidth = componentDimensions.graphWidth-
componentDimensions.titlelength-chartProperties.leftmargin-
chartProperties.rightmargin;
```
Listing 14.71 drawBulletGraph Function Initialization

In the function, the parameter `selection` holds the `div` element from where the function is called. In the first line, the D3 function `.each` is used to chain a function to that `div` element. The parameters (`d,i`) stand for the attached data and the index number of the element, respectively.

You create a variable that holds the D3 function wrapped around `this`. The keyword `this` calls the `div` element, not the root element. You use the `d` parameter to collect the data that belongs to this particular BULLET GRAPH, and then attach the data to a new SVG element with the `bulletgraph` class.

The `currentdiv` is the D3 function wrapped around the calling element. In the final line, the maximum width of the bar is calculated. You'll need to scale the bars later.

In the second part of the `drawBulletGraph` function (Listing 14.72), you build the root element of the graph. Using the D3, enter and update functions. Create a main SVG element and provide functions so when the user hovers over the graph with their mouse, a tooltip will appear.

```
thisGraph.enter().append("svg")
.attr("class","bulletgraph"),
thisGraph.attr("width",componentDimensions.graphWidth)
.attr("height",componentDimensions.graphHeight)
.on("click",function(t){clicked.graphkey=
t.chartKey,that.firePropertiesChanged([
"clickedgraphkey"]),that.fireEvent("onclick")})
.on("mouseover",function(t){if(1==chartProperties.tooltip)
    {tooltip.transition().duration(500).style("opacity",1);var e=
d3.format(",.2f"),o="<br>Current Realization: "+e(t.real)+"</
br>";t.extrap>t.real&&(o+="<br>Period End Prediction: "+e(t.extrap)+"</
br>"),o+="<br>Comparison Value: "+e(t.compare)+"</br>",
tooltip.html(o).style("left",d3.event.pageX-
componentDimensions.position.left+"px").style("top",d3.event.pageY-
componentDimensions.position.top+"px")}}).on("mouseout",function(t){too
ltip.transition().duration(500).style("opacity",0)});
```
Listing 14.72 Drawing the Bullet Graph Main SVG Element

With the `.on` function, you add functions to react to a user's click and mouse hovering. In the function for the click event, use the `firepropertiesChanged` method and the `fireEvent` method from the Design Studio framework. These methods are now chained to the `that` variable because the `this` keyword points to the `div` element that called the function and not the main SDK component.

When a user hovers over the graph, the tooltip element becomes visible, and the location is set based on the location of the mouse pointer using the `d3.event.pageX` and `d3.event.pageY` methods. The top and left positions of the root element are subtracted because the coordinates applied are in reference to the component and not the entire screen.

Next, you need to set up the lines required to create new parts of the graph. First, we'll focus on a few specific parts of the code that we will use, followed by the entire function listing.

In the group settings, the G elements are created based on the property settings:

```
var labelgroup = thisGraph.selectAll("g.label").data(data);
var xaxisgroup = thisGraph.selectAll("g.x.axis").data(data);
var graphgroup = thisGraph.selectAll("g.grapharea").data(data);
```

When you look back to Section 14.2.3, you'll see that the G elements are the first level below the main SVG level. G elements help you provide structure and group elements.

The `header` and `subheader` functions have an almost identical setup regarding the text for the labels. You use the `title` attribute the set the text for the title:

```
header
    .attr("x", 3)
    .attr("y", barheight * 0.45)
    .text(function(d){ return d.title;})
```

One of the powerful features of D3 is the possibility to use functions based on the data and use the results to set attributes of elements. The height is set to almost half of the bar height to ensure that the header is aligned with the graph.

In the next part (Listing 14.73), you need to evaluate whether you need to show an alert; if so, you add a red circle to the beginning of the graph to call attention to an area on the graph. As you may remember, there were numerous options to choose from to set alerts. Due of this, the evaluation is set in a separate function: `showAlert`. The first step is to remove any existing circles, and then evaluate and add the circle if necessary.

```
labelgroup.select("circle").remove();
if (showAlert(data[0])) {
var sparkLineAlert = labelgroup.append("circle")
    .attr("class", "sparklinealert")
    .attr("cx", componentDimensions.titlelength - (barheight * 0.25) )
    .attr("cy",barheight * 0.5)
    .attr("r", barheight * 0.15)
    .attr("class", "alertbad");
```
Listing 14.73 Alert Element Based on a Function

In the last part (Listing 14.74), you build the rectangles and lines to create the visualization of the data. Here, you need to scale the size based on the data numbers.

```
var xScale = d3.scale.linear()
    .range([0,maxBarWidth])
    .domain([Math.min(0,d3.min(data[
0].values, function(d) {return d;})),d3.max(data[
0].values, function(d) {return d;})]);
var xAxis = d3.svg.axis().scale(xScale).orient("bottom");
    xaxisgroup.call(xAxis);
    xaxisgroup.select("path").remove();
    thresholds
 .attr("width", function(d,i) {var returnval = 0; if(i!=0){ returnval = data[0].threshholds[i-1]}; return xScale(d-returnval);})
    .attr("x", function(d,i){var returnval = 0; if(i!=0){ returnval = data[0].threshholds[i-1]}; return xScale(returnval);})
    .attr("y", 0).attr("height",barheight)

    realization
      .attr("width", function(d) {return xScale(d.real);})
      .attr("x", 0).attr("y", barheight * 0.35).attr("height", barheight
 * 0.3);
extrapolation
      .attr("width", function(d) {return xScale(d.extrap-d.real);})
      .attr("x", function(d) {return xScale(d.real);})
      .attr("y", barheight * 0.35).attr("height", barheight * 0.3);
comparison
 .attr("width", 2)
      .attr("x", function(d) {return xScale(d.compare);})
      .attr("y", barheight * 0.25).attr("height", barheight * 0.5);
});
```
Listing 14.74 Building the Bullet Graph

You scale the rectangles and position the line based on the available data. In the first three lines, you define a scale and assign the resulting function to the variable xScale. The parameters are the `range`, that is, the minimum and maximum value, and the `domain`, which is the minimum and maximum value of the data.

Next, you see the function to build the visualization of the *X* scale. The D3 library offers a function where you can set the number of properties, and it will draw a scale for you. First, assign the function and the properties to the variable `xAxis`. In the following line, chain the variable to `xAxisGroup`. The `xAxisgroup` is a variable that holds a `G` element. Chaining the function to the variable is the same as saying "put it here."

The `if` statement is to check whether the designer wanted an axis; if not, it will remove the axis. Finally, you'll draw the rectangles. As previously stated, you use functions to determine the *X* attribute and the width. Let's look at the most complicated one and discuss that function.

You can have up to five thresholds (the gray shaded rectangles). The *X* attribute needs to start at the point where the previous rectangle ended. The width is based on the current threshold. Let's zoom in to the threshold code (Listing 14.75).

```
thresholds
     .attr("width", function(d,i) {var returnval = 0; if(i!=
0){ returnval = data[0].threshholds[i-1]}; return xScale(d-
returnval);})
     .attr("x", function(d,i){var returnval = 0; if(i!=0){ returnval =
 data[0].threshholds[i-1]}; return xScale(returnval);})
     .attr("y", 0).attr("height",barheight)
```
Listing 14.75 Code to Create Threshold Rectangles

In the function tied to the attribute width (Listing 14.75), you first collect the value from the previous rectangle using the index parameter from the function. You can subtract 1 to go to the previous line in the data. If this is the first line, you keep the value at 0. The width of the rectangle is then based on the current value minus the value of the previous rectangle. The value is then scaled using the xScale function defined earlier.

The x attribute, the horizontal position, is based on the endpoint of the previous rectangle. Again, you collect the information using the `i` parameter and set the x value based on the previous value. To set up the right location and width, the position *X* is based on the following:

> *Width based on the current value – Width of the previous value = Total width that the current rectangle needs to be*

To download the source code for the `drawBulletGraph` function for this example, go to this book's product page at *www.sap-press.com/3951*, and scroll down to the PRODUCT SUPPLEMENTS section.

This concludes our discussion of the `drawBulletGraph` function. We'll now address some of the other functions briefly and highlight some of the more complex parts of the supporting functions.

Other Functions

In the first line of the `afterUpdate`, you saw that the function `returnData` was used to return the data. This function checks if there is bound data and returns that bound data if it's available. If it's not available, then there is the option to use random data so that the designer can at least see how it will look.

The bound data is returned by the `returnBoundData` function that is called from the `returnData` function. It molds the bound data into the structure you need to work with for the graphs. You can use SCN community functions to help mold them.

The bound data has a typical structure based on the properties you've set in *contribution.xml*. The initial structure in the example component (Figure 14.25) is a very layered structure.

```
▼ factdata: Object
  ▶ axis_columns: Array[11]
  ▶ axis_rows: Array[54]
    columnCount: 11
  ▼ data: Array[594]
    ▶ [0 … 99]
    ▶ [100 … 199]
    ▶ [200 … 299]
    ▶ [300 … 399]
    ▶ [400 … 499]
    ▶ [500 … 593]
      length: 594
    ▶ __proto__: Array[0]
  ▶ dimensions: Array[4]
    locale: "en_US"
    rowCount: 54
  ▶ selection: Array[4]
  ▶ tuples: Array[594]
```

Figure 14.25 Structure Source Data When Arriving in the Component JavaScript

For this data source, there are four dimensions; that's why you see an array of 4 in the `dimensions` property. If you open this, you'll see that each dimension has a number of attributes, One of these attributes is called `members`. The `members` attribute holds the individual values of the dimension (Figure 14.26).

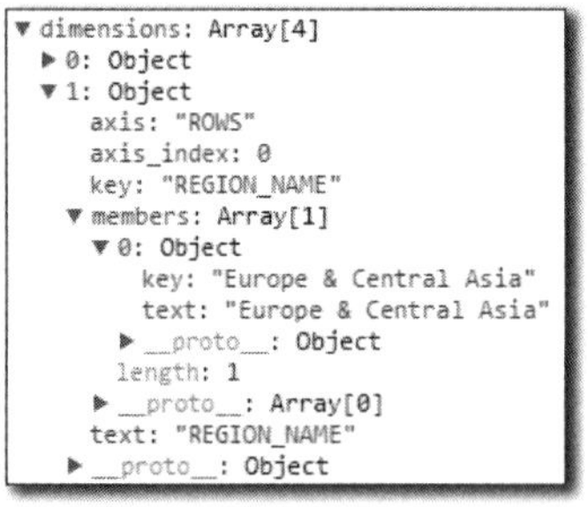

```
▼ dimensions: Array[4]
  ▶ 0: Object
  ▼ 1: Object
      axis: "ROWS"
      axis_index: 0
      key: "REGION_NAME"
    ▼ members: Array[1]
      ▼ 0: Object
          key: "Europe & Central Asia"
          text: "Europe & Central Asia"
        ▶ __proto__: Object
        length: 1
      ▶ __proto__: Array[0]
      text: "REGION_NAME"
    ▶ __proto__: Object
```

Figure 14.26 Dimension Values in the Bound JSON

For the transactional data (Figure 14.27), the numbers are all in the `data` attribute. If you want to relate the data to the dimension value, you look at the tuples. Each tuple holds an array of four numbers. Each number is the index number of the member value in the dimension.

The dimension we showed earlier is the second dimension in the list. Therefore, the second number of the tuple points to that dimension. The number is 0, meaning that it points to the first member, which is "Europe & Central Asia."

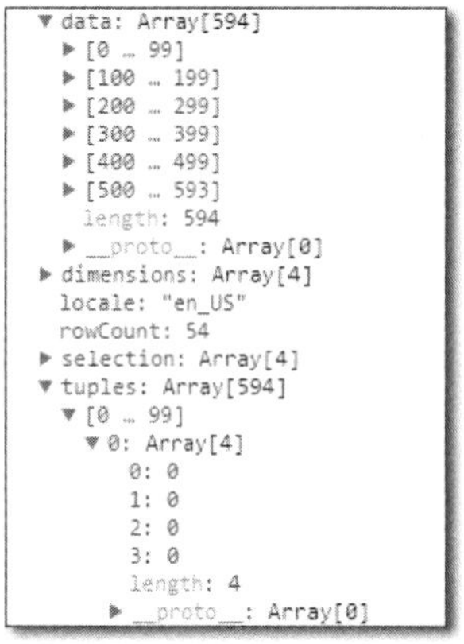

```
▼ data: Array[594]
  ▶ [0 … 99]
  ▶ [100 … 199]
  ▶ [200 … 299]
  ▶ [300 … 399]
  ▶ [400 … 499]
  ▶ [500 … 593]
    length: 594
  ▶ __proto__: Array[0]
  ▶ dimensions: Array[4]
    locale: "en_US"
    rowCount: 54
  ▶ selection: Array[4]
  ▼ tuples: Array[594]
    ▼ [0 … 99]
      ▼ 0: Array[4]
          0: 0
          1: 0
          2: 0
          3: 0
          length: 4
        ▶ __proto__: Array[0]
```

Figure 14.27 Fact Data in the Bound JSON

If there is no bound data, the `returnData` function calls `returnRandomData`. This function creates random numbers and creates the necessary variable structure so that the graphs can be visualized based on this data. The random numbers are generated by the functions `createRandomArray` and `createRandomInt`. The first function creates arrays and calls the second function to provide the random numbers.

14.8.6 Creating Additional Properties

In this section, you'll expand the additional properties to accommodate the selection of dimensions for the `label`, `sublabel`, and `key` dimension (Figure 14.28). This will be helpful because you now have to type in the dimension names manually. Additionally, we'll place a button on the ADDITIONAL PROPERTIES panel to edit the data selection.

Because this is an accordion menu, you can collapse the data group and select the margin group. Now you can set the margins (Figure 14.29). Note how this structure helps store numerous options in the ADDITIONAL PROPERTIES panel without overwhelming the user with options.

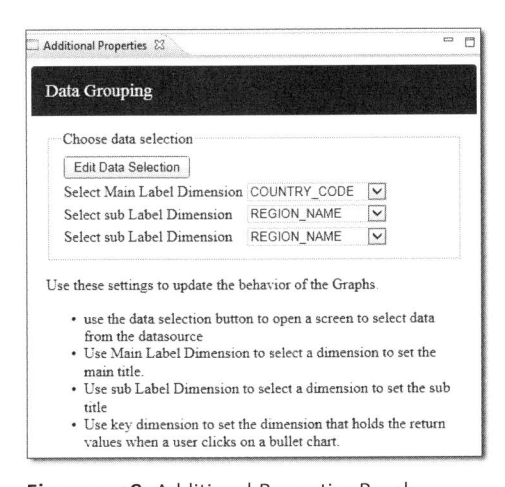

Figure 14.28 Additional Properties Panel

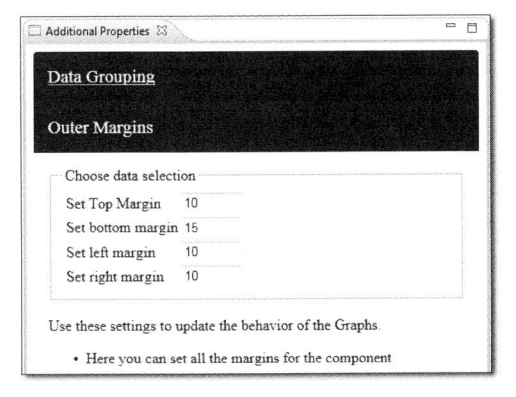

Figure 14.29 Margin Screen with Data Grouping Collapsed

You'll first create the HTML structure to support the menu in the HTML section. Then, you'll add the functionality to open and collapse the groups, populate the options, and finally exchange the property value with the other parts of Design Studio.

HTML

In this section, we'll look at the more elaborate setup of the accordian menu. To create the accordion menu structure, you create a structure to accommodate the two groups. This is a set of embedded `div` elements and `HREF` elements to link to the different groups (Listing 14.76).

```
<div class="accordion">
 <div class="accordion-section">
  <a class="accordion-section-title" href="#accordion-1">Data Grouping</a>
  <div class="accordion-section-content" id="accordion-1">
   </div><!--end .accordion-section-content-->
 </div><!--end .accordion-section-->
  <div class="accordion-section">
   <a class="accordion-section-title" href="#accordion-2">Outer Margins</a>
   <div class="accordion-section-content" id="accordion-2">
   </div><!--end .accordion-section-content-->
  </div><!--end .accordion-section-->
 </div><!--end .accordion-->
```
Listing 14.76 HTML Additional Properties

The outer `div` container holds the entire menu and has the class `accordion`. For each section, there is a `div` element with the classes `accordion-section` and `accordion-section-content`. The sections have a unique ID, and the `A HREF` element point to those IDs.

Each `div` content holds a form with input elements and a list of help texts, as shown in Figure 14.30. Because you already set up the CSS file, the layout is using the CSS classes. If you want to change parts, look at the CSS class of that part, and change the layout of that class in the CSS file.

```
<form id="form" name="form">
    <fieldset>
        <legend>Choose data selection</legend>
        <table>
            <tr>
                <td><input id="editdataselection" type="button" value="Edit Data Selection"></td>
            </tr>
            <tr>
                <td>Select Main Label Dimension</td>
                <td><select id="mainlabeldimension" name="labeldimension" size="1" style="width: 150px"></select></td>
            </tr>
            <tr>
                <td>Select sub Label Dimension</td>
                <td><select id="sublabeldimension" name="sublabeldimension" size="1" style="width: 150px"></select></td>
            </tr>
            <tr>
                <td>Select sub Label Dimension</td>
                <td><select id="keydimension" name="key dimension" size="1" style="width: 150px"></select></td>
            </tr>
        </table>
    </fieldset>
</form>
<p>Use these settings to update the behavior of the Graphs.</p>
<ul>
    <li>use the data selection button to open a screen to select data from the datasource</li>
    <li>Use Main Label Dimension to select a dimension to set the main title.</li>
    <li>Use sub Label Dimension to select a dimension to set the sub title</li>
    <li>Use key dimension to set the dimension that holds the return values when a user clicks on a bullet chart.</li>
</ul>
```

Figure 14.30 Structure of the Content in a Section

For buttons that can open a dialog box, use the following:

```
<input id="editdataselection" type="button" value=
"Edit Data Selection">
```

For dropdown selections, use the following:

```
<select id="mainlabeldimension" name="labeldimension" size="1" style=
"width: 150px">
```

For manual input, use the following:

```
<input id="charttopmargin" maxlength="5" name="top margin" size=
"5" type="text">
```

This sets up the structure that you need for the ADDITIONAL PROPERTIES panel. Next, you'll follow this up by adding the necessary functions to the JavaScript.

JavaScript

You've already implemented the functionality to open and close the groups based on the selection in JavaScript. Now you'll add functions to pass the property values to and from the ADDITIONAL PROPERTIES panel. In addition, you'll create a function to populate the dropdown boxes with dimension names.

For each input field, you'll create two functions: an event listener that informs Design Studio that a new value is available and a `getter/setter` function to pass the values to and from Design Studio.

The first change event listener syntax is as follows:

```
$("#mainlabeldimension").change(function() {that.firePropertiesChanged([
"labeldimension"]);return false;});
```

This example points to the select item with the unique ID "`mainlabeldimension.`" When it changes value, it triggers a function that informs Design Studio to use the `firePropertiesChanged` method. This is used here because the function is linked to the `mainlabeldimension` element, and the `this` keyword now points to another element:

```
this.labeldimension = function(e) {if (e === undefined) {return $("#mainlabeldimension").val();}else {$("#mainlabeldimension").val(e);return this;}};
```

This same function was used for the Component JavaScript. The only difference is that instead of a variable, it now uses a form element to store the value. The button is an exception. Because Design Studio provides dialog boxes to work with some types of properties, you can trigger that dialog box by using an `openPropertyDialog` method:

```
$("#editdataselection").click(function() {that.openPropertyDialog("data");}
);
```

When the `editdataselection` button is clicked, the method is used. Design Studio will determine the property type of "`data`" and open the correct dialog box.

Next, you populate the dropdown boxes with the dimensions from the bound data source. In `init()`, you use the `fillDropDown` function to fill each dropdown box with the following line:

```
fillDropDown("#mainlabeldimension")
```

Further down, you find the `fillDropDown` function (Listing 14.77).

```
function fillDropDown(div_id) {
    var jqDropdownMembers = $(div_id);
    jqDropdownMembers.empty();
    var strMetadata = that.callRuntimeHandler("getMetadataAsString");
    if (strMetadata) {
     var metadata = jQuery.parseJSON(strMetadata);
```

```
        if (metadata) {
          var column1Members = metadata.dimensions;
          for (var i = 0; i < column1Members.length; i++) {
              if ( column1Members[i].axis == "ROWS"){
          var member = column1Members[i];
          var jqDropdownItem = $("<option value=
'" + member.key + "'>" + member.text + "</option>");
            jqDropdownMembers.append(jqDropdownItem);
              }
            }
          }
        }
      }
```

Listing 14.77 fillDropDown Function

In this function, you fill the dropdown box based on the values returned from the Component JavaScript. You can call a function by using the `that.callRuntime-Handler` method.

In the Component JavaScript, you add the `getMetadataAsString` function:

```
this.getMetadataAsString = function() {
    return JSON.stringify(this.data());
};
```

This function returns the contents of a `getter/setter` function that is used for the data bound property. After the values are returned, you only want to use the ROW dimensions to select from, so you insert an `if then` statement in the loop to only add items if the `axis` property is "ROWS." These two sections are a subset of the properties. Feel free to add other properties to the ADDITIONAL PROPERTIES panel.

14.8.7 Adding Methods

Now that you have a component, you can include some interactivity options by adding methods. In this example, you'll create a method that allows you to work with the ID of the clicked graph and a method to change the threshold columns.

In the initial setup, you already have the basic ZTL function:

```
class com.rheinwerk.example.BulletGraph extends Component {}
```

You've already inherited methods from the standard components (Figure 14.31). By only adding the line above, with `extends Component` part already enabled, a standard set of methods become available in Design Studio. You can find these

14 | Building Components Using the SDK

methods when you look in the Script Editor of any component. There, you can look up the component and see the available standard methods.

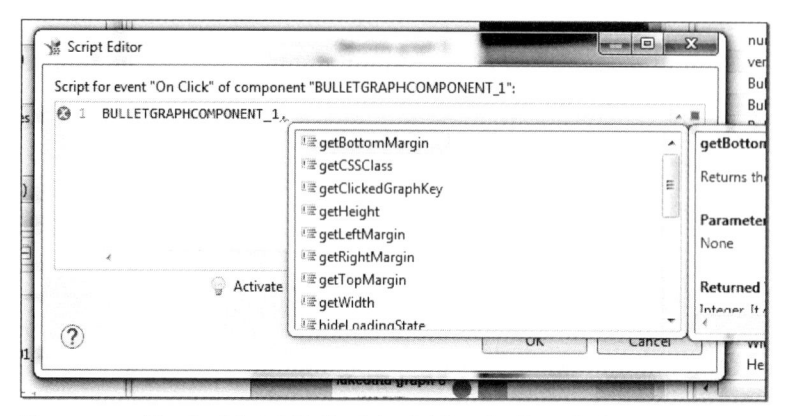

Figure 14.31 Standard Script Methods by Adding the Extends Component

Begin by retrieving the ID of the selected graph using the `getClickedGraphKey` method. This can be used to filter other data sources and provide drilldown capabilities.

The method itself is quite easy to add (Listing 14.78).

```
class com.rheinwerk.example.BulletGraph extends Component {
/* function to return the clicked graph key */
 String getSelectedGraphKey() {*
     return this.clickedgraphkey
  *}
}
```

Listing 14.78 Function to Return Information on a Clicked Bullet Graph

Note that the `getselectedGraphKey` function has some specific syntax requirements. The function content is encapsulated with {* *}.

Now when you return to Design Studio and go into the event Script Editor, you find a new method, which you can use to filter other data sources:

```
Var newFilter BULLETGRAPHCOMPONENT_1.getSelectedGraphKey();
DS_1.setFilter("COUNTRY_CODE", newFilter);
```

The second step is to create a `setthreshold` method, which will allow designers to change the threshold graph and not have to filter the data source. This saves a roundtrip to the backend and increases performance:

612

```
BULLETCHARTCOMPONENT_1.setThreshold("threshold1", "worstperformer");
```

In the *ZTL* file, you add the following code (Listing 14.79).

```
/* set a new threshold column */
 void setThreshold(
/* column to change */
 String thresholdprop,
 /*new value */
 String newThresholdColumn) {*
    if (thresholdprop == "threshold1")
          {this.threshold1 = newThresholdColumn};
    if (thresholdprop == "threshold2")
          {this.threshold2 = newThresholdColumn};
    if (thresholdprop == "threshold3")
          {this.threshold3 = newThresholdColumn};
    if (thresholdprop == "threshold4")
          {this.threshold4 = newThresholdColumn};
    if (thresholdprop == "threshold5")
       {this.threshold5 = newThresholdColumn};
*}
```
Listing 14.79 Methods in ZTL

If you want, you can add an identical function for `realization`, `compare`, and `labels`.

14.9 Summary

In this chapter, we described the steps to build an SDK extension. In the first section, we looked at the SDK framework before diving into the various programming languages. Then, we walked through the basic building blocks of an SDK. After we covered the basics, we moved on to the configuration tasks and internal functionality steps. In the last section before our example, we looked at three JavaScript libraries: jQuery, D3, and SAPUI5. Finally, we put all that information to good use and showed you how to build a BULLET GRAPH component using an SDK.

In the next chapter, we'll discuss another example: the real-time production dashboard.

PART V
Examples

In this chapter, we'll guide you through the process of setting up a pseudo real-time production dashboard based on the usage scenario described in Chapter 3.

15 Building a Real-Time Production Dashboard

In Chapter 3, we described the usage scenario for a real-time production dashboard. In this chapter, we'll guide you through the steps involved for designing and building this application. This chapter integrates many of the topics that you've already seen in this book, such as setting up the data source, using scripts for interactivity, and using Cascading Style Sheets (CSS) classes and styles.

Let's begin with an overview of the application you'll be building before jumping into the step-by-step process.

15.1 Application Overview

In Chapter 3, we discussed how a manager of a production facility can use a real-time dashboard to track certain key performance indicators (KPIs). The dashboard can be switched between a yearly, monthly, daily, and even real-time view of the production data.

When you consider creating a real-time application, you have to set up the back-end system as well to provide the necessary data. There are various options available for this task. In this example, we'll use a BEx query built on an InfoProvider in SAP Business Warehouse (BW). This InfoProvider gets updated every 15 minutes, which means that the data isn't actually real-time, but rather pseudo real-time.

As discussed in Chapter 3, the following are the main KPIs within this dashboard:

- **Availability**
  This tells you how much time the machine spends in production.
- **Performance**
  This tells you how well the machine did in producing its products compared to its normal values.
- **Quality**
  This provides information on the production quality of the product.
- **Operational Equipment Efficiency (OEE)**
  This is a score based on the previous three KPIs and indicates the overall production process.

These KPIs are presented in various views:

- View per hour (real time/nonreal time)
- View per day (nonreal time)
- View per month (nonreal time)
- View per year (nonreal time)

> **Alternatives**
>
> You might consider using SAP HANA views, which may be a better alternative for real-time operational reporting. You can also check out SAP Event Stream Processing, which you can use to trigger actions when certain alerts' conditions are met: *http://www.sap.com/pc/tech/database/software/sybase-complex-event-processing/index.html*.

15.2 Building the Application

In Design Studio, you can use a component called TIMER to simulate the real-time character of the application. In the properties of the TIMER component, you can set a specific time interval, which will trigger a script (you can define this in the properties).

The TIMER component is a new standard components in Design Studio 1.6. Before this version, the TIMER component was available as an SDK component, which could be downloaded as part of a real-time package from the SAP Support Portal (*https://support.sap.com*).

The TIMER component can be found in the OUTLINE view (Figure 15.1) in Design Studio and is one of the available technical components.

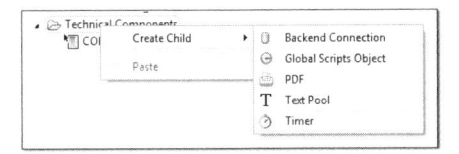

Figure 15.1 Timer Component

The application that you'll develop will consist of four views:

▶ **Real-time view**
Gives an overview of the KPIs for today, displayed per hour. The data will be updated regularly.

▶ **Today**
Gives an overview of the KPIs for today, displayed per hour. The data won't be updated.

▶ **This month**
Gives an overview of the KPIs for this running month, per day.

▶ **This year**
Gives an overview of the KPIs for this running year, per month.

We'll use a single BEx query as data source for the application. As you can see in Figure 15.2, there are four key figures (KPIs) in the COLUMNS section of the query. The Rows section is empty. In Design Studio, you'll modify the view of the BEx query to suit.

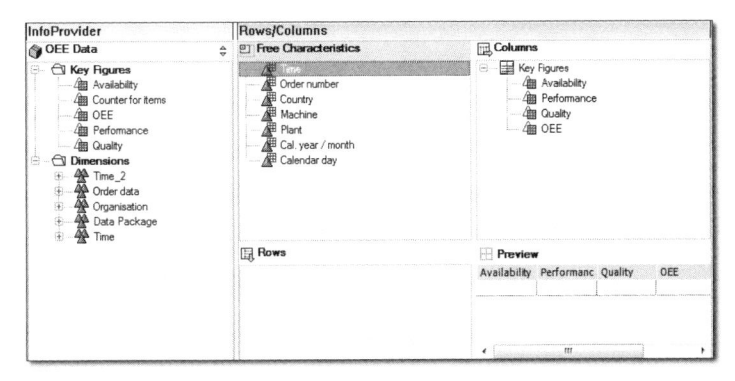

Figure 15.2 BEx Query

15 | Building a Real-Time Production Dashboard

Let's start with the preparation of the views.

15.2.1 Views

In this section, we'll walk you through the process of developing the four views of the dashboard. Follow these steps:

1. Add the BEx query as a data source in Design Studio by right-clicking on the DATA SOURCES folder in the OUTLINE view and selecting ADD DATA SOURCE.

2. After you've added your BEx query as a data source, right-click on the data source, and select EDIT INITIAL VIEW.

3. Now drag the TIME dimension into the rows as shown in Figure 15.3. Rename the data source in its properties to "DS_1_PER_HOUR" (Figure 15.4).

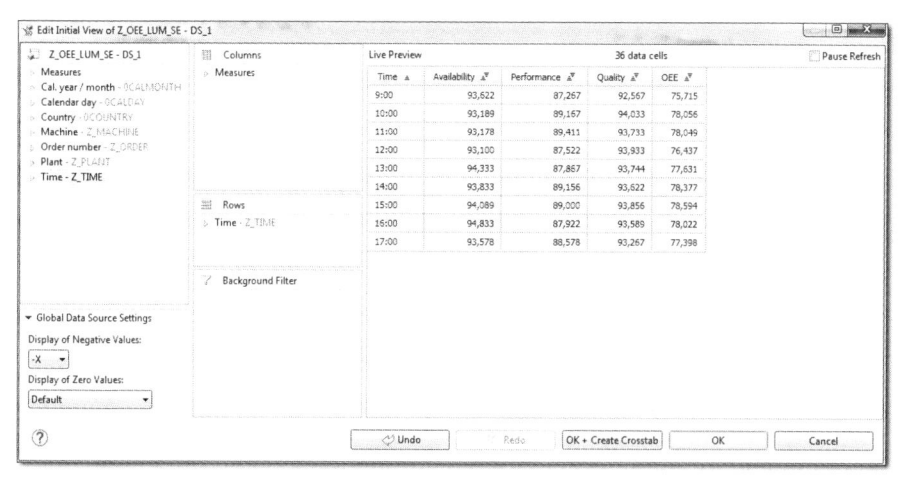

Figure 15.3 Editing the Initial View

Figure 15.4 Data Source Properties

4. Now, copy the data source, and paste it twice.

5. Remove the TIME dimension in both data sources, then add the CALENDAR DAY dimension to the rows in the second data source, and rename the data source to "DS_2_PER_DAY."

6. Add the CAL. YEAR/MONTH dimension to the rows of the third data source, and rename the data source to "DS_3_PER_MONTH." The initial views of the new data sources should look like Figure 15.5 and Figure 15.6.

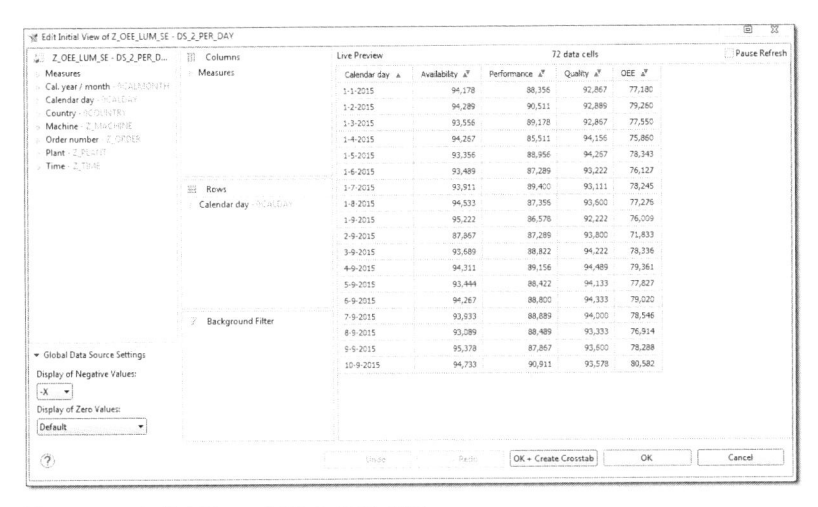

Figure 15.5 Initial View of DS_2_PER_DAY

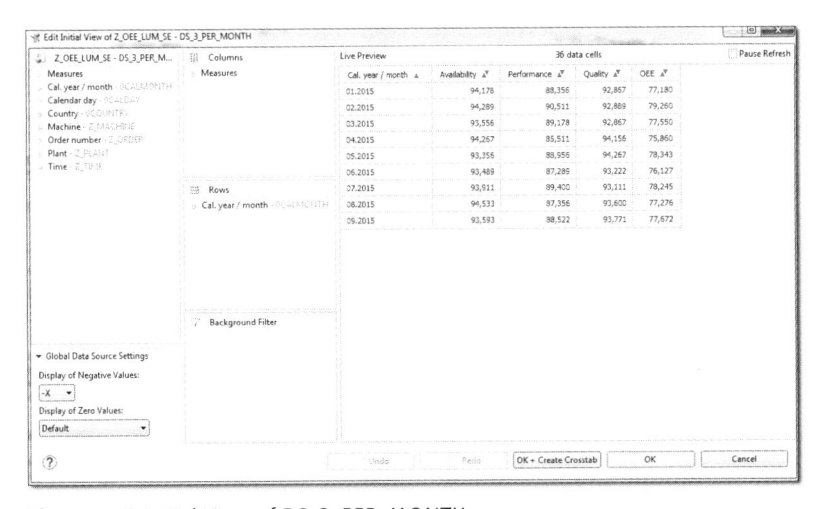

Figure 15.6 Initial View of DS_3_PER_MONTH

7. Create two more views based on the same data source:
   - DS_4_PLANT, with the PLANT dimension as the only dimension in the rows of the data source
   - DS_5_MACHINE, with the MACHINE dimension as the only dimension in the rows of the data source

Now that the data sources and views are ready, let's focus on the layout of the application. The first step is to define the CSS classes and components.

15.2.2 CSS Classes

In this section, we'll walk through how to build the layout of the application. We'll begin by looking at the different CSS classes and then look at the different components you'll be using.

You'll use a simple CSS file in this application in which you'll create four classes. The first class is used for the application title, the second and third class for the buttons in the application, and the last class for the KPI titles. Follow these steps:

1. Create a CSS file named *demo.css*.
2. Copy Listing 15.1 into the CSS file.

```css
.mytitle
{
font-weight: bold;
font-size: 32px;
color: #2E8FFF;
text-shadow: 30px 10px 3px #C7C7C7;
}
.mybutton
{
border: 2px solid;
border-radius: 25px;
text-align: center;
font-size: 12px;
font-weight: bold;
background-color: #2E8FFF;
}
.mybutton_selected
{
border: 2px solid;
border-radius: 25px;
text-align: center;
font-size: 12px;
```

```
font-weight: bold;
color: white;
background-color: black;
}
.mykpi
{
color: #2E8FFF;
font-weight: bold;
text-align: center;
font-size: 16px;
}
```

Listing 15.1 CSS File

3. Link the CSS file to your application.

CSS

You can find more information about CSS in Design Studio in Chapter 10 of this book.

15.2.3 Components and Layout

Now that you have the CSS in place, let's focus on the components that you'll use to build the application. It's a good practice to group your components into PANEL components, as shown in Figure 15.7, to keep a good overview of the layout in your application. Follow these steps:

1. Create a PANEL component, and name it "MAIN."

2. Set the TOP MARGIN, LEFT MARGIN, BOTTOM MARGIN, and RIGHT MARGIN to 0, and set the WIDTH and the HEIGHT to AUTO.

3. Create a PANEL component, and name it "HEADER."

4. Set the TOP MARGIN, LEFT MARGIN, and RIGHT MARGIN to 0. Set the BOTTOM MARGIN and the WIDTH to AUTO, and set the HEIGHT to 100.

5. Create a PANEL component, and name it "BODY." Set the TOP MARGIN to 100, and the LEFT MARGIN, BOTTOM MARGIN, and RIGHT MARGIN to 0. Set the WIDTH and HEIGHT to AUTO.

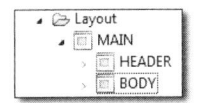

Figure 15.7 Main Layout

You've successfully created the primary components for the application. In the next three subsections, we'll look at the layout of the header, body, and various buttons within the application.

Header

The header of the application will contain a TEXT component that you'll use as the title for the application. You'll create a link to the CSS class that you defined in the CSS file from Section 15.2.2 to make the title stand out.

Follow these steps:

1. Add a TEXT component in the HEADER panel.
2. Set the TOP MARGIN to 20, the LEFT MARGIN to 30, and the BOTTOM MARGIN and RIGHT MARGIN to AUTO. Set the WIDTH to 500 and the HEIGHT to 50.
3. Add the title of your application in the properties of the TEXT component. For this example, name the application "Rotterdam International."
4. In the properties of this TEXT component, use `mytitle` as the CSS class.

The title should now look like Figure 15.8.

Rotterdam International

Figure 15.8 Application Title

Body

The BODY will consist of three GRID LAYOUT components: one for the real-time view and the view for today, one for the view per month, and one for the view per year. In the BODY, we also reserve some room for the filters.

Let's start with the GRID LAYOUT component for the real-time view and the view for today, which should look like Figure 15.9. Follow these steps:

1. Place a GRID LAYOUT component in the BODY panel, and name this component "GRID_1_HOUR."
2. Set the TOP MARGIN and BOTTOM MARGIN to 40, the LEFT MARGIN and RIGHT MARGIN to 0, and the WIDTH and HEIGHT to AUTO.

3. Set the NUMBER OF ROWS to 2 and the NUMBER OF COLUMNS to 3.

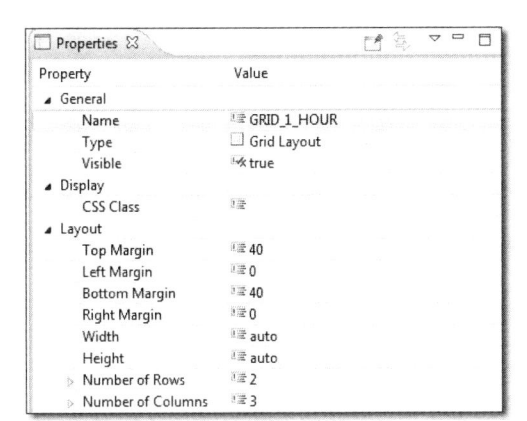

Property	Value
General	
Name	GRID_1_HOUR
Type	Grid Layout
Visible	true
Display	
CSS Class	
Layout	
Top Margin	40
Left Margin	0
Bottom Margin	40
Right Margin	0
Width	auto
Height	auto
Number of Rows	2
Number of Columns	3

Figure 15.9 Grid Layout Properties

We now have a 2 × 3 grid to form a total of 6 blocks. Fill each of these blocks with a TEXT component for the title of the KPI and a CHART component. Use the following settings for the TEXT component:

1. Set the TOP MARGIN, LEFT MARGIN, and RIGHT MARGIN to 0. Set the BOTTOM MARGIN and WIDTH to AUTO, and set the HEIGHT to 40.

2. Use the CSS class `mykpi` to format this TEXT component. The CSS defined in this class is used to center the text, apply the same color blue as the title, and use a font size of 16px.

Next, use the following settings for the CHART component:

1. Set the TOP MARGIN to 40; set the LEFT MARGIN, BOTTOM MARGIN, and RIGHT MARGIN to 0; and set the WIDTH and HEIGHT to AUTO.

2. Go to the PROPERTIES tab, and set the SWAP AXIS option to TRUE.

Now that you've created a TEXT and a CHART component for each KPI, copy these components into each of the remaining five blocks. The structure of the BODY panel should look like Figure 15.10. Rename the KPIs according to Figure 15.10.

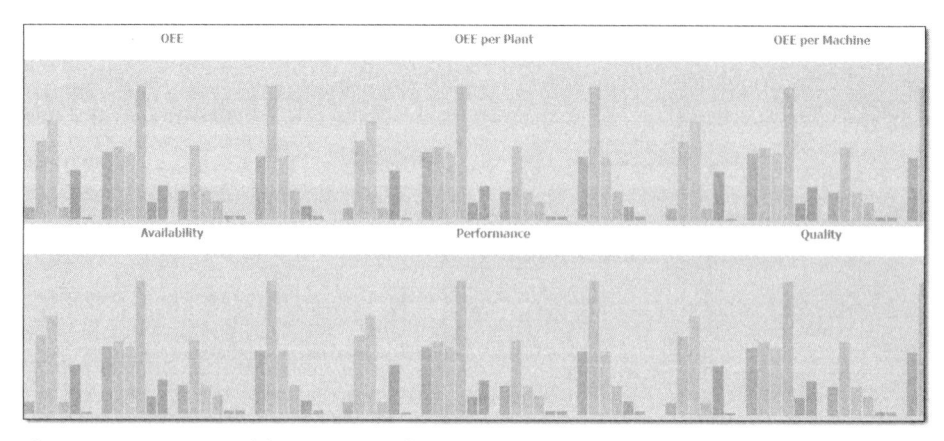

Figure 15.10 Structure of the BODY Panel

At this point, the first view for the real-time overview and the overview for today is ready. The following steps walk through how to create the exact same layout for the view per month (where you see the data per day in the current month) and the view per year (where you see the data per month for the current year). Follow these steps:

1. Copy GRID_1_HOUR.
2. Paste and rename the new GRID LAYOUT component to GRID_2_DAY.
3. Paste it again, and rename the third GRID LAYOUT component to GRID_3_MONTH (Figure 15.11).
4. Set the visible property for GRID_2_DAY and GRID_3_MONTH to FALSE. Only the first grid and the components in it are shown when the application starts up initially. The other two grids are set to VISIBLE when the user clicks on one of the buttons in the menu. The logic and script to handle this interaction are discussed in Section 15.2.5.

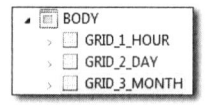

Figure 15.11 BODY Outline

You've completed the outline for the BODY panel of the application. In the next section, we'll look at creating the different buttons of the application.

Buttons

Now you'll apply formatting to the four TEXT components so that they look like buttons. These buttons are used to select and display a different view of the data for the user.

For the real-time view TEXT component, follow these steps:

1. Place a TEXT component in the BODY panel.
2. Set the text to REAL-TIME.
3. Set the TOP MARGIN to 0, the LEFT MARGIN to 21, the BOTTOM MARGIN and the RIGHT MARGIN to AUTO, the WIDTH to 120, and the HEIGHT to 25.
4. Use `mybutton` as the CSS class.

For the view for today TEXT component, follow these steps:

1. Place a TEXT component in the BODY panel.
2. Set the text to TODAY.
3. Set the TOP MARGIN to 0, the LEFT MARGIN to 151, the BOTTOM MARGIN and the RIGHT MARGIN to AUTO, the WIDTH to 120, and the HEIGHT to 25.
4. Use `mybutton_selected` as the CSS class.

For the view of this month TEXT component, follow these steps:

1. Place a TEXT component in the BODY panel.
2. Set the text to THIS MONTH.
3. Set the TOP MARGIN to 0, the LEFT MARGIN to 281, the BOTTOM MARGIN and the RIGHT MARGIN to AUTO, the WIDTH to 120, and the HEIGHT to 25.
4. Use `mybutton` as the CSS class.

For the view of this year TEXT component, follow these steps:

1. Place a TEXT component in the BODY panel.
2. Set the text to THIS YEAR.
3. Set the TOP MARGIN to 0, the LEFT MARGIN to 411, the BOTTOM MARGIN and the RIGHT MARGIN to AUTO, the WIDTH to 120, and the HEIGHT to 25.
4. Use `mybutton` as the CSS class.

The four TEXT components should now look like Figure 15.12. Notice that the second button has another color compared to the other buttons to indicate that this button is selected.

Figure 15.12 Buttons to Select a View

At this point, you're done with the layout. We can now focus on adding data to the components in the application and creating some scripts to handle user interaction.

15.2.4 Adding Data to the Views

In this section, we'll look at adding data to the views and components for GRID_1_HOUR, GRID_2_DAY, and GRID_3_MONTH.

GRID_1_HOUR

Let's focus on the first view, the view per hour for today. Follow these steps to add data to this view:

1. Add DS_1_PER_HOUR to the charts that represent OVERALL EQUIPMENT EFFECTIVENESS (OEE), AVAILABILITY, PERFORMANCE, and QUALITY. You can do this by holding down the Ctrl key and selecting the four charts in the outline of the application.
2. Add the data source in the PROPERTIES section of these components.
3. Select only the first chart where you want to display the OEE data per hour. In the properties of this chart, select DATA SELECTION, and select the OEE key figures, as shown in Figure 15.13.
4. Use the DATA SELECTION option in the remaining three charts as well, and select AVAILABILITY, PERFORMANCE, and QUALITY as key figures in their respective charts.
5. Add the data source DS_4_PLANT to the chart that will display the OEE per plant.
6. Add the data source DS_5_MACHINE to the chart that will display the OEE per machine.

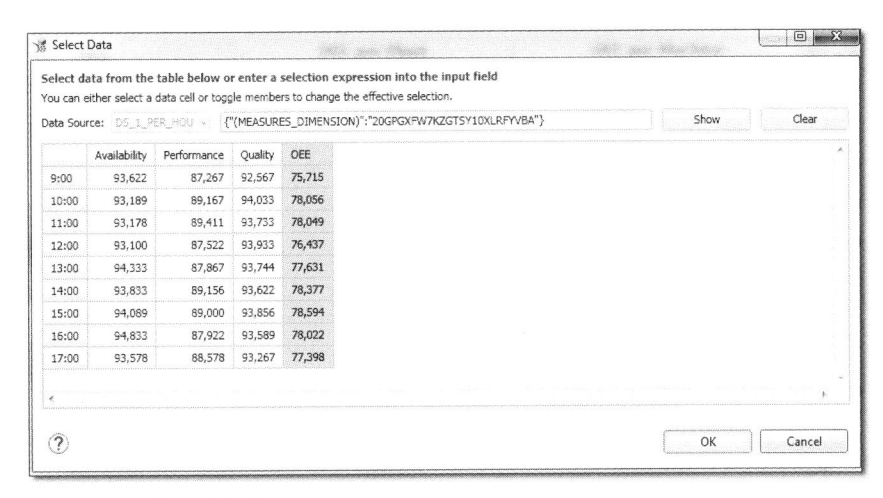

Figure 15.13 Data Selection

7. Choose the DATA SELECTION option to select the OEE key figure in both charts.
8. Change the CHART TYPE to BAR for both charts.
9. Set the SWAP AXIS to FALSE.
10. Save and run the application.

Your application should now look like Figure 15.14.

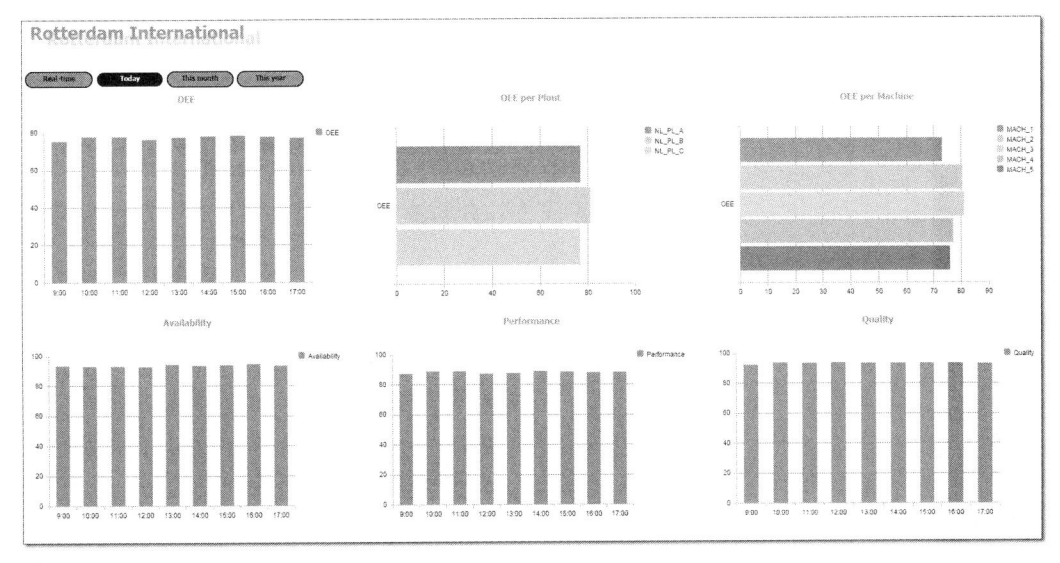

Figure 15.14 First Output

GRID_2_DAY and GRID_3_MONTH

You need to apply the same logic as you did for GRID_1_PER_HOUR, but instead of using data source DS_1_HOUR, use DS_2_PER_DAY in GRID_2_DAY, and DS_3_PER_MONTH in GRID_3_MONTH.

15.2.5 Interaction

When the application starts up, the view for today will be displayed, and the button TODAY will have another color compared to the other buttons, to indicate that it's selected.

When the user clicks either the THIS MONTH or THIS YEAR button, the appropriate view needs to be displayed, and the button should change color to indicate that it's selected. You'll use script to achieve this function.

Follow these steps:

1. Create a GLOBAL SCRIPT OBJECT by right-clicking on TECHNICAL COMPONENTS in the outline. Select CREATE CHILD, and then choose GLOBAL SCRIPT OBJECT (Figure 15.15).
2. Right-click on GLOBAL SCRIPT OBJECT, and select CREATE SCRIPT FUNCTION.
3. Name the GLOBAL SCRIPT FUNCTION, "change_views."
4. Insert two parameters in the Script Editor (Figure 15.16). The first one is called grid and is a type of GRID LAYOUT component. The second one is called button and is of type TEXT component. This last parameter must also be set to ARRAY.
5. Add the code shown in Listing 15.2 in the editor, and click OK.

```
// Hide all buttons
TEXT_8.setCSSClass("mybutton");
TEXT_9.setCSSClass("mybutton");
TEXT_10.setCSSClass("mybutton");
TEXT_11.setCSSClass("mybutton");

// Apply CSS to buttons
button.forEach(function(element, index) {
  element.setCSSClass("mybutton_selected");
});

// Hide all grids
GRID_1_HOUR.setVisible(false);
GRID_2_DAY.setVisible(false);
GRID_3_MONTH.setVisible(false);
```

```
// Make the selected view visible
grid.setVisible(true);
```

Listing 15.2 Global Script Called change_views

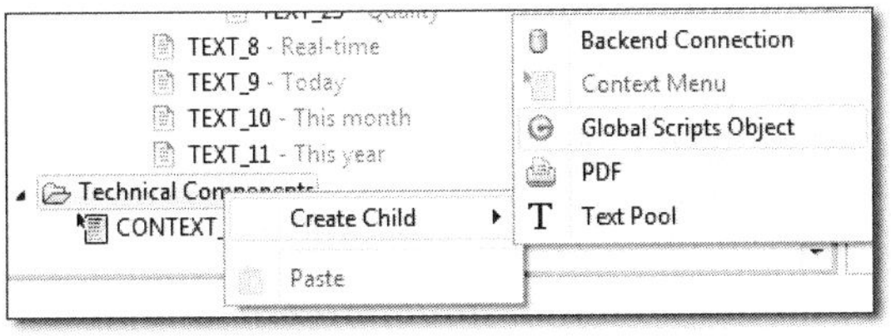

Figure 15.15 Global Script

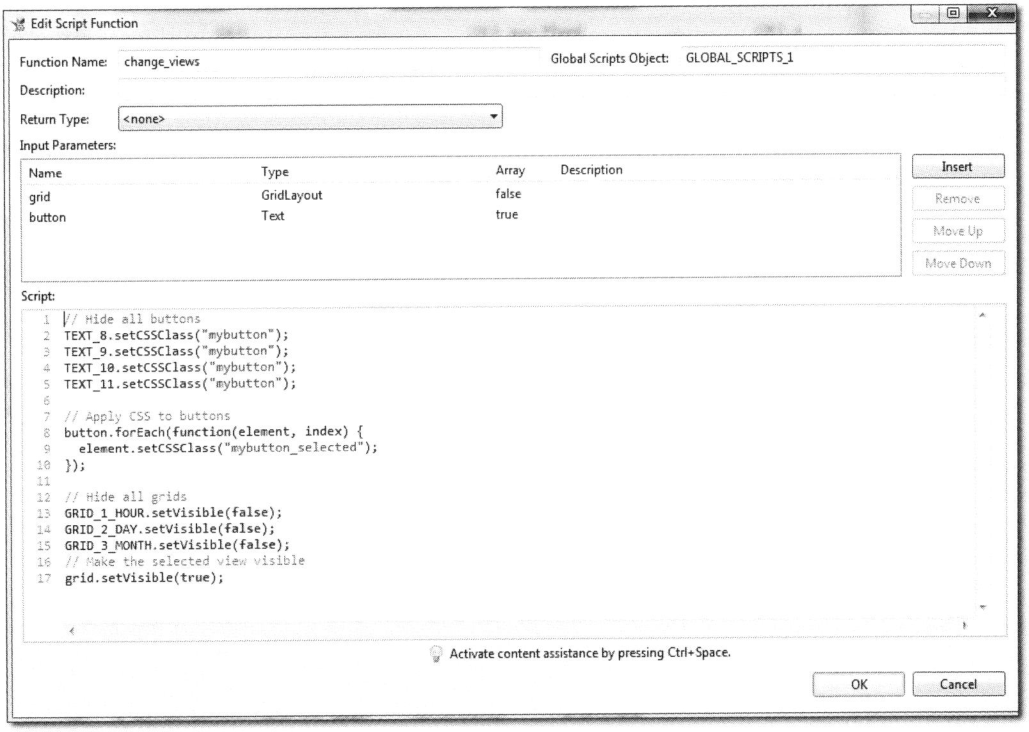

Figure 15.16 Script Editor

The code in the Script Editor sets the `mybutton` CSS class to all the buttons and then sets the `mybutton_selected` CSS class to the buttons that the user clicks on.

The same logic applies to displaying the GRID LAYOUT components. First, all of the grids are hidden, and then the correct one is displayed.

When the user clicks on TODAY, GRID_1_HOUR should be displayed, and the `button_selected` CSS class should be applied to this button. When the use clicks on REAL-TIME, the same GRID LAYOUT component should be displayed, and the `button_selected` CSS class should be applied to both this button and the TODAY button. The logic (script) that handles the changing of the views is now in place. In the next step, you'll call this script in the appropriate buttons:

1. In Design Studio, select the TEXT component for the TODAY button.
2. In the `On Click` property, add the following code to display the correct grid and apply CSS to the correct button:

    ```
    GLOBAL_SCRIPTS_1.change_views(GRID_1_HOUR, [TEXT_9]);
    ```

    GRID_1_HOUR is the GRID LAYOUT component with the view per hour, and TEXT_9 is the name of the TEXT component representing the TODAY button.

3. Select the TEXT component representing the REAL-TIME button. Apply the following code in the `On Click` event in its properties:

    ```
    GLOBAL_SCRIPTS_1.change_views(GRID_1_HOUR, [TEXT_8, TEXT_9]);
    ```

    The same grid will be made visible as with the previous button. The difference is that TEXT_8, which is the button representing REAL-TIME, will also be given the CSS class `mybutton_selected`.

4. The script for the other two TEXT components follows the same logic. For THIS MONTH, use the following script:

    ```
    GLOBAL_SCRIPTS_1.change_views(GRID_2_DAY, [TEXT_10]);
    ```

5. For the THIS YEAR button, use the following script:

    ```
    GLOBAL_SCRIPTS_1.change_views(GRID_3_MONTH, [TEXT_11]);
    ```

When the user clicks on the REAL-TIME button, the view per hour is selected, and the buttons REAL-TIME and TODAY appear in black. As you can see in Figure 15.17, data per hour are displayed on the X-axis of the chart.

When the user clicks on the THIS MONTH button, the view changes to data per day (Figure 15.18). At this point, the data isn't filtered yet to display the correct data, but we'll take care of that when we discuss the `On Startup` script of the application.

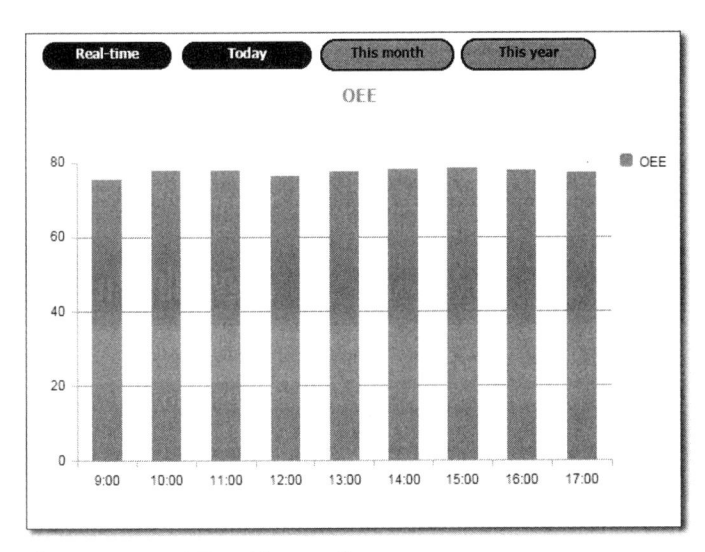

Figure 15.17 Real-Time View per Hour

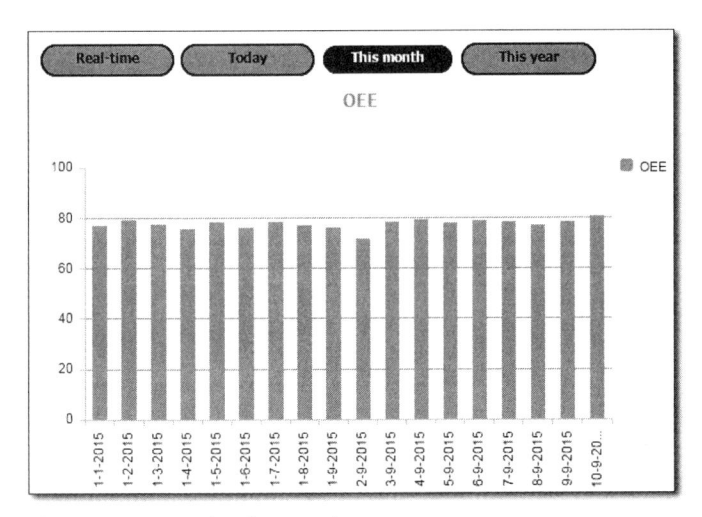

Figure 15.18 View for This Month

15.2.6 Applying Filters at Startup

This example real-time production dashboard application uses five data sources that are based on the same BEx query. Each time a user requests a certain view, the filter values in the application need to be changed.

Let's take a look at the logic:

- When the application starts up or when the view for TODAY or REAL-TIME (which also shows data for today) is selected, the data needs to be filtered to show only today's data.
- When the view for this month is requested, the data for THIS MONTH needs to be shown (per day).
- When the view for THIS YEAR is requested, a filter needs to be applied on the current year.

You'll use variables in Design Studio to store the dates based on the current date. To apply this logic, follow these steps:

1. Create three GLOBAL SCRIPT VARIABLES as shown in Figure 15.19. The first one, `var_this_day`, is used to store the current day. The second one, `var_this_month`, is used to store the current month. The last one, `var_this_year`, is used to store the current year.

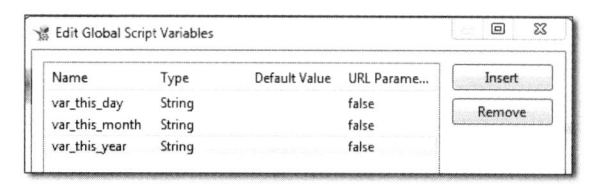

Figure 15.19 Global Script Variables

2. In the `On Startup` script, use the following code to fill the variables with a value computed from the current day, and filter the data sources with these variables:

   - First, get the current date from Design Studio and store it in a local variable called `date`:

     ```
     // Get current date in format YYYYMMDD
     var date = APPLICATION.getInfo().dateNowInternalFormat;
     ```

   - Next, cut the string that is stored in the `date` variable into smaller pieces to get the day, month, and year:

     ```
     var_this_day = Convert.subString(date, 6,8);
     var_this_month = Convert.subString(date, 4,6);
     var_this_year = Convert.subString(date, 0,4);
     ```

   After the variables are filled in, a filter is applied on all data sources using these filter values. Notice that DS_4_PLANT and DS_5_MACHINE are initially also filtered on the current day when the application starts up (Listing 15.3). Because you also use these data sources in the other views, you need the change the filter when another view is selected.

```
// Filter DS_1, DS_4 and DS_5 based on the current day
DS_1_PER_HOUR.setFilter("0CALDAY", var_this_day);
DS_4_PLANT.setFilter("0CALDAY", var_this_day);
DS_5_MACHINE.setFilter("0CALDAY", var_this_day);

// Filter DS_2 based on the current month
DS_2_PER_DAY.setFilter("0CALMONTH", var_this_year+var_this_month);

// Filter DS_3 based on the current year
DS_3_PER_MONTH.setFilter("0CALYEAR", var_this_year);
```

Listing 15.3 On Startup Script

Now that the On Startup script is in place, let's take care of the filtering for this month's view and this year's view for data source DS_4_PLANT and DS_5_MACHINE. Remember that these data sources are initially filtered on the current day because when the application starts, they need to provide data for the current day by default (the application starts up on today's view).

When you change the view to THIS MONTH, the filter on this day needs to be removed before you can apply a filter on this month; otherwise, you will still get data for only today. The same is true when you apply a filter for this whole year. To achieve this, follow these steps:

1. Select the THIS MONTH button, and add the lines of code from Listing 15.4 in the Script Editor.

    ```
    DS_4_PLANT.clearAllFilters();
    DS_5_MACHINE.clearAllFilters();

    DS_4_PLANT.setFilter("0CALMONTH", var_this_month);
    DS_5_MACHINE.setFilter("0CALMONTH", var_this_month);
    ```

    Listing 15.4 This Month Button

2. Select the THIS YEAR button, and add the lines of code in Listing 15.5 in the Script Editor.

    ```
    DS_4_PLANT.clearAllFilters();
    DS_5_MACHINE.clearAllFilters();
    ```

```
DS_4_PLANT.setFilter("0CALYEAR", var_this_year);
DS_5_MACHINE.setFilter("0CALYEAR", var_this_year);
```
Listing 15.5 This Year Button

3. In the On Click script in both the REAL-TIME and TODAY buttons, add the code in Listing 15.6 to filter the data with the current day.

```
DS_4_PLANT.clearAllFilters();
DS_5_MACHINE.clearAllFilters();

DS_4_PLANT.setFilter("0CALDAY", var_this_day);
DS_5_MACHINE.setFilter("0CALDAY", var_this_day);
```
Listing 15.6 Real-Time and Today

In Figure 15.20, you can see the effect via a chart that shows data only for the days in the current month, which in this case is September.

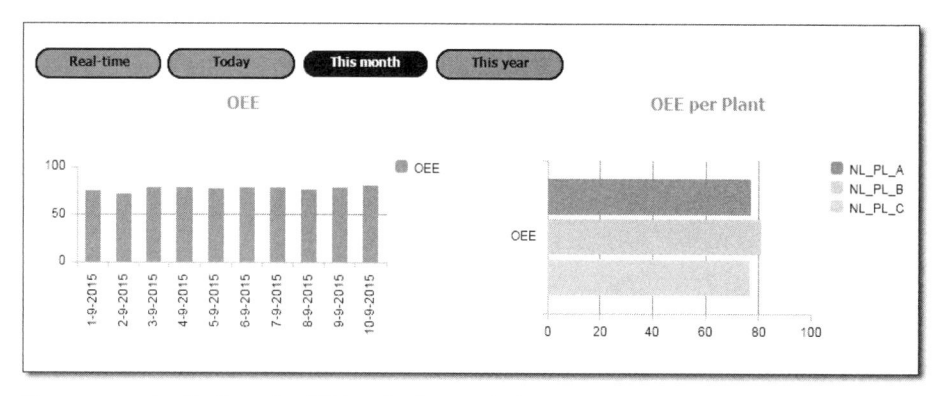

Figure 15.20 Application after Editing the Startup Script

> **Filtering**
>
> For the purpose of this example, we used the setFilter option when the application starts up to apply the correct filters. This works fine for this demo with little data, but for performance reasons, we recommend using BEx variables to set up the data sources initially.

15.2.7 Timer Component

Finally, let's take a look at the TIMER component. The idea is that when the user clicks on the REAL-TIME button, the TIMER component is activated. The TIMER component can be set to a specific amount of time, and when that time elapses, a specific action can be triggered. For this application, you'll set the TIMER to 15 minutes, and when the time passes, the data sources that display data for today will reload. As long as the TIMER component is activated, it will continue to count down and execute the reloading script that you'll define next.

Follow these steps:

1. Using the context menu in the OUTLINE view on the TECHNICAL COMPONENTS, select CREATE CHILD, and then select TIMER. Enter the default name "TIMER_1".

2. In the PROPERTIES screen, set the INTERVAL IN MILLISECONDS to 900000 (15 minutes), as shown in Figure 15.21.

3. In the `On Timer` event property, use the following code to reload the data sources when the timer expires:

   ```
   DS_1_PER_HOUR.reloadData();
   DS_4_PLANT.reloadData();
   DS_5_MACHINE.reloadData();
   ```

4. Add the following line of code in the `On Click` event property of the REAL-TIME button to activate the TIMER:

   ```
   TIMER_1.start();
   ```

5. Add the following line of code in the `On Click` property of the other three buttons:

   ```
   TIMER_1.stop();
   ```

Property	Value
General	
Name	TIMER_1
Type	Timer
Vendor	SAP SE
Display	
Interval in Milliseconds	900000
Events	
On Timer	DS_1_PER_HOUR.reloadData();DS_4_PLANT.reloadData();DS_5_MACHINE.reloadData();

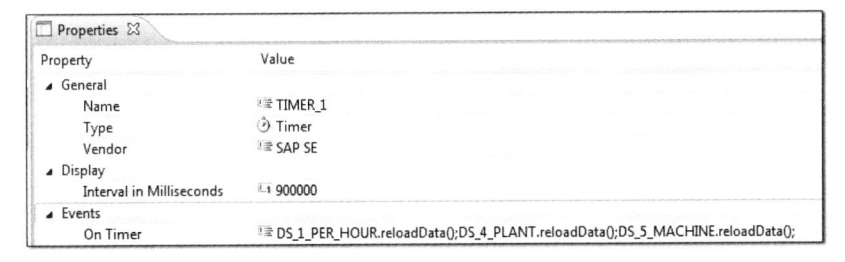

Figure 15.21 Timer Component Properties

You've successfully completed the steps to create a real-time production dashboard! Of course, there is much more you can tweak in this dashboard. For instance, you can play around with the settings of the TIMER component. If your data warehouse (data source) allows this, you can use a more frequent reload schema to increase the real-time frequency of the dashboard.

15.3 Summary

In this chapter, we walked through the steps involved in designing and building a (pseudo) real-time production dashboard. You put into practice the various topics covered in previous chapters, such as applying formatting using CSS and using basic and complex scripts to handle user interaction.

In the next chapter, we'll continue with our expanded use cases by showing you how to set up a sales dashboard.

Expanding on the use case scenario described in Chapter 3 for a sales dashboard application, this chapter describes the techniques used to build the dashboard.

16   Building a Sales Dashboard Application

In Chapter 3, we introduced you to a sales dashboard for the solar installation company, Solar Install Company. In this chapter, we'll take a closer look at the nuts and bolts of the application. In Section 16.1, we'll discuss the techniques for building the main sales dashboard, and in Section 16.2, we'll walk through the process of building the actual sales dashboard.

> **Download Available**
>
> The application is available for download at *www.sap-press.com/3951* if you want to have a closer look.

16.1   Application Overview

In our sales dashboard application, there are two main screens: the main page (Figure 16.1) and the detail page (Figure 16.2). Additionally, there is an option on the detail screen to open a quote creation screen and create a document. The fixed structure of the sales dashboard application is the header, footer, and a right-hand side menu that is visible at all times. The main page dashboard content is placed on the middle left side. When you drill down, this content is replaced by the drilldown report.

16 | Building a Sales Dashboard Application

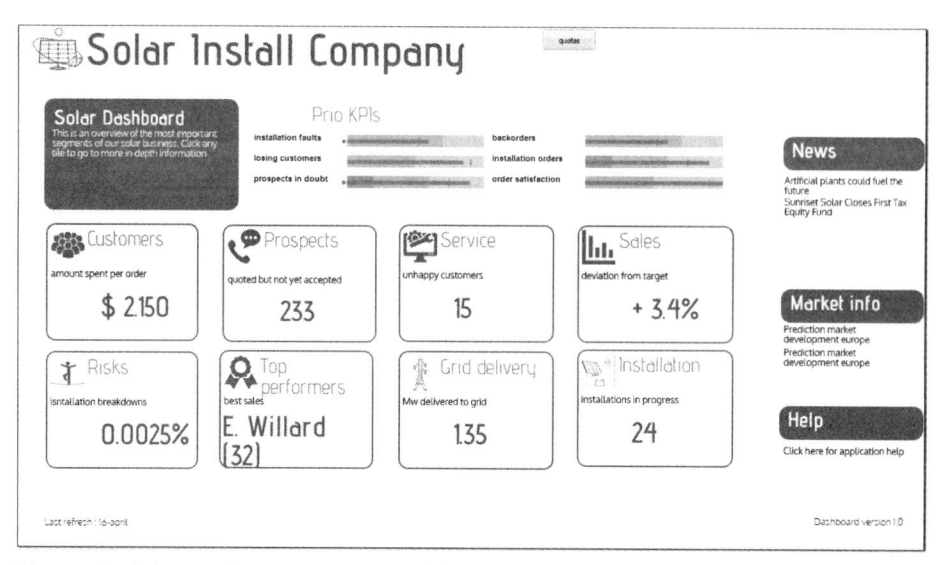

Figure 16.1 Solar Install Company Main Dashboard

As previously discussed in Chapter 3, the main screen is a placeholder for the main key performance indicators (KPIs). At the top of the page in Figure 16.1, you see the PRIO KPIs, which show KPIs that need extra attention. Furthermore, you see eight themes in the middle of the main page (CUSTOMERS, PROSPECTS, SERVICE, SALES, RISKS, TOP PERFORMERS, GRID DELIVERY, and INSTALLATIONS), each in their own panel showing an aspect of the company. In each panel, you see one KPI that is deemed to be the most interesting KPI for that aspect.

The detail screen opens when you click one of the panels (Figure 16.2). Here, you'll find more in depth information about a single aspect of the company. On this screen, you see a number of KPIs, a word cloud graph to analyze customer feedback, and two trend graphs. Note that the header and the right-hand side menu are still the same as shown on the main screen (refer to Figure 16.1).

A third screen is available to create a quote for customers (Figure 16.3). On the QUOTE DELIVERY screen, you can select products on the left-hand side and fill in the name of the customer and an expire date.

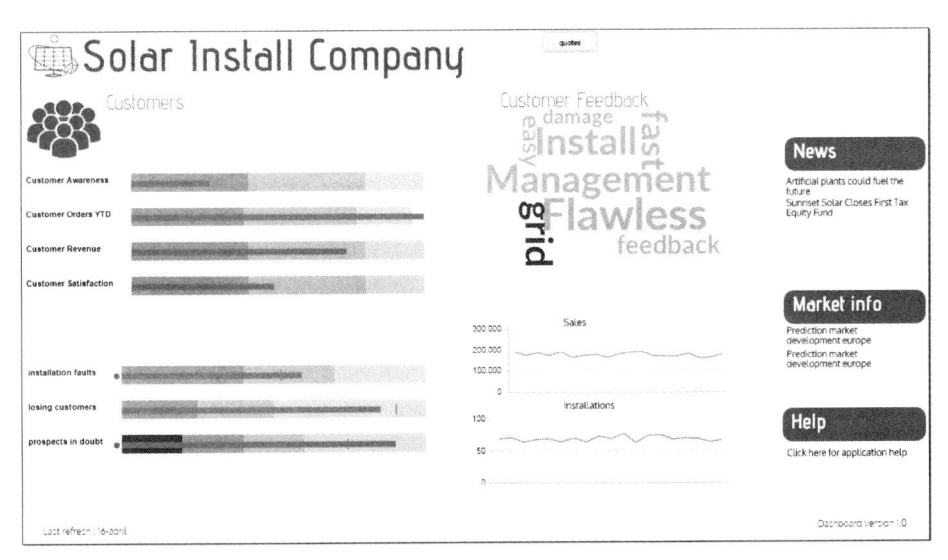

Figure 16.2 Customer Detail Screen

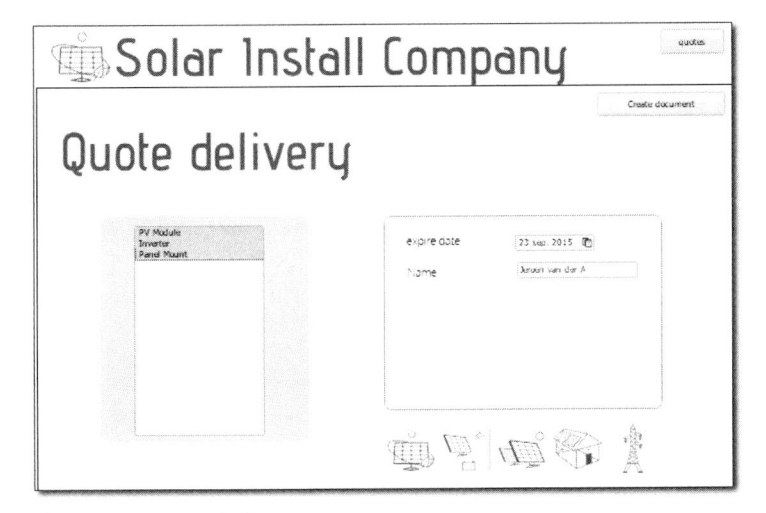

Figure 16.3 Quote Delivery

The information entered here is then used to create a sales quote document that can be printed or sent to a potential customer (Figure 16.4).

Figure 16.4 Quote Document

Now that you've seen what the application should look like, next we'll explain the steps to achieve this.

16.2 Building the Application

Now you'll begin the steps necessary to build each page of the application, starting with the main page you saw earlier in Figure 16.1.

16.2.1 Main Page

In this section, you'll learn how to build the main page of the sales dashboard. The sales dashboard is built for a laptop screen. If the screen resolution is bigger than the dimensions of the dashboard, the outer margins will be increased on all sides to keep the dashboard aligned to the middle of the screen. To keep the main dashboard content in the middle, you'll use a GRID component with three rows and three columns (Figure 16.5).

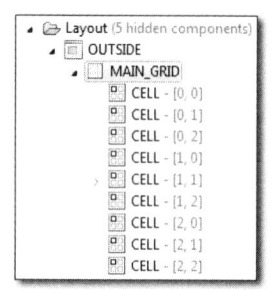

Figure 16.5 Main Grid

In the GRID component, the rows and columns can be set to a relative width so you have control over the size of each cell in relation to the others. To use the GRID component, follow these steps:

1. Drag the main GRID component onto the canvas.
2. Next, set the properties of the component:
   - Set the HEIGHT and WIDTH property to 0.
   - Set the LEFT MARGIN, RIGHT MARGIN, TOP MARGIN, and BOTTOM MARGIN to 0.
   - Set the NUMBER OF ROWS to 3.
   - Set the NUMBER OF COLUMNS to 3.
3. Click on the NUMBER OF ROWS to see each row. Set the first row number to 1, the second to 8, and the third to 1.
4. Click on the NUMBER OF COLUMNS to see each column. Set the first column number to 1, the second to 8, and the third to 1.

With these steps, you've set the properties of the rows and columns in such a way that there is 10% room on the top, bottom, left, and right of the screen (Figure 16.6).

In Figure 16.6, the first and third rows/columns have a value of 1, and the middle row/column has a value of 8. The size of the rows and columns are calculated by using the relative size of the numbers you entered in relation to the total sum. The bottom and top have a value of 1, and the total sum of all rows is 10. The top and bottom row will each get 1/10th of the available vertical room.

Number of Rows	3
Row Height	1
Row Height	8
Row Height	1
Number of Columns	3
Column Width	1
Column Width	8
Column Width	1

Figure 16.6 Main Grid Properties

You can change these properties to any value to order the dashboard to your own requirements. The main dashboard is inserted in CELL 1,1. This is the middle cell in the second row. In the main dashboard, we use panels to structure the layout. In the structure, the header, footer, right-hand menu, and main content are maintained on the same level (Figure 16.7). To structure the main dashboard layout, follow these steps:

1. Insert a panel into Cell 1,1 of the Grid component.
2. Now set the properties of the component:
   - Set the Height and Width of the panel to Auto.
   - Set the margins of the panel to 0.
   - Name the panel "BACKGROUND."
3. After you've added the properties of your BACKGROUND panel, add the two Panel components into the BACKGROUND panel.
4. Set the properties of these two new Panel components:
   - Set the Height and Width of the panels to Auto.
   - Set the Top Margin to 75, the Bottom Margin to 50, the Left Margin to 0, and the Right Margin to 0.
   - Name the first panel "MAIN_DASHBOARD."
   - Name the second panel "SEGMENT_INDEPTH."
   - Name the third panel "ORDERFORM."
5. Add another Panel component into the BACKGROUND panel.
6. Set the properties of the new Panel component:
   - Set the Height to 75 and Width to Auto.
   - Set the Top Margin to 0, the Bottom Margin to Auto, the Left Margin to 0, and the Right Margin to 0.
   - Name the panel "HEADER."
7. Add another Panel component into the BACKGROUND panel.
8. Set the properties of the new Panel component:
   - Set the Height to 50 and Width to Auto.
   - Set the Top Margin to Auto, the Bottom Margin to 0, the Left Margin to 0, and the Right Margin to 0.
   - Name the panel "FOOTER."
9. Right-click on the technical components in the Outline view. Select Create Child • Add a PDF Component.

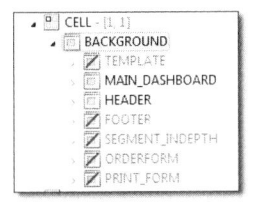

Figure 16.7 Main Dashboard Layout

In this structure, you also see the in-depth dashboard, the order form, and the print form. As users navigate through the application, you hide and show panels based on users' navigational choices.

Now you'll add 10 elements to the MAIN_DASHBOARD PANEL component. Follow these steps:

1. In the first panel, change the following properties:
    - Set the name to "MAIN_TILE."
    - Set the CSS CLASS to INNERPANEL.
    - Set the margins: TOP MARGIN: 37; BOTTOM MARGIN: AUTO; RIGHT MARGIN: 1037; and LEFT MARGIN: 38.
    - Set the HEIGHT to 158 and the WIDTH to AUTO.

2. Add two TEXT components to the MAIN_TITLE panel. For the first TEXT component, enter the following:
    - NAME: "MAIN_TILE_HEADER"
    - CSS CLASS: "innertitle2"
    - TEXT: "Solar Dashboard"

    For the second TEXT component, enter the following:
    - NAME: "MAIN_TILE_TEXT"
    - CSS CLASS: "textinverse"
    - TEXT: "This is an overview of the most important segments of our solar business. Click any tile to go to more in depth information."

3. For the last eight components, name them TILE_1 through TILE_8.

4. In each of these eight TILE components, you'll insert one PANEL component and three additional TEXT components. The following are the properties that need to be entered for the PANEL component in each of the eight TILE components:

- Top Margin and Left Margin: 5
- Bottom Margin and Right Margin: Auto
- Height and Width: 50
- Name: Outer Panel name + ICON (also inside the TILE_1 panel, the name is TILE_1_NUMBER).

5. Provide the properties for the three Text components. Enter the following properties for the first Text component:
   - Top Margin: 5
   - Bottom Margin: Auto
   - Left Margin: 60
   - Right Margin: 21
   - Width: Auto
   - CSS Class: title3
   - Name: Outer Panel name + Header (also inside the TILE_1 panel, the name is TILE_1_HEADER)

6. Enter the following properties for the second Text component:
   - Top Margin: 64
   - Bottom Margin: Auto
   - Left Margin: 4
   - Right Margin: 8
   - Width: Auto
   - Height: 32
   - CSS Class: textstrong
   - Name: Outer Panel name + KPI (also inside the TILE_1 panel, the name is TILE_1_KPI).

7. Enter the following properties for the third Text component:
   - Top Margin: 98
   - Bottom Margin: Auto
   - Left Margin: 80
   - Right Margin: 14

- HEIGHT: 63
- WIDTH: AUTO
- CSS CLASS: title2
- NAME: OUTER PANEL name + NUMBER (also inside the TILE_1 panel, the name is TILE_1_ NUMBER)

8. For each of the eight TILE panels, set the HEIGHT to 167 and the WIDTH to 229.
9. Set up the eight tiles for the different segments. First, set the margins of the PANEL component. Then, set the CSS CLASS of the PANEL component that is inside the current PANEL component:
   - Set the Panel TILE_1 margins to:
     - TOP MARGIN: 219
     - LEFT MARGIN: 41
     - BOTTOM MARGIN: AUTO
     - RIGHT MARGIN: AUTO

   For the inner PANEL component located in Panel TILE_1, set the CSS CLASS to CUSTOMERS.

10. Set the Panel TILE_2 margins to:
    - TOP MARGIN: 219
    - LEFT MARGIN: 310
    - BOTTOM MARGIN: AUTO
    - RIGHT MARGIN: AUTO

    For the inner PANEL component located in Panel TILE_2, set the CSS CLASS to PROSPECTS.

11. Set the Panel TILE_3 margins to:
    - TOP MARGIN: 219
    - LEFT MARGIN: 576
    - BOTTOM MARGIN: AUTO
    - RIGHT MARGIN: AUTO

    For the inner PANEL component located in Panel TILE_3, set the CSS CLASS to SERVICE.

12. Set the Panel TILE_4 margins to:
    - TOP MARGIN: 219
    - LEFT MARGIN: 845
    - BOTTOM MARGIN: AUTO
    - RIGHT MARGIN: AUTO

    For the inner PANEL component located in Panel TILE_4, set the CSS CLASS to SALESNUMBERS.

13. Set the Panel TILE_5 margins to:
    - TOP MARGIN: 406
    - LEFT MARGIN: 41
    - BOTTOM MARGIN: AUTO
    - RIGHT MARGIN: AUTO

    For the inner PANEL component located in Panel TILE_5, set the CSS CLASS to RISK.

14. Set the Panel TILE_6 margins to:
    - TOP MARGIN: 406
    - LEFT MARGIN: 310
    - BOTTOM MARGIN: AUTO
    - RIGHT MARGIN: AUTO

    For the inner PANEL component located in Panel TILE_6, set the CSS CLASS to MEDAL.

15. Set the Panel TILE_7 margins to:
    - TOP MARGIN: 406
    - LEFT MARGIN: 576
    - BOTTOM MARGIN: AUTO
    - RIGHT MARGIN: AUTO

    For the inner PANEL component located in Panel TILE_7, set the CSS CLASS to POWERGRID.

16. Set the Panel TILE_8 margins to:
    - TOP MARGIN: 406
    - LEFT MARGIN: 845
    - BOTTOM MARGIN: AUTO
    - RIGHT MARGIN: AUTO

    For the inner PANEL component located in Panel TILE_8, set the CSS CLASS to CURRENTSETUP.

17. Each panel tile also contains three TEXT components. These TEXT components will contain the header information, the KPI value, and the description. Change the texts in these components to mimic the texts in our example, or replace them with your own texts.

18. Add the following code to TILE_1:

    ```
    MAIN_DASHBOARD.setVisible(false);
    SEGMENT_INDEPTH.setVisible(true);
    ```

If you decide to build more in-depth modules for the other panels, you can continue using either of the following two approaches:

- Build a separate panel for each segment.
- Build one panel and use scripting to populate it based on the chosen tile.

We prefer the second option because you have fewer screens to maintain. If, for example, you want to add a component to the in-depth dashboard, the first approach requires you to add a component for each panel you've created. The second approach only requires one additional component.

So far, you've provided the necessary components for the main dashboard. In the next few subsections, we'll look at the additional content you need to configure.

Bullet Graphs

On top of the main content, you can use BULLET GRAPH components (Figure 16.8) to highlight the most important KPIs. The BULLET GRAPH component is an SDK component, which we discussed in Chapter 14. If you didn't build it, don't worry—you can use the download from the SCN community where we added the BULLET GRAPH component and use that one instead.

16 | Building a Sales Dashboard Application

> **SCN Community**
>
> In the SCN community, you can download a large number of SDK components free that are maintained by volunteers. Remember, however, that if you use them for production, you can't rely on them for maintenance because it's provided on a voluntary basis. Use the following link to access these SDK components:
>
> http://scn.sap.com/community/businessobjects-design-studio/blog/2014/12/10/scn-design-studio-sdk-development-community

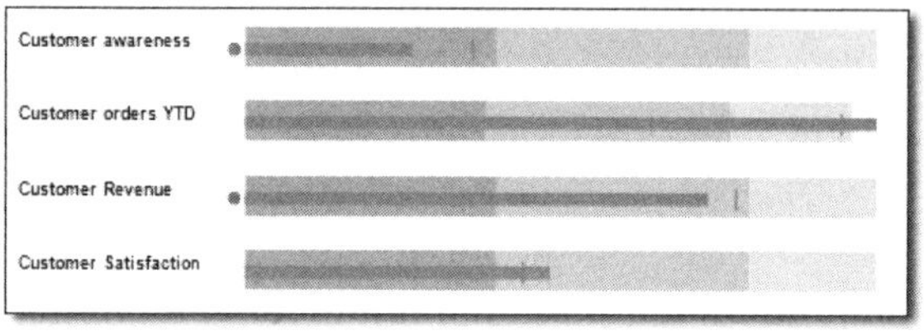

Figure 16.8 Bullet Graphs

For the source data of the BULLET GRAPH component, we used an SDK extension from the SCN community to create a manually inputted data source. The SDK extension contains custom data source components that allow us to work with manual entries. This allows us to include some data that can be viewed in the download of the application that we've provided (go to *www.sap-press.com/3951* to download) because it doesn't require a backend system that is available to you.

You can add the data source component to the technical components. When you select the newly added data source component, you can go to the additional properties. Under the ADDITIONAL PROPERTIES tab, you can add the data as shown in Figure 16.9.

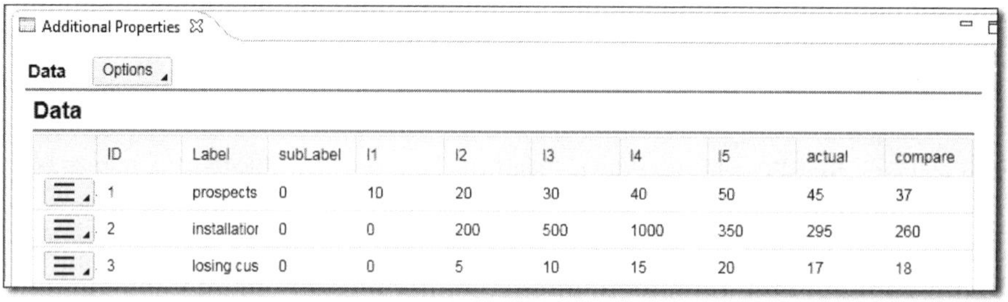

ID	Label	subLabel	I1	I2	I3	I4	I5	actual	compare
1	prospects	0	10	20	30	40	50	45	37
2	installation	0	0	200	500	1000	350	295	260
3	losing cus	0	0	5	10	15	20	17	18

Figure 16.9 Manually Entered Records in a Data Source

Follow these steps to add your own data sources:

1. Go to the OUTLINE panel, and right-click on the subsection DATASOURCES.
2. Select the ADD CUSTOM DATA SOURCE button, and then select BRING YOUR OWN DATA.
3. Name the data source "DS_PRIO_ONE."
4. Set the NUMBER OF DIMENSIONS to 2.
5. Set the MEASURES IN ROWS property to FALSE.
6. Set the SORTING to ALPHANUMERIC ASCENDING.
7. Go to the ADDITIONAL PROPERTIES tab.
8. Select the OPTIONS button.
9. Switch to the CSV view.
10. Add the following data:

    ```
    ID,Label,subLabel,l1,l2,l3,l4,l5,actual,compare
    1,prospects in doubt,0,10,20,30,40,50,45,37
    2,installation faults,0,0,200,500,1000,350,295,260
    3,losing customers,0,0,5,10,15,20,17,18
    ```

Follow the same steps for the second data source, in addition to the following:

1. Name this data source "DS_PRIO_TWO".
2. Add the following data:

    ```
    ID,Label,subLabel,l1,l2,l3,l4,l5,actual,compare
    1,installation orders,0,10,20,30,40,50,45,37
    2,backorders,0,0,200,500,1000,350,300,260
    3,order satisfaction,0,0,5,10,15,20,20,18
    ```

Now that you've set up the data sources, you can add and configure the BULLET GRAPHS because you now have data source to work with.

In the BULLET GRAPH component, you set the properties to use the data you set up in the data source (Figure 16.10). You can see that for this example, we used column l1 to populate the FIRST THRESHOLD COLUMN property, column l3 to populate the THIRD THRESHOLD COLUMN property, and column l5 for the FIFTH THRESHOLD COLUMN property. These column names correspond to the column names we added to the data sources.

16 | Building a Sales Dashboard Application

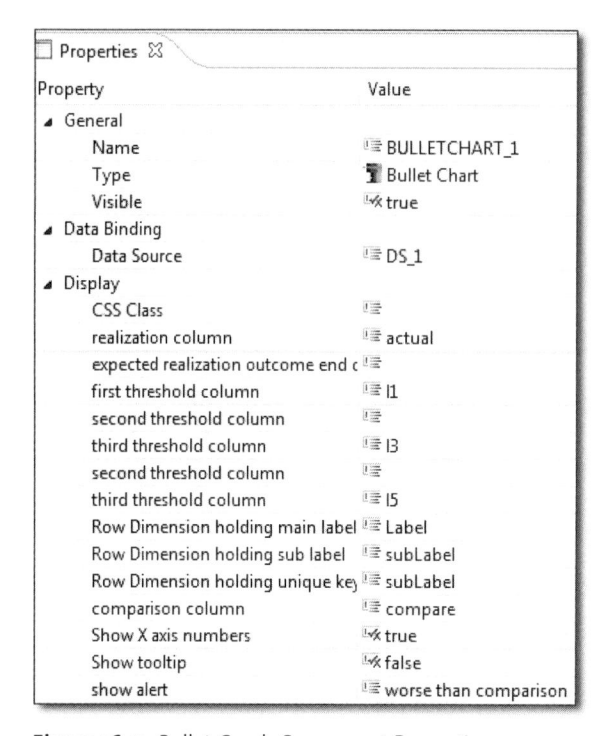

Property	Value
General	
Name	BULLETCHART_1
Type	Bullet Chart
Visible	true
Data Binding	
Data Source	DS_1
Display	
CSS Class	
realization column	actual
expected realization outcome end c	
first threshold column	l1
second threshold column	
third threshold column	l3
second threshold column	
third threshold column	l5
Row Dimension holding main label	Label
Row Dimension holding sub label	subLabel
Row Dimension holding unique key	subLabel
comparison column	compare
Show X axis numbers	true
Show tooltip	false
show alert	worse than comparison

Figure 16.10 Bullet Graph Component Properties

In the main page (refer to Figure 16.1), you see two columns of BULLET GRAPHS. The second column is actually a second BULLET CHART component. In the second component, the property REALIZATION HIGHER THAN TARGET IS BETTER is set to TRUE so alerts will show when the value in the REALIZATION COLUMN is higher. In the first BULLET GRAPH, a lower value in the REALIZATION COLUMN is better.

Follow these steps:

1. Drag two BULLET GRAPH components onto the canvas.

2. Rename the first BULLET GRAPH "BULLETCHART_PRIO_ONE" and the second BULLET GRAPH "BULLETCHART_PRIO_TWO."

After you've named the two BULLET GRAPH components, follow these steps that are common for both of the BULLET GRAPH components:

1. Set the data source to "DS_PRIO_TWO."

2. Enter the properties shown in Figure 16.10.

3. Set SHOW REALIZATION VALUE to FALSE.
4. Set MAXIMUM HEIGHT TO OF SINGLE GRAPH to 20.
5. Set MINIMUM HEIGHT OF SINGLE GRAPH to 20.
6. Set NUMBER OF TICKS to 4.
7. Set HORIZONTAL MARGIN BETWEEN GRAPHS to 0.
8. Set NUMBER OF COLUMNS to 1.
9. Set VERTICAL MARGIN BETWEEN GRAPHS to 10.
10. Set the BULLET MARGINS to 0 (TOP, BOTTOM, LEFT, and RIGHT).
11. Set BOTTOM MARGIN and RIGHT MARGIN to AUTO.
12. Set the TOP MARGIN to 88.

Now that you've gone through the steps that are common for both of the components, you need to define the component-specific properties that differ between the two:

- For BULLETCHART_PRIOR_ONE, set the REALIZATION HIGHER THAN TARGET IS BETTER to TRUE, and set the LEFT MARGIN to 353.
- For BULLETCHART_PRIO_TWO, set the REALIZATION HIGHER THAN TARGET IS BETTER to FALSE, and the LEFT MARGIN to 712.

Tiles

The application also contains TILE components (Figure 16.11). TILES are made up of five components: two PANEL components and three TEXT components (Figure 16.12).

Figure 16.11 Single Tile

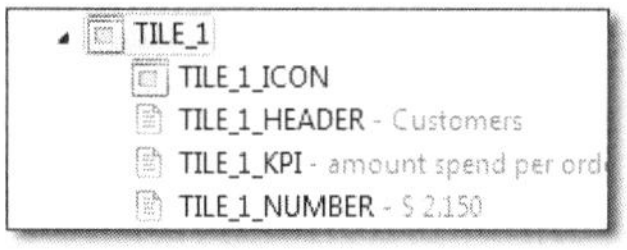

Figure 16.12 Tile Components

The next step to increase the flexibility of the application is to make the title, KPI text, and the customer icon flexible in script. To get the texts for the title, KPI, and so on, first filter a data source on the segment, and subsequently use the dimension values to find the values to populate those components. The same technique is used for cascading filters. Follow these steps:

1. Filter a data source on the segment you want to access: `DS_1.setFilter("SEGMENT", "001");`.

2. You can access different dimensions to retrieve the values and use them to set the component properties. Because the returned values are arrays, you need to use `forEach` statements to get the values (Listing 16.1).

```
var kpi_text = "";
var segment_title = "";
var segment_icon = "";

var KPI_NAME = DS_1.getMembers("Label", 1);
var SEGMENT_TITLE = DS_1.getMembers("Label", 1);
var SEGMENT_ICON = DS_1.getMembers("Label", 1);

KPI_NAME.forEach(function(element, index) {kpi_text =
 element.text;});
SEGMENT_TITLE.forEach(function(element, index) {segment_title =
 element.text;});
SEGMENT_ICON.forEach(function(element, index) {segment_icon =
 element.externalKey;});

TILE_1_ICON.setCSSClass(segment_icon);
TILE_1_KPI.setText(kpi_text);
TILE_1_HEADER.setText(kpi_text);
```

Listing 16.1 Flexible Alternative to Link from the Main Screen to the Detail Screen

Right Side Menu

The right side menu is a collection of texts that link to other resources. There are three headers to categorize those resources into News, Market info, and Help (Figure 16.13).

Figure 16.13 Right Side Menu

Let's set up the structure and the texts and then discuss the possibilities. Follow these steps:

1. Add a PANEL component to the PANEL component MAIN_DASHBOARD.
2. Name the new PANEL component "MAIN_RIGHTHAND_PANEL."
3. For the MAIN_RIGHTHAND_PANEL, enter the following properties:
   - HEIGHT: AUTO
   - WIDTH: 222
   - Set the TOP, BOTTOM, and RIGHT margins to 0 and the LEFT MARGIN to AUTO.
4. Add three PANEL components to MAIN_RIGHTHAND_PANEL.
   - Name the first PANEL component PNL_NEWS, the second PANEL component PNL_MARKET, and the third PANEL component PNL_HELP.
   - Set the CSS CLASS for all three to INNER PANEL.
   - Add a TEXT component to all three PANEL components. Set the margins of the TEXT component as TOP MARGIN 3, LEFT MARGIN 10, BOTTOM MARGIN AUTO, and RIGHT MARGIN AUTO. Set the WIDTH and HEIGHT to 145 and 30, respectively. Name the TEXT components "TXT_NEWS", "TXT_MARKET", and "TXT_HELP."
   - Insert the texts NEWS, MARKET INFO, and HELP.

5. Insert five Text components into MAIN_RIGHTHAND_PANEL. Set the margins for the five text components to the following:
   - Left Margin: 10
   - Right Margin: 11
   - Width: Auto
   - Height: 32
6. Name the first two Text components "NEWS_1" and "NEWS_2."
7. Set the Top Margin for NEWS_1 to 145. Set the Top Margin for NEWS_2 to 176.
8. Name the next two Text components to "MARKET_1" and "MARKET_2."
9. Set the Top Margin for MARKET_1 to 362. Set the Top Margin for MARKET_2 to 396.
10. Name the final Text component to HELP_1, and set the Top Margin to 539.
11. Set the script `On Click` event to `APPLICATION.openNewWindow("www.google.com");`.
12. Set the texts for all the items.

If you find that there are too many news items, and you have a data source with links at your disposal, you can replace the individual Text components with List Box components. You can then populate them based on the dimension values in your data source:

```
LISTBOX_1.setItems(DS_HELP_TEXTS.getMembers(TEXTS, 8));
DROPDOWN_1.addItem("xx", " ");
DROPDOWN_1.setSelectedValue("xx");
```

As you can see, we added an empty line and made it the selected item. This ensures that all the real texts will react when you click them. The List Box component `OnChange` event only works when you actually change the selection to another value.

CSS Classes

You can edit the layout of your application, including the icons, via CSS classes. In the CSS file, we defined a number of classes, and within the application, we tried to do as much as possible using only the classes. In the application itself, there is a Template panel (Figure 16.14) that holds examples of all available classes. Although it's not technically necessary to have a template in place, it makes it a lot easier to find the right font or picture when you have an example at your disposal.

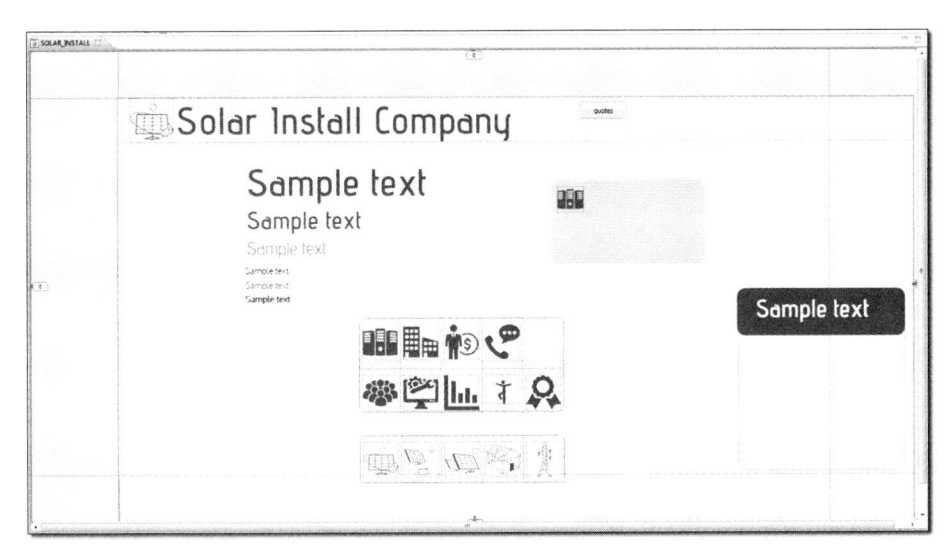

Figure 16.14 Template Page

In the CSS file, you'll find the layout details on the classes. First, you need to read the font files, so the correct font is always displayed, regardless of the component it's shown on. In CSS, you can define the location of the font files, as shown in Listing 16.2.

```
@font-face {font-family: adventprosemibold;
 src: url(advent-pro.semibold.ttf);
}
@font-face {font-family: adventprolight;
 src: url(advent-pro.light.ttf);
}
@font-face { font-family: oxygenlight;
 src: url(Oxygen-Light.ttf);
}
```
Listing 16.2 CSS Loading Fonts

The browser, which is rendering the application, will have the correct fonts to display, independent of the client computer that runs the application.

The next step is to use the fonts for a number of classes that can be reused. In Listing 16.3, we use a number of different classes to define the fonts.

```
.title1 {font-family: adventprosemibold, sans-serif; font-
size: 66px; color: #107896;line-height: 1;}
.title2 {font-family: adventprosemibold, sans-serif; font-
size: 42px; color: #107896; line-height: 1;}
.title3 {font-family: adventprolight, sans-serif; font-
size: 30px; color: #107896; line-height: 1;}
```
Listing 16.3 CSS Classes Defined for the Application

The names `title1`, `title2`, and `title3` are easy enough to remember. A designer will automatically assign them without having to reference documentation for the correct naming.

Notice that if for some reason the `adventpro` font family isn't working, we fall back to a standard `sans-serif` font. If a font isn't available on a client computer, you still have some control over how the application will look because you have something to fall back to.

Free Fonts

The adventpro font is free to use via the SIL Open Font License (OFL). The link can be found at *www.google.com/fonts/specimen/Advent+Pro#charset*.

The next step in defining the CSS classes is to define all the icons. We use CSS classes to get a background picture into the PANEL (Listing 16.4).

```
.logo {background:url('icons/logo.svg') no-repeat left top;}
.server {background:url('icons/servers1.svg') no-repeat left top;}
.building {background:url('icons/urban7.svg') no-repeat left top;}
.financial {background:url('icons/financial.svg') no-repeat left top;}
.financial2 {background:url('icons/financial2.svg') no-
repeat left top;}
```
Listing 16.4 CSS Classes to Set Up Icons

As shown in Listing 16.4, there is a background URL pointing to the image file for each CSS class. These files are Scalable Vector Graphics (SVG) files, which means that they aren't pictures, but rather a set of instructions on how to draw a picture.

The advantage is that the image will resize nicely when you change the size of the panel (Figure 16.15).

Figure 16.15 Resizing Made Easy

In the application, all you have to do is assign a class to a component, and the background image will appear in that box in the right size. Before you can use an SVG image, you have to check whether the `viewbox` is set. In the `svg` tag, you'll find some properties, like those shown in Listing 16.5.

```
<svg
  version="1.1"
  id="Capa_1"
  xmlns=http://www.w3.org/2000/svg
  xmlns:xlink="http://www.w3.org/1999/xlink" x="0px" y="0px"
    viewBox="0 0 425.126 425.125"
>
```

Listing 16.5 Header of the SVG Image

The `viewbox` property sets up a coordinate system, which means that it will create the drawing within these coordinates and then translate them into the actual width and height. You'll want to use this property if you're resizing an image.

> **Flaticon**
>
> This example uses icons from *flaticon*, a free database of icon vectors. You can download them for free if you add the website's link. Or, for a small fee, you can obtain a license for continued usage without needing a reference. You can visit flaticon at *www.flaticon.com/*.

Finally, you'll edit the PANEL that forms the right side menu. This PANEL is used for the news items and the market information that we created in the previous section (Figure 16.16).

16 | Building a Sales Dashboard Application

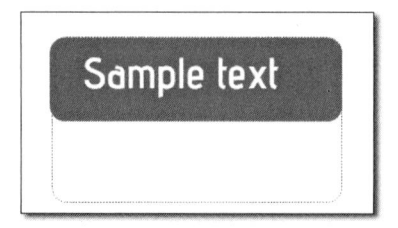

Figure 16.16 Panel Template

This PANEL component contains another PANEL component as the header. The inner component holds a TEXT component for the header text (Figure 16.17).

Figure 16.17 Structure of the Main Panel in the Template

Each part of the PANEL component has its own CSS class. The main outer PANEL has a border with a round edge:

```
.mainpanel { border-style: solid;border-width: 3px; border-color: #107896 ;background: white;border-radius: 15px 15px 15px 15px}
```

The inner PANEL has a round edge to make it look like it's part of the outer PANEL. It also contains a green background:

```
.innerpanel { border-style: solid;border-width: 3px; border-color: #107896 ;background: #107896;border-radius: 15px 15px 15px 15px}
```

The header text is white instead of green to stand out against the background color:

```
.innertitle {font-family: adventprosemibold, sans-serif; font-size: 42px; color: white; line-height: 1;}
```

You've now set up the main page of your sales dashboard application! In the next section, we'll move on to the detail screen.

16.2.2 Detail Screen

The second screen you'll come across in your sales dashboard application is the *detail screen*. In this section, we'll look at the elements that differ from the main dashboard screen. You'll reuse a lot of the same types of components and techniques you used when creating the main page. Generally, this is a good thing.

Our focus will be on those components that we haven't addressed before. The first component we'll look at is the WORD CLOUD GRAPH (Figure 16.18).

Figure 16.18 Word Cloud Graph

The WORD CLOUD GRAPH is an SDK component from the SCN community. The WORD CLOUD GRAPH shows the number of times a particular word is used. You analyze customer feedback by counting words. This graph then will visualize the word count and the mood that is associated to the words. This graph is dependent on a data source where each word is listed with a number representing its relative usage.

We used a manual data source to supply the numbers (Figure 16.19). This will enable you to access the same backend systems as we do. Otherwise, you wouldn't be able to see how the app works!

Label	I1	I2
Install	100	50
Happy	25	30
Flawless	200	10
Management	100	20
problem	20	1
panels	50	70
feedback	20	5000
damnage	10	10
fast	75	1999
easy	20	20

Figure 16.19 Data Source for a Word Cloud Graph

The L1 column is used to determine the size of a word. The L2 column defines the color of a word. You can assign a qualitative value (100 is good, and 0 is bad) to these words. The color will tell you if more positive words or more negative words are uttered in relation to your service. The property settings for the WORD CLOUD GRAPH are shown in Figure 16.20.

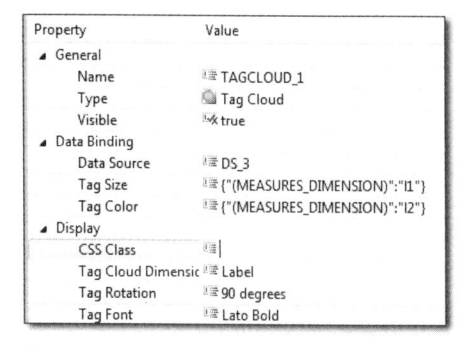

Property	Value
▲ General	
Name	TAGCLOUD_1
Type	Tag Cloud
Visible	true
▲ Data Binding	
Data Source	DS_3
Tag Size	{"(MEASURES_DIMENSION)":"l1"}
Tag Color	{"(MEASURES_DIMENSION)":"l2"}
▲ Display	
CSS Class	
Tag Cloud Dimension	Label
Tag Rotation	90 degrees
Tag Font	Lato Bold

Figure 16.20 Word Cloud Component Properties

To insert a WORD CLOUD GRAPH, follow these steps:

1. Create a new custom data source.

2. Name the new data source "DS_WORDCLOUD." For the new data source, provide the following property values:
   - Set the NUMBER OF DIMENSIONS to 1.
   - Set MEASURES IN ROWS to FALSE.
   - Set the SORT METHOD to ALPHANUMERIC ASCENDING.

3. Go to the ADDITIONAL PROPERTIES tab. Click the OPTIONS button, and select SWITCH TO CSV VIEW.

4. Add the data shown in Listing 16.6.

   ```
   Label,l1,l2
   Install,100,50
   Happy,25,30
   Flawless,200,10
   Management,100,20
   problem,20,1
   panels,50,70
   feedback,20,5000
   damage,10,10
   fast,75,1999
   ```

```
easy,20,20
grid,100,0
warranty,75,40
,0,0
```

Listing 16.6 Dataset for Word Cloud Graph

This is the dataset. The two values next to the different words are the two dimensions of frequency and value of word. One dimension determines the size of the word; the other determines the color.

5. Drag a WORD CLOUD component into PANEL component SEGMENT_INDEPTH. Name the component INDEPTH_WORDCLOUD.

6. For the INDEPTH_WORDCLOUD components, provide the following property values:
    - Set the DATASOURCE to DS_WORDCLOUD.
    - Set the TAG SIZE DATA SELECTION to column L1.
    - Set the TAG COLOR DATA SELECTION to column L2.
    - Set the TAG CLOUD DIMENSION to LABEL.
    - Set the TAG ROTATION to 90 degrees.
    - Set the TAG FONT to LATO BOLD.
    - Set the TOP MARGIN to 50, the LEFT MARGIN to 680, and the BOTTOM MARGIN and RIGHT MARGIN to AUTO.
    - Set the HEIGHT to 260 and the WIDTH to 394.

On the details screen, you also have two trend graphs to create (Figure 16.2). Let's begin by creating the data sources for both the trend graphs:

1. Create a new custom data source, and name it "DS_TREND."

2. Provide the following property values to DS_TREND:
    - Set the NUMBER OF DIMENSIONS to 1.
    - Set MEASURES IN ROWS to FALSE.
    - Set the SORT METHOD to NONE.

3. Go to the ADDITIONAL PROPERTIES tab. Click the OPTIONS button, and select SWITCH TO CSV VIEW.

4. Add the data in Listing 16.7.

16 | Building a Sales Dashboard Application

```
label,1,2,3,4,5,6,7,8,9,10,11,12,13,14,15,16,17,18,19
sales,192500,175000,187250,173250,190750,164500,173250,178500,164500
,180250,189000,192500,171500,169750,169750,182000,159250,164500,1785
00
order,69,71,64,68,69,64,70,64,73,69,77,63,74,75,68,70,69,64,67
```
Listing 16.7 Word Cloud Graph Data

Next, you'll add two CHART components to the PANEL component SEGMENT_INDEPTH. Follow these steps:

1. Name the CHART components "TREND_ONE" and "TREND_TWO." For both the CHART components, provide the following property values:
   - Set the DATASOURCE to DS_TREND.
   - Set the CHART TYPE to LINE.
   - Set SWAP AXES to FALSE.
   - Set SHOW TOTALS to FALSE.
   - Set DIMENSION LABEL to INITIAL VIEW DEFINITIONS.
   - Set the WIDTH to 393 and the HEIGHT to 104.

2. For CHART TREND_ONE, provide the following values:
   - Set the TOP MARGIN and the RIGHT MARGIN to AUTO.
   - Set the LEFT MARGIN to 674 and the BOTTOM MARGIN to 183.
   - Set DATASELECTION as {"LABEL":"SALES"}.

3. For CHART TREND_TWO, enter the following properties:
   - Set the TOP MARGIN AUTO, LEFT MARGIN 674, RIGHT MARGIN AUTO, and the BOTTOM MARGIN 52
   - Set DATASELECTION: {"LABEL":"ORDER"}

Next, you'll add two new data sources: DS_DETAIL_BULLET_1 and DS_DETAIL_BULLET_2. Follow these steps:

1. For both data sources, provide the following property values:
   - Set the NUMBER OF DIMENSIONS to 1.
   - Set MEASURES IN ROWS to FALSE.
   - Set the SORT METHOD to NONE.

2. Go to the ADDITIONAL PROPERTIES tab. Click the OPTIONS button, and go to CSV VIEW.

3. For DS_DETAIL_BULLET_1 data, add the following:
    - `ID,Label,subLabel,l1,l2,l3,l5,actual,compare`
    - `1, Customer Revenue,100,200,300,400,500,367,388`
    - `2, Customer Satisfaction,100,200,300,400,500,243,220`
    - `3, Customer orders YTD,100,200,300,400,500,520,490`
    - `4, Customer awareness,100,200,300,400,500,134,180`

4. For DS_DETAIL_BULLET_2 data, add the following:
    - `ID,Label,subLabel,l1,l2,l3,l4,l5,actual,compare`
    - `1,prospects in doubt,0,10,20,30,40,50,45,37`
    - `2,installation faults,0,0,200,500,1000,350,295,260`
    - `3,losing customers,0,0,5,10,15,20,17,18`

5. Add two BULLET GRAPH components to the PANEL component, SEGMENT_INDEPTH. Name the BULLET GRAPH components "BULLET_DETAIL_1" and "BULLET_DETAIL_2".

6. For both of the BULLET GRAPH components, enter the following properties:
    - Set the REALIZATION COLUMN to ACTUAL.
    - Set the FIRST THRESHOLD COLUMN to L1, the THIRD THRESHOLD COLUMN to L3, and the FIFTH THRESHOLD COLUMN to L5.
    - Set the ROW DIMENSION HOLDING MAIN LABEL to LABEL and the ROW DIMENSION HOLDING UNIQUE KEY to ID.
    - Set the COMPARISON COLUMN to COMPARE.
    - Set SHOW X AXIS NUMBERS to TRUE.
    - Set SHOW TOOLTIP to FALSE.
    - Set MINIMUM AND MAXIMUM HEIGHT OF EACH GRAPH to 30.
    - Set the NUMBER OF TICKS to 4.
    - Set the HORIZONTAL MARGIN BETWEEN GRAPHS to 0.
    - Set the NUMBER OF COLUMNS to 1.
    - Set SHOW ALERT to WORSE THAN COMPARISON.
    - Set the TOP MARGIN, BOTTOM MARGIN, LEFT MARGIN, and RIGHT MARGIN to 0.

7. For just the BULLET_DETAIL_1 BULLET GRAPH component, provide the following property values:
   - Set the DATASOURCE to DS_DETAIL_BULLET_1.
   - Set REALIZATION IS HIGHER THAN TARGET to TRUE.

8. For the BULLET_DETAIL_2 BULLET GRAPH component, provide the following property values:
   - Set the DATASOURCE to DS_DETAIL_BULLET_2.
   - Set REALIZATION IS HIGHER THAN TARGET to FALSE.

For the icon and the text on the top left, copy the text and icon of the CUSTOMER tile, and paste them into the SEGMENT_INDEPTH panel. Then, follow these steps:

1. Set the name of the icon panel to PNL_DETAIL_ICON.
2. Provide the following property values for PNL_DETAIL_ICON:
   - Set the TOP MARGIN to 16, the LEFT MARGIN to 18, and the BOTTOM MARGIN, and RIGHT MARGIN to AUTO.
   - Set both the WIDTH and HEIGHT to 110.
3. Set the name of the text to TXT_DETAIL_HDR.
4. Provide the following property values for TXT_DETAIL_HDR:
   - Set the TOP MARGIN to 16, the LEFT MARGIN to 136, and the BOTTOM MARGIN and RIGHT MARGIN to AUTO.
   - Set both the WIDTH and HEIGHT to 110.

You've now completed the steps for the details screen. In the next section, we'll look at a third screen where you can create quotes for customers.

16.2.3 Quotes

In this section, we'll look at how the quote page is made and how the PDF document is generated. In Figure 16.21, you can see a form where you can fill in the expiry data and customer name. Furthermore, you can select the products that you want to include in your quote. When you're done, a PDF document is created using the entered values.

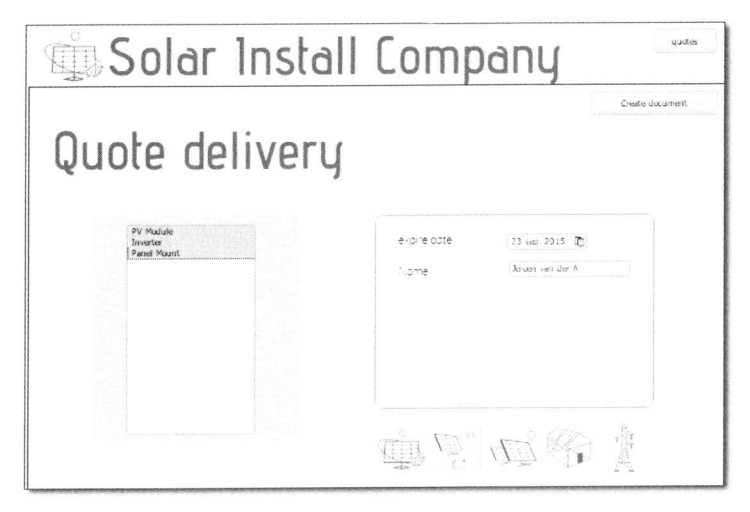

Figure 16.21 Quote Delivery Form

In this section, we'll explain how to script so the PDF document will contain all the information necessary for the customer quote and ensure that it's printable in a standard print format.

The information in the quote letter (Figure 16.21) is a combination of direct information from the form and information derived from data sources based on the product input. Most of the data on the printed document is derived directly from the form, but pricing has to be invoked using scripting. On the left side of the screen, you'll see a LIST BOX component with the products listed. The LIST BOX component uses *property binding* to link a component to a data source dimension. When the user changes the product selection, a script is run to change the contents of the document accordingly. In the script, the first step is to collect the selected product keys and texts.

Let's begin by setting up the components for the order form. Follow these steps:

1. Create a PANEL component, ORDER_FORM, within the BACKGROUND component.

2. Provide the following property values:
    - Set the TOP MARGIN to 75, the BOTTOM MARGIN to 50, the RIGHT MARGIN to 0, and the LEFT MARGIN to 0.
    - Set both the HEIGHT and WIDTH to AUTO.

3. Add a TEXT component, and name it "ORDERFORM_TITLE." Provide the following properties for ORDERFORM_TITLE:
   - Set the CSS CLASS to TITLE1.
   - Set the TOP MARGIN to 50 and the LEFT MARGIN to 30.
   - Set the HEIGHT/WIDTH to 410 and 65, respectively.
   - Set the TEXT to QUOTE DELIVERY.

4. Add a PANEL component and name it "PNL_PRODUCT_SELECT." Provide the following property values for PNL_PRODUCT_SELECT:
   - Set the TOP MARGIN to 160, the BOTTOM MARGIN to AUTO, the LEFT MARGIN to 80, and the RIGHT MARGIN to AUTO.
   - Set the HEIGHT to 165 and the WIDTH to 250.
   - Set the CSS CLASS to PANEL2.
   - Set the CSS STYLE to `border-color: #fff600;`.

5. Add a LIST BOX component to PNL_PRODUCT_SELECT, and name it "PRODUCT_SELECTION". Provide the following values to the PRODUCT_SELECTION component:
   - Set MULTIPLE SELECTION to TRUE.
   - Set the TOP MARGIN to 10, the BOTTOM MARGIN to AUTO, the LEFT MARGIN to 40, and the RIGHT MARGIN to AUTO.
   - Set the HEIGHT to 260 and the WIDTH to 274.

Next, you'll need a data source from a backend system. You need to create this yourself. The following values should be at least in the data source:

- `ID,Name,Price`
- `1,PV module,895`
- `2,Inverter,719`
- `3,panel mount,40`

To create your own data source, follow these steps:

1. Add your own data source to the application.
2. Continue to configure the LIST BOX PRODUCT_SELECTION.

3. Click the EDIT PROPERTY BINDING button on the right side of the property ITEMS. Now expand the ITEMS property, and set the SOURCE property. Expand the SOURCE property to set the data binding.

4. Set TYPE to DIMENSION MEMBER BINDING.

5. Set DATASOURCE to the data source you added yourself.

6. Set DIMENSION to the dimension in the data source where the product texts are located.

7. Set the MAXIMUM NUMBER OF MEMBERS to 30.

8. Set MEMBER DISPLAY to TEXT.

9. Set ALL MEMBER TEXT to ALL PRODUCTS.

10. Create a PANEL component, PANEL_QUOTEINFO, inside ORDERFORM. Provide the following property values for PANEL_QUOTEINFO:

    - Set the margins: TOP MARGIN 160, LEFT MARGIN 440, and BOTTOM MARGIN and RIGHT MARGIN AUTO.
    - Set the WIDTH to 350 and the HEIGHT to 240.
    - Set the CSS CLASS to PANEL.

11. Insert a DATE FIELD component, an INPUT FIELD component, and two TEXT components into PANEL_QUOTEINFO.

12. Name the DATE FIELD component "EXPIRY_DATE." Provide the following property values for the DATE FIELD component:

    - Set the margins: TOP MARGIN 22, LEFT MARGIN 166, and BOTTOM MARGIN and RIGHT MARGIN AUTO.
    - Set the HEIGHT to 50 and the WIDTH to 100.

13. Name the INPUT FIELD component, "INPUT_CUSTOMER_NAME." Provide the following property values for INPUT_CUSTOMER_NAME:

    - Set the margins: TOP MARGIN 55, LEFT MARGIN 170, BOTTOM MARGIN AUTO and RIGHT MARGIN AUTO.
    - Set the TOOLTIP to WRITE DOWN THE FULL CUSTOMER NAME.

14. Name the first TEXT component "EXPIRY_LABEL."

15. Provide the following property values to EXPIRY_LABEL:

    - Set the CSS CLASS to TEXT.
    - Align the label with EXPIRY_DATE.

16. Name the second Text component "CUSTOMER_LABEL". Provide the following property values to CUSTOMER_LABEL:
    - Set the CSS Class to Text.
    - Align the label with EXPIRY_DATE.

17. Create a Panel component PRINT_FORM inside ORDER_FORM. Provide the following property values:
    - Set the Width to 1190 and the Height to 1684. These particular sizes are chosen to align with the standard paper format A4.
    - Set the margins: Top Margin and Left Margin to 0, Bottom Margin and Right Margin to Auto.

18. Add five Text components to PRINT_FORM.
    - Name the first "SALESQUOTEDATE," and set the following properties:
        - Set the CSS Class to title3.
        - Set the Text to Sales Quote.
        - Set the margins: Top Margin 100, Left Margin 175, Bottom Margin Auto, and Right Margin Auto.
        - Set the Height/Width to 30 and 400, respectively.
    - Name the second "TXT_INTRODUCTIONS," and set the following properties:
        - Set the CSS Class to Textstrong.
        - Set the text to We're happy to deliver this sales quote.
        - Set the margins: Top Margin 226, Left Margin 30, Bottom Margin Auto, and Right Margin Auto.
        - Set the Height/Width to 380 and 22, respectively.
    - Name the third "TXT_INCLUDING," and set the following properties:
        - Set the CSS Class to Textstrong.
        - Set the Text to The installation included the following:.
        - Set the margins: Top Margin 288, Left Margin 30, Bottom Margin Auto, and Right Margin Auto.
        - Set the Height/Width to 380 and 22, respectively.

- Name the fourth "TXT_ADDRESSING," and set the following properties:
  - Set the CSS Class to Text.
  - Set the Text to Dear:.
  - Set the margins: Top Margin 197, Left Margin 30, Bottom Margin Auto, and Right Margin Auto.
  - Set the Height/Width to 380 and 22, respectively.
19. Name the fifth "PRINT_TITLE," and set the following properties:
    - Set the CSS Class to Title1.
    - Set the Text to Solar Install Company.
    - Set the margins: Top Margin 18, Left Margin 11, Bottom Margin Auto, and Right Margin 400.
    - Set the Height/Width: Auto,60
20. Add a formatted Text view to PRINT_FORM.
    - Set the margins: Top Margin 280, Left Margin 290, Bottom Margin Auto, and Right Margin Auto.
    - Set the Height/Width to 450 and 125, respectively.
21. Add a Panel component PNL_AMOUNT to PRINT_FORM, and set the following properties:
    - Set the margins: Top Margin 432, Left Margin Auto, Bottom Margin Auto, and Right Margin 481.
    - Set the Height/Width to 480 and 80, respectively.
22. Add two Text components to PNL_AMOUNT.
    - Name the first "TXT_AMOUNT," and set the following properties:
      - Set the CSS Class to Textstrong.
      - Set the margins: Top Margin 13, Left Margin 14, Bottom Margin Auto, and Right Margin Auto.
      - Set the Height/Width to 380 and 22, respectively.
    - Name the second "TXT_EXPIRE," and set the following properties:
      - Set the CSS Class to Textstrong.

- Set the margins: Top Margin 35, Left Margin 14, Bottom Margin Auto, and Right Margin Auto.
- Set the Height/Width to 380 and 22, respectively.

23. Go to the Technical Components section in the Outline panel.
24. Add a PDF component in the Outline panel on the Technical Components subsection. Right-click on the subsection, and select Add Child • PDF.

Now that you've added the relevant items, next you'll add script for the full functionality. Follow these steps:

1. Go to the PRODUCT_SELECTION component.
2. Add the following script parts (Listing 16.8, Listing 16.9, and Listing 16.10 in order) to the On Select event.

```
var products = PRODUCT_SELECTION.getSelectedValues();
var productText = PRODUCT_SELECTION.getSelectedTexts();
var htmlText = "";
var totalprice = 0.0
```

Listing 16.8 Initializing the Values

3. The next step is to loop through those products and find the product text and the product price. The price is determined by using a getData method on a data source using the current product ID as a filter.

```
products.forEach(function(element, index) {
    var ProductText = "";
    productText.forEach(function(element, ID_index) {
      if (ID_index == index){ProductText = element;}
    });

    var price = DS_7.getData("Price", {"ID": element });

  htmlText = htmlText + "<li>" + element + " -
" + ProductText + " " + price.formattedValue + "</li>";
  totalprice = totalprice + price.value;
});
```

Listing 16.9 Calculating the Total Price

4. You might notice that we included HTML tags in the string variable. We're using a formatted text view to list the products. Insert these HTML tags to create bullet point lists in the text.

5. Each time a price is found, it's added to the variable `totalprice`. Finally, after looping through all the products, set the text to the total amount using that variable (Listing 16.10).

```
htmlText = "<ul>" + htmlText + "</ul>";
ITEMLIST.setHtmlText(htmlText);
TXT_AMOUNT.setText("the Total amount is : $" + totalprice);
```

Listing 16.10 Setting the Texts

In the customer entry, you add script that updates the PRINT_FORM component after changing the value.

Next, you ensure that the data entered by the user will result in a text suitable for reading in a quote. In the first part, take the data selected by the user and change it to a sentence that uses the day, month, and year. Follow these steps:

1. Add the script in Listing 16.11 to the `On Select` event of EXPIRY_DATE.

```
var year = EXPIRY_DATE.getDate().substring(0,4);
var month = EXPIRY_DATE.getDate().substring(5,6);
var day = EXPIRY_DATE.getDate().substring(7,8);
TXT_EXPIRE.setText("expires on : " + day + " - " + month + " -
 " + year);
```

Listing 16.11 Apply to the On Select Event

In this script, we split the date into year, month, and day and then use it to build the text in the PRINT_FORM component.

2. Add the following script to the `afterChange` event of INPUT_CUSTOMER_NAME:

```
TXT_ADDRESSING.setText("Dear " + INPUT_CUSTOMER_NAME.getValue());
```

Next, you need to set up the application so the quote letter (refer to Figure 16.21) will scale to A4 paper. To do this, you need to use a PANEL component that has the same relative dimensions as an A4. Follow these steps:

1. Use the following dimensions to set up standard A4:
   - 72 dpi (web): 595 × 842 pixels
   - 300 dpi (print): 2480 × 3508 pixels
   - 600 dpi (print): 4960 × 7016 pixels

2. Set the VISIBILITY of the page to TRUE, so only visible PANELS can be printed.

3. Print the PDF using the now visible PANEL. Set the PANEL back to NOT VISIBLE again so the rest of the application is available once more.

4. Next, create a separate button to print.

5. Add the BUTTON component BTN_CREATE_PDF to ORDERFORM.

6. Change the TEXT to CREATE DOCUMENT. Then enter the following properties:

    - Set the margins: TOP MARGIN 8, LEFT MARGIN 710, BOTTOM MARGIN AUTO, and RIGHT MARGIN 481.
    - Set the WIDTH/HEIGHT to 160 and 30, respectively.
    - Set the On Click event:
      ```
      PRINT_FORM.setVisible(true);
      PDF.exportPanelScreen(PRINT_FORM);
      ```

16.3 Summary

In this chapter, we discussed the different steps to create the sales dashboard application. We highlighted the techniques used to create the structure, the layout, and the functionality.

In the next chapter, we'll look at building an OLAP application using a template.

In this chapter, we'll use one of the Design Studio templates to build an OLAP application.

17 Building an OLAP Application Using a Template

Online Analytical Processing (OLAP) applications are great for end users who want to discover insights into their datasets. They can do this by slicing and dicing data sources and applying filters and calculations. In Chapter 3, we described such a scenario.

Although various tools are available for building OLAP applications, such as SAP BusinessObjects Analysis, edition for Microsoft Office, and SAP BusinessObjects Analysis, edition for OLAP, setting up your own OLAP application allows you to have full control over the behavior of the application. It also allows you to customize the look and feel of the application based on your own company's style.

Another benefit of setting up your own OLAP application is that you can integrate this application into your existing dashboards. You can easily create your own OLAP application in Design Studio. In this chapter, you'll set up a simple dashboard with two tabs. On the first tab, you'll put two charts to display the data graphically, and on the second tab, you'll create an OLAP application where the user can slice and dice through the dataset, apply some filters, and use different chart types to display the data.

17.1 Creating the Application

You've already seen in Chapter 3, Section 3.3, how this application looks and what users can do with it. Figure 17.1 displays the OLAP application on startup. In the top-left corner of your screen, you see that the CHARTS tab is selected. When the user clicks on a point in either one of the charts, the application will go

17 | Building an OLAP Application Using a Template

to the second tab (Analysis), and the OLAP application will become available (Figure 17.2).

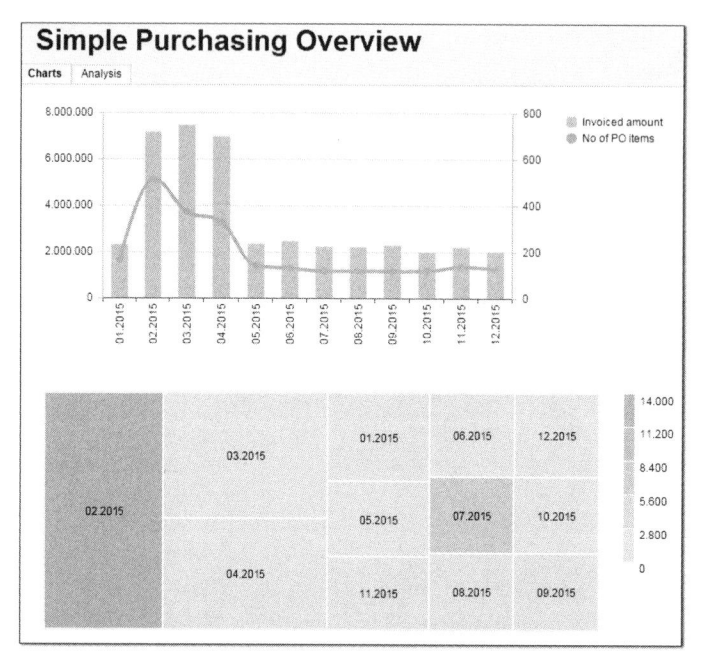

Figure 17.1 Purchasing Dashboard with Two Tabs

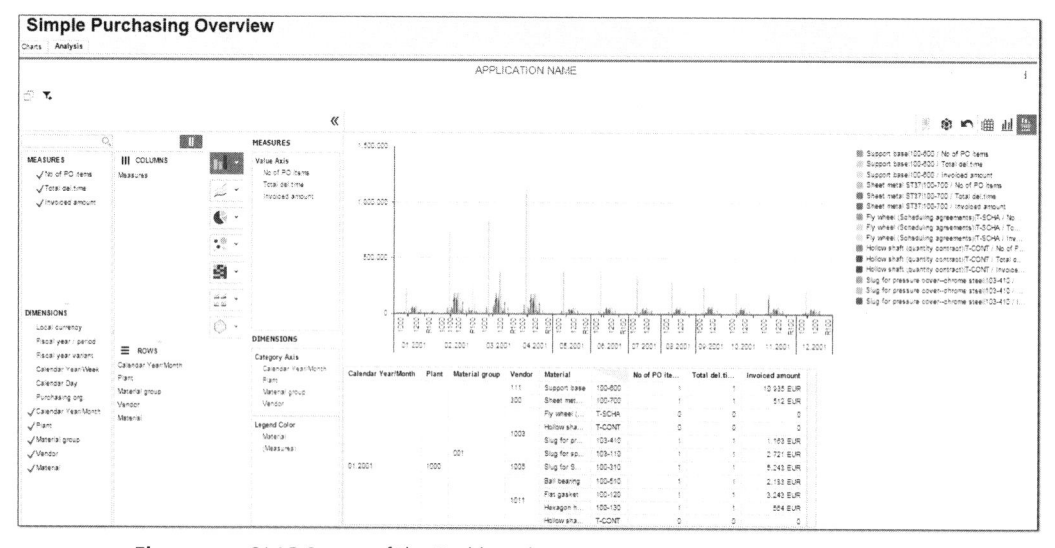

Figure 17.2 OLAP Screen of the Dashboard

Let's start building the application. In this example, you'll use one of the ready-to-run application templates (GENERIC ANALYSIS). The GENERIC ANALYSIS template offers the application developer a complete working application that can be used to perform slice-and-dice analysis on any available dataset.

Using this template, you don't have to set up the OLAP application from scratch. You only have to make some minor adjustments to the template. Along the way, we'll explain some of the more important properties that are set for some components and some of the scripts that are used in this application.

Creating an OLAP application with a GENERIC ANALYSIS template is very simple. To create a new Design Studio application, press Ctrl+N. Then select the GENERIC ANALYSIS template that is available in the READY-TO-RUN section of the TEMPLATE SELECTION screen (Figure 17.3). Give your application a name, and click CREATE.

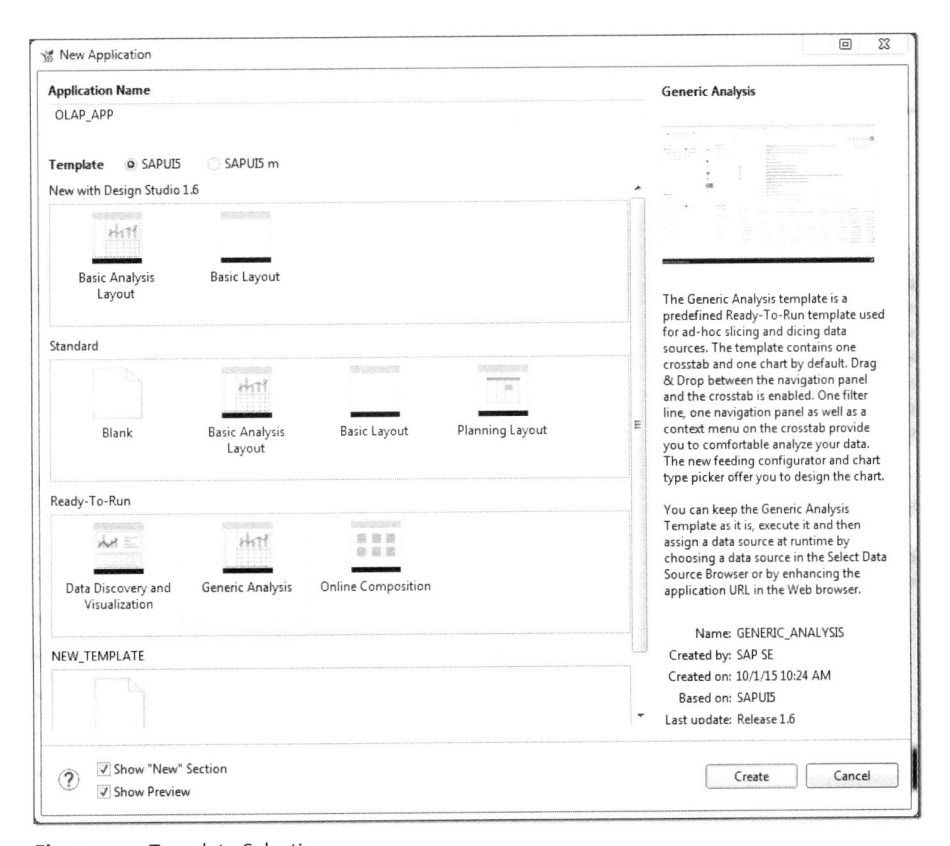

Figure 17.3 Template Selection

At this point, you can execute the application because the template that you've used is a fully functional application. However, in this example, we want to integrate this OLAP application into our own dashboard. Let's look at how that is done.

We want to have to separate tabs in the application. The first tab is for the dashboard, and the second tab is for the OLAP application. You'll also reserve some room on the screen to create a header where you'll display the name of the application.

The components that are used in the template are grouped by functionality in panels such as those shown in Figure 17.4. The LAYOUT_CONTAINER contains all components used for displaying data in the application.

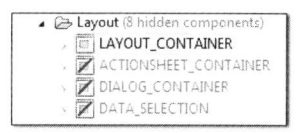

Figure 17.4 Layout of the Application

To create room for the header and divide the application into two tabs, follow these steps:

1. Right-click on the LAYOUT folder, and select CREATE CHILD. Select the PANEL component. Name this panel "MAIN_APP," and set the TOP MARGIN, LEFT MARGIN, BOTTOM MARGIN, and RIGHT MARGIN to 0. Set the WIDTH and the HEIGHT to AUTO.

2. To create the header, right-click on the MAIN_APP panel, and select CREATE CHILD. Select the PANEL component. Set the TOP MARGIN, LEFT MARGIN, and RIGHT MARGIN to 0. Set the BOTTOM MARGIN and WIDTH to AUTO, and set the HEIGHT to 50 to create a header of 50 pixels high starting at the top of the screen.

3. Create a title for the application by right-clicking on the APP_HEADER component. Select CREATE CHILD, and choose TEXT component. Set the TOP MARGIN and LEFT MARGIN to 20, the BOTTOM MARGIN and RIGHT MARGIN to 0, and the WIDTH and HEIGHT to AUTO. Use the text SIMPLE PURCHASING OVERVIEW as TEXT in the properties of this component. Use the following CSS code in the CSS STYLE property to make the size of the text bigger:

```
font-weight: bold;
font-size: 32px;
```

4. Now let's move on to creating the tabs. Right-click on the MAIN_APP panel, and select CREATE CHILD. Select the TABSTRIP component. By default, two tabs will be created, which is perfect for this example application. Set the TOP MARGIN to 50; the LEFT MARGIN, the BOTTOM MARGIN, and the RIGHT MARGIN to 0; and the WIDTH and the HEIGHT to AUTO. This way, the tabs will cover the whole screen except for the top 50 pixels, which is used for the header.

5. At this point, you can create the simple dashboard. You'll divide the available screen into two rows. Right-click on TAB_1, and select CREATE CHILD. Select the GRID LAYOUT component. Set the TOP MARGIN, LEFT MARGIN, and BOTTOM MARGIN to 0. Set the RIGHT MARGIN and HEIGHT to AUTO, and set the WIDTH to 750. Set the NUMBER OF ROWS to 2, and the NUMBER OF COLUMNS to 1.

6. Before you can display information, you need to add a data source to the application. In the OUTLINE view, right-click on the DATA SOURCES folder, and select ADD DATA SOURCE. Select a data source for your dashboard. This application uses a BEx query containing some purchasing information. Figure 17.5 shows a view of the data.

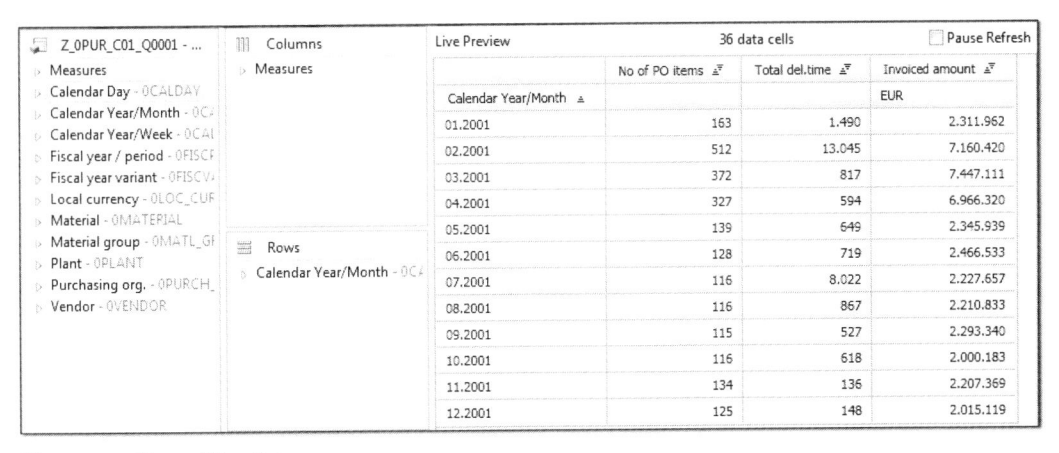

Figure 17.5 View of the Data

7. Now add an INFO CHART component to CELL – [0,0]. You can use the CHART CONFIGURATION option in the properties of this component to create a COMBINED COLUMN LINE CHART WITH 2 Y-AXIS, as shown in Figure 17.6. To position

the chart, set the TOP MARGIN, the LEFT MARGIN, the BOTTOM MARGIN, and the RIGHT MARGIN to 0. Set the WIDTH and HEIGHT to AUTO.

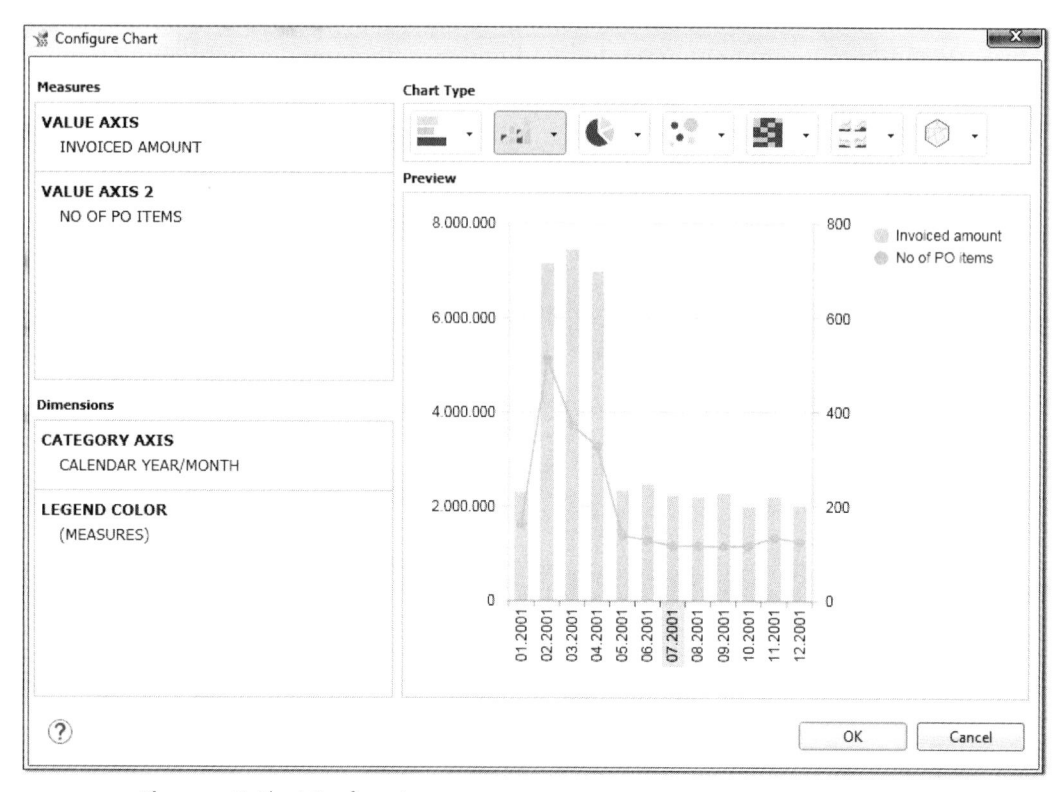

Figure 17.6 Chart Configurator

8. Copy the INFO CHART from CELL – [0, 0] into CELL – [1, 0]. Use the CHART CONFIGURATION option to create a heat map, as shown in Figure 17.7.

9. The dashboard containing purchasing information is now ready. You now need to move the LAYOUT_CONTAINER panel to TAB_2, so that the OLAP application is displayed on the second tab of the application. You can simply drag and drop this panel into the desired tab in the OUTLINE view. The final layout of the application should look like Figure 17.8.

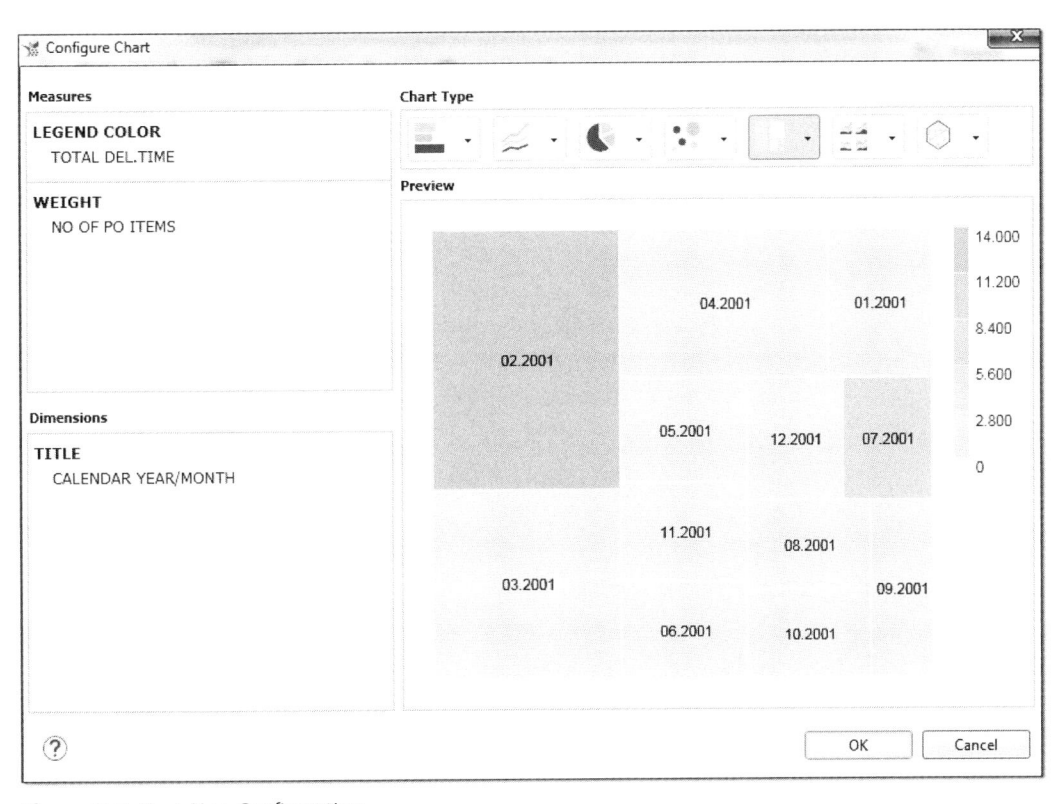

Figure 17.7 Heat Map Configuration

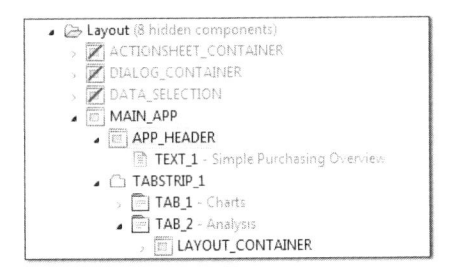

Figure 17.8 New Application Layout

10. Before you can run the application, you need to make sure to clear the script that was added by default in the On Startup property of the application. There is only one line of code. Remove this line of code or place it in comments by adding two slashes in front of the code (//START_FUNCTIONS.on_startup();).

11. When the user clicks on a certain point in one of the charts, the OLAP application will be show on TAB_2. To achieve this, select both charts, and open the Script Editor by clicking on the ON SELECT property. Add the following lines of code:

```
DS_1.assignDataSource("2 -
 SAP BW 7.40 on HANA", DataSourceType.QUERY, DS_2.getInfo().query-
TechnicalName);
TABSTRIP_1.setSelectedTab("TAB_2");
```

DS_1 is the data source that is used in the OLAP application. The first line in the code makes sure that the BEx query that is used in the charts gets assigned to DS_1. In the second line of the code, TAB_2 gets selected.

12. You can also choose to pass a filter from the chart to the OLAP application. Let's say, for instance, that you want to remember the month that a user selects from the chart and pass this month on to the OLAP application to use as a filter. This can be done by adding the following lines of code below the code in the previous step:

```
var month = this.getSelectedMember("0CALMONTH");
DS_1.setFilter("0CALMONTH", month);
```

At this point, you've set up a simple purchasing dashboard with two charts. The dashboard also has a second tab where the user can perform slice-and-dice analysis on his dataset. By using one of the available templates, you immediately have other functionality available such as bookmarking and choosing different datasets. In the following section, we'll explore different parts of the template to get you more acquainted with the different properties and script you can use in Design Studio.

17.2 Application Properties

Figure 17.9 and Figure 17.10 show the application's properties, as described here:

▶ GENERAL
In the GENERAL part of the properties, you'll find some basic information about your application such as the name, when it was created, and by whom. The CUID is a unique identifier in your SAP BusinessObjects Business Intelligence (BI) platform that remains the same in all deployments in your landscape (development, test, and production).

- BEHAVIOR

    In the BEHAVIOR area, you see that the MAXIMUM NUMBER OF STEPS BACK is set to 20. This means that the application remembers up to 20 navigation steps, and the application designer can implement a function to go back up to 20 navigation steps sequentially, or reset the application at once. You can also turn on/off the drag and drop functionality between components here, and you can enable or disable offline recording of the application.

- DISPLAY

    In the DISPLAY area of the properties, you find information about what theme and rendering mode are used (see Chapter 10 for more information). In the CUSTOM CSS option, you can upload your own CSS file. You can also define whether or not you want to see error and warning messages.

- PROMPTS

    In the PROMPTS area of the properties, you see that the MERGE PROMPTS option is set to TRUE. This means that when a value for a BEx variable is changed, the application will trigger all the queries that use this variable. When the MERGE PROMPTS option is set to FALSE, the application designer can control which query needs to be triggered.

- PLANNING

    The PLANNING properties aren't used in this application.

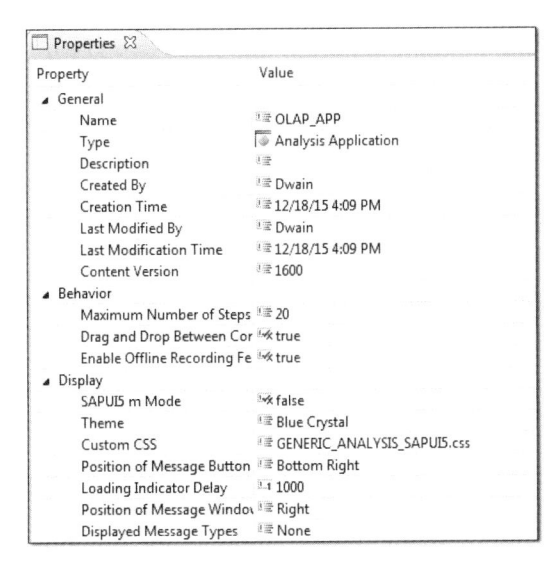

Figure 17.9 Application Properties (Part 1)

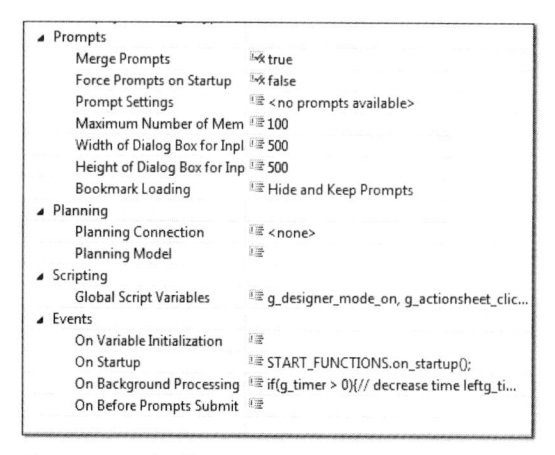

17 | Building an OLAP Application Using a Template

Figure 17.10 Application Properties (Part 2)

- SCRIPTING

    In the SCRIPTING area of the properties, the GLOBAL SCRIPT VARIABLES option shows all the global script variables that are used in this application (Figure 17.11). The most important variables in this list will be explained later in the chapter when we explain the different scripts that use these variables. Note that some variables are defined with the value TRUE for URL PARAMETER. This means that variables can be passed through the application by adding them to the OpenDocument link of the application.

- EVENTS

    In the EVENTS area, you can see that an `On Startup` script is defined.

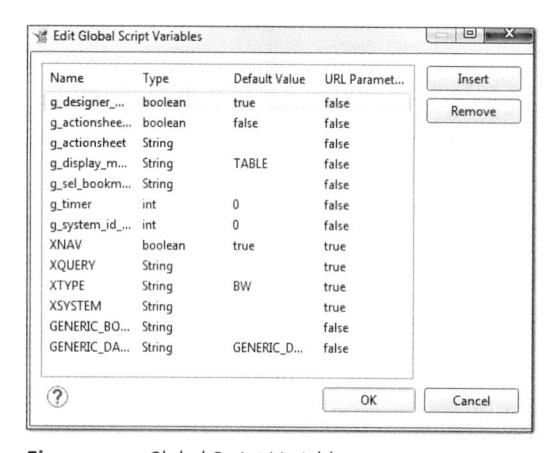

Figure 17.11 Global Script Variables

684

17.3 Application Components

This OLAP application uses numerous components. In Figure 17.12, the components are grouped together by functionality. The following list provides an overview of what components are used in the application and how they are grouped:

- LAYOUT_CONTAINER
  All components that are presented to the user on the screen are grouped inside this PANEL. The LAYOUT_CONTAINER is divided into a HEADER, BODY, FILTER_AREA, FOOTER, and TOOLBAR.

- HEADER
  In this PANEL, two TEXT components are used to display information about the application.

- FILTER_AREA
  The filter components, such as the FILTERLINE, are stored inside this PANEL.

- BODY
  This PANEL contains ANALYTICS COMPONENTS such as CROSSTAB components and CHART components.

- TOOLBAR
  This PANEL groups various ICON components that are used as buttons in the application toolbar.

- FOOTER
  This PANEL holds some TEXT components that have some extra information about the application.

There are also technical components used in this application:

- CONNECTION
  This component is used to store information about the source system that will be used.

- CONTEXT MENU
  This component is used to enable the right-click menu in CROSSTAB components. You can even define your own menu items here.

- GLOBAL SCRIPTS
  Global scripts are grouped together in a specific category. Grouping scripts based on the function they execute is useful for application designers and for

those who maintain the application. The global scripts in this application handle, for instance, the logic when the application starts up or what should happen when an application gets bookmarked.

- PDF

   This component is used to export to a PDF.

- TEXT_POOL

   This component is used to create text mappings (translations) in your application.

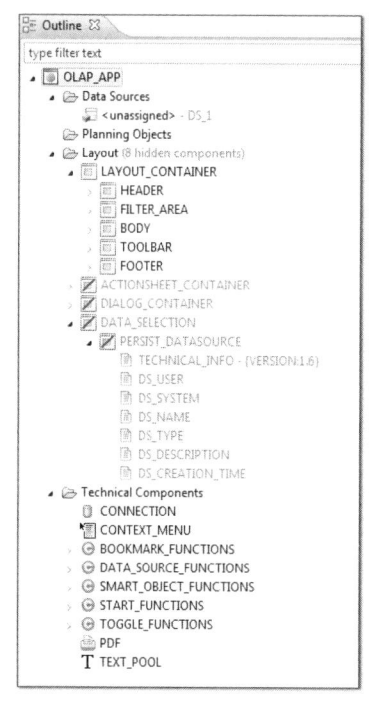

Figure 17.12 Application Outline

You may notice from Figure 17.12 that many components are hidden. It's a good practice when you develop large applications to hide components that you don't need to see at that moment during the development process. This way, they aren't rendered in your development canvas, which saves time and system resources.

Now that we've touched on the main group of components, let's zoom a little bit deeper on each group.

17.3.1 Header

This HEADER component isn't the header that we've previously created. This HEADER is created by default when you use the template. The HEADER is a bar 35px high starting on the top of the application. In Figure 17.13, you can see that one ICON component and two TEXT components are used in this header. The HEADER_BACKGROUND is a TEXT component expanding across the whole header. It's linked with the CSS class `myHeader`. The following CSS code is defined in the `myHeader` CSS class:

```
.myHeader {
background-color: #e5e5e5 !important;
border-top: 5px solid #007cc0;
}
```

This CSS class gives the HEADER a gray background with a blue top border of 5px. By using the CSS editor in the application properties, you can take a look at all the CSS classes and edit them the way you like.

The TEXT_HEADER_TITLE text component is a placeholder for the title of your application. This component will be filled when the `On_initialization` function from the `START_FUNCTIONS` global script is called. The `On Startup` script is triggered every time the application is executed. We'll discuss this script in more detail later in Section 17.3.4. The CSS class that is linked to this component is called `myHeaderTitle` and contains the CSS code shown in Listing 17.1.

```
.myHeaderTitle {
font-family: Arial, Helvetica, sans-serif !important;
font-size: 18px !important;
font-weight: normal !important;
color: #333333 !important;
text-align: center !important;
}
```

Listing 17.1 CSS Code That Handles the Header Style

> **!important Statement**
>
> As you can see in the CSS code, the `!important` statement is used in almost every line. A component can inherit CSS markup from various sources, so a text can get more than one color assigned to it. With the `!important` statement on a specific property, you can define a CSS statement that overrules all others.

This CSS code indicates that the text should have a gray color with size 18px and center alignment.

The last component in the HEADER is an ICON component. With this component, you can choose from a list of available icons to use in your application. In the properties of this component, you can set its color, its background color, and its size.

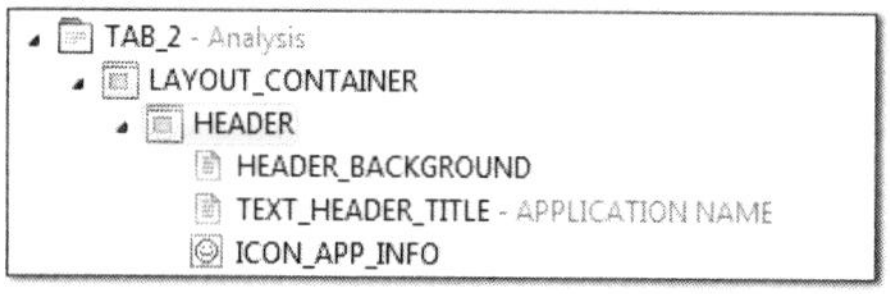

```
▲ 🗋 TAB_2 - Analysis
    ▲ 🗋 LAYOUT_CONTAINER
        ▲ 🗋 HEADER
            🗋 HEADER_BACKGROUND
            🗋 TEXT_HEADER_TITLE - APPLICATION NAME
            🗋 ICON_APP_INFO
```

Figure 17.13 Application Header

17.3.2 Body

The body of the application is where most of the information is presented to the end user. Figure 17.14 gives an overview of the most important components that are used in the body of the application.

You may recall from Chapter 3 that there are three views available for the user to switch to:

▶ A view of the data in a CROSSTAB
▶ A view of the data in a CHART
▶ A view of the date in both a CROSSTAB and a CHART

The user can select one of the views by clicking on one of the buttons in Figure 17.15. A variable called `g_display_mode` gets filled with the value CHART, TABLE, or CHART_TABLE, depending on which view is desired. Next, a global script function called `toggle_diplay_mode` is executed to handle this user interaction. See Listing 17.2 with explanations provided.

```
//In this block of code, all the CSS is removed from the three //
icons.
ICON_CHART.setCSSClass("");
ICON_TABLE.setCSSClass("");
ICON_CHART_TABLE.setCSSClass("");

//In the second and third block of code, the chart and crosstab //
component are set to invisible to reset all previous //styling.
CHART.setHeight(Layout.AUTO);
```

```
CHART.setTopMargin(0);
CHART.setBottomMargin(0);
CHART.setVisible(false);

CROSSTAB.setTopMargin(0);
CROSSTAB.setHeight(Layout.AUTO);
CROSSTAB.setVisible(false);

//Now, depending on which view is selected, either the //
crosstab, chart, or both are displayed on the screen. This //
logic is handled by if statements. You can also see in the //
code that the icon that is clicked will get a CSS class //
assigned to indicate that this icon was clicked.

// display mode CHART
if (g_display_mode == "CHART") {
    ICON_CHART.setCSSClass("ICON_ACTIVE");
    CHART.setVisible(true);
}
// display mode TABLE
if (g_display_mode == "TABLE") {
    ICON_TABLE.setCSSClass("ICON_ACTIVE");
    CROSSTAB.setVisible(true);
}
// display mode CHART/TABLE
if (g_display_mode == "CHART_TABLE") {
    ICON_CHART_TABLE.setCSSClass("ICON_ACTIVE");
    CHART.setVisible(true);
    CROSSTAB.setVisible(true);
    CHART.setHeight(400);
    CROSSTAB.setTopMargin(400);
}
TOGGLE_FUNCTIONS.toggle_designer_mode();
```

Listing 17.2 Script to Toggle Displays

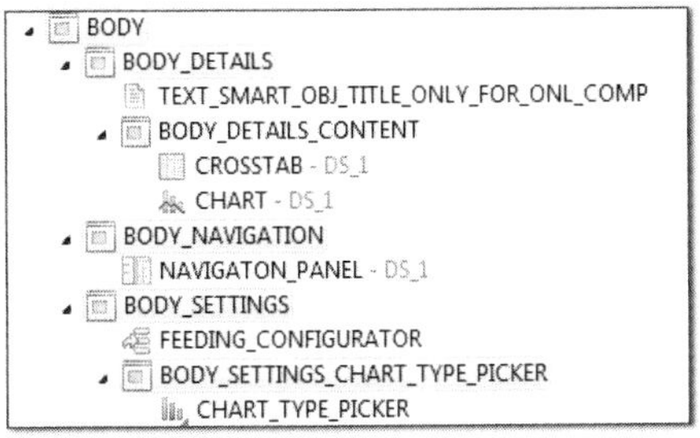

Figure 17.14 Application Body Component

The BODY_NAVIGATION and BODY_SETTINGS panels (Figure 17.14) hold a NAVIGATION_PANEL and FEEDING_CONFIGURATOR component, respectively.

Only one of these views can be visible at a time. The user can switch views by clicking one of the view buttons in the menu on the right side of the screen (Figure 17.15).

Figure 17.15 Three Available Views to Choose From

Each time a user clicks one of the buttons, two of the panels that are mentioned previously are set to `invisible`, and the appropriate panel is set to `visible`. You saw in Listing 17.2 that the icons in Figure 17.15 have an assigned CSS class depending on whether or not they are clicked. The name of the CSS class is `.ICON_ACTIVE`. You can check out the CSS code by opening the default style sheet that comes with the template used for this example application:

```
.ICON_ACTIVE {
    background-color: #0080C0 !important;
    color: white !important;
}
```

When an ICON component gets the `ICON_ACTIVE` class assigned, the icon will become white, and the background will become blue, indicated by the color code #0080C0.

17.3.3 Buttons

The PANEL component ICON_GROUP_ANALYSIS contains the buttons just below the header of the application (Figure 17.16). These buttons are actually ICON components, three of which you've already seen.

Figure 17.16 More Icon Components

This PANEL contains six buttons. It's interesting to see what scripts are executed when each one of these buttons is clicked.

Bookmark

The first button in Figure 17.16 is the BOOKMARK button. When this button is clicked, the options shown in Figure 17.17 become available to the user.

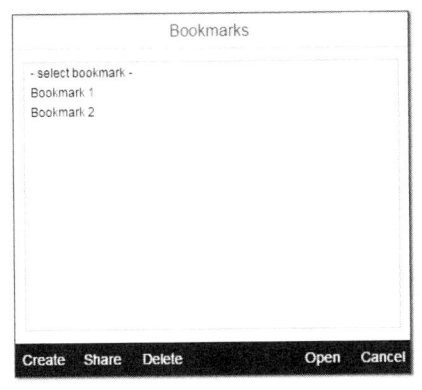

Figure 17.17 Bookmark Options

In the `On Click` event, the global script `BOOKMARK_FUNCTIONS.bookmark_list_refresh` is used to display all bookmarks in a LIST BOX component (Figure 17.17). Next, two PANEL components are made visible, DIALOG_CONTAINER and DIALOG_BOOKMARK, as shown in Figure 17.17. This uses the following code:

```
DIALOG_CONTAINER.setVisible(true);
DIALOG_BOOKMARK.setVisible(true);
```

Open Data Source Browser

The second button in Figure 17.16 opens a new window where the user can select a data source such as a BEx query from one of the available source systems (see Figure 17.18).

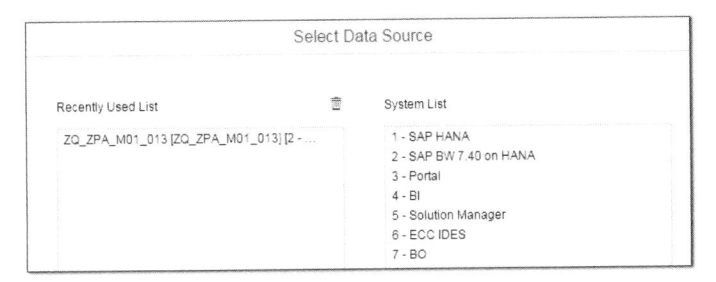

Figure 17.18 Data Browser Window

On the `On Click` event, the LAYOUR_CONTAINER, which is the screen containing the crosstabs and charts, is hidden, using the following code:

```
LAYOUT_CONTAINER.setVisible(false);
```

After that, the DIALOG_CONTAINER, the PANEL component containing various user interaction components, is set to `visible`, along with some other panels that make up Figure 17.18:

```
DIALOG_CONTAINER.setVisible(true);
GRID_DIALOG_CONNECTION.setVisible(true);
DIALOG_CONNECTION.setVisible(true);
BUTTON_DIALOG_CONNECTION_BACK.setVisible(true);
```

The important part of the code happens in the `DATA_SOURCE_FUNCTIONS` global script. In the first script function, `load_system_ids()`, all available source systems are fetched and displayed in a LIST BOX component (see the system list in Figure 17.18):

```
DATA_SOURCE_FUNCTIONS.load_system_ids();
```

The `load_recently_used_datasources()` global script function loads the recently used data sources in a LIST BOX component and displays them in a list as shown in Figure 17.18, using the following code:

```
DATA_SOURCE_FUNCTIONS.load_recently_used_datasources();
```

BUTTON_UNDO

The third icon in Figure 17.16 is the UNDO button. The script that executes this functionality has only one line of code:

```
State.backOneStep();
```

Remember that in the application properties, the number of MAXIMUM NUMBER OF STEPS BACK was set to 20 (see Section 17.2). One of the methods of the `State` object is `backOneStep()`, which sets the application one navigation step back.

BUTTON_HEADER_INFO

The INFO icon that is located in the top-right part of the screen will open the PANEL called PANEL_INFO, which contains a large amount of information (Figure 17.19). There is a lot of code in the `On Click` event of this button. Let's look at some interesting pieces of this code.

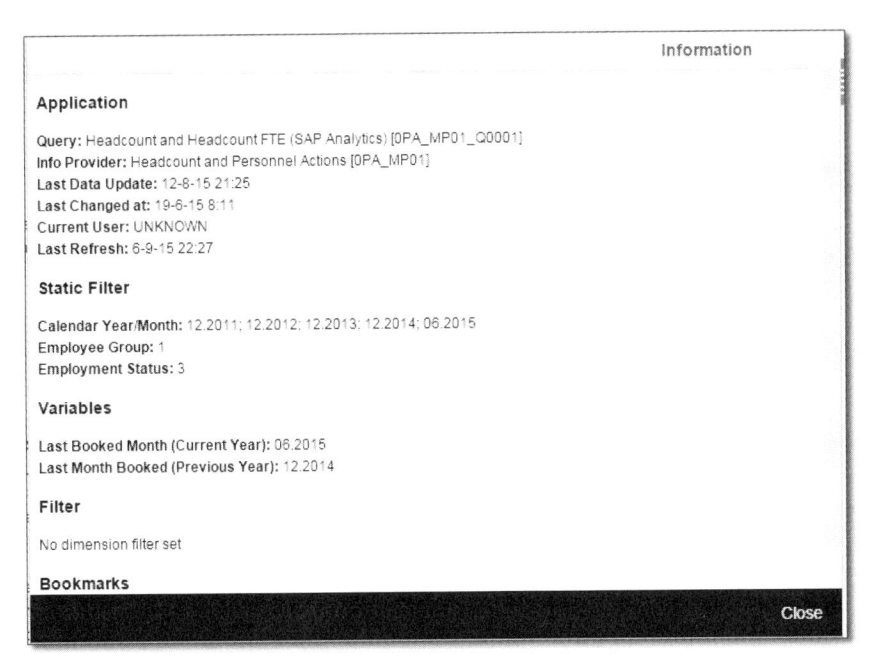

Figure 17.19 Info Button

The component used here is a special kind of TEXT component, called a FORMATTED TEXT VIEW component. The text for this component is built up in the script. Take a look at the following lines:

```
INFO_CONTENT.setHtmlText(INFO_CONTENT.getHtmlText() + "<h3>" + TEXT_
POOL.AppInfo + "</h3>");
```

INFO_CONTENT is the name of the FORMATTED TEXT VIEW component. With the `setHtmlText()` method, a text will be set in this component. Each time this method is called, the text that is already set will be overwritten. That is why the `getHtmlText()` method is used to set the text that was previously added again. After the previously set text, some text is added such as the HTML tags `<h3>` and `</h3>` indicating the text should be marked as heading 3, and the value in the TEXT POOL component called TEXT_POOL with KEY and APPINFO. In Figure 17.20, you can see the mapping for the items in the TEXT POOL component.

Figure 17.20 Entries in the Text Pool Component

In Listing 17.3, the same logic is used. Each time the `setHtmlText()` method is called, the previously added text will be set first. You can see that the word "Query:" is added to the text, along with the query description (obtained by the method `DS_1.getInfo().queryDescription`) and the technical name of the query (`DS_1.getInfo().queryTechnicalName`).

```
INFO_CONTENT.setHtmlText(INFO_
CONTENT.getHtmlText() + "<strong>" + TEXT_POOL.Query
+ ": " + "</strong>" + DS_1.getInfo().queryDescription + '
  [' + DS_1.getInfo().queryTechnicalName + ']' + "<br>");
```
Listing 17.3 Info Icon On Click Event

The whole text in this component is built using the same logic. The rest of the text is filled with the values for the static filters, variables, and dimension filters.

ICON_PROMPTS

The ICON_PROMPTS icon is located in the top-left of the screen. When clicked, the following line of code is executed:

```
APPLICATION.openPromptDialog(700, 700);
```

This code opens a default window where the values for BEx variables can be entered if they are available.

17.3.4 On Startup

As the name indicates, the `On Startup` script is executed when the application starts. This script can be viewed and edited by opening the Script Editor in the PROPERTIES of the application (Figure 17.21).

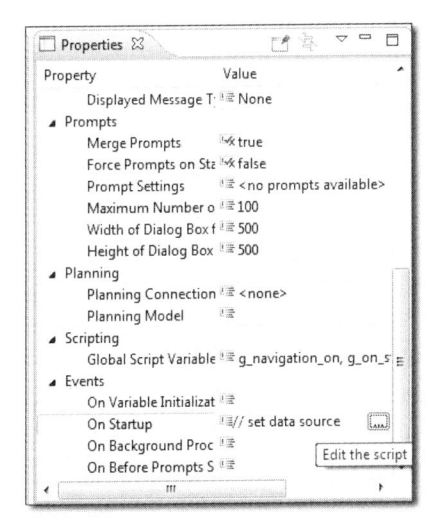

Figure 17.21 Application Properties

You can control the initial setup of your application in the `On Startup` script. For instance, it's possible to select which data sources is loaded at startup. You can also set values for BEx variables at this point.

Let's take a look at the code in the `On Startup` script. We'll break the code down into smaller pieces. Remember that in the beginning of this chapter, we removed the code in the `On Startup` property. Initially, we used `START_FUNCTIONS.on_startup()`, which is actually a call to a global script function. This function again calls another function called `START_FUNCTIONS.on_initialization()`. The code is broken down into smaller pieces in the following.

First, a check is done to see whether or not a data source is loaded using the following code:

695

17 | Building an OLAP Application Using a Template

```
if (DS_1.isInitialized()) {
```

If this is true, the available variables from the data source are collected and stored in an array called `variables`. When there are variables available, the icon to choose variables will also be enabled as shown in Listing 17.4.

```
/
* check variables and disable Prompt Icon, if no input ready variables
are available */

var variables = DS_1.getVariables();
var prompt_possible = false;
PROMPTS_DISABLED.setVisible(true);

variables.forEach(function(variable, index) {
    if (variable.inputEnabled == true) {
        prompt_possible = true;
        PROMPTS_DISABLED.setVisible(false);
    }
});
```
Listing 17.4 Variables

Next, the query description is used as a title for the application, and the technical name of the query is used as a `tooltip`, as shown in Listing 17.5.

```
/* get DataSource information for Header Title */
if (DS_1.getInfo().queryDescription) {
TEXT_HEADER_TITLE.setText(DS_1.getInfo().queryDescription);
TEXT_HEADER_TITLE.setTooltip(DS_1.getInfo().queryTechnicalName);
}
else if (DS_1.getInfo().queryTechnicalName) {
    TEXT_HEADER_TITLE.setText(DS_1.getInfo().queryTechnicalName);
}
else {
TEXT_HEADER_TITLE.setText(XQUERY);
}
```
Listing 17.5 Query Description

Finally, the bookmarking menu is set up. First, the bookmark menu is hidden, and the bookmark icon's style is reset. Then the initial view of the data is set to TABLE (note that the user can choose from TABLE, CHART, or CHART_TABLE), as shown in Listing 17.6.

```
/* enable Bookmark Icon */
BOOKMARK_DISABLED.setVisible(false);
ICON_BOOKMARK.setCSSClass("");
```

```
/* set initial mode */
g_display_mode = "TABLE";
g_designer_mode_on = true;
TOGGLE_FUNCTIONS.toggle_designer_mode();
TOGGLE_FUNCTIONS.toggle_display_mode();
}
```
Listing 17.6 Bookmark Menu

17.3.5 Adding Filters

Next to the prompts icon in the top-left part of the screen, you'll find a FILTER LINE component. Users can add filters to the application by clicking on the ADD FILTERS icon (Figure 17.22).

Figure 17.22 Adding Filters

Clicking this icon brings up a DIMENSIONS list (Figure 17.23). Users can select a dimension to apply a filter value.

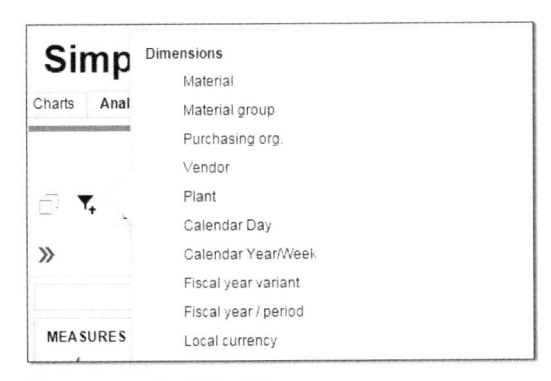

Figure 17.23 Available Filters

When a dimension is chosen, the user can then set a value in the window that opens (Figure 17.24).

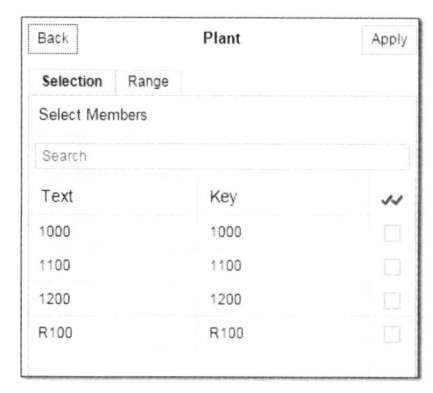

Figure 17.24 Available Filter Values

When a filter value is set, the FILTER LINE is updated with the new applied filters (Figure 17.25).

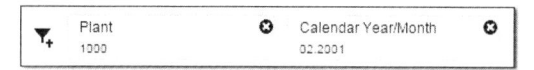

Figure 17.25 Applied Filters

17.4 Summary

In this chapter, we discussed how you can integrate your own dashboard application with a ready-to-run template to create a dashboard application where the users can also perform OLAP functions. In addition, we looked at the important components, properties, and scripts that are used in the OLAP application. You've seen that the different views (table, chart, or both) are grouped into panels, and that these panels are made visible or invisible when needed. Finally, we explored what happens when the On Startup script is called, and how global script functions are grouped together and used in the application.

In the previous two chapters, you've seen how two other applications are developed. This application is the last of the examples in this book. In the next chapter, we'll provide an outlook for Design Studio.

A lot has changed in Design Studio up until version 1.6. In this chapter, we'll see what's in store for future developments based on SAP's strategy and roadmap.

18 Outlook

Having walked through the features currently available with Design Studio, in this chapter, we'll look ahead, towards the future, to see what other developments are in store. Please be mindful that the content in this chapter is our opinion based on the current information and statements made by SAP. While these changes have been mentioned, they aren't set in stone.

That being said, in this chapter, we'll look at the current SAP BusinessObjects Business Intelligence (BI) strategy, and then walk through a roadmap of how Design Studio will continue to evolve.

18.1 SAP Analytics and Platform Strategy

Before we go into the future of Design Studio, we have to look at SAP's main business intelligence strategy. The business intelligence strategy has two fundamental pillars on which product development takes place: *lead the cloud* and *innovate the core*.

"Lead the cloud" refers to developing all applications for usage in the cloud. In terms of SAP BusinessObjects BI, this means developing and consuming SAP BusinessObjects BI software products using browsers instead of the installed Design Studio software on your computer. This is the future direction that SAP is looking at.

However, SAP is aware that many customers are still interested in taking a traditional approach (software installed on a computer) to their business intelligence. This is supported by the second piece of the strategy puzzle: "innovate the core." In this strategy line, the current portfolio will be developed further.

Design Studio is part of the core in the "innovate the core" strategy. There are three value propositions within that frame:

- **Leverage enterprise assets**
  This means that you should be able to connect to the data you have available for analytical purposes. This includes SAP Business Warehouse (BW), SAP HANA, or any other data source with the use of existing data models (such as third-party enterprise data). You'll be able to access the latter using either SAP HANA Smart Data Access or a Universe (UNX) built on the SAP BusinessObjects BI 4.x platform.

- **Leverage future investments in the SAP BusinessObjects BI 4.x platform**
  The SAP BusinessObjects BI 4.x platform will be further improved for performance and reliability. Design Studio will be enabled to use those improvements.

- **Leverage investments in the SAP BusinessObjects BI 4.x client suite**
  Design Studio isn't an application unto itself. It's developed with interoperability in mind with SAP Lumira and SAP BusinessObjects Analysis, edition for Microsoft Office. This means that you can link to documents created by these other programs and pass information that enables filters, navigation, and so on. Additionally, you're able to create documents in these two applications and transfer them to Design Studio and continue to develop there.

  This can, for example, allow users to prototype reports, stories, and visualizations in SAP Lumira and transfer that design to Design Studio to create a more robust version that is equipped with more refined authorization and that handles more options, and then is released to a larger number of users.

In the SAP BusinessObjects BI portfolio, there are a lot of software tools to choose from (Figure 18.1). Each tool has its strengths and weaknesses and is geared toward a particular function.

SAP Lumira is for discovery and analysis. Users can combine data, perform calculations, and visualize results to create a compelling story. Design Studio is made to create dashboards and applications. SAP BusinessObjects Analysis, edition for Microsoft Office, is for more advanced analysis and Microsoft Office integration. For standard reporting, you have SAP Crystal Reports or SAP BusinessObjects Web Intelligence, where you can create reports with a fixed layout that are sent to a group of users at regular intervals.

SAP Analytics and Platform Strategy | 18.1

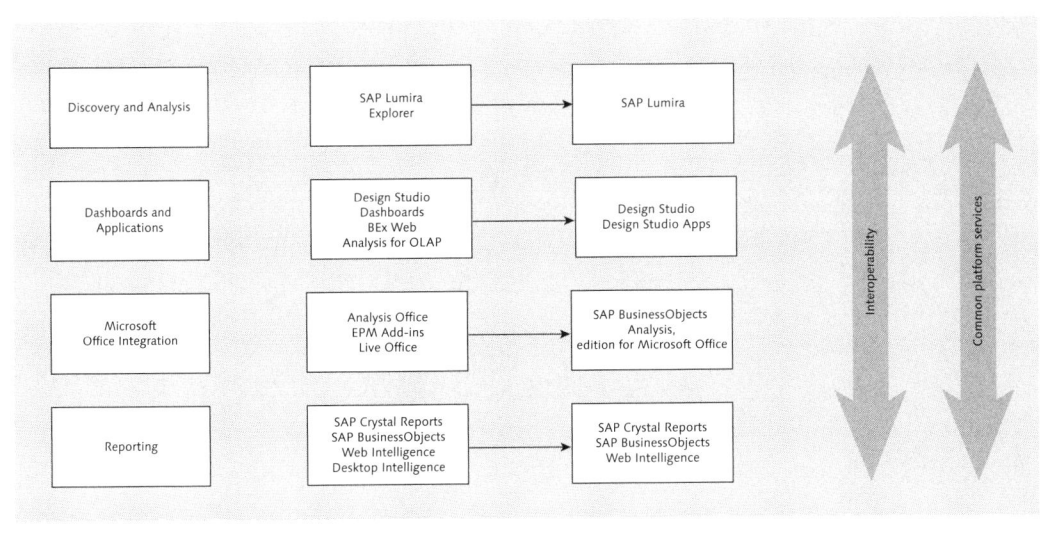

Figure 18.1 Design Studio's Place within the Portfolio

The question many organizations face is which tool to choose. The answer depends heavily on the kind of business intelligence service you want to offer. Do you want people to be able to do their own analysis and present their findings? Then SAP Lumira is probably the answer. Do you want more advanced options and freedom? Then SAP BusinessObjects Analysis, edition for Microsoft Office, should be your tool of choice. Do you want to offer a portfolio of SAP BusinessObjects BI products centrally managed? Then Design Studio might be what you're looking for. Whatever you choose, be sure to carefully evaluate your options.

In the future, the BEx Web Application Designer and SAP BusinessObjects Dashboards will continue to be maintained for bug fixes. You can't expect many (if at all) new developments. What we see is SAP making Design Studio into a large toolkit to make all kinds of reports that can serve self-discovery, analysis, standard reporting, and dashboards. The sum of their capabilities together with the new technologies make Design Studio a product that can function as a jack of all trades because it can serve as a development tool for many types of reports.

If you continue to work with either the BEx Web Application Designer or SAP BusinessObjects Dashboards, note that you won't be able to automatically migrate them to Design Studio. The programs fundamentally differ too much to be able to do so.

701

SAP will invest most of its resources into the development of Design Studio on the SAP BusinessObjects BI platform. This is in line with the core strategy we discussed previously. On the SAP BusinessObjects BI platform, Design Studio is able (with help from UNX) to harness all available backend databases and show the results in the applications. If you currently run on SAP NetWeaver or SAP HANA, but you don't have an SAP BusinessObjects BI platform in your organization, you should think about moving to the SAP BusinessObjects BI platform. In the future, we expect there to be more and more functionalities that are only available via this platform.

Having looked at SAP's general SAP BusinessObjects BI strategy, next we'll turn our attention to the current available roadmaps for Design Studio and how we expect the software to evolve.

18.2 Roadmap

The Design Studio roadmap (Table 18.1) is often the best place to identify how a product will continue to evolve. Ideally, you should check on the Design Studio roadmap often (i.e., every two to three months). Sometimes the changes between versions are more telling than the current version itself because they can indicate direction changes and functional overhauls.

In Table 18.1, the current Design Studio roadmap is laid out based on present, planned, and future innovations divided by the type of user the feature is intended for. The today column indicates what the newest available version has to offer. The planned innovations column typically indicates advances planned in the next version or release. The future direction column provides information on long-term plans for the software. These can indicate either features next in line or a few years away from release.

	Today	Planned Innovations	Future Direction
End User	▸ Geo map and chart enhancements. After the first introduction in 1.5, this is the next step. ▸ Visualization components: SCORECARD, SPREADSHEET (for planning with copy/paste), TIMER (was already available an SDK example), TREE. ▸ Export to PDF. ▸ Right-to-left language support.	▸ Scheduling and broadcasting (depending on how this evolves, it would do much to replace reporting functionality from SAP Crystal Reports). ▸ Annotations and comments. ▸ Improved mobile experience: responsive layout, chart scrolling, and chart zooming. ▸ Enhanced interoperability with SAP BusinessObjects Analysis, edition for Microsoft Office.	▸ Enhanced schedule and broadcasting. ▸ Export to PDF enhancement. ▸ Enhanced annotations and comments. ▸ Offline mobile dashboards.
Analyst	▸ CROSSTAB component: drag and drop. ▸ Custom measures and Top N filters for runtime. (This will be very handy as a lot of developers had to resort to complex queries to achieve this in Design Studio.) ▸ Chart context menus.	▸ Ad hoc currency conversion; switch between currencies. (You'll probably need a connection to a currency table.) ▸ Threshold filters at runtime (the kind of filter where you can, say, present only those orders of $40,000 or more).	▸ Variant support. Variants are typical SAP BW features where you can save filter settings to easily re-apply them the next time.

Table 18.1 SAP BusinessObjects Design Studio Roadmap (Source: SAP)

	Today	Planned Innovations	Future Direction
Designer, Developer, Administrator	▸ Rapid prototyping for CSV data. (This allows you to insert data without having a backend database and start creating applications faster.) ▸ SAP Fiori component library. ▸ Context menu customization. ▸ UNX connectivity. ▸ Enhanced standard apps. ▸ Improved design experience. ▸ Extended language support.	▸ Component enhancements. ▸ Component composition and reuse. ▸ Enhanced interoperability with SAP Lumira (including importing stories) and Velocity support. ▸ Improved design experience.	▸ Local calculations and projections: data manipulation and mash-ups for SAP BusinessObjects Dashboards. ▸ Improved design experience. ▸ Extending administrative capabilities.

Table 18.1 SAP BusinessObjects Design Studio Roadmap (Source: SAP) (Cont.)

In this section, we'll focus on the current planned innovations and the expected future direction SAP has set out for how the product will evolve.

> **Roadmaps**
>
> If you want to look at the most recent version of the roadmap, go to *http://scn.sap.com/community/product-and-solution-road-maps*. You can find the updates on the roadmaps of the SAP products and solutions there.

18.2.1 Planned Innovations

In the Planned Innovations column of Table 18.1, we see many continuations of current features that build upon their capabilities. We expect that the SAPUI5 and SAP Lumira applications will be further developed to incorporate Design Studio features. Furthermore, we see the mobile experience and capabilities being improved as well. This will benefit many customers as these problems are often solved now using SDK components.

Another interesting feature coming up is the enhanced PDF and Excel exports capabilities. With this feature in place, you can combine parts of your application into a single export. This would allow an advanced print option where your key performance indicators (KPIs) could be rendered into an official monthly or quarterly report.

18.2.2 Future Direction

In the future, all the development investments will be directed to the SAP BusinessObjects BI platform, which means if you use Design Studio on top of SAP NetWeaver or SAP HANA, you'll be missing out on a lot of options.

In addition, we see that Design Studio components are being rebuilt using the SAPUI5 m library. This is done to add the same kind of components as in SAPUI5 apps and SAP Fiori apps. The disadvantage of this is that every dashboard you've built up to version 1.5 will need to be converted in the foreseeable future.

18.3 Summary

In this chapter, we discussed SAP's current strategy for SAP BusinessObjects BI platform and Design Studio. Based on this information, we can see that SAP places Design Studio firmly in the core as a tool that should be able to combine all the information that you have in house for analytical purposes. Second, SAP has advised customers to use the SAP BusinessObjects BI platform for their analytical needs. This fits with the strategy because the SAP BusinessObjects BI platform is built to connect to multiple sources from all kinds of backend systems.

Finally, we see a lot of advancements that are continuations of current features already available. Particularly, we're curious about the SAPUI5 and SAP Fiori apps you can create and how Design Studio will adapt to these new technologies.

Appendices

A Tips for Using SAP BusinessObjects Design Studio and SAP BusinessObjects Analysis, Edition for Microsoft Office 709

B SAP BusinessObjects Mobile and SAP BusinessObjects Design Studio 715

C The Authors 723

A Tips for Using SAP BusinessObjects Design Studio and SAP BusinessObjects Analysis, Edition for Microsoft Office

SAP BusinessObjects Analysis, edition for Microsoft Office, is part of the SAP BusinessObjects BI portfolio, and it allows advanced multidimensional analysis of OLAP sources. It is the successor to the BEx Analyzer and runs, just like the BEx Analyzer, as a plugin within Microsoft Excel. It is also possible to use SAP BusinessObjects Analysis from within Microsoft PowerPoint. Besides the Microsoft Office version of SAP BusinessObjects Analysis, there is also an online web version available, called SAP BusinessObjects Analysis, edition for OLAP. This application is integrated into the SAP BusinessObjects BI platform and can be accessed from the BI Launch Pad.

> **Note**
>
> This appendix is devoted specifically to the Microsoft Office edition of SAP BusinessObjects Analysis. We will refer to the product as simply SAP BusinessObjects Analysis, but know that we are specifically referring to the Microsoft Office, not the OLAP, edition.

There are two hidden features in SAP BusinessObjects Analysis that can be useful when you want to develop a Design Studio application:

- Creating a Design Studio application
- Smart copying data sources

SAP BusinessObjects Analysis also has a few features that are not available in Design Studio yet. You can, for example, add calculations, conditional formatting, and exceptions in a data source—all features that we can make use of in Design Studio. In Design Studio, you can now add calculations in the CROSSTAB component. However, changing data sources is still not possible. In this appendix, we will show you how to take advantage of the two hidden features we mentioned.

A | Tips for Using Design Studio and SAP BusinessObjects Analysis

> **Future of Smart Copy**
>
> We expect that the missing functionalities will be added directly to Design Studio in future versions. Until that time smart copy ist he way to tweak datasources and use them in Design Studio

A.1 Creating a Design Studio Application

It is possible to transfer the components of an SAP BusinessObjects Analysis workbook to a new Design Studio application. The following components are supported:

- CROSSTAB components
- CHART components (pie, line, column, bar, surface, radar, bubble, and scatter charts)
- FILTER components

> **Creating OLAP Applications**
>
> Instead of using the CREATE DESIGN STUDIO funtionality you can also work with the templates offered in Design Studio for creating OLAP applications. Given that the support for creating an application from SAP BusinessObjects Analysis is limited to a few components, we recommend using a template to get a better head start.

To transfer components, follow the steps below:

1. Open SAP BusinessObjects Analysis.
2. Open an existing workbook or create a new one (Figure A.1).
3. Check whether the CREATE WEB APPLICATION icon is present in the ANALYSIS ribbon (Figure A.2).
4. If this icon is not available, go to SETTINGS • ADVANCED SETTINGS and select the option for SHOW "CREATE WEB APPLICATION" IN TOOLS GROUP (Figure A.3). Click OK.

Creating a Design Studio Application | **A.1**

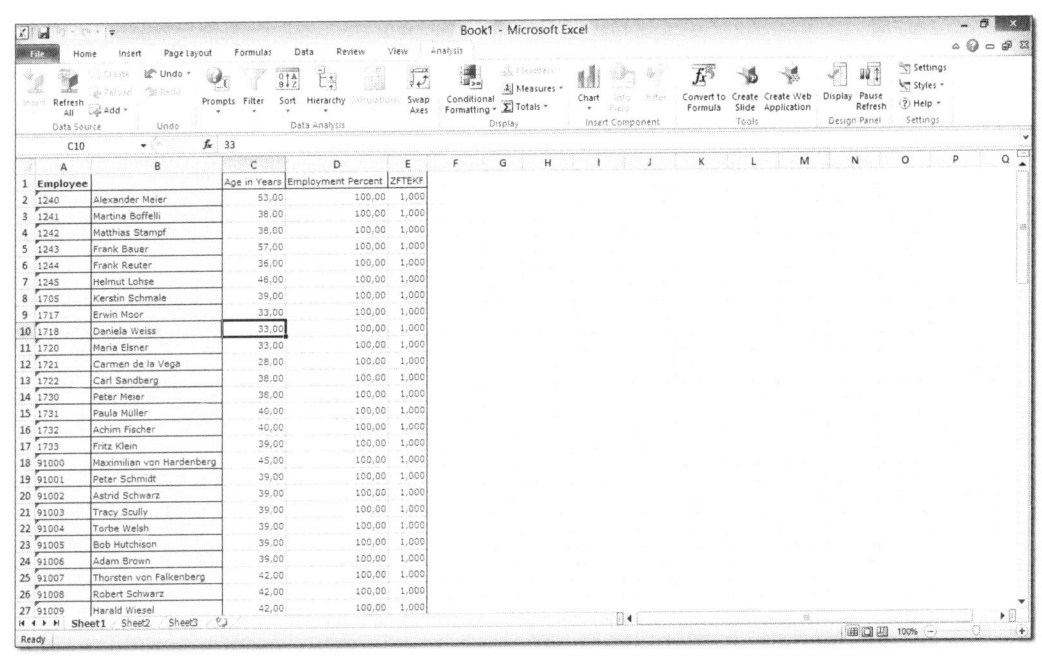

Figure A.1 SAP BusinessObjects Analysis

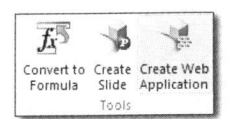

Figure A.2 Create Web Application Icon

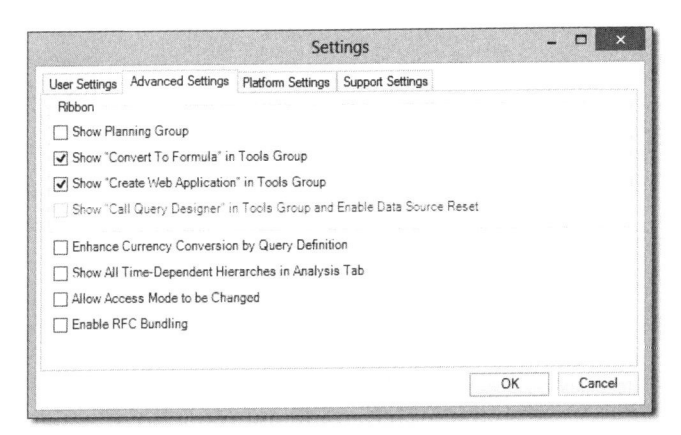

Figure A.3 SAP BusinessObjects Analysis Settings

711

A | Tips for Using Design Studio and SAP BusinessObjects Analysis

5. Make sure that Design Studio is not currently running. If it is, save your work and close Design Studio.
6. Select the workbook sheet you want to transfer to Design Studio.
7. Click the CREATE WEB APPLICATION button in the ANALYSIS ribbon (Figure A.2).
8. Design Studio starts now. Enter your credentials and click OK to log on to Design Studio.
9. You will now see a new Design Studio application based on the Analysis workbook, including the components and data sources (Figure A.4). You can continue working on this application from here.

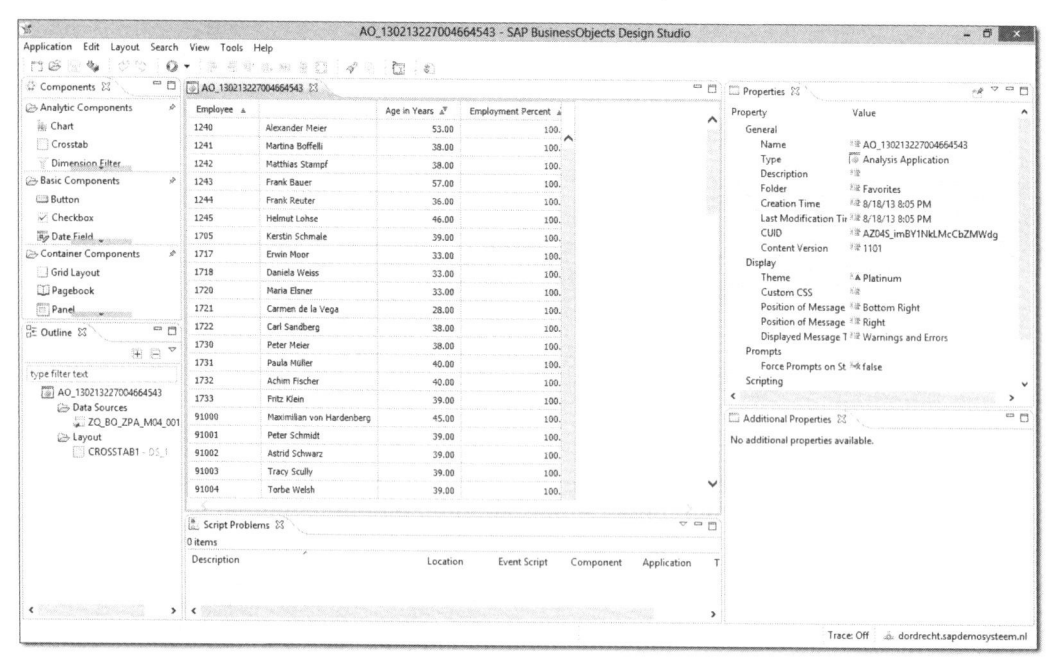

Figure A.4 New Design Studio Application Based on SAP BusinessObjects Analysis

A.2 Smart Copying Data Sources

Instead of transferring a whole workbook from SAP BusinessObjects Analysis, we can also copy the data source from the workbook.

There are two prerequisites that you need to be aware of before using this feature:

- You need an local installed copy of both SAP BusinessObjects Analysis, edition for Microsoft Office and Design Studio.
- Both tools need to be used in either local mode or with an SAP BusinessObjects BI platform. Only then you will be able to insert an exported data source.

Proceed witht the following steps to use smart copying:

1. Open SAP BusinessObjects Analysis.
2. Open an existing workbook or create a new one.
3. Now right-click the result table and select SMART COPY from the context menu (Figure A.5).

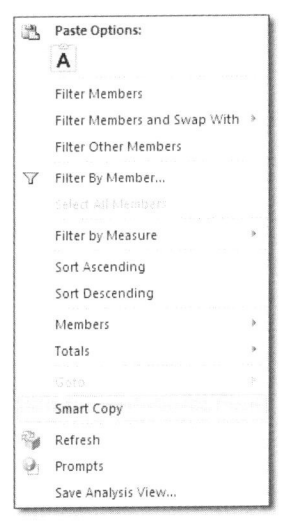

Figure A.5 Smart Copy Option in SAP BusinessObjects Analysis

4. In Design Studio, right-click the DATA SOURCES folder in the OUTLINE view (Figure A.6). Select SMART PASTE. The data source is now added to the Design Studio application.

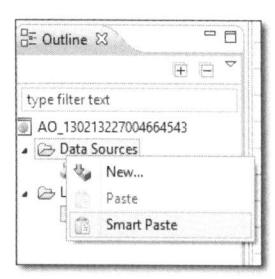

Figure A.6 Smart Paste Feature in Design Studio

Another option is to right-click the Layout folder in the Outline view and select Smart Paste. In this case, not only the data source is added to the Design Studio application, but also a new Crosstab component is added and already assigned to the new data source.

B   SAP BusinessObjects Mobile and SAP BusinessObjects Design Studio

In this appendix, we will introduce SAP BusinessObjects Mobile (Figure B.1). With the SAP BusinessObjects Mobile application, users of mobile devices can get access to several content types of the SAP BusinessObjects BI platform from a single mobile application. Besides Design Studio applications, this includes content from SAP Crystal Reports, SAP BusinessObjects Web Intelligence, and SAP BusinessObjects Dashboards. Additionally, you can access SAP BusinessObjects Explorer information spaces.

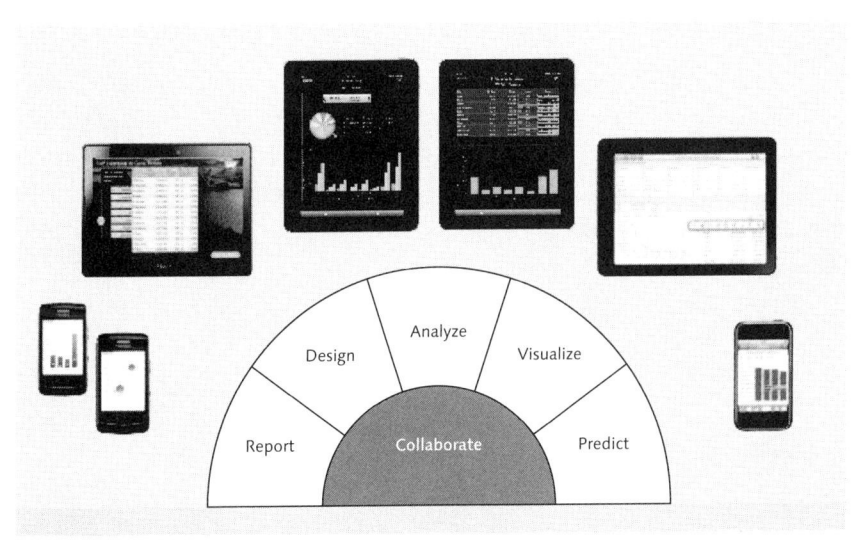

Figure B.1 Mobilizing the SAP BusinessObjects BI Suite

In this appendix, we will take a quick look at the features of this mobile application. Please note that we are using version 6.3.8.

B.1   Supported Platforms

The SAP BusinessObjects Mobile application is currently available for iOS devices (iPhone and iPad) and Android smartphones and tablets. The applications can be downloaded for free from the Apple App Store and the Google Play Store:

715

▶ **SAP BusinessObjects Mobile 6 for iOS**
   https://itunes.apple.com/us/app/sap-businessobjects-mobile/id441208302?mt=8

▶ **SAP BusinessObjects Mobile 6 for Android**
   https://play.google.com/store/apps/details?id=com.sap.mobi&hl=en

> **Mobile Server on the SAP BusinessObjects BI Platform**
>
> To connect to an SAP BusinessObjects BI platform and use its content on the mobile applications, the SAP BusinessObjects Mobile Server needs to be installed and configured on the SAP BusinessObjects BI platform. More information about the Mobile Server can be found at https://help.sap.com/bomobilebi.

B.2 Connectivity

Connecting the SAP BusinessObjects Mobile application to an SAP BusinessObjects BI platform requires that you have set up a connection in the application. This can be done via BROWSE • SETTINGS (the gear icon) • APPLICATION SETTINGS • CREATE NEW CONNECTION. In this screen, you can enter the connection name, provide the server URL and CMS name, and set the authentication mode. You also have to enter your user credentials (Figure B.2).

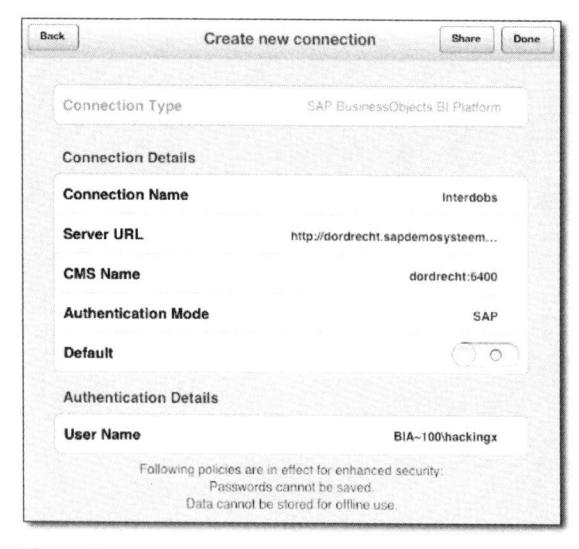

Figure B.2 Connection Setup

B.3 Using Content

Before you can use content from the SAP BusinessObjects BI platform, you have to make that content available for mobile usage. This should be done by filing the content documents—for example, a Design Studio application—in the MOBILE category. This is explained in Chapter 4, Section 4.4.4.

B.3.1 Browsing the Application

After connecting to the SAP BusinessObjects BI platform, the available content shows up on the home screen of the application (Figure B.3). Here you can open a report, dashboard, or application and refresh it. You can also view information about a document by tapping the information icon in the bottom right part of the tile.

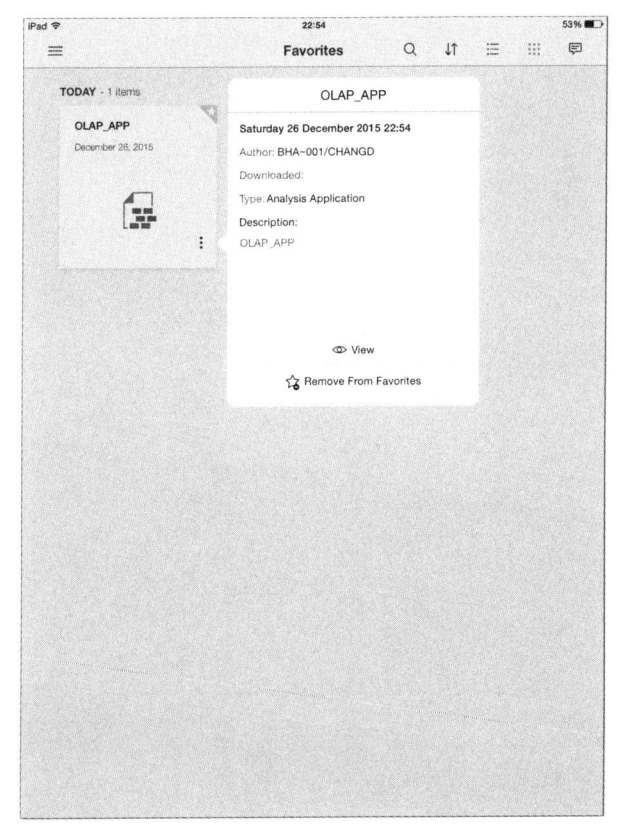

Figure B.3 Mobile Content

B.3.2 Running SAP BusinessObjects BI Content

When running a Design Studio application in SAP BusinessObjects Mobile, the exact same functionality is available as when you execute the same application in a browser. The only difference is that now you use your fingers instead of the mouse to interact with the components.

In Figure B.4, you can see the first tab of the Design Studio application that we created back in Chapter 17. The data is displayed in two charts, a combination of a line and column chart and a heat map chart.

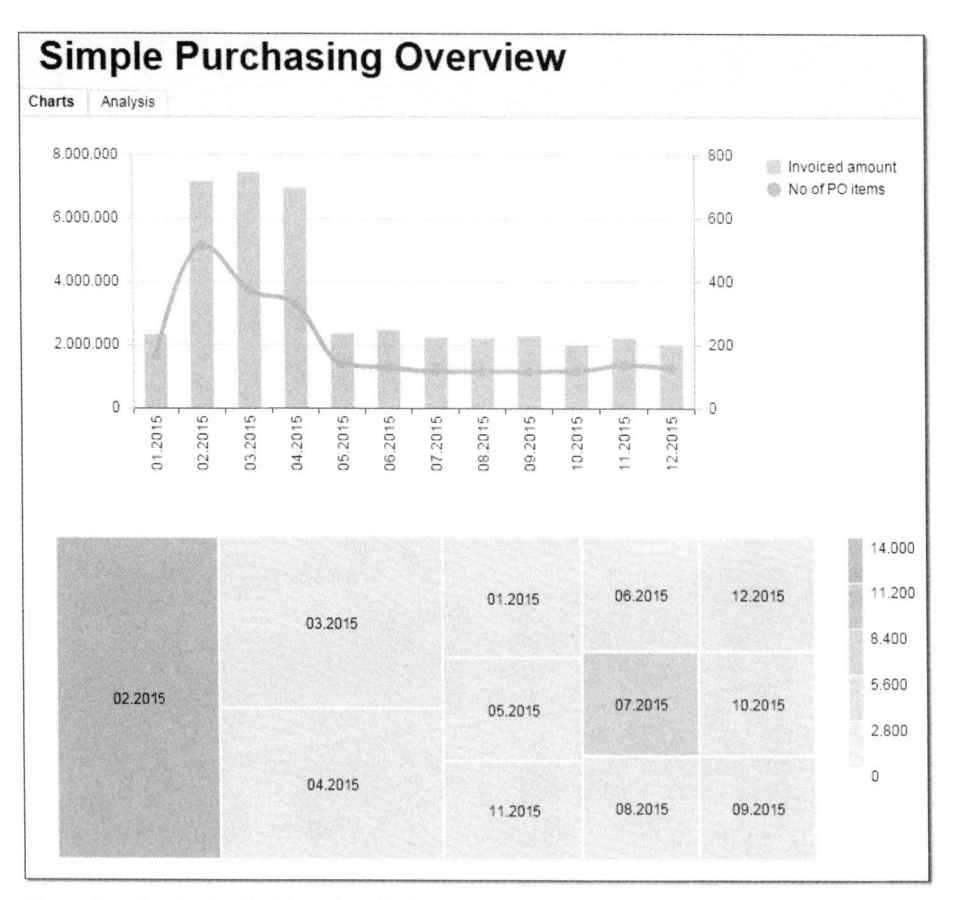

Figure B.4 Purchasing Dashboard on iPad

When the user selects a point in either one of the charts, the application will go to the second tab, where he/she can perform OLAP functionality on the dataset.

Figure B.5 shows the data in tabular form, but as you may recall from Chapter 17, the data can also be displayed in a chart.

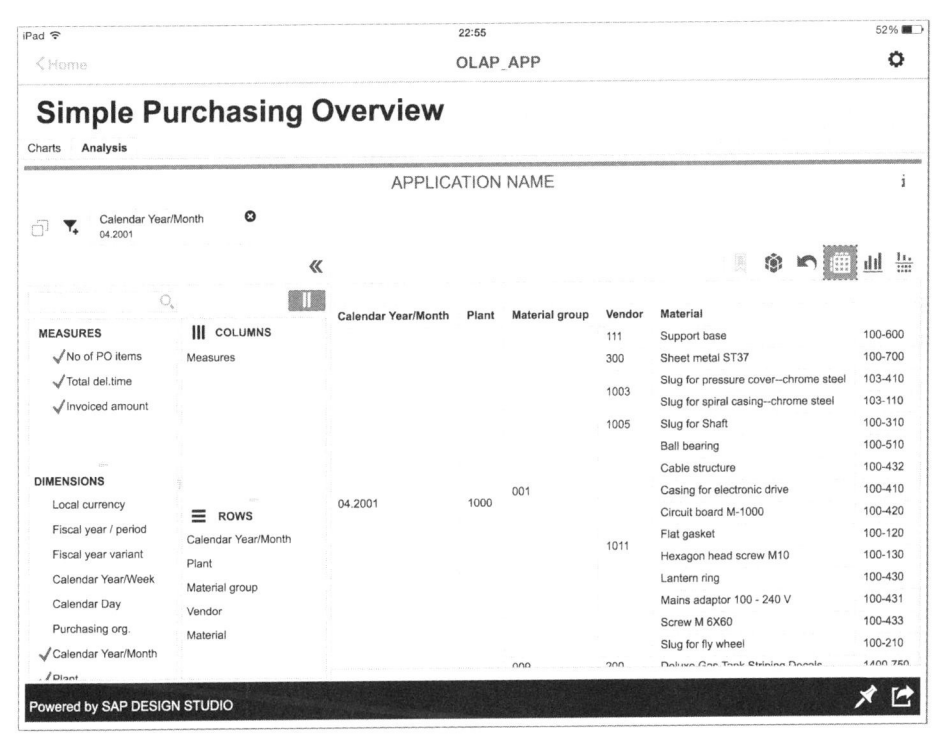

Figure B.5 OLAP Application

B.3.3 Collaboration Features

When a report, dashboard, or application is running, a settings toolbar can be made visible by tapping the SETTINGS button in the upper-right corner of the screen (Figure B.6). This gives you access to some interesting collaboration features.

The content can be shared and discussed with colleagues over the SAP Jam collaboration platform. If you want to add some texts, lines, or boxes; blur parts of the content; or crop the output of the content, you can use the ANNOTATION option (Figure B.7). You can even record a voice memo as an annotation (Figure B.8). Finally, you can send an email that contains a screenshot of the content (annotations included), with links to the content (Figure B.9).

B | SAP BusinessObjects Mobile and SAP BusinessObjects Design Studio

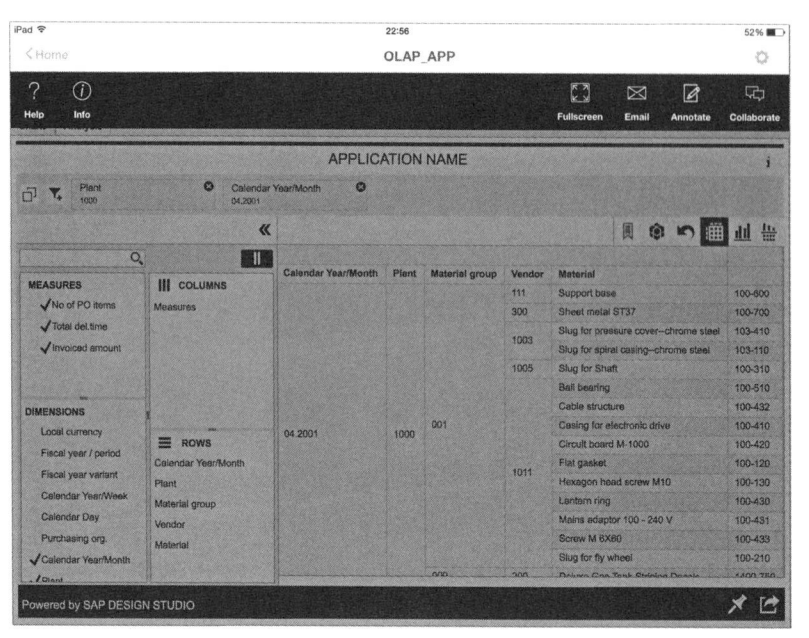

Figure B.6 Settings Toolbar

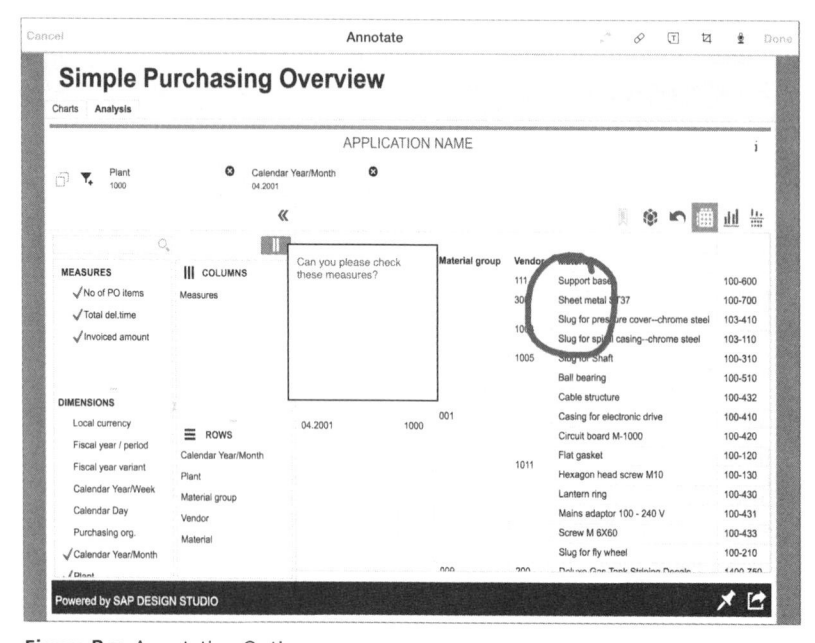

Figure B.7 Annotation Options

720

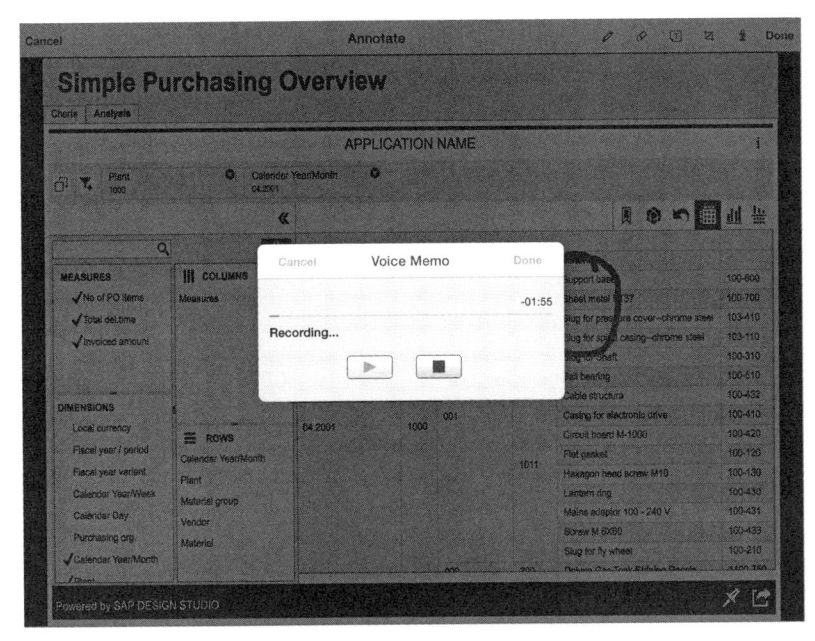

Figure B.8 Voice Memo

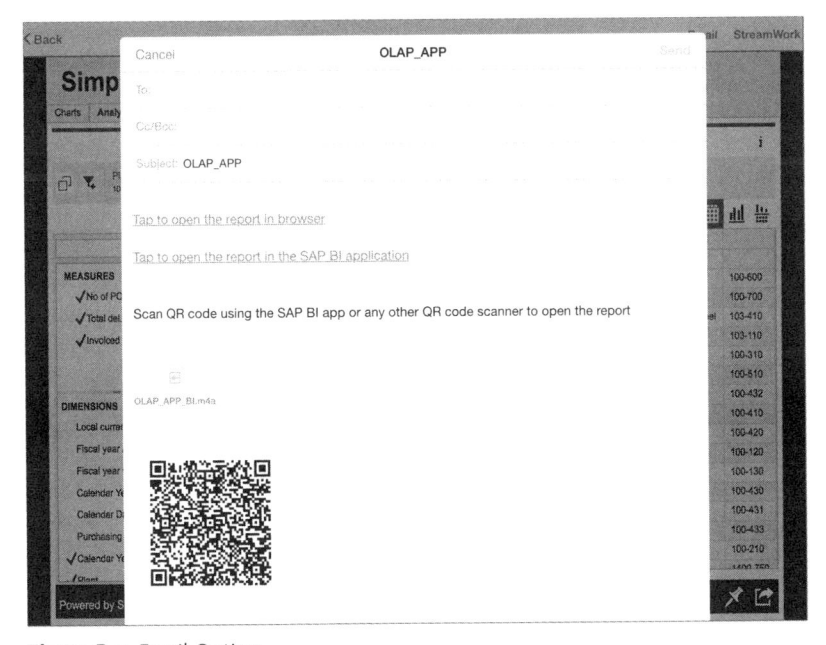

Figure B.9 Email Option

C   The Authors

Xavier Hacking is an SAP BI specialist from Eindhoven, the Netherlands, and works as a consultant for Interdobs. He has a master's degree in industrial engineering and management science from the Eindhoven University of Technology. He has worked with a wide range of products from the current SAP BW and SAP BusinessObjects BI toolset, with a focus on dashboard development within SAP environments.

Xavier co-authored *SAP BusinessObjects Dashboards 4.1 Cookbook*, *Getting Started with SAP BusinessObjects Design Studio*, and SAP *BusinessObjects Dashboards 4.0 Cookbook*, and is a writer for *SAP BusinessObjects Expert* magazine. He is also part of the Dutch BI Podcast, and blogs on all sorts of business-intelligence-related topics at *http://www.hackingsap.com*. You can follow him on Twitter at *@xjhacking*. Photo taken by Sander van Dillen.

Jeroen van der A is a passionate SAP BI consultant from the Netherlands working for Interdobs. He has over 18 years of experience with business intelligence and started using SAP products in 2005. Jeroen is focused on finding innovative ways to use business intelligence products to create added value, and uses a broad range of products to achieve this goal.

Jeroen is an international speaker on Design Studio, a writer for the Dutch SAP user magazine *VNSG* and is part of the Dutch BI Podcast. He writes regular blogs on *http://scn.sap.com* and on *http://www.interdobs.nl*. You can follow him on Twitter at *@hyronimous*. Photo taken by Sander van Dillen.

Dwain Chang is an SAP BI consultant, originally from Surinam, who currently lives in the Netherlands. He has a master's degree in informatics and economics as well as a degree in marketing from the Erasmus University Rotterdam. Dwain started his professional career in 2011, and has participated in various SAP backend and frontend development projects. Dwain has done a number of Design Studio implementations at a wide range of clients in the fields of Logistics, Finance, PM, and HR, to name a few. Photo taken by Sander van Dillen.

Index

!important, 687
.concat, 512
.exit(), 564
.getselectedvalue, 306
.save, 394
.splice, 513
@media, 415
100% stacked bar chart, 439
100% stacked column, 441

A

Action Sheet component, 301
activateHierarchy, 325
Active Provider, 171
Ad hoc
　currency conversion, 703
Adaptive Processing Server, 109, 477
　create, 111
Additional properties, 508, 529, 530, 607
afterDesignStudioUpdate, 572
afterUpdate, 545, 547, 549, 562, 596
alert, 522
Analysis Application Design Service, 305
Analysis Application Service, 105, 109
　initializing, 109
Analysis tab, 82, 676
Analytic component
　Scorecard component, 242
　Spreadsheet component, 251
Analytic view, 123
Android, 715
Anonymous functions, 565
Anscombe's quartet, 435
ap_bulletgraph.css, 580
API, 559, 571
AppInfo, 693
Application, 29, 92
　add data source, 150
　building principles, 453
　building tips, 454
　close, 149
　complex, 453

Application (Cont.)
　create new, 145, 197
　delete, 149
　execute locally, 153, 214
　execute on SAP BusinessObjects BI, 154
　exit, 155
　open, 148
　open recent, 148
　output, 361
　preferred startup mode, 155
　recovery, 165
　responsive, 414
　save, 149
　size, 455
　template, 167
　title, 624
Application component, 329, 356
　custom CSS, 218, 220
　displayed message types, 219
　force prompts on startup, 219
　global script variables, 219
　On Startup, 220
　position of message button, 218
　position of message window, 218
　properties, 218
Application design process, 195, 196
　adding data, 202
　executing the app, 214
　formatting, 211
　interactivity, 208
　UI and visualizations, 197
ApplicationInfo Object Component, 331
Architecture, 92
Archius, 487
Area chart, 442
Arguments, 307
Array, 315, 512, 539, 554
　elements, 512
　JSON object, 514
　length, 513
　nested, 513
　object, 512
Assignment statements, 306, 308
attachChange, 572

Index

Attribute, 182
   function, 570
   selectors, 526
Authorization, 463
Auto apply, 257
Automated planning, 392
Availability, 69, 72
Availability KPI, 618, 628

B

Backend connection, 169
Backend Connection component, 294
Bar chart, 570
Bar combination chart, 439, 443
Base folder structure, 575
Basemap, 339
Basic analysis layout, 146
Basic component, 261, 345
Basic layout, 147
Basic selectors, 526
beforeDesignStudioUpdate, 572
beforeUpdate, 545, 547, 577
Behavior, 683
BEx query, 33, 167, 386, 619, 679
   exception, 371
   setup, 203
BEx Web Analyzer, 37, 59, 709
BEx Web Application Designer, 37, 701
   design environment, 60
   functionality, 58
   publishing, 64
   setup, 60
   vs. Design Studio, 49, 64
   web item, 62
BI Action Language (BIAL), 305
BI Excellence, 487
BI Launch Pad, 35, 39, 65
BI tool comparison
   application examples, 67
   component adjustment options, 65
   components, 65
   data connectivity, 66
   data input options, 66
   layout development flexibility, 65
   mobile, 66

BI tool comparison (Cont.)
   output format, 65
   platform, 65
   SAP HANA, 66
   scripting options, 66
   SDK, 66
BIAL
   operators, 309
   syntax, 306
BICS, 56
Binding, 262
Blocks, 418
Blue Crystal theme, 401, 403
Body, 624, 688
Body panel, 416
Bookmark component, 331
Bookmarking, 331, 380, 691
Boolean expression
   call statement, 308
   comparison, 308
   constant, 308
   multiple comparisons, 308
Boston Consultancy Matrix, 444
Bottom margin, 336
Broadcasting, 703
Browser, 96
Bubble chart, 444
Built for comparison, 444
Bullet Graph component, 81, 573, 579, 586, 588, 589, 597, 649, 650
Button component, 265, 337
   icon, 266
   properties, 266
   text, 266
BUTTON_HEADER_INFO, 692
BUTTON_UNDO, 692
By Reference, 515
By Value, 515

C

Calculation view, 123
Calculations, 463
Call statements, 306
Cascading Style Sheets -> see CSS, 34
Cell locks, 386

Index

Central Management Console (CMC), 93, 109, 169, 477
Central Management System (CMS), 105
Centralized code, 461
Certificates, 474
Chaining, 560, 567
changeBy, 523
Characteristics, 552
Chart, 231
  area, 234, 237
  configuration, 679
  highlight, 236
  reference, 378
  view, 367
Chart component, 86, 231, 238, 337, 367
  chart type, 232
  data source, 232
  On Select, 233
  properties, 232
  show totals, 232
  swap axes, 232
Chart Type Picker component, 267
  properties, 268
Chart types
  100% stacked bar chart, 439
  100% stacked column, 234, 441
  additional, 236
  area chart, 442
  bar, 233, 437
  bar combination chart, 439
  bubble, 234
  column, 233, 440
  column combination, 234, 441
  column dual axis, 234
  comparison, 450
  crosstab, 443
  dual line, 233
  horizontal area, 234, 442
  horizontal line, 233, 437
  horizontal waterfall, 234, 445
  line, 233, 436
  multiple pie, 234, 447
  multiple radar, 235, 448
  pie, 234, 446
  radar, 235, 448
  scatter, 235, 450
  stacked bar, 233, 438

Chart types (Cont.)
  stacked column, 234, 440
  stacked waterfall, 234, 446
  waterfall, 191, 234, 444
Checkbox component, 268, 340
  properties, 268
  text, 268
Checkbox Group component, 341, 421
  properties, 270
Child, 517
Class name, 410
Classes, 525, 526
  variables, 593
Clean, 502
clearFilter, 393
Client tool, 92, 135
  required components, 96
clientReset, 395
Closures, 522, 523
Column, 83
Column chart, 440
Column combination chart, 441
Column margin, 595
Column sizing, 343
Combination chart, 82
Common layout properties
  bottom margin, 230
  height, 230
  left margin, 229
  right margin, 230
  top margin, 229
  width, 230
Complex applications, 453
Component, 32, 217
  analytic category, 180, 231
  Application component, 217
  arrange, 186
  basic category, 180
  composition and reuse, 704
  container category, 180
  CSS class, 224
  distribute, 186
  elements, 535
  global script variables, 225
  hide, 185
  level, 535
  methods, 306

727

Component (Cont.)
  On Startup, 225
  reload, 154
  show, 185
Component CSS, 531, 584
Component JavaScript, 528, 544, 550, 555, 571, 577, 578, 610
  adding functions, 546
  create, 592
  outline, 592
componentDeleted, 545, 549
Components
  internal formatting, 462
  types, 311
Concatenates, 309
Conceptual rules, 451
Condition, 521
Conditional formatting, 237, 249, 325
Conditional statements, 306, 307, 519
Configuration, 91
Connection, 685
Constructor, 516
Container component
  properties, 283
Content Assistant, 313, 314, 531
Context menu
  enabled, 248
Context menu component, 335
contribution.xml, 496, 509, 527, 531, 549, 575
contribution.ztl, 531, 558
Convert component, 323
copyFilter, 393
copyVariableValue, 393
Counter object, 523
Create
  child, 679
  new, 175
Crosstab component, 84, 247, 390, 426
  column limit, 248
  CSS class, 248
  data source, 248
  OLAP application, 83
  pixel-based scrolling, 248
  properties, 248
  row limit, 248

CSS, 34, 218, 305, 399, 401, 414, 581
  additional properties, 239
  advanced, 413
  attribute selectors, 526
  basic selectors, 526
  browsers, 414
  class, 253, 257, 266, 272, 336, 404, 413, 532, 622, 658
  color codes, 407
  custom classes, 408
  font size, 407
  group classes, 414
  hiding panels, 416
  include, 537
  layout, 461
  loading fonts, 657
  style, 282, 404
  style properties, 462
  themes, 401
CSS Style Editor, 405, 410
CUID, 372
Currency table, 703
Custom
  data sources, 133, 134
Custom Chart component, 77
Custom measures, 703
Customer feedback, 640

D

D3, 507, 559, 561, 601, 602, 604
  adding columns and rows, 563
  adding elements, 561
  data binding, 563
  functions, 599
  library, 518, 537, 561
  scales, 569
  transitions, 566
D3.selectAll, 594
Dashboards, 29, 30, 50
Data
  binding, 52, 262, 541
  bound, 536, 540, 555, 586, 587
  cell binding, 262
  discovery, 147
  grouping, 607
  manipulation, 359

Data (Cont.)
  preparation, 361
  selection, 629
  series, 239
  visualization, 29, 147
Data Field component, 271
Data Runtime JSON, 549, 553, 554
Data source, 152, 169, 181, 202, 328, 464, 679
  add, 150, 203
  browser, 456
  manually entering records, 650
  pause refresh, 183
  show prompts, 152
Data Source Alias component, 227, 314, 324
Databound component, 231
Date Field component, 343
  properties, 271
deactivateHierarchy, 325
Declarations, 413
decrement, 523
Deep copy, 515
Design principles
  control your screen, 432
  don't make users think, 430
  don't make users wait, 430
  emphasize features, 431
  keep it simple, 432
  use conventions, 432
  user focus, 431
Detail screen, 660
Dimension, 83, 182, 255, 256
  array, 551
  filters, 334
  hierarchy, 325
  items, 274
  member binding, 263
  name, 255
Dimension Filter component, 254, 344
  data source, 255
  display mode, 255
  properties, 255
  target data source, 255
Display, 683
div, 525, 549, 608
Documentation, 461
DOM, 509, 558, 564

drawBulletGraph, 600
drawKPIBarChart, 549
Drilldown report, 639
Dropdown Box component, 271, 345, 355, 363
  properties, 272
DS_1, 682
Dynamic properties, 568

E

Eclipse, 31, 491, 494, 557
  application, 503
  environment, 495
  installation, 487, 491
Edit menu, 156
  copy, 157
  delete, 157
  paste, 157
  redo, 156
  undo, 156
Elements, 512, 524, 559
enter(), 564, 568, 599
Enterprise assets, 700
Enum, 311
Event handler, 312
Events, 684
Execute, 393, 394
  locally, 153, 214
  on SAP BusinessObjects BI platform, 154
exit, 568
Export as Template, 167
Expression, 309
  types, 310
Expressions, 307
Extends, 558
Extension level, 533
External parameter, 225, 455

F

Fact data, 552
Fact Data Runtime, 552
Fake data, 573
Federated, 408

fillDropDown, 610
fillMetadataProperty, 543
Filter Line component, 146, 252
Filter Panel component, 256, 344
   data source, 257
   dimensions, 257
   on apply, 257
   properties, 256
   target data source, 257
Filters, 85, 87, 255, 257, 325, 633, 636
   area, 685
   cascading, 654
   values, 87
firepropertiesChanged, 602
Fixed structure, 639
flaticon, 659
Float, 310
   number, 324
Follow-up, 454
Font file, 657
font-weight, 408
Footer, 685
   panel, 416
For each – for each – loop over array, 315
for statement, 521
Forecasts, 392
Formatted Text Field component, 273
Formatted Text View component, 693
Fragment Gallery component, 146, 273
Full time equivalent (FTE), 195
Function call, 544
Functions, 546, 557

G

Galigeo, 487
Generic Analysis template, 147, 677
Geo Map component, 258, 339, 703
   properties, 259
GEoJSON file, 261
GeoJSON Mapping Property, 261
getDimensions, 557
Getter/setter, 511, 547, 595
Getting started, 175
Global script object, 296, 321, 630
Global script variables, 225, 312, 634

Global scripts, 312, 459, 630
Global variables, 458, 511, 522
Graph column, 246
Graphomate, 487
Grid Layout component, 285
   column width, 285
   name, 285
   number of columns, 285
   number of rows, 285
   properties, 285
   row height, 285
Guidelines, 453

H

handlerType, 571
hasClientChanges, 395
Header, 249, 624, 685, 687
   panel, 416
Heat map, 681
Height, 336
Help menu, 175
Hierarchy, 182
Hierarchy node, 552
High Contrast Black theme, 401, 403
Highlight, 235
Highlight outliers, 443
Horizontal area chart, 442
Horizontal line chart, 437
Horizontal waterfall chart, 445
hover, 581
HTML, 509, 525, 608
HTML5, 31, 525
HTTP protocol, 170

I

IBCS, 432, 434, 451
Icon component, 274
   properties, 275
ICON_GROUP_ANALYSIS, 690
ICON_PROMPTS, 694
Icons, 532, 536, 585, 666
IDs, 525, 526
if – if –else block with compare, 317

if – if statement, 316
if statement, 512
Image
 file, 658
 resizing, 659
Image component, 275, 346
 CSS class, 276
 image, 276
 properties, 276
includeData, 544
increment, 521, 523
In-depth dashboard, 645
Index number, 513
Info Chart component, 240, 339
Info Chart Feeding Panel component, 241
InfoAreas, 380
InfoProvider, 341
InfoProviders, 33
Init(), 546, 561, 577, 594
Initial values, 591
Initialization, 521
Input and output parameters, 298
Input Field component, 277, 347
 CSS class, 278
 properties, 277
 value, 278
Input-ready, 327
Installation, 91, 96
 Analysis Application Support for Mobile Services, 105
 Analysis Application Web component, 104
 document guides, 96
 extract files, 98
 full or custom, 104
 software components, 97, 98
 wizard, 102
Instance, 516
Integrated development environment (IDE), 143
Interactivity, 305
Inverse scale, 569
iView template, 130

J

Java, 493
 uninstall, 493
Java Development Kit (JDK), 491
 install, 491
Java Runtime Environment (JRE), 96
JavaScript, 34, 508, 509, 529, 609
 classes, 516
 conditional statements, 519
 inheritance, 517
 libraries, 559
 methods, 517
 object-oriented, 516
 properties, 516
JavaScript Object Notation (JSON), 318
jQuery, 507, 559
 library, 510, 518
 manipulating elements, 560
 selecting elements, 559
 selections, 559
jsInclude, 531, 537
JSON, 310, 318, 320, 514, 548, 553, 556
 dimension members, 556
JSON Grabber, 557

K

Key, 85
Key figures, 552
KPI, 43, 69, 72, 76, 573, 618, 640
 quality, 618, 628
 title, 622

L

Language support, 703
Layout Editor, 179
Layout menu, 157
 aistribute, 158
 align commands, 157
 Maximize Component, 158
LAYOUT_CONTAINER, 678, 680
Lead the cloud, 699
Leverage investments, 700

Lifecycle Management Console (LCM), 93
Line chart, 378, 436
Linear scale, 569
List Box component, 278, 345, 363, 691
   CSS class, 279
   items, 279
   on select, 279
   properties, 279
   vs. Dropdown Box component, 278
Load in script, 227, 228
Loading state indicator, 336
Local, 409
Local file installation, 478
Local mode, 139, 154
   repository folder, 154
Local variables, 311, 511
Log level, 173
Logical name, 410
Loops, 521

M

Machine analysis, 70
Main
   layout, 623
   page, 640
MANIFEST.MF, 576
Manual planning, 390
Mash-ups, 704
Math component, 332
Maximum number of members, 257, 669
Maximum widths of header area, 249
Measures, 83, 182, 326
Measures in rows, 651
Members, 326, 551
   selection, 165
Menu bar, 143
   application menu, 143
Merging, 463
Metadata, 550
   dimension levels, 551
Metadata Runtime JSON, 542, 550
Method chaining, 518
Methods, 306, 307, 322, 330, 517, 519
   adding, 611
   Application component, 329

Methods (Cont.)
   ApplicationInfo object, 331
   Bookmark component, 331
   Button component, 337
   Chart Component, 337
   Checkbox component, 340
   Checkbox Group component, 341
   common, 335
   create, 557
   Crosstab component, 342
   Date Field component, 343
   Dimension Filter component, 344
   Filter Line component, 344
   Filter Panel component, 344
   Image component, 346
   Input Field component, 347
   Math component, 332
   Navigation Panel component, 345
   Pagebook component, 348
   Panel component, 348
   Popup component, 348
   Scorecard component, 340
   Spreadsheet component, 340
   Tabstrip component, 349
   Text component, 349
Microsoft Excel, 51, 709
MIME repository, 411
Mobile, 31, 35, 118, 703
   category, 118
   content available, 717
   dashboards, 703
   device, 177, 215
   running Design Studio content, 718
   server, 119, 716
   theme, 402, 404
Modes, 536
Multidimensional arrays, 513
Multiple pie chart, 447
Multiple radar chart, 448
Multisource relational UNX, 134
myBodyPanel, 416
mybutton, 631
myCheckBox, 422
myFooterPanel, 416
mytitle, 415

N

Naming conventions, 456, 458
Navigation, 257, 465
   items, 350
   menu, 350
   popup, 353
Navigation Panel component, 345, 374
Network connections, 171
Nodes, 524
Notepad++, 410
Number of dimensions, 651

O

Object constructor, 516
ODBC Data Source Administrator, 170
OLAP application, 81, 373, 675
   adding charts, 376
   additional options, 88
   bookmarking, 88, 691
   chart options, 86
   component, 685
   connection, 93, 379
   create, 675
   dashboard, 82
   editing views, 83
   filters, 87, 697
   layout, 678
   navigation panel, 83
   output, 85
   properties, 682, 695
   selecting a data source, 379
   tabs, 82, 676
OLAP connection, 120, 123
   define authentication method for SAP BW, 122
   SAP HANA, 123
On Click, 632
On Startup, 681, 695
OnChange, 656
Online Analytical Processing (OLAP), 81
Online somposition, 147
OnTimer, 637
Opacity, 276
Open data source browser, 691
OpenDocument, 214, 312
Operators, 309
Ordinal scale, 570
Outline panel, 456
Overall Equipment Efficiency (OEE), 69, 70, 618
   per plant, 71

P

Pagebook component, 287, 348, 375
   CSS class, 287
   page caching, 288
   properties, 287
   selected page index, 287
   transition effect, 287
Panel component, 284, 289, 348, 456
   CSS class, 290
   CSS style, 290
   properties, 289
Parameter, 546
Parent, 517
Part-to-whole relationship, 439
Performance, 70, 463
   KPI, 618, 628
   measurement, 330
Pie chart, 446
Planning, 683
   applications, 147
   connection, 219, 387
   function, 387, 389, 392
   functionality, 394
   layout, 147
   model, 219
   object, 388
   prerequisites, 385
   sequence, 387, 389, 392, 393
Planning application
   building, 395
Planning component, 333
Planning Function component, 333
Platinum theme, 402
Popup component, 146, 290, 348
   animation, 291
   autoclose, 291
   model, 291

Popup component (Cont.)
  name, 290
possiblevalue, 540, 591
Predefined
  statement, 315
  statement templates, 317
Preferences menu, 163
  application design, 163
  scripting, 163
Primitive types, 310, 515
Product Availability Matrix (PAM), 94
Production, 70
Project
  import, 499
  importing, 500
Prompts, 152, 683
Properties, 217, 405, 516, 538
  common layout, 229
  custom CSS, 220
  description, 218
  theme, 218
Properties panel, 534
Property
  binding, 667
PropertyPage, 530
prototype.constructor, 518
Prototyping, 704
Purchasing dashboard, 82

Q

QR code, 177
Quality, 70, 73
Quote
  delivery form, 79
  document, 642

R

Radar chart, 448
Radio Button component, 345
Radio Button Group component, 280
  columns, 280
  CSS class, 280
  items, 281
  on select, 281

Radio Button Group component (Cont.)
  properties, 280
Range, 254
Readability, 457, 460, 518
Ready-to-run, 147, 677
Realization column, 652
Real-time
  view, 619, 633
Real-time production dashboard, 69, 617
  components and layout, 623
  interactivity, 630
Redundant selections, 257
References, 459
Regression test, 485
Relational UNX, 134
Rendering mode, 146
Reports, 29
Reset, 395
ResultCellList, 553
returnData, 605
Reusable functions, 587
Right margin, 336
Row-based data models, 463
Rows, 83

S

S_RS_ZEN, 130
  authorization fields, 130
Sales dashboard, 75, 639
  CSS class, 656
  detail screen, 77
  headers, 654
  icon, 658
  main page, 75, 642
  PDF document, 79
  quotes, 79
  quotes page, 666
  right side menu, 654
SAP Business Objects BI
  promoting, 483
SAP Business Warehouse, 33, 92, 93, 95, 147, 170, 214, 411, 478, 491, 700, 703
  BEx Analyzer, 709
  BEx query, 150, 152, 202
  connecting to multiple systems, 125

Index

SAP Business Warehouse (Cont.)
  InfoArea, 151
  InfoProvider, 150
  Java Portal, 65
  OLAP connection, 120
  query view, 150
  role, 151
  setup for Design Studio, 124
  supported versions, 95
  transporting, 483
SAP BusinessObjects Analysis, 42
  creating a Design Studio application, 710
  smart copy, 709, 712
SAP BusinessObjects Analysis, edition for Microsoft Office, 37, 40, 42, 81, 675, 700, 703, 709
SAP BusinessObjects Analysis, edition for OLAP, 40, 42, 147, 709
SAP BusinessObjects BI, 33, 92, 93, 214, 379, 385, 411, 477, 700
  add-on for Design Studio, 100
  client session, 113
  configuration for Design Studio, 108
  log, 113
  mobile server, 716
  prerequisites, 94, 102
  public folder, 223
  strategy, 699
  supported versions, 94
  types, 310
  user authorization, 114
SAP BusinessObjects BI tools
  dashboarding and application creation, 43
  discovery and analysis, 40
  reporting, 38
SAP BusinessObjects Dashboards, 30, 37, 43, 704, 715
  chart types, 53
  components, 53
  container component, 55
  data connectivity, 56
  design environment, 52
  example, 50
  map, 55
  publishing, 57
  SDK, 57
  selectors, 54

SAP BusinessObjects Dashboards (Cont.)
  setup, 51
  single-value component, 55
  vs. Design Studio, 49, 64
SAP BusinessObjects Design Studio, 43
  and SAP BusinessObjects BI, 37
  BEx Web Application Designer and Dashboards, 37
  client tool, 92, 93, 96, 135
  components and properties, 217
  configuration, 91
  future direction, 703, 705
  installation, 91
  mobile, 715
  outlook and future developments, 699
  planned innovations, 703, 704
  roadmap, 702, 703
  SAP BusinessObjects Mobile, 715
  supported browsers, 96
  usage scenario, 69
  vs. BEx Web Application Designer, 49, 65
  vs. SAP BusinessObjects Dashboards, 49, 64
SAP BusinessObjects Explorer, 37, 40, 715
SAP BusinessObjects Mobile, 35, 118, 715
  annotation, 719
  collaboration, 719
  connectivity, 716
  iOS, 715
  supported platforms, 715
  voice memo, 719
SAP BusinessObjects Web Intelligence, 37, 40, 700, 715
SAP BW Integrated Planning (SAP BW-IP), 64
SAP Consulting, 487
SAP Crystal Reports, 37, 39, 700, 703, 715
SAP Enterprise Portal, 93, 95, 130, 478
  prerequisites, 95
  setup for Design Studio, 124
SAP Event Stream Processing, 618
SAP Fiori, 146, 705
SAP HANA, 33, 66, 93, 95, 123, 147, 151, 170, 214, 478, 491, 700, 702, 705
  analytic view, 150
  calculation view, 150
  transporting, 484
  view, 618
SAP HANA Smart Data Access, 700

735

SAP HANA Smart Data Streaming, 135
SAP Jam, 719
SAP JCo, 173
   trace, 173
SAP Logon, 93, 170
SAP Lumira, 37, 40, 81, 147, 700, 704
SAP Notes, 98, 125
SAP Predictive Analytics, 37
SAP Promotion Management, 93
SAP Service Marketplace, 96, 97, 98
SAP Software Download Center, 97
SAP Transport Management System (TMS), 94
SAP Visual Intelligence → SAP Lumira
SAPUI5, 95, 507, 536, 559
   common mode, 146
   components, 146
   functions, 572
   library, 536, 571
   m category template, 147
   m mode, 146
Scales, 569
Scaling factor, 249, 327, 329
Scatter chart, 450
Scheduling, 703
Scorecard component, 242, 370
   graph columns, 246
   text column, 245
Screen size, 421
Script, 34, 173, 305, 313, 455, 457, 684
   contributions, 530, 584
   errors, 320
   methods, 300, 530, 558
   navigating between applications, 357
   OLAP application, 373
   readability, 272
   variables, 311
Script Editor, 313, 631
SDK, 33, 57, 66, 507
   building an extension, 573
   Bullet Graph component, 573
   certificates, 474
   code, 524
   component, 470
   component level, 535
   configuring an extension, 533
   deployment, 491
   extension, 470, 507, 508

SDK (Cont.)
   extension building blocks, 527
   extension files, 587
   extension level, 533
   framework, 507
   installation and deployment, 487
   installing extensions, 471
   installing extensions on other platforms, 476
   internal functionality, 544
   licenses, 473
   lower version, 481
   main structure, 528
   moving through the landscape, 482
   new install, 471
   programming languages, 509
   testing extensions, 484
   third-party extensions, 485, 488
   uninstalling, 480, 481
   updating extensions, 478
   vendors, 487
Search menu, 158
   find references, 160
   search application, 159
selectAll, 562, 599
Selection components, 345
Shallow copy, 515
shift(), 513
Shorthand code, 413
Show
   realization value, 653
   scaling factors, 233
Single number, 436
Single sign-on (SSO), 122
Single-source UNX, 134
Size factor, 275
Smart paste, 714
Solar Install Company, 639
Source code, 420, 426
Split Cell Container component, 146, 293
Spreadsheet component, 340, 390
Stacked bar chart, 438
Stacked column chart, 440
Stacked waterfall chart, 446
Standard components, 421, 618
Standard method, 584
Startup
   filter, 633

Index

String, 310
stringLength, 323
stringToInt, 324
Support, 176
   settings, 172
SVG, 525, 546, 567
   elements, 567, 601
   files, 658
   groups, 568
   image, 659
Swap axis, 629
switch, 520
Synchronization, 464
Syntax
   coloring, 173
System ID, 294

T

Table, 696
Tabstrip component, 291, 349
   on CSS class, 292
   properties, 292
   selected tab index, 292
Tags, 524, 525, 526, 672
Target platform, 502
Technical components, 293, 619
Template, 34, 146, 167, 461, 498
   download, 496
   page, 657
   scripting, 174
   selection, 677
Testing, 482
Text, 85
Text column, 245
Text component, 281, 349, 359
   CSS class, 282
   on click, 282
   properties, 282
   style, 282
Text pool, 686
text-align, 408
that keyword, 578
Theme, 34
this keyword, 516, 523, 524
This month, 74, 619

This year, 74, 619
Threshold columns, 651
Tick count, 330
Tiles, 76, 653
Timer component, 618, 636
Today, 619
Toggle displays, 689
Tomcat, 107
Toolbar, 177, 178, 685
   command descriptions, 178
   send to mobile device, 177
   seven command groups, 177
Tools menu, 162
Tooltip, 237, 278, 337, 340, 535, 539, 601
Top margin, 336
Top N filters, 703
totalprice, 673
Transaction
   SE80, 411
   STMS, 412
Tree
   component, 283
   map, 82
Trend graph, 78
Trigger, 312
Tuples, 554

U

Undefined, 511
Universes (UNX), 56, 133, 704
Update, 568
URL installation, 479
URL parameter, 312, 357
use strict, 578

V

Values, 405
Variables, 218, 309, 311, 458, 463, 510, 696
   changing values, 522
   declaration, 593
   flexibility, 373
   input, 361
   placeholder, 458

Index

Velocity, 704
Vendor, 533
View, 620
   additional properties, 190
   properties, 186
   script problems, 193
View menu, 160, 180
   additional properties, 161
   components, 161, 180
   error log, 162, 192
   outline, 161, 181
   properties, 161, 187
   reset layout, 162
   script problems, 161
   search results, 162
Visual components, 229, 335
Visualization, 429, 603
   method, 434

W

W3schools, 405
Waterfall chart, 444
WDeploy, 107

Web Application Container Services (WACS), 107
Welcome page, 139, 175
What-if scenario, 51
while-statement, 521
Widtth, 336
Word cloud graph, 78, 661
   data source, 661
Workspace, 502
WYSIWYG, 32, 143, 179

X

Xcelsius, 51
XML, 524, 537, 567
   catalog, 499
   definition, 495
   elements, 524
   nodes, 524
   registering definition, 498
   setup, 498, 499
   tags, 524
xScale, 604

- Master the basic principles and concepts of SAP BW
- Learn how to perform data modeling, ETL, reporting, and more with detailed instructions and screenshots
- Follow along with a real-life case study to see SAP BW in action

Palekar, Shiralkar, Patel

SAP BW 7.4—Practical Guide

Don't just read about SAP BW—get your hands dirty with this updated, must-have guide. Tackle all of the common tasks you'll encounter when working with SAP BW, from creating objects, to extracting and transforming data, to mastering the BEx tools. Keep your skills sharp with information new to this edition, including updates for SAP BW 7.4 and SAP BW powered by SAP HANA. Throughout the book, follow along with a comprehensive case study to cement your knowledge.

852 pages, 3rd edition, pub. 4/2015
E-Book: $59.99 | **Print:** $69.95 | **Bundle:** $79.99

www.sap-press.com/3733

Rheinwerk Publishing

▶ Learn how to model and visualize data to tell a story

▶ LExplore the entire design process, from accessing data sources to using the SDK

▶ Find out your options for deployment, installation, and configuration

Christian Ah-Soon, Peter Snowdon

Getting Started with SAP Lumira

Take your data viz up a notch with SAP Lumira! In this book, get the whole story on using SAP Lumira to create compelling infographics, storyboards, and more. Learn how to access and query data sources, create new objects, export and publish data, and use the SAP Lumira SDK to enhance and extend data sources and visualizations. With step-by-step instructions, screenshots, and detailed examples, you'll learn how to make each picture—or chart—worth a thousand words.

540 pages, pub. 11/2014
E-Book: $59.99 | **Print:** $69.95 | **Bundle:** $79.99

www.sap-press.com/3645

- Explore your SAP BW on SAP HANA implementation options
- Get step-by-step instructions for migration, including pre- and post-steps
- Learn how SAP HANA changes data modeling, reporting, and administration for an SAP BW system

Hügens, Merz, Blum

Implementing SAP BW on SAP HANA

If you're making the leap from SAP BW to SAP HANA, this book is your indispensable companion. Thanks to detailed pre-migration and post-migration steps, as well as a complete guide to the actual migration process, it's never been easier to HANA-ify your SAP BW system. Once your migration is complete, learn everything you need to know about data modeling, reporting, and administration. Are you ready for the next generation of SAP BW?

467 pages, pub. 4/2015
E-Book: $69.99 | **Print:** $79.95 | **Bundle:** $89.99

www.sap-press.com/3609

- Your one-stop reference for all things WebI
- From report creation to publication, and everything in between
- Updated for release 4.1, SAP HANA, and more

Marks, Sinkwitz, Brogden, Orthous

SAP BusinessObjects Web Intelligence

The Comprehensive Guide

Report creation. Data display via charts. Report sharing. Get both the basic concepts and the actionable details to advance your work with SAP BusinessObjects Web Intelligence! Updated for WebI 4.1, this third edition includes UI and functionality changes and coverage of new topics like SAP HANA and mobility. Work smarter in WebI!

691 pages, 3rd edition, pub. 8/2014
E-Book: $69.99 | **Print:** $79.95 | **Bundle:** $89.99

www.sap-press.com/3673

www.sap-press.com

Interested in reading more?

Please visit our website for all new
book and e-book releases from SAP PRESS.

www.sap-press.com

SAP PRESS